Winn L. Rosch

Your Old
PC

The Complete Upgrading and Renovating Guide

Winn L. Rosch

Your Old PC

The Complete Upgrading and Renovating Guide

////Brady

New York   London   Toronto   Sydney   Tokyo   Singapore

Brady Publishing

A Division of Prentice Hall Computer Publishing
15 Columbus Circle
New York, NY 10023

ISBN: 1-56686-104-7

Library of Congress Catalog No.: 93-29814

Printing Code: The rightmost double-digit number is the year of the book's printing; the rightmost single-digit number is the number of the book's printing. For example, 93-1 shows that the first printing of the book occurred in 1993.

96 95 94 93   4 3 2 1

Manufactured in the United States of America

Credits

Publisher

Michael Violano

Acquisitions Director

Jono Hardjowirogo

Managing Editor

Kelly D. Dobbs

Acquisitions Editor

Michael Sprague

Copy Editors

John Burek
Tyrone Prescod

Editorial Assistants

Lisa Rose
Yana Strutin

Illustrator

Bruce Sanders

Book Designer

Kevin Spear

Cover Designer

Jay Corpus

Imprint Manager

Scott Cook

Production Analyst

MaryBeth Wakefield

Indexers

Jeanne Clark
Joy Dean Lee

Production Team

Diana Bigham, Katy Bodenmiller, Tim Cox,
Meshell Dinn, Mark Enochs, Howard Jones,
Tom Loveman, Roger Morgan, Beth Rago, Joe
Ramon, Carrie Roth, Marc Shecter,
Greg Simsic

Marketing Director

Lonny Stein

Marketing Coordinator

Laura Cadorette

About the Author

Winn L. Rosch has written about personal computers since 1981 and has penned nearly 1,000 published articles about them—a mixture of reviews, how-to guides, and background pieces explaining new technologies. One of these was selected by The Computer Press Association as the best feature article of the year for 1987; another was runner up for the same award in 1990. He has written several other books about computers, the most recent of which are *The Winn L. Rosch Hardware Bible* (Brady, 1992), *The Winn L. Rosch PC Upgrade Bible* (Brady, 1991), and *The Micro Channel Architecture Handbook*, co-authored with Chet Heath (Brady, 1990). At present, he is a contributing editor to *PC Magazine*, *PC Week*, *PC Sources*, and *Computer Shopper*. His books and articles have been reprinted in several languages (French, Italian, German, and Portuguese).

Besides being a writer, Rosch is an attorney licensed to practice in Ohio and holds a Juris Doctor degree. He was appointed to, and currently serves on, the Ohio State Bar Association's Computer Law committee.

In other lifetimes, Rosch has worked as a photojournalist, electronic journalist, and broadcast engineer. For 10 years, he wrote regular columns about stereo and video equipment for The Cleveland Plain Dealer, Ohio's largest daily newspaper, and regularly contributed lifestyle features and photographs. In Cleveland, where he still lives, he has served as a chief engineer for several radio stations. He has also worked on electronic journalism projects for the NBC and CBS networks.

In his spare time, Rosch conducts experiments on spontaneous generation in his refrigerator and is researching a definitive study of Precambrian literature.

About the Illustrator

Bruce Sanders has been living and working as an illustrator and art director in Boston with his wife Ellen for the last 15 years. Bruce started drawing early in life and never stopped. Educated as an architect, he discovered that he would rather build drawings than draw buildings.

Contents

FOREWORD

By Bob Vila

Computers aren't as much part of our lives as are the homes in which we live, but with every passing year we are becoming more and more dependent on our personal computers. I've seen the changes in my own work and life. When I started in my career as a contractor, having a computer on your desk was as absurd as building a blast furnace in your backyard. Computers were huge monster machines meant only to be used by big business. One machine took a whole crew of people with special skills to operate. Today, I have a computer on my desk. Like you, I've read the comparisons that put the power of my desktop PC somewhere beyond the capabilities of those blast-furnace-size machines. But for me, however, the most important changes have been that now I run my own computer and that I couldn't run my business without it.

In fact, computers have changed faster than anyone 20 years ago might have thought possible. More surprisingly, in my own experience they've changed faster than anyone even a couple of years ago might have thought, too. Had you bought a PC two years ago with the idea that it would be all the computer you'd ever need, today you know how mistaken you could be. It's not only that the machines have changed. What we want and need to do with them has changed, too. It's like buying a bungalow. Start a family, and in a few short years your life changes and you outgrow your old house. You need more bedrooms, a playroom, and a place to get away from the kids. Soon you're looking for a new house or some way to add on to what you have to get the space you need.

I've seen the same kind of change affect my needs in a computer. A couple of years ago, the PC I used in my business was little more than a calculator and bookkeeping machine. We poured numbers in, and new numbers gushed out — a work schedule, the payroll, or the bill of materials for a project. That's not enough for what I need to do anymore. PCs now have graphics power that I couldn't even imagine — let alone imagine using — when I bought my first machine. Today, I'm reviewing design changes on my monitor screen that have been sent to me in electronic form by architects. I'm sketching my own ideas and drawing blueprints directly on the screen. I never could do any of that on the numbers-oriented PC I bought two years ago.

Probably the most amazing thing that I've found in watching the changes in personal computers and just using them is how adaptable they are. The small network of PCs I bought two years ago never could have handled all that I do now — the high-resolution graphics and all — but I'm still using basically the same equipment. I was able to keep my computers current by a clever strategy that's developed in the PC industry, one that's called upgrading. Add in a few parts and an older PC becomes better than new. You can give an old machine new capabilities so that it can tackle today's demanding software.

For example, to give my desktop PC the capability to View, to Create, and to Exchange complicated graphic images and drawings, I upgraded its microprocessor, memory, and graphics system, and I was able to do it for far less than the cost of a new machine. And I did it all in little more than an hour's time. Well, almost.

Anyone seeing me on television knows that I appreciate a job well done, usually by someone else. On TV, I'm the host, the narrator, the guide. I explain what you can do while other hands are at work. After all, you can always hire someone to help with or do the physical labor, but you can't hire out making the decisions on what to do. With upgrading my PC, the situation was no different.

Winn Rosch visited my Cape Cod company and did the mechanical work of upgrading my desktop system for me. It was a revelation. Not only did I gain the power of a new PC, the computer that seemed so unapproachable before took on a new, more familiar aspect. Upgrading a PC, I discovered, was hardly different from what I had been doing for years as a contractor — renovating homes, adding life to old structures, making the dilapidated the envy of the neighborhood. All the elements of the job of home renovation and PC upgrading are the same. The hands-on work with tools can be easier than you would suppose, but the preparation and decision-making could range from headache to torture — almost too many tough calls to make about equipment and technologies about which you might have little experience.

As Winn points out in this book, the similarity between home renovation and PC upgrading starts when you have the first inkling that you need to make a change. With a home and PC the initial issue is the same: should you renovate or tear everything down and start over? The issue is never simple because it's rarely just a matter of economics. You may be sentimentally attached to what you have, or you may want the novelty of something new. With a house, the decision may be further clouded by zoning restrictions and historic designations. PC and upgrade purchases, too, can be confounded by corporate policy or family dictates.

But the tough decision-making doesn't end there. After you've made the choice to go ahead with your renovation or upgrade, you need to sort through another range of options — the technologies to use and the specific products that are available. It's not easy. In fact, finding the product that best suits your renovation plans or upgrading needs is generally where you'll need the most guidance. That's what I give you when you want to change your home. In my television shows and videos, I concentrate on letting you know what you can do and how to do it. That way you'll know what you're getting yourself into and what you can get out of your renovation work.

In this book, Winn does exactly the same thing for upgrading your PC. He goes beyond simply telling you to hit the nail with your hammer or whatever you need to do to plug in your PC upgrade. He starts by telling you about all the options you have available to you so that you can choose the right one. Beyond just that, he concentrates on providing you with all the background information that you need so you can make your own, personal decision about the form your upgrade will take. He explains the technologies available to you and the strengths and weaknesses of each. Only then does he give you the step-by-step instructions that you need to follow to update your PC.

Probably the best part of approaching a renovation or upgrade yourself is the confidence that it brings. When you work on your own house, you begin to feel more intimately connected with it. You understand it better, and you know your own skills better. You're less afraid to try something new a second time, to do more work yourself, to get more done, and to get more value for the money you invest in your home and renovation.

Working on your own PC brings you the same benefit. I know. For my first PC upgrade, I had the best guidance available, Winn at my side with his hands in my system. Next time, I have no doubt that I can make the upgrade my PCs need myself, and I may just do it. At least as long as I can't convince Winn to give it another try for me.

If you don't have an expert you can blackmail into helping you make your first upgrades as I did with Winn, you can do almost as well with this book to guide you. The most important lesson that it teaches is the same as the one I give. You can do it yourself. All it takes is the right background knowledge and less work than you'd suppose. Who knows? Maybe you'll build enough confidence working on your old PC to tackle a more daunting job — like your old house.

Marston Mills, July, 1993

Preface

Personal computers are great, better than dogs in fact, to the extent of taking over the role of man's best friend, or at least the best friend of authors. Second editions show the PC's talent for making life easier. Using the search-and-replace feature of your word processor, you can find all the old buzzwords and replace them with the hot-button terms of today. Out goes the ST506 and in comes the SCSI.

Were life and writing only so simple, I'd have enough free time to figure where my sanity went. But crafting a book—even a mere second edition—is inevitably slow and tedious, at least if you have the dueling goals of completeness and correctness. The electronic speed of the fast 486-based PC responding to the pressure of my fingertips is held back by the slow spin and grind of the gears in my brain.

Although there's a lot to be said about the leisurely life, in today's high-tech world, most of it must be speculation. Writing a book like this one is always a race, one that pits the plodding turtle of writing against the quarterhorse of technology. The winner never is in doubt. The deliberate accuracy of authorship always ends in second place. The hard-won words of the computer book slip out of date faster than the book can slide out of its slipcover (were computer book publishers only to bless their volumes with slipcovers). What was once current technology turns to history in a year, ancient history in two.

So has it been with the *Winn L. Rosch PC Upgrade Bible*. Only two years have passed, yet most of that book seems as relevant to today's PCs as an alchemical text. So much has changed in the last couple dozen months that even the column and magazine on which that first effort was based—the "Upgrade Clinic" in *PC Sources*—have both disappeared into the purgatory of suspended publication.

In revising this book, I've followed three guiding principles: if explanations could be made clearer, they were; if data were out-of-date, they were updated; and if jokes were old and dated, so much the better.

In the two years since I finished the original Upgrade Bible, PCs have changed in several major ways which have had direct effects on their upgradability. Upgradability has developed its own promotional value. A few years ago, an upgradable PC was a notable curiosity, generally a dinosaur unaware it was dead, leftovers from the days of CP/M-based S100 bus computers. Then the business people who invested in PCs to give themselves a competitive edge found those edges dull and their computers likewise. Machines hardly two years old had the same status and value as day-old bread. The computer industry responded to their despair and began to promote machines as upgradable; and they were—providing you were willing to pay more than a price of a replacement PC for the upgrade parts.

These machines have given upgrading a bad name—too much money for too little added life and performance. They were also red herrings. Upgradability has in fact been a virtue of PCs since IBM sold its first machine. Only this feature was rarely promoted before the advent of the upgradables. It was something understood and recognized only by the computer cognoscenti, the hardware geeks with pocket protectors and week-end evenings to spare. Like some secret society, they kept hidden a mystery of the ages, that any PC is easy and inexpensive to upgrade.

As upgradability has become respectable, even reaching the status of a buzz word, more and more people are realizing that a simple upgrade can add years to the life of their aging PC. More importantly, thanks to the pioneering efforts of columns like the now-defunct Upgrade Clinic, upgrading is recognized as a viable do-it-yourself job, one that takes little time and brings big rewards.

That's the key to PC upgrades: it's one job you can do yourself and expect results on par (if not better than) you could get from a professional. All you needed was a bit of information to help you choose and make your upgrade.

Then came the big reverse—in 1992, the bottom fell out of the PC market. For less than the cost of most upgrades at the time you could buy a new PC with the latest, greatest, and most-talked-about microprocessor and enough performance-enhancing peripherals to make Star Wars sound modest.

With prices like that, why bother upgrading? Because the price plummet has run through the entire PC industry and includes the supplies you need for upgrading. Although PCs have never been cheaper, upgrades have never been cheaper, either. An astute upgrade makes even a bargain PC look like a bad deal. After all, if you need or want 486 power, which makes more sense—a $2,000 system or a $500 upgrade?

Moreover, the low prices haven't stopped the rush of technology. So even if you buy a top of the line PC today, by this time next week, it will be second-rate and in need of an upgrade. Technology is still on the side of the upgrader—and the author who writes about making upgrades.

But that same technology has made revising an upgrade book a challenge equivalent to rewriting from the ground up. So many changes have happened in such a short time that virtually none of the chapters in the original Upgrade Bible could survive untouched. In fact, this book has grown by several new chapters. It's also given me the need for new track shoes just to keep up with the rate of change.

In little more than a year, Intel released more new microprocessor models than it had in its entire previous history. A number of them were designed as replacements—that is, upgrades—for older Intel chips. Where replacing your PC's microprocessor was once a risky task and one that would benefit few PCs, Intel's OverDrive line makes just about every 486 PC upgradable. As a result, the microprocessor chapter has almost doubled in size and gained a new name (Microprocessors and Motherboards) to document those changes and what they mean to you and your aging PC.

High-performance technologies have swept through the graphics world. Now any PC without a graphics accelerator and a local bus connection is out-of-date. Fortunately, the former is easy to add to any PC, and upgrading the latter requires less skill and cash than you might think. As a result, the graphics chapter has been totally revised. A discussion of local bus motherboard upgrades has been added to the microprocessor chapter.

Mass storage demands are higher than ever—which is okay because disk capacities are larger and more affordable than ever, too. More importantly, the confusion of disk interfaces is clearing up and only two connection schemes now deserve your serious attention—providing you're not trying to revive a PC caught in a glacier during the last ice age. These changes have required not only a rewrite of the hard disk chapter but the addition of a new one, Chapter 8, "Cartridge Disk Drives," to cover read/write removable media technologies (other than floppy disks), both magnetic and optical.

Multimedia came from nowhere to become today's buzziest of PC buzz words. Where once PCs and television mixed together about as well as oil and environmentalists in Prince William Sound, video and hi-fi sound are now essential elements of the PC's latest application. This edition now sports a new discussion in Chapter 13 to deal with multimedia issues such as sound boards and CD ROM players.

Just in case the acres of text is too daunting or confusing, Bruce Sanders has added a wealth of new illustrations to clarify the more complex aspects of every upgrade.

After all of that, search-and-replace journalism sounds even more intriguing—a way that I might be able to sleep nights as well as on the job. But in the end, this revision proved to be no small task—and the result, no small book. It's more complete, even more accurate, and I hope, even more fun than its predecessor. If you plan to upgrade your PC or just understand the upgrade you're having someone else make for you, I don't think you'll find a better guide.

Introduction

Do-it-yourself projects can go a long way by saving you money and by building confidence. Upgrading your PC yourself is no different. Unlike some do-it-yourself projects, however, a PC upgrade takes little time and effort. Even if you have no special computer or electronic skills, you can get results in every way equivalent to the work of a professional. One tough job anyone can do is plan an upgrade carefully to achieve a predetermined goal, such as more speed, storage, or versatility. Along the way, you will discover the upgrade that makes the most sense—or whether to skip the upgrade process entirely by replacing your PC.

What should you do when time takes its inevitable toll; when what once was brand new is forlorn and faded? Old age comes quickly to the computer. Machines only two years old are approaching geriatric. At five, they are fossils; at 10, they are curiosities, antique artifacts that can hardly be considered serious computers.

The PC has a singular strength in its inevitable trip over the hill—most computer hardware has been engineered with add-in hope. Only your home is like the computer, with its innate capability to be revived and updated.

The potential for your home or PC does not stop at mere renovations, however. Along with the wear and tear that time drags along with it come new technologies and other improvements. Not only can you restore your home or PC, you can make it better. Just as you can string new wiring through a century home, you can plug state-of-the-art capabilities into an aging PC.

Of course, nothing comes for free. Getting that old house into shape calls for an investment, often a substantial one. But self-reliance is changing the complexion of home renovation. Where once only a dedicated few struggled to make home repairs and renovations themselves, the number is growing almost astronomically. The do-it-yourself revolution is fueled by economy and education. By doing it yourself, you can save a bundle on building, redecorating, or restoring. Education plays just as important a role in changing the face of home repair. Ability, awareness, and even just knowing that you really can do it yourself and succeed are key.

When it comes to your PC, the same renewal possibilities are present, albeit the realities are somewhat different. With PCs, upgrades not only are

Old age comes quickly to the computer. Machines only two years old are approaching geriatric.

needed more but also can be easier and generally more affordable. You do not need a second mortgage to renovate your PC. Better still, unlike carpentry, plumbing, and electrical work, you need no special skills to rejuvenate almost any PC. The payoff is greater, too, because an upgraded PC does not keep you at the status quo but pushes you into the future.

Your first challenge in upgrading your PC is coming up with a goal. You need to know what you want to achieve before you can do it. Then you need to accept the harsh reality that renovation is not always the answer. After you consider all your options, you may find it more effective to forego the upgrade and to opt for replacement.

Although upgrading your PC sounds like the economical move, buying a new machine may make more sense. Without a doubt, replacing your old PC is the easiest task; there are fewer decisions and an irreversible change that removes all doubts.

The alternative path—the upgrade—has a lot going for it, too. Upgrading means less waste, which is easier on the environment and on your pocketbook. You get the benefits of new technologies without the pain of adjusting to major changes. If you are lucky and make a wise upgrade, you are likely to squeeze enough life out of your existing PC to enable you to skip an entire generation of new machines.

You can advance a PC three generations in the time it takes you to spread a gallon of paint on the wall of an aging house.

Best of all, you have nothing to fear in upgrading your PC. Unlike remodeling your house, updating a computer is quick and easy; a PC is designed to be upgraded. No other modern tool or toy can be upgraded as easily or as well as a personal computer. For example, you can take the oldest IBM PC, blow the cobwebs out, spin a screwdriver a few times, and in half an hour upgrade it into the equivalent of the fastest, most capable computers on sale. But try turning a century home into a modern living space without creaking floors, shoe-box-sized rooms, and plumbing that tints every drink orange. You can advance a PC three generations in the time it takes you to spread a gallon of paint on the wall of an aging house.

A PC represents the ultimate in interchangeable parts. Using off-the-shelf components, you can increase the speed of an ancient system by a factor of 50 or more. You can add megabytes to its memory; speed up its hard disk access by a factor of 10; increase mass storage capacity by a hundredfold; add bright new graphics, a loud and pure multimedia voice, and fax capabilities; and add tape backup—all in the time it takes to change the washer in a faucet.

The best part of making a PC upgrade is that you really can do it yourself. Take just a little care, and you are practically guaranteed success. If you think before you do, luck will not be an issue. In addition, when you make an upgrade yourself, you learn a lot along the way.

Do not think of making an upgrade to your computer as something unusual or exotic. Personal computers are designed to be upgraded. You are not exposed to dangerous voltages inside a PC when the top of its case is removed, even if you forget to switch off the power or pull the plug. Expansion slots await the addition of new peripherals in nearly every machine. Each slot is designed to make the effort of adding an expansion board minimal. The most you need to do is twist a screwdriver a couple of times. In fact, many PC makers have virtually eliminated the need for tools for basic upgrades. To add an expansion board or disk drive to some PCs, you only need a finger and a thumb. In most systems, cables are keyed so that you cannot plug them in wrong.

To add an expansion board or disk drive to some PCs, you only need a finger and a thumb.

Of course, all this simplicity and ease begs an important question: Why is a book on upgrading your PC necessary if anyone can handle it? As with anything you do, upgrading your system is easiest the second time around. In making the first upgrade to your PC with the help of this book, you will learn enough to become an expert in your own right. This book provides the guidance you need to decipher how things come apart and fit together again, what parts go where, which corners you can cut, and which details demand your particular attention. Having a guidebook at your side will make everything go more smoothly. Instead of discovering secrets too late, a guidebook can warn you before you waste time and have to retrace several steps. Just a little hint—such as, attach the cable to a disk drive before you screw it into place—can save you much pain.

The hard part of making an upgrade to your PC is not the actual installation of peripherals; rather, the brain work, or deciding what to upgrade, may be harder. To make the right decision, you have to analyze your computer system and the software you run to determine where you face bottlenecks. You have to find the weak links that determine the strength of your data processing chain, the slowest parts of your computer that ultimately limit its top speed. Identifying the bottlenecks helps you make the most cost-effective upgrade to your computer.

You also have to choose from the thousands of products on the market. You have to know what issues are important and which ones you can ignore. Cares and concerns in PC upgrading have changed substantially in just a few years, during which time most popular interfaces have changed completely, the issue of access time has almost evaporated, and capacities have burst through the roof. Although microprocessor upgrades were once a dream, now they can be the most effective reality around. If you do not consider all the issues and have the most current information, you can make a big, and expensive, mistake. In fact, an unwise upgrade choice could even slow down your system or leave you with a worthless hunk of hardware.

*With the back-
ground this book
provides, you can
determine the best
upgrade strategy
by observing how
your PC works.*

Fortunately, as confusing as all the issues may be, they are not impossible to sort through. With the background this book provides, you can determine the best upgrade strategy by observing how your PC works. Finding the right product then becomes a matter of matching features to your needs.

The big secret is knowing what to look for, how things work (and work together), and how to install your upgrade. In truth, most people do more worrying about upgrades than work while installing them. With a little knowledge, you can smooth out the effort. Upgrading will become, at worst, a learning experience. More likely, it will be a mere 10-minute pause that stretches between ordinary work and performance computing.

Why Upgrade?

The reason for upgrading can be summed up in a single word: *more.* With an upgrade, you get more memory, which enables you to handle bigger programs and huge blocks of data, and you can run more features, like multimedia and multitasking. The right upgrade can unlock the potential of your old or new PC by giving it the memory and storage it needs for the latest operating systems—or the voice it needs for audio/video displays. In the end, any upgrade means getting more done in less time with a more useful tool, an upgraded computer.

*Most PCs and
applications have
at least one weak
spot that makes
them candidates
for an upgrade;
the change can
result in an exhila-
rating improve-
ment.*

The most effective upgrade is a selective one. Instead of replacing every-thing in your PC with something that is faster, you update only the part that is holding back your computer's performance the most. After all, upgrading everything translates into buying a new PC with all the atten-dant costs and virtues. Most PCs and applications have at least one weak spot that makes them candidates for an upgrade; the change can result in an exhilarating improvement. Moreover, the selective upgrade is the best way to add a single new technology to a PC to help it keep up with the times.

The selective upgrade keeps the cost of your dreams affordable. After all, almost everyone would like to have the fastest, most powerful computer available, but that is rarely possible. Even with the big plummet in PC prices of the early 90s, few individuals can afford the real heavyweight machines. Even the most munificent corporate budget may be strained by the cost of acquiring the newest, most powerful machines. But, if you upgrade selectively, you will get most of the benefits of the highest end at a cost closer to the bottom.

Making a selective upgrade enables you to ease your way into greater power. Instead of gouging your purse for a new microprocessor, new memory, a new hard disk, and a new display system at the same time, you can add what you need as necessary or as you can afford it. For example, you can add a larger, faster hard disk today to accommodate a growing database. A month or a year later, you can upgrade your microprocessor to give you more speed in processing information that you have stored.

Another reason to upgrade selectively is to keep up with developing technology. For example, with the right choice of upgrade, you can keep abreast of current display technologies. In the last couple of years, innovations in video systems have followed in quick succession—first graphics coprocessors, then graphics accelerators and local bus connections—all meant to wring every last microsecond from your PC's video response time, while sharpening its on-screen image. As display standards of graphics adapters have improved, monitors have become sharper, more colorful, and easier on your eyes.

When it comes to monitors, there is another angle that makes a selective upgrade a superior choice. More recent monitors are also safer. For example, concern is growing about whether extremely low frequency magnetic fields—commonly called ELF—are a health hazard. Many of the latest computer monitors have been redesigned to minimize such fields. Upgrading your display system to take advantage of one of these products could be the best preventive medicine that you can buy.

Although the specific issues are different, the situation is the same with many of the other aspects of your PC. Just about any innovation that has popped up in new PCs can be added into your machine as a selective upgrade. Most often, the upgrade can be the cheapest way to put new technologies to work for you.

Developing a Plan

Before considering any upgrade, you need to have a plan. Your goal will help determine what part of your system you need to upgrade—or whether there is a more cost-effective alternative to making a change. Upgrading just for the sake of it is foolish and wasteful. You could invest thousands of dollars on your PC—more than the cost of a new computer—and get improvements in your actual productivity that are too small to measure. Without a good idea of what you want to accomplish, you cannot determine what you need to upgrade.

Upgrading just for the sake of it is foolish and wasteful.

Step One: Define Specific Goals of Upgrade

Your plan involves four distinct steps. First, set a goal by deciding the specifics that you want your upgrade to accomplish. Ask yourself which part of your PC bothers you the most; which have you outgrown? Do you need more speed to make answers snap onto your screen or more capacity to hold your burgeoning database? Do you need faster answers in statistical calculations? Do you want to take advantage of the advanced features of the latest microprocessors? Do you just want to make your PC better? Do not forget the timing of multiple upgrades. If two or more parts of your system need help, which needs it most immediately? Do you want to make the entire upgrade immediately or stagger the cost over several months?

Step Two: Analyze Your System

Analyze your system to see exactly what stands between you and your goal. Your PC may suffer from one or more bottlenecks, constituents of your computer that constrict the performance of the rest of its circuitry. While part of your PC may be cruising along, unchallenged by any task that you give it, some other part may be panting and straining every time you press a key.

Step Three: Determine How Much You Want To Spend

Sometimes, a hardware upgrade is not the most efficient change you can make; new software or a new computer system can make more financial sense.

You need to determine how much you want to spend, how much you can afford, and how much of an upgrade actually makes sense. Sometimes, a hardware upgrade is not the most efficient change you can make; new software or a new computer system can make more financial sense.

After you have determined what you want to upgrade, you must select the best product to fit your needs. For example, if you determine that your system would benefit most from a new hard disk, you have to consider how large the capacity of a new drive must be, what kind of interface it uses, how much performance it delivers, and even how large it is physically. You need to consider what manufacturer supplies the product you want and where to buy it—from your local dealer, from a parts distributor, or from a mail order vendor.

Step Four: Install the Product into Your PC

In many ways, installation is the easiest of all upgrading chores. The actual installation should take a fraction of the time it takes to make your upgrade plans.

Setting a Goal

Setting a goal does more than help you decide what to upgrade to; it reveals whether you need to upgrade at all. If you cannot set a goal, chances are that you do not need an upgrade. Although you are the only one who knows what the best goal for your upgrade might be, most PC owners have similar ideas and aims. Some of these goals are discussed in the following sections.

Running Particular Applications

Many programs have particular hardware requirements, without which they will not run on your PC. Other programs need to take advantage of particular hardware features to develop their full power. For example, some engineering and scientific applications absolutely demand that you have a math coprocessor—either as a separate chip or built into your PC's microprocessor. Most of today's best applications also demand that your PC have a graphical display system. And if you want to get the most from such programs, you will probably want higher resolution abilities than those that came with your PC. If you want to advance beyond DOS to a new operating system like OS/2 or Windows, you will probably have to add more RAM to your system—especially if you want to optimize your system's speed. Even the latest versions of DOS, starting with the now passé Version 5.0, need memory in excess of the 640K to maximize what is available to your programs.

Sometimes, a particular application area demands a hardware feature that your PC lacks. For example, multimedia and information retrieval applications nowadays lean toward a reliance on optical-based storage systems, such as CD-ROM. Adding a CD-ROM drive to your PC will help you snare the information you need—both pictures and sounds—with on-line speed.

Typically, a simple upgrade will satisfy the special needs of most programs—and for a lot less than the cost of a new computer. If all your
system lacks is a single feature to bring your favorite advanced application
to life, you have got a clear-cut upgrade goal, one that will probably be the
least expensive way to running your application.

This sort of goal is easy to set. Compare the list of system requirements on
the box of software you are eager to take home from the computer store
and then subtract what is already in your PC. Odds are you will come up
several megabytes short somewhere in your PC. You may also be off by a
factor of 100 when it comes to your microprocessor. (Your ideal program
may demand a 386 microprocessor when your PC only has a 286 to offer.)
Graphics adapters, coprocessors, high-resolution monitors, CD-ROM
players, and tape drives are all candidates for your most wanted list.

Achieving Better Performance

The biggest difference between the latest personal computers and those of
10 years ago is speed. Today, you can buy a machine that costs the same as
the first IBM PC but runs between 25 and 100 times faster. That makes
the latest computer hardware a great bargain. But, you can upgrade your
old PC to the same performance level for a fraction of the cost of a new
machine. That makes the upgrade an even bigger bargain.

Achieving a noticeable speed increase is not as straightforward as it seems.
In PCs, speed is not a singular thing; there are several aspects to system
performance, and each can be individually upgraded.

*Getting better
numbers does not
always mean that
your work gets
done faster.*

When most people compare the speeds of computers, they talk about
microprocessor performance or how quickly the brains of the computer
can solve a given problem. They bandy about terms like *clock rates,*
megahertz, MIPS (millions of instructions per second), *megaflops* (millions
of floating-point operations per second), *whetstones, dhrystones,* and
Winmarks as if they know what the terms mean (and as if the terms have
some absolute meaning in themselves). Getting better numbers does not
always mean that your work gets done faster.

Nevertheless, a faster, more powerful microprocessor will help your PC
carry out some operations more quickly. Your PC will be able to calculate
numbers in spreadsheets with less waiting, find and replace text in documents faster, and even respond to your commands faster. Sorting through
database records, loading large graphic images, and copying big files may
result in a substantially larger speed increase by upgrading your hard disk
drive. The hard disk in your computer determines its mass storage speed.

(If you do not have a hard disk, your first upgrade should be to add one. No contemporary computer is complete without one.)

If you use your computer for a lot of high-level mathematics (computing statistics, computing complex formulae, generating engineering drawings), adding a math coprocessor may boost its speed even more than a new microprocessor. Most graphic applications, too, benefit from extra math prowess, because they have to compute the color and brightness of every dot on your monitor screen. Math coprocessors carry out some complex functions hundreds of times faster than ordinary microprocessors do. In fact, the benefits of math processors are so great that Intel now builds coprocessor circuitry into its top-of-the-line microprocessors like the 486DX/2 and Pentium.

Most people hardly strain their computer's microprocessors; the chores microprocessors have to do are trivial compared to the power of even a simple 16-bit microprocessor chip. However, they still appreciate one aspect of having a faster computer because such machines respond faster. The people who use those quicker systems feel like they are getting more done.

Most of the apparent speed of a computer is determined by its display system. The faster the display system can put images on your monitor, the quicker your computer seems. Adding an improved display adapter (the board that generates the signals to operate your monitor) can give the most satisfying of performance increases to your computer. Any PC that lacks today's twin video innovations—graphics acceleration and a local bus interface—is a second-class citizen in the world of graphics performance. The acceleration these technologies achieve can mean more than faster response, however, even though most of the extra speed boost is hidden by the snappier screen. A quicker display system actually can make the rest of your computer work faster, too, by *offloading* much of the work that is required to create an on-screen image. That gives your microprocessor more time to do its own work and eliminates its wait while the screen updates. A quick display can thus deliver both the illusion and reality of performance computing.

If speed is what you are after, take a good look at what is holding you back.

Increasing speed is such a complex issue that this book devotes Chapter 2 to finding the main constraint in your system. If speed is what you are after, take a good look at what is holding you back.

Adding More Mass Storage

Many applications require huge amounts of disk storage space, and some software is sneaky, starting with minimal demands on your system and then growing and growing until you need dozens, even hundreds of megabytes to store data files alone. Even if you do not have a particular application that eats up storage space, your everyday use of your PC can easily spin off so many files that soon the hard disk that once was adequate is now reaching its capacity.

When the IBM PC XT was introduced in 1983, its 10M was revolutionary with more capacity than anyone could imaginably need—at least for the first 10 minutes of operation of the machine. Today, the most popular hard disk size is about 200M, and even casual PC users worry about filling them up.

If your PC has less than 100M of hard disk, you are already a candidate for an upgrade.

If your PC has less than 100M of hard disk, you are already a candidate for an upgrade. That is barely over the minimum needed for OS/2 and scarcely a workable amount for Windows. Opt for Windows NT, and you will need at least twice as much space.

If less than about 20 percent of your present hard disk's space remains unused, you probably should be thinking about an upgrade, too. If you are responsible for a file server, every time you add a new user, you should carefully consider whether now is the time to upgrade.

Choosing mass storage upgrades is becoming increasingly complicated by the availability of a number of new mass storage devices. Although your choice once was merely among different hard disks, now you can select between fixed-media and removable-media hard disks, optically enhanced floppy disk storage (so-called floptical drives), high-density flexible media magnetic cartridge drives—primarily Iomega Corporation's Bernoulli Box, Write-Once Read-Many times optical disk drives (WORM drives), and rewritable magneto-optical (MO) disk drives. Each of these drive types has its own strengths and weaknesses in particular applications.

Getting More and Sharper Colors

All the hottest new applications for PCs (some of which have already begun to cool off) involve graphics: desktop publishing, graphical user interfaces (GUIs), such as Windows and OS/2, presentation preparation, interactive video, and multimedia systems. All of these applications—as well as many others at the edge of the microcomputer mainstream, such as Computer-Aided Design and Drafting—benefit from better display systems. After all, graphic systems are designed to convey information more efficiently through visual communication. The more information that can be displayed and the more easily it can be distinguished, the better these systems work.

Today, the VGA (IBM's Video Graphics Array) that has become standard equipment in almost every PC is essentially passe. Ordinary 640-by-480 pixel resolution is only about enough to whet your appetite for Windows. A sharper display system—one with higher resolution—puts more detail and thus more information on the screen.

Higher resolution is great, but getting realistic images also requires color—and the more the better. After all, 256 colors of the VGA fall far short of the millions you can see. Even if you have the most base artistic abilities, you can probably distinguish a million different shades. Mimicking reality, or just coming close, takes hundreds of thousands of color choices.

Having a range of hues also makes images appear sharper at a given resolution level. That is why television, which has resolution hardly on par with a primitive PC's color graphics adapter display system, can look sharper than a good VGA image.

Another reason to upgrade to a sharper, more colorful display is that it is easier on your eyes. If you have ever woke up in the morning with an eyestrain headache, you will certainly appreciate a sharper display system.

Unfortunately, the sharper and more colorful an image, the more data it contains, and the slower it will display. All other things being equal, with every notch you move your PC's display system toward the ideal, the slower it will become. Consequently, performance is a primary issue with any new graphics systems you add.

All other things being equal, with every notch you move your PC's display system toward the ideal, the slower it will become.

Exchanging Information with Other PCs

PCs should not be an island unto themselves, without a single link to other computers around them. You often will want to exchange files with friends, coworkers, and the like. If both of you do not have similar disk drives, you may find exchanging files rather difficult. By adding a second floppy disk drive, however, you can give your PC plenty of swapping capabilities.

Some of the latest programs require that you have a high-density drive just to get started. For example, applications delivered on high-density floppy disks require that your system have a high-density drive to read them. With the growing popularity of graphics, the ordinary floppy disk is proving to be an inadequate exchange medium. A single graphic file may require more bytes than even the biggest floppy disk holds, forcing you to live with the oddities of DOS's backup program to split the data among several disks.

Upgrading to a tape drive with a standard data format or an optical drive can enable you to exchange megabytes as easily as floppy disks exchange a few kilobytes.

Building Backup Security

The digital data that you have spent years amassing is vulnerable to every quirk of fate.

Although your computer can put megabytes of data on-line, it also can put what could be your most valuable possession on the line. The digital data that you have spent years amassing is vulnerable to every quirk of fate. Lightning, stupid mistakes, and even the well-meaning but ill-informed meddling of helpful friends and coworkers can wipe out every byte stored on a hard disk in a fraction of a second.

Your first, and typically only, line of defense is a backup system. High-density floppy disks, high-technology removable disk media, and tape cartridges all afford you the luxury and security of keeping several copies of your valuable files. Upgrading your system to work with one of these mediums can be your best bet against disaster. You can keep not one, but several copies of your most important records just in case your PC is stolen or fire or disaster strike your home or office.

You also can add to the security of your system and its data by ensuring that your PC can still run, even if the utility that supplies your home or office with power fails. Adding a standby power system can eliminate the system crashes and loss of data that inevitably follows a power failure.

Determining the Bottlenecks

The most effective speed enhancement, of course, is the most cost-efficient one.

The next step in your planning process is determining what you want to upgrade and where you want better performance. For most people, the goal of the upgrade is to get the most out of their computer. The most effective speed enhancement, of course, is the most cost-efficient one. That means breaking the bottlenecks that constrict the performance of your PC. In other words, to make the most effective upgrade, you must determine which part of your computer performs the slowest. If your system is harnessed by a slow hard disk, even the fastest microprocessor upgrade will yield a disappointing improvement. If you can make your system more responsive by just upgrading its display adapter, you may save the thousands of dollars it would cost for a new system board or PC.

The challenge in finding system bottlenecks is that they are not the same in every PC. Not only do bottlenecks vary with computer model, but the performance constraints also depend on the options and peripherals connected to the PC as well as the applications that are being run. A word processor, for example, faces entirely different bottlenecks than a database. The principal factor in determining where bottlenecks arise, in fact, is often not with the computer but with its operator.

What you do with your PC has the greatest influence on what part of the system is sluggish. You have your own personal demands, and you set your own performance criteria. You can optimize your PC to do one thing well, or you can make it best at juggling a dozen applications at the same time.

If your system is harnessed by a slow hard disk, even the fastest microprocessor upgrade will yield a disappointing improvement.

Finding bottlenecks is thus a multi-step process. You have to assess how you work with your PC and what you do with it. Then you need to determine which part of your PC you stress most when you use it. Finally, you have to verify whether that part is actually constraining the performance of the system or whether something else has caused the burden to shift elsewhere.

Odds are, you can answer most of those questions with just a few moments of thought. If you want to be absolutely sure, a few tests or a bit of careful observation may suffice to confirm your suspicions.

Armed with that knowledge, you can make an intelligent choice about what part of your PC to upgrade. You also face what is perhaps the most difficult part of any upgrade process: determining which of the thousands of upgrade components of a particular type will be best for your upgrade.

Selecting an Upgrade

The major concern with selecting an upgrade is cost. After all, if you did not have to worry about the cost of making an upgrade, you would have the wherewithal to scrap your old computer and buy the best and latest model for your desktop.

The next concern is the level of performance you need to achieve to make your upgrade worthwhile. You may want a speedy 16-bit interface from a graphic adapter or a 15-millisecond average access time from a hard disk, but your budget may not allow it. Match your needs with your budget and see if any products can conform with both. Three hundred dollars, for example, might not buy much of a hard disk, but it does open up a wide range of high-quality VGA display adapters.

The cheapest video board may not seem like such a great buy if it starts turning the brightest colors into grayish pastels the day after its warranty runs out.

Next, you must find the product that gives you the most for your money. You could choose from a dozen disk drives in the 100M range, all with access speeds that make your current drive look slow. You face a hard decision because you need to consider every aspect of every product—not just the numbers that appear on the specification sheet, but the intangibles, like the manufacturer's and dealer's reputation, services offered, and the length of the warranty. The cheapest video board may not seem like such a great buy if it starts turning the brightest colors into grayish pastels the day after its warranty runs out.

Finding the one product that is right for your upgrade will not be easy, but after you finish this book you will know what to look for, what is important, and what is not.

Installing the Upgrade

When your dealer does the work, you need not fear that an errant slip of the screwdriver will short something out or bring down the local power grid.

The actual mechanical work of putting a new peripheral inside your PC is not hard; even your computer dealer can do it. In fact, if you buy your upgrade from a local dealer, having the dealer do the installation for you can be a real bonus. Odds are your dealer will have had experience installing other upgrades, so he has already learned how to do everything. The dealer also can relieve your worries about making the upgrade yourself. When your dealer does the work, you need not fear that an errant slip of the screwdriver will short something out or bring down the local power grid. Instead, you shift responsibility into the dealer's hands. Thus, in the unlikely case that your upgrade does not work the first time it is switched on, your dealer can probably quickly diagnose the problem or substitute an identical upgrade to get you going.

However, you have a great deal of incentive to do the installation yourself—such as the great deals that are available through mail-order vendors. They pass along to you at least some of their savings by not needing to spend their time holding your hand and a screwdriver.

Deciding Not To Upgrade

Even if you have paid good money for this book, you will come out ahead if the book helps you avoid an unnecessary upgrade.

Every story has at least two sides, and the upgrade saga is no different. Although an upgrade can bring many benefits, it is not a panacea. In some cases, you may be better off not upgrading your PC and either sticking with what you have or buying an entirely new system. Even if you have paid good money for a copy of this book to help you make an upgrade, you still come out ahead if the book helps you avoid an unnecessary upgrade.

1

Bottlenecks and Brick Walls

W hy might you renovate a part of your home? Maybe you
don't have enough room, or perhaps the plumbing
knocks, the attic creaks, or the charm of Castle Dracula
architecture has worn thin. Maybe you just have grown tired of the
same old same old. If one part of your house particularly bothers
you, improving that part alone can change your attitude about your
home faster and with less expense than bulldozing and rebuilding.
Bricking up the back of the wine cellar can put bad memories and
past-its-prime amontillado to their final rest.

Similarly, if one part of your PC is holding back its performance,
replacing just that part makes more sense than emptying your bank
account or stretching your credit limit to buy a new computer.
Target the one place where your system chokes up, and you may
discover new life in your old PC. This chapter helps you discover
what is holding back the performance of your system—the bottlenecks—and what the limits are to what it can do—the brick wall.

A constraint on the performance of your PC is often termed a
bottleneck. Like the neck of a ketchup bottle, a bottleneck restricts
the flow of the goods. In your PC, a bottleneck slows the flow of
information. A bottleneck could result from a physical narrowing of
a data path—such as when a 32-bit word of data must squeeze
through an 8-bit bus—or it could stem from a more obscure source.
A peripheral that can't accept information as fast as your PC
generates it can send out signals that slow down your system's
operations. A lackadaisical hard disk can make your microprocessor

*This chapter helps
you discover what
is holding back the
performance of
your system—the
bottlenecks—and
what the limits are
to what it can do—
the brick wall.*

wait—and wait and wait—for the data it needs. A slow video system can stop the whole PC while it paints the screen.

For most PCs, the brick wall is built by today's technology.

If speed is what you want from your system upgrade, you first must determine what's slowing up your PC's performance. By identifying your system's primary bottleneck, you can upgrade selectively, eliminating the bad without needlessly replacing the good. And you can keep breaking bottlenecks until you run into the brick wall that marks your system's ultimate performance level.

Looking beyond the final bottleneck, the performance of your PC faces an ultimate limit, as immovable as a brick wall. This wall represents the top end of a computer's capabilities—the point at which no upgrade will make a difference. For most PCs, the brick wall is built by today's technology. You could upgrade every part of your PC, creating an entirely new system from microprocessor to serial port. You could slip in a new motherboard with the latest microprocessor, the best bus, and the most memory money can buy. Add to that the biggest, quickest hard disk and an array of peripherals you can only imagine, and you begin to see the fuzzy form of the ultimate brick wall.

Most people face more realistic brick walls, such as the funds they have available. Although you could replace every part of your PC, you probably could replace the entire system more cheaply. Also, even some selective upgrades leap the bounds of good sense, and those become a personal brick wall that you build in your own PC. In modern computers, that brick wall often can be glimpsed just a few bottlenecks away. Therefore, the secret to a successful upgrade is finding the right bottlenecks to break, choosing the proper order in breaking them, and knowing when to stop.

Most modern PCs can accommodate at least one microprocessor upgrade, so the logical first bottleneck to attack might seem to be the chip. Often, however, some other bottleneck is choking your system well below your PC's data processing capacity. Moreover, a microprocessor upgrade is one of the most expensive improvements you can make to a computer. Older systems not originally designed for microprocessor upgrades push the practical brick wall even closer. The best way to upgrade one of these PCs—replacing its old system board—is the equivalent of stuffing a new computer in an old case. If something else is holding back your existing microprocessor, you probably can break the bottleneck more cheaply and effectively.

Perhaps the most common bottleneck is the performance of your PC's hard disk. The information that the microprocessor works with is electronic, and the chip processes it electronically at lightning speed. Disks, on the other hand, are mechanical, and they move that same data mechanically, suffering all the handicaps imposed by the laws of physics. The spin of the disk itself must be finite and modest if its not to fly apart from centrifugal stress. The mechanism that reads and writes the data on the disk must shuffle back and forth at a lazy rate imposed by inertia. Just finding a byte of data needed in a calculation might take the disk a thousand times longer than the microprocessor. However, in moving large blocks of data in and out of storage, disks are better matched to microprocessors. In some systems, particularly older ones that seem to have microprocessors chipped from flint instead of silicon, disks are actually quicker than the microprocessor. In today's fast computers, however, disks definitely lag behind, delivering data at one-tenth the rate that it could be used. A slow disk means that your microprocessor spends a large amount of its time waiting.

Another performance-robbing bottleneck can be your PC's display system—your computer could create a screen of multicolored graphics and then have to wait while your display adapter sorts out the pattern of pixels for your monitor to display, or your system could spin its wheels idly, waiting for memory to catch up with its operations. Dial the phone, and your modem may slow everything down to its touch-tone rate.

Although most of these system bottlenecks are well known, a few are obscure and seem related only tangentially to system performance. For example, bus mastering—the technology that aids network servers—can speed up your PC's printing response considerably. If you want to get the best value for your computer investment, you can't afford to ignore any possible bottleneck, no matter how offbeat it might seem.

If you want to get the best value for your computer investment, you can't afford to ignore any possible bottleneck, no matter how offbeat it might seem.

Unfortunately, you just can't look up the make and model of your PC on some chart and point your finger to its slowest part. Bottlenecks don't arise out of hardware alone. They are a result of interaction between your computer's circuitry and the application software you run. Some programs stretch your system's microprocessor to the limits, demanding every last megahertz they can lay their greedy digits upon. Others leave the system's brain as idle as a bureaucrat's daytime hours.

Remember, the first step in any upgrade is making a plan, and finding your bottlenecks is an essential part of that plan. Consequently, before you make any upgrade, you need to identify the bottlenecks in your PC.

The first step in any upgrade is making a plan, and finding your bottlenecks is an essential part of that plan.

Bottleneck Causes, Effects, and Cures

Performance bottlenecks have no single cause. Some result from poor component choices that took place when your system was being designed. Some occur when certain applications make demands that cannot be fulfilled by ordinary, general-purpose hardware. Some simply result from using your PC.

Poor component choice is perhaps the easiest to diagnose and improve—and the existence of which seems the least justifiable. You would expect the manufacturer of your PC to give you the best possible components for working with one another. That's rarely the case, however. Often the manufacturer had no choice. Even the quickest hard disk can't keep up with the best of today's microprocessors.

When starting your search-and-destroy mission for system bottlenecks, it's best to know what you're looking for.

Sometimes, however, the reason for the mismatch is more mundane. Performance costs a premium, and to trim the original price of your computer, its manufacturer may have slighted you when choosing components—slower RAM chips or a cheaper hard disk. The technology just may not have been available. For instance, the introduction of cached hard disk controllers lagged behind the development of computers that could benefit from them by several years.

When starting your search-and-destroy mission for system bottlenecks, it's best to know what you're looking for. Understanding how bottlenecks arise in the various components of your PC makes identifying and correcting them easier. The following sections detail the causes of most system bottlenecks and the effects that they have on the operation of your PC.

Microprocessor Bottlenecks

The microprocessor is often the principal bottleneck.

The microprocessor in a PC should be more like the bottle itself rather than a bottleneck. The microprocessor does all the work, setting the pace for the rest of the computer and determining the speed limit for whatever your PC does. In top-of-the-line PCs, the microprocessor dictates the ultimate performance limit. When you buy the latest and fastest Pentium-based PC, you don't expect the microprocessor to hold you back. When you buy the best, you can't do better (at least until Intel releases its next generation of performance-enhanced Pentium chips).

Unfortunately, not everyone can afford a Pentium—right now, anyhow. In lesser PCs, the microprocessor is often the principal bottleneck. Upgrading it with a more powerful chip does wonders for most applications.

The older your PC, the more its microprocessor needs to be upgraded. Microprocessor performance has taken great leaps, improving on the order of a hundredfold in the last decade. Other parts of computer systems have been hard pressed to keep up. Hard disk access and disk data transfer speeds, for example, have increased by about a factor of 10. Most modern PCs, however, incorporate the latest technologies regardless of their microprocessor power, making the slower chips bottlenecks waiting to be upgraded. Consequently, the microprocessor in your computer can be the single biggest factor holding back its performance. Tasks can be processor-bound, unable to accelerate regardless of improvements you make to the rest of your system.

Tasks can be processor-bound, unable to accelerate regardless of improvements you make to the rest of your system.

The types of problems the first computers were designed to solve— calculations—are the most likely to exacerbate microprocessor limitations. Not that computers haven't gotten better at calculating, we've just demanded they solve ever-tougher problems—and more of them. The math in engineering calculations, scientific data analysis, and the geometric equations needed to process images on your monitor all stress the capabilities of your system's microprocessor.

The Intel-architecture microprocessors that IBM-standard PCs are based upon contribute to this bottleneck. Except for the latest generations—the 486DX, 486DX2, and Pentium—Intel's chips just aren't very good at math. Intel's other microprocessors are the glorified equivalent of four-function calculators squeezed onto a silicon wafer. (In fact, the first hand-held calculators were based on the predecessors of these garden-variety microprocessors.) The only mathematical functions included in their instruction sets—the repertory of commands that the microprocessor knows how to carry out—are addition, subtraction, multiplication, and division. The vast majority of commands in their instruction sets are for general-purpose operations such as manipulating data bits, comparing values of bytes and strings of characters, and following the steps of a computer program. Tough math problems, like calculating a sine or tangent function, are approximated by repeatedly carrying out simple arithmetic commands. Figuring a sine value might, for example, take tens of thousands of rudimentary steps. Suddenly, even a microprocessor that can handle millions of instructions per second strains, and system response correspondingly slows.

How to break through this kind of bottleneck? You have two strategies: make the microprocessor carry out its appointed tasks more quickly or make it more efficient at evaluating transcendental and other high-level math functions. You can use both strategies to make practical PC upgrades.

With most newer PCs, you can upgrade your present microprocessor to a faster one with an Intel OverDrive upgrade, but most older PCs make no provision for exchanging microprocessors; nor can you just speed up the existing microprocessor with an electronic form of amphetamines (at least in most cases), because every microprocessor has a maximum rated speed. Most computer makers exploit the top speeds of the solid-state components they put in their PCs, and some less reputable manufacturers may actually operate chips at speeds in excess of their ratings, sacrificing reliability. When a chip is already running at top speed, you can't (or at least shouldn't) push it faster.

A more practical alternative is to upgrade to a microprocessor that can handle higher speeds. Just popping out a microprocessor and inserting another works only with OverDrives and a few other special cases. You can make an effective upgrade by swapping out all the speed-determining circuitry in your system and microprocessor in a single swipe by replacing its system board. Alternately, you can plug a new microprocessor and its support circuitry into an expansion slot. Chapter 3, "Microprocessors and Motherboards," discusses these strategies in greater detail.

Although you can't saw off the top of a microprocessor and tinker with its insides to make it more efficient, you can augment its math capabilities by adding a numeric coprocessor (or "floating-point unit") to your older system if it's based on a 486SX or any microprocessor less than a 486. Because of production and pricing concerns, Intel in effect sliced most of its old microprocessors in half. One half is the general-purpose microprocessor that your PC is based upon. The other half, the numeric coprocessor, performs all those transcendental operations that the general-purpose circuitry cannot fathom. The two halves were meant to work together, but in the early days, microprocessors were not cost-effective to produce as a single chip. The resulting piece of silicon would have been too big to be affordable and would offer benefits only to users needing transcendental functions. Only with the introduction of the 486 were these functions finally mated again. If you don't have a coprocessor in your PC and the work you do involves transcendentals, the coprocessor is the quickest and most useful (though hardly the least

When a chip is already running at top speed, you can't (or at least shouldn't) push it faster.

expensive) upgrade you can make. Chapter 4, "Coprocessor Upgrades," tells you more.

Bus Bottlenecks

Sometimes, other bottlenecks prevent your PC's microprocessor from fully stretching its legs. Slower parts of your system may be unable to supply the microprocessor with data as fast as it can process it, so the microprocessor must wait for the rest of the system to catch up. The problem might lie with peripherals that can't find, create, or transmit the data before the microprocessor yearns for more.

Because most applications you're likely to run on your PC use data that must be moved from place to place, instead of data that stays strictly within the microprocessor, the transfer of information can be a significant performance limit. The more the microprocessor needs to access information, the more constraining the data transfer bottleneck becomes.

The more the microprocessor needs to access information, the more constraining the data transfer bottleneck becomes.

In most PCs, that delivery system is the *expansion bus*. The bus gives the microprocessor access to expansion board circuitry and all the peripherals connected to it including input/output ports, the monitor (through display memory), the hard and floppy disks, and sometimes even expansion memory. In these systems, the speed at which information is transferred across the bus *could* be a bottleneck.

In traditional PCs—those that use the XT or AT expansion bus rather than innovations such as Micro Channel Architecture, Enhanced Industry Standard Architecture (EISA), or local bus designs—the microprocessor takes command of system operation and expects the rest of your PC's circuitry to serve its needs whenever it wants. When the microprocessor needs a particular byte of data—whether from memory, disk, or keyboard—it single-mindedly waits until that data is dished up to it. The rest of the system comes to a halt without the microprocessor telling it what to do.

The support circuitry around the microprocessor serves these obstinate, single-minded demands without delay because it is designed to match microprocessor speed and always be ready when a request is made. But when the microprocessor or the support circuitry has to send out for data (or send data out), it waits patiently for it as if it were a home-delivery pizza. Eventually, the order comes, but it invariably arrives later than you want it. In the meantime, the processor cools its heels instead of its dinner.

Most of these requests are made through the system's input/output (I/O) bus, which roughly corresponds to your PC's expansion bus where peripherals plug into your system. The speed at which information moves across the expansion bus is controlled by two principal factors: the clock frequency of the bus and the number of bits of data that can be transferred in each clock cycle. Before 1992, most of the highest performance PCs had buses that operated at frequencies much lower than the clock speed of the microprocessor, as low as one-sixth its speed. Although microprocessors tick along at 50 MHz and faster, the clock speed of the buses of most PCs is slower, about 8 MHz. The reason is standardization: buses that meet the AT expansion standard never were designed for higher speeds. A faster bus would make a PC's slots off-limits to a variety of expansion boards. This standardized speed limit handicaps many systems by a factor as high as six.

The conventional AT expansion bus—the most popular PC expansion bus—has another drawback, providing only a 16-bit connection with peripherals. This is half the data-handling capacity of today's 32-bit microprocessors and one-quarter that of the 64-bit Pentium. This narrow connection can slow the movement of data by another factor of 2 or 4. As a result, when a program makes any significant use of the I/O bus, the bus speed rather than the microprocessor speed limits system performance. Such applications are called input/output-bound or I/O-bound.

In 1992, a new concept called *local bus technology* became popular. Finally, bus speed was pushed up to (or closer to) microprocessor speed. In addition, local bus designs have broadened the standard data path to a full 32 bits, matching all but the latest microprocessors, with options to embrace 64-bit Pentium data. PCs made before 1992—and even many new machines built without thought to local bus technology—can break through the bus bottleneck by converting to a local bus using a motherboard upgrade. See Chapter 3, "Microprocessors and Motherboards."

Special circuitry can be designed into the bus master that's actually faster than the general-purpose microprocessor at transferring data.

Factors other than bus speed and width often have a greater influence on I/O performance. In conventional systems, the microprocessor controls the movement of each byte across the bus. That in itself can be a speed limit because the overhead associated with each byte transferred can be many clock cycles. When printing, for example, moving a single byte across the expansion bus can require 500 to 1,000 separate microprocessor operations. This overhead can swamp all the other factors constraining bus performance, making the bus bottleneck actually a microprocessor constraint—but one best solved by improved bus technology rather than a new microprocessor.

The trick is to break the linkage between the microprocessor and the bus, putting some other component in control rather than the microprocessor. A technique called *bus mastering* does exactly that. When an expansion board needs to shift data, the board itself is permitted to take control, becoming the master in control of the bus and taking over responsibility from the microprocessor. Special circuitry can be designed into the bus master that's actually faster than the general-purpose microprocessor at transferring data. Moreover, while the bus master is doing the data transfer work, it's possible for the system microprocessor to engage in another task. With such a design, your PC could do two things at the same time.

The only way around a bus bottleneck is to replace one expansion bus with another that's faster and provides more features. Any bus more advanced than the AT bus gives your PC the capability to handle bus mastering.

Despite all the vile canards spread about the shortcomings of the old AT expansion bus, except in a few particular cases (video and mass storage) it is usually not the biggest I/O bottleneck in most PCs. Even though the AT bus is slower than the microprocessor, things connected to the bus drag down performance even further. Most PC peripherals are hard pressed to achieve even the data transfer rate of the 16-bit AT expansion bus, let alone the rates achieved by the latest local bus designs. Systems with such peripherals are also I/O bound, but by the peripherals themselves rather than the expansion bus. They require a different speedup strategy—replacing the slow peripheral.

Any bus more advanced than the AT bus gives your PC the capability to handle bus mastering.

Memory Bottlenecks

Memory is generally considered an extension of the microprocessor. The two are intimately connected, both electrically and logically. Nearly everything that the microprocessor does involves memory, but your system's microprocessor and its memory are not necessarily matched optimally. The memory in some machines can be the biggest bottleneck in the path to better performance.

Memory bottlenecks arise because all memory is not the same. It varies in how it is connected to the microprocessor and how fast it can operate. In old-fashioned PCs, memory chips were connected almost directly to the microprocessor. Only a few support chips stood in the way of a direct connection. With such an arrangement, the memory was essentially an extension of the microprocessor, reacting at the same speed as the chip and holding back nothing.

The memory in some machines can be the biggest bottleneck in the path to better performance.

Even when memory was relegated to the expansion bus instead of being nestled next to the microprocessor on the system board, performance impact was minimal. After all, in early machines the bus operated at the same clock speed as the microprocessor.

Faster 286-based PCs and all 386-based and more powerful machines pushed the microprocessor clock well beyond the rate that the expansion bus could reliably operate. Consequently, when memory is dropped into an expansion slot in one of these machines, it hits processing throughput hard. This memory slows the system every time the bus in which the card is mounted is accessed.

The only way around this problem is to avoid using the slow expansion bus for memory expansion. Modern PCs do exactly that, locating all memory on the system board if possible. Because system boards are limited physically in the number of memory chips or modules that they can accommodate, computer manufacturers devised special proprietary expansion boards for memory that operated at microprocessor speed. For top performance, these slots rather than normal expansion slots must be used for memory expansion.

Not all memory chips can operate at the same high clock speeds as the fastest microprocessors. In fact, the most common dynamic RAM chips lag far behind microprocessors. Although some exotic strategies have been used to better match slow chips to fast microprocessors, they are far from perfect. Some systems enable you to improve this match by adding memory cache boards—blocks of high-speed memory that insulate the microprocessor from slower RAM. The larger the memory cache, the better the performance you can expect from your system. Adding a memory cache to a system with support for it helps bring the system up to its potential. You'll find other memory optimization strategies discussed in Chapter 5; memory caching is considered along with microprocessor upgrades in Chapter 3.

Disk Bottlenecks

Hard disk systems are notorious for the delays they add when you want to access information. Most of the sluggishness in the response of a disk system can be attributed to the mechanical basis of disk storage. Unlike solid-state memory such as your system's RAM, all disks impose a slight delay period (called *latency*) while they spin around to find the byte the system requires. The read/write head hangs over the disk, and the disk itself must spin each bit into position under the head. On average, the desired bit is half a revolution away. At the once-standard spin rate of 3,600 rpm, that works out to about 13 milliseconds, compared to the nanoseconds (billionths of a second) required to find a bit in solid-state memory. Even today's quickest disks struggle to spin twice as fast as the old 3,600 rpm standard, which still makes their latency thousands of times longer than that of all-electronic RAM.

In addition to this initial latency, the hard disk causes more waiting as its head meanders laterally across the disk to zero in on the track containing the needed information. This delay, called the average access time of the disk, may range from a dozen to a hundred milliseconds. Compare, again, the nanosecond-level access time of solid-state memory. At best, locating a byte on disk is at least a thousand times slower than finding it in electronic memory.

At best, locating a byte on disk is at least a thousand times slower than finding it in electronic memory.

As a result, on applications that require repeated access to random disk information, disk access delays can swamp other aspects of system performance. Your system's microprocessor could be racing along, executing tens of millions of instructions per second. When it bumps into a command to read from the hard disk, sparks fly from its brakes as the system grinds to a halt and waits until the disk drive responds. Thousands of instructions might have been carried out in the same length of time. Instead, your system whiles away its time and any investment you've made in a faster microprocessor.

After the disk head locates the information your microprocessor needs, the disk drive still needs to transfer the data to the microprocessor. Most disks are linked to their system hosts through the expansion bus and suffer all the constraints imposed by the bus. Even worse, the disk signals must traverse an often slower data link, the hard disk interface. Although today's fastest interfaces achieve transfer rates up to about 10M per second, with 40M per second possible in the future (under new SCSI standards), the latest local bus designs boast rates three times as fast, and top-of-the-line microprocessors are faster still. Put an old-technology hard disk in a 66 MHz 486DX2 system with an AT-style expansion bus, and the microprocessor might be able to handle information about 16 times quicker than the bus and up to 50 times quicker than the hard disk. The result of such a mismatch is that the performance of your entire system can be bottled up by the disk when loading large programs or retrieving or saving big files.

A faster bus alone won't speed up disk data transfer performance. Upgrade to a twice-as-fast hard disk, and you'll cut your waiting time nearly in half.

Note that the disk transfer rate bottleneck is lodged squarely in the disk subsystem rather then in the expansion bus. A faster bus alone won't speed up disk data transfer performance. One solution is simply to get a faster disk. Upgrade to a twice-as-fast hard disk, and you'll cut your waiting time nearly in half. You can gain similar improvements by upgrading to a hard disk that uses an advanced interface with a higher data transfer rate.

Some applications lend themselves to another form of disk acceleration: disk caching (not to be confused with memory caching, previously discussed). The disk cache is a block of solid-state RAM that dynamically duplicates some of the contents of the disk. If your system's microprocessor requires disk-based data that's duplicated in the disk cache, the disk cache can deliver it at RAM speed rather than the mechanical speed of the disk drive. The increase in speed can be dramatic, potentially a thousandfold improvement.

A disk cache is not a perfect panacea for disk bottlenecks in all applications. Your disk-based data must be loaded into the cache, and the cache can fill no faster than the disk is ordinarily read. When your applications repeatedly read the same information from disk, your data can be lodged there and almost instantly relayed. But when new matter must be read from disk memory, the cache offers little improvement. In other words, the cache can provide big benefits when your software is fixated on particular pieces of disk data (reading a library file when compiling a program or sorting a database) but fails if you need long tracts of file information that you use only once (for example, moving a bit-image graphics file from disk to screen).

Typically, the faster cache is the smarter one, anticipating the data you'll need by judging from your past information requirements.

One of the principal differences between disk caches is how they get information from disk to RAM. Typically, the faster cache is the smarter one, anticipating the data you'll need by judging from your past information requirements. Two main types of disk cache have found favor in PCs: software caches and hardware caches.

Software caches run in the background on your PC and appropriate a block of your system's extended or expanded memory for data storage. Software caches are inexpensive, generally simple to install, and easy to use. Sometimes, however, they are incompatible with certain programs. Software caches are discussed in Chapter 2, along with other speed-up strategies that don't require a hardware investment.

Hardware caches are usually built into so-called *caching disk controllers*, more properly called *caching host adapters* when using modern interface disk systems. These expansion boards use their own RAM to store disk information and, typically, use a microprocessor to manage the disk cache and keep the most often-demanded data in the cache. Caching disk controllers tend to be expensive because they use large blocks of RAM but can be very effective in agreeable applications. Caching controllers are discussed along with hard disks in Chapter 7.

Display Bottlenecks

One unexpected bottleneck is your PC's display system. Far from being an innocent spectator in the race for better PC performance, the display system is right in the middle of the track—and too often lying there lifelessly. Although you might think your monitor merely reflects what your PC is accomplishing, it actually may be slowing the rest of the system down.

Although you might think your monitor merely reflects what your PC is accomplishing, it actually may be slowing the rest of the system down.

The images on your monitor originate deep inside your programs and PC. The conventional VGA display system of most older PCs requires your PC's microprocessor to determine one-by-one exactly which pixels on the screen light up and, in color systems, what hue each has. Old PCs with more primitive display systems—monochrome MDA, CGA, or EGA—work the same way. With VGA, your system has 307,200 dots to control. The display can change up to 60 times a second, and the microprocessor must manage it all while juggling everything else it has to do, from running the bus to executing programs. Push on-screen resolution up to today's popular 1,024-by-768 level, and you have 786,432 dots to move.

The problem is compounded because, to put any image on your monitor, your PC must route the data through its I/O bus. That means more bus-control instructions and sometimes squeezing through an eight-bit interface to get to the screen, an interface that often adds dozens of wait states to your microprocessor. Worse, putting characters on the screen and moving them is a complex process involving many layers of software instructions, piled on by both your system's Basic Input/Output System (BIOS) and DOS, which together force your microprocessor to grind through an arm's length list of code to display each character. That's more work and more waiting.

The killer is that video slowdown is the most visible ill that can afflict your PC. Even when it takes a fraction of a second longer to paint an image on the screen, you'll notice it. When the characters start popping on the screen as if they were fired by a machine gun stuck in molasses, you'll realize your PC isn't running as fast as it could.

*Video slowdown is
the most visible ill
that can afflict your
PC.*

Almost every program uses your PC's display system, but different applications put different demands on it. Text-based programs take the least work, minimizing the amount of data that must be manipulated by limiting it to 4,000 characters and attributes per screen. Graphics programs (and text-based programs that run in graphics mode), take a very heavy toll on your system's processing time. Heavy-duty graphics, including desktop publishing, computer-aided drafting (CAD), and presentation graphics require the most from your system and are most likely to contribute to the display system bottleneck. Your system's performance when running these applications is likely to be limited by your display system or combination of display system and microprocessor.

Several different approaches can help speed up on-screen displays as well as your system. You can substitute optimized display instructions for the laggardly commands in your BIOS or a display list driver for CAD programs, as noted in Chapter 2, or you can install a new display adapter with a wider interface for faster operation. You can add a graphic accelerator to relieve your system's microprocessor from dot-moving detail, or you can opt for the latest local bus technology to break the bus bottleneck—at the price of installing a new system board.

Printing Bottlenecks

*When you turn
your computer
loose on a print
job, it wastes most
of its processing
power just waiting
for your printer to
catch up.*

Printers suffer an overhead affliction similar to that of graphic displays, but printers compound the problem with their own physical limitations. In a PC, moving a single character to your printer using the system's built-in BIOS instructions can take a series of 500 commands. Multiply that by the amount of information on a full page of bit-mapped laser-printed graphics, and the entire processing capacity of an older generation microprocessor such as a 286 is used up quickly.

As with hard disks, printers are mechanical devices and suffer mechanical delays. For example, most printers can deal with data only as fast as they can pound, burn, or blaze it on paper, as much as one thousand to ten thousand times slower than your computer can generate it. When you turn your computer loose on a print job, it wastes most of its processing power just waiting for your printer to catch up.

Any application that makes you sit and watch an unchanging screen while your printer putters along likely suffers from a printing bottleneck. A faster printer is the most straightforward cure, but also probably the most wasteful. Software often can free up your microprocessor for other tasks while data slowly is reeled out to your printer. A print spooler utility divides your system's time between printing and other applications so that you can do two things at the same time. Print spoolers are so useful that all of the latest operating systems (Windows, OS/2 and most network operating systems) have built-in spooling capabilities. Software-based print spoolers, however, don't do anything about the overhead required by printing instructions. Moreover, they penalize you because the time required to manage the spooler is stolen from whatever other application you want to run.

Hardware solutions are often better and faster at eliminating printing bottlenecks. An external print buffer, often packaged as part of a printer sharing device, can make your printer look lightning-fast to your PC. A properly designed buffer accepts data output from your PC as fast as it can be ushered to your printer port. If you have an advanced expansion bus in your PC, you also can cut the microprocessor overhead by upgrading to a bus master printer adapter. These upgrade options are discussed in Chapter 2.

Network Bottlenecks

Networks typically compound PC performance problems because information shared on the network is handled by at least two PCs en route to being used. For example, should you need a specific record from the corporate database, you'll have to wait while a command to retrieve that record is sent from your PC through the network to its server. Then the hard disk in the server searches out the record (imposing its average access delays) and copies the record to the server's network adapter—through the server's expansion bus. Then the record travels down the network pike, which operates at a fraction of the speed of the typical system board expansion bus, perhaps waiting along the way for other network traffic to clear. Finally, when it arrives back at your PC, the record traverses the expansion bus again from the network adapter to your microprocessor. Any one of these steps holds a potential bottleneck.

Far and away the slowest part of any network is the wiring linking the nodes or the server. Except for fiber optics, all network wiring schemes operate at transfer rates many times slower than even system board bus speeds. Most Ethernet systems have a peak transfer rate of 1.25M per second but cannot sustain lengthy transfers at that rate

The bus speed of an ancient AT-style computer is more than four times faster than basic Ethernet.

across an active network line. Other less sophisticated networking schemes like Arcnet, StarLAN, and zero-slot (serial- or parallel port-based) systems are even slower. The bus speed of an ancient AT-style computer is more than four times faster than basic Ethernet.

Moving up to a quicker network architecture is usually impractical, in most cases requiring a complete rewiring of the entire network. Network performance can be improved, however, by taking advantage of individual PC upgrades on the nodes and servers in the network. You can work around the wiring bottleneck itself by changing your usage strategies on your PCs, cutting network traffic by keeping more tasks within the node instead of reaching out across the network line.

Human Bottlenecks

When the patience of your PC is being tried, usually the system is waiting not for memory or a disk to respond but for a touch of the keyboard.

The most nagging of bottlenecks in the day-to-day operation of most PCs is the one over which you have the most control but the least potential for improvement: you. Your typing, your decisions about each keystroke and each move of the mouse, the thoughts that surge and course and curse through your mind, all slow down your PC more than the anchor of an XT hard disk or a video system left over from Lee de Forest's vacuum tube experiments. When the patience of your PC is being tried, usually the system is waiting not for memory or a disk to respond but for a touch of the keyboard. When you press a key, maybe a million circuits swing into action and for a fraction of a second, your computer is filled with electronic excitement. Then, as quick as the flurry of activity begins, the character is recognized, the system determines whether it needs to carry out some advanced action, and most likely falls back into a semiconductor slumber, quietly awaiting the next disturbance of its nap.

When you use some word processing or spreadsheet applications, the performance of your system is limited by how fast you can move the cursor around the screen. Hold down the cursor key and see how long it takes to move between cells or paragraphs. Each repeat of the keystroke comes at a predefined interval that can be devilishly long when you're at the bottom-left cell and want to be at the top right. Although you might be able to make movements more quickly using a mouse, the delays are still substantial compared to the possible performance of your computer's microprocessor. You still may spend a fraction of a second on a simple movement, during which your microprocessor might have carried out a million instructions.

Breaking through the bottleneck at the human interface can be a ticklish job. A serious dose of caffeine—say a double espresso—may quicken your reactions, but it never will get you up to electronic speed. You can try thinking faster, and eventually you can learn to type faster, but there are a few better ways of broadening the human bottleneck even if you can't break through entirely.

Software can help speed up repetitive tasks. Write a macro, and you can run your weekly analyses with 1-2-3 at superhuman speeds. Macros—as well as style sheets, canned paragraphs, and letters—also help speed up text entry and printing with your word processor. You also can speed up the response of your keyboard or send your mouse ballistic. Although these tricks (and others in the next chapter) won't get you quite in step with the fleet thoughts of your PC, they'll help you get more done faster. And that, of course, is what you bought your PC for.

Macros—as well as style sheets, canned paragraphs, and letters—also help speed up text entry and printing with your word processor.

Locating the Bottlenecks

Before you can uncap a system bottleneck, you need to find out what computer demon is holding up the job. There's often little evidence to go by (other than your computer being slower than you want it to be). It's like identifying a perpetrator from fingerprints left after a snowball fight: the process takes time, observation, insight— and more than a little inspired guesswork.

The process takes time, observation, insight—and more than a little in- spired guesswork.

On the other hand, your intuition can be surprisingly accurate. If you feel like you're waiting too long for things to happen—for numbers to pop up in spreadsheet cells, for files to open and save, for your screen to change, for your life to go on—something in your PC may benefit from an upgrade. Also, you may know that you need something more just by looking at the various computer magazines. You might realize that you need the latest and best microprocessor, disk, and display.

Sometimes, these intuitive feelings expose a real need for an upgrade, but none are as definitive as testing your PC for weak spots. You can round up all the suspects and start the paper rolling through the polygraph, questioning them all until the instrument points to the prime suspect. Likewise, you can be sure where the bottlenecks are by scientifically monitoring the operation of your programs using special software tools.

No matter how you elect to locate your system's bottlenecks, the starting place is the same: your applications. Determine which program you use most, the one whose faster operation would benefit you most. Consider how that application uses your PC. You need to know what your primary program is doing, what system resources it requires, and how you use the program. What follows are several tests and observations that can help you find where the bottlenecks in your PC lurk.

Verifying Processing Bottlenecks

Only after you eliminate the other possibilities can you be sure that you're suffering from a processor bottleneck.

To determine whether your PC is plagued by a processing bottleneck, start by checking the response of your system using the software you normally run. If, after you press a keystroke that initiates a recalculation or computation, you can play a round of golf before an answer appears, the program probably is testing the microprocessor power of your system. If your system doesn't do anything else while performing the calculation—the display doesn't change and the disk activity light does not come on—you almost certainly have an application limited by processor performance. Often, however, other forces conspire to slow your system down. In many cases, they may have more of an effect than your system's microprocessor. Only after you eliminate the other possibilities can you be sure that you're suffering from a processor bottleneck.

Checking Your Disk

If you don't have a hard disk, your system is old enough to require a complete replacement to get you up to speed.

One likelihood is a disk bottleneck. Some statistical packages may require reading data from disk, and language compilers may require constant access to disk-based libraries. Loading and saving large files such as presentation graphics and the audio and video parts of multimedia displays also demand fast disk access. A slower drive often can be the major cause of your interminable waiting. To find out for sure whether inadequate disk-access performance is holding back your PC's potential, watch the red drive light on your hard disk drive or the drive light on the control panel of your PC. (If you don't have a hard disk, your system is old enough to require a complete replacement to get you up to speed.) If the drive light flashes on and off more than occasionally—perhaps so often and fast that it appears to be continuously though dimly lit—your disk is likely one of the big bottlenecks in your system.

Other types of software are notorious for their disk use and should prompt you to begin your search with a look at the drive light. In general, any application that is based on a common database package like Access, dBase, FoxPro, or Paradox is almost always more disk-intensive than processor-intensive and benefits from a low access time. Any application that creates or manages fat files stuffed with more than a few dozen kilobytes—including bit-image graphics, large CAD drawings, full-motion video, high-quality sound— demands the best disk transfer rate.

A disk with a faster access time and transfer rate also can make your system more responsive when you launch programs. If you're bothered by the slight delay between when you press a key and when your PC reacts with an on-screen change or a flutter from the disk light, a faster drive can help.

Determining Display Delays

Some bottlenecks are not restricted to a single class of software or the given operating mode. In particular, slow output can drag down the performance of nearly any application. Often, your display system is responsible for slow system response that you might attribute to the processor or disk.

Depending on how a program uses your display, your computer's video system can strangle execution speed in two ways. Watching how your software displays data on your screen helps you select the right microelectronic miracle drug.

Watching how your software displays data on your screen helps you select the right microelectronic miracle drug.

If characters appear on your screen one at a time or one line at a time (other than in response to typing on the keyboard), the program you are running likely uses DOS and your computer's BIOS to generate its display. Such programs are constrained by software overhead and will respond to add-on speed-up software. On the other hand, graphics programs and those that display screens of data in blocks typically sidestep DOS and the BIOS by writing directly to video memory. These programs are slowed by the video hardware in your system and may require new display adapter hardware to accelerate.

Any graphics program benefits from a faster display adapter.

Any graphics program benefits from a faster display adapter. If you use a graphic environment like Windows or OS/2 and your PC does not have a graphic accelerator, you may be amazed by the extra zip one can provide. When your PC is running in graphics mode, an accelerator can increase the speed as much as a notch or two up the microprocessor hierarchy. With today's software, a graphic accelerator can be considered mandatory equipment. If you don't have one, you'll want to make an upgrade.

Checking for External Delays

Applications that rely heavily on external system peripherals can face bottlenecks inside and outside of your computer. Printers handle only a few dozen to a few thousand characters per second, but computers deal with millions. Characters wanting to fly out your parallel port get bottled up waiting for your printer to peck its way through the characters preceding them. On the other hand, some print jobs, particularly those involving heavy-duty full-page graphics, draw upon your PC's full power to generate images.

Most modern software helps you avoid the system slowdown that a lagging printer creates. Many programs and most advanced operating systems incorporate built-in print spoolers designed to enable you to keep working while the print job is fed to your printer slowly and invisibly. For example, many word processors enable you to start a document printing and to resume editing. Windows and OS/2 both include their own spooling programs that organize print jobs and operate your printer in the background.

The purpose of spoolers is to return control of your system to you quickly so that your PC has more time to accept your input. Although they help hide printer-induced slowdowns, they can't completely eliminate them. As software subsystems, they steal substantial processing time from your PC. Editing may go much slower when a document is printing, for example. Because print processing must be done whether it appears in the foreground or background, the overhead does not change appreciably when a spooler is running. If your system almost stops during printing because of this overhead, improving the external connection won't help, although upgrading your microprocessor might.

On the other hand, if the software you use most often turns your PC into an unresponsive vegetable when you're printing, you may be able to cut your losses by adding a software-based print spooler or a hardware-based external printer buffer. Either breaks the printer bottleneck by simulating a faster printer.

To see how much faster your print jobs finish by using a spooler or buffer to break the printer bottleneck, note the time it takes the program you use most often to print to a file. Compare that figure to the time it takes to create hard copy directly on the printer. The difference is a good indication of the improvement you can expect from an add-in spooler or external print buffer.

Modem performance can perplex new and even some experienced PC users. What many people blame on a slow computer more often results from a slow modem connection. Determining whether your computer or your modem is aging while you wait for a screen update is simple. If you're staring helplessly at your screen while characters pop up one at a time, you're waiting for your modem. However, if you experience periods in which nothing appears on the screen—for instance, during a search or while the remote system pores through your mail—the computer at the far end of the modem connection is the cause of the delay. A faster modem can't eliminate such a delay.

Even if you are willing to put up with the slow performance of a 1,200 bps modem, an increasing number of bulletin board services (BBSs) won't.

Even if you are willing to put up with the slow performance of a 1,200 bps modem, an increasing number of bulletin board services (BBSs) won't. Many are setting their minimum speed at 2,400 bps, and some are moving to 9,600 bps or higher speeds. If you plan to stay on-line with your favorite BBS, you eventually will have to upgrade to a high-speed modem. Do it today; you'll not only be ready for the future, but you'll be able to download more files and send messages faster while waiting for the future to arrive.

Checking the Human Interface

Although the class of software you run is a rough guide to the slow spots in your system, how you use your programs also affects where bottlenecks appear. For example, databases only bottle up during sorts and other reporting functions. Many database operations (such as input and revision) won't strain your disk system much—they are limited by how fast you can press keys to enter data or make commands.

Any application that requires you to type in large amounts of data will be limited by the speed of your fingers on the keyboard.

In fact, any application that requires you to type in large amounts of data—be it a mailing list or other database, spreadsheet, statistical analysis, or word processor—at some time or another will be limited by the speed of your fingers on the keyboard. At other times, however, these same keyboard-intensive applications may demand other system facilities. For example, you might use a word processor just to search for keywords, paste together boilerplate paragraphs, or

If you use your computer chiefly to type in original materials, you and your fingers are the likely the bottleneck.

If you use your software merely to read or pull large blocks of data together, don't blame the keyboard for keeping you in low gear.

check spelling. Instead of the keyboard, your disk then might limit the performance of your system. Instead of being keyboard-bound, your system may put your disk into action as the machine scans for obscure words. What you do most with your system determines where shattering the bottleneck is most effective.

Here are a few simple rules. If you use your computer chiefly to type in original materials—that is, you deal in data input—you and your fingers are the likely bottleneck. Typing lessons, practice, or hiring a pair of faster hands are your best bet for speeding up throughput. If you do more editing than input, the keyboard could still hold you back, particularly if you press a lot of cursor keys. However, speed-up software or an alternate input device—mouse, trackball, or digitizing tablet—may help accelerate your thoughts. (Of course, if you work in a modern graphics environment, you *need* a pointing device.) If you use your software merely to read or pull large blocks of data together, don't blame the keyboard for keeping you in low gear.

Scientific Determination of Bottlenecks

If casual but informed observation still leaves you guessing where your system bottlenecks are, you can try some tests to determine their location.

Many users take the manufacturer's word on system performance. They get a 33 MHz system but don't realize that it adds 20 wait states, null processing cycles programmed to allow components to catch up with the CPU, to all video accesses or 4 or 5 wait states to every memory access on bus. Without some benchmark or another system to compare to, there is no real way to judge your system's performance unless it's something very noticeable. Benchmarking programs, therefore, can lend a hand.

The leading commercial benchmarking application is Power Meter, published by DiagSoft, Inc. (Scotts Valley, California). This package includes a full spate of tests for every aspect of system performance. One of its features, its database for managing your evaluation results, is particularly helpful in comparing systems.

Another commercial program, Personal Measure from Spirit of Performance (Harvard, Massachusetts), also provides clear points of reference. When run in the background, this inexpensive program monitors the operation of any application you select and gives you a graphic display as well as printed reports of the time spent using your microprocessor, disk, keyboard, printer, and auxiliary ports. One look, and you can tell exactly where the bottlenecks are.

A number of benchmarking programs are available for free; Ziff-Davis Labs provides some of the best. Ziff-Davis Labs is the testing arm of Ziff-Davis Publishing, which publishes *PC Magazine, PC Computing, Computer Shopper*, and several other computer magazines. Their latest benchmarks are available at little or no cost through ZiffNet (the electronic publishing arm of Ziff-Davis) and often from local bulletin board services. Besides the Ziff-Davis Labs benchmarks, your local board may offer other benchmarking programs.

Benchmarking programs help you identify the slower components in your system, although they cannot locate the actual hardware-software interactions that cause true bottlenecks. Nevertheless, if you find a slow hard disk or display system in your otherwise fast computer, you've found a candidate for upgrade.

Although identifying system slowdowns sounds complex, you can probably sort through the candidates in less than an hour, faster with the aid of this specialized software. The short time you spend in your search will reap you a large reward. Your system will be more responsive, and you'll get more done every minute you use it. Your PC just may become fun to work with again.

The Usual Suspects

Every application uses a different mix of the resources available in your PC. Different applications may run into different bottlenecks. Although removing all bottlenecks so that you're blocked only by the final brick wall certainly speeds up your PC, selective upgrading is more cost-effective—if you can narrow down the number of upgrades that you need. As most people regularly use a small number of applications—from one to eight, depending on the source you believe—a selective upgrade aimed at one or two specific applications may be all you need.

A selective up-grade aimed at one or two specific applications may be all you need.

If a scientific look at where your PC resources are strained yields unsatisfying results—maybe it tells you that *everything* in your PC is slow—or if you would just rather work with your PC than diagnose and measure it, some general guidelines can help you zero in on the likely bottlenecks in your system and its software. After you eliminate the usual suspects, you'll be on your way to renewing your beautiful friendship with your PC.

Microsoft Windows

Once upon a time, Microsoft thought Windows could run on any and every PC in the world. Version 3.0 would give a valiant try on any system with at least 1M of memory, extended or expanded, and just about any microprocessor. Not that you would be happy running the program on your ancient machine, but at least it would work. Since Version 3.1, however, the hurdles are higher—and often out of the range of older systems.

Windows greedily sucks up just about any upgrade you give your PC.

To start 3.1, you need a 386SX, about 4M of RAM, and a hard disk. Starting Windows and being happy with it are two different ideas. Windows greedily sucks up just about any upgrade you give your PC. Some, however, still reward you with pleasantly enhanced speed.

There are four critical areas for Windows upgrades: memory, microprocessor, disk, and graphics. Which yields the most improvement for the least expense depends on what you do and expect with Windows.

If you do a lot of context-switching—moving between Windows applications—then a memory upgrade should be the first step to take. Windows relies on virtual disk technology when it runs out of memory, using a *swap file* on your hard disk to hold what won't fit in your system RAM. You end up waiting however long the disk takes to respond. Add more RAM, and Windows won't have to do the swapping. Switching between applications then occurs at RAM speed. Windows' response time substantially improves with about 8M of memory. For most people, 16M should be sufficient for today's Windows applications.

The general rule is to give Windows the fastest microprocessor you can afford.

A faster microprocessor speeds up all aspects of Windows. The general rule is to give Windows the fastest microprocessor you can afford. Often, however, the expense of a microprocessor upgrade may override your making it. An OverDrive upgrade may nearly double Windows' speed, but the price may be dear—on the order of $500. You can get as much or more *apparent* improvement in other ways.

A faster disk loads Windows and its applications more quickly. It also speeds up switching between applications if you don't add to Windows' basic memory requirements. Give Windows memory to spare, however, and a faster disk benefits only those applications that are traditionally disk dependent: programming, bit-image graphics, and databases.

Because Windows is a graphic operating environment, it can be constrained severely by the performance of your PC's display system. A graphic accelerator (with or without a local bus connection) can help. The added visual snap often makes Windows seem like you've upgraded its microprocessor, but there's an important difference. The graphics accelerator only speeds up what you see, but a faster microprocessor accelerates what you see *and* what you get from your programs. With a quick chip, programs find results and respond with greater dispatch.

The graphics accelerator only speeds up what you see, but a faster microprocessor accelerates what you see and what you get from your programs.

OS/2

Like Windows, OS/2 has developed an increasing appetite for system resources as it has evolved. The latest versions have much the same requirements as Windows 3.1 (although you'll need more memory to get going). OS/2 also benefits from the same upgrade strategies as Windows: memory, microprocessor, disk, and graphics.

Just to get OS/2 off the ground, you'll need at least a 286 microprocessor for Versions through 1.4 and a 386SX for 2.0 or later. You'll also need 2M of RAM for Version 1.3, 8M for 2.0, and 4M for Version 2.1. If you can afford more, you'll get better response, particularly when you engage in multitasking. Although you may not need a larger, faster hard disk, the High Performance File System of OS/2 Versions 1.2 and later help you take advantage of greater capacity. A graphic accelerator speeds response when you run in graphics mode.

Word Processing and Desktop Publishing

Ask any writer—working with words strains your mind more than your PC. A brain transplant might yield the most acceleration, but improving your PC could remove enough frustrations to enable you to think more clearly.

If all you do is type, think finger exercises instead of system up-grades.

Most word processors are used as data-entry programs. Most of what you do is thus limited by your own very human typing limitations. Even the slowest 8088-based computers are fast enough to keep pace with your keystrokes. If all you do is type, think finger exercises instead of system upgrades.

Today's word processors do more than just accept your keystrokes. Previewing documents takes processor and display horsepower to put all those dots on the screen. Graphics-based word processors—any that run under Windows, for example—take substantially more power than traditional text-based ones and benefit from anything you do to improve Windows overall. You'll need more than 8088 or 286 power just to get them running, and a faster microprocessor helps make these programs more responsive. A faster display system helps improve the response time of graphics-based word processors.

If you work with large documents or often switch between small files, a faster hard disk may help. Word processors, however, are capable of loading most documents entirely into memory, so the only time you feel the pinch of a slow disk is when you save.

Activities ancillary to word processing can demand greater system power. For example, most spell-checkers still scan a disk-based file when they encounter an abstruse word. A quick disk (or a large disk cache or RAM disk emulator) can speed up the spell-checking process.

Move up to print preparation and genuine desktop publishing, and word processing changes character entirely. After you start moving text around, wrapping it in a graphic display, and pulling in drawings and pictures, you're dealing with graphical editing rather than word processing. Anything that improves graphic perfor-mance—which means darned near anything you do to your PC—speeds things up. The needs are essentially the same as Windows. After all, most publishing programs now run under Windows (or pretend like they do!).

Databases

Databases are the preeminent example of disk-intensive programs. Most computer gurus tell you that a typical database sort causes more activity than a fire in a popcorn factory. Sorting sends the disk head hopping everywhere across the disk platter, making a hard disk with a low average access time best.

Although it is true that a database sort is one of the most disk-intensive things you can do with your PC, most of the time your database program won't be sorting. Before you can sort data, you have to add it to your database, and that means typing it. The program will be sitting around waiting for *you*. As with word processors, when typing into a database, you probably won't strain even the most long-in-the-tooth PC. You can get by with a slow PC for data entry, and it even may work for sorting if you do it only occasionally and don't mind spending your afternoon shopping or fishing while your computer completes its job.

If you keep your databases under a megabyte or two, you can gain much more speed from memory than from a faster disk. Devote the memory to a software disk cache, and you can sort at near-RAM speed. A faster microprocessor accelerates the sort further.

If you jump between records when entering or editing data, a faster disk may do the trick. You'll get a quicker response finding the record you need.

The one upgrade you're likely to need with a database is a bigger hard disk to accommodate the ever-growing mass of records you'll generate. One rule of thumb is to buy a hard disk roughly twice as large as you think you'll need so that you'll run out of capacity after a few weeks rather than immediately. Today, that may mean hundreds of megabytes, but along with the extra capacity, you'll get a bonus. By moving up to a modern, large-capacity hard disk, you can gain access and transfer speed to trim sorting and reporting time.

By moving up to a modern, large-capacity hard disk, you can gain access and transfer speed to trim sorting and reporting time.

Spreadsheets

If any program would benefit from a numeric coprocessor, you would think it would be the spreadsheet. Look deeper, however, and you'll see that most spreadsheet data involves integers and simple math—that is, dollars and cents that you try to make add up. Math coprocessors, however, excel at manipulating floating-point numbers, in which the decimal moves around as needed so that significant digits are taken into account in the calculation. They work better with complicated transcendental operations than simple addition. The math match between spreadsheets and coprocessors simply isn't very good.

Philosophical differences aside, a coprocessor can be a worthy addition because they bring some improvement in overall perfor-mance, and they are cheap. For example, a floating-point processor

*A faster micropro-
cessor cuts the time
your spreadsheet
takes for recalcula-
tions—and just
about everything
else you do with
the spreadsheet.*

*Except when
you've got an
ancient absurdity
like an 8088 with
128K, you should
have no problem
exploring the
reaches of today's
spreadsheets.*

like a 387 can be a worthwhile investment in speed. For about $100, you can get 30 to 80 percent more speed from most spreadsheets with a math chip, at least on operations that are not limited by some other bottleneck (such as your data input speed).

Microprocessors handle integer operations just fine, so a faster microprocessor cuts the time your spreadsheet takes for recalculations—and just about everything else you do with the spreadsheet. The only drawback is that microprocessor upgrades are generally more costly than coprocessors (except with the 486 when they are essentially the same thing).

Another reason you might want to upgrade your PC is if you are running out of cells in your spreadsheet. More memory might seem like a quick way of getting more space on your spreadsheet. Unfortunately, that's rarely the case. Except when you've got an ancient absurdity like an 8088 with 128K, you should have no problem exploring the reaches of today's spreadsheets. Most now use virtual memory or related techniques to reach where your RAM can't go. Moreover, if your spreadsheet data starts straining at the periphery of your program, you're better off restructuring the spreadsheet instead of rebuilding your PC. A spreadsheet beyond the reach of a state-of-the-art program is probably also beyond human comprehension. Break it up into logical pieces that you can link—upgrade your thinking instead of your system.

Application Development

If you write software, you probably know what you need—the biggest, best, and most powerful computer possible. Compiling programs is a microprocessor-intensive task. If you've been writing software for a while, you probably know all the tricks, like putting your compiler and libraries on a fast solid-state RAM disk. If you do that, you probably want as much memory as possible in your PC to allow for the largest possible disk (or at least one large enough to contain your language files).

If you prefer to work from your hard disk or are forced to because of the size of the libraries involved, you want to upgrade to a hard disk with a low average access time. Your compiler will be digging for data from what you've written, and to the compiler, your writing will look random.

Computer-Aided Design

Drafting and drawing programs tax your PC more than any other kind of software. Design programs dig deeply into graphics to show you what you're doing but also tax your PC's math capabilities because they have to compute every dot they display as well as the details of every stroke you draw. Because a drawing quickly gets huge, CAD programs need memory and disk space galore when you need to save your work. Every aspect of your PC can be pressed to its limit by CAD.

Because CAD programs are number-intensive applications—both in the data they generate and the need to calculate individual pixels— they need the calculating horsepower only supplied by the quickest numeric coprocessors. Most CAD programs require a coprocessor just to load. To take care of the rest of the details of their operation—all those non-numeric operations, of which there will be many—you also want the fastest microprocessor you can fit in your system. If your PC is one generation behind in microprocessor, upgrade or replace it immediately. The new microprocessor's faster response will help you get more done in your working day.

Upgrade to as much memory as you can afford. Many CAD programs have threshold memory values. Although the programs operate with less RAM (often by using virtual memory, substituting disk space for RAM), after you reach a certain level of RAM, performance improves dramatically. That's why CAD programs often have listed minimum and recommended memories. You'll want at least the recommended amount.

CAD programs are also display-intensive. After all, you have to see your work—and in as much detail as possible. Most people want the sharpest possible displays with their CAD programs, and they want display speed. Updating the screen is often the most time-consuming part of using a CAD program. All of these needs add up to one thing—an accelerated graphics adapter of some kind. Adding a graphic accelerator or coprocessor board often speeds up a CAD program more than stepping up to the next most powerful microprocessor. Local bus isn't a big advantage for CAD because most CAD programs don't move bit-images across the expansion bus. They shift only drawing commands, which a graphic accelerator or graphic coprocessor manipulates in a local frame buffer. (A frame buffer is memory on the display adapter for holding and processing certain graphc functions.)

Every aspect of your PC can be pressed to its limit by CAD.

Adding a graphic accelerator or coprocessor board often speeds up a CAD program more than stepping up to the next most powerful microprocessor.

If you plan on using CAD, you'll want the most powerful upgrades of every type for your PC.

Because CAD programs naturally create huge files, fast disks can benefit them, too, particularly disks with high data transfer rates. You want a large capacity to store all those files.

If you plan on using CAD, you'll want the most powerful upgrades of every type for your PC. If you have to buy your upgrades in order, get the display system first, then the disk, and finally the microprocessor, because by the time you get ready to buy it, a faster one probably will have come out.

2
Before You Upgrade

Odds are, you are not squeezing the best performance out of your computer in its existing configuration. A few simple tricks can help you tune up your PC without having to upgrade its hardware.

Sometimes, you can sidestep the need for a PC upgrade. For instance, you can eke out more speed from your system when it is slowed by some undesirable part. You can even gain more mass storage space without a hard disk replacement. In some cases, the improvements—often without cost—can be so dramatic that you might forget about making an upgrade.

These simple solutions rely on software. No matter what hardware you have in your PC, it will not work at its optimum if you do not take advantage of all the software features that are available. If you just boot up DOS and run your applications, you may be missing out on some of your operating system's built-in performance and storage enhancements. Installing them and turning them on takes just a few minutes but can add immensely to the power of your PC. In many cases, you can go further by taking advantage of specific commercial software.

You may be missing out on some of your operating system's built-in performance and storage enhancements.

In the long run, software features are temporary solutions; they do not enhance your system by leaps and bounds the way a microprocessor upgrade can. More importantly, they help you get more from what you have—especially after you upgrade.

*Features in the
latest versions of
DOS make tricks
that are worthwhile
with older versions
meaningless.*

Most of these tricks offer the biggest improvements for older
systems. You stand to gain more if you have an old hard disk, an old
system unit, or old software. The newest PCs and software already
incorporate advanced hardware features that take over the same jobs
as some of these software tricks but do them even better. Features in
the latest versions of DOS make tricks that are worthwhile with
older versions meaningless.

If you have been more occupied with using your PC rather than
tinkering, you may have missed some opportunities to tweak out a
bit more speed. Even if you have made an upgrade, you will probably be even more interested in getting everything you can from
your PC.

Increasing Disk Capacity

Because files can grow rampantly, the most important reason to
upgrade a hard disk is to gain storage space. Soon, even the largest
hard disk can overflow with megabytes of data. If money is an issue,
you will want to squeeze as much storage as you can from the hard
disk that is already in your system.

*Be a savage
housekeeper. Use
a hatchet instead
of a broom when
clearing disk
space.*

Take a bit of time, and you can be very successful at increasing your
disk capacity. You can easily double the amount of storage you have
available on your PC by taking advantage of even just one DOS
feature. If you are willing to devote more time to trimming, you can
gain even more storage.

The easiest, cheapest, and fastest way to get more disk space is to be
a savage housekeeper. In other words, use a hatchet instead of a
broom when clearing disk space. Delete all the files you do not use
regularly, destroy all those backup files that clutter your hard disk,
and discard those temporary files left by big programs when you exit
them with a system reboot—destroy every unnecessary byte.

Of course, if you are near the limits of your hard disk, you probably
have done that already. Maybe you do not want to delete files
because you like the convenience of having everything available on
disk whenever you need it. Maybe you know that those backup files
are there for a reason, and you want the reassurance that they can
give. Whatever the reason, you can still squeeze more space from
your disk—even without deleting files.

Disk Compression

DOS now sanctions a near-miraculous cure from crowded disks called disk compression. The free lunch of mass storage, disk compression is an elusive phenomenon with undeniable allure—run some software, and your shortage of mass storage disappears. Adding an invisible software driver to your PC can double its hard disk capacity. Compression means that you can forestall the next increment of hard disk upgrading, and when you do decide to buy, you can save a few hundred dollars by opting for a smaller capacity to get the same level of storage. Better still, compression stretches your budget so that you can get more for the same money.

The free lunch of mass storage, disk compression is an elusive phenomenon with undeniable allure.

DOS 6 makes file compression an optional feature that is easy to add. Under DOS 6, file compression is essentially invisible—you do not have to tangle with your system setup files. Because compression is now part of DOS, it is an industry standard. You can exchange compressed disks and be sure that your correspondents can read them (providing, of course, that your friends are not using a version earlier than DOS 6).

Besides DOS 6, you have several other choices for disk compression. Three major add-on compressors are available as free-standing utility packages: SuperStor Pro from Addstor Corporation; Stacker 3.0 from Stac Electronics; and XtraDrive software, XtraDrive Plus hardware, and DCP compression processor chip from Integrated Information Technology.

These compression programs work on-the-fly; that is, they intercept the data that is being sent to your disk for storage, compress it to a more compact form that takes fewer bytes to store on your hard disk, and then send the compressed data back to the disk. When you read from your disk, the compression software reverses the process. The intermediate processing step can be carried out using nothing but an add-in software utility or through a special hardware upgrade. (For example, special circuitry to handle the file compression can be built into your hard disk controller.)

The software compression scheme is less expensive but in some systems—particularly older, slower PCs—compression software can slow down disk reading and writing operations because of the extra processor overhead it imposes. Hardware compression systems, though rare and more expensive than software, increase transfer speed rather than overhead.

The magic underlying data compression is not the work of mounte-banks but conservative engineers. Most mass storage systems were designed for convenience and speed rather than maximum capacity. They store information in the form that your programs can most readily use so that your applications can read it directly without time-consuming conversions. Although that design made sense long ago when microprocessors were hard-pressed to keep up with disk drives that spun about as fast as windmills, such primitive storage strategies do not make sense in a modern world of fast 486 micro-processors.

Today, the big wait is for the disk to deliver data. With a 386 or better microprocessor, there is usually no penalty for preprocessing data to maximize storage capacity. In fact, compression processing can actually speed up data transfer, cutting the amount of data your disk drive needs to deal with. Trim the amount of data that needs to be sent to disk in half, and the effective transfer rate doubles without altering the underlying hardware. In reality, the overhead of com-pression steals into the potential acceleration, but increases of 50% in transfer rate are possible with highly compressible files.

One down side of file compression is that it puts data on your disks in a non-standard format. You cannot exchange it with coworkers and friends unless they, too, use the same compression system. (Some systems give you the option of not compressing data that is bound for floppy disks so that you can readily exchange disks with others who do not have a data compression system.) The compressed format also can be worrisome if you do not have explicit faith in the software; if the compression system makes a mistake while automati-cally extracting your files, you might lose contact with all your files on the disk. On the other hand, compression can comprise a simple security system. Even if someone steals your hard disk, they will not be able to easily read through your confidential files when they are in non-standard, compressed form (other than DOS 6).

Because data compression is a form of coding, files are stored in a form that is unreadable without the decoding algorithm. In other words, after you have squeezed your data onto disk, you need the original software (or something compatible) to pull it off. That can be worrisome to individuals who do not want to trust their data to the vagaries of computer software companies. Moreover, a single bit-error in a file can multiply and make reconstruction difficult or impossible. Fortunately, these three products are accepted well enough that such worries should be unnecessary.

Compression processing can actually speed up data transfer, cutting the amount of data your disk drive needs to deal with.

In reality, the overhead of compression steals into the potential acceleration.

Conventional disk utilities do not take well to the vagaries of compression programs; they do not know the odd disk structure they use and cannot properly defragment files. Consequently, SuperStor Pro, Stacker, and Xtradrive include the needed utilities, including defragmentation.

The secret formula used by all disk compressors is pattern matching. The compression program scans the data you send to disk for recurring patterns at the byte or block level and assigns each complex pattern a simple token (or symbol). After the token and its definition (the original pattern) is stored, further occurrences of the pattern are saved as the token alone. When decompressing the data, the program simply substitutes the original data for its token.

The effectiveness of this strategy varies with the data being compressed. Bit-image graphic files often have large areas with little detail that compress by factors of eight or more. Compressed graphic files (for example, the GIF files you might download from a bulletin board) already have the fat rendered out, so they do not compress at all. In fact, precompressed files can give compression software indigestion, often doubling the time it takes to transfer the data to and from your disk drive.

Still, the storage increases are intriguing. On the average, you can expect to come close to the capacity-doubling increase promised by the data compression vendors. Some graphic files squeeze down to 10 percent of their original size. Documents, help files, and executable programs often fit in half the space.

All compression programs—including DoubleSpace in DOS 6—use a roundabout method for making more file space. They take the bulk of your disk (or any smaller amount that you designate) and convert it to a single file that holds all the compressed data. A software driver makes the file look like another disk to your PC programs. Another drive swaps drive letters so that the fake drive appears in place of the old, uncompressed drive (which gets a brand new drive letter, such as F:). Typically, you add an entry or two to your PC's CONFIG.SYS file to bring the compression system to life. One reason for the need of this strategy is to enable your PC to read the disk compression program code. If your entire hard disk were compressed, the compression code itself would be compressed, too. Your system would be unable to read the code to determine how to decompress the code to read it. Not only must the code itself be kept in the clear, so does the CONFIG.SYS file that loads the code into DOS. So, part of your hard disk must not be compressed.

Precompressed files can give compression software indigestion, often doubling the time it takes to transfer the data to and from your disk drive.

DOS 6 DoubleSpace differs from the other compression utilities only in detail. Because it was engineered as part of DOS, its driver can be added in a special, no-hassle place. It loads automatically and invisibly even before your PC reads its CONFIG.SYS file. Oddly, the DOS engineers did not take advantage of the intimate connection between file compression and the operating system to entirely eliminate the need for an uncompressed disk and driver software. Nevertheless, the DOS method is the least obnoxious among commercial compression systems.

All disk compression systems increase the complication of using your PC. With new compression programs, that penalty is fading, but it still can take a toll on your patience. The big complication of compression is the hassle of dealing with software drivers and utilities that have to be properly loaded and managed. Interaction among drivers can make every change to your system setup files a headache as the compression package tries to outmanage your setup efforts. You also get the pleasure of "mounting" and "unmounting" drives on occasion—for instance, when swapping floppy disks in and out of a drive—a complication otherwise abandoned with mainframe computers.

Some compression programs are more obnoxious than others, making system configuration changes an interesting and frustrating experience. Stacker 3.0 is the most obnoxious in this regard; it automatically undoes the changes you make to your setup files if you are not careful. (You can avoid much of the hassle by customizing your setup, but the extra steps make the complex software even more forbidding.) Version 3.1 is much improved.

Because of the unique DOS 6 architecture, it adds less trouble than other compression systems. No wonder other compression vendors are adapting their programs to replace DoubleSpace and load in exactly the same hassle-free manner.

Actually, the biggest problem you may encounter with disk compression is not how it works but getting to know it. Many essential details of disk compression software have been left undocumented— such as capacity limits. Most disk compression programs do not work with disks larger than half a gigabyte (528MB), but they do not warn of this constraint. SuperStor Pro only warns that the disk is too large during setup and refuses to do anything without ever telling you of a limit. DOS 6.0 dutifully builds the biggest compressed volume it can but does not tell you why. Only Stacker

Versions 3.0 and later expand the capacity of disk partitions, up to two gigabytes. With other disk compression systems (including DOS 6), you will have to break your hard disk into multiple partitions and compress each separately.

All disk compression systems aim to make squeezing your files easy. Run any installation program, and it will check out your hard disk, add the necessary drivers to your PC's configuration files, and compress your files down to size. DOS 6 follows this pattern. All compression programs will warn that you should back up your hard disk before you start the compression process, lest something should go awry.

If you do backup your hard disk first, you will save time and headaches by reformatting your hard disk, running the compression installation program, and then restoring all of your files back to your hard disk. The compression on-the-fly programs compress your files quicker than the first-time squeeze-what-is-there installation process and shave the defragmentation utility that DOS 6, for example, runs after the compression process. Newly restored files do not need defragmentation.

If you follow the official Microsoft installation process, you will first copy all of your DOS files to your hard disk in normal, uncompressed form and then compress them when you install the DoubleSpace software. If you try to circumvent the standard DOS installation process, you encounter error messages because DoubleSpace will not be able to find some of the program files it requires. Some of the necessary files may be unexpected. You need to make sure that the following files are in your current path to make a DoubleSpace installation:

> CHKDSK.EXE
>
> DBLSPACE.EXE
>
> DEFRAG.EXE

You probably will find it handy to keep a boot disk with these files as well as COMMAND.COM, FDISK.EXE, FORMAT.EXE, and SYS.EXE.

The actual DoubleSpace installation process is entirely push-button controlled. After you type DBLSPACE (with the above programs either on your hard disk or in the search path) the software prompts you for all the information it needs.

File Compression

Most of the wasted space in files that compression squeezes out results from redundant information.

Many people have ungrounded fears about disk compression, but there is one good reason to avoid the technology: the power of redundancy. Most of the wasted space in files that compression squeezes out results from redundant information. That is where the patterns that can be *tokenized* come from. Redundancy, however, serves a grander purpose than repeating itself over and over; it provides more secure storage. If one redundant copy is destroyed, the rest are left intact. If the master table of patterns and tokens gets corrupted, errors spread like the plague through your data. An error to a single token might get copied thousands of times throughout a file in odd and unpredictable places. The difference could be between recovering important data and losing it when a single sector is damaged on a disk.

If the master table of patterns and tokens gets corrupted, errors spread like the plague through your data.

People truly afraid of disk compression simply forego the technology and buy larger disks. They do not, however, have to entirely give up the benefits of compression. They can put it under manual control to keep command of what gets compressed and what does not. By opting to compress only the files that need to be stored, they can still save megabytes of hard disk space.

The manual alternative to disk compression is called file compression. The principal is the same as disk compression; just as you could squeeze the air out of the cereal box, you can squeeze the wasted space out of your files. Some files can be reduced to 10 percent of their original size without losing the sense of their contents.

In general, file compression works much like disk compression. But because file compression does not need to occur in *real time*— actually in a tiny slice of real time between when a program generates data bound for disk and the disk accepts it—file compression programs can use a number of alternatative squeezing techniques to crunch files down to a fraction of their initial size. The commercial file compression programs give their own delightful names to the file size reduction technologies they use—squeezing, crunching, and imploding. Of course, the name of the technique does not matter as long as it works and can be undone to restore the compressed files to their original condition.

If you need to use a file often, do not bother archiving it.

You need to be able to reverse the file compression process because compression changes the data format of the file, and thus renders the file unusable by the application that created it. The compressed files become *archive files*. Like paper archives, they are accessible only through certain methods. Accessing a paper archive means searching out some long-lost file cabinet, carefully pulling open the rusty drawer, and gingerly lifting out the papers hoping they do not turn to dust. Archive files are somewhat less trouble; you only need to extract them before you can use them with your program again. But the file archiving and recovery process does involve several manual steps: running a program to make the archive, storing the archive (and eliminating the redundant and space-wasting original), and extracting the file to use it again. If you are only keeping files just to have them and not to use them regularly, file archiving can make a lot of sense, despite the bother. If you need to use a file often, however, do not bother archiving it.

Minimizing the bother means making the compression and extraction process as quick as possible. File compression programs have made such great strides in the last few years that a typical 386 computer can compress hundreds of kilobytes in a few seconds. File archiving programs also differ in their compression efficiency. Some pack data more tightly than others, sometimes with a sacrifice in speed.

The best part of file archiving software is that some of the best programs for it are available for free or as shareware—programs that you can test for free, paying for them only when you decide you want to use them. They are generally available on computer bulletin boards. Two of the most highly regarded shareware programs are ARC from System Enhancement Associates and PKZip from PKWare.

If you decide to use file archiving software, you should take one precaution: make several backups of the software that does the file extraction. If you lose the software, all your archived data will be inaccessible.

Optimizing Available Storage Space

Whether or not you decide to compress disks or files, you can still save space by managing your storage resources. Take a bit of time to eliminate the chaff, and you will be surprised at how much wasted space you can recover from your hard disk.

Find Lost Clusters

Lost clusters subtract from the capacity of your disk without bringing you any benefit.

Sometimes, even the best programs go wrong. They may create temporary files while they operate and delete them when they are done, but sometimes the files do not get completely deleted. Although the offending name is removed from your disk's directory, the clusters used by the files may not be freed for reuse. Early versions of programs and odd combinations of software sometimes create this problem. Unfortunately, the evil process and its results are almost entirely invisible. You may never know that anything is wrong, yet space on your disk will disappear at an alarming rate. The problem is that your disk has developed a number of *lost clusters*, unused space that DOS cannot use because it thinks (erroneously) that the space is actually allocated to files. Lost clusters subtract from the capacity of your disk without bringing you any benefit.

The best way to detect lost files is with the CHKDSK utility supplied with DOS. Among the other statistics it derives from your disk is the number, if any, of lost clusters and the capacity they consume.

If CHKDSK actually finds lost clusters, it warns ominously that its /F option was not used and asks whether to convert the lost clusters into files. Without the use of the /F (for Fix) option, CHKDSK just reports on what it finds on the disk, so even if you choose to convert lost clusters into files, nothing on your disk changes. CHKDSK only reports what would happen should it make the conversion.

If you run CHKDSK and discover lost clusters, the only thing you need to do is use the /F option, typing the following command at the DOS prompt (assuming that you are logged into the drive you want to check and that the CHKDSK program is located within the reach of your current search path):

CHKDSK /F

When CHKDSK asks for your choice, tell it to convert the lost chains into files. The result will be one or more (maybe hundreds of) strangely named new files in your root directory, starting with FILE0000.CHK. The number will be incremented for each subsequent file. You then can examine the contents of these files to see whether they contain any data you want using any editor you have handy. You can even use the DOS TYPE command if you do not mind seeing a strange, hesitant display accompanied by beeps as your system attempts to echo control codes as well as text.

After you are satisfied, you have no need for the recovered files, delete them. The space they occupied—the lost clusters—will then be freed for use by other programs. In extreme cases, tens of megabytes of new file space may become available on your disk.

Archive Inactive Files

The information stored in disk files can be arranged in any of a number of different formats—at times it seems that every application uses its own. If you have ever tried to exchange files between word processors, you know the frustration of it—a letter written using one word processor when opened by another turns into a collection of smiley faces, musical notes, and playing card suits. Although some standard file formats have arisen in some application areas (dBase files, Lotus 1-2-3 files, and so on), all of these file formats have one thing in common—none is optimized to pack information on your disk as efficiently as possible. In fact, disk files are often like boxes of cereal—even when they are full, you pay for a lot of air space inside.

Disk files are often like boxes of cereal—even when they are full, you pay for a lot of air space inside.

Speedup Tricks for Old Disks

PCs can suffer from adding too many applications; as soon as you start piling on them, you never seem to have enough speed. Inadequate disk performance is such a nagging problem that whole classes of software and entire industries have been created to fight it. As a result, a huge array of hardware and software products are available to crack through different disk bottlenecks. The software solutions are relatively quick and easy. The most that you need is some idle-time on your system—up to a few hours—and extra memory to devote to disk work.

Inadequate disk performance is such a nagging problem that whole classes of software and entire industries have been created to fight it.

The place to begin is with what DOS offers you. DOS includes capabilities ranging from rudimentary to advanced that can help you boost the performance of your system. Add or edit some entries in your system's configuration files, and you can wring some waste out of your disk's access time. Spend some time reorganizing your disk structure, and you can get better performance from your system by making it easier for DOS to deal with.

Improving access time makes the most dramatic change in older PCs.

These speed-up techniques affect the two disk bottlenecks—access time and data transfer rate—differently. Transfer rate is the least amenable to improvement. But that is okay, because improving access time makes the most dramatic change in older PCs. When your hard disk has a faster access time, it reacts more quickly and makes your PC more responsive to your keystrokes. Consequently, improving access time makes the biggest difference in the apparent speed of your PC. Moreover, although a handful of tricks help you squeeze more access speed from a disk drive, only one improves its apparent data transfer rate: disk caching—although you can create a new, equally fast disk drive using a disk emulator. In fact, disk caching is the most important disk speedup tool available, and you should consider using it for any and all disks in your system, new or old, hard or floppy, magnetic or optical.

Software-Based Disk Caching

The big performance problem with any disk drive is that it is a mechanical device that is expected to keep up with an electronic device. The race is hardly fair; it is like the average person sprinting against an Olympic-trained runner. Inside your PC, the head in a hard disk drive is fortunate indeed if it can change direction 66 times per second. The electronics in a PC are easily a million times faster; pulses there change direction as often as 66 million times per second. When a computer expects a response in nanoseconds, it is lucky to get results from a disk in milliseconds. A disk cache bridges this millionfold difference, isolating the electronics of your PC from the mechanical bottleneck of your hard disk.

The larger the disk cache, the more likely the data you need will be in the disk cache and the faster the overall system will perform.

All disk caches work by moving the memory contents from mechanical storage into a temporary electronic holding area—fast, solid-state RAM (random-access memory). The temporary storage area is the disk cache itself. Special circuitry or software called the disk *cache controller* performs several important functions. It copies data from the mechanical disk drive into the solid-state memory, where it can be retrieved more quickly. Because a disk cache almost always holds less information than the device it speeds up (otherwise, the slow device could be tossed out completely with the disk cache taking over its entire function), the disk cache controller must also check every request for disk data to see whether the information that is needed is available in the fast disk cache memory. If it is, it quickly fills the request with data from the disk cache. If the disk cache does not have the information that is needed, the controller must forward the data request to the disk, in which case your system suffers normal disk-based delays.

Obviously, you get faster response if all the data you need is located in the disk cache so that your system never has to dip back into disk storage. Two fundamental rules of caching performance directly follow from this principal: the larger the disk cache, the more likely the data you need will be in the disk cache and the faster the overall system will perform. Overall, disk cache performance will also depend on the ability of the disk cache controller to anticipate what information you need and to fill the disk cache with the corresponding data.

The first rule, which essentially reduces to "the more the merrier," begins to break down when the numbers get large. You have already noted the maximum practical size for a disk cache—the size of the disk being cached. Enlarging a disk cache gains nothing further because everything on the disk would fit neatly inside a disk cache that is bigger. Below that maximum, however, the effectiveness of a disk cache does not increase linearly; you use some storage areas of your disk more than others. Obviously, the free space on your disk need not be cached, because the disk cache controller will not find any data you need lurking there. You also are likely to have piles of files that you are storing for future reference that you do not access every day. In fact, most of the time you will be working from a very limited area on your hard disk. A disk cache storing one to two megabytes embraces most normal disk use, often from 70 to 90 percent of what you do. Doubling the memory in the disk cache obviously does not double the percentage of what is available in the disk cache, so you necessarily face a law of diminishing returns.

In that your disk cache is necessarily smaller than your disk, the disk cache controller must somehow be able to determine what data gets stored in the disk cache and what does not. The disk cache controller follows a set of rules called the *caching algorithm* to decide. The algorithm also sidesteps the logical inconsistency of the disk cache; that is, since data has to be read from disk into the disk cache anyway, how can the disk cache cut down on disk access time and improve throughout speed?

Most caching algorithms take care of both of these issues by anticipating what you will need based on simple rules. Almost all algorithms start by simply saving what you have already read from your disk. Although that does not save any time in the initial access to your disk, it eliminates any further need to refer to the disk the next time the same information is required. Much of the time your

Disk cache performance also depends on the capability of the disk cache controller to anticipate what information you need and to fill the disk cache with the corresponding data.

system calls for the same data over and over again, so this method is the most beneficial (and widely used) disk speedup technique. In addition, most caching algorithms read ahead from your disk, knowing that after you read one cluster from a file, you are most likely to read the next one. Reading ahead requires somewhat more time to transfer data but does not add much (if any) access time because the disk drive head is already in place. Extra bytes can quickly be transferred from disk to disk cache.

Eventually, the data you read from your disk and the data read ahead by the disk cache piles up until it exceeds the capacity of the disk cache. At that point, the real black magic of the individual disk cache kicks in. The caching algorithm must be able to predict which data you will want again and which you are finished using. The latter can be discarded to make room for new information. Most disk caches retain the data that you have most recently accessed, in the belief that it is the freshest and that which you will most likely want again. Some disk caching algorithms retain the data that has been used most often instead of most recently; some balance the two considerations. How effectively the algorithms match how you work determines how much acceleration a particular disk cache will deliver.

One important difference between disk caching algorithms is how the disk cache handles writing to disk. Most early disk caches ignored write operations and let you wait while every write was completed. Because most disk operations require only reading, these disk caches were effective but hardly optimal.

The makers of disk caches avoided write operations for two reasons. For one, sidestepping writes is easier, thus making a product require less effort, and less can go wrong. Disk write caching puts disk-bound data at risk. For a period ranging from milliseconds to several seconds, disk cached information may be stored solely in solid-state memory. With a disk write cache, between the time your program attempts to write to your disk and when the disk cache finally copies the data onto disk, that information is vulnerable to the vagaries of your PC's programs and power. A system crash will wipe out everything in the cache, including data that has not yet been physically written to the disk. Should you switch off your PC during this critical period or should your power fail, the data will disappear even though you and your program think that it was safely written to disk.

Disk caches that handle write operations do attempt to minimize the danger period. Generally, a disk cache only waits until your disk is no longer busy to carry out the write operation. Usually, the disk cache has an override that ensures that the disk cache will never wait too long before ensuring the safety of your data to be written. Better disk write caches even intercept the infamous three-finger salute (Ctrl-Alt-Del) that reboots your system. They force the cache to write all the information it contains to disk before they allow your reboot command to be processed. Even so, when you use a disk cache that takes care of write operations, you should be very careful. In particular, never switch off your PC immediately after you save a file.

On the other hand, caching disk write operations gives more apparent speed than caching read operations because you get instant response. Press the "save" button, and the cache absorbs the information in an instant, enabling you to resume work immediately. This acceleration is particularly valuable when extended to floppy disk drives. You can save a file to disk and instantly go on to another job while the disk cache spends several seconds copying your file to the slowly spinning floppy disk.

Better disk write caches even intercept the infamous three-finger salute (Ctrl-Alt-Del) that reboots your system.

Hardware versus Software Disk Caches

Disk caches come in two types, hardware and software. Adding a hardware-based disk cache requires a physical upgrade to your system. You must add either a new disk host adapter or a new hard disk to get hardware disk caching if your system currently lacks it. Software caching requires only running a program. Most PCs already have the software they need to take advantage of disk caching, and a multitude of disk caching programs are available commercially from dealers or as shareware.

A great deal of debate surrounds whether hardware or software disk caching is better. There is no argument about the usefulness of caching in general. Any cache (of a reasonable size) is better than none.

Any cache (of a reasonable size) is better than none.

The biggest shortcoming of the software disk cache is that it steals memory from your system that could otherwise be used by your applications. Some programs try to mitigate the damage. For example, DOS and Windows SMARTDRV and the latest versions of PC-Kwik dynamically share cache memory with the EMS needs of other programs, shifting memory from one purpose to the other as it is required, helping minimize the memory impact of the disk cache. Disk caching software also requires a slice of your microprocessor's performance to manage its memory operations, but this typically has only a slight impact on the overall speed of your system.

Both hardware and software disk caches can lead to compatibility problems.

Software disk caches hold the potential of operating faster than the more expensive hardware disk caches. The software disk cache operates in your system's memory, so it can keep up with your PC's microprocessor no matter what type of microprocessor it is or what speed it operates at. Hardware disk caches in general are connected to your system through its expansion bus and consequently suffer from the bus-speed bottleneck. On the other hand, hardware caches do not require your microprocessor's time to read ahead. They do not have to transfer across the expansion bus all the data the disk-caching algorithm thinks you want but have not asked for.

Both hardware and software disk caches can lead to compatibility problems. Earlier generations of hardware disk caches proved to be incompatible with older versions of popular disk utility programs. The hardware used by the disk cache prevents the utilities from getting the direct control of the disk that they require. Both the program developers and hardware makers took note of these problems and worked to eliminate the incompatibilities, so you are not likely to encounter them with current products.

Early software disk caches also demonstrated incompatibilities with some applications. For example, early versions of software disk caches did not follow the XMS standard that has emerged for managing extended memory. As a result, these older caching programs would interfere with other software that attempted to use extended memory. The introduction of Windows 3.0 brought this problem to a head, and most disk cache writers have adapted to the new standards. Although the wide use of software disk caching has forced program developers to fix problems with their products, incompatibilities occasionally surface with new program or cache versions.

The biggest advantage of the software disk cache is that it is often the least expensive disk speedup you can add to your PC. For more than six years, most PCs have included disk-caching programs. The IBM and Compaq made a software disk cache standard with their systems in 1987, although they required you to install the disk caching software yourself. The most recent versions of DOS and Windows also include their own software caches, which are dramatically improved over the early products included with computers and even their own early versions.

DOS 6.0 and Windows 3.1 include the same program, SMARTDRV.EXE, that is among the fastest software disk caches available. SMARTDRV.EXE caches both disk read and write operations and works with any DOS disk device—hard disks, floppy disks, and even optical drives. It makes older cache programs included with PCs or operating systems obsolete, including the SPEEDISK.SYS software driver included with earlier DOS and Windows versions.

Besides SMARTDRV.EXE, you can choose among several commercial disk caching programs, such as Flash from Software Matters, Inc., Indianapolis, Indiana; PC Cache, included as part of the PC Tools utility package from Central Point Software, Beaverton, Oregon; and Super PC-Kwik from Multisoft Corporation, Beaverton, Oregon. The chief difference between the commercial programs and SMARTDRV.EXE is their increased configurability and features. The commercial programs promise extra speed but getting it requires carefully tuning the cache to match your system.

SMARTDRV.EXE is among the fastest software disk caches available.

The most important factor in determining the performance of a software disk cache is the amount of memory available to the cache. Although a small disk cache, on the order of 64K, may improve the response of your PC, really benefiting from a disk caching program requires huge amounts of RAM. In other words, you should devote as much of your system's memory to your disk cache as you can, up to the point of diminishing returns. Most of the time, you will have to make a trade-off between the memory demanded by your applications and that used by the disk cache. In general, after devoting a megabyte to disk caching, you are better off giving excess megabytes to Windows should you plan to load multiple applications.

When shifting between loaded applications in systems without adequate RAM, Windows streams the temporarily unused program code from RAM to disk. Caching does not help the moving of data because after the code is shifted to disk, it is not used again until it gets loaded back into RAM. Although a cache big enough to hold all the information would eliminate the mechanical delays, the same memory could more usefully be devoted to Windows itself and could eliminate the need for unloading memory and transferring data in the first place.

Although a small disk cache may improve the response of your PC, really benefiting from a disk caching program requires huge amounts of RAM.

Older software disk-caching programs give you a choice of the memory that you want to use for running them—DOS, expanded, or extended RAM. Modern caching programs automatically use extended memory because that is what most systems have. Expanded memory is becoming obsolete, and there is simply not enough DOS memory available to make a reasonable-sized cache. In older systems and with older caches, you may have to make do with one of the older memory choices. When it is available, however, extended memory remains the best choice, particularly if you use a software EMS emulator (sometimes called a LIMulator) to add expanded memory to your system. It just does not make sense to use two layers of memory management when one will do. SMARTDRV.EXE draws all the memory it uses from the extended memory area. If you need to use expanded memory, you will need another disk cache.

The cache you are most likely to use is SMARTDRV.EXE, because you probably have it already and because it is hard to beat for all but the most specialized applications. It is also among the easiest disk caching programs to use.

Unlike older disk caches, SMARTDRV runs as a terminate-and-stay resident (TSR) program. You run it once, and it stays in operation in your system until you reboot or switch off your PC. Most people add SMARTDRV.EXE to the AUTOEXEC.BAT file of their PCs. In fact, Windows and DOS 6.0 automatically make SMARTDRV the first entry in your AUTOEXEC.BAT file if it is not there and you do not tell the DOS or Windows setup programs not to add it in.

In its default configuration, SMARTDRV opts for one megabyte of memory (if you have enough in your system) and configures itself to cache both the read and write operations of your hard disk. It also defaults to caching only the read operations of your floppy disk. Although the memory that SMARTDRV uses is set when the program first loads, you can alter whether read or write caching is used for any particular drive at any time.

Other Disk Acceleration Alternatives

Disk caching is an all-in-one solution that eliminates the need for several other speedup strategies. Load SMARTDRV.EXE, and you will not have to worry about other technologies such as RAM disk emulators, the FASTOPEN program, or properly setting the number of buffers in your CONFIG.SYS file. SMARTDRV handles all of these functions or their equivalent in a single step, in most cases doing the job better.

In the last six years, software disk caching has proven itself to be an effective and reliable method of improving disk performance. However, some people remain leery of it, for disk write caching can definitely lead to lost data if you do not take the proper precautions. The chances that read caching alone will cause problems are small. But because there can be no guarantee that a cache will not eventually send one or more bytes awry or crash your system, a few prefer to avoid the technology. If you are one of them, you can still take advantage of a few tricks to get more speed from your hard disk.

The chances that read caching alone will cause problems are small.

DOS Buffers

Perhaps the simplest speedup caching you can use is the DOS BUFFERS statement in your CONFIG.SYS file. Under the DOS definition, a buffer is part of your system's RAM that is devoted to storing additional information read from or written to your system's disks. As DOS reads information from your disk, it stores the data in RAM while it passes the information along to your program. If your program needs that information again, DOS can quickly read the data directly from the buffer memory instead of waiting for the disk to catch up. In writing, buffers work exactly the same way. When DOS writes something to disk, it also preserves a copy in its buffers, ready to be read back instantly should your program need to take another look.

DOS always stores the most recently read or written data in its buffers. Once the buffers are filled, it discards the oldest data as it reads or writes something new. Thus, the buffers are kept fresh with all the latest information. This description sounds much like a disk cache, and in fact DOS buffers work like a rudimentary cache. Missing, however, is the overall intelligence of a disk caching algorithm. Moreover, DOS buffers are much more limited in size than a cache and are thus more limited in acceleration potential.

DOS buffers are much more limited in size than a cache and are thus more limited in acceleration potential.

Look-Ahead Buffers

Since DOS 4.0 was introduced, DOS also includes secondary buffers or look-ahead buffers. They add a twist to ordinary buffers by continuing to read a file while finishing delivery of the part of the file that a program wants. The next second of the file is kept waiting in the look-ahead buffer, ready to be delivered to your program at RAM speed.

Buffers are assigned in sector-size blocks, each holding 512 bytes. Because each buffer requires a bit of system overhead, each one steals from 528 bytes to more than 532 bytes (depending on your DOS version and whom you believe) away from the DOS memory that is otherwise available to DOS applications. The more buffers DOS uses, the more likely the information that it needs will be located in them—and, of course, the more memory you will have to devote to buffering. If you use a DOS version older than 4.0, you will have to carve this buffer memory from the memory that is otherwise available for running your DOS applications. DOS 5.0 and later automatically use RAM from the 64K above the one-megabyte real-mode memory range (which Microsoft calls the High Memory Area) if you have a 286-, 386-, or 486-based PC, and the rest of DOS loads into HMA. If you do not have any RAM in the HMA, DOS 5.0 uses conventional memory for itself and its buffers. That way, memory will not be taken away from your DOS programs for buffering, although you will still lose some RAM that might otherwise be usable by your system.

DOS 4 enables you to move buffers into expanded (EMS) memory, if you have enough EMS installed in your system. To use EMS memory with BUFFERS under version four of DOS, you have to add a switch, /X, to the BUFFERS statement in your CONFIG.SYS file.

You can specify how much memory you want DOS to devote to buffering using the BUFFERS statement in CONFIG.SYS. The statement is easy to use. With DOS versions previous to 4.0, you indicate the number of sector-size buffers you want to assign following an equal sign after the BUFFERS statement. You can specify anywhere from 1 to 99 buffers, which will steal from 528 to 52,272 bytes from other purposes. A typical BUFFERS statement would look like this:

```
BUFFERS=20
```

Later versions of DOS enable you to specify normal buffers and look-ahead buffers. Just add the number of look-ahead buffers after the primary buffer number, using a comma as a separator. For example, the following command would install 30 conventional buffers and 8 look-ahead buffers:

```
BUFFERS=30,8
```

To make DOS 4.0 use expanded memory for its buffers, you would modify this command to read:

```
BUFFERS=30,8 /X
```

Buffers do the most good with applications that randomly access your disk drives—applications such as databases. Programs that read and write large files to disk do not benefit much because as they course through a large file they constantly read new data from disk, updating the buffers and discarding old data. By the time you go back to read or write the file again, most of it will have been discarded from the buffers. The largest file that can fit totally inside DOS-based buffers is one accommodated when using the BUFFERS=99 statement, about 50K bytes, which is not very big in today's world of bit-image graphic files.

The largest number of buffers is rarely the best number to use, however. With a large number, like 99, DOS spends more time searching for what it wants in the buffers than it takes to access a moderate performance hard disk. As a result, a moderate number of buffers—such as the 20 given in the previous example—is usually considered the optimum number.

There is no one perfect number of buffers to use in all situations because the optimum number varies with the applications that you use and how you use them. Microsoft makes its own recommendations, based on the size of your hard disk. Remember, however, these numbers are not golden. In some situations, other figures may work better. The only way to determine the best figure is by trial and error. Consequently, most people stick with 20 to 30 buffers.

The penalty for not including a BUFFERS statement in your CONFIG.SYS files also varies with the version of DOS that you use. Early versions of DOS defaulted to a small number of buffers, so adding a moderate number to your CONFIG.SYS file made a big difference. Since DOS Version 3.3, however, the number of buffers DOS assigned by default has varied with the equipment in your system. If you have a PC with less than 128K of RAM and only 360K floppy disk drives, DOS automatically assigns you a measly two buffers. If you have the same paltry memory but upgrade to a larger floppy disk drive (720K, 1.2M, 1.44M, or 2.88M capacity), DOS adds an extra buffer.

Memory makes a bigger difference, however. If your system has more than 128K but no more than 256K, DOS assigns five buffers.

Buffers do the most good with applications that randomly access your disk drives—applications such as databases.

If your system has more than 256K but not more than 512K, you get 10 buffers. With more than 512K of RAM, DOS automatically assigns 15 buffers, very close to the preferred compromise.

Most PCs today have the DOS maximum memory of 640K, often more. For these systems, the BUFFERS=20 statement is not going to make a lot of difference in how your system operates. However, you can tweak the number of buffers to get slightly better random access performance from your disk if you decide not to use a cache.

There are situations in which you will definitely want to use a BUFFERS= statement but reduce the automatic allotment that DOS assigns you. The pre-eminent case is when you add a third-party disk-caching program to your system. A good disk cache can augment the speed of your disk system substantially more than loading your PC with all the buffers DOS allows (99). But although buffers are good and caches are better, using them together is a waste. Because disk caching is just a more intelligent form of buffers, you are stacking two layers of work to accomplish one job. You might see a little extra benefit, but it probably will not be worth the work. It is like taking money from one pocket, putting it in another, then pulling it out again to pay for a newspaper. The extra movement does not add anything to the transaction but time. Moving bytes from disk to buffers to cache to memory (or disk to cache to buffers to memory) takes one step more than is necessary.

The basic rule is to minimize the number of buffers your system uses when you have a cache available. Many programs advise that you simply eliminate the BUFFERS statement from your CONFIG.SYS file when you use a hardware or software-based disk cache. However, you may still be stuck with 15 buffers if you have a system with a reasonable RAM endowment. The better alternative is to specify a minimal number of buffers, say two. In actual use, you may see little difference in performance, but you will gain the space that DOS would have otherwise allocated to unnecessary buffers.

The only other time you may want to reduce your buffers statement (but not necessarily eliminate it entirely) is when you use memory-hungry programs that need every byte you have. Remember, the more buffers you specify, the fewer bytes of DOS memory will be available for your applications. A really memory-hungry application might not run if you have a substantial number of buffers. If you encounter such an insufficiency, reduce the number of buffers in your CONFIG.SYS until the greedy application runs.

A good disk cache can augment the speed of your disk system substantially more than loading your PC with all the buffers DOS allows (99).

The basic rule is to minimize the number of buffers your system uses when you have a cache available.

The symptoms of insufficient memory are difficult to ignore. Some programs warn you in a straightforward manner when your system lacks sufficient RAM to get the program running. They may send you a self-explanatory error message such as `Insufficient Memory`. Some applications, however, merely jam up when loading in a system with insufficient RAM. Typically, you hear some exercises from your hard disk with nothing appearing on your screen but a flashing hyphen prompt. After a while, the disk activity stops—the program has loaded all of itself it could into your PC's RAM—but nothing else happens. The flashing prompt continues to flash, but no program ever appears, and no amount of frantic key pressing returns your system to life.

A really memory-hungry application might not run if you have a substantial number of buffers.

FASTOPEN

DOS is not the smartest operating system in the world. In fact, it has a tendency to be quite forgetful. For example, when you give DOS a command to load a program, it must search for the file that you want, even if it has carried out that same search just a few seconds earlier. Even if you give DOS a hint in finding a file by explicitly telling it which subdirectory the file is located in, DOS must read down the directory tree, opening each subdirectory to see how to get to the next one down, until it finally finds the program that you want and locates it on the disk. Even when you give the same command twice back-to-back, DOS goes through this same search, like a creature of habit rather than an inspired worker.

You can add a bit of inspiration to DOS using its FASTOPEN command, which has been available in all versions of DOS since 3.0. FASTOPEN tells DOS to remember where it found files so that it can find them again without stepping through the tedious search yet another time.

A FASTOPEN command applies only to one hard disk drive. If you keep programs or regularly used files on more than one disk drive, you will need to issue the FASTOPEN command for each disk you want to accelerate. To indicate which hard disk drive you want FASTOPEN to work with, you need to specify the drive letter (followed by a mandatory colon) after the command name.

FASTOPEN gives you one option, a choice of the number of directory entries or files to remember. As with the BUFFERS command, FASTOPEN has a set capacity. After its memory is full, it dumps the least recently used directory entry from its memory, replacing it with the most recently accessed directory entry. You can set the number of filenames that FASTOPEN remembers between 10 and 99. (These figures are not quite as arbitrary as they look—FASTOPEN can only read two-digit numbers. Even with FASTOPEN, DOS is not very bright.) If you do not specify a number, FASTOPEN defaults to memorizing 34 directory entries.

To buffer the default number of directory entries, type FASTOPEN followed by the letter of the disk drive to which you want the command to apply. For example, to make FASTOPEN work with drive D:, you would type this:

```
FASTOPEN D:
```

To specify the number of directory entries for FASTOPEN to memorize, append an equals sign after the drive on which you want FASTOPEN to work and follow that by the number. For example, the command to remember the 45 most recent file accesses on drive C: would look like this:

```
FASTOPEN C:=45
```

The optimum number to use with FASTOPEN depends on how you use your hard disk. You can experiment to determine a value that works best.

The FASTOPEN command can be given like any other DOS instruction on the command line or, better, it can be included in your AUTOEXEC.BAT file so that it leaps into action as soon as you boot your PC.

You are better off avoiding FASTOPEN and relying instead on your disk cache.

Many users reported problems with early versions of the FASTOPEN command. Even before SMARTDRV became part of the DOS and Windows default configuration, FASTOPEN had fallen from favor. With a disk cache, running FASTOPEN is entirely unnecessary. Moreover, it is undesirable because it wastes memory and may add a bit of instability to your system. In other words, you are better off avoiding FASTOPEN and relying instead on your disk cache.

RAM Disks

Like a write-enabled disk cache, the RAM disk is volatile and puts your data at risk.

Long before PC users had disk caching, they could take advantage of a technology based on the same RAM-is-faster-than-disk principal—the RAM disk. Sometimes called a *disk emulator* or *virtual disk*, this technology simply takes a block of RAM and makes it act like a disk drive, using a special program called a software driver. Because the entire storage of the RAM disk is made from fast solid-state memory, the RAM disk has RAM speed; it can be as fast as your system's microprocessor. There is no waiting for mechanical delays or transfer times, and there is no worry about caching algorithms. At that level, the RAM disk is sort of a simplified disk cache. In fact, along with cache speed the RAM disk carries with it all the disadvantages of a software disk cache. Like a write-enabled disk cache, the RAM disk is volatile and puts your data at risk. When you switch off your PC, your RAM disk and its entire contents irrevocably vanish. You lose not just the few kilobytes nestled in your cache but the whole capacity of the RAM disk. The RAM disk also requires management. Because it is created fresh every time you boot up your PC, you must load the files you need into the RAM disk every time you boot up your PC. For safety's sake, you will also have to copy all the data forms from the RAM disk to a real disk drive before you switch off your PC. Three, like a disk cache, the RAM disk demands RAM, usually in prodigious amounts. The RAM disk requires as many megabytes as its entire capacity. A cache can get by with as few as you want to offer it.

According to Microsoft, SMARTDRV is as effective for most purposes, as is any RAM disk (including the one that Microsoft itself packaged with its products). People who regularly compile and link programs or check the spelling of documents often would copy their libraries and dictionaries to RAM disk to minimize the wait for disk access. For them, spell-checking and program compilation run with lightning-like speed. In that nothing new is ever created on the RAM disk, using this strategy, the volatility of the storage is not a problem. Should a power failure wipe out the contents of the RAM disk, the same library files can be quickly copied back into place.

SMARTDRV is as effective for most purposes as any RAM disk.

In all versions of DOS since 2.0, a RAM disk driver has been included as standard equipment. Earlier versions of DOS used the driver VDISK.SYS, and more recent versions (including DOS 5.0) use a new program called RAMDRIVE.SYS. Either one loads as a device driver in your system's CONFIG.SYS file.

For years, nearly every new AT system had a VDISK-driven RAM disk. The reason was that VDISK was just about the only program that could take advantage of the extended memory those systems offered. It also can use ordinary DOS memory, but that is in such short supply in most systems these days that few people hack out a hunk for RAM disk use. RAMDRIVE.SYS can use conventional, extended, or expanded memory.

Because RAM disks could take advantage of otherwise worthless memory, they initially became very popular. Now they are superseded by caches. Disk-caching programs offer nearly the same speedup without the need to setup a RAM disk or copy files to it. Nevertheless, a RAM disk can still be useful if you have an application that matches its virtues. Typically, you will want to create an entire system revolving around the RAM disk. Along with the commands necessary for bringing the RAM disk to life, you will also want to put instructions in your AUTOEXEC.BAT file to copy the files you will use to your RAM disk automatically when you boot up. You also will have to install those programs to use the drive letter assigned to your RAM disk rather than the physical disk on which they are stored.

To create a RAM disk, load the VDISK.SYS or RAMDRIVE.SYS driver using the DEVICE= statement in your system's CONFIG.SYS file. VDISK and RAMDRIVE allow several options to be included on the line that loads the driver.

For VDISK, these options include the number of directory entries allowed on the RAM disk, the sector size of the RAM disk, and the total size of the RAM disk. Of these, only the last will be a major concern when setting up your RAM disk. You specify the RAM disk size by including the option B= (or the words Buffer Size=) followed by the RAM disk size in kilobytes. In its current form, VDISK can create RAM disks ranging from 64K to 4MB in size, providing your system has sufficient RAM to accommodate it. The only other important option is /E, which tells VDISK to use extended memory for creating its RAM disk.

The command to create a 360K RAM disk in extended memory would look like this:

```
DEVICE=VDISK.SYS B=360 /E
```

After VDISK is loaded, it stays in memory until you reboot your system. So, carefully consider how much memory to assign to it lest you should not be able to load programs later on.

RAMDRIVE.SYS works similarly. After the driver name on the command line you specify, the disk size you want to create (in kilobytes), the sector size (if you want something other than 512 bytes, the only other valid values being 128 and 256 bytes), and the number of entries possible in the disk's root directory, from 2 to 1024. The default is 64. In addition, the /e option indicates you want your RAMDRIVE to use extended memory; /a indicates to use expanded memory.

A typical RAMDRIVE entry in your CONFIG.SYS file to create a one megabyte RAM disk in expanded memory would look like this:

```
DEVICE=RAMDRIVE.SYS 1024 /a
```

You also could specify a two megabyte RAM drive in extended memory with 256-byte sectors and 512 directory entries with this entry:

```
DEVICE=RAMDRIVE.SYS 2048 128 512 /e
```

If you are operating from a RAM disk like the DOS VDISK or RAMDrive program for a substantial amount of the work that you do, buffers will not do much good either. Again, you are already using fast RAM to handle your disk information, so buffers become an additional RAM step, slowing things down instead of speeding them up. When you work exclusively from a RAM disk, minimize the number of buffers you assign with an explicit BUFFERS statement. If you work from both a RAM disk and a physical disk, you will probably want to set up a compromise value—and the default of 15 offered by DOS is not such a bad place to start (and finish).

Disk Management for Improved Performance

No matter whether you choose disk caching, some other acceleration technique, or nothing at all, you can still improve the performance of your hard disk by properly managing the data that you store.

Defragment Your Disk

Every time you use your hard disk, it gets a little slower—slightly, almost imperceptibly, but slower nevertheless. This sluggishness is nothing mechanical but is caused by an interaction between software—specifically DOS—and the head actuator (the mechanism that moves the read/write head of your disk drive). It is not really a problem but a result of how your disk is organized and how files are managed by DOS.

The source of this age-induced disk speed degradation is DOS's method of packing files onto disk. Because DOS was written when capacity was more important than speed, it tries to pack files on disk as stingily as possible by dividing them into clusters and squeezing them as tightly as it can, with hardly a space between.

Unlike files, which vary in length, these clusters are interchangeable units of a standard size, (from 512 to 8096 bytes, depending only on disk type, format and DOS version). The contents of a single file may be spread among dozens or hundreds of these clusters, each one located anywhere on the disk and not necessarily physically near any of the other clusters in the file.

With earlier versions of DOS, a simple rule governs which clusters are assigned to each file. The first available cluster, the one nearest the beginning of the disk, is always the next one used. Thus, on a new disk, clusters are picked one after another, and all the clusters in a file are contiguous.

When a file is erased, its clusters are freed for reuse. These newly freed clusters, being closer to the beginning of the disk, are the first ones chosen when the next file is written to disk. In effect, DOS first fills in the holes left by the erased file. As a result, the clusters of new files may be scattered all over the disk.

More recent versions of DOS first work to the end of the disk before trying to squeeze new data in clusters that were previously erased. But after it has written to the entire disk once, even newer DOS versions try to squeeze data into freed-up clusters scattered across the disk.

Every head motion wastes time, and the more scattered the clusters are, the slower the drive performs.

When you read or write to a file, DOS automatically and invisibly strings all of the clusters together, using a map of disk space called the file allocation table or FAT. No matter how scattered over your disk the individual clusters of a file may be, you—and your software—only see a single file no matter how the clusters are scattered.

Although simple for DOS, this cluster sorting is a nightmare for the disk drive. The read/write head must jump all over the disk to shuttle between the scattered clusters. Every head motion wastes time, and the more scattered the clusters are, the slower the drive performs.

Although Microsoft recognizes the value of optimizing your disk, only DOS 6 provides one.

By reorganizing your disk to optimize the interactions of DOS and the head actuator, you can make your system perform substantially faster—so much faster that you will be able to see the difference when you load programs or files. Programs that carry out the necessary reorganization are called *disk optimizers*, *disk defragmenters*, or (as Microsoft prefers, *disk compactors*). Although Microsoft recognizes the value of optimizing your disk, only DOS 6 provides one. Fortunately, what earlier versions of DOS missed the market supplied in profusion. A number of special-purpose programs are available for disk optimization, and most hard-disk utility packages also include one. The DOS 6 program to use is DEFRAG, which works with DOUBLESPACE. Alternatively, you can defragment your disk's files using your hard disk backup system (streaming tape, cartridge disk, or even floppy disk) to back up and restore all your hard disk files.

The latter choice is cheaper (if you already have the backup hardware but not DOS 6) and has a side benefit that may save you a lot of pulled out hair and profanity if disaster strikes later on. It guarantees that you will have at least one backup copy of your disk files that you might never have otherwise made. The former method of defragmentation—using the DEFRAG (if it came with your version of DOS) or a commercial program—is easier, faster, and thus somewhat safer.

If you opt for the backup technique, the first step is to make a backup copy of your hard disk that can be restored file-by-file (rather than as a disk image) using your normal backup system. Even the DOS BACKUP utility and floppy disks, though time-consuming, can be effective. Remember to have a stack of formatted disks (which need not be blank) ready when you use BACKUP.

Just to be safe, you may want to make two backups (particularly if you use the DOS BACKUP program) because the next optional but recommended step—reformatting your hard disk—can be frightening when you have megabytes on the line.

The formatting process gives DOS an effectively new disk to write your files back to by wiping the disk clean (and, of course, wiping out your original files). Reformatting may incidentally save you from some future disasters by spotting disk clusters that may have gone bad since you put the drive into service.

Although all disks deteriorate and develop bad clusters as they age (from magnetic decay or from small, unnoticed head crashes), DOS only checks for bad clusters when the disk is formatted. Therefore, sometimes your important data may be written to a cluster that has gone bad since formatting, and that data is lost forever. (This occurs principally with programs that by-pass DOS's disk-writing safe-guards to gain extra speed.) Reformatting your disk again when you optimize it finds such deteriorated clusters and flags them so that your data will not be trusted to them. After your hard disk is reformatted, the next step in optimization-by-backing-up is to

Reformatting may incidentally save you from some future disasters by spotting disk clusters that may have gone bad since you put the drive into service.

restore all your files to it using your backup system's file-by-file restoration option. During the restoration process, all files are copied back to your disk so that their clusters are contiguous.

Another method for reorganizing scattered clusters is to use one of the commercial programs expressly designed for that purpose. Most disk utility packages (for instance, Central Point Software's PC Tools and Semantec's Norton Utilities) include disk optimizing features. These programs work by temporarily copying data from one area of the disk to another, freeing up a contiguous area of free clusters, and copying the data back to the newly freed clusters. At least one copy of your data is always safely recorded on the disk, so you do not risk losing anything if the power fails or the system crashes during the optimization process. They are easy to use—you just type a command at the DOS prompt or make a menu selection—and they automatically run to completion without your intervention. In fact, these programs are generally safe enough to run overnight, giving you an optimized disk the next day.

Trim Your Search Path

Speeding up your disk is often not a matter of adding to your system but organizing what you have. DOS's tree-structured directory is a primary case in point. One of the great conveniences of the later versions of DOS is its capability to search through multiple paths on your disks to find the programs that you want to run and even the files needed by programs. By nesting subdirectories, you can organize your disk logically so that you can easily remember where each of your files is.

Although the tree-structured directory system used by DOS versions since 2.0 are a great way of organizing your hard disk, they also can slow down the performance of the system. To find the starting cluster of a file (which is where DOS always must start reading a file), DOS needs to read through each layer of all the subdirectories along the way to find the file. This research can involve lots of head movement on your disk drive when a file is buried deeply, several layers of subdirectories down. That means your disk drive's read/write head must scamper from track to track—and with each leap it incurs a performance penalty statistically equal to the average access time of the drive. Five subdirectories and five leaps of a 40 millisecond drive imposes a delay of 200 milliseconds, a noticeable and

By nesting subdirectories, you can organize your disk logically so that you can easily remember where each of your files is.

To take advantage of all the speed your hard disk has to offer, be sure that your most frequently used files are nearest the root directory.

bothersome one-fifth second wait. Obviously, if you want to take advantage of all the speed your hard disk has to offer, be sure that your most frequently used files are nearest the root directory.

There is another complication: DOS is able to find devices, including disk partitions, that are given their own drive letter faster than it can dig into subdirectories. Although DOS must search for subdirectories, it remembers where each root directory of each disk is. Hence, if you organize your files by partitioning (using FDISK) rather than using subdirectories (using MKDIR), you can speed access to them, trimming those hundreds-of-milliseconds waits. Note that using the SUBST command to give drive letter designations to subdirectories does not enhance disk speed, because although the process is invisible to you, DOS still must search through the SUBST-ed subdirectories despite their drive letter designations.

Nearly everything you do to enhance the convenience of using your hard disk slows its performance.

The subdirectory slowdown illustrates a sad fact: Nearly everything you do to enhance the convenience of using your hard disk slows its performance. One particular case in point is the PATH command through which you tell DOS where to look for programs it cannot find in the current directory. Whenever you ask DOS to run a program and it cannot find it in the current directory, it searches through all the directory and subdirectory names listed in the last PATH command you gave it.

Obviously, the fewer alternate paths you specify, the less time it will take DOS to zero in on the program that you want (or give you the message that the program cannot be found). If you must specify more than one directory in a PATH command, put your most often used programs in the first directory specified. Better yet, specify disks instead of directories. Best of all, keep your most often used commands on a high-speed RAM disk emulator (like DOS's VDISK) and list the RAM disk first in your PATH command. Never put a floppy disk in your search path. Floppies are not only slow, but you stand the good chance of not having the right disk in your drive. Should that happen, DOS triumphantly announces File Not Found (or Drive Not Ready if you have no disk in the drive), wasting even more of your time. This problem is particularly annoying when you mistype a command and you have to wait for DOS to exhaust all its path options before issuing an error.

Never put a floppy disk in your search path.

Improving Memory Speed

Although you cannot make the memory in your PC run faster, you can make sure that it is running at its maximum speed. The speed of memory in your system is determined by the clock that drives your microprocessor, the configuration of the memory, and the operating limits of the solid-state memory chips themselves. Although any of those factors can be altered with hardware upgrades, such changes are inevitably expensive.

Sometimes, however, you may not be taking advantage of all the performance potential that is built into your system. By making a slight change in how you work with memory or how you set it up, you may be able to coax more speed from what you have without investing in hardware changes.

Extended versus Expanded

The first place to look is at the kind of memory you have installed in your system. All PCs start with DOS memory, the basic memory that comes with your system and stretches upward to 640K. Beyond that range, in most systems you have your choice of using extended memory or expanded memory (EMS). The only exceptions are PCs based on the original 8088 microprocessor and those closely related to it: the 8086, 80C86, NEC V20, and NEC V30. Because of the limited addressability of these chips, they can be augmented only with expanded memory and that must take the form of a special expanded memory board that slides into an expansion slot.

Systems based on the 286 and more recent microprocessors have the option of using extended or expanded memory. The latter can be created using special EMS boards in expansion slots or through using EMS emulation software to change extended memory into expanded memory. Some programs, particularly those designed for the 386 and new microprocessors, also have the capability of using extended or expanded memory. Whichever you choose can affect the performance of your system. If you have made the wrong choice, correcting it can give you a modest performance boost without the cost of an upgrade.

The simple rule is to use extended memory with any programs that
will accommodate it. As noted concerning the VDISK disk emulator, using emulated expanded memory with programs that can use
extended memory makes no sense because it results in the use of two
redundant layers of memory management. In 286 systems, expanded
memory emulation often means copying large (64K) blocks of data
from one area of memory to another to simulate the switching of
memory banks. The overhead of this operation makes these expanded memory simulators particularly slow. Use them only when
you need to run a specific program that is worth sacrificing performance.

Note that IBM's 286-based Micro Channel PS/2s have their own
bank-switching capabilities that eliminate this overhead when using
expanded memory emulators. Extended or expanded memory
usually delivers equivalent speed in those systems.

The makers of some early Micro Channel memory expansion boards
add another twist. A few such boards were designed to operate as
expanded memory boards and came with special driver software that
emulated extended memory. Because of this emulation, these boards
delivered abysmally slow extended memory performance that should
be avoided whenever possible. If you have a Micro Channel expansion board that refers to it using an "extended memory emulator,"
try using the product only to provide expanded memory, avoiding its
emulated extended memory whenever possible.

Another exception to the extended-memory rule is in PCs that have
EMS memory boards in expansion slots as well as matching microprocessor clock and expansion bus speeds. In these systems, and
these systems only, expanded memory actually can perform faster
than extended because the bank switching that is built into EMS
memory boards can move a block of memory instantly.

Trimming Wait States

The only way to truly increase the memory performance of today's
highest speed PCs is to augment their memory caches with more
high-speed cache memory—an expensive hardware upgrade.
Sometimes and with some systems, you can improve memory
performance by eliminating unneeded memory wait states that have
been accidentally programmed in.

The chipsets used by a large number of 386- and some 286- and
486-based computers make the number of memory wait states

*Sometimes and
with some systems,
you can improve
memory perfor-
mance by eliminat-
ing unneeded
memory wait states
that have been
accidentally
programmed in.*

programmable. Using either a utility supplied with these systems or built into their Basic Input/Output System (BIOS) code, the number of wait-states imposed per clock cycle can be altered. If your system is not set to use the optimum number, reducing this setting will improve performance. Some systems provide hardware jumpers to alter the number of wait states used.

The process of altering wait states through your PC's setup procedure is very risky. If you lower the number of wait states too far, your system may not operate—even to let you switch the number of wait states back to a workable value. Before you begin changing wait states, be sure that your system provides some means of resetting itself to its factory default settings. For example, some systems instruct you to move a jumper from one position to another to totally reset the machine. If you cannot reset your PC, do not change its wait state settings.

If your PC does not work after you change the setting, you can always change it back to get it going again.

When the wait states used by your system are set by hardware jumpers, you have fewer worries. If your PC does not work after you change the setting, you can always change it back to get it going again.

To be on the safe side, before you attempt any alterations to your system's hardware or software setup, write down all the current setup values so that you can be reassured that you will be able to restore them manually. Taking a little time before you begin will save you worries, headaches, and telephone calls when you try to put all the pieces back together again if something goes awry.

To alter the number of wait states in systems that support changing waits states through setup, you will only need to enter your PC's advanced setup menu. (If your system does not have such a menu in its setup system, you probably cannot change its wait state setting through software.) Among the options available to you may be "wait states." For more speed, reduce the number that is listed there. Zero wait states is as fast as any system can go.

The settings for hardware jumpers in systems that use them are usually given in the instruction manual of the machine or system board upon which the machine is based. You are most likely to find the settings given in an appendix.

Going the other direction—slowing your system down by adding wait states—is not at all dangerous. If the world is spinning too quickly for you, just add another wait state to your PC's present settings. You can also find programs to slow down your system on most bulletin boards. These programs work by adding wait states or their equivalent to your system. You will find them particularly handy when you try to run an old game on a new computer, and after a blur of beeps and screen activity, the game ends before you can even touch the keyboard.

Maximizing Memory

The only way to get more memory in your system is to add more memory. You can, however, squeeze more useful memory from the RAM you have, and perhaps forestall the inevitable memory upgrade. By managing your system's memory, you can make your PC behave as if it had more RAM at its disposal.

Your goal is to bring memory-hogging programs under control. Although you cannot trim the RAM required by king-size applications, you can cut down the contention among other programs and features for the memory you have.

By managing your system's memory, you can make your PC behave as if it had more RAM at its disposal.

Managing TSRs

One place to begin is with taming your TSR programs. Using a TSR management program, you can load and remove your favorite TSR utilities from memory as needed, freeing up RAM for other applications. Some TSR programs also have their own capabilities to remove themselves from memory. Typically, they are required to run the TSR program again with a special command-line option to pop them out of memory. There is one restriction to unloading TSR programs in this way; you must remove the utilities in the reverse order from which they were loaded.

TSR management programs unify the unloading process so that you do not have to type a half-dozen different commands to clear out your RAM. They enable you to load TSRs when you need them and dump them when you do not. In particular, when you want to run a gargantuan application, you can free up nearly all of your system's 640K for the program by ejecting the TSRs. Of course, you will not be able to run TSRs while the gargantuan application is running— but at least the application will run. Later, you can pop your TSRs back into place by loading them as you normally would.

Be careful about the order that you load your TSRs. Load the more expendable utilities later.

TSR managers face the same restriction as unloading utilities individually. You can never remove a TSR that was loaded into memory before another one that is still resident. It is like a stack of dishes only turned upside down; you cannot pull one out from the middle without making the whole stack crash down. In practical application, this limitation means that if you want to unload one TSR, you also will have to dump any other TSRs you have loaded since that one. The moral is to be careful about the order that you load your TSRs. Not only do you need to worry about which ones must be loaded in which order to work, you also want to take advantage of whatever flexibility remains to prioritize your utilities. Load the more expendable utilities later.

Another way of managing TSR utilities is to use a virtual memory system; that is, a program that enables you to spool your TSRs to disk by making part of your hard disk appear like added RAM. Memory management programs with virtual memory capabilities not only give you more control over your TSR software, they take over control from the TSR. Under their management, TSRs stay out of normal DOS memory except when you want to use them—even though they still act like they are memory-resident. Press a key, and the memory manager finds the TSR and puts it back into memory and brings it to life. After you exit the TSR, the memory management program puts the TSR away on disk (or in expanded or extended memory should your system have some of either). Instead of letting a TSR program hog up DOS memory, the memory manager shifts it out of the way until you need the program. Of course, the shuffle adds a little time and slows the instant response of pop-up programs, but that can be a small price to pay for an extra 100K or more for your other applications. Two programs that handle these memory management tasks are Headroom from Helix Software and Extra from Delta Technology International.

The only way to cut the memory used by drivers and other continuously running programs is to fine-tune your system.

These programs, like any TSR manager, cannot move everything out of DOS memory. Software drivers, RAM disks, or continuously running utilities like screen blanking programs need to stay in conventional memory because they are always working. Move them to disk and the applications will halt, likely stopping your system at the same time. The only way to cut the memory used by drivers and other continuously running programs is to fine-tune your system. For example, some drivers (such as caches and RAM disk emulators) enable you to select the amount of RAM they use. You can trim what you give them to the minimum that enables them to work to gain RAM for other applications. Similarly, you can judiciously reduce some of your DOS options—for example, the number of buffers, files, and environment size set in CONFIG.SYS—to gain a few extra bytes or kilobytes. Although those seem like paltry sums, they can make the difference between running the latest version of Lotus 1-2-3 and sitting around staring at a blank screen.

Improving Display Performance

Today's top-performing applications write directly to video memory by merely transferring bytes from your system's normal RAM to the video memory in your display adapter. This transfer is limited by the performance of your system's input/output bus.

The vast majority of programs rely on DOS or BIOS firmware to put characters on the screen rather than writing directly to memory. These applications are limited by the bus bottleneck and by the overhead imposed in the extra instructions. A further complication is that the BIOS video instructions are often held in ROM, which in most systems is substantially slower than system RAM. Several strategies and software utilities can help you avoid some of these slowdowns.

Video Speedup Programs

The most visible improvement you can make in your PC is accelerating its display performance. A snappier screen makes a snappier, more responsive PC. But you do not have to go to the expense of upgrading your display system to get faster displays. By attacking the weaknesses in the way programs use your display system, you can make great improvements in display speed without an equally great investment in an upgrade.

By attacking the weaknesses in the way programs use your display system, you can make great improvements in display speed.

The place to begin improving your display system is with your system's BIOS. DOS and many applications use routines in your PC's BIOS to put text and graphics on the screen. In the original design of the PC, the BIOS was supposed to be the primary connection between software and your PC hardware. But the BIOS routines are conservatively written to be easy to use and compatible with the widest range of programs. They are decidedly not written to be compatible with impatient human beings. Worse, DOS provides its own display routines that the programmer can use, routines that dip down and use the BIOS code, adding a second layer of overhead (and second insult) to display speed. Many programmers have, in frustration, bypassed the DOS and BIOS display routines to write bytes directly to video memory (the chips on your display adapter card), giving their systems a discernible speed boost. But many, many applications stick by the rules and write video with BIOS or DOS routines.

For these programs as well as DOS, a little magic is available— software that alters the BIOS codes to kick in the display adrenaline. Altering your system's BIOS may sound like a drastic step but it can be accomplished quickly and easily. A TSR program can intercept the interrupts used by the DOS and BIOS routines and substitute lean, mean, and high-speed display codes. Pre-eminent among these programs is the screen portion of PC-Kwik Power Pak from Multisoft. It adds new snap to your video displays as well as a screen review feature. With applications that use DOS video routines, PC-Kwik Power Pak actually can make a bigger difference than shifting from an 8-bit to a 16-bit video board.

Video Shadowing

One of the most pernicious display bottlenecks is actually a memory problem. Programs that use BIOS routines must, of course, access the memory holding the code for those routines. In most systems, that code is stored in ROM (read-only memory), which is notoriously slow. Accessing ROM adds extra wait states to the microprocessor. Moreover, most 32-bit systems use 16-bit ROM memory, slowing the routines stored there to half speed.

The 386 and later microprocessors have built-in capabilities to remap memory—software that can convince the chips to look at different memory locations than those indicated by applications for data that those applications need. When DOS or software attempts to read a BIOS routine, memory remapping enables the request to be redirected to some other memory location.

A technique called *video shadowing* copies the BIOS routines from slow ROM memory into fast RAM and then redirects the system (DOS and all programs) to look in RAM when it needs video routines. Shadowing can speed up display routines by a factor of two or more. Many of the latest high-performance computers have built-in ROM shadowing capabilities. They automatically copy the code in slow ROM memory to fast RAM to speed up execution.

As with replacement TSR video routines, video shadowing runs from within the fastest RAM in your system. In that way, it is redundant. In fact, if you use speed-booting replacement video routines, you should avoid using video shadowing. The RAM memory that is allocated to shadowing will be wasted because the display routines copied in the shadowing process are bypassed like any other BIOS display routines by the speedup program. This is one case where the advantage of two acceleration methods do not add up. Combining them only results in wasted RAM. Video shadowing also may limit your maximum RAM expandability.

Display List Drivers

With Computer-Aided Design (CAD) programs, the actual work putting an image on your screen is easy compared with the process of producing the image. The CAD program must compute exactly which dots on the screen to illuminate by mathematically calculating every line and curve to be drawn. Although an image in video memory can be flashed on the screen in one-sixtieth of a second, filling the video memory with the image can take several minutes or more.

Every time the screen changes, the CAD program must calculate every dot all over again—a process called *regeneration*—because the image is built up from the very beginning. Regenerations are often the most time-consuming part of using a CAD program.

Regenerations are often the most time-consuming part of using a CAD program.

With AutoCAD from AutoDesk Corporation it is possible to sidestep the regeneration process in many cases by using a display list driver. This add-on program remembers all the calculations that were done to generate a screen and regurgitates them to redraw the screen when necessary. With all the calculation time saved, updating the screen becomes a much faster process, often cut from minutes to seconds.

Adding a display list driver to AutoCAD is no more difficult than installing the driver needed to match any other display system to the drafting program. The driver is executed before AutoCAD is run. The AutoCAD program itself is set up to use its ADI display method. Many recent VGA boards include their own display list drivers to accelerate AutoCAD's performance. A general-purpose AutoCAD display list driver is available from Vermont Microsystems under the name AutoMate.

Printer Spooling

Too many PCs turn themselves into vegetables when they print. After you issue the print command to your database or spreadsheet, your computer single-mindedly concentrates on shifting characters from its memory onto paper. Printers, being mechanical devices, can rarely keep up with the rate that your PC can generate data. As a result, when printing, your PC must constantly wait while your printer laboriously pecks away. Meanwhile, you are stuck watching an immutable screen while the whole chore drags along. You could regain control of your PC from a print job more quickly if you could dump all the data out of your computer at its speed rather than the printer's. That way your PC never has to wait for the printer to catch up.

A device that enables you to regain control is a printer spooler, or printer buffer. The spooler can be a separate hardware upgrade or a software program.

The software solutions are the least expensive, particularly since the programs that you need are usually free. Nearly every memory expansion board at one time or another included a "free" bonus printer spooler. Some operating systems (such as OS/2 and UNIX) and some operating environments (such as Windows) and many applications (particularly word processors) also include spoolers as standard equipment. Spoolers are also available on most computer bulletin board systems.

Software spoolers have an advantage over the hardware variety because they can acquire data as fast as your applications generate it, while data bound for hardware buffers must first squeeze through a communications port. But software spoolers can consume prodigious amounts of your PC's microprocessor power—and lots of disk or RAM if you let them. In 8088 machines, for example, a spooler slows down your system to a fraction of its normal speed, sometimes making it take agonizing seconds from the press of a key to a character appearing on the screen. Although 286, 386, and 486 computers take less of a hit because they have greater performance reserves, the slowdown may still be noticeable. Nevertheless, when the choice is doing nothing while printing and working more slowly than usual, low speed can come up the big winner.

Note that adding a print spooler does not speed up the rate at which your printouts are finished, nor do you regain control of your PC instantaneously. Processing files for printing still takes time.

Keyboard Quickeners

The toughest bottleneck to beat is one that lies not in the electronic realm but in the human. Although you cannot do anything to quicken your thoughts, you can do something about communicating them faster to your PC. Without changing either your keyboard or adding more hardware (such as a mouse or trackball), you can boost the speed with which you can interact with your computer. You can make improvements in two places: navigating through menus and applications and keying in data.

You can make improvements in two places: navigating through menus and applications and keying in data.

Navigational Speed

Applications that require you to repeatedly press the cursor keys to move around in an editing display are particularly amenable to acceleration. By increasing the typematic rate—the speed at which a key that is held down squirts out a series of characters to your PC— you can make the cursor fly through applications. A faster cursor accelerates the rate at which you can choose words and characters for editing or race through a data input template.

Some programs, notably Microsoft Windows, have their own, built-in keyboard quickeners. Or you can buy a quickener as part of a generalized speedup utility package. The keyboard-enhancer in Multisoft's PC-Kwik Power Pak is particularly useful.

Some computers do not require software keyboard quickeners. Instead, they may have built-in facilities for altering the keyboard's built-in typematic rate, often making it part of your system's setup procedure (check your owner's manual). Several keyboard speedup programs are also free and available on local electronic bulletin board services.

Keyboard Macros

Much of the typing that you do is likely to be repeated time and again. For example, every letter you type probably has an address block at the top and your name at the bottom. Or, you may issue a series of commands every time you use your PC to collect your E-mail, open a spreadsheet, and pull down the latest update from the corporate database. It is foolish for you to have to type these same words and commands over and over again when a device with a better memory than your own—your PC—can do the work for you.

A macro is a facility that enables your PC to read, write, or process a predefined sequence of text or data when given a simple command. A keyboard macro simulates the keystroke you type at your keyboard. The keyboard macro sends letters to your PC and the application it is running, as if you had typed them in directly. The keyboard macro can send blocks of text to your word processor, commands to DOS, or data to a spreadsheet exactly as if you had typed it all.

Versions of DOS more recent than 5.0 include a rudimentary keystroke macro program called DOSKEY. It enables you to recycle old command lines and to save strings of characters for later reuse.

Commercial keyboard macro programs go farther and are easier to use. Most include a simplified way of defining your macros called "learn mode." To create a macro, you hit a hot-key combination— the keys you later press to cause the macro to send keystrokes to your computer—and then you just type the sequence of keystrokes you want the macro to remember. Pressing a special key stops the learn mode and causes the macro to remember everything. Thereafter, each time you press the hot key, the macro dutifully echoes your previous keystrokes. You can save all the macros you make to disk so you can later read them back into memory without having to go through the learn process all over again.

The macro program itself is a TSR utility that lodges itself in your computer's memory every time you execute it. Although the program permanently remembers the macros you type by storing them on disk, it typically keeps them in RAM after you start the macro program running. Consequently, the macro steals not only enough memory to hold its own code, but also enough RAM to store the output of all the macro commands.

Most powerful programs and operating environments like Quarter-deck Systems' DESQview have their own, built-in macros that minimize the need for external keyboard macros. As a result, this software has fallen from favor over the last few years, and many products have been discontinued. The advent of DOSKEY as part of DOS will likely accelerate this trend. Nevertheless, keyboard macros remain useful should you want to automate lesser programs that lack built-in macro support.

3

Microprocessors and Motherboards

The most radical change you can make in your PC is upgrading its microprocessor. A microprocessor upgrade gives you extra processing speed, the capability to handle greater amounts of memory, and access to new environments and operating systems. But an upgrade can be costly, and tinkering with your system's innermost circuits can be worrisome. However, you will find that the benefits easily outweigh the risks.

Replacing a microprocessor is essentially a brain transplant, resulting in a complete change in the personality of your system.

Replacing a microprocessor is essentially a brain transplant, resulting in a complete change in the personality of your system. Whereas before your system may have been lazy (or at least lackadaisical), a new brain makes it a willing and speedy worker. Once shirking from such tasks as running multiple programs at the same time, with a new personality it can juggle programs like bowling pins. Better yet, transforming your system from woebegone to whippersnapper need not take more than an hour of your time.

Although changing microprocessors can improve the performance of your system dramatically, upgrading your chip is not just a matter of speed. Your computer's microprocessor not only does all the work, it also determines what work gets done and what programs you can run. It dictates whether you can use the latest operating systems or forever are stuck relying on EDLIN for word processing. If you have an older PC, an upgrade to the current generation of microprocessors allows your PC to use today's utilities that expand the amount of memory available to your DOS applications. Thanks to the advanced memory handling capabilities of the latest microprocessors, you can stretch the addressing range of DOS and move memory-resident drivers and utilities out of the way of your programs. Moreover, the repertory of programs that your PC can handle expands to embrace nearly everything available, including powerful multitasking operating systems like OS/2 2.1, Windows/NT, and beyond.

The best part about upgrading the microprocessor in your PC is that you can do it yourself with a lot less trouble and danger than changing a light switch, let alone installing a new light fixture. If you know which way to spin a screwdriver and have managed to slide an expansion board into your PC without eliciting fireworks, you can handle the job. Even the most difficult microprocessor upgrades can be completed in under an hour. If you have a 486-based PC, the job is even easier because you need plug in only a single chip. The latest machines just as quickly can switch to Pentium technology. The only tough part is deciding which microprocessor to install and which of the available upgrade methods to use.

If you know which way to spin a screwdriver and have managed to slide an expansion board into your PC without eliciting fireworks, you can handle the job.

Chip Choice

The first decision you must make—which microprocessor to upgrade to—might seem to be the easiest. Like every other PC owner, you probably want the kind of secret super-chip that mainframe computer makers have suppressed in fear of wiping out their own sales, something like the long-awaited 500 MHz 80986, only faster. Today, the minimum to set your sights on is the 486-level chip, the highest increment that most machines—except for the very latest models—now allow. Moreover, choosing a 486 means fewer regrets and second guesses later. Pentium upgrades—scheduled for availability in late 1994—will only work on a select few machines released since the end of 1992, hardly the ones in greatest need for an upgrade.

Although you may aspire to a 486 or better microprocessor, you can't always get one. With some PCs, a 486 simply won't fit, or the 486 might not fit your budget. Unfortunately, you might have to lower your aspirations.

To make the most intelligent upgrade, you should consider what each microprocessor offers you and your PC. You also should know where your current chip fits in the overall scheme of microprocesors.

In other words, before you decide what you need, you must know what you have and where you can go. To help you get acquainted with the choices available to you, here is a brief "chipography" of the microprocessors currently compatible with today's PC standard.

The 8088 Family

The place to begin is with the minimum microprocessor you will find in any PC, the Intel 8088, the chip that ignited the fireworks of the PC revolution. As glorious as it once was, in today's world of Pentium atom bombs and 486 dynamite, the 8088 has all the bang of a soaked cap gun. In fact, on a scale of microprocessor performance from zero to one hundred with a Pentium at the top, the 8088 only rates a fraction.

Different models of 8088 chip are available. The fastest 8088 that's widely available runs at about 10 MHz, twice as fast as the standard microprocessor in IBM PCs and XTs, which are throttled back to 4.77 MHz.

Those numbers don't sound too far off today's top chips. At 10 MHz you might expect an 8088 to be only one-third the speed of a good 33 MHz 486, but the clock speeds of different microprocessor families are not directly comparable. The actual processing speed of a microprocessor is dependent on a number of factors, of which clock speed is only one. For instance, each chip architecture has an efficiency factor that roughly equates to the number of clock cycles required to carry out a single instruction. Various chip instructions can require from one to more than one hundred clock cycles. Moreover, microprocessors also differ in the number of data bits that they can handle at a time. A chip that can process 32 bits at a time (like a 386 or 486) carries out operations 4 times faster than one limited to 8 bits at a time, all else being equal. A greater bit-width also enables the chip to acquire instructions and data more quickly. When all these factors are taken into consideration, the 8088 pales in comparison to newer chips. For example, its direct descendant, the 80286 microprocessor, runs between 4 and 5 times faster than an 8088 at the same clock speed. In other words, as a comparison *between* microprocessor families, megahertz are meaningless, relevant only to comparisons *within* a family of chips—such as when comparing one 8088 to another.

The 8088 is not a microprocessor anyone would upgrade *to*—but it is certainly a chip anyone would want to upgrade *from*. It serves as a reference point to compare other microprocessors in its family (that is, those that use Intel's architecture). All such microprocessors are defined by three characteristics—the bit-width of its internal registers (which carry out all of the microprocessor's instructions and calculations), the bit-width of the data lines used for acquiring data and instructions, and the number of address lines that determine the maximum memory that the chip can handle.

The 8088 chip contains 4 principal registers, each of which is 16 bits wide. Its connections with the outside world are limited to a width of 8 bits. And because the 8088 has 20 addressing lines, it can address a maximum of 1M of memory directly (that is, 2^{20} bytes of memory).

Because DOS was written to run on the 8088 series of microprocessors, it confines itself to the addressing limits of the 8088. To retain compatibility with 8088 microprocessors, DOS never attempts to address more than 1M of memory. In fact, some programs take advantage of the 1M addressing limit and wrap addresses "around" the limit, knowing that when the limit is exceeded, the 8088 starts counting again from the beginning.

The more familiar 640K DOS limit is a result of IBM reserving the last 384K of the 8088's addressing range for fixed internal functions of the original PC. Because IBM didn't want programs interfering with these functions, a line was drawn at 640K that programs weren't allowed to cross.

The 8088 family has two close relatives. One is a low-power version, the 80C88. Low-power Complimentary Metal Oxide Semiconductor (CMOS) construction makes the 80C88 consume much less power (and contributes the "C" in its name). The other, the V20 microprocessor, is a clone of the 8088 made by NEC. It has the same register width, data path, and addressing limits of the 8088. However, the internal structure of the V20 is somewhat more efficient than the 8088, resulting in slightly better performance on some applications.

The 8086 Family

The 8088 microprocessor is actually an offshoot of another chip, the 8086. The difference is that the 8088 has an 8-bit connection with external data while the 8086 has a 16-bit connection. The 8088 was derived from the 8086 to reduce costs. At the time the 8088 was developed, microprocessor support circuits that used 8-bit data paths were substantially less expensive than those using 16-bit paths.

Internally, the 8088 and 8086 use identical register structures. The two chips have the same 20-bit addressing capability and also use the same instruction sets. The 8088 and 8086 run the same software, but, because of the differing number of data connections, they are not pin-for-pin compatible. You cannot substitute one for the other.

The wider external connection of the 8086 means that it can read and write to memory and peripherals somewhat faster than the 8088, approaching (but never quite reaching) a twofold performance improvement over the 8088 when the chips operate at the same clock speeds. The performance improvement was sufficient that some manufacturers once offered 8086 upgrades for 8088 systems. Most (if not all) of these have been discontinued not only because of the modest speed gain but also because the 8086 is limited to 1M of memory handling. It cannot run the protected-mode programs or operating systems that have become so popular today. In other words, the 8086 has changed from an 8088 upgrade to a chip that itself needs to be upgraded.

Like the 8088, the 8086 is available in a low power version. NEC also offers its own clone of the 8086 called the V30. Another Intel chip, the 80186, is essentially an 8086 with some of its required external support chips grafted into its silicon. Unless you have the barest minimum—and most aged—PC, you won't want to consider any of these as candidates for your next upgrade.

The 80286 Family

In the early 1980s, Intel created the 80286 (now shortened in general use to the 286) as its *tour de force*. The new chip offered much greater inner efficiency than its 8086 predecessor and broke asunder the older chip's memory-handling barrier. The 286 was to be the chip that would revolutionize how personal computers worked. The 286 did change computers, but not in the way expected. The 286 was chosen first by IBM for its powerful Personal Computer AT, which set the industry standard for future PCs, a standard only now wavering, but the 286 proved to be only a part of that new standard. The design work on the 286 started before DOS dominated the world of personal computers. The 286 was created to be the powerhouse behind a new operating system. Unfortunately, at the time the world was behind DOS and no new operating system was delivered for the 286 for three years (and it—OS/2—had a chilly initial reception indeed). The 286 was stuck running DOS, and its memory-handling capabilities were hardly tapped because DOS couldn't do the tapping.

In a major break with the past, the 286 was designed to operate in two mutually exclusive modes. In *real mode* it emulates the 8086 but runs substantially faster. As with the 8086, it has 16-bit internal registers and 16-bit data connections. Although the 286 has 24 address lines (allowing it to directly address 16M of RAM), the chip is limited to addressing 1M of RAM in real mode.

The other operating mode of the 286 is *protected mode.* Protected mode allows programs to use all 16M that the chip can address. Several programs can run simultaneously in this memory without interfering with each other. However, the 24-bit addressing of protected mode and the 16-bit addressing used by DOS don't mix, so DOS cannot run in protected mode.

Worse, the designers of the 286 envisioned real mode as a springboard to leap into protected mode. They thought that after all that memory was made available, no one would want to go back to the memory confines of real mode. So the switch between real and protected modes was designed as a one-way street. The 286 can not switch modes at will. The 286 must boot up in real mode, and in most cases that's where it stays, running DOS applications.

The 286 has been termed "brain dead" by any number of industry commentators, its vegetative state caused by its incompatibility with DOS, but the 286 doesn't have a completely flat EEG. It functions fine at a primitive—that is, DOS—level. It can run DOS applications at high speeds, particularly in the chip's 20 MHz version. But that's about all it can do for your DOS applications. It runs only one at a time, and they only can touch addresses in the first megabytes of its memory range. If all you want to do is run DOS, the 286 does it handily. It also manages some versions of Novell Netware, UNIX, and OS/2. If you have higher aspirations, —like Windows 3.1, Windows NT, or OS/2 Version 2.1. Consider the 286 (and its low-power CMOS twin, the 80C286) another chip to upgrade from rather than to.

The 80386 Family

Large corporations learn from their mistakes, and the 80386 family of microprocessors—now termed the 386 family—is proof of the learning experience at Intel. Instead of ignoring DOS, the 386 embraces it. Not only does the 386 excel at running DOS, it runs multiple DOS programs simultaneously.

Like the 286, the 386 has both real and protected modes. The two modes operate exactly as they do in the 286, with the exception that the 386 can switch back and forth between real and protected modes.

The 386's multitasking capability comes from a third operating mode. The new mode, virtual 8086 mode, allows the 386 to divide available memory into areas that each operate like a separate 8086 microprocessor running in real mode. These memory areas are isolated from one another so that errant code from one cannot interfere with another. As with an actual 8086, the 386 can address up to 1M of RAM in each of these memory areas. The result is that an individual DOS program can run in each memory area as if it were in its own computer. In fact, each division behaves exactly like a separate computer, allowing a full regimen of TSRs and drivers to operate as if in multiple PCs.

Virtual 8086 mode is the key feature required by DOS multitasking systems. It allows DESQview, Windows, and OS/2 to run several ordinary DOS applications at a time. If you want to do multitasking with DOS applications, you need at least a 386 microprocessor. Although true Windows and OS/2 applications don't use virtual 8086 mode, they too require at least a 386 microprocessor to take advantage of other advanced features, such a 32-bit programming instructions.

Virtual 8086 mode isn't the only reason you'll want to make the 386 your minimum microprocessor choice if you depend on DOS applications. The 386 also has advanced memory management features. It can remap memory through its own internal hardware, allowing the 386 to alter the logical address at which it recognizes physical memory. Memory remapping tricks programs into running elsewhere, allowing computers to shadow their ROM memory for added speed and to increase the memory area available to DOS applications. Although some 286 computers allow ROM shadowing, this feature must be implemented in external memory management circuitry. To increase the memory available to DOS, memory re-mapping relocates drivers and TSR programs out of the DOS 640K addressing range and into high memory. This memory-managing capability is needed to take advantage of all the power of the latest versions of Windows as well as DOS Versions 5.0 and later.

The 386 also incorporates dramatic improvements, the value of which only becomes apparent in the long run. Intel extended the addressing range of the most powerful 386 chips to a full 32 bits, putting up to 4 gigabytes of memory within its direct reach. The 386 also can address virtual memory—RAM that's simulated by disk memory—up to 16 trillion bytes of virtual RAM.

In addition, the 386 is a full 32-bit microprocessor, capable of running applications twice as fast as the 16-bit 286. However, this performance advantage is not meaningful when you only run DOS programs, OS/2 through Version 1.3, or Windows through Version 3.1. DOS was written as a 16-bit operating system, and its code uses only 16-bit instructions. When operating at the same clock speed, the 386 executes DOS applications and other 16-bit applications at about the same rate as a 286 (some 286-based systems actually earn a performance edge over the 386 when running DOS). However, Intel makes 386 chips that run at substantially higher clock speeds than 286 chips, giving the 386 the performance lead.

Beyond DOS, there's no comparison between the 286 and 386. The 286 cannot run programs based on the 386's 32-bit instructions. A program recoded with 32-bit instructions often runs twice as fast (or faster) on a 386 PC than its 16-bit equivalent running on a 286. As more and more applications and operating systems are written using the 386's native 32-bit instruction set, you'll have even more reason to upgrade to the 386.

You have two 386 upgrade choices, the 386DX and 386SX. The 386DX is the original 386 under a new name, a full 32-bit chip in all regards—32-bit registers, 32-bit addressing, and 32-bit input/ output data path. The 386SX is a more recent down-market version of the original 386. It cuts the input/output data path in half to 16 bits while retaining the same 32-bit addressing and 32-internal registers of the 386DX. Although the narrow data path reduces some speed capabilities, it does enable the 386SX to work with 16-bit peripherals, which are in general less expensive than their 32-bit counterparts. The 386SX is thus designed as an alternative for computer manufacturers that enables them to build less expensive machines. The 386SX recognizes the same 32-bit instruction set as the 386DX, and it operates in the same three modes and so can run any program written for the 386DX and lesser microprocessors.

Another addition to the 386 family is the 386SL, a chip with the same internal architecture as the other 386s but using a different cir- cuit technology and design goal. The 386SL was created to be an

energy skinflint, conserving power in a variety of ways to allow laptop and notebook PCs to run as long as possible on a single charge.
As far as applications are concerned, the 386SL is just another 386.
Everything that runs on a 386—from the tiniest utilities to high-
powered graphics bombshells using 32-bit instructions—happily
executes in a 386SL.

The 386SL is not a chip to plan an upgrade around, however. To
computer hardware, the 386SL is an unusual beast, more a set of
chips than a single microprocessor. Taking advantage of its energy
management capabilities requires special computer designs, and
there is little reason to squeeze more from the watts in your PC. The
power demands of the support circuits and peripherals in desktop
PCs are many times greater than those of the microprocessor.
Although the 386SL gives your PC the same program-running
capabilities as any other chip in the 386 family, the 386SX is a much
cheaper way to achieve that goal.

When you have a choice of upgrading to a 386DX or 386SX, if all
things are equal, the 386DX is the hands-down choice because it's
the bigger, faster chip. The 386DX is also available in higher speed
ratings than the 386SX. However, the 386DX is more expensive; a
386SX chip costs much less. The only disadvantage to choosing the
386SX over the 386DX is speed. There is no difference in the
applications that the two chips run or in their advanced features.

Although the 386 family boasts an impressive list of features, the
entire family now rates as another to upgrade from, not to. The 486
is simply a much more effective upgrade. The only time to consider
adding a 386 to your PC is when you already have a more modest
microprocessor—an 8088 or 286—and you cannot readily upgrade
further. But with the availability of a low-end version of the 486 for
existing 286 systems, consider upgrading to that level of performance
rather than settling for a "mere" 386.

The 80486 Family

Intel's 80486, colloquially the 486, is both a slimmed-down and
beefed-up version of the 386. It's slimmed down in that its circuitry
has been made more efficient, able to carry out many operations 15
to 25 percent faster than a 386 running at the same clock speed. At
the same time, it has been beefed up with its own modest (8K)

memory cache and a math coprocessor. The price of the chip, too, has been beefed up to match—the cost of a 486 hovers close to that of a 386DX with a matching 387DX math coprocessor. Because the 486 family has proven so popular, several manufacturers have created clones. Both Advanced Micro Devices and IBM offer versions that legally borrow Intel's basic design. Cyrix Corporation and Texas Instruments offer their own versions of code-compatible 486 chips.

Regardless of the manufacturer, all 486 chips are at heart the same as the 386, so the 486 family runs most of the same programs that the 386 will. The few exceptions are the work of clever programmers who attempted to modify the contents of the system's cache and unwittingly thwarted the 486's capability to keep the contents of memory and its internal cache congruent. Note that the number of incompatible programs has decreased to insignificant as programmers have had their transgressions pointed out to them.

Beyond these few exceptions, all programs, multitasking operating environments, and operating systems that run on 386 chips run on the 486. The two chips understand the same 32-bit (as well as 16-bit and 8-bit) instructions, and have the same operating modes and memory-handling capabilities. Programs like AutoCAD that require a Intel-style math coprocessor also run on systems equipped solely with a 486 microprocessor. Stepping up to a 486 won't add extra capabilities to your PC—it won't run any programs that it could not before. The reason to make the 486 upgrade is performance. The 486 is just that much faster than preceding chips.

The 486 has proven so popular that you'll find more variety within the 486 family than among all lesser microprocessors. The official Intel 486 family is bifurcated somewhat like the 386 family. Like the 386DX, the high-end 486 chip, dubbed the 486DX, has its own poor re-lation, the 486SX. The difference between the two 486 chips is not the bus connection, however. Both the 486DX and 486SX are full-blown 32-bit chips. Rather, the 486SX is stripped of the built-in numeric coprocessor of the 486DX. As many applications don't take advantage of the coprocessor in the 486DX, the 486SX delivers streamlined 486 performance at a more affordable price. AMD's 486 clones follow the Intel model with DX and SX versions.

At first the favorable pricing of the 486SX was believed by some to be just clever marketing—Intel was thought to be selling 486DX chips in which the coprocessor was defective (termed "floorsweepings" by some). Today, however, Intel runs a separate production line for the 486SX, making it a true chip in its own right.

In 1991 Intel expanded its 486 line with its clock-doubling micro-processors, the 486DX2 line. These chips hark back to the old 8088/8086 split that divided microprocessors into low-performance versions for inexpensive motherboards and high-performance chips for more advanced motherboards. Where the 8088 cut back on bus interface to allow the use of inexpensive 8-bit components, the clock-doubling chip trims the operating frequency of external circuits to minimize motherboard expense. By internally doubling the frequency of the circuitry of the motherboard, the 486DX2 chips process data faster than the motherboard clock frequency would ordinarily allow. An old motherboard designed for 33 MHz operation can thus take advantage of 66 MHz technology. The slower external connections of the 486DX2 family mean that the chips don't deliver the same performance as ordinary DX chips that run with full speed motherboards; the clock-doubled chips excel at internal calculation but lag when it comes to accessing memory. Overall, they deliver about 70 to 90 percent of the processing throughput you would expect from their internal clock rate. Note that to put the best spin on this technology, these clock-doubling chips are rated at their higher internal processing speed.

Intel offers a special line of 486 clock-doubling chips designed to replace older chips that operate at the same speed internally as externally. Called *OverDrive* microprocessors, they plug into special sockets or in place of older chips to bring clock-doubling technology to older systems. The OverDrive chips are one of the most effective upgrades available and are discussed separately.

Intel (as well as IBM and probably most other chip vendors) is working on clock-tripling microprocessors, pushing clock-doubling technology up to the next increment. They have the same strength—faster processing on slower system boards, but they also have same weakness—slow memory and input/output response.

Cyrix's 486 chips actually rate below Intel's. The Cyrix 486SLC is more like a 386SX than a 486. The Cyrix chip has many of the features of a 386SX—16-bit external data connections with 32-bit internal registers. In fact, the 486SLC is designed to plug into a 386SX socket without modification. However, the 486SLC understands the full 486 command set. Like the Intel 486 family, the Cyrix chip includes an internal cache, but it's limited to 1K of memory. The 486SLC also lacks an internal math coprocessor. Although the 486SLC fits a 386SX socket, it is not a direct replacement for the older chip. Activating the internal cache (and thus the full performance potential) of the 486SLC requires BIOS modifications.

The system board, sometimes referred to as the mother-board, is the main computer circuit board containing the CPU, the microprocessor support circuitry, random access memory, and expansion slots.

The Cyrix 486DLC has most of the same features of the 486SLC—full 486 command set, no coprocessor, and 1K internal cache—but it matches the 386DX pin-out with a 32-bit external data bus. (A *pinout* is the number of pns connecting the chip to its environment.) As with the 486SLC, a 486DLC cannot be substituted directly for a 386 chip because controlling the cache requires a BIOS change. Both Cyrix chips are designed to make the job of motherboard manufacturers easier—their 386 designs can be easily (and cheaply) modified to Cyrix 486 technology.

Although the Cyrix chips lack integral coprocessors, Cyrix makes up for this by pricing the combination of its 486-level microprocessors and its 387-style numeric coprocessors favorably. Motherboard makers pay little (maybe $20) if anything extra for the coprocessor. The difference to you, however, is more substantial. The Cyrix processor/coprocessor combination lacks the tight integration of the Intel 486DX microprocessor, so the two chips cannot exchange data as fast as the single-chip Intel design.

IBM was not satisfied with Intel's designs and re-engineered the 486 to suit itself, developing the 486SLC2 (sometimes called the 486SL2). Using its advanced chip design technology, IBM cleaned up the Intel chip layout and added some innovations of its own to the basic 486 technology. At heart, the 486SLC2 is a 486SL chip enhanced with clock-doubling technology and a 16K internal memory cache. As a result, it handily outperforms Intel chips with the same speed rating.

IBM licensed Intel's 386 and 486 technology and thus can manufacture Intel's own designs. IBM's license prohibits the company from selling IBM-made chips as such to other computer makers, but it can sell the 486SLC2 as part of finished assemblies. In recent years, IBM has become a multifaceted vendor of PC components, among them complete motherboards, so you'll find the 486SLC2 chip inside a variety of computers with common and uncommon brand names. All are likely to include IBM motherboards along with the IBM-manufactured microprocessor.

The Pentium Family

In 1993, Intel introduced its ultimate microprocessor—for the time being. Although long expected to be termed the 586, the company opted for the contrived name *Pentium*. The unusual nomenclature probably stems from a federal court ruling that the 386 numeric designation was generic, describing a type of product rather than something exclusive to a particular manufacturer. Intel chose a specific name so that when other companies cloned its new chip, they could not use the same name as the original.

Pentium sports a 64-bit interface rather than the 32-bit connections of the older microprocessors. However, inside the Pentium is still a 32-bit chip, albeit an unusual one. In essence, it is two 486 chips linked together to divide the work between them.

To help match the Pentium to your PC, Intel has built a 16K internal cache into the chip. This cache is arranged quite differently from that of the 486. It is effectively split in half, with 8K used for managing program instructions and the other 8K for buffering data. The bifurcated design is a more efficient way of dividing data for processing by the microprocessor. The result is that the cache of the Pentium is much more efficient than that of the 486, even after allowing for its increased size.

The cache of the Pentium is much more efficient than that of the 486, even after allowing for its increased size.

The Pentium carries on the Intel tradition of backward compatibility. Despite its revolutionary design, the Pentium still runs all the same programs that execute on the 386 and 486 in exactly the same operating modes. The Pentium boots up in real mode and then can switch to (and back from) protected and virtual 8086 modes. The Pentium instruction set includes all the commands used by the 486 and adds new instructions of its own.

The primary—and most interesting from an upgrade perspective—difference between the Pentium and its predecessors is speed. The initial Pentium chips were supposed to start at about twice top-of-the-line 486 speed (that is, about twice as fast as a 66 MHz 486DX2). Although the first Pentium chips operated at a top speed only matching the internal 66 MHz of Intel's quickest clock-doubling 486 chips, they did turn in results about 80 percent faster when running DOS applications. The unusual Pentium design isn't particularly well-suited to running ordinary DOS applications. Its dual nature requires programs to be optimized to be split between its processing sections, and DOS is a one-thing-at-a-time operating system. Windows and OS/2 have the potential to exploit the power of the Pentium, but for best effect even they require changes in application software. Considering the slow market acceptance of full 32-bit software (32-bit OS/2 appeared a full five years after the introduction of the 32-bit 386 chip), new Pentium-optimized programs may be a long way off.

According to Intel, the most powerful enhancement to the Pentium is not its microprocessor circuitry but its internal coprocessor. According to Intel, the Pentium coprocessor is three to five times faster than the floating-point unit in a 486 running at the same clock speed. As with other coprocessors, this advanced Pentium feature only comes into play when you run applications that use complex math functions. Oddly, the most popular Pentium application—network servers—doesn't tap this capability.

There's no hope of plugging a current Pentium chip in place of a 486.

The initial Pentium chips connect to their computer hosts through a full 64-bit address bus. This wide link allows the Pentium to acquire and save data twice the speed of a chip with 32-bit connections. (Internally, parts of the Pentium are linked with connections as wide as 256 bits!) For reaching memory, the Pentium uses the same 32-bit addressing system as the 386 and 486 family, allowing it to reach 4 gigabytes of system RAM.

The increased number of connections used by the Pentium has one important implication for upgraders: There's no hope of plugging a current Pentium chip in place of a 486. However, Intel has promised (for late 1994) a version of the Pentium that works in 486 computers. Code-named the P24T, the upgrade chip is not pin-compatible with the 486 chips it supersedes and requires a special upgrade socket, one with 268 pins. Most new 486-based PCs built since Intel released the P24T pin-out specification in 1992 have included upgrade sockets. However, as this is written, the general upgradability of these PCs is clouded.

A big problem is heat. The initial Pentium chips dissipated about 17 watts of power—on the order of a small light bulb. Because they are based on the same Pentium design, P24T chips probably dissipate a similar magnitude of power. That heat has to go somewhere. If it doesn't, the result may be a meltdown (or at least a system shutdown). A problem may arise in that many so-called Pentium-upgradable PCs with P24T sockets were not designed with cooling in mind. That is, although these machines may have the necessary socket for a P24T chip, they don't provide the cooling the high-powered chip requires. A P24T upgrade in such a system would be doomed to failure. Intel tried to prevent such a problem by publishing the cooling requirements of the P24T, but a number of manufacturers did not heed them. Intel is working on a solution to the problem—for example, P24T chips with different cooling technologies (such as built-in fans) for different systems and a selection chart to help you pick the right chip for your PC. In any case, Intel hopes to have a means of providing a functional P24T upgrade for all systems that sport a proper socket.

Which Chip To Pick

When you decide to upgrade your PC's microprocessor, the initial temptation is to get the most powerful chip available. You can't always do that because the most powerful chips—like the initial release of Intel's Pentium—simply won't fit most PCs. The next best selection is to upgrade to the fastest chip that fits into your system. For most people, that's the best overall upgrade choice. If you get the best, you'll have less to regret. Ultimately something faster will be available, and you won't be as far behind as you would with a lesser choice. You'll get the maximum life out of your PC as well. The economics of upgrading your PC once are sometimes dubious. If you try to eke two upgrades out of a single PC, you won't have any doubts about the economics—you'll be better off opting for something new.

There's one exception to the go-for-the-most rule, and that's when you try to stretch your system too far. If your PC is more than five years old or has one of the more rudimentary microprocessors, forget the upgrade or aim modestly with your eye focused on economy. When you put a high-power microprocessor in your old system, it's likely to suffer from the laggardly capabilities of older disks and expansion boards that date back to the years technology forgot. Upgrade the rest of an older PC to match a new top-of-the-line microprocessor, and you can easily exceed the cost of a new computer.

Upgrade the rest of an older PC to match a new top-of-the-line micro-processor, and you can easily exceed the cost of a new computer.

Even some economical upgrades are difficult to justify. For example, the relatively inexpensive move from the 8088 to a 286 microprocessor is probably not a wise move today. Although you gain 3 to 10 times more speed, as well as the capability to run early versions of OS/2, your system still lacks all the 386 features that make power users drool. It also lacks the memory capabilities needed to take advantage of today's advanced applications that can run several DOS programs at the same time.

The best price-to-features compromise for older computers based on 8088, 8086, and 286 microprocessors is upgrading to the 386SX or 486SLC microprocessor. Although both chips deliver only slightly better overall speed than the original 286, both make your PC capable of running any 80386-specific application. You'll gain the advanced memory-mapping capabilities of the 386 family which,

If you move from a 286 to a 386SX, you probably won't need a new set of peripherals to reap the new chip's benefits.

among other things, enable you to relocate TSRs out of DOS's 640K and give you more memory for your regular programs. You'll gain the 386's virtual 8086 mode that supports true multitasking, and your newly enhanced system understands the 32-bit 80386 instructions of high-powered programs like AutoCAD 386.

The cost of a 386SX or 486SLC upgrade may be $100 to $200 more than a 286, a result of the price differential charged by Intel for the chips. For what you get, the difference is well worth it. Moreover, if you move from a 286 to a 386SX, you probably won't need an new set of peripherals to reap the new chip's benefits.

You can upgrade your system to include an Intel i860 RISC microprocessor as easily as moving to a new 286 or 386.

Should you want uncompromising high performance and have a budget to match, you'll find upgrades that equal the capabilities of the best complete computer systems you can buy today. You don't have to stop with just a 486. You can buy some upgrade products that take you into the realm of Reduced Instruction Set Computing (RISC). Although RISC-based microprocessors won't run DOS, they can run more powerful operating systems—in particular UNIX. Today, you can upgrade your system to include an Intel i860 RISC microprocessor as easily as moving to a new 286 or 386.

Microprocessor Upgrade Alternatives

As compelling as microprocessor upgrades are, if your upgrade goals are more specific, you might be able to find a few better alternatives. For example, if you want to wring as much performance as possible from your PC and don't mind experimentation or tempting fate, you can push your old microprocessor beyond its rated speed. If you just want to give your favorite DOS applications a few extra kilobytes on your 286, you could add extra memory-controlling hardware to your PC to relocate driver programs and TSRs as you could with a 386 and a memory manager.

When you compute the cost of an upgrade with all the improvements you want, you may find that the price is awfully close to that of a new PC. In such a situation, you may find it more logical to leave your old machine alone—keep it as a spare—and buy a new (and more powerful) PC instead.

Increasing Clock Speed

Some people approach home improvement as if it were a virulent disease. If they do indulge, they want quick, proven, and hassle-free solutions. Others like to tinker until they've exhausted all the options or—they hope—found the right one along the way.

Your approach to accelerating your microprocessor can take similar form. When it comes to altering computer circuitry, most people have a fear of frying their expensive silicon and instead opt for time-tested solutions. But the inveterate tinkerer knows that computer circuitry is a lot more rugged than the other folks think—that nothing short of a welding torch and blasting caps can damage computer electronics. The tinkerer is apt to try anything just to see what it does and doesn't mind temporary setbacks when there's the slightest glimmer of getting extra performance.

If you're of this class, you may want to see just how far you can push the computer hardware you already have. Wind up your system as tight as it will go, and see if it actually runs faster. Although PCs don't have clockworks and springs, they all have something akin to a mechanical governor—the crystal that sets the speed of operation for the entire system. Changing this crystal—a part that often costs less than $5—can yield a 25 to 50 percent speed improvement in some systems. The important word is "some." Most systems already are pushed to the limit when you buy them. Upping the clock speed likely won't win anything with such PCs. On the other hand, there's little to lose other than time, so the avid tinkerer is always willing to give it a try.

One class of system is almost guaranteed to give you a 25 percent performance improvement. The very first ATs that IBM sold operated at a clock frequency of 6 MHz. That limit appears to be artificially imposed. The computer's circuitry is capable of handling higher speeds, and some believe that the original AT was slowed purposefully to avoid competing with the more powerful and more expensive computers that IBM offered. In fact, the schematic diagrams of the original AT in some IBM technical reference manuals indicate a speed not of 6 but 8 MHz. These original ATs—and a very few clones—willingly accept higher speed crystals that accelerate processor throughput.

Unfortunately, this strategy is sure-fire only with the first (and slowest) AT generation. It does not apply to newer ATs that are set by the factory to operate at 8 MHz—these machines are limited by their BIOS software as well as their crystals. When these newer ATs boot up, their test routines examine the system clock speed and prevent the computer from completing the boot process if their speed is altered from the factory spec. For a while, some companies offered kits that let you tiptoe past these speed restrictions. The kits held back the speed of the clock during the boot-up process and then unleashed performance once the check was completed. Unfortunately, after IBM halted production on the AT line, the market for these kits dried up, and they are difficult (if not impossible) to find today.

Most 286- and 386-based AT-compatible computers are not good candidates for crystal swapping because they are designed, manufactured, and sold with their circuits operating at maximum speed. Any increase in clock speed decreases the reliability of these systems.

In the 486 generation of PCs, however, the crystal acceleration strategy has found new advocates. Some chips—486SX chips in particular—appear to accept higher speed operation with gusto. The reason is the way these microprocessors are speed rated. Most 486SX chips are manufactured identically, and higher speed chips are tested more stringently to ensure their higher ratings. Chips are not tested to discover their limits; they're tested at the rate at which they will be put to work. Any extra potential isn't investigated. If you're willing to take the time, you may be able to exploit this untested range. Of course, testing is not without its risks, but the risks don't necessarily include damage to your microprocessor. With a bit of care, you have nothing to fear.

The only systems that are not amenable to clock tampering are the first generation 8088 and 8086 machines with 8-bit expansion buses.

If you're venturesome, you can tinker with the clock crystal in almost any PC. In fact, the only systems that are not amenable to clock tampering are candidates for the antique shop—the first generation 8088 and 8086 machines with 8-bit expansion buses. They don't take well to clock change because of the peculiar motherboard timing circuit design they use. One crystal controls all timing in the system. Some programs won't operate properly, and your system clock definitely won't keep proper time. Such a change is at best disorienting.

A chip that gets too hot is likely to generate errors that halt your PC and soon stops working.

Whenever you tamper with a clock crystal to boost system performance, the principal risk you face is heat. The faster a microprocessor runs, the more heat it generates. Its circuits must switch faster, but the time available for dissipating the heat does not change. If a chip gets too hot, it can damage itself, melting its critical silicon junctions into amorphous globs of sand, but microprocessors generally stop working long before they melt down. A chip that gets too hot is likely to generate errors that halt your PC and soon stops working. After a cooling period, however, it starts back up and works just fine.

When you try a faster clock speed, watch for such errors. If your system locks up after working for half an hour, you have pushed it too far. Either back off the speed or add a cooling apparatus to keep your system running. People who hot-rod PCs usually mount a tiny fan adjacent or physically attached to their microprocessors to get maximum cooling and performance. Don't trust a PC you've pushed beyond its ratings until it has proven itself reliable for an hour or more of steady operation in the environment you plan to run it. Don't run critical applications—anything that will cause you to lose valuable time or data should your system crash—until your PC has shown itself stable at a given speed.

The microprocessor is not the only element in your PC that has a speed rating and might falter at faster operation. The support chips, memory chips, and etchings of the motherboard all have limited operating frequency. No matter which circuit element is first to fail when you try to boost your PC, the symptoms of pushing too far are the same. First come the errors and then the shutdown without physical damage. The rule is the same—after your system shuts down on its own, back off the crystal frequency or add extra cooling.

Also, running circuits hotter is known to shorten their lifetimes. So, upping the speed of your system could shorten the life of its circuitry. However, adding adequate cooling—such as an additional fan—drives the temperature down to the same as it was before you upped the speed. Besides, most PCs prove to last well beyond their useful lives.

Should you want to tinker with the clock speed of your system, the only thing you need is one or more replacement crystals. Most manufacturers set the speed ratings of their microprocessor at increments 25 to 50 percent apart, as in Intel's speed steps—20 MHz, 25 MHz, 33MHz, and 50MHz. The odds favor you getting at least half an increment more speed, so that's one place to begin. Most people speed up their microprocessors to the next full notch, primarily because replacement crystals are most easily available at the standard speeds. Although you'll be tempted to get a crystal that takes you all the way to 50 MHz, you're more likely to succeed with modest increases. A true tinkerer tries several crystals, working his way up the performance spectrum. You can find the necessary crystals by mail order or sometimes as close as your local Radio Shack.

If you're trying to hot-rod a 286-based PC like IBM's old AT, you need to select a speed-determining crystal that oscillates at twice the frequency at which you want your system to run. The circuitry of your AT cuts the crystal frequency in half. For example, the crystal in a 6 MHz AT actually runs at 12 MHz, so you'll want to upgrade to a 16 MHz crystal to get an 8 MHz AT. Computers based on 386 and 486 typically have full-speed crystals that oscillate at the same rate the microprocessor runs. For example, to soup up a 20 MHz 486SX, start with a 25 MHz crystal.

Some machines lock their bus clock to the microprocessor crystal, so upping the microprocessor oscillator also may boost bus speed. If you keep your change modest—say only 25 percent—kicking up microprocessor speed also gives you better bus throughput. Go for too much, however, and expansion boards may become unwilling to keep up. Many such machines have jumpers that trim the microprocessor clock to a reasonable bus speed (generally 8 MHz). Changing a jumper often enables you to keep the bus speed constant with increases in crystal frequency. Check your system's owner's manual.

The speed-determining crystal in most modern PCs is a small silver can that measures less than an inch across and high. It is vaguely rectangular with the narrow sides rounded. In 6 MHz ATs, the crystal is found near the rear of the system board, to the left of the power supply when looking from the front of the computer. Other computers locate their crystals elsewhere on the system board. Many machines have several crystals, so you should look for the one clearly marked with a speed rating that matches the operating speed of your PC. The quick change of clock crystal assumes that your crystal is socket-mounted. If the clock crystal in your PC is soldered in place, however, don't bother with this speedup strategy.

Note that the leads from most PC clock crystals are thick, and some replacement crystals use very thin leads that make poor contact with many crystal sockets. If you find yourself in such a predicament, bend the leads double to make a better connection before sliding the crystal into its socket.

Memory Tricks

Another way of squeezing more performance from an existing computer and microprocessor is to speed up its memory. Most microprocessor operations involve memory in one way or another—bytes must be loaded into the microprocessor's registers from memory before they can be worked on and must be dumped back when the calculations are done. Only the calculations themselves are free from the influence of memory. Thus, reducing the time required to access memory can accelerate system performance much as a faster microprocessor would.

The three memory tricks that have the greatest effect on system performance are caching, wait states, and memory interleaving. Where you can take advantage of these performance gains depends on the design of your PC. The caches in today's 486 machines affect performance most, isolating slower memory from the fast microprocessor. Enhancing the cache on these systems usually yields the biggest performance boost. With older (386 and earlier) systems that lack memory caches, other alterations give the biggest change. Not all PCs allow you to toy with each of these parameters. For example, older 8088-based computers can't benefit from these strategies; AT-class 286-based PCs rarely use caching; and most modern PCs ignore memory interleaving.

Expanding Cache Memory

The most significant performance difference between PCs with like microprocessors is memory caching. Without a memory cache, today's fastest microprocessors would be held back to the sluggish rate of most Dynamic Randam Access Memory (DRAM) chips, and systems with full-speed DRAM would be prohibitively expensive. (See Chapter 5 for a complete discussion of memory types.) As good as caching is, more caching is often better; many PCs can benefit by adding to their existing caches instead of undergoing a full microprocessor upgrade.

Every Intel 486 chip has a built-in 8K static RAM cache—a *primary* memory cache—which helps match the fast microprocessor to slower external memory chips. Some manufacturers, such as Cyrix (1K in its 486SLC and 486DLC) and IBM (16K in its 486SLC2) put different size caches in their 486 versions. You cannot alter the internal memory cache.

The three memory tricks that have the greatest effect on system performance are caching, wait states, and memory interleaving.

Reducing the time required to access memory can accelerate system performance much as a faster microprocessor would.

Most quicker 486 machines supplement their internal memory caches with an external (*secondary*) cache. Many 386 PCs also have memory caches, which necessarily are external to the microprocessor. In many of these 386 and 486 systems, the external memory cache can be expanded. A number of manufacturers have incorporated expandable or *scalable memory caches* in their systems so that they can be sold at a low price with a small endowment of expensive cache memory and later enhanced. The larger the cache, the greater the likelihood of making a cache "hit" on each memory request and the lower the effective number of wait states suffered by the system.

Some experts recommend at least a 256K memory cache for serious multitasking work.

As with other upgrades, the improvement from upgrading your PC's external memory cache varies with what you do. If the only programs you run are old DOS applications, increasing your external cache has minimal effect. Multiuser and multitasking applications, however, benefit greatly from enlarged caches. Some experts recommend at least a 256K memory cache for serious multitasking work.

PC memory caches are described as direct-mapped, set associative, write-through, and so on. These terms describe the technology used by the cache. In general, although some of these technologies are more effective than others, you cannot alter what the maker of your PC has decided to use. One architectural difference in secondary memory caches is important when making an upgrade, however. In some PCs, the entire memory cache works with whatever amount of RAM you have installed in your system, but in other PCs, the maximum effective size of the cache depends on your RAM. For example, some PCs can support a 256K external memory cache only when you've filled all motherboard SIMM sockets. That may mean you need 16M of RAM to take full advantage of the memory cache. Install less RAM, and a smaller slice of the memory cache is used. This problem is aggravated by a lack of standard terminology— neither design alternative has a distinctive name. To avoid buying cache memory you cannot use, check your owner's manual before you buy or give your PC vendor a call.

Adding cache memory depends on your PC's physical design. Sometimes, you add cache chips as loose chips that install like any other chips, as discussed in Chapter 6. Other systems put their add-on caches on special, proprietary boards that plug into place.

Memory caches require special high-speed static RAM chips. Ordinary RAM chips won't work. These static RAM chips are often quite expensive and more difficult to find than regular RAM chips. Unlike main memory, for which you can buy as many identical chips or SIMMs as you can afford, PC memory caches often require two or three different chip types. Some manufacturers also require that you change special support chips like Programmable Logic Arrays (PLAs) to make an enlarged cache work. The result is that you face a shopping problem. Larger memory dealers often offer upgrade kits for the PCs of larger machine manufacturers, but if you have a PC from a more obscure maker, you'll need to check your manual for chip type. You may have to contact the manufacturer to secure PALs or other upgrade parts.

While you're reading the manual, check what other alterations you need to make to bring the larger cache to life. You may have to reset jumpers or run your system's setup program. Whatever the case, your system or motherboard manual is your bible.

Trimming Wait States

Most dynamic RAM chips—the least expensive kind of memory—cannot keep up with today's fastest microprocessors and cache controllers, so PCs now add wait states when memory is accessed. That is, the microprocessor or cache controller waits for one or more clock cycles between memory accesses. The number of clock cycles that it waits—the wait states—is a function of the design of the computer, and some designs make this number flexible. As noted in Chapter 3, you can alter it relatively easily.

The number of wait states required depends on the speed of your microprocessor, the speed of the memory, and your system design. Although you cannot change your system design, you can alter your microprocessor and the memory speed ratings. Raise your microprocessor speed, and you may have to increase the number of wait states used by your PC. Invest in faster memory—with a lower microsecond rating—and you may be able to reduce the number of wait states your system uses. Today's PCs are often equipped with 70 or 80 nanosecond (ns) SIMMs. Replacing them with faster, more costly 40, 53, or 60 ns parts may help you reduce the number of wait states used to improve performance several percent (depending on the effectiveness of your cache). In older, non-cached systems, reducing wait states can boost system performance by as much as 50 percent.

Caching helps isolate the modern 486 from the effects of wait states, but it cannot eliminate them. Every cache miss must reach into main memory and endure the wait states that the system demands. The smaller the memory cache in your PC, the greater the effect of wait states on overall performance.

Note that most PC makers today claim zero wait-state operation. In most modern systems, such statements are misleading. The microprocessor sees zero wait states because it sees memory only through its cache controller, which transfers data to the microprocessor with zero wait states. The underlying memory, however, is still hampered by wait states. It has to be—only the most expensive memory modules can keep up with today's 33 MHz and 50 MHz microprocessors.

In PCs that allow user-configurable wait states, your PC can use one of three methods of control: software, hardware, and automatic. Software control relies on software use to change a register in the chips used to implement the computer's electronics. Hardware control uses a jumper or DIP switch setting to achieve the same result. Automatic control senses the maximum operating speed of the memory in the system and adjusts wait states to match.

The software wait state settings are accessed most often during the system's advanced setup procedure. You should be familiar with the procedure from the first time you switched your computer on—it asked for the correct time and date as well as the type of disks you had installed. Every time your system battery gets low (and often at random times of your system's own choosing) you're confronted with this menu.

Some systems offer an adjunct to this menu, typically called *advanced setup*. This procedure allows you to select more intimate operating parameters such as EMS simulation and the shadowing of BIOS and video memory. Among the selections often available is the number of system wait states. By pressing a couple of keys, you can trim the number of wait states used by your PC from 2 to 1 or 0. But don't do it—at least before preparing for the worst. Selecting too few wait states makes your PC operate erratically, if at all. If you choose too few, as soon as your system tries to boot up it bumps squarely into a memory error. You don't pass Go, and you may end up forfeiting $200 to your dealer to jump-start your PC again.

Most computer manufacturers have anticipated your transgressions. Typically, a system with software setup provides for some means of making the system revert to its factory settings should your adjustments go awry. For example, you may have to move a jumper from one position to another or ground a specific terminal as the computer boots up. Before you tinker with wait states—or any other advanced setup parameter—be certain you can undo any possible damage. Only then should you venture cautiously (and with enough spare time to work your way through potential problems) into adjusting wait state settings with software.

You have fewer worries with the hardware setup of wait states. All you need do is look up the proper jumper settings in your computer's manual (or the system board manual that some vendors include) and move the jumper to the number of wait states you want to try. If your system doesn't work, move it back.

Normally, your system won't work when you reduce its wait state value. The manufacturers usually have made your system as fast as they think its memory will allow. However, you can always upgrade to faster memory and then trim the number of wait states. Chapter 5 discusses upgrading your PC's memory.

There is one special case in wait-state reduction: IBM's 1987 PS/2 Models 50 and 60. These machines were designed with one state (for every two-step memory cycle) that slowed performance by about a third. The later Model 50Z eliminated the wait state—its Micro Channel design allows motherboard memory to be switched off. Special Micro Channel memory expansion boards support zero wait-state operation; installing one in your 50 or 60 and switching off motherboard memory endows the entire machine with true zero wait state operation.

Interleaving Memory

In many 286 and 386 PCs, computer makers reduced the number of wait states by interleaving memory, dividing the system RAM into two or more banks, then alternating the data in the memory so that every other byte was in one bank and the remainder in the other. When the microprocessor went to fetch sequential bytes, it first accessed one bank and then the other. Although one bank was being accessed, the other could be refreshed so that on the next memory request the microprocessor could address that bank without wait states.

Some 486 machines use memory interleaving, but most PC makers have abandoned the technology for 486 and Pentium products because the small improvement it offers after other speed-enhancing technologies (principally memory caching) are used cannot justify the complications it adds. For example, gaining one or two extra percent of memory speed using interleaved banks require that all SIMMs be the same size. You would have to fill your PC completely with 1M or 4M SIMMs. Most people prefer the flexibility of mixing different SIMM sizes.

In systems that use interleaving without memory caching, however, the technique can be very effective. Although interleaving saves waiting only on sequential transfers and every other random transfer (the odds are 50 percent that the next byte will be in the other bank when transfers are made at random), it can substantially reduce the waiting.

Even PCs capable of taking advantage of memory interleaving often don't come equipped with all the SIMMs they need to bring it to life.

Even PCs capable of taking advantage of memory interleaving often don't come equipped with all the SIMMs they need to bring it to life. Most PC makers included only a token amount of memory in their products, the minimum they could offer without seeming too chintzy. In general, that means they equipped their systems with a single bank of memory, depriving interleaving of the multiple banks it requires. To gain the extra speed of memory interleaving, you have to add another bank of memory. Making a memory upgrade not only gives you more room for running your programs but also accelerates the system's overall performance.

The best way to determine whether your system supports interleaving and whether the feature is actually used in your system as it is currently configured is to check its instruction manual under "memory." You could also query the manufacturer's customer service department. Chapter 5 provides step-by-step memory upgrade assistance.

Adding Memory Management

Of the two watershed changes in microprocessors—the breaking of the 1M barrier when moving from 8088 to 286 and the four-way change (more memory, memory management, virtual 80386 mode, and 32-bit instructions) when moving from 286 to 386—by far the more important is the latter. You need all that a 386 (or its 486 and Pentium derivatives) offers to use today's software.

Not everyone wants Windows and multi-megabyte applications that tear through resources with the same abandon as Godzilla rampaging through Tokyo. For practical souls—labeled Luddites by more progressive types, such as the salespeople representing the publishers of the multi-megabyte applications—DOS was good enough for Grandma, so it's good enough for them. Many people, in fact, see little need to abandon an old spreadsheet, database, or word processor when they haven't even come close to tapping the full potential of their existing software.

These people eye today's supercharged microprocessors with one thing in mind—more memory for the programs they have. They run so many TSR programs and software drivers that they end up with little room left for running their favorite applications. They might get away with a TSR-managing program that unloads from memory the pop-up programs not currently in use, but the performance hit when all that code is copied to disk is bad—especially with the molasses-filled hard disks built into most AT-class machines. A more satisfactory (and functional) solution is to add memory management capabilities to the 286. Because the 8088 doesn't handle enough memory to worry about and 386-and-better microprocessors have built-in memory management, this strategy applies only to 286 systems.

The only impediment to adding memory management circuitry is that it requires modifications to your PC's hardware. A few commercial products, the major one being the ALL ChargeCard from ALL Computing, Toronto, Ontario, provide all the necessary add-on circuitry on a small circuit board that plugs in between your system's microprocessor and its socket. Special software is supplied with the board to handling the actual relocation of your TSRs and driver software.

Installing a ChargeCard is relatively simple—at least for those who don't mind tinkering with the microprocessor in their system. First remove your system's 286 microprocessor from its system board. Next you plug the chip into the socket waiting for it on the ChargeCard. Finally, you only need to plug the entire assembly back into the microprocessor socket on the system board of your PC. Figures 3.1 through 3.3 illustrate these steps.

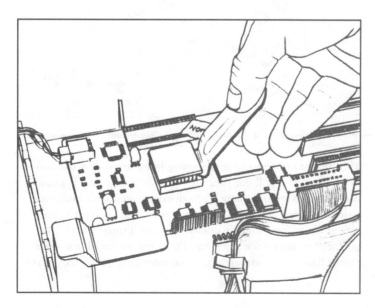

Figure 3.1
First, remove your old 286 chip.

Figure 3.2
Next, line up the
ChargeCard with the
notch on the board.

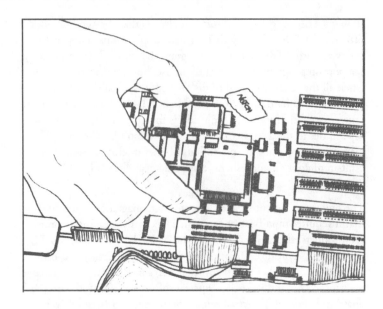

Figure 3.3
Finally, press the
ChargeCard into
place.

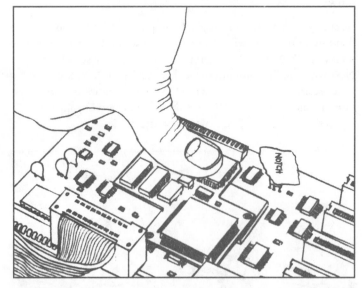

This process can be more complicated, however. Seldom can you
just reach in and pull out your system's microprocessor. Typically,
you'll need to remove many if not all expansion boards from your
system to gain access to the microprocessor. After you get a good
look at the socket, you may discover to your dismay that all 286
microprocessors are not the same. The chips are available in three
physically different packages, and you must match the ChargeCard

you want to use to the type of chip package it is supposed to work with. Be sure that the salesman knows what kind of computer you have so that you can get the right adapters.

Moreover, the ChargeCard is not a panacea. For example, it does not change the performance of your 286, so you'll gain only enhanced memory capabilities with the ChargeCard. The real downside of the ChargeCard is cost—you probably can buy a fully equipped 386SX system board for the price. Moreover, 386SX and 486SLC upgrades for your old 286 bring memory management along with even more significant benefits (32-bit instructions and virtual 8086 mode), and many of these chip upgrades are less expensive than the ChargeCard. Of course, you'll still need the software to remap your programs with a chip or motherboard upgrade, but these alternate strategies improve the overall performance of your system, too. Choose the ChargeCard and similar memory-mapping enhancements for their ease of installation, but for performance and compatibility you might want to make a different upgrade.

Choose the ChargeCard and similar memory-mapping enhancements for their ease of installation, but for performance and compatibility, you might want to make a different upgrade.

Replacing Your Entire PC

Certainly the idea of upgrading is compelling—it's an ecological alternative, the electronic equivalent of recycling. You replace only a chip and not all the accompanying accouterments—the case, keyboard, power supply, expansion boards, mass storage, and memory. From that perspective, an upgrade should be less expensive than buying a replacement PC.

The economics of upgrading may not be so straightforward. A microprocessor upgrade only improves a portion of your system, while a new PC may bring multiple improvements. For example, the allure of upgrading your microprocessor may be that you won't have to write off your investment in the hard disk you've already got in your PC. Retaining your old disk can be a mistake—it may not be up to the speed needs of your new microprocessor (or even your old one). You could upgrade your disk when you switch microprocessors, but that can up the upgrade cost considerably. Plus, your upgrade requirements might not stop at a microprocessor and disk. Opting for a new PC could bring a multitude of other benefits, such as new floppy disk drives, a faster, sharper video system, and a heftier power supply.

Opting for a new PC could bring a multitude of other benefits.

After upgrading, you're left with one computer system—albeit a better one—and you also have a microprocessor and its associated circuitry left over, neither of which likely has any value to you. Choosing a new system instead leaves you with two PCs—one that you can use as a spare, hand down to someone else in your business or at home, or sell off to help recover your investment in new hardware. With so many improvements made in the last couple of years—new disk interfaces, local bus video, graphics acceleration— a new PC might make more sense than the few dollars you could save with an upgrade.

Generally, the newer your PC, the more likely it can benefit from a microprocessor upgrade. That's because less of the rest of your system is likely to be behind the times. A PC bought in the last couple of years probably has a fast display system and a large, quick hard disk. A newer PC might have been designed to be upgraded, either with upgrade boards or with a socket for one of Intel's OverDrive chips. With little effort or skill and only a moderate expense, you can upgrade your system's microprocessor to keep it performing among the best.

A microprocessor upgrade is not an alternative to a new computer. Rather, the upgrade should be viewed as a means of breaking through a particular bottleneck or of adding specific features to the system you already have. For example, if you have a PC that's first class in every way but lacks local bus expansion, upgrading the motherboard (which automatically brings a new microprocessor) can be a cost-effective solution.

Microprocessor Upgrade Method

After you've decided to upgrade your microprocessor and you have a good idea what chip to upgrade to, all that's left is to choose *how* to make the upgrade. Upgrading your PC's microprocessor can be as straightforward as switching chips, but also it can involve replacing your system's motherboard. You might be tempted to take the easy way out, but the simplest upgrade method is often the most expensive and may not deliver the same benefits as the more demanding method.

You face practical considerations, too. If you have an older PC based on 386 or earlier technology, you almost never can pull out one microprocessor and slide another in its place. Even if you want to upgrade the easy way with a factory-authorized assembly, you may be frustrated that your particular computer manufacturer never foresaw your desire to upgrade and never made an upgrade module—or simply didn't factor upgrades into the design. Fortunately, even the PC least willing to accept upgrades can be updated with just a little more work.

Four basic upgrade strategies are available. Some systems enable you to take advantage of any of these alternatives. Others may restrict you to only one. Each has its own strengths and weaknesses, be they performance, installation ease, accessibility, or cost.

- *Direct microprocessor replacement* is usually cost-effective only at the edges of the PC spectrum—the oldest and newest machines. 8088 upgrades are cheap but slow, and 486 upgrades are expensive but effective. Chip upgrades for the vast middle ground of 286 and 386 PCs often are expensive and add only marginally to performance.

- *Turbo boards* are favored by many because they sometimes make the microprocessor upgrade as easy as adding another expansion board to your system. You may be able to plug in a turbo board and blast through programs double-time—in theory, at least.

- The *replacement motherboard* is generally considered the most radical, the most difficult (it really isn't, as you will see), and the most worthwhile change. It's often a panacea for whatever lethargy your PC currently suffers.

- *Proprietary upgrades* are the easiest to install and manage but are often as expensive as replacing your PC entirely.

Although the various upgrade types require different installation methods, deciding among them is more than just a matter of how to install the hardware. You need to balance factors such as the degree of performance improvement you expect, the smoothness with which your system will operate, the skill required in making the transplant, and the bottom line—whether you can afford it, and whether it's worth your investment.

Replacing Your Microprocessor

To upgrade your microprocessor, the straightforward thing to do would be to pull out your old chip and plug in a new one. Although the idea seems logical, until 1992, it was not really possible. The problem was that microprocessor types are, generally, not directly interchangeable. Before the introduction of Intel's OverDrive chips in 1992, the only chips that would plug in place of others were clones. Such a switch involved replacing one manufacturer's chip with a souped-up twin from another. The only direct clone chips available took the place of Intel's venerable 8088 and 8086 micro-processors. Clones of Intel's 286 didn't merit a second look because the other companies were licensed to build chips that were an exact match of Intel's. The 386 clone chips developed by Advanced Micro Devices and IBM were designed for manufacturers to buy and install (for example, the AMD chips soldered in place) so you weren't likely to try swapping one in.

Only when some marketing genius at Intel figured out that upgrades can provide a continuing source of income from existing PCs did upgrade chips come of age. Intel designed its OverDrive series for its 486 line. In effect, the company discovered it could sell two micro-processors for every PC—one as original equipment and a second as an upgrade. Suddenly chip-level upgradability made sense for Intel.

8088 and 8086 Chip Upgrades

If you blow the dust off your old IBM PC or XT, you'll find an Intel 8088 chip lurking inside. With 10 minutes and about $10, you can add more than 10 percent to its performance. Although that's not much improvement—it won't make your PC rival a 486—it's not much money or work, either. If you have a 8086-based machine like the original Compaq DeskPro, you can follow a similar strategy and get similar results.

The replacement processors for the Intel 8088 and 8086 chips are the near-clones made by NEC. That company's V20 and V30 microprocessors were engineered to duplicate the functions of the 8088 and the 8086, respectively. Having the benefit of hindsight and reverse engineering, NEC was able to design its chips to cal-culate somewhat faster than their Intel forebears at the same clock speed.

Although NEC makes similar replacements for other microproces-sors, the chips have been tied in legal knots by Intel's legal efforts to prevent their sale. Intel believes that NEC chips infringe on its patents. As a result, the other NEC chips are difficult (if not impossible) to find. Currently, they are not widely available on the U.S. market.

286 and 386 Chip Upgrades

No direct plug-in replacement microprocessors that deliver performance improvement are available for Intel's 286 or 386 chips.
Other manufacturers' 286s are exact matches for the Intel products,
duly licensed and made using the same production masks. At the
386 level, Advanced Micro Devices cloned Intel's 386 (using Intel's
own microcode under a disputed technology-sharing agreement).
Although AMD increased the speed of its chips (offering a 40 MHz
386 chip versus Intel's 33 MHz), at the same clock rate, each
manufacturer's chip delivers essentially the same performance.
There's no point to replacing an Intel chip with an AMD or vice
versa.

A better alternative if you have a 286-based PC is adapting another
microprocessor to fit its socket. Although the 386 and 486 have
different pin-outs and socket requirements from the 286, with a
moderate amount of external circuitry, some varieties of these chips
can be adapted to fit in. The two candidates for 286 upgrades are
the Intel 386SX and Cyrix 486SLC.

Several companies now offer plug-in assemblies that mate a 386SX
microprocessor to 286 sockets. Included among these makers is
Intel, whose Snap-In product line gave legitimacy to this upgrade
strategy. The various 286-to-386SX products demonstrate philosophical differences. Some boards opt for the simple treatment,
aiming only to bring the advanced features of the 386 to 286-based
PCs (including 32-bit compatibility, advanced memory management, and virtual 8086 mode). Performance improvements are
modest in 8 MHz AT-style systems and negligible in faster computers. Other boards (among them the Snap-In) start with those
benefits and add some degree of performance enhancement. They
speed up the 386SX and add cache memory to minimize the drag
imposed by the slower memory installed in your system. At best,
you may see a two-time performance improvement.

Because the 486SLC is essentially an updated clone of the 386SX,
it offers the same upgrade potential. Because it has its own 1K cache,
it doesn't need an external RAM cache to even up performance.
Consequently, 486SLC upgrades are potentially less expensive for a
given level of performance improvement. ALL Computers—the
ChargeCard company—offers a plug-in 486SLC product, the ALL
SX 486-25. Although these 486SLC upgrades move your system two

*There's no point to
replacing an Intel
chip with an AMD
or vice versa.*

notches up the microprocessor scale, the performance gains you'll see are not much different from a cache-enhanced 386SX.

The real reason for choosing a 386SX or 486SLC upgrade for your 286 is to gain the full repertory of features of the 386 microprocessor family. Your old PC will be able to run all the latest software (if, of course, you have the disk space and memory you need), but they will run so slowly that you will be tempted to try another upgrade method should you ever wake up.

Another reason for having second thoughts about replacing your 286 is that not all 286 microprocessors are the same, coming in great variety with a number of different housings, each requiring a different kind of socket. Because a plug-in 386SX or 486SLC board plugs into your 286 socket, the kind of socket you have is important when you order this kind of upgrade. You should specify the make and model of your computer when you order the upgrade board to ensure compatibility. Alternately, should your vendor never have heard of your particular brand of computer, you can describe the kind of microprocessor you have. The three principal types of 286 microprocessors are the Pin-Grid Array (PGA), the Leadless Chip Carrier (LCC), and the Plastic Leadless Chip Carrier (PLCC).

When viewed installed in its socket, the PGA looks like a dark gray square of epoxy. No socket is visible except in side view because the chip completely overhangs it. When pried from its socket, the bottom side of the PGA chip has two parallel rows of gold pins parallel to each of its edges.

The LCC chip is a black square in a plastic socket, typically held in place by a wire at one end. If you look at the slight gap between the edge of the chip and the socket, you won't see any connecting pins. If you pry up the wire and pop the chip from the socket, you'll see that its contacts are flat traces of gold on the bottom face of the chip.

The PLCC has silvery pins folded around its perimeter. When the chip is in its socket, you can see these pins in the gap between chip and socket. Out of the socket, the leads run around the edge of the chip and curl underneath.

OverDrive chips are your best bet for updating your 486 outside of replacing your entire motherboard.

486 Chip Upgrades

The once top-of-the-line 486 chip that had no need for upgrades now is the most upgradable of microprocessors, thanks to Intel's clever introduction of its OverDrive processor line. With an

OverDrive, you can nearly double the performance of a 486DX or blast a 486SX even further ahead quickly and easily. In fact, as long as your PC came equipped with an Intel 486 microprocessor, you can upgrade it with an OverDrive no matter what the machine's make and model. OverDrive chips are your best bet for updating your 486 outside of replacing your entire motherboard.

The secret to this upgrade strategy is how OverDrive chips work. By using the same clock-doubling technology as Intel's 486DX2 microprocessors, the OverDrive allows your PC to double its thinking speed without affecting the other circuits inside your system. In addition, all OverDrive chips include a built-in floating-point coprocessor, adding fast math capabilities to PCs built around the 486SX.

Of course, the overall performance of your PC won't double with the addition of an OverDrive because its memory circuits and the rest of the machine remained unchanged after the upgrade. The 8K memory cache built into every OverDrive chip helps minimize the memory slowdown. In most PCs, you can expect to get a 60 to 80 percent increase in overall speed by installing an OverDrive.

How much benefit the OverDrive brings depends on the applications you run most often. Software that makes the heaviest demands on microprocessor power—statistics, graphics, and the like—sees the biggest performance increases; memory and I/O intensive applications like databases and bit-image editing gain the least. Nothing ever slows down from an OverDrive upgrade, so you've much to gain and nothing to lose by chucking out your old chip.

Nothing ever slows down from an OverDrive upgrade, so you've much to gain and nothing to lose by chucking out your old chip.

The only drawback to an OverDrive upgrade is that only PCs designed for Intel 486 microprocessors can benefit. Today's 486-compatible chips from other makers—the Cyrix 486DLC and 486SLC and IBM 486SLC2—have different pin-outs and require different sockets from Intel chips. Thus PCs based on existing non-Intel 486 chips cannot be upgraded with OverDrive processors. In addition, PCs that were originally equipped with Intel's 486DX2 microprocessors already use clock-doubling technology so they won't benefit from an OverDrive.

An OverDrive upgrade is not for everyone. The chips are expensive, about the same price as their 486DX2 chip equivalent. The two-inch square of silicon can cost nearly $500. The one case in which choosing an OverDrive upgrade is the only smart decision is when you have a 486SX and need math coprocessor power. For example, to run a math-hungry CAD program, a floating-point processor like the 487SX would vastly increase the speed of high-level calculations and accelerate drawing and CAD-based screen painting. A coprocessor can cut the time required for difficult calculations by a factor of 1,000. Figure in system overhead (calculations are only a small part of even the most number-hungry programs), and you can still see an impressive double or triple speed improvement on math-based applications.

OverDrive is not a single product but an entire line of chips designed to upgrade PCs based on any Intel 486DX or 486SX microprocessor. Three different chips, each with a number of speed ratings, are available to match PCs with different native 486 microprocessors. All PCs based on the 486SX microprocessor are upgraded with Intel's OverDrive ODP486SX chip, which is available in three speed ratings. The 20 MHz version upgrades or replaces 16 MHz and 20 MHz 486SX chips, and the 25 MHz and 33 MHz versions upgrade or replace 486SX microprocessors with matching speed ratings.

Selecting the right ODP486SX only means matching the speed rating of your existing microprocessor to that of the OverDrive chip. You always can install an OverDrive with a higher rating than you require—that's why the 20 MHz OverDrive can replace 16 MHz and 20 MHz 486SX microprocessors—but the higher speed rating won't add extra performance to your system. It indicates only the maximum clock rate at which the OverDrive chip will operate reliably. Its actual operating speed is set by your PC.

Even though all 486SX systems use the same OverDrive chip, different system units require their own upgrade procedures.

Even though all 486SX systems use the same OverDrive chip, different system units require their own upgrade procedures. With some, you plug the OverDrive chip into the coprocessor or OverDrive socket. Others may require you to change jumper settings after you put the OverDrive into the coprocessor socket. A few machines require that you remove your old 486SX microprocessor and replace it with the OverDrive (as well as changing jumpers to reflect the brain change).

For PCs with native 486DX microprocessors, Intel offers two OverDrive chips to match different system designs. The OverDrive ODP486DX slides into the empty OverDrive upgrade socket (in PCs that have them). For PCs that don't have the right vacant sockets (a Weitek coprocessor socket won't work), your choice is the OverDrive ODPR486DX, which replaces your existing 486DX microprocessor. Both styles of 486DX OverDrive are offered with 25 MHz and 33 MHz speed ratings.

You can use any of several methods to determine the proper OverDrive chip to upgrade your 486DX. You can check with the manufacturer of your PC—scan through the manual or call technical support. Or you can open up your PC and look for an OverDrive socket on its motherboard. If you find an OverDrive socket, your system likely uses an ODP486DX chip; if there are no vacant sockets or only a Weitek coprocessor socket, you'll need an ODPR486DX chip. As with 486SX chips, you'll also have to match the speed of the OverDrive to that of your system.

As with all microprocessors, the faster an OverDrive chip operates, the more heat it generates. Because of its double-time internal clock, an OverDrive replacement generates more heat than the chip that it upgrades. In fact, some OverDrive chips get so hot that the faster ones need additional cooling. All 25 MHz and faster OverDrive chips (which operate at 50 MHz or faster) come with built-in heat sinks—instead of the top of the chip being smooth ceramic, it is covered with rectangular black fins that increase its surface area and allow more heat to dissipate.

In some systems, these fins may interfere with expansion boards that run above the microprocessor or upgrade sockets. In some systems with inadequate airflow, even the heat sink fins might not be sufficient to properly cool the high-speed OverDrive adequately. Although even in the worst of cases, an OverDrive chip probably won't get hot enough to self-destruct, temperature problems can destroy what you're working on. The chip may make errors in calculations or other operations, inevitably crashing your system, possibly in the middle of your work.

In PCs designed to have proper airflow across the microprocessor, you should not need to worry about overheating. However, in the tightly-packed homebrew PCs used for an OverDrive test installation, the chip was cramped under a drive bay and could not cool itself properly. As a result, the machine crashed about half an hour after the OverDrive was installed.

As with 486SX chips, you'll also have to match the speed of the OverDrive to that of your system.

Turbo Boards

The logical place to put any upgrade for your system is its expansion slots, and turbo boards do exactly that, putting a new microprocessor on an expansion board. Therefore, you can upgrade a microprocessor as easily as adding a serial port—at least sometimes. Other times, turbo boards require more work than a microprocessor upgrade.

Turbo boards actually come in two styles, coprocessor board and microprocessor replacement, and they differ in the results they deliver and the mechanical skill required to put them to work.

The coprocessor is the purest form of turbo board, earning its name from how it works, cooperating with the microprocessor already in your PC. The coprocessor takes over all the tough work—the calculations and computations—and uses your PC's original microprocessor to handle your system's video display, hard disk, and other peripherals.

The coprocessor has three important benefits. First, it's easy to install—you just slide it into any vacant expansion slot, run some software, and go to work at higher speed. Also, coprocessors include their own memory, so they are not limited by the slow RAM chips that may be in your PC. In most cases, the coprocessor board doesn't care how much memory is installed in your PC. Finally, because you don't remove your original microprocessor when you install the coprocessor-style turbo board, you always can revert to using the old chip when your software proves persnickety or the coprocessor (heaven forbid) fails.

On the other hand, the coprocessor-style turbo board has some severe drawbacks. Because it connects to your system through an expansion slot, it suffers all the limitations of your PC's expansion bus—and then some. Not only does the bus connection limit turbo board performance when accessing the memory on your motherboard, but it also handicaps communication with other expansion boards. Traditional PC designs—those machines not built with advanced expansion buses like Micro Channel and EISA—don't expect to be controlled by a microprocessor in an expansion slot and throw roadblocks in its general direction. Video and disk performance cannot be any better than before the upgrade and often is worse with jumpy video displays. (Advanced bus coprocessor turbo boards, on the other hand, sidestep the roadblocks and often deliver excellent performance.) Coprocessor turbo boards are also relatively expensive because each one is essentially a complete computer built onto an expansion board. The coprocessor board duplicates many of the functions (such as memory) already in your PC. For these and other reasons, coprocessor-style turbo boards for conventional PCs are becoming as rare on the market as absinthe, buggy-whips, and affordable housing.

Bus mastering, however, makes a coprocessor turbo board extremely effective. A coprocessor turbo board can take direct bus control and substitute itself for your PC's native microprocessor. In a Micro

Channel computer, the coprocessor turbo board delivers speed, easy installation, and tight integration, shorting only on cost-effectiveness. Micro Channel turbo boards cost more than replacement motherboards or entire PCs. They make sense only where convenience counts over all else—for example, where you need to make the least possible change in someone's desktop PC because unfamiliarity can breed contempt, particularly among those who work on PCs only grudgingly.

The other kind of turbo board, the microprocessor replacement, exchanges installation ease for performance improvement. Besides fitting into an expansion slot, this form of turbo board has a tentacle-like connecting cable that latches onto the socket belonging to your system's original microprocessor. You have to pop out the microprocessor and replace it with the connecting cable and, through it, the turbo board.

By usurping your old microprocessor's socket, this kind of turbo board can take direct control of your PC, meaning smoother operation. In many cases, it also means that the turbo board handicaps itself by making do with the circuits already installed on your motherboard, among them memory that probably was challenged even to keep up with your pokey old microprocessor. Better replacement-processor turbo boards avoid the restrictions of your system's old circuitry by including on-board memory caches or their own RAM. Fast, on-board RAM means that the turbo board never needs to stoop to the slow speed of motherboard memory.

Although replacement-processor turbo boards are expansion boards and do slide into expansion slots, they really aren't as easy to install as most people suppose. The installation job may require removing all other expansion boards from inside your PC to get at the microprocessor socket. You also need to install the plug on the turbo board's cable very carefully into the microprocessor socket—one bent lead and your PC won't work. As with 386SX boards, you'll also have to make sure that the turbo board you choose mates with the socket of your microprocessor: PGA, LCC, or PLCC. After the board and cable are in place, you must then painstakingly bend and fold the wide, flat connection cable inside your computer (easier said than done) so that it doesn't get in the way of expansion boards.

Turbo boards often require extensive software setup and support. To make them work properly, most turbo boards require software drivers that need to be installed in your system's CONFIG.SYS file. As with all memory-resident software, these drivers can have odd effects on some applications—and you never know until they do.

These software drivers also steal some memory for their own purposes, cutting into what is available to your programs. Of course, you've got to install the drivers just right to make the entire system work properly.

The killer for any turbo board—the factor that has skewered the industry—is cost. A state-of-the-art turbo board is essentially a complete computer system board that you slide into an expansion slot, so the turbo board costs nearly as much as an entire system board to manufacture. In fact, a turbo board often costs *more*. The advantage of the turbo board is thus its perceived (but often not actual) ease of installation and its reversibility. Most of your PC is unchanged by the installation of a turbo board, so you can restore your system more readily to its old configuration when things go awry. Although it seems strange that one of the selling points of a technology is the ease with which you can avoid using it, such is the case of the turbo board.

All that said, a turbo board can make a significant improvement in the throughput of your PC. Short of a replacement motherboard, a turbo board is the only way to add 386 performance and memory features to an decrepit 8088 machine. It also can boost the performance of a 286 or 386. Although adding a 486-based turbo board doesn't push your PC into the same performance realm as a new computer, it significantly increases your system's processing speed. More importantly, it can give your system all the features of a 386 or better microprocessor, which, for most people, are even more important than raw speed.

Replacement Motherboards

The chief difficulty with replacing a microprocessor or adding a replacement-style turbo board is that you often end up disassembling your PC. You may need to pull out all the expansion boards, and in some cases, you must pull out your system board to access chips hidden under the drive bays. After you have the system board out, it's no more effort to replace the board as it is to reinstall the old one. Replacing your motherboard can be less dangerous than a microprocessor or turbo board replacement because you never deal with the delicate pins on integrated circuits or loose chips that are particularly prone to damage from static electricity. In fact, replacing your entire motherboard is a more elegant solution than a turbo board from a software and hardware standpoint. A new motherboard takes over and runs like any other computer. You won't need new software drivers. Moreover, installing a motherboard is hardly a dreadful task—in many systems, the entire motherboard replacement involves removing about two screws and a few cables.

Motherboards are probably the biggest bargains available in the personal computer industry, making them an excellent microprocessor upgrade choice.

Replacing your motherboard does more than just update your PC's microprocessor. It changes memory to equal your microprocessor's speed, thus avoiding the mismatch bugaboo of other chip upgrades. Better still, a motherboard upgrade can endow your PC with a new expansion bus, one incorporating local bus technology.

New motherboards are surprisingly inexpensive, too, tending to cost less than a turbo board. Even though they should be more expensive to make, generally requiring more materials and components than turbo boards, greater competition among motherboard makers drives down prices. In fact, motherboards are probably the biggest bargains available in the personal computer industry, making them an excellent microprocessor upgrade choice.

Upgrading an 8088-based XT to a full 32-bit (internally) 3865x, only costs about $100 for a new motherboard plus the cost of memory. Upgrading to 486 technology can cost as little as $150 plus the microprocessor and memory of your choice. Nothing else can enhance your PC's performance so much for so little.

The only downside to the motherboard replacement is that it makes your old computer into a new one, one with its own idiosyncrasies. You'll have to relearn the personality of your machine should you swap its motherboard. For example, if you pull the system board out of an IBM computer and replace it with another maker's product, you won't have an IBM machine any more. It won't run the IBM BASIC interpreter because it no longer has an IBM BIOS. Your old setup and configuration utilities may not work on your PC after the upgrade, because the software may think that you have an entirely new machine. Fortunately, most motherboards come equipped with all the setup software you need.

What You Can Keep

When you upgrade your motherboard, you'll try to keep as many components from your old board as you can. After all, why buy new ROM and RAM if you can recycle what you have? Unfortunately, little of what's on your old board can be used to make a major improvement in system performance. For example, in moving from a 286 to 486, you'll probably find that your old memory can't keep up with a faster microprocessor—or it might not fit on a higher performance motherboard. The latest motherboards use Single In-Line Memory Modules (SIMMs) rather than individual integrated circuits for memory. Those using individual RAM chips usually prefer chips with 1M or greater capacity. Your old PC or XT's chips held no more than 64K. Fortunately, your memory losses in making a motherboard upgrade are generally minimal. Typically, you'll lose about 640K of RAM (about $25 worth) because that's about all most old motherboards hold. You can't move the ROM chips that hold your PC's BIOS, either. An old BIOS won't work in a different environment; if it did it would inhibit performance. But not to worry—almost every system board comes with its own BIOS chips already installed. Most also come with the setup software you'll need, either on disk or written into ROM.

On the other hand, if your goal in upgrading your motherboard is more than a simple microprocessor change—for example, upgrading your 486 motherboard to gain local bus technology—you might be able to recycle much of what you have. You can add local bus by installing a bare $150 motherboard without microprocessor or memory modules and then moving all those expensive parts from your old motherboard to the new.

Choosing a Motherboard

You already know everything you need to know to select the right motherboard upgrade. Most of your concerns are identical to choosing a PC—microprocessor, power, memory capabilities. You should look for the same features you'd want in a new PC. Because you've bought at least one PC already—why else would you need to upgrade?—you know how to buy a motherboard.

Physical Considerations

The only special concern when considering a new motherboard is that it actually fits into the case that you have. For the most part, that's easy because most motherboards are made in standard sizes. The two preeminent forms match the motherboards of the IBM XT (8.5 x 12 inches) and AT. Most standard-size computers used motherboards of one of these two sizes. If you're not sure what size current system is, take out a ruler, measure it, and get a replacement of the same dimensions. Figure 3.4 shows the essential dimensions of these motherboard styles.

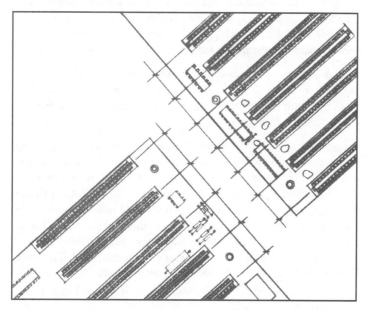

Figure 3.4
Expansion slots in PCs and some compatibles are spaced at one-inch increments; XTs and newer computers use 0.8-inch spacing.

If you've put off upgrading for a decade too long and still have an original PC to update, you'll find fitting a new motherboard difficult because of slot spacing. The expansion slots in PCs and some very early compatibles are spaced at one-inch increments. XT, AT, and later expansion slots are spaced at 0.8-inch increments. XT and PC system boards are nearly the same size, but if you try to put an XT-size motherboard in a PC chassis, the slots and cutouts won't line up properly. Moreover, the locations of the screw holes that secure the motherboard to the chassis are slightly different for PC and XT motherboards. Most replacement board makers avoid this problem by drilling enough holes in their boards that mice might mistake them for Swiss cheese. These extra holes accommodate PC, XT, and even AT mounting arrangements and hardware.

A few motherboards use the PC spacing for their expansion slots. These are usually so much more expensive that you likely are better off moving everything from your PC's case into a new XT-size case. Use this strategy, and you'll also get more expansion slots along with the new microprocessor.

Computer cases from vendors other than IBM may be more difficult to match with new motherboards when you are upgrading. For instance, Compaq Deskpros uses a different mounting scheme than IBM, and replacement motherboards designed for IBM computers won't fit in Compaq cases. Fortunately, one company, Hauppauge Computer Works, makes high-performance replacement motherboards for Compaq Deskpros.

The proliferation of small-chassis computers makes finding a replacement motherboard even more difficult. With these machines, you often must improvise on the case with a hacksaw and drill or choose another form of microprocessor upgrade.

Low-priced 386SX replacement motherboards and a growing variety of more powerful products are now made even smaller than XT size, some about eight inches square, hardly large enough to accommodate their expansion slots. Although you won't have difficulty fitting these in larger cases, you may find that your old motherboard and its replacement have their mounting holes in different locations. There are two solutions to this problem: Buy a new case or modify your own to accept the hole spacing of your new motherboard. The latter involves drilling holes in the proper places in the chassis of your old computer. Make too many mistakes, and you'll have to buy a new case, anyway.

If your old motherboard is not a standard size, you usually can adopt the same strategy as with fitting XT products to PC hardware. Get a case along with your motherboard and move all your old peripherals into the new case. You may also need a new power supply. All told, the $50 to $100 cost of a case is a small penalty for the new features you'll get.

Most motherboards use the same mounting hardware IBM used for its motherboards, and most aftermarket cases use the same strategy. That means only two screws are required to hold the board in place. All the necessary holes are predrilled.

You'll be much happier with a motherboard that includes all the necessary spacers.

On all official IBM products and many compatibles, you also have to tangle with spacers in addition to the screws. That's good news because the spacers pop right into place on the motherboard and let you slide the board into position inside the chassis. However, you may need to move the spacers from your old mother-board onto the new board, a more than minor bother. In theory, you can squeeze a spacer out by pinching its wings with a long-nosed pliers, then pushing it out. Often, however, the spacers don't come off intact, leaving you with useless pieces. You'll be much happier with a motherboard that includes all the necessary spacers. You may even want to buy new spacers when you buy your new motherboard. At least ask about them.

Some compatibles don't use spacers. Worse, some computers, although they have enough room for a standard-size motherboard, don't use the same spacing as IBM chose for its motherboard mounting holes. Again, you'll have to improvise the mounting, drilling holes where necessary and making your own spacers with parts from your local hardware store.

Memory Considerations

Memory is important when considering a new motherboard for your PC, both in the amount delivered on any product and how it can be expanded. Many motherboards are advertised at low prices with 0K, that is, no memory. Be sure to factor in the cost of adding memory chips or SIMMs to those boards when comparing them to products already stuffed with RAM.

More memory on the motherboard—or the capability of accommodating more memory—is better. Motherboard memory is typically the cheapest and fastest to add, so it pays to fit the most you can on the motherboard itself.

Be sure to consider how much memory your system can accommodate. The 286 microprocessor and motherboards using it top out at 16M. The least microprocessor you're likely to upgrade to, the 386SX, potentially can handle the same 4 gigabytes as other 386, 486, and Pentium chips. However, many motherboards limit you to 16M. One reason is that the standard AT expansion bus, Industry Standard Architecture (ISA), can address only 16M. Many system boards stop there, despite the fact that memory on the motherboard does not have to heed the bus limit.

You also may encounter other barriers in exceeding 16M. Many systems that use ROM shadowing require their BIOS to locate the shadow memory at 16M. Because most operating systems require all of their memory to be contiguous, shadow memory acts as a roadblock, preventing memory beyond 16M from being used. To take advantage of greater RAM using this sort of motherboard, you must switch off shadowing, typically part of the motherboard's x advanced setup procedure and usually not a major loss. The primary reasons you need more than 16M—advanced operating systems like Windows and OS/2—don't make much use of the BIOS, so they

Motherboard memory is typically the cheapest and fastest to add, so it pays to fit the most you can on the motherboard itself.

won't miss the ROM shadow. System speedup utilities like disk caches and video enhancers also bypass the BIOS and reduce the need for shadowing.

ISA motherboards with certain peripherals may be limited to less than 16M no matter how much RAM they can accommodate physically. Many new peripherals, such as graphics accelerators, use *memory apertures*, reserved address areas used for transferring data to and from the peripheral. Technically speaking, the memory aperture is the address range used by an address-mapped input/output device. Because ISA systems have only 16M of addresses on the expansion bus, the memory aperture must appear in this range. The aperture steals from the useful memory the motherboard can use, and if the memory aperture is not located at the uppermost available address range, any memory above the aperture is non-contiguous and thus inaccessible by DOS. Motherboards with properly designed advanced expansion buses like EISA, PCI, and VL Bus don't have this problem because they permit full 32-bit addressing for peripherals; their apertures can be located anywhere in a 4-gigabyte address range.

Most of today's replacement motherboards have 8 SIMM sockets and limit capacity only by the size of the SIMMs you install. Theoretically, with 16M SIMMs, you could pack a PC with 128M— enough RAM for most single-user PCs for a long time to come. Many motherboards are more limited in their memory handling, but total capacities from 16M to 64M on the motherboard are not unusual.

A steadily declining number of replacement motherboards require proprietary memory expansion boards to hold their RAM. If the motherboard you're thinking of buying uses a proprietary memory board, check the availability of the memory board (with or without RAM) when you order the motherboard. Sometimes manufacturers rush their motherboards to the market and only later (if ever) produce the memory expansion boards that they need. Most of the time you're best off buying a memory expansion board without memory when you buy your motherboard. That way your opportunity for memory expansion is not dependent on a board maker that may go out of business.

Also remember that all memory is not created equal. Although Chapter 5 discusses all the types at length, you should be aware that several types of memory can be used on a motherboard. At one time you had to consider whether a motherboard used DRAM chips or

SIMMs, the latter being more compact and convenient. For the most part, that choice is gone as SIMMs are now standard. But there are still several types of SIMMs to choose from. Some boards use 36-bit SIMMs, others use 9-bit, and a rare few use 8-bit.

The most economical choice is a motherboard that uses 9-bit SIMMs, because 9-bit memory modules are more widely available and, generally, less expensive. Although 36-bit SIMMs may be more costly and difficult to find, they make incremental upgrades easier because you only need one 36-bit SIMM per memory bank in 386 and 486 PCs (which use 32-bit memory buses). You'll need four matched 9-bit SIMMs for a single 32-bit bank.

Eight-bit SIMMs are used on motherboards that lack parity checking. In general, eight-bit SIMMs aren't any cheaper than the nine-bit variety and result in a less reliable PC. You probably don't want a motherboard that uses them.

Another memory concern is speed. The faster the memory your new motherboard requires (measured in nanoseconds, the lower the number the faster), the more it is likely to cost. Most motherboards make do with 70 ns SIMMs, but some require 53 ns or faster memory, which can be much more expensive. To get the most speed, a growing number of memory boards require page-mode memory chips, which are also more expensive and more difficult to find than standard DRAM chips. Because they have the same pin-out, however, page-mode and linear SIMMs are interchangeable (but not within a memory bank). Selecting page-mode for a motherboard that supports page-mode operation may yield a slight improvement in overall performance.

The important thing is to find out what kind of memory your system requires, particularly if you are ordering expansion memory when you buy your new system board.

Bus Considerations

No matter what else your new motherboard does, you want it to enable you to expand your PC, and you want the expansion to be as invisible as possible. After all, you don't want to add yet another bottleneck to your PC.

When you move a lot of information between your PC's memory and an expansion board, the expansion bus can be the chief constriction in your system. In most PCs, video data must crawl across the expansion bus to get to a display adapter and your monitor screen. *Crawl* can be a very apt word. Compared to the rate at which your graphics board races data to the screen, the bus hardly moves.

By connecting to the microprocessor in a computer, local bus can move bytes from memory to screen at microprocessor rather than bus rate.

Local bus is indeed key to the expansion of any new motherboard, meaning more transfer bandwidth and thus the fastest video performance. The promise of local bus technology is an end to the bottleneck holding back quick screen updates—the input/output bus of PCs. By connecting to the microprocessor in a computer, local bus can move bytes from memory to screen at microprocessor rather than bus rate.

Bandwidth figures make the best case for local bus. The I/O bus connection used for the video systems of most PCs (that is, Industry Standard Architecture or the AT bus) operates at 8 MHz with a 16-bit channel width, which multiplies out to a 16M per second rate. A typical 486 microprocessor operates at 33 MHz with a 32-bit channel width—that's 132M per second. Take these numbers at face value (which is how local bus advocates usually present them) and a local bus connection could be more than 8 times faster than today's standard video systems.

As always, reality falls far short of the computed values. Data transfers generally take at least two cycles each—one to establish the address of the data to be moved and another to transfer the data, cutting those high megahertz rates in half. Dig deeper, and other factors trim the computed values. No PC can sustain those data rates because it has to take care of a number of tasks just to continue operating. With today's PC designs, about six to ten percent of microprocessor time is devoted to refreshing its memory. Add timer service and other system overhead, and those peak rates plummet further. In most PCs, the microprocessor generates the image, too—and that's usually more work than moving the results to the screen.

The data rate across the I/O bus and the local bus suffer equally from these factors, but real-world throughputs don't approach the numbers bandied about by local bus advocates.

There are more buses to select from than ever before. In fact, you have four primary bus choices in a new system board—ISA, EISA, VL Bus, and PCI. The last two aren't available by themselves but may be combined individually with either of the first two, making six distinct possibilities (ISA or EISA alone; ISA or EISA combined with VL Bus, and ISA or EISA combined with PCI). Trailing far behind is Micro Channel, which has proven scarce among replacement motherboards. If you are desperate to upgrade your old PS/2, however, you can buy IBM motherboards to upgrade some systems. For example, you can install a Model 65SX motherboard in your

Model 60 case to update from 286 to 386SX technology. However, a turbo board or microprocessor replacement may deliver equal or more performance. Some third-party vendors also offer Micro Channel motherboards. As of this writing, however, none are available with local bus slots.

ISA

Odds are that Industry Standard Architecture, the classic AT expansion bus, is where you're upgrading from. ISA is the most popular expansion bus. More peripherals are available with ISA connections than any other, and, in general, they are the cheapest expansion options available. If there is any universal standard in PC expansion, good old ISA is it.

Besides popularity, ISA has one more factor in its favor: simplicity. ISA motherboards are simple, thus cheap to make, which helps to keep their prices low. But ISA, although once adequate, is at a distinct disadvantage in today's world of high-performance computing—it's slow. In a world where an entry-level 33 MHz 486 microprocessor can move data around at a peak transfer rate of about 66 million bytes per second, ISA can push no more than 8M per second. It just can't keep up with the thinking speed of today's PCs.

That's not always as big a disadvantage as it sounds. Even memory can't keep up with a fast microprocessor. Moreover, most of what you attach to an expansion bus has no problem with the basic ISA transfer rate. Consider today's fastest modems, which may squeeze 57,600 bits per second down your telephone line. Allowing for normal asynchronous data words, that's a transfer rate of only 5,760 bytes per second or 0.00576M per second, no strain for ISA. Printers and plotters push harder, but hardly past the limits of ISA.

Choose ISA for the low cost and the wide availability of expansion boards.

ISA does present two kinds of throughput problems. One is raw bandwidth—32-bit memory at 33 Mhz with an 8-Mhz bus—with certain system components that can operate faster than ISA allows. These include display systems, hard disk drives, and some networking host adapters. With these devices, ISA is the bottleneck.

The other is that ISA is limited by the performance of your microprocessor and vice versa. The design of ISA requires your microprocessor to take on most of the work in moving data. For most transfers, your microprocessor must indicate the source and destination addresses of every byte that moves across the expansion bus.

*For the utmost in
performance,
choose a bus
besides ISA.*

Choose ISA for the low cost and the wide availability of expansion
boards. It delivers adequate speed with most AT Interface (IDE)
hard disks and video boards with graphics acceleration. However,
for the utmost in performance, you'll want to investigate an alternate bus.

EISA

First proposed in 1988 and delivered in PCs the next year, EISA
was the backward-compatible version of IBM's Micro Channel
developed by an industry consortium. It attacked the three chief
shortcomings of ISA. To increase data throughput, it broadens the
bus to a full 32 bits using an ingenious connector that interleaves the
contacts with the traditional ISA pin-out so that an EISA slot can
accommodate both ISA and special EISA boards in a connector the
size of a standard AT expansion slot. In addition, EISA adds three
new transfer modes that break the old rule that two bus cycles are
required for each word transferred. By adroitly rearranging the
timing of the bus signals, EISA can move data words as quickly as
two per bus clock, effectively quadrupling data throughput. This
timing alteration is necessary because the actual bus clock speed must
be maintained at a relatively slow 8 MHz to maintain compatibility
with old ISA boards. EISA supports fully arbitrated *bus mastering*,
which allows an expansion board to take control of the bus from the
microprocessor to manage its own data transfers. Arbitration
provides a means by which multiple bus masters can take control of
the bus without interfering with one another. To break through the
16M addressing limitations of ISA, EISA brings its total address lines
to 32, allowing the full 4-gigabyte memory space of a 386 or 486
microprocessor to be directly addressed. EISA also breaks through
the ISA interrupt roadblock—15 interrupts that must be shared by a
wide variety of motherboard and expansion slot-based devices—by
allowing interrupt sharing. Using level-sensitive interrupts, multiple
devices can use a single interrupt to take care of all their system
service needs.

EISA and IBM's Micro Channel are often compared. Although
Micro Channel earns the award for being first, EISA, a smart copy,
is definitely the better choice for system upgrades. Although it lacks
the technical elegance of Micro Channel, it has something more
important—general usefulness. And its backward compatibility—
perhaps a dubious virtue in a new PC that would be held back by the
performance of old peripherals—is a definite advantage because you
can move more of your peripherals to your upgraded motherboard.

EISA has subtler advantages for motherboard upgrades. Because EISA motherboards are designed for full 32-bit addressing, most of the memory problems of ISA vanish. Shadow memory typically does not locate itself directly atop the 16M ISA range, and memory apertures can be located anywhere in the full 4-gigabyte address range. Generally, EISA motherboards handle more memory than their ISA counterparts.

EISA has a few negatives, however, Traditionally, it has been more expensive than ISA. EISA motherboards initially cost nearly $1,000 more than ISA equivalents, but that difference has fallen to less than $200. Of course, in most cases you can plug the ISA alternatives into your EISA system and forget about the problem. EISA also adds a complex software setup procedure that can be time-consuming to run from floppy—not a great concern if you're upgrading one PC but a vicious assault on your free time if you maintain dozens of PCs. Moreover, taking advantage of the advanced, cycle-saving transfer modes requires that you install driver software. That's not a big deal if you have a lot of PC experience, but it can be troubling if not.

Despite its shortcomings, EISA would be today's expansion bus of choice were it not for the development of local bus. Link the leading local bus alternative to ISA, and all of ISA's shortcomings are eliminated without adding the hassles associated with EISA. Although there's nothing wrong with combining EISA and local bus—many manufacturers have chosen to do so—little of practical value is gained, while the hassles and price inevitably increase. The combination is unnecessary for all but network servers that require multiple network adapter cards with fully arbitrated bus mastering.

Local Bus Technology

Local bus is the hottest buzzword in PC expansion. Instead of running at some arbitrarily reduced rate, local bus runs at microprocessor speed via direct connections to the microprocessor (or it should, from the sound of it). When your PC needs data, instead of slowing down to the rate of an ordinary expansion bus, local bus allows it to keep running full speed ahead.

However, none of the local buses built into PCs truly fit this direct-connect design. Both of today's standard local buses—PCI and VL Bus—are at least one step removed from the microprocessor's actual connections, but that doesn't prevent them from being the fastest interconnection systems available for PCs. Moreover, being local

Generally, EISA motherboards handle more memory than their ISA counterparts.

buses only in name is an advantage, not a disadvantage. Today's top two local buses share many advanced features with the fully arbitrated Micro Channel and EISA buses but have even more throughput potential.

Local bus started out as a video design, integrated into the motherboards of a select few PCs. That's because video stands to gain the most from local bus technology. The reason a more direct connection is important dates back to IBM's first PC, which was in fact closer to a true local bus than any of today's standards. No one thinks of it as such because the PC expansion bus was so slow—and otherwise an exact match for the PC's 8088 microprocessor.

When this first PC was introduced, its display system was groundbreaking—memory-mapped, although most small business computers used teletype displays. In the PC, part of video memory was configured as a *frame buffer* in which the memory addresses directly corresponded to character or pixel (picture element) positions on the monitor screen. The display systems on these machines were managed by the main microprocessor, which moved data to specific addresses in video memory to form screen images.

Inherent in this design is the need for the frame buffer to be addressable by the microprocessor. Original PCs made the connection between microprocessor and memory through the input/output bus—essentially the expansion bus of the machine. A direct connection between microprocessor and memory was impossible because of insufficient room on the motherboard for the required video circuitry. Video could fit only in a slot. Moreover, putting the display adapter in an expansion slot gave the purchasers the option of adding a color or monochrome display system. This was not a hardship because the PC's bus was just an extension of the 8088's external connections, buffered and demultiplexed—that is, the strength of the signals from the chip were increased and the signals combined on a single microprocessor pin were separated out to their own connections. The entire PC expansion bus was effectively a local bus, but the term had not arisen because there was nothing to contrast it to. It was just the bus.

When microprocessors got faster and the bus could not keep up with their fast system clocks, the bus was split from the microprocessor and operated at a slower speed more compatible with existing expansion boards. That slower rate typically amounted to whatever fraction of the microprocessor's clock came closest to 8 MHz.

When the split came, video stayed on the expansion bus. Even when display circuitry was moved to the motherboard, the connection was made through the I/O bus controller rather than directly. The microprocessor had gotten too fast for most video circuits to handle a direct connection. The I/O bus provided a convenient channel for addressing video memory, one that required no extra circuitry, added engineering work, or newer, high-speed chips. Most important, there was no perceived need for a quicker connection, at least among important PC manufacturers. A full 3 years after IBM introduced 16-bit expansion, the company introduced its first motherboard-based display system—one using an I/O bus connection constricted with an 8-bit bus width.

As general program interfaces have shifted to graphics, however, the amount of data handled by the display system has increased dramatically—and relative performance has slowed commensurately.

In 1991, NEC was first to break through the old barriers by sidestepping the I/O bus bottleneck with a local bus video connection. Others manufacturers (such as Micronics, Orchid, and CSS Labs) followed suit by adopting their own, proprietary versions of the local bus display systems integrated on their motherboards.

Although each of these independent designs achieves a similar result in regard to overall performance, each company has approached the problem of linking video circuitry to the microprocessor's local bus differently. As a result, compatibility (or the lack of it) is the most troubling characteristic of these systems. This shortcoming is understandable in that no major company such as IBM or Compaq had even hinted at a preferred method of making a local bus connection when these designs were created.

Although all of these systems work as advertised and hold through-put potentials substantially higher than the I/O bus (though not as high as the most fanciful claims), they impose a penalty when it comes to upgrading. Because the proprietary designs are supported only by their own manufacturers, most upgrade options must originate from the original manufacturer (each model of machine holds such a modest market share that third party support is unlikely).

Even in situations where upgrading is possible because the PC manufacturer had the foresight to connect the local bus and video circuitry, your future local bus options undoubtedly will be restricted and expensive. You can upgrade these systems by plugging a display adapter with a conventional host interface into the standard expansion bus, but you forego any throughput advantage the proprietary local bus system offers.

Local bus itself does not require a specific circuit technology, but the logical way to make the connection is through the PC's chipset. After all, the chipset already handles bus-related features such as memory and I/O bus control. Consequently, chipset makers began incorporating local bus potential in their products.

One chip maker went further. OPTi, Inc., not only added local bus connections to its DXBB chipset (which itself comprises its 82C496 System/Data Controller and 82C206 Integrated Peripheral Controller) but also produced a specification outlining an expansion connector for local bus add-ons. OPTi contributed the design to the public domain, providing the first local bus standard.

OPTi proved not to be a strong enough market force to create a standard, however. Instead, two standards arose: one from an industry committee (VESA's VL Bus) and another from a powerful hardware manufacturer (Intel's PCI).

VL Bus

The "local bus" concept sneaked onto the market in 1991 inside NEC's PowerMate desktop PCs. The motherboard-mounted display systems of these machines were connected to a new third bus connected almost directly to the microprocessor, augmenting its Compaq-style separate memory bus and conventional ISA expansion bus. Termed "local bus" by NEC, the bus link enabled the PowerMate to move pixel data at (or near) the speed of the microprocessor instead of the lower rate imposed by the expansion bus.

The major drawback to the NEC design was that the local bus connection was embedded in the motherboard circuitry with no possibility of external connections. Improving the display system in an older PowerMate (for example, for higher resolution) meant foregoing local bus performance because no connector was available for local bus boards.

The video local bus design provided a definite benefit—about a 30 percent overall improvement in video speed. To keep up, many PC makers copied the NEC design, making their systems upgradable by putting their local buses on proprietary expansion connectors. Unfortunately, the profusion of proprietary standards hindered wide support. Although OPTi, the maker of PC chipsets, proposed an open local bus standard based on its products, the proprietary design never found wide adoption.

Recognizing the need for a standard for interchangeable local bus products, an industry consortium called the Video Electronics Standards Association (VESA) began work on a local bus standard in early 1992. (Hardly coincidentally, NEC was one of the founders of VESA.) The VESA Local Bus standard—VL Bus—was formally announced on August 28, 1992. Industry acceptance was instant. In fact, because preliminary specifications had been circulating for months, compatible products were announced immediately.

VL Bus gave the PC industry a standardized connector and protocol for PC local bus expansion systems. Inherent is the potential for interchangeable display adapters (and other expansion boards), allowing for a free and open market for new peripherals. Although originally targeted at advanced video systems, the resulting specification was made broad enough to be equally adept at handling other peripherals requiring high-bandwidth transfers, such as mass storage and network interfaces.

VL Bus was designed around the needs of Intel microprocessors, specifically the 486. It duplicates the signal needs of that chip, except that a few signals are more broadly defined to allow compatibility with 386 microprocessors. Other microprocessor families are accommodated using bridge logic, circuits that translate signals and protocols.

The most important innovation of VL Bus is its high operating speed. Although the VL Bus specifications set no maximum or required speed, technical considerations put the maximum at 66 MHz. The best combination of features and performance come with 33 MHz operation. Coupled with its full 32-bit design (with the capability to handle 16-bit operations), the 33 MHz speed gave the VL Bus a claimed peak throughput of 132M per second.

VL Bus is quick, but not *that* quick. The fastest at which it can transfer data is in burst mode, which follows Intel's definition of the term for the 486 chip. A burst is a single address cycle followed by 4 data cycles—5 clock cycles for the transfer of 4 double-words (each of which is 4 bytes or 32 bits). At a 33 MHz bus speed, that's 105M per second, not counting other overhead. For other (non-burst) transfers, VL Bus requires 2 clock cycles (address, then data) for each transfer, yielding a peak throughput of 66M per second.

Even that figure is generous. At operating speeds above 33 MHz, at least one wait state is added to each read and write operation; at

33 MHz and below wait states are waived for write operations only. One wait state reduces non-burst throughput by 50 percent; the 66M per second peak transfer rate effectively becomes 44M per second. Burst speed is nearly halved (9 cycles for 4 32-bit transfers or 58M per second). Moreover, individual VL Bus devices may add still more wait states by sending signals to the bus controller indicating they are not ready for the next cycle.

Architecturally, VL Bus approaches a true local bus in design, and in simplest form provides little more than a set of unbuffered address, data, and control signals that are directly connected to the host microprocessor. PC makers can add buffering to extend the reach of the bus (that is, more slots), sacrificing speed. More connectors mean more capacitance, which enforces a lower speed limit.

The original VL Bus specification recommended designers use no more than three local bus devices in any system operating at speeds of 33 MHz or lower. The recommended limit did not distinguish between slot-mounted devices and those integrated into the system board. Therefore, a PC with local bus video built into its motherboard likely would be constrained to a maximum of two VL Bus connectors. Higher speeds limit the count further. At 40 MHz, only two devices (one of which could be a slot) were recommended, and at 50 MHz, only one VL Bus integrated into the system board was recommended.

The small count of bus connectors was not seen as a handicap because few devices can benefit from local bus speed. Most PCs would need only the three high-speed connections recommended for 33 MHz operation—one each for video, mass storage, and network host adapters.

The physical embodiment of VL Bus is a 16-bit Micro Channel-style connector with 0.05-inch spacing of its 112 contacts in two rows of 56. Obviously that connector cannot handle all the signals on 168 pins of a 486 microprocessor. Therefore, the signals of the 486 that are redundant or irrelevant to an expansion bus are not carried to the VL Bus.

In addition to the 486-derived signals, the VL Bus specification adds several signals of its own. Status signals on four pins outline the system's microprocessor architecture for the benefit of devices attached to the VL Bus. Two pins reveal the type of microprocessor in the host. Of four possible definitions, two were reserved for future designations, while the other two indicate 386 or 486 chips. Another pin indicates whether the host PC can accept high-speed writes (those without wait states). The fourth pin indicates whether the host PC operates lower, equal to, or higher than 33 MHz.

VL Bus allows for bus-mastering operation following the capability built into the 486, but using slightly different signaling. When a bus master wants to take control of the bus, it sends a special signal to the host system. It then takes command only upon receiving a confirmation signal from the system host. Unlike Micro Channel or EISA, the VL Bus specification does not set the priorities of bus mastering devices. Arbitrating competing requests to use the bus is left to the motherboard and the proclivities of its designer.

As with microprocessors, the VL Bus includes signals to indicate whether addresses on the bus refer to memory or input/output ports and whether a read or write operation should be carried out. It also distinguishes data from program instructions using another signal, a distinction irrelevant to the 486 but useful to the Pentium (which uses separate internal caches for code and data).

Although a PC could be built with nothing but these few VL Bus slots, the VESA design aims to add instead of replace a conventional expansion bus. The VL Bus connector fits the same slot positions as a traditional ISA, EISA, or Micro Channel bus connector, collinear with it. VL Bus expansion cards themselves are permitted (but not obligated) to include two connectors, one for the VL Bus and one for the traditional bus. The latter enables VL Bus peripherals to take advantage of the resources of the other expansion bus—interrupts, DMA control, and the like—which are not provided by VL Bus. The VL Bus includes only one hardware interrupt control line.

Automatic configuration is not part of the VL Bus specification. Board makers can design products that are set up traditionally—that is, with jumpers and DIP switches—or devise their own software setup systems. In either case, VL Bus is invisible to software. No drivers need be used for your PC and its peripherals to take advantage of the higher speed transfers possible with the VL Bus design. Used in conjunction with ISA, VL Bus provides higher performance than EISA or Micro Channel with none of the compatibility worries.

Reflecting the introduction of the 64-bit Pentium in 1993, VESA is working on a second-generation VL Bus standard (Version 2.0) which was in preliminary form at the time of this writing. The revised specification redefines the maximum number of VL Bus slots

Used in conjunction with ISA, VL Bus provides higher performance than EISA or Micro Channel with none of the compatibility worries.

permitted in a single circuit. VESA recommendations allow for up to three slots at 40 MHz and two slots at 50 MHz if low capacitance is maintained in the design. PCs can sidestep these limits by using multiple VL Bus subsystems—separate VL Bus controllers, each handling no more slots than recommended.

The 2.0 specifications add bits as well as slots, defining a 64-bit interface based on a 32-bit Micro Channel connector. The wider bus and higher clock push theoretical throughput up to 400M per second, subject to the same real world adjustments as the 132M per second claim of the VL Bus original. The 2.0 update also includes support for write-back caching.

The VL Bus 2.0 specification requires backward compatibility. Boards designed to the new standard work in old VL Bus PCs and vice versa. In fact, 64-bit boards operate in 32-bit systems as 32-bit cards. Ratification of the new standard is expected in the fall of 1993.

PCI

In July 1992, Intel Corporation introduced its own concept of local bus, a specification called Peripheral Component Interconnect (PCI). The final design proved to be both more and less than the industry had hoped for. The first PCI specification defined mandatory design rules and included hardware guidelines to help assure proper circuit operation at high speeds, but it fell short where the industry wanted the most guidance: the pin-out of an expansion bus connector that would allow the design of interchangeable expansion boards. PCI actually is not a local bus at all, but a high-speed interconnection system a step removed from the microprocessor, running closer to microprocessor speed than would a traditional expansion bus.

Although, in initial form, PCI was compatible with VL Bus, in May 1993, Intel positioned its design as a VL Bus alternative by introducing PCI Release 2.0. The new specification extended the original in two primary ways. It broadened the data path to 64 bits to match the new Pentium chip, and it gave a complete description of expansion connectors for both 32-bit and 64-bit implementations of a PCI expansion bus. The new design is incompatible with VL Bus.

The original purpose of the PCI design was to make the lives of those who engineer chipsets and motherboards easier. Whereas each new family of Intel microprocessors required the makers of chipsets and motherboards to redesign their products, PCI promised a common standard, one independent of the microprocessor generation or family.

Intel also felt that the PCI standard would help simplify circuit design. A stated goal of the standard is to eliminate "glue logic," the pesky profusion of integrated circuits required to match big VLSI (very large scale integration) chips to one another. All PC chips that follow PCI can be joined on a circuit board without glue logic. In itself, that could lower PC prices by making designs more economical, while increasing reliability by minimizing the number of circuit components.

Intel also intended PCI to be an open industry standard around which chip makers could design their products. Such a standard would foster the creation of a wide variety of chips with specialized functions that could easily attach to PCI—not just video but also SCSI controllers, LAN adapters, and audio and video products for multimedia systems.

As with VL Bus, PCI is designed to work inside PCs based on more traditional buses such as ISA, Micro Channel, or EISA. Unlike VL Bus, however, PCI is self-contained and need not affiliate with another bus. The standard envisions PCI boards connecting only to the PCI bus and getting all the signals they need from the PCI connector.

A key tenet of the PCI design is processor independence—circuits and signals not bound to the requirements of a specific microprocessor or family. That alone removes PCI from being a true local bus. Even though the standard was developed by Intel, the PCI design is not limited to Intel microprocessors. In fact, some computers based on DEC's Alpha chip are expected to use PCI.

That said, the speed of operation of the PCI bus is dependent on the host microprocessor's clock. PCI components normally are synchronized with the host microprocessor. The standard foresees operation in a frequency range from 20 to 33 MHz, although PCI is designed for operation down to 0 Hz, a dead stop.

To accommodate devices unable to operate at the full speed of the PCI bus, the design incorporates three flow control signals indicating that a given peripheral or board is ready to send or receive data. Thus PCI transactions can take place at a rate far lower than the bus speed would imply.

The PCI design provides for expansion connectors extending the bus off the motherboard but limits such expansion to a maximum of three connectors (none are required by the standard). As with VL

Bus, this limit is imposed by the high operating frequency of the PCI bus. More connectors would increase bus capacitance and make full speed operation less reliable.

To attain reliable operation at high speeds without the need for terminations (as required by the SCSI bus), Intel chose a reflected rather than direct signaling system for PCI. To activate a bus signal, a device raises (or lowers) the signal on the bus to half its required activation level. As with any bus, the high-frequency signals meant for the slots run down the bus lines and are reflected back by the unterminated ends of the conductors. The reflected signal combines with the original signal, doubling its value to the required activation voltage.

The high bus speed of PCI makes the layout of circuit traces on the motherboard itself critical, and the PCI specification gives guidelines for the physical configuration of components on the motherboard. Intel believes that PCI devices should be arranged as close as possible so that connections to the high-speed parallel bus (which Intel calls the "PCI speedway") are spaced about an inch apart. Normal device spacing is seen at two-inch increments, staggered on each side of the speedway. This design minimizes the length of the bus and the capacitive effects that would limit its operating frequency.

The basic PCI interface requires only 47 discrete connections for slave boards—boards that cannot exert control over the system— with two more on bus-mastering boards. To accommodate multiple power supply and ground signals and blanked-off spaces to key the connectors for proper insertion, the physical 32-bit PCI bus connector actually includes 124 pins. Every active signal on the PCI bus is adjacent to (either next to or on the opposite side of the board from) a power supply or ground signal to minimize extraneous radiation. The 64-bit implementation of PCI uses a 188-pin connector. As with VL Bus, PCI connectors are patterned after those used by Micro Channel with 0.05 inches between pins.

To give more speed to the PCI system, Intel endowed it with its own burst mode that does not suffer the 4-cycle, 16-byte limit of VL Bus's burst mode. During burst-mode transfers, a single address cycle can be followed by multiple data cycles that access sequential memory locations.

Burst mode and multiplexing are managed by a single signal. Activating the signal indicates that a valid address is on the bus. This burst mode underlies the 132M per second throughput claimed for the

32-bit PCI design. (With the 64-bit extension, PCI claims a peak transfer rate of 264M per second.)

Even though PCI anticipates all devices following the standard will use its full 32-bit bus width, the standard allows for transfers of smaller widths. Separate signals indicate which of four byte-wide blocks of PCI signals contain valid data.

As a self-contained expansion bus, PCI naturally provides for hardware interrupts. Its four hardware interrupt signal lines allow for interrupt sharing as with EISA and Micro Channel, but the PCI specification does not itself define what the interrupts are or how they are to be shared. Even the relationship between the four signals is left to the designer (for example, each may indicate its own interrupt or may define up to 16 separate interrupts as binary values.) Typically, they are implemented in a device driver for the PCI board.

The basic PCI design supports arbitrated bus mastering, much like VL Bus. It also has its own bus command language (a four-bit code) and supports secondary cache memory.

To ensure that addresses and data sent across the bus are not corrupted in transit, PCI incorporates parity checking. Unlike Micro Channel, PCI parity checking is mandatory and must be implemented in every board and system. One parity bit is provided for the combination of the 32 bits of bus width and the control signals that indicate which four bytes of the data bus contain valid information.

The PCI specification also anticipates an eventual switch from standard 5-volt logic to power-saving 3.3-volt operation. To accommodate the development of low-voltage "green" PCs, PCI specifies two connector types and three different connector regimes—a 5-volt connector for today's prevailing circuit designs, a 3.3-volt connector for low-power designs, and the capability to combine both connectors on a single expansion board for a smooth transition between designs. A key on 5-volt sockets (that is, a tab that blocks two pins) prevents the insertion of 3.3-volt boards. Five-volt boards are slotted at the key's position so they slide in unimpeded. A different key on 3.3-volt sockets restricts the insertion to corresponding 3.3-volt boards. Boards capable of discriminating the two voltage regimes have slots in both places.

As with Micro Channel and EISA, PCI contemplates system configuration without the need to set jumpers or DIP switches. Under the PCI specification, expansion boards include registers of configuration information that can be tapped to set up systems automatically. PCI requires 256 registers for configuration information on every board.

Although both claim the misleading title "local bus," VL Bus and PCI are very different. Most people see them as competitors with one eventual winner (and one loser). However, the future of the two buses will likely differ as much as their technology.

VL Bus has taken an early lead in the number of PCs using it—the first commercial PCI machines will not appear until late 1993 or early 1994, because the chipset Intel designed to implement PCI proved flawed.

Machines based on VL Bus likely will be less expensive than those using PCI because VL Bus simpler. It has fewer signals, fewer rigid requirements, and no need for new technologies or chipsets. Many PC makers even price their VL Bus machines the same as machines using a more conventional expansion bus.

Regarding performance, there's really no way to compare. No existing local bus PC seizes all of the potential of either VL Bus or PCI. Without a doubt, either outperforms any older bus. VESA has published higher claimed peak transfer rates than Intel, but whether these claims carry through to real products remains to be seen.

PCI is technically more advanced than VL Bus; PCI likely has more future potential.

PCI is technically more advanced than VL Bus. PCI was developed from the ground up, but VL Bus is more a patchwork. PCI likely has more future potential. It may be the more enduring standard.

Both give you more responsive video in your next PC, and either can accelerate the speed of mass storage transfers. Both work invisibly in simple situations. Taking advantage of bus mastering or interrupt sharing requires, however, the same confusion of setup and drivers as the older advanced buses.

If you're buying a PC today and want the highest performance expansion option, you'll want VL Bus.

If you're contemplating buying a new PC, don't avoid VL Bus because you suspect PCI will be the longer-lived standard. The PC industry has already made an extensive commitment to VL Bus, and peripherals using it likely will be available for more than the lifetime of your next PC. PCI is something to worry about tomorrow. If you're buying a PC today and want the highest performance expansion option, you'll want VL Bus.

Proprietary Upgrades

The final choice for upgrading your PC's microprocessor is the proprietary upgrade, a board or assembly specifically designed by a particular PC manufacturer to upgrade its products (and its products only). Proprietary microprocessor upgrades combine the installation ease of a turbo board with the smooth integration of a replacement motherboard. Their only disadvantages are limited availability—not all manufacturers and PCs support proprietary upgrades—and expense. There's little competition for proprietary products, so manufacturers charge what the market will bear, which can be a surprisingly high price. Twice the cost of a similar but more generic upgrade is the general rule.

Exactly which proprietary upgrade options are available depends on the computer you have. Some computers, such as early Zenith machines, had most of their critical circuitry installed on special expansion boards that could be easily replaced. One expansion board held the microprocessor, its support circuitry, and often memory, too. Swapping this board for a newer and faster one is the equivalent of replacing an entire system board but without the hassle. Other manufacturers adopted similar strategies with different mounting hardware. In its PowerVEISA systems, Advanced Logic Research puts its microprocessor and cache circuitry on small daughter cards. For its early 386-based PS/2s, IBM offered a "Power Platform" that fits flat atop the system motherboard in its Model 70. Later, IBM switched to a Zenith-like expansion board for updating the micro-processor circuitry of its Models 90 and 95. Tandon put the micro-processor in a plug-in cartridge that didn't even require you to open the case to replace.

Because the choice of proprietary upgrades is limited—few man-ufacturers even offer them, and those that do provide few options—your choice of power ranges is limited. You can follow only the upgrade trail blazed by the system's maker. On the other hand, you are ensured of compatibility with your hardware, and that's the biggest recommendation for proprietary upgrades.

Often, it's cheaper and easier to upgrade a machine in a way other than its manufacturer intended. For example, although a proprietary upgrade module may sell for $2,000, the entire motherboard could be replaced for less than $750. These dubious economics and Intel's OverDrive chips have made proprietary upgrade modules increasingly rare.

Step-by-Step Upgrade Guides

However you upgrade your system's microprocessor, a faster microprocessor can enable your system to zip through programs, blast through compilers, and cost you less time waiting. The following sections detail how to go about your upgrade, whether you're switching microprocessor chips, installing a turbo board, or replacing your motherboard.

Microprocessor Replacement

Upgrade procedures for your PC's microprocessor at the socket level are basically the same with whatever chip you have. Except in the case of the 486SX (and 486DX systems with upgrade sockets), you pull out your existing microprocessor and replace it with the upgrade. The procedure is simple, straightforward, and poses little danger (none to you, just a little to the chip) if you are careful.

Following is more specific guidance for chip-level upgrades for each of the three major microprocessor families (8088, 286 and 386/486).

8088 or 8086 to V20 or V30 Upgrades

To upgrade a 8088 or 8086 microprocessor with a V20 or V30 chip, you first need to identify the chip to replace. The 8088 and 8086 are packaged in 40-pin Dual In-line Pin (DIP) cases, usually made from black epoxy. The microprocessor is usually one of the largest integrated circuits in the computer, measuring about 2 inches long and 0.8 inches wide. After you locate this big, black chip, you can verify your find by the pale gray silk-screen lettering on top of it. Amid all the code numbers, you'll find the numbers "8088" or "8086," usually with a prefix of few letters and a suffix of "1" or "2."

You can tell where the microprocessor is only by opening your system and taking a look. Some systems hide the microprocessor underneath the drive bays or in other inconvenient locations. The only sure way to upgrade when the chip is so placed is to remove the system motherboard, replace the chip, and reinstall the motherboard. If you're going to all that trouble, you're better off spending the few extra dollars to replace the whole system board. You should take a preliminary glance before investing in a new chip.

After you're sure that you can get to the microprocessor, you're ready to begin. Start by switching off your PC. To be safe, unplug the power cable from your system so it doesn't get switched on accidentally. Pull off the cover of your system's case and access your microprocessor by removing the expansion boards covering it. On general principle—the desire to avoid scratched and bloodied fingers—you may want to remove them all so there's nothing to get in the way.

Take out a pad and pen and sketch the area where the microprocessor is located. Mark down the orientation of the existing microprocessor, noting whether its notched end points to the front, back, left, or right side of your PC. After you're sure that you won't forget the orientation of the chip, remove your old microprocessor. Special tools called *chip pullers* are available to make the job easier. In a pinch, you can use a blank card-retaining bracket from an expansion slot as a level. Put the short end of its L under one edge of the chip and pry up slightly. Move the bracket to the opposite edge of the chip and pry up. Alternate ends of the chip, prying a bit at a time until the chip comes free. Then pick up the chip, being careful not to touch its leads (if you can avoid it) so you don't risk damaging the chip. Someday, you might need to plug it back in.

Before going further, prepare your new microprocessor for the socket by bending its leads perpendicular to the body of the chip. Grasp the chip by its ends and press down on a hard surface such as a tabletop, forcing the leads of the chip from being splayed slightly out to exactly square with the chip.

After the leads on the new chip are ready, position the chip in the socket, ensuring that the orientation of its notch matches that of your old microprocessor. All 40 leads (legs) of the new chip must line up exactly with the holes that they match. Press the chip straight down into its socket. Now inspect your work—make sure that all the leads go into their holes and do not fold under the chip or slide outside the socket.

Only after you're sure that all the leads are set properly, begin reassembling your PC. Start by putting your expansion boards back into their sockets, then reconnecting all cables to your PC, including the power cable. Switch your PC on and verify that it works properly. If you're certain all is well, turn it off and replace the cover. Your upgrade is finished.

286 to 386SX (or 486SLC) Upgrades

Replacing the microprocessor in any PC is a delicate operation— after all, it *is* brain surgery. Sterilize your work area by clearing space around your PC so you have room for parts, tools, and instructions. Before you make your first incision, anesthetize your PC—park its hard disk and switch off the power. Remove the power cable from the machine so there's no chance that an accidental bump on the on/off switch will lead to disaster. Then open your PC's case.

After the lid is off, and you can see inside, locate your system's microprocessor. Its appearance varies, but no matter the package, the microprocessor is one of the larger chips on your PC's system board, square and dark gray or black. Don't settle for the first big chip you find—most of today's PCs have a number of large, square Application-Specific Integrated Circuits (ASICs) to confuse you.

In the case of 286 microprocessors using the PGA package, the main chip is easy to locate. It's the one that looks like it doesn't have a socket. The big, gray chip hides the socket beneath it.

Chips using the PLCC package are doppelgangers for ASICs, so you're forced to rely on the stenciling on the chip for absolute identification. A 286 microprocessor bears identifying numbers typically in the form "80286-12" with the last digits representing the speed rating of the chip. The manufacturer's name, Intel, appears on many 286 chips, but that is not a sure sign because several other companies also make the 286.

Chips using the LCC socket have a retaining wire or wires holding them down or a heat sink atop them. You can't see the chip's legend because often it's hidden underneath the chip or its heat sink. Only after you pull an LCC microprocessor from its socket can you identify it.

After you've located your system's 286, you need to access it. Inevitably, the microprocessor is somewhere difficult to reach, often covered with expansion boards. You'll need to remove them to replace the chip.

Generally, it is better to remove more boards than fewer. You'll have more room to work and will be less likely to injure yourself (it's easy to cut yourself on the short, sharp wires that stick out from most expansion boards) or damage your system by trying to squeeze something in place. Scribble down which board came from which expansion slot. Don't forget to record all the associated cables that you disconnect.

After you have access to the area around the microprocessor, you have one more preparatory step—note the alignment of the microprocessor in its socket. Square chips can have any of four possible alignments, only one of which works. Chips are keyed so that you cannot misalign them inadvertently. However, with little effort you can overcome these preventive measures and make a chip fit in a socket any which way. As three out of four alignments are wrong, applying force is not a good idea.

Most microprocessor packages have a notch or beveled corner, which should correspond to a matching feature in the microprocessor's socket. In some cases—many IBM PS/2s being archetypical—the necessary keying or indication of alignment on the socket is absent. Carelessness in these cases can lead to the destruction of your upgrade by improper alignment. So take all possible precautions. Draw a sketch or put a temporary marker on the system board to indicate which direction the notch points. Intel provides self-adhesive tabs with the SnapIn 386 to make such indications.

After the preparation is done, remove the last obstacle standing in the way of plugging in your 286-to-386SX upgrade board—your old microprocessor. Be careful removing it so that you can slide it back in should (heaven forbid) your upgrade fail or your favorite vintage software package prove incompatible.

PGA chips must be extracted from their sockets cautiously. Most manufacturers supply a helpful tool with their upgrade. The tool resembles a small rake with fingers designed to slide under the chip, fitting between its leads. You push down on the arm of the tool to lever the chip up. If you don't get such a tool with your upgrade, use an ordinary L-shaped retaining bracket from an unfilled expansion slot in the same way.

When you start prying your chip up, be extremely careful to insert the fingers of the tool between the chip and its socket, not between the socket and your system board. If you wedge the tool too far down, you might pry the socket off the system board. If, when trying to lift your microprocessor, you feel inordinate resistance, stop. Make sure that you're not trying to lift the socket as well as the chip.

Don't try to pry one side of the chip free with one push. Instead, gradually work the chip up by lifting one side a bit, then alternating sides. By taking this balanced, gradual approach, you'll avoid bending the leads of your microprocessor so you can reuse it more easily.

Chips in LCC sockets are easier to remove. Push off the one or two retaining wires holding the chip down. The best way is to use two hands. Lock the upper corners of the retaining wire under the fingernail of your index finger, put your thumbs against the side of the socket, and pull the wire toward the closest edge. Use slow, steady pressure rather than a quick push. If you cannot get your hands deep inside your computer, you can use your thumbs to move the wire while holding your hand in place with your fingers against the side of the socket. In either case, move both ends of the retaining wire at the same time. After one wire is off, remove the other in the same way. Be careful that the wires don't come off the socket and get lost in your PC.

PLCC sockets hold their chips tenaciously. The easiest way to remove them is with a special tool that may accompany your upgrade board. If not, you need to pry the chip from the socket using a small screwdriver (a pair of them is better). The chip comes out easiest if you lift as close to straight up as possible.

After your old chip is free, remove it from your PC entirely. To avoid damage to the sensitive semiconductor inside the chip, avoid touching the chip's leads. Hold PGA and LCC chips by their edges; hold the PLCC chip by pinching its flat faces between your fingers.

Put the old chip in a safe place. Often vendors of upgrades include a container for storing the old chip. Even an envelope is okay— providing it's not plastic (to avoid static) and that you keep it in a safe place where you won't drop an unabridged dictionary on it.

The next step is to plug in your upgrade. First determine which corner is keyed to match the socket. Align this corner with the socket, relying on your notes or tape marker you made earlier. Loosely fit the upgrade board in the waiting socket. With PGA installations, take a good look and make sure that all of the leads of the upgrade are aligned with matching holes in the socket.

After you're sure that everything is properly lined up, press the upgrade board into place. If you feel unusual resistance or if the board tends to lean to one side, stop. Examine the fit between board and socket, realign the two if necessary, and press on.

After the upgrade board is in place, reassemble your PC. Be careful should any expansion boards extend over the upgrade board. Because the new board is undoubtedly somewhat thicker than the original microprocessor, it may interfere with one or more expansion slots. If necessary, move any expansion board that would use the slots above the upgrade to another slot, reserving the obstructed slots for short boards.

If you need to use the slots directly above the upgrade for expansion, be cautious when you slide the boards into place. Ensure that they sit properly in their sockets without pressing down on the upgrade and that the upgrade does not hold the boards up at a slight angle to the expansion connector. The pressure of the expansion board may stress the upgrade and any resulting misalignment can lead to a bad connection or even the failure of the either board.

After you've reinstalled all the expansion boards and are otherwise satisfied with your installation, plug your PC back in—without putting the cover back on the case. Turn on the power and let your PC boot up to be certain it is working properly.

If you don't see anything on your screen, make sure that you've plugged in and turned on your monitor. If it's working and you still see no message, check your installation. If you can find no obvious errors, it's time to call technical support.

If your PC boots up—which it most likely will—run the installation software that came with the upgrade board. Part of that installation process is a diagnostic that determines whether you made your upgrade successfully—although your PC booting at all is a good preliminary test! After you pass the manufacturer's test, you can switch off your PC, reinstall the cover, and run the latest software releases on your newly enhanced PC.

486 to OverDrive Upgrades

If you're not certain of your abilities in chip-level circuit surgery, you can use Intel information to decide whether to handle the upgrade process yourself. Intel believes that anyone can put an OverDrive chip into an upgrade socket, but recommends people with less PC hardware experience not tackle pulling out their old microprocessor. Even so, the company includes a chip removal tool with its OverDrive replacement processors.

Intel believes the best strategy is to have your dealer switch processors for you.

Intel believes the best strategy is to have your dealer switch processors for you, but that can be difficult when the vendor you bought from is 3,000 miles away. Fortunately, the extra step of removing your old microprocessor is easy.

What's not always easy is getting access to the microprocessor in systems not designed to be upgraded. Most PCs from major manufacturers have their upgrade sockets located in the open—that is, not hidden under the disk bays or power supply—so you can open up your PC and press the OverDrive right into a waiting upgrade socket. Smaller vendors, however, usually design their systems for low cost instead of easy accessibility. Not only do their systems often lack upgrade sockets, but microprocessors in such low-end PCs may be hidden anywhere on the motherboard. In many systems, the microprocessor socket is buried under the drive bays, where no amount of cramped-finger prying gives you sufficient access.

If you cannot see the entire 486 microprocessor in your PC, you'll have to remove the motherboard to make the replacement. Yikes! That's major surgery for what was supposed to be a simple chore. Unlike open-heart work, however, this operation adds only about half an hour to the total upgrade time, and the chances of survival are near certain.

Because microprocessor accessibility can have a major effect on the work and skill involved in making an OverDrive upgrade, the best first step is to determine what you're getting yourself into. Before you order your OverDrive chip, check your motherboard. Locate the microprocessor and the upgrade socket (if any) to see how difficult they are to access.

Actual 486 microprocessor chips are easy to identify—they have the name "Intel" and the "486" designation silk-screened in large white letters on top of the chip package. They are usually the biggest circuit components on a motherboard, measuring 1.7 inches square and made from a dark gray ceramic compound.

Upgrade sockets take two forms, conventional and ZIF (Zero Insertion Force). A conventional socket is a chip-size square decorated with three parallel rows of silver donuts in a square array. There is a large hole in the middle of the plastic socket that enables you to see the (typically green) circuit board underneath. The tiny hole in the center of each silver donut accommodates one of the pins on the chip.

ZIF sockets are big black squares perforated with three rows of holes arranged like the donuts on ordinary sockets. The socket usually covers the circuit board, so you cannot see any of the green board under the socket.

At one side of the ZIF socket is a lever; when you lift it, you can drop a chip into the socket by lining up its pins with the holes—there's no need to press it down. Hence, the force required is zero (thus the name of the socket). Swinging the lever flat against the motherboard locks the chip in place and ensures that its leads make secure contact.

After you've identified your microprocessor and any upgrade sockets, determine whether you have the access you need to make your upgrade. If you do not—if the socket is located under the drive bay of your PC or is so close to a side of your PC that you cannot access all sides to use the chip removal tool—you'll need to remove the motherboard to make the upgrade.

Generally, although motherboard removal sounds daunting, it's easier than you would expect and only adds about 15 minutes to your OverDrive upgrade. Begin motherboard removal by taking all the standard PC upgrade precautions. Park your hard disk, switch your system off, and unplug all cables—the power cable and all signal cables going to your peripherals. Record where each cable went. Then slide off the cover of your system's case.

Pull out all your expansion boards, noting in which slots they were installed. Disconnect all cables attached to your old motherboard. Typically these include two power supply cables, a speaker cable, and one or more cables for the system lock, backup battery, and turbo or reset switch. Note where each of these cables went, too.

Finally, remove all the screws holding the motherboard in place. If your system follows standard AT practice and packaging, you'll find only two or three. One is usually near the keyboard connector and another near the center of the motherboard. Some makers are more generous, however, and require you to remove six to ten screws. You'll know you've gotten all the screws out when the system board slides around inside your system.

Many system boards lift right out of your PC, but some use special white nylon spacers that slide into slots, so you'll have to push your board to the left about an inch before you can lift it out. In any case, after your system board is out, lay it flat on your work surface.

If your PC motherboard requires that you remove its existing 486 microprocessor, that should be your next step. Before you remove your old 486 chip, examine it closely. You'll note that one corner has been lopped off to indicate its proper orientation. Take a piece of masking tape and stick it on your motherboard near this corner. This mark will help you install your OverDrive chip.

Intel supplies a rake-like pry bar with its OverDrive chips that simplifies chip removal. The teeth of the rake slip between the pins on the bottom of the microprocessor so that you can lever it out of its socket.

To remove your old 486, hold the rake with its long arm angled upward and its teeth horizontal, pointing toward the side of the 486. Slide the teeth of the rake under the edge of the chip so that they interleave with the chip's pins—slide the rake parallel to the edge of the chip while pressing the rake under it until the teeth slip into place.

Apply downward pressure to the long arm of the tool until you feel the chip give. Lift the side of the chip very slightly—trying to pry a whole side up at the same time bends the connecting pins and makes the chip impossible to reuse.

Move the tool to the opposite side of the 486 and pry the side slightly upward. If the chip lifts easily, return the tool to the first side and pry a bit more. If the chip is reluctant, move the tool to an adjacent side and work your way around all four sides of the chip, prying each one upward in turn. In most cases, you'll need to pry each side about three times before you've loosened the chip enough to lift it out.

If your PC has a ZIF socket, all you have to do is raise the lever at the side of the socket and lift the 486 from the socket.

However you pop your 486 from its socket, hold the chip only by the edges. To store your old 486, press it into the black foam inside the OverDrive package. This foam is specially treated to prevent static damage to semiconductors.

With most PCs, finding the OverDrive socket is no big deal. The only critical part of the installation is alignment. The OverDrive must be oriented in the proper direction and all its leads must properly engage their matching holes in the socket.

Intel indicates the orientation of the OverDrive chip in several ways. The most obvious of these is a notch or bevel of one corner of the square package. Turn the chip over; one of the pins has a square base. There is also a small gold ray on the central square of the package. All indicate the same corner of the chip.

One corner of every OverDrive socket is also specially marked. Many sockets have an outside corner notched to match the chip; some have one of their inner corners partly filled; others require investigation of the motherboard itself where you'll find a silk-screened outline of a beveled corner. Orient your chip to match the alignment indicated by your PC's OverDrive socket.

With a ZIF socket, raise the lever and the chip should drop into place. Press down the socket lever to lock the chip in place, and your OverDrive is installed.

With conventional sockets, lower your head so that you can peer between the OverDrive and its socket. Ensure that all the leads of the OverDrive match holes in the socket. In particular, be sure that you haven't offset the chip by one or more rows in any direction.

When you are absolutely certain that the OverDrive is aligned, press it down into the socket. Start with firm, even pressure from your thumb or forefinger on the center of the chip. If it does not slide smoothly into the socket (most chips won't), work it down by pressing each side down a little bit at a time.

Do not press down hard on the center if your OverDrive is reluctant to fit. Too much pressure can bend your motherboard, breaking connections in the inner layers of the printed circuitry. Ease the chip down until the bottom of the chip nearly touches the top of the socket. Then inspect your work, checking that none of the chip's leads have been bent.

Do not press down hard on the center if your OverDrive is reluctant to fit.

After your new OverDrive chip is in place, put your PC back together—install the motherboard back into the chassis if you've removed it, slide all expansion boards back into their slots, and reconnect all cables. Switch your PC on as you normally would. It should boot up faster than before. It may race through its diagnostics in double-time and dash through your configuration files.

Turbo Board Upgrades

Adding a coprocessor-type turbo board is just like adding any other expansion board—you open your PC, scope out an empty slot, slide the board in, and button everything back together.

Replacement microprocessor boards, however, take more work. The first step is to open up your PC and survey the territory. Of course, don't forget to switch off your PC and disconnect the power cord for safety's sake. See the Appendix for case-opening instructions.

After you're inside, locate your system's microprocessor and determine which expansion board—even one that's currently occupied—is nearest the microprocessor. Just as you would in replacing the microprocessor with a new chip, take out a pad and pen and sketch the area where the microprocessor is located so that you have a record of the orientation of the old chip.

Then commit yourself to the upgrade by removing your old microprocessor. Again, a chip puller is the best tool to use, but a blank card-retaining bracket will serve as well. You can work PGA-packaged chips up by putting the short end of its L-shape under one edge of the chip and prying slightly, then moving the bracket to the opposite edge of the chip and prying again. Alternate ends of the chip, prying a bit at a time until the chip comes free. PLCC chips can be pried out with a thin screwdriver. LCC chips require you to remove the retaining wire at the top of the socket, freeing either a cover plate, heat sink, or the back of the chip itself. You can lift out the chip after it's free. Be careful not to touch the leads or the gold connector pads on the chip—nearly all replacement microprocessor turbo boards require that you plug the old chip into the turbo board itself.

Next, hold one end of the turbo board's adapter cable over the vacant microprocessor socket and ensure that the orientation of the connector matches that of your old microprocessor (see fig. 3.5). After you're sure that all the leads of the connector are properly lined up with the holes they match, press the connector into place. Inspect your work, making sure that all the leads go into their holes and do not fold under the connector or sneak outside the edge of the socket.

If your turbo board requires it, plug your old microprocessor into the socket waiting on the board. If you plan to install a coprocessor on the board, do so now, too.

Now you're ready to slide the turbo board into the expansion slot you've chosen. Judge whether it is easier to plug the other end of the adapter cable into the turbo board before, during, or after you seat the turbo board in its socket. After you've made up your mind, slide the board into place and plug in the other end of the adapter cable.

While your PC's case is still open, reconnect all cables to your PC, including the power cable. Switch your PC on and verify that the system boots. Then install the turbo board software and check the complete operation of the board. After you've assured yourself that your system is operating properly, turn it off and replace the cover. Your upgrade is finished.

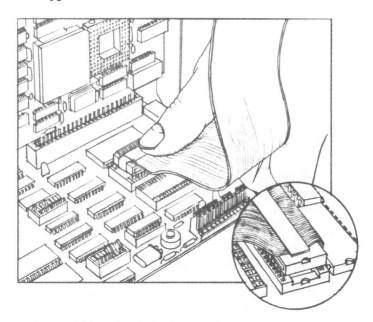

Figure 3.5
Be sure the notch on the cable lines up with the notch on the socket and be careful not to bend the connector pins.

Motherboard Upgrades

Before you begin to replace your motherboard, ensure that you have adequate working room. You're going to need a place to put all the expansion boards from your system and a convenient place to put your old system board.

Start by switching off your PC. Unplug all cables connected to your system, power, and signal. If you doubt your memory, make a note of where each cable went. You can use pieces of masking tape to label each cable and matching connector. Then pull off the cover of your system's case.

Remove all expansion boards from inside your PC. Again, note where each was so that you can duplicate the arrangement with your new motherboard.

Now disconnect all cables attached to your old motherboard (see fig. 3.6). Typically, these include two power supply cables, a speaker cable, and, on newer machines, one or more cables for the system lock, backup battery, and turbo or reset switch. As you remove each cable, such as the power supply shown here, be sure to write down which went where. Check the board twice to ensure you haven't missed anything.

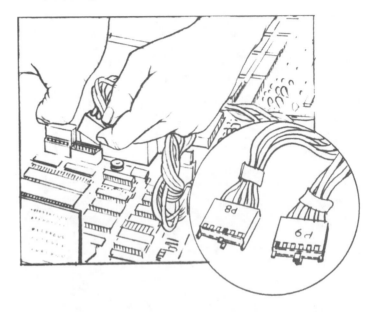

Next remove all the screws holding the motherboard in place (see fig. 3.7). You'll be surprised at how few there are. PCs and XTs, for instance, only have two. Draw yourself a map and mark which holes the screws went into.

When the screws are out, the motherboard is loose inside the case but not free. If your old system board was secured by three or more screws, it may lift right out after you've removed the screws. Slide the old motherboard to the left about an inch until you can move it no further, releasing the spacers that hold the board in place (see fig. 3.8). Lift it out of your PC while continuing to move it to the left.

After you have the old board out of your system, play vulture. Recycle whatever parts you can. For example, remove the spacers used for mounting the old motherboard, noting which holes in the old board had screws and from which you removed spacers. Pinch the "wings" at the top of each spacer with long-nosed pliers and push it down through its hole (see fig. 3.9). Snap them back in the identical positions on the new board.

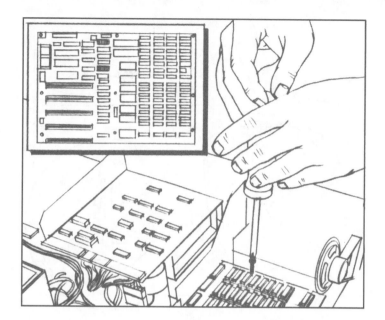

Figure 3.7
Removing the screws that hold the motherboard in place.

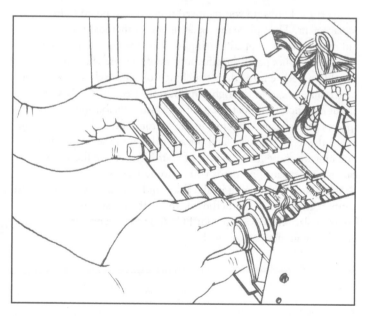

Figure 3.8
Slide the board about an inch to the left. It then should pivot up and out.

Figure 3.9
Removing the
spacers from your old
system board.

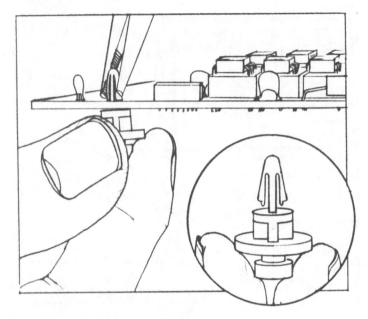

Transfer the hardware you removed from the old board to its
replacement. Then place the replacement motherboard where your
old motherboard stopped moving to the left when you removed it.
Check that it lies parallel to the bottom of the case. The spacers
should properly engage their matching slots in the chassis. Slide the
new motherboard to the right until it stops (see fig. 3.10). When it is
about one inch from its final position, ensure the bottoms of the
spacers have engaged the slots in the bottom of the chassis. Slide the
board the rest of the way, and the screw holes in the board should
line up with those in the chassis of your PC. Replace the screws,
cables, and expansion boards you removed from your system.
Reassemble the case, plug in all cables, and switch on your system to
verify that your new motherboard works. If your system successfully
boots, replace the cover on your PC. You've made one of the most
effective upgrades you can make.

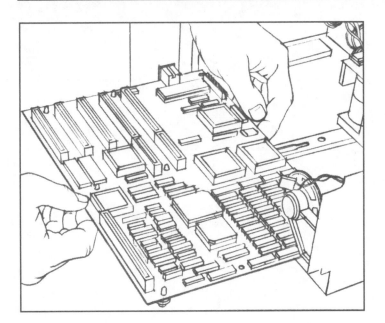

Figure 3.10
Slide the new system
board in to the right.

4

Math Coprocessors

When you need quick answers to complex math problems, a floating-point unit or math coprocessor delivers answers faster than any other PC enhancement. Adding a math coprocessor to any PC lesser than a 486 DX or Pentium is truly the most trouble-free upgrade you can make; however, it only helps certain applications. To do the job right, you must match the right chip to your needs and your PC.

Adding a math coprocessor to any PC older than a 486 is truly the most trouble-free upgrade you can make.

Once prohibitively expensive, coprocessors have fallen to the level of affordability. In addition, they have almost become a necessity—one that is built into all of today's most powerful PCs.

When upgrading, you must decide whether or not a math coprocessor is for you. In top-of-the-line PCs, the most common math coprocessors—the Intel floating-point units—are unnecessary because every Intel 486DX, 486DX2, OverDrive, and Pentium chip has all the coprocessor circuitry built in. No separate math coprocessor is needed to upgrade 486SX systems because the standard OverDrive microprocessor upgrade includes the coprocessor circuitry—and it costs about the same as an add-in 487SX math coprocessor.

With the exception of the specialty Weitek family, the math coprocessor is a product that only benefits older generations of PCs. In that these machines need the most help to keep up with today's software, a coprocessor is an excellent upgrade candidate. You may see an improvement of 2 to 10 times with some applications.

Sorting through which applications do or do not benefit from a coprocessor is not easy. Moreover, before you can make your coprocessor upgrade, you must sort through a variety of chip models. For 286 and 386 microprocessors, there are several coprocessor choices. At least six different vendors—Advanced Micro Devices, Cyrix Corporation, Integrated Information Technology, Intel Corporation, ULSI, and Weitek Corporation—offer chips that plug into various PCs and accelerate their performance on some math-intensive tasks. The odds of picking the best one at random from this group are even worse than those against winning at Three-Card Monte.

Coprocessor Fundamentals

A *coprocessor* is something that simply works in cooperation with your PC's microprocessor. Its goal is performance won by greater efficiency through specialization and division of labor. To divide the labor, the coprocessor takes charge of some particular tasks normally relegated to the general purpose microprocessor. At the same time, the coprocessor is a specialist, designed to handle one particular task. In sacrificing the need to be all things to all software, it can be trimmed down to the bare essentials required to perform its task most efficiently.

Math coprocessors, also called numeric coprocessors and floating-point units (or FPUs), specialize in manipulating numbers. In particular, they are designed to handle all the complex functions that gave you nightmares while you were daydreaming in high school: long division, trigonometric functions, roots, and logarithms. These operations yield floating-point numbers, the type that math coprocessors are most adept at handling.

Floating point describes a way of expressing numbers. At that, a *floating-point number* is not a mathematically defined class of numbers like integers, rationals, and real numbers. Rather, a floating-point number can represent (or approximate) any of these. The essence of a floating-point number is that the decimal point floats between a pre-defined number of significant digits rather than being fixed in place the way ordinary dollar values always have two decimal places.

Mathematically speaking, a floating-point number has three parts: a sign, which indicates whether the number is greater or less than zero; a significant (sometimes called a mantissa), which comprises all the digits that are mathematically meaningful; and an exponent, which determines the order of magnitude of the significant, essentially the location to which the decimal point floats. Think of a floating-point number as one represented by scientific notation, the compact way of expressing huge numbers. But where scientists are apt to deal in base 10—the exponents in scientific notation are powers of ten—math coprocessors think of floating-point numbers digitally in base two, all ones and zeros in powers of two.

In carrying out complex mathematical operations on floating-point numbers, the math coprocessor works in much the same way as a general-purpose microprocessor. Using digital logic, it processes patterns of bits containing information (the floating-point numbers) under the control of other bit patterns making up instructions. These operations are carried out in registers, special internal memory areas inside the coprocessor.

To make a computation, the math coprocessor first loads one of the numbers that it is to work upon into one of its registers and then loads the second number into another register. Next, it reads the program instruction, which tells the chip what particular operation it should carry out on the two numbers. The instruction starts another, miniature computer program running inside the coprocessor chip, and that program causes the circuitry of the coprocessor to actually calculate the desired answer. The entire set of programs inside the math coprocessor that respond to the various instructions that the chip understands are called its *microcode*, just as in an ordinary microprocessor.

After a result has been calculated, getting the answer out of the coprocessor requires the execution of another instruction. Alternately, the next instruction can make the coprocessor carry out another operation on the results of the first.

General-purpose microprocessors operate exactly the same way. The math coprocessor earns its speed advantage over microprocessors in handling floating-point numbers because its command set includes high-level mathematical operations and because it has more internal circuitry devoted to carrying out those instructions. For example, a general-purpose microprocessor can compute an irrational root, but it might have to execute a loop of simple instructions hundreds of times to come up with the answer. The coprocessor solves the same problem with a single instruction.

Certainly, a microprocessor could be designed to carry out all of the complex instructions handled by a math coprocessor; the Intel 486DX and Pentium microprocessors do exactly that. In effect, the 486DX and Pentium each combine a general-purpose processor and a numeric processor on a single piece of silicon. In other microprocessors (including the low-cost 486SX implementation), the coprocessor exists as a separate element for reasons tied to the standardization of floating-point calculations and the technology of integrated circuits.

Applications that Benefit

Before you even begin to consider which microprocessor you should add to your PC, you need to know whether a math coprocessor will do you any good.

When the manufacturers of math coprocessors talk about performance gains their products can give you, they usually talk up some special benchmark programs that they have written. Run the program, and before your very eyes, you see performance race ahead. When you try to run an actual application, however, you see that the benefits of a math coprocessor can be quite elusive. Most programs that you are apt to run do not gain any extra speed from the addition of a math coprocessor.

The fundamental explanation for this is that most programs simply do not use the complex math operations at which coprocessors excel. Even the number crunching that most business people use their PCs for benefit little, if at all, from using a math coprocessor. The only chores that really stand to gain from a coprocessor are those that are computationally intense—applications used in chores like statistics, engineering, and graphics.

Coprocessor benchmarks are designed to give the chip a real workout, allowing no time for the chip to catch its breath.

If you do have a program that uses the advanced math that is the lifeblood of a numeric coprocessor, you will probably discover that the performance improvement won by adding the chip will not be nearly as great as that demonstrated by the benchmarks written by the coprocessor providers. Coprocessor benchmarks are designed to give the chip a real workout, allowing no time for the chip to catch its breath. The benchmarks are nothing but wall-to-wall math problems. The coprocessor loves the challenge, racing through at blinding speed.

Normal applications, however, are typically only lightly sprinkled with high-level math problems. Most of the time, the typical application program is involved in input/output (I/O) operations—waiting for keystrokes, moving data around, putting numbers on the screen. The coprocessor cannot help with I/O, so the potential of the math chip is hardly tapped. It just sits around, waiting for its next assignment.

Exactly how big an improvement you can expect in performance varies with the specific application that you run. For example, spreadsheets generally benefit to some degree from the addition of a math coprocessor, but the real benefit shows up only when the spreadsheet is involved in heavy-duty math work. Calculations, however, are only a small part of what a spreadsheet does.

Beyond spreadsheets, the performance increase you can expect from a coprocessor is still dependent on the math functions required. To gain any performance improvement from a coprocessor, you must have a need for transcendental functions. Typical accounting programs have no need for such calculating; engineering and scientific chores more likely do. The stranger the symbols look in the math you want to do—sines, cosines, derivatives, integrals, logarithms, exponents—the more likely a coprocessor can help.

Computer-Aided Design programs all benefit from the addition of a math coprocessor, but again the advantage gained varies with the operation carried out. Loading images and screen regenerations can be handled in about half the time when a coprocessor is available. Hidden-line removal benefits only a little more than 10 percent.

Loading images and screen regenerations can be handled in about half the time when a coprocessor is available.

Although math coprocessors do not help with normal data entry, that is not to say that they are overrated. If you have a job that can take advantage of one, there is no more cost-effective advantage you can give your PC.

Coprocessor History

To understand the relationship between the various available math coprocessors and why you might need a one, you need to understand some history of the technology. Coprocessors were not a sudden inspiration to some obscure design engineer; rather, they were a solution to a problem brought about by using precise digital technology to find answers to questions that arose in an irrational world.

In the mid-1970s, math coprocessors did not exist as they are known today. Computers were all mainframes and minicomputers. They all did floating-point operations and, oddly enough, they all came up with different answers. Not that they added two and two and deduced different results, but when they calculated irrational numbers and rounded them off, the last few decimal places varied depending on what make and model of computer did the calculating. The problem was that real-world irrational numbers like pi have an infinite number of decimal places, but computer memories are finite. Irrational answers can only be approximations, and different computers used various methods of approximating and rounding off irrational numbers.

Scientists were not thrilled to have the results of their calculations vary with the hardware on which they were computed, so the Institute of Electrical and Electronic Engineers (the IEEE) formed an industry committee to develop standards for floating-point calculations.

At the same time the IEEE was standardizing, Intel Corporation was developing a successor to its successful 8080 and 8085 microprocessors and decided that it should develop a hardware implementation of the IEEE floating-point standard as part of that microprocessor program. Not that Intel foresaw the tremendous demand for personal computers that would develop; rather, they saw the new microprocessor chips finding use in things like robotic and numeric-control applications—commanding lathes, grinders, and milling equipment in machine shops and factories. The advanced math capabilities of a silicon-based implementation of the IEEE floating-point would be a boon to the design of such equipment.

The IEEE floating-point unit was first conceived as part of a microprocessor, but practical matters stood between that idea and reality. The microprocessor that Intel was working on eventually would become the 8086, the immediate predecessor of the 8088 that served as the foundation of the IBM PC. At the time the 8086 was being developed in the years before its introduction in 1978, creating an integrated circuit was much more difficult than it is today. The size and number of components that could be grown and etched onto a wafer of silicon limited the complexity of possible (or at least affordable) integrated circuits. Ordinary microprocessors like the 8086 were the most complex circuits ever designed up to that time.

One of the rules of chip-making is that the larger the chip, the more likely it is to contain some defect that would make it unusable. Yet manufacturers cannot arbitrarily make chips smaller because the state of the art in silicon fabrication constrains how small the details of a chip can be. If the chip layout is too small, it will more likely suffer manufacturing defects, reducing the yield of the manufacturing process so that producing the chip is uneconomical. For example, the smallest possible details in the 8086 microprocessor measured 5 to 10 microns across. Today, chips are made with details as fine as 0.6 micron.

Together, the rule and the limit conspired to put an effective lid on the complexity of the new 8086 chip. Adding the IEEE floating-point circuitry to it would have far exceeded the level of complexity permitted by the technology of the times. Moreover, there was little incentive to try. Coprocessors for the 8080 and Z80 chips that were popular in the rudimentary desktop computers available at the time were unavailable. Hobbyists were only beginning to figure out what to do with the normal functions of those microprocessors; they had no concept of what to do with a coprocessor. And, just as today, most applications did not need or could not use a floating-point processor that followed the evolving IEEE standard.

Weighing all these considerations, Intel elected not to include the IEEE processor as part of the 8086 or any other microprocessor chip. Instead, the circuitry was relegated to a separate element, which eventually was produced as a commercial product in 1980—the 8087 math coprocessor.

In historic perspective, the 8087 was to become only the first product in a family of IEEE floating-point processors. As microprocessor technology developed, the 8087 was first revamped to keep up. When Intel came up with the 80286 microprocessor, the 8087 was revamped into the initial incarnation of the 80287 (known as the 287) coprocessor. Later, the internal circuitry of the 8087 and 287 was redesigned to create the more efficient 80387 (or 387). Finally, technology reached a point at which it became practical to incorporate the IEEE circuitry on the same piece of silicon as the regular microprocessor circuitry, achieving the original floating-point design goal. The all-in-one chip resulted with the first 486. And for people who bought the 486SX and discovered that a coprocessor was necessary after all, Intel reworked the 387 circuitry into a new chip, the 487SX.

But Intel was not satisfied with the performance delivered by the 387 level of coprocessor. The internal math circuitry of the Pentium has been redesigned from the circuitry of the 486SX. The result is the fastest math circuitry on the planet for Intel-based computers.

*To get the fastest
possible math, the
real route is to
follow the Pentium.*

According to Intel, the math circuitry in the Pentium is three to
five times faster than the circuitry in a 486DX. In that Intel has in
the past adapted its newer coprocessor designs to replace older
coprocessor chips, there is a possibility that you might be able to
add part of the Pentium to your existing PC. But to get the fastest
possible math, the real route is to follow the Pentium.

Coprocessor Communications

No matter the part number or speed, all Intel math coprocessors
share the same architectural elements. Except in 486DX, 486DX2,
OverDrive, and Pentium chips, the Intel design makes a math
coprocessor a separate piece of hardware that is nevertheless logically
integral to the main microprocessor. Even the Intel microprocessors
with integral coprocessors devote an area of their silicon to coprocessor functions. In operation, however, the math coprocessor is seen
by programs as part of the main microprocessor. In fact, with Intel
systems, the only thing that changes when you add a math
coprocessor to your system is that the microprocessor understands a
wider repertory of commands, and these commands elicit answers to
mathematical questions at great speed.

Because the coprocessor works with its microprocessor host, the two
chips must communicate in some manner to exchange data and
instructions. There are, in fact, two ways of linking microprocessor
and coprocessor chips together that have been realized in commercial
products. Some coprocessor chips link to the main microprocessor
through a direct connection of input and output ports through
which they send and receive data and instructions. Other coprocessors use a memory range to exchange data and instructions with
the main microprocessor. The first type of coprocessor, which
includes the Intel coprocessor family, are often termed *I/O-mapped
coprocessors*. The second type, called *memory-mapped coprocessors*, are
more exotic chips that are less often encountered.

Besides all the math coprocessors made by Intel, all chips that claim
compatibility with the Intel coprocessor chips use I/O-mapped
technology. Included among these chips are the Cyrix 83D87, IIT
387, ULSI 83C87, and the various 287 chips from numerous
manufacturers. The pre-eminent example of memory-mapped math

coprocessors are those made by Weitek Corporation, the 1167 multi-chip platform as well as the 3167 and the 4167 single-chip implementations. Another math coprocessor contender, the Cyrix EMC87, has characteristics of both of these types of coprocessors. This Cyrix chip works both as an I/O-mapped chip for compatibility with software written for the Intel 387, yet it can accelerate to memory-mapped speed with applications written especially for it.

I/O Mapping

In the Intel I/O mapped design, both the microprocessor and the coprocessor are connected to the data lines that carry information— program instructions as well as the data that they work on—inside your PC. Normally, the main microprocessor executes all of the instructions in most computer programs. Certain instructions, however, are recognized by the math coprocessor as its own, and it can calculate them out directly.

In a way, the Intel I/O-mapped math coprocessor is like a leech, a parasite that cannot live without the microprocessor it clings to. Only the microprocessor has circuitry to control your PC's address lines to find information; therefore, proper operation of the coprocessor requires careful coordination of its work with that of the main microprocessor. The effort of the two chips is kept together through a direct hardware linkup—wires connecting the two chips— that are electrically controlled through I/O ports. These ports are internal to the two chips and, unlike the I/O ports used by your PC's peripherals, cannot be accessed directly by you.

The Intel I/O-mapped math coprocessor is like a leech, a parasite that cannot live without the micro-processor it clings to.

Both the main microprocessor and the coprocessor have their own registers (in which all calculations take place) and internal control circuitry. As a result, the two chips can operate somewhat independently and simultaneously. In other words, while your math coprocessor is wrestling with a particularly difficult problem, the microprocessor can do something else.

In theory, this design could add a degree of parallel processing to your PC. But in reality, it often does not. Most programs send the math chip scurrying off in search of an answer and leave the microprocessor waiting until the results are found. A few applications on the other hand, Borland's Quattro Pro, for example, take advantage of this parallel-processing capability. By carefully hand-coding assembly language routines, Borland was able to achieve a high degree of parallel processing when a coprocessor is present. That is why Quattro Pro shows a greater performance increase when a coprocessor is present than most other spreadsheets do.

Memory Mapping

Memory-mapped microprocessors communicate with your programs and microprocessor by using memory addresses as mailboxes. A small range of addresses (typically a 4K page) in far off paragraphs of your system's RAM (random-access memory)—well above the 16 megabytes that most 386-based computers can use for physical RAM, but within the four-gigabyte addressing range of the micro-processor—is cordoned off for such communications. (All available memory-mapped coprocessors are designed to work with 386 and more powerful microprocessors.) The microprocessor pushes instructions for the coprocessor to one group of addresses and data to be worked on to other addresses. The coprocessor gathers up the data and instructions, carries out the appropriate operations, and responds with its results in the same manner. No actual RAM chips are installed at the memory locations used for these communications. Rather, the memory for holding the commands and data are part of the coprocessor's circuitry.

One obvious requirement of the memory-mapped design is that the coprocessor chip must have access range to the address lines used by the microprocessor. In that I/O-mapped coprocessors have no need for this address information, address lines are not available at coprocessor sockets designed for 387 chips. Memory-mapped coprocessors thus require larger sockets with more pins to accommo-date all the address lines they need access to. That is why memory-mapped coprocessors have sockets the size of those used by 386 microprocessors, but 387 sockets are smaller. These special sockets for memory-mapped coprocessors are termed EMC sockets because they use an Extended Math Coprocessor interface. (It is quite possible that other uses for these sockets might be found beyond coprocessing. Any advanced function requiring direct memory addressing could take advantage of a memory-mapped coprocessor socket.)

The big disadvantage of the memory-mapped coprocessor is that the interface has not been standardized. Each memory-mapped coprocessor family has its own commands and uses its own distinct address range. For example, although the Cyrix ECM87 and the

Weitek 3167 plug into the same socket, the two chips are completely incompatible, and each is unable to execute programs written for the other chip. Hence, to take advantage of the coprocessor, programs must know the secrets particular to each coprocessor. As a result, each memory-mapped math coprocessor requires its own version of a particular application. That need creates a huge burden for the software publisher, who must distribute a profusion of similar but incompatible programs should he want to take advantage of any available coprocessor. Few programs actually have such built-in support for any memory-mapped math coprocessor, let alone support for more than one family.

The sad fact is that although memory-mapped math coprocessors can be quicker, they do not often offer a speed advantage because most programs cannot use them. Memory-mapped coprocessors are only an effective solution if your everyday work relies heavily on a single application and that application has specific support for the memory-mapped coprocessor that you chose.

Intel Architecture

The I/O-mapped coprocessors in the Intel family each share some common traits. Beyond the 8-, 16-, and 32-bit registers of microprocessors that you are used to dealing with, the Intel-style coprocessors work with 80-bit registers.

Eighty bits seems somewhat arbitrary in a computer world that is based on powers of two and a steady doubling of register size from 8 to 16 to 32 to 64 bits. But 80-bit registers are exactly the right size to accommodate 64 bits of significant data with 15 bits left over to hold an exponent value and an extra bit for the sign of the number held in the register. The registers in Intel coprocessors are not limited to this single data format, however. They can calculate on 32-, 64-, or 80-bit floating-point numbers, 32- or 64-bit integers, and 18-digit binary coded decimal (BCD) numbers as well. (Binary coded decimal numbers simply use the specific 4-bit digital code to represent each of the decimal digits between zero and nine.)

Each Intel chip has eight of these 80-bit registers in which to perform their calculations. Instructions in your programs tell the math chip what format of numbers to work on and how. The only real difference is the form in which the math chip delivers its results to the microprocessor when it is done. All calculations are carried out using the full 80 bits of the chip's registers, unlike Intel micro-processors, which can independently manipulate its registers in byte-wide pieces.

The eight 80-bit registers in an Intel coprocessor also differ from those in a microprocessor in the way they are addressed. Commands for individual microprocessor registers are directly routed to the appropriate register as if sent by a switchboard. Coprocessor registers are arranged in a stack, sort of an elevator system. Values are pushed onto the stack, and with each new number, the old one goes down on level. Stack machines generally are regarded as lean and mean computers. Their design is more austere and streamlined, which helps them run more quickly.

In the original design of Intel's first coprocessor, the company's engineers had the foresight to divide the chip's circuitry into two functional elements: a *bus interface unit* and a *floating-point unit*. The former links the chip to the rest of the system in which it is installed (the microprocessor in particular), and the latter performs the actual calculations. This division of labor gives chip designers great flexibility, which Intel has exploited in improving its original coprocessors. Each part of the coprocessor can be upgraded as the need arises and technology develops. This step-by-step improvement method has enabled Intel to match coprocessors to microprocessors much more quickly than would have otherwise been possible.

The 8087

Stack machines generally are regarded as lean and mean computers.

The 8087 was Intel's first IEEE floating-point unit, designed to complement its 8086 microprocessor. Although the two chips were conceived as a unified whole, the math coprocessor was not released until 1970—two years after the microprocessor it supported. Difficulty in designing the 8087 led to this lag, because it just was not easy to make. In fact, according to Intel, the 8087 was the most complex large-scale integrated circuit ever produced at the time of its introduction. It adds a full 68 machine language instructions to the instruction set found in the 8086/8087 level instruction set.

The 8087 was the most complex large-scale integrated circuit ever produced at the time of its introduction.

The 8087 fits into a 40-pin DIP socket that provides the chip with the same addressing and data-handling capabilities of the chips it was to match, including 20 address lines. Although the 8087 can accept data from a 16-bit bus, it also can step backwards without modification and connect up with the 8-bit bus of the 8088. The 8087 automatically adapts itself to 8-bit operation as necessary. Besides the 8086 and its 8-bit cousin, the 8088, the 8087 math coprocessor also can operate in conjunction with the other Intel microprocessors that are derived from the 8086. These include the 80186 and 80188.

The 8087 is designed to operate at the same speed as its host microprocessor and ordinarily shares the same clock frequency with its microprocessor. Intel still offers three models of the 8087 chip, each of which is rated at a different operating speed. The best match for IBM PCs and compatible computers that run at 4.77 MHz is the 5 MHz 8087. Versions of the 8087 that operate at 8 and 10 MHz are also available. The nomenclature describing these chips is somewhat odd, however. A chip labeled with nothing more than a plain 8087 operates at system clock speeds of up to 5 MHz. A chip bearing the identification 8087-2 operates at a speed of up to 8 MHz, and the 8087-1 operates at up to 10 MHz.

You should never try to skimp by adding a slower 8087 than your system calls for.

As with other chips, the speed rating defines the maximum rated operating speed of the chip and does not necessarily affect the speed at which the chip will operate (or how fast it can calculate). That speed is set by the clock inside the computer host. You can plug an 8087 into a system that calls for a chip with a lower speed rating, but you should never try to skimp by adding a slower 8087 than your system calls for. In other words, using a 10 MHz 8087 in a PC that calls for half that speed is wasteful but does not result in any operational problems. Putting a 5 MHz chip in a 10 MHz computer, however, is an invitation to miscalculation, a system crash, or the catastrophic failure of the chip.

Putting a 5 MHz chip in a 10 MHz computer is an invitation to miscalculation, a system crash, or the catastrophic failure of the chip.

The 287

The 80287, usually abbreviated to just 287, was introduced in 1985 by taking advantage of Intel's split-chip strategy. It retains the floating-point section of the 8087 but couples it with new interface logic to match Intel's 80286 microprocessor chip.

As with the 8087, the bus control logic of the 287 is designed to link to a 826 and to rely on the microprocessor for system support. Unlike the 8087, the 287 coprocessor chip does not even have access to the address lines of the computer in which it is installed, so all memory-related operations are handled by the main microprocessor. This design enables the 287 to deal with the real and protected modes of the 286 processor, enabling the 287 to address the full 16 megabyte range of that microprocessor. The 8087 operates only in real mode. Although the 8087 and the 287 are packaged in a 40-pin DIP socket, the two chips are not pin-for-pin compatible and cannot be substituted for one another. This incompatibility should be obvious because the 8087 requires a full complement of address lines while the 287 depends on its microprocessor host to handle all addressing functions.

Unlike the 8087, the 287 is designed to operate asynchronously. This means that the coprocessor does not necessarily operate at the same speed as its host microprocessor. The two chips, microprocessor and coprocessor, know how to adjust their operations, waiting as necessary, to match their data transfer cycles.

Ordinarily, the 287 is connected with the same oscillator that runs the rest of a PC. However, an internal divider slows down the clock frequency entering the 80287 to one-third its original speed before it reaches the floating-point circuitry. Hence, a 287 operates at one-third the clock speed that is presented to it.

In most 286-based systems, the clock that runs the microprocessor is divided in half before being connected to the 286. Typically, the original double-speed clock is connected to the 287 so that the coprocessor effectively operates at two-thirds the microprocessor speed. For example, in an 8 MHz IBM AT, the 287 coprocessor runs at 5.33 MHz.

Using a dedicated clock can boost the data throughout the 287 substantially.

Some systems give the 287 a dedicated clock of its own, allowing the engineer designing the system to operate the coprocessor at whatever speed he wants, thanks to the asynchronous possibilities of the chip. Using a dedicated clock can boost the data throughout the 287 substantially.

Although Intel at one time offered four different speeds of 287, the company's lineup was trimmed to two in 1990, versions that operate at 8 and 10 MHz, eliminating versions that operated at 5 and 6 MHz. A new design, discussed later in this chapter, has now made those two surviving 287 models obsolete as well. Nevertheless, you may still encounter these discontinued versions of the 287 in older PCs and on the market, so identifying them is important.

A chip labeled only as an 80287 or that bears the identification 80287-3 is rated to operate at up to 5 MHz. The suffixes on the other discontinued 287s give the maximum speed rating of the chip in megahertz. Thus, the 80287-6 runs at up to 6 MHz; the 80287-8 runs at up to 8 MHz; and the 80287-10 goes all the way to 10 MHz.

Because the 287 is based primarily on the 8087 floating-point circuitry, the chip is almost completely backwardly compatible with the 8087 and executes most of the same software—but not all software, because the floating-point unit is not a gate-for-gate copy of the 8087 but was improved somewhat in the upgrade. Differences in the two chips show up primarily in the way that they handle errors. Software can compensate for the differences in the chips, so a well-written program will run interchangeably on either coprocessor.

The Intel bus-control-logic design of the 287 that makes the coprocessor rely on its microprocessor for addressing information earns the 287 an extra degree of flexibility. The chip is not inherently limited by any of its own addressing constraints nor by the 16M memory-handling capabilities of the 80286. As a result of this versatile design, the 287 is also able to operate with 386 microprocessors. For two years, in fact, it was the official Intel coprocessor for the 386.

However, the 287 had been left behind by technology and the evolving IEEE floating-point standard. Only after the 287 had been put into production was the IEEE floating-point standard finally written in its final form, now known as ANSI/IEEE 754-1985. In some subtle ways, the 287 and the finalized standard were at variance. Moreover, the 287 was designed with a 16-bit databus interface, which handicapped newer microprocessors that used 32-bit databuses. Consequently, the 287 is not the ideal math coprocessor, particularly for 386-based PCs. Nevertheless, a slow 287 is faster on floating-point operations than a 386 by itself, so even a lowly 287 can be a worthy addition to a PC that will accommodate one.

Eventually, Intel totally redesigned the floating-point unit of the 287 to create a coprocessor more in line with the capabilities of the 386. The new floating-point unit design proved to be about five times faster than the original 287 on some operations and was first used in the 387 coprocessor. But in January, 1990, Intel adapted this new technology to the 80287 chip, in the process producing the two new, faster chips: the 287XL and 287XLT. The former is a direct, pin-compatible replacement for the 287 of days gone by. The 287XLT is designed for new PCs, primarily low-power laptop and notebook computers, and uses a PLCC (Plastic Leadless Chip Carrier) case that makes it incompatible with the sockets designed for other Intel coprocessor chips. Either of these advanced coprocessors operate at speeds up to 12.5 MHz with either 80286 or 386 microprocessors designed to accommodate them. Because of the more efficient design

Because of the more efficient design of the new chips, they can calculate about 30 percent faster than the old 287s at the same clock speed.

of the new chips, they can calculate about 30 percent faster than the old 287s at the same clock speed.

The 287XL now entirely replaces Intel's old 287 line, giving you one chip to fit all existing applications—no more worries about matching chip speeds. In addition, the new floating-point unit in the 287XL and 287XLT easily outperforms the one in older 287 chips, giving a bit of extra zip to math-intensive operations (though perhaps not enough to make replacing a plain 287 with a 287XL worthwhile).

Beside the more efficient circuitry and compliance with the final IEEE floating-point standard, the new chips were also designed using a different silicon technology. They use Complimentary Metal Oxide Semiconductor (CMOS) technology rather than the N-Channel MOS (NMOS) of the original. As a result, the new chips consume much less power than any of the old versions of the 287. Although the old NMOS 287 chips were offered at the same time as their new revisions, the old and new versions were priced similarly—obviously, Intel's intent to rid itself of the older chips and to rely on the new one.

Your choices are not limited to Intel coprocessors for 286- and early 386-based computers.

Your choices are not limited to Intel coprocessors for 286- and early 386-based computers, however. Advanced Micro Devices, which was licensed by Intel to manufacture the 286 microprocessor and (or so the AMD contends, there is a lawsuit on this issue) to use the Intel's microcode in other products, offers its own version, the AMD80C287. Built using low-power CMOS technology, the AMD chip was initially offered in two speeds, 10 and 12 MHz. In that these chips use Intel's own microcode, compatibility is not an issue with them. You can use an AMD chip anywhere an Intel chip fits, providing you observe the proper speed rating.

Integrated Information Technology also offers its own versions of 287-compatible coprocessors. These chips are based on IIT's own design rather than the Intel microcode, which is both an advantage and disadvantage. They hold the potential of calculating faster but may miss achieving complete compatibility. Of course, any speed benefit is swamped by the I/O overhead of programs. And compatibility is likely a similar non-issue. The IIT chips are as compatible with the 287 as the 387 is, so you are unlikely to run into problems with any normal application.

The 387

When Intel began to design a coprocessor to match the 386, it chose to develop both a new bus interface unit and a new floating-point unit. The project fell behind schedule, and Intel hedged its bets by enlisting the 287 as the coprocessor for some early 386-based PCs and by hiring Weitek Corporation to develop a version of its three-chip floating-point package, eventually named the 1167, for the 386.

All along it was carefully designing the 387 in Israel to implement the newly written IEEE standard floating-point standard. The design was totally fresh and blessed with the virtue of hindsight. Consequently, Intel was able to design the 387 floating-point unit to be faster than the one in the 8087/287.

The design was totally fresh and blessed with the virtue of hindsight.

After introduction of the new floating-point unit in 1987 as part of the 387 math coprocessor, it became the foundation of all later Intel math coprocessors, including the 387SX, 287XL, 287XTL, and the coprocessor section of the 486DX microprocessors. (The 387SX is essentially the same chip as the 387 but is designed to work with the 16-bit bus of the 386SX instead of a full 32-bit data bus.) Much of its design is also carried over into the 486 microprocessor's floating-point section.

The 387 promises a similar degree of backward compatibility with the 287 as the 287 does with the 8087. The primary differences appear in error handling, mostly because of changes in the IEEE standard. These differences are easily managed by properly written software. On some problems, the 387 or 387SX may, in fact, deliver slightly different answers than a 287 would—not to the extent of adding two and two and getting twenty-two but deriving transcendental functions that may differ in the far right decimal place. Not that either microprocessor is wrong; the 387 and 387SX just conform better to the current IEEE standard.

Another change Intel made in updating the floating-point units of the 387 was endowing the chip with a greater range of transcendental functions, including sine, cosine, tangent, arctangent, and logarithmic functions. Thus, although the 387 and 387SX should be able to run all programs written for the 287, the reverse is not necessarily true. Programs that take advantage of all the power of the 387 or 387SX may not run on the lesser chip. In general, however, code meant for the 8087 and 287 run on either the 387 or 387SX.

Although the 387 and 387SX should be able to run all programs written for the 287, the reverse is not necessarily true.

The speed ratings of different 387 chips can be identified by the part number on the chip.

Although it can operate asynchronously, a 387 generally operates at the same speed as the 386 it is installed with. Available versions have tracked the speed of the 386 as that microprocessor has become available in faster versions, all the way up to 33 MHz. (Cyrix and ULSI offer or have offered clones of the 387 rated at 40 MHz.) The speed ratings of different 387 chips can be identified by the part number on the chip. The 387 legend is followed by a hyphen and a two-digit number indicating the rating in megahertz. Consequently, a 387-25 operates at speeds up to 25 MHz.

The 387 even looks like a 386, only smaller. Its square 68-pin PGA (Pin Grid Array) case has the same slate-like appearance as the microprocessor.

The 387 design has not been static. When it became necessary to boost the 387 to 33 MHz, further design improvements became necessary. Intel switched from NMOS technology to CMOS and used new manufacturing processes that allowed details as fine as one micron to be etched in the chip's silicon. (Older 387s were limited to 1.5 micron details.) These improvements along with some tinkering in the floating-point unit itself yielded a performance improvement of about 20 percent.

The 33 MHz 387, introduced in April, 1989, incorporates all of these advanced features. On October 1, 1990, the 16, 20, and 25 MHz versions of the 387 were also upgraded to the new technology. You can distinguish old technology 387s from new technology chips by the numeric code under the part number. Old 387s always begin this line of 10 numbers with the letter "S." New technology chips do not. Use the chips without the "S."

Recently, Intel compressed the speed ratings of 387 chips. From diversity, Intel went to a one-size-fits-all philosophy. The company now makes only the quickest chips (33 MHz), which can be used in any PC that uses an Intel 386 microprocessor.

The 387SX, a math coprocessor complement for the 386SX microprocessor, was introduced in January, 1990, and all versions of it use the new technology. Again, a single version is now available for all 386SX systems. Older chips may still bear the ratings of their maximum operating speeds—from 16 MHz up. You can tell the difference between the ratings of these older chips by examining the numbers silk-screened on the chip's case. As with the 387, the rating follows the chip designation and is given as two digits representing the megahertz rating.

387-Compatible Chips

Unlike the 286 and 287, Intel chose not to license its 386 and 387 chips. Therefore, no company except Intel could legally produce its 387 design (AMD, in its lawsuit against Intel, claims to be licensed to use Intel's designs), forcing companies to *reverse-engineer* chips. Companies start with a list of all the functions the chip is to carry out and then create entirely new circuitry to handle those functions. Several companies have followed this approach—Cyrix Corporation, Integrated Information Technologies, and ULSI (the products of which are marketed by Specialty Development Corporation). Advanced Micro Devices also is likely working on such chips.

According to the various manufacturers, their designs are both hardware- and software-compatible with the Intel products. Because the 387-compatible chips are not slavish copies of the 387 itself, the various manufacturers have taken advantage of the design freedom to innovate. Most claim that they have added improvements to make their products more desirable than those made by Intel.

Cyrix Corporation

Although not originally conceived as a coprocessor company when founded in 1988, Cyrix Corporation quickly decided to make coprocessors its first product because they saw a ready market for the chips that lacked significant competition. The first of Cyrix's FasMath series of coprocessors were introduced in October, 1989, as the 83D87, a pin-compatible replacement for the Intel 387. A lower cost version for 386SX computers, the 83S87 was introduced in March, 1990.

The Cyrix products are designed to be completely compatible with the Intel 387 family.

The Cyrix products are designed to be completely compatible with the Intel 387 family, although they are not copied from the chip through traditional reverse-engineering methods (X-raying a chip to determine its internal layout). Instead, Cyrix engineered its coprocessors with an entirely different logic design based on the documented and undocumented functions of the Intel products.

Perhaps the most important difference is that the Cyrix chips rely more on hard-wired logic than microcode.

Perhaps the most important difference is that the Cyrix chips rely more on hard-wired logic than microcode. From this alternate design direction, they can achieve substantially greater speed than Intel's chips on floating-point operations.

Hard-wired logic is exactly what it sounds like; the bit-patterns that make up commands directly trigger state-changes in the solid-state circuitry of the chip. Each pattern—each logical instruction—must be specifically designed into the hardware of the coprocessor.

In microcode designs, instructions sent to the microprocessor cause the chip to run through several steps that make up the miniature internal program. The internal program tells the more general-purpose logic of the chip to carry out the function required of it.

The microcode design is the more structured approach. It gives the designer greater flexibility and can help get products to the market faster. It also allows complex instruction sets to be handled by general-purpose circuits. But microcode can slow down the thinking process of the chip. Executing the microcode imposes another layer of overhead on every calculation.

In real-world applications, I/O demands trim the Cyrix speed advantage dramatically.

On tasks that involve nothing but floating-point calculations, the hard-wired Cyrix chips can obtain answers in roughly half the time as the microcode-based Intel chips. Of course, only benchmarks (and not all of them) do nothing but floating-point operations. In real-world applications, I/O demands trim the Cyrix speed advantage dramatically. Even on the most math-intensive tasks, you should expect only about a 10% difference in the performance of the Cyrix 83D87 compared to the Intel 387 on commercial applications.

Cyrix offers its 83S87 for 386SX computers in both 16 and 20 MHz versions. Four models of the 83D87 are available, rated at 16, 20, 25, and 33 MHz.

Beyond these pin-compatible I/O-mapped chips, Cyrix hopes to set a new high-performance coprocessor standard with its own line of memory-mapped coprocessors. The first of these products was the EMC87, which combined I/O-mapped instructions for compatibility with Intel's 387 with its own proprietary memory-mapped design for improved performance. Internally, the EMC387 is based on the same processor architecture as the 387, with eight 80-bit registers, and it has essentially the same command set.

Free code converters are of no value to you as an end user.

Understanding the need for availability of software to create a demand for the chip, Cyrix offers a code converter that adapts assembly language code from I/O-mapped to memory-mapped instructions for the EMC87. This code-converter works with any assembly language file, including those produced by higher level language compilers, such as Pascal or C. Although these free code converters may be interesting for software developers, they are of no value to you as an end user. They cannot convert commercial applications to make them compatible with the EMC87.

Until software publishers opt to take advantage of the EMC87 and write programs to match, the chip will remain more a curiosity than an added enhancement. However, because it is code-compatible with the Intel 387 and was originally priced at the same level as both the Cyrix 83D87 and Intel 387 (at the same speed ratings), the EMC87 could be a no-penalty hedge for optimists who believe in memory-mapped technology.

Integrated Information Technology

At its heart, Integrated Information Technology is a coprocessor company. Founded in 1988 by two engineers who left Intel to work for competing coprocessor-maker Weitek Corporation, the company now offers chips compatible with Intel's 80287 and 387. As with the Cyrix products, those from IIT were developed from the ground up rather than reverse engineered. Both are CMOS designs based on 1.2 micron technology.

The IIT coprocessor design differs from the Intel original in that the IIT 3C87 has thirty-two 80-bit registers instead of a mere eight. These registers are divided into four banks and are designed to facilitate 4-by-4 matrix math, which can accelerate drawing performance in graphics applications. Using just one of those four banks simulates an Intel-architecture coprocessor. Using all four requires specially written programs that use the IIT 4-by-4 matrix instruction. So far, only a handful of programs take advantage of the 4-by-4 matrix instruction. As with the Cyrix memory-mapped chip, the matrix capability should be viewed as an optimist's hedge: if it costs nothing, it does not hurt. It may even bring future benefits should programmers ever decide to take advantage of the feature. Because of a better internal design to its floating-point unit, IIT claims that the 3C87 can calculate 50 percent faster than an Intel 387 in its math functions. Independent tests confirmed a speed advantage on benchmarks and commercial software from 3 to 36 percent.

IIT claims that the 3C87 can calculate 50 percent faster than an Intel 387 in its math functions.

ULSI

The initials stand for Ultra Large Scale Integration, and that is the company's specialty—developing tiny products full of lots of circuitry. One of its products is a clone of the Intel 387, which ULSI

Reverse-engineered, the ULSI chips differ from Intel chips in construction and performance.

calls the MathCo 83C87. The ULSI products are entirely socket-compatible with the various Intel chips that they mimic.

Reverse-engineered, the ULSI chips differ both in construction and performance. The ULSI products use CMOS technology and claim to be more efficient in their processing than the Intel products, requiring fewer clock cycles for each calculation. For example, although it takes an Intel chip 18 clock cycles to carry out a simple add instruction, the ULSI chip needs only 3. Division, which takes an Intel chip 80 cycles, is handled by the ULSI chips in 40.

The best part of the ULSI line is that it extends the frontiers of speed to match faster microprocessors such as AMD's 40 MHz 386. Five versions of the 83C87 are or have been available, rated at 16, 20, 25, 33, and 40 MHz. In addition, the company offers 387SX clones as well, the 83C87SX line. These chips have been available with rated speeds of 16, 20, and 25 MHz.

Weitek Corporation

Formed in 1981 by former Intel engineers, Weitek Corporation has concentrated on making math coprocessor chips for a variety of computer platforms. It does not offer chips directly compatible with Intel's I/O-mapped designs. Instead, it has developed its own line of memory-mapped coprocessors.

By 1985, Weitek was producing floating-point coprocessors for a variety of workstations, including those based on Motorola 68020 and Sun SPARC microprocessors. Around that time, Intel contracted with Weitek to develop a coprocessor for the 386 microprocessor. According to Weitek, the in-house Intel 387 program was behind schedule, and Weitek developed its product parallel to the 387 team.

The 3167 and 4167 are offered with ratings to match the speeds of the Intel coprocessors with which they work.

Those efforts led to the Weitek 1167, the first of the Abacus line. The 1167 was not a single coprocessor chip but a small circuit board that combined two of the company's coprocessor elements used in 68020 computers along with interface logic to match the 386. The 1167 board actually included a socket into which you could plug a 387 to outfit your PC with both coprocessors. The 387 could then run I/O mapped instructions while the Weitek chips would handle memory-mapped instructions.

Although effective, the board-based design was hardly elegant, and in April, 1988, Weitek introduced a single chip equivalent to the 1167:

the 3167. As with the 1167 board, the 3167 was designed to enhance Intel 386 microprocessors. In November, 1989, Weitek introduced its 4167, a math coprocessor designed to enhance the Intel 486 microprocessor. The 4167 maintains compatibility with the Abacus 3167 and gives 486-based PCs the capability to run programs written with Weitek memory-mapped coprocessor instructions. Both the 3167 and 4167 are offered with ratings to match the speeds of the Intel coprocessors with which they work.

All Weitek chips plug into the 132-pin EMC sockets in computers that have them. They are not hardware compatible with Intel coprocessor designs; nor do they run Intel I/O-mapped instructions. In fact, even according to Weitek, only a handful of commercial programs have built-in support for the company's Abacus series of coprocessors, about 38 applications at the time this book was written. Most of those are specialized scientific packages, high-end CAD programs, or developmental software not exactly in the same product mainstream as Excel, Quattro, and 1-2-3. Unless you have software that explicitly supports one of the Weitek Abacus coprocessors, you will not see any speed improvement using one. The expensive chips just do not do anything.

The 487

One of the major advances made by the Intel 486 microprocessor was its inclusion of coprocessor circuitry on the same silicon chip as the microprocessor. Far more than just a convenient package, the intimate relations between the two functions means intimate communications. The processor and coprocessor can toss instructions back and forth much more quickly than separate processor/coprocessor designs. In fact, on real-world tasks, you might see a two-times improvement between the performance of a 486DX and a 386/387 combination operating at the same speed. Obviously, if you want the ultimate in math performance, forego a 386 and any coprocessor and opt for a 486DX instead. The introduction of the 486SX in 1991 complicated matters. The chip, lacking a coprocessor of its own, was designed to be complemented with Intel's 487 math coprocessor. Of course, using two chips for the same purpose of the one-chip 486 undermines the 486's benefit of using internal communication between the processor and coprocessor. The Intel solution is surprising. The 487 is basically a complete 486DX dressed in different garb. When installed in your PC, it takes over the function of the 486SX and math calculations, leaving the 486SX

If you want the ultimate in math performance, forego a 386 and any coprocessor and opt for a 486DX instead.

essentially idle. But the 487 is packaged differently from the 486—it has an extra pin—and is therefore not socket-compatible with it. You cannot substitute one chip for the other. Moreover, the 487 does not work without a 486SX, so do not even think about trading in your microprocessor when upgrading to a 487.

Intel offers 487 chips in speeds to complement its various models of 486SX chips. Again, these chips can be identified by the speed rating, which is silkscreened on the chip itself after its model designation. But there is no point in looking for the ratings, because an OverDrive microprocessor upgrade gives your 486SX-based PC clock-doubling technology along with a math coprocessor for about the same price as an Intel coprocessor alone.

Making the Upgrade

Adding a coprocessor to your PC can be the easiest hardware upgrade you can make. Practically, all you need to do is slide a new chip into a socket. Before you can do that, however, you must find the right chip, perhaps prepare it to be inserted, orient it properly, and then finally plug it in. Afterwards, you also may have to set up your system to recognize the new chip.

Finding the Right Chip

Adding a coprocessor to your PC can be the easiest hardware upgrade you can make.

The correct coprocessor for your PC must match your system in several ways: the chip must be of the right variety to match your microprocessor; it must have packaging and pin-out that are accommodated by your system; and it must be rated at the proper speed.

Your microprocessor is the first guide to your chip choice. If your PC is based on the 8088, 8086, 80186, 80188, V20, or V30 microprocessors, you must use an 8087 coprocessor. PCs based on 80286 microprocessors must use chips in the 287 family, such as Intel's 287 and 287XL. PCs based on the 386 microprocessor are best enhanced by the 387 coprocessor or one of its clones. However, some 386s also may be able to use the 287 family of coprocessors or a memory-mapped coprocessor. Computers based on the 486SX can be enhanced with the 487 coprocessor, but an OverDrive is the better choice. Although 486-based PCs do not ordinarily need coprocessors because of the built-in circuitry of the 486 chip itself, in most cases you can add a memory-mapped coprocessor to them. When this was written, no math coprocessors of any type were available for enhancing PCs based on Pentium chips.

The owners' manual of your PC should outline your microprocessor options. If you cannot find your manual, the available sockets are a sufficient guide.

The coprocessor socket or sockets inside your PC determines which coprocessors you can physically add. All computers that use 8087 coprocessors have 40-pin DIP sockets for that chip. Nearly all 286-based PCs have the same socket, although some newer machines may have a square PLCC socket for the 286XLT coprocessor.

The chip must be of the right variety to match your microprocessor.

PCs based on the 386 microprocessor are likely to have the most socket options. Early machines have both a 40-pin DIP socket to accommodate 287-family microprocessors and square 68-pin PGA sockets to accommodate 387-style coprocessors. Later machines may have either a 68-pin PGA for the 387 family or 112-pin PGA sockets for memory-mapped coprocessors. An examination of your PC's system board will reveal which options are available to you. (You do not have to count all the pins with a PGA socket. A 68-pin PGA coprocessor socket has two rows of pins around its perimeter; a 112-pin socket has three rows of pins.) PCs equipped with 386SX chips have PLCC sockets to accommodate the coprocessor. Machines accepting a 487 have a PGA socket.

The chip must have packaging and pin-out that are accommodated by your system.

Matching coprocessor speeds in 8088, 386, 386SX, and 486SX systems is easiest. In most cases, you need a coprocessor that runs at the same speed as the microprocessor. An original IBM PC needs a 5 MHz 8087 to match its 4.77 MHz clock speed. A 386-based PC that runs at 25 MHz requires either an older 25 MHz or the newer one-speed-fits-all model, and so on.

Speed issues arise with 80287 chips; in both 80286-based and 386-based PCs, coprocessors are likely to run at speeds at variance from the microprocessor speed. In all cases, the 287 chips run slower than the microprocessor. How much slower is too important to guess. The only way to be sure of the speed required from an 80287 coprocessor is to check the instruction manual of your PC or system board. Use a chip rated at the speed designated by your manual.

The chip must be rated at the proper speed.

Intel publishes a very complete list of which of its chips it recommends for upgrading various PCs. Generally, you can substitute the equivalent chips from other manufacturers providing you abide by the basic speed rules: install a chip rated at the speed required by your PC or faster.

System Preparation

All coprocessors are installed internally inside PCs, so the first installation step you need to make is opening up the case of your PC. First, switch off the power to your computer, then pull out the power cord just in case you accidentally switch it on while you are working. Then slide off the top of the case.

When you can see inside, locate the coprocessor socket. In most computers, it is the only vacant socket on the system or microprocessor board. In some systems, you will find two vacant sockets for expansion ROMs (read-only memory). The easy way to tell the difference between ROM and coprocessor sockets is that most ROM sockets—full or empty—come in pairs; coprocessor sockets come alone. ROM sockets almost always use the DIP pin arrangement. Only 8087 and 287 coprocessors use this kind of socket. Generally, coprocessors have more pins, 40 versus the 28 or so typical of ROMs. In systems that accommodate both a 287 and 387, the 287 socket is DIP and the 387 socket is PGA.

At this point, you should do whatever is necessary to gain easy access to the coprocessor socket. In most cases, that means removing one or more expansion boards. Be liberal in the number that you remove to give yourself as much room as possible. If you have to scrunch your hand to fit in, you are likely to misalign the coprocessor and skin your knuckles. Be sure to write down which boards went where so that you can put everything back where it came from when you reassemble your system.

You are now ready to prepare and install your coprocessor.

Preparing a Coprocessor

Before coprocessor chips packaged in DIP cases can be installed, the chips need to be prepared. Chips that need preparation include the 8087, 287, 286XL, and 80C287. Preparation is required because DIP chips are usually sold with their legs splayed out. That is, the two rows of pins spread slightly apart. The spacing where the pins make the bend where they leave the chip's case matches the spacing of the holes in the chip socket. The spreading of the pins makes them difficult to insert properly.

You need to ensure that each pin is bent at exactly a 90-degree angle. To do this, grasp the two ends of the chip between your index finger and thumb. Hold the chip with one of its rows of pins against a hard surface (see fig. 4.1), such as a desktop, with the main body of the chip perpendicular to the surface. Apply pressure to the pins while holding the main body perpendicular so that the pins and the body of the chip form a right angle. Turn the chip over and do exactly the same thing with the other row of pins. When you are done, the pins should no longer be spread apart. The chip is then ready to be plugged in.

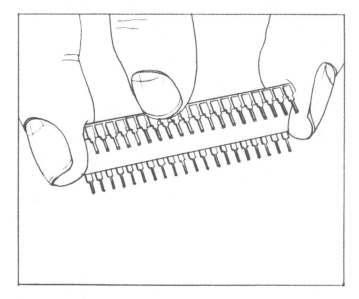

Figure 4.1
Before inserting an 8087 or 80287, straighten the pins on the chip by pressing each row flat against a hard, smooth surface.

PGA chips like the 387 and 487 as well as PLCC chips like the 287XLT and 387SX need no preparation. They can be pushed directly into their sockets.

Chip Orientation

In many PCs, the hardest part of installing a coprocessor is finding the socket into which the chip goes. Better PCs put the coprocessor socket in an easily accessible area. A few manufacturers lack the foresight to understand that you would want to install a coprocessor and hide the socket in some unreachable place, perhaps under the power supply or drive bays. If you cannot reach the socket for your coprocessor, you can either take the easy way out and have your dealer do it, or you can remove the drive bays or system board to gain access to the socket.

Better PCs put the coprocessor socket in an easily accessible area.

Before you slide the chip into its socket, you must be certain that the coprocessor is oriented properly—that the right end points in the right direction and that pin one on the chip goes into the socket hole meant for pin one.

A notch (see fig. 4.2) at the end or corner of DIP-packaged coprocessor chips indicates the pin one end, and a corresponding notch at the end of the socket indicates its pin one end. Other chip styles have similar notches or other indications to help you identify pin one. In addition, most chips also indicate pin one with a recessed dot directly above or adjacent to the pin. All you have to do is match pin one on the chip with pin one on the socket.

Figure 4.2

The proper orientation of 8087 and 80287 coprocessors is indicated by a notch at the end of the chip that matches a notch at the end of its socket.

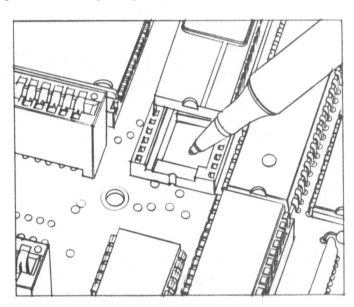

Typically, DIP sockets have a notch at one end to correspond with the notch on the chip. Align the notches, and your chip is oriented properly.

Always double-check the alignment of a chip before pressing it in place.

Always double-check the alignment of a chip before pressing it in place. Improper alignment can result in bent pins and, if not discovered before you switch the power on, the demise of an expensive coprocessor chip.

Matters are not quite so simple with some of IBM's early ATs, which were manufactured with their DIP-style coprocessor socket oriented backwards. The sockets were put on their system boards by machines that had neither the eyes to detect a difference nor the motivation to care whether there was one. Consequently, if by chance you have such an AT and follow the standard notch code, your expensive coprocessor could still go up in smoke.

Here is how to know you are inserting your coprocessor correctly in an AT. The silk screening, the white lettering on the green circuit board, on the system board (when it is visible) shows the correct orientation with the notch in the correct position. The blind insertion machine could not alter the silk-screened image. In most ATs, that means that the socket should have its notch at its end toward the front of the system unit. Make sure that the notch on the top of your 287 also points toward the front of the computer case if you have that kind of machine.

Note that most IBM PCs and XTs are just the opposite—the notch of the 8087 coprocessor that fits into those machines should face toward the rear of the case, matching the notch of the DIP socket it plugs into.

The 387 coprocessors and their clones also require proper orientation. The square PGA chip has one corner truncated more than the other three, corresponding to the location of pin one. You also may find a printed or embossed dot above this corner of the chip. The PGA socket (see fig. 4.3) for these chips should show a similar marking on their pin one corner—either the outside edge of the socket will be similarly truncated or the socket may be donut-shaped and its inner edge will show a slight bridging over corresponding to the pin one corner. That is, you will find that three of the four inside corners of the socket will be square and the fourth angled at 45 degrees. The angle marks the orientation (see fig. 4.4) of the beveled corner of the coprocessor chip. Just line everything up and press the chip in place.

When fitting a 387 coprocessor into a 112-pin EMC socket, you will notice that there is an extra hole in the socket in the bridged-over pin one area. Ignore this hole. On the EMC socket, the 387 fits into the two rows of holes closest to the center of each side of the socket. It is normal for the outer row to remain vacant all the way around the chip. Make sure that it looks the same on all four edges of the chip. If one edge is wider and shows two rows of pins and the opposite side shows none, you have installed the chip too far over by one row.

Figure 4.3

The proper orienta-
tion of 387SX chips
is indicated by a
flattened corner of
the chip that matches
a flattened corner of
its socket.

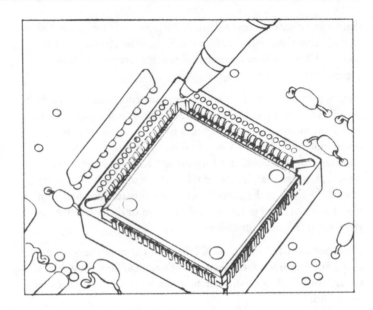

Figure 4.4

A 387 chip matching
its socket.

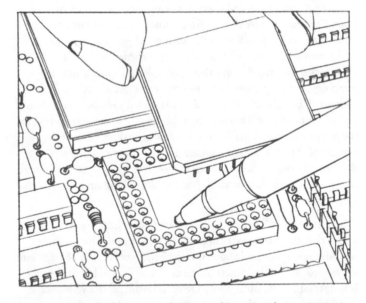

Memory-mapped chips cannot be inserted improperly into 112-pin
EMC sockets because they have an extra pin corresponding to the
extra hole in the EMC socket. Of course, you can try to force a chip
into its socket improperly and damage it, so it is best to be sure that

you have the chip oriented properly before you insert it. Again, the truncated corner of the chip corresponds to the pin one placement. Match it with the truncated or bridged-over corner on the socket.

PLCC chips like the 387SX also have a beveled corner. Inside the PLCC socket, you should notice that one corner corresponds to the beveled chip. As with PGA sockets, you will see three square corners and one angled at 45 degrees. The angled corner shows the proper orientation of the beveled corner of the PLCC chip.

When your coprocessor is properly lined-up with its socket, you can press it in place; however, your job is not yet done. Carefully inspect your work. Chips in DIP cases are particularly irksome. Their legs are apt to bump into the side of the hole for which they were meant and then curl under the chip or slide outside the socket entirely. With DIP chips, you should always check that all leads are properly inserted into the matching holes. Be on the lookout for leads that fold invisibly under the chip. Should you locate one or more leads that are not making good contact with the socket, you will have to pull the coprocessor out of your PC and straighten the leads. Figure 4.5 shows the easiest way is to squeeze the leads flat—with long-nosed pliers.

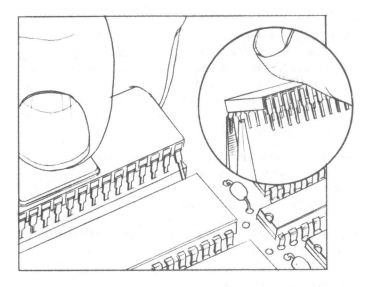

Figure 4.5
Straighten leads with long-nosed pliers.

Coprocessor chips in PGA packages pose few problems. Their pins are much more substantial and rigid than those of DIP chips. They bend only under the most severe forces.

PLCC chips just require steady pressure to push them down into their sockets. They are designed so that neither you nor an automatic insertion machine can damage the pins when you slide the chip into place. Just be sure to orient the chip properly before you press down. PLCC chips are difficult to remove after you have pushed them into place.

Coprocessor System Setup

The equipment flag is not set to indicate the presence of a coprocessor unless you tell your system that the chip is there.

Even after you install a numeric coprocessor in your PC, it may not do you any good until you tell your computer that the chip is there. Although a coprocessor can be found using only software, IBM has tried to make coprocessor detection easier. Programs can avoid testing for a coprocessor by checking an *equipment flag*, a special memory location where system information is stored, to determine whether a coprocessor is present. The equipment flag is not set to indicate the presence of a coprocessor unless you tell your system that the chip is there.

Depending on the model of your computer, you tell it about a coprocessor either with a hardware setting or through software. The IBM PC and XT require that you throw a switch (see fig. 4.6), one of many in a bank of DIP switches. The AT and all models of PS/2 learn about coprocessors through the software setup routine. In general, compatible computers follow the scheme used by the IBM model they emulate.

Software setup means running the setup program on the "Setup" or "Reference" disk accompanying your computer or entering the setup routines built into the BIOS of your PC. You need to reinstall all the expansion board that you removed for access to the coprocessor socket before you attempt the software setup. When the boards are back in, slide the power cord back into its socket and then boot up your PC. If your system uses hardware setup, make the appropriate DIP switch adjustment, reseat all the expansion boards you removed, and plug your system back in.

To set up the coprocessor through software, you follow the same setup procedure as you did when your originally bought and configured your computer. Just change the coprocessor option from No to Yes after you have installed your new chip.

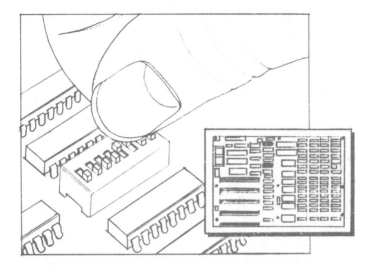

Figure 4.6
Indicating a
coprocessor's
presence by flipping a
DIP switch.

Machines designed to use Weitek memory-mapped coprocessors
make a special provision for it, either a DIP switch setting or a
special entry during software-controlled setup. Simply follow the
instructions in your PC's owners' manual to make the correct
adjustment to reflect installation of a Weitek chip. If you install a
387 on the WTL 1167 board, you must indicate its presence to your
computer, too, just as you would indicate that the 387 was your
principal coprocessor. When you have made the adjustments to your
computer to show that you have installed a coprocessor, you need
not do it again (unless the setup memory of your AT or PS/2 loses
power—in which case you will have to go through the entire setup
process).

Check out your coprocessor before you completely reassemble your
PC. Run a program that you know uses the coprocessor to be sure
that everything is working properly. When you are happy with the
results, switch off your PC, put the top of the case back on, and
screw everything back together. Your PC is now ready to race
through numbers as if it had been born a prodigy.

5
Memory

Of all the upgrades you're likely to make, the most inevitable is adding more memory, which helps your PC do more of what you bought it for. To add the versatility of a multitasking system, the glamour of a graphical user interface, or the utmost in speed, you'll want to stuff your system with every megabyte it can manage. Memory makes software work, and with today's big programs and huge operating systems, you need more than ever.

Step beyond DOS as your operating system, and your memory needs start where the native endowments of most systems leave off. You'll want 4M just to open your first Window, or to start with OS/2 -8M to get up to speed, or 16M to climb into Windows/NT. The latest DOS versions not only sidestep the old memory barriers but also demand more memory than ever to bring their advanced features to life.

More memory also means more speed. Switching between applications with a multitasking operating system is quicker when you can keep the entire program and its data in memory. Maximum cache performance requires multiple megabytes of RAM. Scrimp on RAM, and you'll shortchange your system's performance.

Although you might think that bytes are bytes, with today's computer systems it's not so simple. You can't just pick up your phone and order a dozen megabytes. Memory comes in more flavors than ice cream, and choosing the wrong one gives you something worse than a tummyache—you can get stuck with useless memory modules. You have to worry about bits, banks, and bytes, count pins on SIMMs, deal with page mode and linear addressing, and think in nanoseconds. Moreover, even two identical memory modules can be seen differently by your PC. In fact, some installed memory can act invisible, inaccessible by your programs, making your upgrade as valuable as used lottery tickets.

Memory makes software work, and with today's big programs and huge operating systems, you need more than ever.

You'll want 4M just to open your first Window, or start with OS/2, 8M to get up to speed, or 16M to climb into Windows/NT.

With a little advice and patience, however, anyone can escape this memory morass. Making the right buying decision can be as simple as a two-piece jigsaw puzzle—as long as you know the kind of microprocessor in your computer and the provisions made in your machine for adding RAM, both pieces should fall right into place.

Types of Memory

All the megabytes inside a PC are not the same. There are four types of memory that can be used by your programs: conventional, extended, expanded, and cache. In addition, DOS versions later than 5.0 single out several address ranges of memory for special purposes, adding new names to the memory glossary—names like *upper memory blocks* and *high memory area*. Although made from the same chips and modules as ordinary memory, these areas of memory have new, unconventional purposes, breaking old memory barriers with clever subterfuge.

The four basic kinds of memory differ primarily in how they are accessed by your PC and its software. Although today's operating systems ease your need to know (and care about) some of these differences, some applications require a particular memory type. Moreover, older systems may make some kinds of memory off limits.

Conventional Memory

At one time, the only kind of memory installed in PCs, *conventional memory* refers to the 640K that can be used directly by DOS and ordinary DOS programs. It's called "conventional" because it's the only kind of memory accessible by the computers that came before the "advanced" IBM AT was marketed in 1984. (AT stands for "Advanced Technology.")

Conventional memory goes by several other names. Conventional memory is often called *DOS memory*, or sometimes *real-mode memory* because it is directly addressable in the real operating mode of Intel microprocessors. Strictly speaking, however, conventional memory comprises only the first 640K of the 1024K of real-mode memory; the remainder is called *high DOS memory* or simply *high memory*. Conventional memory is also called *base memory* because every PC has at least a small amount (most now have a full complement) that serves as a foundation of the system. This base memory must be present because Intel microprocessors boot up in real mode and need some memory available in real mode to carry out operations.

Although conventional memory is probably the most useful in your PC, it's also the most limited. The original PC design pegged the maximum at 640K, forcing any machine wishing to remain compatible to do likewise. This limit was partly imposed by the 8088 microprocessor of the original IBM PC. Although the chip could handle one full megabyte of memory (1024K), IBM reserved 384K of the total addressing range for use by system functions such as the Basic Input/Output System (BIOS) and video display.

The reserved 384K earns the name *high memory* because it is the upper end of the 8088's addressing range. In most PCs, the entire allotment of high memory is never used as intended. Only the upper 64K is usually given to your PC's BIOS (and in IBM computers, the built-in cassette BASIC interpreter language); another 64K is relegated to use by display systems; and another 8K or so is devoted to the extra BIOS code needed by hard disks. Networks and other peripherals also may steal some of the high memory addresses for their own BIOS codes. The remaining high memory cannot be used by DOS because video memory is located at the bottom of the high memory range, making the rest of high memory not contiguous with the lower 640K.

Even before memory management was built into DOS 5.0, software designers sidestepped the rules of reserved memory with customized software that could check which addressing ranges were used and which lacked associated ROM or RAM. If no physical memory was assigned to a particular range, that range could be used for extending conventional memory in computers capable of memory remapping. Such computers include those with a 386 or better microprocessor or specific hardware support such as Micro Channel Architecture or an ALL Charge Card. Design features in these systems allow memory addressed in one range to be logically addressed as if it were in another range. In most cases, this remapping is done by special memory management software that also enables you to allocate non-adjacent address ranges in the high memory area to driver software and TSR programs.

Under DOS 5.0 and later, this high memory gains the more specific name *high DOS memory* because the DOS memory manager can use it to run utilities. As with other programs, however, utilities require contiguous memory addresses. Each hole in high DOS memory unused by BIOS and video is suited for running background utilities that will fit. These filled holes are then called *upper memory blocks*.

Special hardware and software enables you to blur the dividing line between conventional memory and high memory. With some work and a willing system configuration, you can add up to an extra 96K to the 640K quota. If all you run is DOS (the technique won't work with Windows), you can squeeze in some extra kilobytes for your applications and utilities. Although still useful in special cases, the usefulness of this manipulation disappears as you shift from DOS to Windows and beyond.

The secret behind expanding the conventional memory boundary is capitalizing on the address allocation of the EGA and VGA frame buffers.

The secret behind expanding the conventional memory boundary is capitalizing on the address allocation of the EGA and VGA frame buffers. Free up those addresses, and you can extend DOS higher. But to do so, you have to send your PC back to the video stone age by pulling out your VGA board. By recovering the address range normally assigned to VGA—the first 64K on top of the DOS 640K—you can shift those addresses to application memory with special memory boards or a system that allows memory remapping with the right software.

The memory range used by a monochrome display adapter (MDA) starts 64K above the 640K conventional memory limit, so if you use MDA instead of VGA, you might be able to recover this address range. Better still, opt for bad video under the color graphics adapter (CGA) standard. The range used by CGA starts another 32K above MDA, so systems with only a CGA adapter can host 96K of memory beyond the DOS 640K—with the proper combination of memory board, microprocessor, and software.

Whatever extra conventional memory you add must be contiguous with all the bytes in the normal range—no gaps permitted.

Note that when using special hardware to gain extra addressing ranges for conventional memory, the conventional 640K range must be completely filled before you allocate more DOS bytes above 640K. Whatever extra conventional memory you add must be contiguous with all the bytes in the normal range—no gaps permitted.

Extended Memory

When new microprocessors were added to PCs to improve performance—the 80286 in 1984, the 80386 in 1987, the 80486 in 1989, and the Pentium in 1992—they brought the side benefit of greatly broadened addressing ranges. The 80286 has an addressing potential of 16M. The 386 (SX and DX), the entire 486 family, and the Pentium all are equipped to handle 4,096M. These larger memory areas, piled on top of real-mode memory, are directly accessible to their respective microprocessors.

Although adding more memory might seem as simple as increasing the number of sockets that accept chips, things aren't so easy for the designer, who must devise a means of accessing the new memory. The design process for each new chip was progressively more difficult because Intel strove to make each new microprocessor backward-compatible with its predecessors. Without careful planning, old chips wouldn't be able to control the new address lines, and instructions for the new lines would confuse older chips. To prevent problems, when Intel's engineers added more address lines to their newer microprocessors, they restricted the use of the new lines to new operating modes, thus eliminating most hardware compatibility problems.

The memory addressed by the new lines required the use of protected mode, thus the name *protected mode memory*. This term never caught on among PC people, because for several years protected mode remained off limits to PCs for lack of software that recognized it. Because the new memory extended the address range of the PC, it instead assumed the name *extended memory*. When the 386 came along and extended memory further, no new name was necessary.

All the memory that you add to a modern PC beyond the first megabyte is extended memory. Because most PCs now come equipped with more than 1M, all memory upgrades to newer systems become extended memory. All 386-specific programs and operating systems use extended memory, so you won't have to worry about memory types or compatibility problems.

However, if you're upgrading an older PC, you'll run into complications. Computers based on the 8088 and 8086 microprocessor are incompatible with extended memory—they can't reach it because they don't have the necessary address lines. They can address only the first megabyte of real-mode memory.

All 386-specific programs and operating systems use extended memory, so you won't have to worry about memory types or compatibility problems.

Expanded Memory

The memory-handling shortcomings of 8088 microprocessors were apparent even before 286-class microprocessors came into wide use. By 1983, just two years after the IBM PC made older computers with 64K effectively obsolete, the PC's own addressing limits hampered the use of more complex programs and large amounts of data. All machines were effectively limited to the 640K addressable by DOS.

To break through the DOS memory barrier, a consortium of companies led by Lotus Development Corporation, Intel Corporation, and Microsoft Corporation developed a new memory access method, *expanded memory specification (EMS)*. Sometimes called simple expanded memory or LIM memory (for the names of its developers), EMS took advantage of bank-switching to enable 8088 microprocessors to address memory otherwise beyond their reach. Although the standard was designed for 8088 microprocessors, it also works for more modern chip designs because of Intel's backward-compatible design. In fact, only with the acceptance of protected mode operating systems and the wide use of extended memory has EMS lost favor.

Bank-switching works by dividing additional system memory into a number of blocks or memory banks not directly linked to the microprocessor. Rather, each bank is connected to a software-controlled hardware switch. Software commands switch individual blocks into the addressing range and control of the microprocessor. The total memory held in the memory banks thus can be accessed through a small range of addresses called a *page frame,* which enables even a primitive microprocessor like an 8088 to access multiple megabytes of memory.

Using the latest incarnation of EMS (version 4.0), up to 32M can be shifted into the conventional addressing range in 16K banks. Although the original EMS design used a 64K page frame located in high memory, EMS 4.0 enables bank-switching to take place within the DOS 640K addressing range. The difference is important because it puts EMS 4.0 within the contiguous addressing range of DOS and enables program code to be bank-switched. This permits specially-written programs larger than 640K to run on 8088 systems. The earlier EMS 3.2 specification only allowed the storage of data in bank-switched memory.

Expanded memory doesn't come free. It requires hardware and software additions to your system. Nearly all 8088, 8086, and 286 machines require a special EMS memory board to take advantage of EMS 4.0 expanded memory. That's because most earlier PCs can't bank-switch by themselves, lacking the hardware to disconnect and reconnect banks of memory. The EMS board adds the necessary control circuitry along with bank-oriented memory.

In addition, you need a software driver to match applications to the EMS facilities in your system. Among other things, the driver tells programs which EMS features are available and how to use them, the location of the page frame (which can vary to allow for systems with different configurations), and the amount of available memory. The page frame used by the EMS board reserves a 64K range of high memory for its exclusive use.

Some 286 computers and all 386 and later machines can simulate bank-switched expanded memory using extended memory and their built-in memory mapping abilities. Recent versions of DOS and most memory management software packages include the driver software necessary to convert extended memory into bank-switched EMS. The DOS expanded memory manager for 386 or newer microprocessors is called EMM386.EXE, and it loads as a device driver through your CONFIG.SYS file.

Most memory management software packages include the driver software necessary to convert extended memory into bank-switched EMS.

Expanded memory emulation programs, sometimes called *LIMulators*, can nearly mimic EMS even on 8088 machines. On 286 computers, this software simulates EMS using extended memory. On 8088 machines, the software uses disk memory to simulate EMS. In either case, the LIMulation software copies code from the page frame to the available disk or extended memory as needed. The copying operation can slow performance severely, but it offers you more RAM for using larger data sets when you really need it.

Note that neither 8088 nor ordinary 286-based computers can exactly duplicate EMS 4.0 with software alone. Some EMS 4.0 functions require specific hardware features, so some programs may not operate with simulated EMS. However, most virtual memory managers come close enough to the standard that you can expect most of your expanded memory applications to accept virtual EMS.

Some EMS 4.0 hardware has limitations traceable to its design, a cooperative effort among manufacturers each looking out for their own best interest. If you think a camel is a horse designed by committee, EMS 4.0 will look like it was crafted by an entire congress. EMS 4.0 was designed to eliminate the shortcomings of previous versions, but some memory boards that conform to the EMS 4.0 standard are incapable of multitasking. This incongruity results from how the EMS 4.0 standard specifies page-mapping registers.

Page-mapping registers indicate which bank of RAM stores the bits used by a program or task. When a certain piece of code or data is required, the register points to its physical location in the memory hardware. Although one set of registers is necessary on an EMS 4.0 board for it to function, multiple sets enable multitasking. When the supervisory software transfers control from one task to another— typically on the order of 18 times per second—it only needs to peek at the second set of registers to see where it can find the needed code in memory.

The weakness of EMS 4.0 is that it allows a conforming product to have one *or* more sets of page-mapping registers. Boards with one set only have enough hardware to track one task. EMS 4.0 skirts this issue by simulating multiple registers. The EMS 4.0 driver included with expanded memory boards supports function calls made by programs using EMS 4.0 memory. These calls comprise a miniature BIOS, matching software to the specific hardware.

One such call shifts between registers. With expanded memory boards that have one set of page-mapping registers, the call executes a complicated pirouette each time a multitasking system shifts between tasks. It must copy the values from its registers to reserved RAM, find the next set of register values elsewhere in RAM, and transcribe them into the registers. This lengthy process can make true concurrency untenable.

EMS boards with a single set of page-mapping registers fit the EMS 4.0 standard because of the committee nature of the specification. The companies that promulgated the EMS 4.0 standard all had existing products, some designed for an intermediate kind of memory called *Enhanced Expanded Memory Specification (EEMS),* requiring two sets of page-mapping registers, and others conforming to EMS 3.2, requiring only one. By not specifying the number of registers to be used and by using driver software, makers of both kinds of boards instantly had products that could be sold under the new EMS 4.0 banner.

If you plan on multitasking, be sure that any EMS 4.0 board you buy supports multiple page-mapping registers.

Therefore, you should be careful when buying an EMS 4.0 board. Most new boards support multiple page-mapping registers, but some older ones, legitimately labeled as following the EMS 4.0 standard, do not. If you plan on multitasking, be sure that any EMS 4.0 board you buy supports multiple page-mapping registers.

Only in a few cases do you have to worry about expanded memory. If you have programs that specifically require expanded memory and cannot use extended memory, you need to emulate EMS on your 386 (or better) PC. On a 286 machine, your best bet is to install an EMS board. If all you have is an 8088 machine to upgrade, your only choice for adding memory beyond the 640K is expanded memory. Of course, this upgrade works only with software written for EMS. In all other situations, you want only extended memory in your PC after you've filled its conventional memory quota.

If all you have is an 8088 machine to upgrade, your only choice for adding memory beyond the 640K is expanded memory.

Cache Memory

Cache memory (also called a *memory cache* to distinguish it from a disk cache) is used by programs and directly accessed by microprocessors, but it differs from ordinary RAM in that your programs don't really know it's there—it's functionally invisible. Cache memory matches a high-speed microprocessor to slower RAM memory chips. Some caches are upgradable, and upgrading your PC's cache can yield a substantial performance boost. But cache memory is better considered part of your PC's microprocessor than its memory system. Upgrading cache memory is discussed in Chapter 3. No matter how many bytes you install in your PC's cache, none of them add to your system's capability to run programs—except to run them faster—and cache bytes are never figured into the number of megabytes of memory.

Some high-performance PCs have a separate hardware disk cache made up of ordinary memory chips or modules. This memory is located on the disk controller or host adapter. As with a memory cache, it has no effect on the storage used by your programs, and its bytes are never counted when totaling system RAM—except when you need to mislead someone about how much memory with which your PC is equipped.

High Memory Area

A design quirk in the design of the 286 microprocessor created a special block of extended memory that Microsoft called the *high memory area.* Although in the extended address range, the high memory area has an odd characteristic—it can be addressed in real mode. The area is located in the first 64K (minus 16 bytes) of extended memory above the 1M addressing limit of the 8088 microprocessor. It's higher than any other real mode memory, hence the name.

With 80286 and more recent microprocessors, software can use this memory as if it were real mode memory. For example, DOS versions after 5.0 use the high memory area (when available) for loading most of its kernel—its essential operating code. This gives you more of the lower 640K for your programs.

The reason this area exists is linked to the way Intel designed its microprocessors. Normal memory addressing in 8088 computers wraps around; if your program tries to address a memory area located above the 1M limit, the microprocessor ignores the part of the address above 1M and starts counting at the beginning of conventional memory again. The 80286 (and later) microprocessors don't wrap around because they can address memory above the conventional memory area. When a program meant for the 8088 attempts to wrap around, it ends up trying to access memory above the conventional limit which, strictly speaking, is extended memory.

Some memory management programs can use this extended memory as if it were conventional memory, giving memory management software an extra 64K in which to relocate drivers and TSR programs. DOS versions before 5.0 and application software (even when running under DOS 5.0) can't use this memory because it is not contiguous with the lower 640K of conventional memory.

Choosing a Memory Type

Nearly all PCs sold today are filled to their conventional memory capacity, and expanded memory can be considered passé. Only if your PC is older do you want to tangle with the confusion of conventional, expanded, and extended memory. Which of these you choose to add depends on your PC and your software.

When you choose, base your decision on the programs you run. If your software works with expanded memory, choose that; if it uses extended, use that. Nothing tough about that decision. Plus, most memory expansion boards enable you to configure them as extended *or* expanded by throwing some switches or running setup software.

To upgrade an 8088-based machine, the decision is even easier—
your only choice is expanded memory.

If you have a 386 or later PC, you don't have to worry about
selecting extended or expanded memory. With the EMM386.EXE
software driver supplied with DOS, you can turn extended memory
into expanded easily. Only with 286 and more primitive PCs is the
difference worth worrying about—and then it's usually a better idea
to upgrade the machine completely rather than waste money on slow
memory in a slow PC.

Application Considerations

If you're stuck with a 286 and have to decide between extended and
expanded memory, the software that you want to run should make
the decision for you. In most cases, opt for expanded memory; the
programs that demand extended memory also want a 386 or better
microprocessor.

In any case, check your software before deciding. You may be
surprised to find that your software cannot take advantage of more
memory (or the kind of memory you can add), making any upgrade
fruitless. Most ordinary DOS applications do *not* recognize EMS or
extended memory. The only programs that can take advantage of
memory beyond the conventional addressing range are those
specifically written to do so. In other words, EMS is valuable only
when you have software that needs it. Do not consider enhancing
your PC with EMS memory if you do not have an application that
needs it.

*Most ordinary
DOS applications
do not recognize
EMS or extended
memory.*

Performance Considerations

In some systems, software-based EMS can be two to four times faster
than a dedicated EMS board. In others, the board beats the software.
The determining factor is the relationship between the speed at
which your PC's microprocessor operates and the speed of its
expansion bus.

If your computer is based on a 386DX or 486 microprocessor,
always add extended memory directly to the system board or use
proprietary memory expansion boards. Plugging any memory board,
extended or expanded, into a slot in one of these machines degrades
its performance because the expansion buses of these computers are

slower than their microprocessors and proprietary memory expansion slots. If you need expanded memory in such a computer, add extended memory and use a LIMulator to convert the extended RAM.

The 286 and 386SX microprocessors create more complex matters. System board and expansion board memory are equally quick in models in which the expansion bus operates at the same clock speed as the microprocessor. Examples of such machines include genuine IBM ATs, non-Micro Channel PS/2s, PS/1s, and compatibles operating at microprocessor speeds of 10 MHz or less. In these machines, true EMS boards generally work faster than a software-based LIMulator.

In similar machines with quicker clocks, however, memory added directly to the system board or through proprietary boards is faster than expansion slot memory. Should you have one of these computers, as well as software that works with extended or expanded memory, add extended memory to your PC. Ordinary extended memory will be faster than expanded memory emulated with software, and you'll have one less driver stealing memory from your system. If, however, your favorite programs demand expanded memory, use a LIMulator. The emulated expanded memory it creates outperforms memory handicapped by expansion bus speed.

Upgrading an ancient PC based on an 8088 or 8086 microprocessor, you can add only expanded memory, and it must be in the form of an EMS board installed in an expansion slot. Nothing else works—or fits. The overall performance of your PC won't change for better or worse.

Hardware Considerations

Of course, any memory upgrade you add to your PC must pass one further test—it must be physically compatible with your computer.

Matching a memory board is more than a matter of finding one that slides into a slot. After all, even a 10-year-old 8-bit memory card fits nearly every available PC (except, of course, Micro Channel machines), but it hardly would be a good match for a fast EISA-based super-server. It probably would not work.

The first hardware issue is where to put additional memory. You have three basic choices: on the system board, on proprietary memory expansion boards, and on conventional expansion cards in system expansion slots (slotted memory). The choices are arranged in order of desirability (most to least).

System board memory is generally the fastest in any PC. It's connected more directly to the microprocessor, suffering only a slight detour through the control logic that organizes its addresses and keeps its contents fresh. In most PCs, system board memory matches the width of the microprocessor input/output channel, so it is almost always the best match for microprocessor speed.

Most PCs prefer system board memory. Most of today's fastest PCs enable you to install *only* system board memory; the rest typically require that you fill the system board memory sockets to capacity before accepting other types, ensuring you the best performance. Generally, if the manufacturer of your PC provides empty sockets on your system board for memory expansion, fill them before exploring other options.

Proprietary memory expansion uses special boards to add more RAM. The boards are unique to each manufacturer, sometimes even to each PC, because they use the same memory architecture as system board memory, matching the microprocessor in bus width, connection method, and as closely as possible in speed. Because there's no standard for memory architecture, computer makers are forced to go in their own directions.

These boards are fast, matching system board memory in performance. The proprietary nature of these boards, however, makes them obtainable only from the manufacturer (or vendor) of your PC. The exceptions are the products of the largest computer makers, such as Compaq and IBM. Their machines have achieved sufficient distribution that some companies have found it profitable to make and sell accessories for them.

The rule is simple in buying a proprietary memory board—get what fits from whoever sold you your PC. If boards are offered with different capacities, opt for the highest. Eventually you may want as much memory as you can squeeze into your PC. You might have to toss out a low-capacity board to increase your PC's memory in the future.

The rule is simple in buying a proprietary memory board— get what fits from whoever sold you your PC.

Generally, proprietary memory boards use standard memory chips and modules. When the boards are available with and without their full memory quotas, be sure to evaluate the price charged for the chips installed on the board. If the premium for buying memory is negligible (some vendors charge little or no markup as a sign of goodwill), buy the boards stuffed with memory. However, some computer makers see memory boards as a profit center—even an exploitation center—and levy heavy premiums on preinstalled chips.

In this case, buy the board with no chips installed—a so-called 0K RAM board—and install your own.

Slotted memory fits your PC's standard expansion slots, the same slots that accommodate everything from hard disk adapters to game ports. Today, slotted memory boards are nearly commodity products, fitting a wide variety of PCs without regard to concerns such as memory architecture.

In the original IBM design of the PC and XT, slotted memory was the prime—and only—expansion choice. The expansion buses of these machines were designed to match the performance of the system microprocessor. Adding memory to the expansion slot thus was no performance hardship. However, as microprocessor clock speeds increased, bus speeds stayed nearly constant to accommodate old expansion boards, and slotted memory became penalty memory. Every access to the bus meant a waiting period for the system microprocessor. The faster the microprocessor, the worse the idea of putting memory in expansion slots.

The slot penalty is minimal for PCs, XTs, and other machines of their class. In fact, putting memory in an expansion slot is the only option for many machines. For AT-class computers that operate at 8 MHz or less and many 10 MHz machines (including IBM's low-end PS/2), slotted memory is equally effective. At microprocessor speeds in excess of 10 MHz, however, the slots run more slowly than the microprocessor, and the wait states begin to add up. The higher the microprocessor clock speed, the longer the wait for slotted memory.

No manufacturer currently offers a memory board that follows either the VL Bus or PCI local bus standards.

Today's local bus computers run their expansion slots at the same speed (or nearly so) as their microprocessors, but that doesn't make local bus a good choice for memory expansion. Most local bus systems add extra wait states to accesses across the bus, and these additional wait states slow down the memory in your system's local bus slots, often substantially. There's another reason to avoid memory in a local bus slot: no manufacturer currently offers a memory board that follows either the VL Bus or PCI local bus standards.

Sometimes you can't avoid adding to your PC's memory through ordinary expansion slots, particularly if you have an older PC with inadequate motherboard memory provisions. For example, when expanding an XT or adding real EMS to a fast AT, you'll need to use a memory expansion board. In such situations, you'll have to follow a few rules to be sure that your memory board will be compatible with your PC.

First, make sure that the bus of the memory board matches the widest expansion bus available in your system. This match is important for two reasons. The widest possible bus ensures that memory transfers are made as quickly as the expansion bus permits. With a wide-bus board, although you may have to endure some wait states, wait states are minimized. In addition, a wider bus gives the expansion board a wider potential address range. Boards designed for the 8-bit XT bus cannot be addressed outside the 1M range of conventional memory because only 20 address lines are available on the narrow bus. Similarly, 16-bit memory boards designed for AT-style computers cannot range beyond the 16M addressing limit of the 24 address lines of the AT bus. Boards that use the 32-bit EISA bus have the full 4-gigabyte 386 address range available to them, as do modern 32-bit Micro Channel boards. Some early 32-bit Micro Channel memory boards were, however, limited in their addressability to the 16M AT range.

Even though a board uses a wide bus, you have no guarantee that it takes advantage of the full range and flexibility of the bus's addressability limits. A memory board needs to be versatile enough to locate its memory anywhere in the available address range so that it can extend the contiguous memory of your PC. Most memory boards provide some method of indicating the starting address for the memory they hold, either through DIP switch settings or non-volatile latches set with a software configuration routine. Boards with adjustable capacity typically enable you to set the starting and ending addresses of the board. Be sure whatever slotted memory board you buy can locate its memory in the range you require.

Early PC, XT, and AT expansion boards usually included additional functions beyond mere memory so that you could add ports and possibly a clock (for PCs and XTs) to a single expansion slot. As long as these extra features can be switched off or relocated to avoid conflict with the ports already installed in your PC, there is no reason not to take advantage of such multifunction boards. In fact, they can be a good value, but don't pay extra for ports you don't need.

The trend today is for boards to offer memory alone—lots of it. As with proprietary boards, the ultimate chip capacity is your primary concern. Be sure to get a board that allows for as much memory as you need today and for the foreseeable future. Check the price of installed memory and make sure that you can't do better by buying and installing the RAM chips yourself.

Avoid boards that only emulate extended memory unless you're sure that you'll only need expanded memory.

Slotted memory boards vary in how they enable you to choose whether their bytes are configured as extended or expanded RAM. The best boards are those that handle this selection through board hardware by assigning memory banks to one or another function. Other boards may offer a viable alternative in RAM that's configured only as extended memory but include an expanded memory emulator as standard equipment. A few boards come with their entire capacity designated as expanded memory and use an extended memory emulator. Simulating extended memory with expanded causes performance to suffer dramatically, so avoid boards that only emulate extended memory unless you're sure that you'll need expanded memory.

Laptop and Notebook Memory Considerations

Adding memory to a laptop computer raises entirely different issues than does an upgrade for a desktop PC—issues that you might not want to deal with. Most notebook computers are a lot like toothpaste tubes—both are built into packages that can be infuriating to fill. After you know the secrets, however, neither job is truly tough.

Memory upgrades can be as easy as changing the battery in your TV remote control.

Rather than using a small funnel and a vast amount of patience to squeeze Gleem through the nozzle end of the tube, you stuff the empty tube full through the big end, sealing with a crimp when you're finished. With a notebook computer, you don't have to disassemble the PC into a pile of parts resembling the debris from a battle between aliens. Memory upgrades can be as easy as changing the battery in your TV remote control, never much more difficult than adding an expansion board to a desktop computer. All you need are a few hints at access, and the right memory to make the upgrade.

Given an adequate dose of RAM, your notebook PC will be as adept at shifting between tasks as the biggest desktop behemoth.

Odds are that if your laptop or notebook computer is more than a year or two old, when you bought it 1M of RAM appeared to be a generous endowment. The memory demands of applications and your expectations have risen in lockstep, and that big megabyte is no longer enough. Today you can (and want to) load the same memory management programs onto your laptop or notebook PC that you run on your desk. Windows and other multitasking systems are now standard equipment. After all, when you're on the road, you face more distractions and more reasons for quickly shifting between modes and applications than you do when in your office. Given an adequate dose of RAM, your notebook PC will be as adept at shifting between tasks as the biggest desktop behemoth.

Upgrading laptop and notebook memory is not the same as with desktop RAM, however. System capacities are lower, most expansion designs are proprietary, chips and modules cost more, and the means of making the upgrade seem as obvious as the solution to a four-dimensional Rubik's Cube. Making the upgrade means approaching each of these issues head-on.

Portable computers face more architectural memory expansion limits than desktop machines. Although the memory capacities of many desktop systems now start at 32M, it's rare for portable machines to aspire that high. The limits are dictated by size and power considerations. More memory might not fit inside a smaller machine. Moreover, manufacturers know that adding too much RAM can drain battery power fast.

As with desktop PCs, the microprocessor in a laptop or notebook PC also affects memory handling. Some recent notebook computer introductions still use 8088 or 80286 microprocessors (or their equivalents), chips essentially obsolete in desktop machines. As a result, these notebook PCs suffer the same memory-handling limits of discredited microprocessors. Adding RAM may not bring the benefits you intend.

On the other hand, you probably can put more laptop memory to work, even in an 8088-based laptop. Many of the aging notebook computers based on this microprocessor or its derivatives (for example, the original NEC UltraLite and the Toshiba T1000 series) enable you to use more memory—typically an additional 2M—as a solid-state substitute for the hard disks they may lack. Although this extra RAM won't enable you to run bigger programs, it adds speed by cutting disk delays and enabling you to keep important programs and data resident in the machine. However, be sure to back up anything you store in a RAM disk on a laptop—although the machine's memory may be preserved when you switch it off, the rigors of travel can result in temporary power losses that make data on electronic disks vanish.

If you use the memory of your laptop or notebook computer as a RAM disk, you can expand it without investing in more chips or modules. By running disk compression software like that discussed in Chapter 2, you can make your machine think it has twice the RAM in its disk emulator it actually does, just as you can double the storage space on a hard disk.

How Much To Add

In an ideal world, you would have an unlimited budget and unlimited memory in your PC. Unfortunately, the real world quickly eats into your budget with the cost of your mortgage, groceries, college loan, and beer nuts. You have to be practical about the memory you add to your system, unless you plan to work on your PC starving out in the cold, uneducated, with the bitter essence of hops lingering on your tongue.

Money is only one of the constraints on how far you can expand your PC's memory. The kind of microprocessor in your PC, the architecture of your system, its BIOS, even the peripherals you add all influence how much of the memory in your PC is useful to your applications. The limits can be surprisingly modest. Even the grandest 486 system can bump into a memory expansion roadblock before you've installed enough RAM to make Windows/NT take off.

Because the memory that's best for one system board may not work in another, plan how far you eventually want to go with your PC before adding more memory. After all, if your plans are to some-day—when your budget allows—move to 32M, you won't want a system limited to 16M. Stock up today with the full 16M and you might be able to transfer your memory investment to the system into which you someday plan to move. You're better off making the move now—to a new microprocessor or system board—before making your first upgrade.

Before you outline your memory growth plans, you need to understand the various restrictions on RAM. Their origins can be diverse.

Whatever memory you add to your PC must be usable and used. That can be a problem because not all programs take advantage of every byte that you add to your PC. Moreover, computers cannot handle unlimited amounts of memory. Practical design factors limit capacities, sometimes severely.

Both limits arise from a common cause—addressability. For memory to be used by programs, it must be addressed. Logical and mechanical design factors limit how much memory a given PC can address.

Five factors limit the addressability of the memory in a PC—your programs, your operating system, your microprocessor, your system's architecture, and the aperture mapping used by your system's BIOS and peripherals. The maximum amount of memory that you can put to work is set by the smallest of these constraints.

Program Limits

The strictest limit on memory usage is inherent in your software. In particular, applications written for ordinary DOS are severely constricted in the amount of memory they can use: 640K.

On the surface, you would assume that a simple rewrite of DOS would eliminate the 640K barrier and give even your oldest programs full access to more megabytes. If pushing beyond the 640K limit were so easy, someone would have done it long ago.

The underlying problem is that nearly every program ever written includes some internal reference to memory. For example, every DOS program assumes the DOS environment that operates in your microprocessor's real mode, so every reference to memory includes space for only 20-bit addresses. DOS-based programs just don't know how to reach beyond the basic 1M. The only way that multitasking systems can move these applications into extended memory is to break the vast range of available RAM into blocks no larger than 1M that DOS programs can manage.

In some cases, you can add operating environments that let programs written only to work with DOS memory take advantage of other memory types. They make your programs see and use the other kind of memory as ordinary DOS RAM. However, when run under such an operating environment, the power of your programs is not enhanced even though the power of your PC may be. The program can use no more memory than it could without the operating environment.

In recent years, some programs have been written with an eye beyond DOS, but these programs also are limited in the kinds of memory that they understand. The memory must be the kind that they are specifically written to use.

Operating System Limits

The amount of memory you can use effectively is also constrained by your operating system, especially if you use DOS. After all, an operating system is nothing more than a set of computer programs that do some of the housekeeping involved in running your computer.

DOS is a particular culprit because the original versions were written when real mode was all there was. Inherent in its design was a limitation based on PC architecture, that your PC can address no more than 1M of memory, of which 640K at most is available to it. When new PCs with gigabytes of memory potential finally began to dominate the market, the designers of DOS were saddled with a dilemma: not taking advantage of more memory would shortchange most PCs, yet radically changing DOS would make it incompatible with most programs.

One attempt to solve this problem was OS/2. When originally introduced in 1987, OS/2 tried to give the world a protected-mode operating system with a degree of backward compatibility. It put the full range of protected-mode RAM at your disposal, yet included a "compatibility box" for running DOS applications. The compatibility box, unfortunately, earned the nickname "penalty box" for its performance penalty. Worse, the world linked OS/2 with IBM's PS/2 line and thought the latter was necessary for the former. Developers saw tens of millions of copies of DOS on desktops and hundreds of thousands of copies of OS/2 and opted for the larger market.

With that inspiration behind them, the designers of DOS opted for a less radical course for the world's favorite operating system. Instead of dramatic changes, they tinkered and gradually added memory-enhancing features. Since Version 5.0, DOS has acknowledged that's there's more than 1M in most PCs, but it still gives you few tools for helping your programs take advantage of more RAM. The kernel of DOS itself can nestle itself in a special 64K block of protected memory, and some DOS utilities can use protected memory. Ordinary DOS applications, however, remain locked to the real mode megabyte. Although DOS from Version 5.0 knows new memory-handling tricks, your DOS applications are all old dogs. They refuse to learn anything new—and they may bite you if you try to outsmart them.

Programs with DOS extenders that address more than 1M of RAM can run under DOS because they forego most of what DOS offers. The applications use DOS only to load themselves into memory. After a special *loader* routine has been moved into memory and starts executing, it takes over from DOS and finishes moving the rest of the program. Because DOS is no longer involved, code can be moved into areas not normally addressable by DOS. After all the code is loaded, the program runs by itself, ignoring DOS and its memory constraints. Programs without DOS extenders typically rely on DOS for support in reading and writing files and the like. Programs with DOS extenders handle these operations themselves, acting as their own operating systems while in control of your PC.

Microprocessor Limits

Every Intel microprocessor has explicit memory-handling limits dictated by its design. The limit is defined by the number of address lines assigned to that microprocessor and its internal design features. Ordinarily, a microprocessor can address directly no more memory than its address lines permit.

A microprocessor needs some way of identifying each memory location it can access. The address lines permit this by assigning a memory location to each pattern that can be coded by the chip's address lines. The number of available patterns then determines how much memory can be addressed. These patterns are, of course, a digital code.

The on/off patterns of the 20 address lines of the 8088 and 8086 microprocessors can define 2^{20} addresses, the 1M addressing limit of DOS, a total of 1,048,576 bytes. Because 286 microprocessors have 24 addressing lines, they can directly access up to 2^{24} bytes of RAM, 16M or 16,777,216 bytes. No PC with a 286 microprocessor can address more than 16M of RAM directly. With a full 32 address lines, 386, 486, and Pentium microprocessors can directly access 4 gigabytes of memory—that's 4,294,967,296 bytes. You're unlikely to need more than that amount of addressability soon, considering most programs are still written with DOS constraints in mind. If you could find RAM at $25 per megabyte, reaching the limit of the Pentium would cost you $102,400 for memory alone. Inserting it would make an interesting upgrade—you would be plugging in SIMMs for the better part of a day, if you could find a PC with enough sockets.

Architectural Limits

Not all computers can use all the memory that their microprocessors can address. For example, many 386-based PCs that use the class AT bus for expansion generally permit the direct addressing of only 16M. The reason for this memory-addressing shortfall is that the AT bus was designed with only 24 addressing lines rather than the full 32 of the microprocessor. Newer classic-bus computers break through this limit by forcing you to keep all memory in proprietary expansion. Once no longer constrained by the bus, memory capacity could be expanded to the limits of the PC's microprocessor. Hardly any ISA machines give you that option. A nagging few still maintain the 16M bus limit on motherboard memory because designing and building PCs with such limits is easier and cheaper. Most others restrict you to 32M or so because of constraints built into their support chips.

The advanced PC expansion buses, EISA and Micro Channel, extend their address buses to a full 32 bits. (Although you are well advised not to use these buses for memory expansion—more on that later.) Other aspects of computer design still may limit internal addressing to levels below those allowed by the system's microprocessor. For example, most of the initial 386-based EISA computers allowed up to 32M of RAM to be installed—more than AT-bus machines but well within the 4-gigabyte constraints imposed by their microprocessors. Many machines now available have pushed the limit to 64M. A few have no inherent limit except for the number of memory sockets they provide.

Some special architectures enable micropro- cessors to address more memory than the amount for which they were designed.

Some special architectures enable microprocessors to address more memory than the amount for which they were designed. The most popular of the techniques is the bank-switching method used by EMS. Note, however, that the expanded memory standard restricts bank-switched memory to far less capacity than today's top micro- processors can address directly. Consequently, bank-switching as a RAM upgrade method has fallen into disfavor.

Aperture-Created Limits

Nearly all applications and operating systems assume that your system's memory range is contiguous. One reason is that most programs contain instructions called relative jumps—the instruction tells the program to leap from one point in memory to another. The distance to jump is defined as the number of bytes separating the old point of execution from the new rather than as exact memory addresses. This system works wonderfully because it doesn't matter where in the address range of a program the instruction occurs. Programs can load at different points in RAM without a problem. If there is a hole in memory—if the RAM addresses are not contigu- ous—there's always a chance that a relative jump will drop program execution in the middle of nowhere, where there is no waiting instruction. Not knowing what to do, the program stops or does something unexpected—usually crashing your system.

Ordinarily, your PC satisfies this need for contiguity, but problems arise in a couple of cases: ROM shadowing and memory apertures.

ROM shadowing is a popular PC speed-up technique. Most PCs put their BIOS code into ROM (actually EPROM—Erasable Programmable Read-Only Memory) chips. In most PCs, this ROM memory is handicapped in two ways: the ROM inherently responds slower than RAM, and ROM is typically arranged in 16-bit data words which take twice as long to wield as the 32-bit double words of most RAM. Compounding the slowdown, the system BIOS in the slow ROM is some of the most often-used code in the PC.

To speed up the BIOS code, ROM shadowing takes advantage of the memory mapping abilities of 386 and new microprocessors. The ROM shadowing system copies all the BIOS code to fast 32-bit memory drawn from the extended addressing area and then remaps the copied BIOS code to the original BIOS addresses. When the PC runs a piece of BIOS code, it grabs it from the copy in fast RAM instead of the original in slow ROM.

Of course, the extended memory used for ROM shadowing has to come from somewhere. Most machines steal 256K or so of extended memory from the very top of the available addresses. But many assume that the top will occur at the 16M border. If you stuff such a PC with more than 16M of RAM, shadowing still steals what it needs from just under the 16M limit, leaving a hole in the machine's address range. Operating systems and programs can go no farther no matter how much more memory is installed in the system.

Sidestep this limit by switching off shadowing using your PC's advanced setup procedure. Memory likely benefits your system more than shadowing.

Memory apertures are address ranges used by PC peripherals for memory-mapped input/output operation and control. Your PC sends data and control signals to a memory-mapped device by writing to a given range of memory addresses. The device picks up the data there and does its thing, whatever that may be. A Weitek math coprocessor is one example of a memory-mapped device. Another example—one that's more likely to pop into your PC soon—is a direct memory aperture video board.

Until IBM introduced its XGA system in 1991, most display adapters followed the VGA standard for memory use. Their frame buffers were bank-switched from a 64K frame within the real-mode address range. But bank-switching complicates the programming of graphic software and slows down video speed. IBM's XGA added a direct memory aperture which reserved a range in extended memory for directly addressing the XGA frame buffer. Although other manufacturers have been slow to adopt the XGA standard, they have taken advantage of the direct memory aperture concept. Many graphics adapters now use direct memory apertures to address their frame buffers in their higher resolution modes.

Because display adapters include their own video memory, these memory apertures don't steal any of the RAM you install in your PC. Moreover, because the frame buffer memory is not used by your programs for execution, it need not be contiguous with the rest of RAM. In theory, there should be no problem.

If you have an ISA system and a display adapter that uses a memory aperture or are planning to buy one, do not plan to expand beyond that.

With advanced expansion buses that can address a full 4 gigabytes, there almost never is a problem with a memory aperture. So many addresses are available, there's no chance of conflict. With old ISA, however, the memory aperture can restrict your RAM expansion severely. Because you are forced to install display adapters in an expansion slot and because ISA is limited to 16M, the memory aperture used by a display adapter in an ISA system must appear somewhere below the 16M border. Wham! The aperture blasts a huge hole in your RAM address range somewhere below the 16M border. Memory above 16M cannot be reached by most operating systems, the aperture itself steals a megabyte or two, and you're left with a PC that can give your programs no more than about 14M no matter how much RAM you install. Worse, because most PCs have 8 SIMM sockets, the only way of getting more than 8M is by using SIMMs that hold 4M each, yielding 32M. You can't use 4M SIMMs when you have a display adapter that uses a memory aperture in an ISA system because the aperture overlaps system RAM and conflicts. You'll be restricted to 8M. The bottom line is that if you have an ISA system and a display adapter that uses a memory aperture or are planning to buy one, do not plan to expand beyond that.

This aperture limit ordinarily does not occur with Micro Channel, EISA, VL Bus, or PCI because all four buses permit 32-bit addressing and do not force the aperture below the 16M border.

Special Portable PC Considerations

Nearly all laptop and notebook PCs leave you stuck with the memory limit ordained by the manufacturer.

Although desktop systems that lack a full 16M capacity on the system board enable you to stuff that much RAM in expansion slots, most laptop and notebook PCs lack true AT-style expansion slots, substituting proprietary connectors for modems and memory. Consequently, nearly all laptop and notebook PCs leave you stuck with the memory limit ordained by the manufacturer.

Although the design of a notebook computer sets the maximum amount of memory you can install, the amount that you *should* plug in is another issue entirely. Because notebook memory often is so much more dear than desktop memory, think twice before going for the limit. All you may be doing is subsidizing the computer maker, who probably makes a bigger cut on expansion accessories (like boards and modems) than on the system itself.

If your system only allows the additional memory to be used as a RAM disk, you'll want as much as your program and data files require (after factoring the capacity you can gain from disk compression). Because most systems have minimal memory capabilities —typically 3M max—you'll probably want to go all the way.

More powerful machines require more thought. You may be willing to forego the memory-hogging luxuries you have on your desktop computer, such as a huge software disk cache. You even may want to forego Windows (or other graphic environments) because of the inconvenience of using a pointing device while crammed into a coach-class seat. Start stripping out the software luxuries and you could get away with as little as 1M—you may not need to upgrade.

Ability and desirability are not the same. Odds are that you, like nearly everyone else, expect to get the same level of performance from your notebook computer as you get from your desktop PC, and you probably want to run the same applications the same way on each. After all, your notebook PC could be your only computer. For full functionality, expect to install as much RAM in your portable as in your stationary PC.

Selecting Memory Chips and Modules

After you know where you want to add expansion memory, you need to consider how to fit the memory in. If you've opted for a proprietary or slotted memory board that's already stuffed, your decision is already made. If you've opted for a bare board with 0K of RAM, or you are adding chips directly to your system board, the tough work begins—finding the right modules and chips. Four factors separate the available types of memory chips: packaging, capacity, technology, and speed. You've got to make the right match for each of the four; otherwise your chip investment will be wasted.

Packaging

How a memory chip physically installs and how it interconnects with your system's electrical circuitry is determined by its packaging. Most PCs today use memory packaged on small plug-in circuit boards called *memory modules*. Old PCs of the last generation (and before) used memory in the form of *loose chips*, the component parts of memory modules.

Loose chips are integrated circuits, small wafers of silicon that remember the data you want to store. Each loose chip has a separate package, usually a shell of black epoxy plastic with a number of silver-colored leg-like leads extending away from it. Several chips—usually three or nine—linked together make a memory module.

The shift from chips to modules has a very practical basis. Today's multi-megabyte PCs would require a prodigious number of chips for realistic memory capacities. Installing the necessary number of chips would be like playing poker with them—a big gamble. Potential memory installation problems increase each time you push a chip into a socket—you have a greater chance of bending or breaking the lead of a chip. Moreover, the effort can get time-consuming, when you have more chips to install than patience, and the space required for chips can become outrageous. Putting a few megabytes of loose chips on a system board can take a quarter or more of the available board surface.

Modules offer greater capacities and easy installation. Otherwise, a module is no different from a bunch of chips. In fact, a memory module is a small circuit board that typically holds three, eight, or nine chips as a single, easy-to-plug-in assembly.

To make contact with their sockets, most memory modules use either edge connectors similar to those on expansion boards or projecting pins like the leads of integrated circuits. By convention, a module of the former type is called a *single in-line memory module (SIMM)* and the latter a *single in-line pin package (SIPP)*. While arguments can be made as to which is better (SIPPs can be soldered directly to circuit boards, SIMMs work better in sockets) the only important issue is that you get the correct package to match your computer. Most PCs use SIMMs.

Although SIMMs are standardized to some extent, two types are popular in PCs—9-bit and 36-bit. A rare few PCs use 8-bit SIMMs. Most Apple Macintosh computers use 8-bit SIMMs.

The number of bits refers to the bus width of the SIMM. Nine-bit SIMMs have a data path 9 bits wide, corresponding to a single byte and a parity-check bit. In contrast, 36-bit SIMMs have a data path that's 36 bits wide. The difference is significant: four 9-bit SIMMs are required to make one modern 32-bit memory bank. One 32-bit SIMM constitutes a complete 32-bit bank.

When you are expanding the memory of your 386 or better PC, you'll need to add 9-bit SIMMs four at a time, but you can add 36-bit SIMMs one at a time. Generally, you can expand a machine that uses 36-bit SIMMs in smaller increments. Moreover, 36-bit SIMMs also can be addressed more narrowly, so they also are compatible with 16-bit and 8-bit systems.

Most PCs use 9-bit SIMMs, and where there's popularity there is often favorable pricing. Most vendors sell 9-bit SIMMs at the lowest cost-per-megabyte of any memory product they offer.

If you have an older PC that uses loose chips for memory expansion, you have many of the same concerns as with memory modules—for example, packaging and pins—except that they are multiplied because you need so many more chips to make up a memory bank.

As with memory modules, the arrangement of connecting leads on a chip gives each type its name. The most common chips have two parallel rows of leads with the wide flat surface of the chip parallel to the circuit board they plug into. These are called *dual in-line packages (DIP)*. Some chips have a single row of pins or leads, earning them the name *single in-line package (SIP)*, and install perpendicular to their host circuit board. A third variant has two rows of leads, like a DIP, but put them on an edge like a SIP, and arranges the leads so that the two rows are offset. This pattern of pins gives its name to the package, the *zig-zag in-line package (ZIP)*. Figure 5.1 illustrates the various types of memory.

Although the chips with the same package style may look similar, there can be some big differences between them. For example, the number of leads (pins or legs) that sprout out of the chip can vary. DIP circuits, for example, have anywhere from 6 to 80 leads, memory chips typically from 14 to 20.

Figure 5.1

Figure 5.1
Memory comes in a
variety of packages.
Clockwise from
upper left: a DIP
chip, a ZIP chip
(between fingers),
another DIP, a SIP, a
SIMM, and a SIPP.

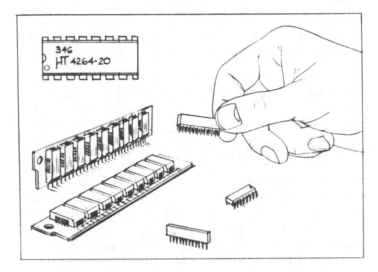

The most important consideration with chip packaging is that the chips you buy fit the sockets in your computer. A chip with too many leads just won't work in a smaller socket. Some systems, however, give you options, enabling you to put smaller 16-pin chips in 20-pin sockets. In such situations, it's important to be sure you install the chips in the correct end of the socket.

Before you order chips, check what package you need and how many leads there are per chip. The manual accompanying your PC or system board should describe the type of memory used. If not, you'll have to look inside your PC.

Chips are traditionally rated by the number of bits of data they can store. For example, a 256-kilobit memory chip stores about 256,000 bits of data or about 32,000 bytes. In most computers, each byte of memory is stored on several memory chips connected in parallel. The byte is divided into its constituent 8 bits, and each bit is stored at the same address in a separate memory chip. Consequently, the smallest practical increment of memory expansion involves 8 chips, often called an 8-bit bank of memory.

*Chips are gener-
ally added to PCs
in one or more
groups of nine.*

Most personal computers add a ninth chip to each bank for parity checking. The ninth chip verifies that the data coded by the other eight is correct and has not changed since it was originally stored. Hence, chips are generally added to PCs in one or more groups of nine.

Today's high-powered 8086, 286, 386, and 486 microprocessors require an even larger increment of memory expansion. The 8086, 286, and 386SX normally move data to and from memory 16 bits at a time. (They are said to have a *16-bit data path*.) Consequently, the minimal expansion for these systems is two 8-bit banks at a time (a total of 18 chips—don't forget the parity chips). The 386DX, 486SX, and 486DX microprocessors use a 32-bit data path and require memory to be added in 36-chip banks. If you're buying loose chips for your 386 PC, you must get 36 at a time. You'll learn firsthand why memory modules are so popular.

If you're buying loose chips for your 386 PC, you must get 36 at a time.

Capacity

The amount of information a chip or memory module can store is its capacity. The capacity you need is easy to determine: just get chips that store the number of bits (or bytes, in the case of memory modules) that your system uses. With memory modules, you select the number of bytes—usually megabytes—per module.

Among loose chips, your basic choices are 64K, 256K, 1M, 4M, and soon 16M per chip. Your computer or memory board manual should tell you what size chips to use.

Note that today's larger chips come in two different styles. In the most familiar arrangement, the entire capacity of the chip is addressed as a single bit-wide unit. Other chips internally divide the capacity of the chip into four independent banks. The former, single-bank chips can be more specifically described as 1×256 kilobit, 1×1 megabit, and 1×4 megabit chips, and the four-bank chips are 4×64 kilobit, 4×256 kilobit, and 4×1 megabit. The four-bank chips are useful in some system designs.

Some systems, particularly those manufactured by IBM, use oddball chip sizes. For example, in some PS/2s there are 768K chips in hermetically-sealed metal cases. These were designed to be 1M chips but didn't pass the necessary quality assurance tests—in each chip one 256K bank proved bad. There's nothing wrong with the three remaining internal banks, so don't think you're getting a second-rate chip. Although these chips are not available on the open market, they are used for standard system memory only—never for expansion memory.

Early ATs used another oddball memory size, 128K modules. These were double-decked 64K chips, soldered together to put 128K in a single DIP socket. In that ATs were sold without their full 640K system board quota, you may encounter a need for these two-story integrated circuits should you want to expand your AT's memory. Unfortunately, they are difficult to find, especially at a good price. But many AT memory boards enable you to backfill your system's conventional memory area from the RAM chips on the board. Look for such a memory board if your AT uses 128K modules and you want to upgrade it.

All chips in a single bank must be the same size.

In many clone computers and older PCs, you'll find a jumper or switch that enables you to select between two or more chip types. Note that chips of different capacities don't mix well—all chips in a single bank must be the same size. There is an exception, though. Some systems build a bank of memory from two 4×256K chips (for eight bits of data) and one 1x256K chip (one bit for parity). This arrangement, though, is most often used for soldered-down standard-equipment memory.

Memory modules, too, are available in various sizes. Currently popular sizes include 256K, 1M, 2M, 4M, and 8M, with 16M modules coming. Memory modules—SIMMs or SIPPs—store bytes rather than bits of data, and are rated in their byte capacity. Only one SIMM is needed for an 8-bit memory bank.

Advanced microprocessors may require 16 or 32-bit banks to optimize their data connections. Rather than using wider memory modules, most of these computers use multiple 9-bit SIMMs to make wider banks. A 16-bit wide memory bus uses two modules; a 32-bit bus uses four. As with loose chips, all memory modules within a given bank must be the same capacity. Many computers enable you to mix capacities of memory modules on a single memory board or on the system board, but even in these PCs each bank is made from modules with the same capacity rating while the different banks may vary in the module capacity they use.

When upgrading the memory of any PC, the cardinal rule is to make sure that you match the capacity of chips to the needs of your system. Check the manual accompanying your PC or its system board to determine the type of chips or memory modules that it uses as well as whatever steps may be required to match different capacities of chips and modules.

Technology

The manner in which a chip functions electrically is called its technology. Most memory chips are *dynamic random access memory* or *DRAM* chips. They are "dynamic" because they store data as electrical charges that slowly bleed off and must be periodically replenished or refreshed to maintain the accuracy of their contents.

With ordinary DRAM chip designs, each chip requires a recovery period between successive read or write operations, possibly imposing a delay between repeated accesses. The time required for this recovery is called the *access time* of the chip, and it is the principal limit on memory speed.

Alternative memory chip designs have been created to minimize this delay. *Page-mode memory* chips allow repeated accesses within a single block of memory on the chip—the block being called a page—to be made without imposing a recovery period. A similar chip called a *static-column RAM* chip allows repeated access within a column (another memory block arrangement) to be made without the recovery delays. Either kind of special DRAM chip can speed up the operation of the host computer by minimizing microprocessor wait states. Memory modules are similarly classed.

From an upgrade standpoint, the most important consideration with these special chip and module designs is that they are not interchangeable with ordinary ones. If your computer calls for one of these technologies, be sure you get matching memory. With memory modules, addressing mode is particularly confusing because page-mode and linear-addressed SIMMs look identical. (They are wired much the same electrically.) Page-mode SIMMs offer your PC extra control lines without changing their essential pin-out.

Most modern PCs relieve you of some of these interchangeability worries. They are designed to use page-mode SIMMs but accommodate ordinary linear-addressed memory modules. Although you lose the potentially faster operation of page-mode memory when installing linear SIMMs in these machines, your memory does operate.

You may encounter the terms PROM, EPROM, EEPROM, flash memory, and interleaved memory when scouring ads. In general, you do not have to worry about them. *PROM, EPROM,* and *EEPROM* are all forms of ROM, hence their suffixes. By nature they are not compatible with the working memory of your PC—ROM chips have their contents fixed inside them when they are made.

ROM chips and RAM chips cannot be substituted for one another in an upgrade.

PROM chips can be programmed at a later date, thus the "P" in the name. EPROM chips can be reused, erased, and reprogrammed as necessary. The "E" stands for "Erasable." Erasing generally means shining bright ultraviolet light through a window in the top of the chip. EEPROM ("Electrically Erasable PROM") can be erased with electrical signals. ROM chips and RAM chips cannot be substituted for one another in an upgrade.

Flash ROM is a special kind of EEPROM designed for repeated erasing and reprogramming. While flash ROM chips work much like RAM, they require different kinds of signals to update their contents. As a result, you cannot substitute one for another.

Interleaved memory is not a kind of chip but an arrangement of memory banks. By halving the memory of a computer so that one half is refreshed while the other is being used, a designer can reduce the wait states imposed by the system. On average, half of the memory in the computer is ready for use at any time without waiting, having been refreshed during the previous memory access. As long as memory accesses alternate between the two halves of memory, no waiting is imposed. Some systems use a four-way interleave, splitting memory into four parts, which can statistically trim wait states to one quarter what normally would be required by a given speed of DRAM chip.

Memory interleaving can be important when upgrading, particularly if your PC is an older design based on a 286 microprocessor. Although interleaving won't influence the technology of the chips or modules you need, it may determine how many. For a two-way interleave, you need twice as many banks as with non-interleaved memory—and the banks must be the same size. This need can put important restrictions on what upgrades you can make. You may not be able to add just 1M each time you want to expand the memory of your system. For example, 386 computers that use two-way interleaving may require memory upgrades in increments of 2M using 256K SIMMs and 8M using 1M SIMMs. Many systems make memory interleaving optional. With an odd number of memory banks, they operate without interleaving. With an even number, they use interleaving. If you have such a PC, be sure that when you're finished with your memory upgrade your system is equipped with a number of memory banks that puts memory interleaving to work.

Two other memory technologies that you might encounter in upgrading your PC are *static RAM* (SRAM) and *video RAM* (VRAM or dual-ported RAM).

Static RAM represents an entirely different memory technology that stores data in the positions of electronic switches called flip-flops. SRAM chips do not require refreshing and usually operate at higher speeds than DRAM. This kind of memory is rarely used in the main memory banks of PCs because it is more expensive, but its speed makes SRAM the top choice for cache memory. SRAM and DRAM chips are not interchangeable.

Video RAM chips are a special type of DRAM chips designed with two ports. Although data is being written to the chip from one port, it can be read from the other. This design allows the screen image to be updated while the data in the chips is sent to the monitor screen, making display systems faster. Again, VRAM chips are not interchangeable with standard DRAM chips.

Speed

All memory chips and modules are rated to operate at a given speed. The rating indicates how long the chip or module needs to recover between successive operations and describes the maximum rate at which the memory reliably operates. Unlike microprocessor speeds that are given in megahertz, however, memory ratings are in the reciprocal value nanoseconds (ns). The higher the megahertz of a chip, the lower the nanosecond rating of the memory it requires.

The higher the megahertz of a chip, the lower the nanosecond rating of the memory it requires.

Typical ratings for dynamic memory are 40, 53, 60, 70, 80, 100, 120, 150, and 200 ns. Static RAM chips may be rated at 15, 25, or 35 ns. Lower numbers indicate faster memory. In most cases faster memory is more expensive. Sometimes, however, you may find an insignificant price difference between memory of different speed ratings. Choose the faster memory when you have the option.

The basic speed rules are simple. Memory chips must be able to operate at least as fast as your system requires them to. Faster chips work in place of slower chips but not the other way around. Faster chips do not, however, make your computer run quicker—the speed at which memory operates is set by the host PC's internal clock and the number of wait states set by your system's circuitry. Faster chips have a higher speed potential; you can install them later in a quicker computer should you upgrade your system or system board. Moreover, with faster memory you may be able to reduce the wait states imposed.

To determine what chip speed you require, look at the chips already installed in your PC. Memory modules appear like small circuit boards projecting up from your system board. Chips and memory modules are marked with a speed rating—the last digit of the identifying number silk-screened on top. Note that for speeds of 100 ns or slower, the right-hand zero is usually not printed, so a chip ending with the suffix -12 is rated at 120 ns while -80 indicates 80 ns.

Memory modules often have ratings stenciled on their circuit boards. If not, the speed ratings of the individual chips on the modules should be visible. Most modules are rated at the same speed as their individual chip ratings.

Your PC's micro-processor clock speed is not a reliable indication of its memory speed.

Because computers vary in the number of memory wait states they impose, your PC's microprocessor clock speed is not a reliable indication of its memory speed. Two computers with identical microprocessors operating at identical speeds may require two different memory speeds. Altough a memory cache tends to isolate main memory from the speed needs of the host microprocessor, it does not eliminate speed concerns. Even cache-isolated memory must operate at a minimum speed, albeit one lower than if no cache were present.

Generally, 386 and 486 comput-ers require 80 to 60 ns memory—the fastest DRAM that's widely available.

Generally, however, 4.77 MHz PCs and XTs operate with 200 ns memory, AT-class machines based on 6 or 8 MHz 286 microproces-sors typically require 150 or 120 ns memory, and quicker computers require quicker memory. Generally, 386 and 486 computers require 80 to 60 ns memory—the fastest DRAM that's widely available.

Portable PC Issues

With laptop and notebook PCs, you face several specialized memory-upgrade issues different from those of desktop systems. Many of the most popular laptop and notebook PCs require proprietary upgrades, special RAM chips, or special packages holding the chips. Others make do with conventional SIMMs.

Proprietary modules are generally easier to install but also substan-tially more expensive than SIMMs. Part of the additional expense can be justified by the extra design work required to create the modules, but it also can have more pragmatic motives. When memory upgrades are proprietary you have a more limited source of supply—often only the computer maker and its authorized dealers—so the manufacturer and not the market sets the price. That can make upgrades a big money maker for the PC manufacturer.

Fortunately, a few laptops have become so popular that they have become standards in their own right. Vendors have begun to stock memory from third-party sources for these machines, and along with multiple vendors has come price competition. Although you still should not expect proprietary laptop memory at ordinary RAM prices, the penalties aren't as high as they were a few years ago. For example, upgrades for Toshiba's (now discontinued) T1000SE cost $500 for 2M when first introduced; the same expansion now costs $169.

Machines that use SIMMs eliminate such worries and enable you to shop for the best deal. Although you still need to be concerned with the type of module (for example, 9-bit versus 36-bit), you won't need to pay more than general market price.

Check your owner's manual to determine what forms and amounts of upgraded memory you can absorb. Many manuals list compatible modules. Moreover, most large RAM vendors can tell you what you need if you tell them the make and model number of your PC.

Chip and Memory Module Installation

The first step in upgrading the memory of your PC is to determine what kind of memory you need. You can work from the chip designation (the numbers printed on the chip), but every manufacturer uses individual designations for its products.

After your new memory-enhancement accessories are delivered, you have to install them. With boards that you buy with memory already in their sockets, that's easy—just plug them in. With loose chips you have to install yourself, either on your system board or on a memory board, you have to be careful. Each chip must be prepared and aligned before you press it into place.

Preparing Chips

Most loose chips used for memory upgrades are packaged as DIPs. DIPs are usually delivered with their leads spread slightly apart, although chip sockets take leads aligned at right angles to the chip case.

The more difficult method of making the chip fit is by pressuring it into its socket. Partially insert the leads on one side of the chip into one side of the socket and then press the chip toward that side until the opposite leads can be pressed into the socket. If you've not inserted chips before, this method can be frustrating and dangerous, potentially resulting in broken leads. If you don't get the first side far enough into the socket, some of the leads will pop out. If you press the chip down, errant leads project from the socket, and the chip won't work. If you press the chip too far into the socket to begin with, you won't be able to fit the opposite leads into the socket. Remember—each bad bend of a lead increases the likelihood that it breaks off.

The easier method is to prepare each chip by bending its leads. Unlike with larger chips (such as numeric coprocessors), you may need to use a tool. An ordinary pencil works well. Hold the two short ends of one chip between your finger and thumb with the leads on one side resting against a tabletop and the body of the chip perpendicular to the surface. Press with the pencil on the leads on the other side until both sets of leads are parallel to the tabletop (see fig. 5.2).

Figure 5.2

Before you install a DIP chip, bend the leads perpendicular to the body of the chip.

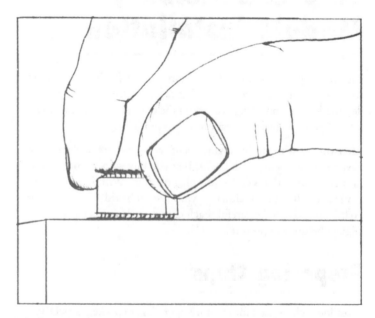

The best alternative in chip installation requires a chip insertion tool. The tool holds each chip securely without your needing to touch the leads (and risk static damage), bends the legs into the proper position, and gives you a longer reach. If you have a tool, use it. If you plan to do a lot of upgrading with discrete memory chips, buy one.

Generally SIP and ZIP chips need no preparation. Sometimes, however, the leads of these chips may be bent slightly when the chips are delivered. Rather than trying to work a chip with bent leads into a socket, first make sure all the leads are properly aligned. Use long-nosed pliers to grip the flat width of the entire length of the lead. Squeezing the pliers flattens most leads straight. You can make further adjustments by bending leads gently.

Finally, in first-generation PCs, indicate that you are adding memory to the system by adjusting the appropriate DIP switch or jumper (see fig. 5.3). Check your system's manual for guidance.

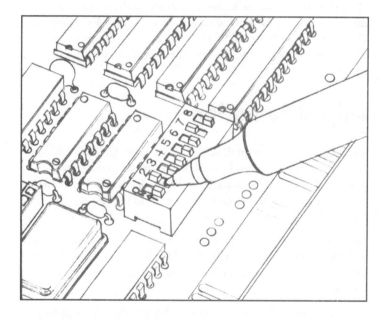

Figure 5.3
In first-generation PCs, indicate that you've added memory to the system by adjusting a DIP switch or jumper.

Which Sockets?

Just as all memory chips and modules are not created equal, neither are their sockets. Most computers assign addresses to chips and modules based upon the sockets in which they are placed. For memory to be contiguous, the memory modules and chips have to be installed in the sockets assigned the next highest addresses in the computer.

In most—but not all—cases a bank of memory chips on a system board or memory expansion board comprises a single row. The rows are numbered zero upwards, and the instructions for your PC or board mention in what order to fill the banks. As long as you fill all the banks needed for a certain memory level, it doesn't matter what order you put the chips into their sockets. Note that some systems divide the banks into odd and even numbers to complicate things. The only sure-fire rule is to follow the instructions.

Although memory modules eliminate the worries about rows of discrete chips, they still may require that you fill their sockets in a particular order, one that may not correspond to their numbering. Again, the only way to be certain is to check your manual.

In only two cases do you not have to worry about which sockets you fill—when you fill all the sockets and when you have a system smart enough to detect what kind of chips you've installed. For example, IBM's PS/2 Models 90 and 95 enable you to plug any memory module in any socket, and the computer configures itself to accept what you do.

Chip Orientation

The alignment of chips in their sockets is critical.

The alignment of chips in their sockets is critical. Chips fit easily in either of two orientations. Pointed in one direction, the chips work properly. Pointed in the other, they might self-destruct the moment you switch on your PC. Clearly, you'll want to be certain your chips are oriented properly.

Fortunately, determining the proper orientation is easy. All you need to do is be careful, observant, and double-check your work. There's only one rule—pin one of each chip goes into the pin one hole in each socket.

Two indications of pin one are used, either separately or together. Most of the time, pin one on the chip is marked by a small depression or dimple in the plastic on the top of the chip's package adjacent to pin one. The pin one end of the chip also may be indicated by a notch at the end of the chip package.

Chip sockets are usually marked for pin one by a notch at their ends (see fig. 5.4). Sometimes, however, other indications are given. For example, a socket may have pin one marked by a tiny notch near the pin one hole itself. Other indications to look for are silk-screened numbers on the circuit board itself. Possibly, on the bottom of the circuit board, pin one may be indicated by a differently-shaped tab on which the socket pin is soldered, or the bulk of the pin pads may be rounded while the pin one tab is square. The basic rule is that if a single solder tab is different from the rest, it marks pin one. Generally, all the chips in a bank of memory should be oriented in the same direction.

Generally, all the chips in a bank of memory should be oriented in the same direction.

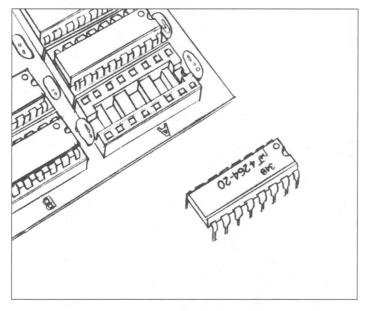

Figure 5.4
Ensure that pin one is aligned with the corresponding end of each socket.

Place the chip lightly in its socket, making sure that the notches line up and that all the leads fit properly in the socket. In particular, be sure that no leads bend over the edge of the socket or under the chip (see fig. 5.5).

After you're certain the chip is aligned properly and all leads are correctly started in their holes, press it into the socket with firm, even finger pressure (see fig. 5.6).

Figure 5.5

Ensure that no leads bend over the edge of the socket or under the chip (as shown here).

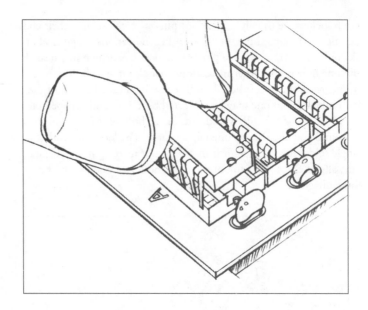

Figure 5.6

After you're certain that the chip is aligned properly and all leads are correctly started in their holes, press each chip into its socket with firm, even finger pressure.

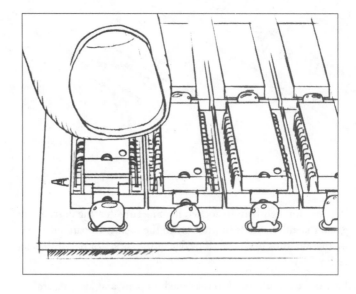

Plugging in Modules

An advantage of SIMMs is that you cannot install them improperly
and thereby destroy them. A tab on each SIMM prevents it from
being snapped into its socket backwards. SIPPs, alas, are like chips
and can be improperly installed; you have to observe the markings
on SIPPs and their sockets. Fortunately, few systems use SIPPs for
memory expansion.

Installing a SIMM is easy after you know how—and pretty confusing until you learn. Hold SIMMs and SIPPs only by their edges.
Instead of inserting it into the socket at the angle at which it will
rest, you slide a SIMM into its socket at an angle and press down
until it engages the contacts at the bottom of the socket (see fig. 5.7).
After the SIMM is as far down in the socket as it will go, lean it back
into place (see fig. 5.8).

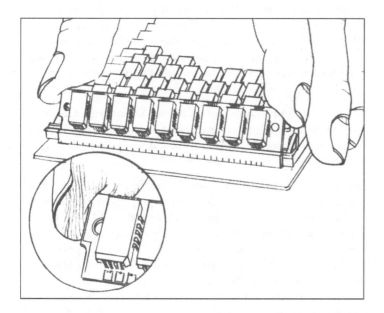

Figure 5.7
When installing a
SIMM, press it down
at an angle into the
socket. Note that a
notch at one end of
the SIMM (inset)
will ensure that it is
correctly aligned.

Figure 5.8

After you've pressed the SIMM down against the contacts as far as it will go, press backward on the SIMM until each end snaps into place.

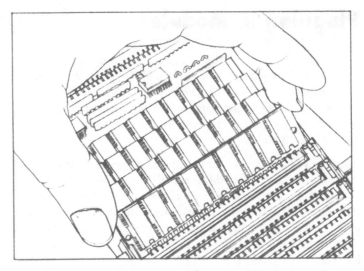

At the two ends of each SIMM socket are posts that prevent it from being pressed further backwards. These posts indicate which way a SIMM is to face when you insert it. When a SIMM has memory chips solely on one side, the side with the chips faces away from the posts. Sockets that hold SIMMs at an angle always put the component side of single-sided SIMMs upward.

SIMMs with chips on two sides are trickier. Examine the SIMM and you'll see that one side has an extra bit of circuit board that acts as a keying tab. Examine the SIMM socket, and you'll see a matching part of the socket into which the key fits.

At either end of a SIMM socket you'll note the fail-safe scheme that ensures that you've got each SIMM seated properly. A plastic finger at either end of the socket snaps into a hole in the SIMM. If the finger doesn't engage, the SIMM isn't deep enough. Also at each end is another finger that snaps over each of the two short edges of the SIMM to latch it in place. If you have to move a SIMM, unlatch these fingers by pushing them outward one at a time until you can push the SIMM forward. After you do one side, unlatching the other frees the whole SIMM.

A mistake with a SIPP can ruin nine or more chips simultaneously.

Determining the alignment of SIPPs is more problematic. The best guide is the numbering of pins. The pins of the SIPPs and the holes in its socket should be numbered with silk-screen identifications on the circuit board. In most PCs, all the SIPPs face the same direction, so you can use existing rows of SIPPs as your guides. In any case, double-check your work even more carefully than when installing loose chips. After all, a mistake with a SIPP can ruin nine or more chips simultaneously.

Installing Laptop and Notebook Memory

The methods of upgrading laptop and notebook computers range from the trivial to the trying. The easiest method is the memory upgrade card. Some systems offer ready access to memory sockets with pop-off hatches in their cases, putting memory installation on par with installing batteries in a TV remote. Tougher upgrades sometimes require you to remove your system's keyboard, a task no more difficult than opening the case of a desktop PC. But in other machines, adding memory may require a total disassembly of the computer—a task to give even Mr. Goodwrench nightmares.

Memory Cards

Upgrading with a card is hardly more trying than grabbing some cash from a bank teller machine—just slide the card in and pray you have the resources you need. The card upgrade is trivial but not worry-free. In fact, it can be dangerous without the right precautions. Most proprietary memory cards, as opposed to more general Personal Computer Memory Card International Association (PCMCIA) expansion products, must be installed with your system switched off. Some proprietary upgrades may be damaged by sliding them into an electrically active socket. Others may not care, but they certainly won't be harmed if installed with your PC off.

Consequently, rule number one is to switch off your system before you begin. You can play it even safer by removing the battery. Also, if you have a semi-permanent RAM drive in your system, back it up. Most systems destroy the contents of RAM drives when you expand their memories.

Most systems destroy the contents of RAM drives when you expand their memories.

Remove the cover to the memory expansion slot. Typically this cover is held in place by a plastic latch that you free by pressing down on the cover itself (see fig. 5.9). The place to push is usually indicated by a pattern molded into the plastic of the cover.

Press down on the hatch and slide it open. Put the loose hatch in a safe place so you don't lose it in the 10 seconds it takes to slide in the memory card. (Don't laugh so smugly. This writer often spends longer trying to locate a misplaced cover than for the rest of the memory-card upgrade.)

Figure 5.9

Many laptops can be opened with a simple plastic latch to access the memory expansion slot.

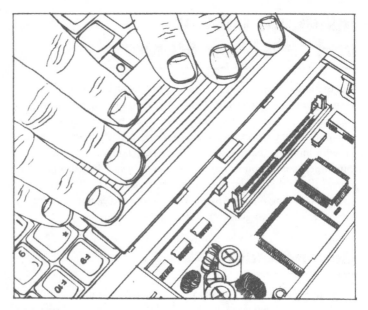

With the slot in plain sight, it's easy to see how to slide the memory card into place. Be sure that the card is properly oriented and that it correctly engages the guides at its edges.

The connector end of the memory card goes into the slot first. That still leaves two possible orientations—one correct, one upside down. Check the instructions accompanying the memory card or your PC to verify the correct orientation.

After you're sure of the proper orientation, slide the card as far as it will go into its slot. At the end of its travel, the card should engage its connector. The required insertion force increases slightly, and the card should slide in another fraction of an inch. If the card is reluctant, stop! You may have oriented it improperly. Forcing it may damage the connector or the card. Be gentle.

After the card is as far as it will go into its slot, replace the slot cover. If the cover doesn't fit back on, the card has not properly engaged its connector. Pull it out slightly to realign it and try again. If it still refuses, check again to be sure that you've oriented it properly.

SIMM Upgrades

Better notebook designs use standard SIMMs or chips and make the sockets easily accessible. The AST Research Premium Exec 325C is a good example. Pop open the hatch at the lower-left edge of the keyboard, and you have direct access to the entire expansion area. Both modem and memory can be added without tools or disassembly.

To add SIMMs to your notebook PC, take the cautious approach. Switch off the system, unplug it, and disconnect the battery. Then remove the access hatch. Again, apply thumb pressure to the marked area and slide the hatch toward the front edge of the system and off.

Inside, you'll see either the modem—if you have one installed—or the SIMM sockets waiting for your upgrade. If you have a modem, temporarily remove it to give you access to the memory sockets. Lift the modem up and out of the system, prying carefully from the connectors on the motherboard.

Although the hatch gives you access to the SIMM sockets, the area is tight around them. You need to be careful. Add memory from the socket closest to the front edge of the keyboard first. Press the first SIMM firmly into the socket with the chips facing away from the hatch area. When it is as deep as it will go, rotate it backward until it snaps in place.

Put the second SIMM into the socket behind the first, following the same procedure—press down, then rock the SIMM back until it snaps into place. Because the Premium Exec 325C is a 16-bit PC (it has a 16-bit 386SX microprocessor), you'll need to add two 8-bit SIMMs to fill a bank. Most 32-bit PCs require four SIMMs to complete a bank.

After the SIMMs are installed, replace the modem if you removed one. Ensure that the gold header posts on the modem engage the sockets, then press it down as far as it will go. Replace the hatch cover, and you're finished.

Many PCs provide an access hatch that's not quite as straightforward as that of the Premium Exec but is larger and provides ready reach to most of the system components: the keyboard. In these PCs, the keyboard is a single assembly that can be removed to reveal most of the motherboard and often the sockets for memory expansion. Because the keyboard is a single unit, you have no worries about destroying it by removing it—if you're careful.

Machines with removable keyboards have a thin crack separating the keyboard from the rest of the PC. The entire keyboard assembly measures about 3/8 inch thick, excluding the height of the keys. To remove the keyboard, twist out the screws holding it in place. Generally, you'll find several screws on the bottom of the system, located in the corners. Keep a sharp eye—sometimes manufacturers hide the screws underneath the rubber foot pads. Also, some systems affix their keyboards with screws above the top (function) key row underneath the panel or plastic strip that accommodates function key legends.

In any case, you need to remove from four to six screws to free up the keyboard (see fig. 5.10). Put the screws in a safe place—you don't want to leave your keyboard flopping in the wind after your upgrade.

Figure 5.10

The keyboard from your laptop is often held in place by screws from beneath.

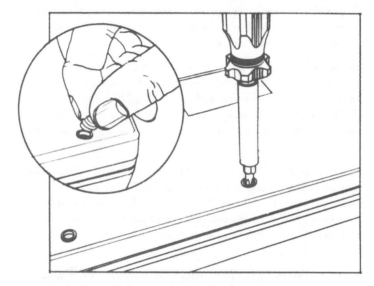

After the screws are removed, gently lift the keyboard (see fig. 5.11). You should be able to raise it an inch or so without any resistance. You cannot lift up the keyboard and put it in a safe place, however. It's probably tethered by a flat ribbon cable. Generally, you can set it to one side of the system or angle it up against the monitor screen.

After you've removed the keyboard, you'll have a grand view of either the motherboard of your notebook PC or of nothing. Some systems put disk drives under the keyboard, and you may see the unrelieved nothingness of their sealed tops. Others put the drives toward the back. If you have one of the latter, you should be able to find the memory sockets in a few seconds. They look exactly as they would in a full-size PC.

Figure 5.11
After removing the screws, gently lift out the keyboard.

When the memory sockets aren't under the keyboard, you've got to look elsewhere, and that means more disassembly (see fig. 5.12). Typically you'll find SIMM sockets in these more troublesome machines hiding under the cover behind the screen hinges. With most cases, you'll have to remove this cover and the screen as a single assembly.

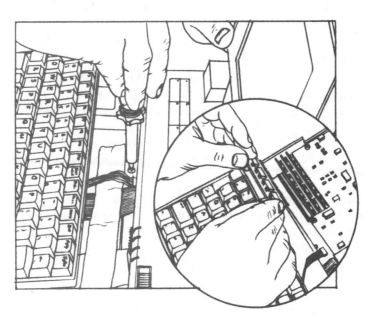

Figure 5.12
Some laptops require still more disassembly to reach the memory sockets.

Your first challenge is to find all the screws holding the rear section of your PC's shell in place. You might find them on the rear panel or at the rear edge of the bottom panel of your PC. The front of this rear cover probably is held in place by two or three screws at its forward edge which may be accessible only after you've removed the keyboard.

With your laptop screen closed, remove the rear screws and carefully open the screen to a near-vertical position. Remove the front screws while holding the screen upright.

After all the screws are out, carefully lift the screen and the case cover. Most of the time you can pivot this entire assembly backward and lay it flat on your work surface. Be careful; its cables may limit travel. Don't stress the wires connecting the screen to the motherboard.

If you cannot move the screen to a safe position, disconnect it from the motherboard. The cable holding the screen to the motherboard ends with a connector at the motherboard end. Note its orientation—because this connector is not designed to be user serviced, it may not be keyed. Consequently, you could install it backwards accidentally, with devastating results.

After you find the SIMM sockets (few laptops use loose memory chips these days), you'll need to determine which sockets to use for your upgrade. Most 32-bit systems (that is, those equipped with 486 or 386DX microprocessors) require you to install SIMMs in matched groups of four. Systems based on 16-bit microprocessors (286, 386SX, or 386SL) typically require two matched SIMMs per memory bank (see fig. 5.13).

If you find more sockets than you have SIMMS to install, your notebook PC's instruction manual should document which sockets to use first. Should you not be able to find that information (or the manual), check the system board. Sockets are often identified with silk-screened lettering or marks etched in the copper trace of the board itself. Fill the lower numbered banks first, starting with zero if that bank is empty.

Laptop and notebook SIMMs install exactly as they do in desktop machines. Most notebook PCs use angled SIMM sockets to make expansion memory as compact as possible.

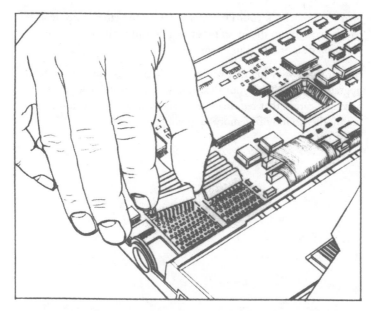

Figure 5.13
Some laptops still
require individual
chips.

After you're satisfied that you've properly installed all the SIMMs,
you can replace the screen assembly and the keyboard. Carefully slide
each piece back in place above the motherboard. Both screen and
keyboard should find their home positions easily, aligning themselves with the edges of the case. Reinsert the screws you removed
and loosely screw in each one. After all of the screws have been
started for each subassembly (screen and keyboard), tighten all those
of the subassembly one by one. Never tighten them enough to
distort or break the case.

Reinstall the battery and power up. Most systems automatically
detect the new RAM you've installed but may report a memory error
because their CMOS settings won't agree with the new endowment.
Running your system's setup procedure should cure the problem and
take advantage of the upgrade.

System Setup

After you've installed all the chips and boards, you have to tell your
computer what you've done so that it can recognize its new memory.
With early computers—PCs, XTs, and their clones—you have to set
DIP switches or jumpers. Because each model of computer has its

own settings, check your PC's manual. ATs and later computers require you to run the setup program that came with the machine, either on disk or stored in its memory.

As you relax, knowing that you've done a good job and successfully upgraded the RAM of your PC, soon you'll find that you need some new application that requires even *more* memory. And you'll be in for another round of memory upgrading.

6

Floppy Disk Drives

G iven three wishes, the first two that most advanced PC users might make would be to eliminate the A: prompt and eliminate the B: prompt. The third likely would be to do away with floppy disks entirely.

Like everyone else, you probably depend on floppies for essential chores: data exchange, backup, program distribution, sometime even active storage. But floppies are their own penalty. They are clumsy, slow, and nearly always store just a few bytes less than you need.

Programs don't fit on a single floppy any more. In fact, you're lucky if you can fit a Windows application on a stack of floppies that won't overload the trunk of a compact car. Running a program from floppy disk is like dragging an anchor through an ocean of molasses. Use floppies for backup, and you get a worn-out elbow from shuffling the disks in and out of your drive slot.

Floppies are the steam-driven technology of the all-electronic information age. Despite advances in microprocessor speed and hard disk capacity that have pushed both ahead by factors of nearly a hundred in the last decade, floppies still spin in the same circles as when the first PC was introduced. Certainly floppy disks and their drives are now smaller and hold more, but in the race of technology, floppy disks caught their stirrups in the starting gate.

A PC without a floppy disk drive is useless. Only through the drive slot can most PCs load programs and data from the outside world. When your system first boots up, the floppy disk is first to supply its operating system. If you ever corrupt DOS or its startup files on your PC, the floppy drive slot is your only savior. Finally, floppies

Floppies are their own penalty; they are clumsy, slow, and nearly always store just a few bytes less than you need.

Use floppies for backup, and you get a worn-out elbow from shuffling the disks in and out of your drive slot.

Floppies are the steam-driven technology of the all-electronic information age.

are cheap and—though not indestructible—fairly reliable repositories of data.

Only when you have a 370K file to store and a 360K disk or, worse, a 3.5-inch disk from a friend and a 5.25-inch drive, do floppies show their unfriendly side. If you have data on a floppy that doesn't fit your drive, you are no better off than not having any data. To confuse matters further, floppy disks come in a variety, and the ones you want to use most are generally the kinds your drive can't handle.

The unchanging nature of floppy technology is one of its graces, ensuring compatibility across vast distances and times. Even though floppy disks aren't always compatible with different floppy drives, most floppy drive types are compatible with most PCs—or can be made that way. You can add a floppy drive to a vacant slot inside your PC, or you can oust an old floppy drive for one with greater storage or one that enables you to exchange files with your friends, associates, or your laptop computer.

Owing to the uncertain future of floppy disk technology, the newest formats may never catch on.

The story of the floppy disk drive is a twisted one. In the six years between the first PC and the watershed introduction of the PS/2, IBM launched six floppy drive standards. In the same number of years after the introduction of the PS/2, several new floppy styles have been unleashed, and the only one to survive is not an ordinary floppy—and one that has yet to win widespread use. Owing to the uncertain future of floppy disk technology, the newest formats may never catch on. Nevertheless, in order of appearance, the most popular seven include: single-sided, double-density 5.25-inch; double-sided, double-density 5.25-inch; double-sided, high-density 5.25-inch; doubled-sided 3.5-inch; double-sided, high-density 3.5-inch; double-sided, extra-density (or quad-density) 3.5-inch; and the odd but interesting half-breed 3.5-inch Floptical disks.

Capacity is perhaps the most distinguishing characteristic of these floppy disk drives. The single-sided drives of the first PCs held 160K of data under DOS 1.0 and 1.1, extended to 180K by the slightly different format used by DOS Versions 2.0 and later. The newer DOS versions packed nine 512-byte sectors on each of the disk's 40 tracks. The old DOS versions could only fit 8.

Double-sided 5.25-inch disks doubled disk capacity. With 8 sectors per track, they hold 320K; with 9 sectors per track, they hold 360K. In that the same disk media holds either 320K and 360K, dependent only on how you format them, you can guess which is more popular—and the default capacity when you format.

High-density 5.25-inch disk drives can read single- and double-sided, double-density disks. At high density, they pack 1.2M on a single disk (with no bad sectors). All double-density 3.5-inch disks are double-sided in the IBM scheme and hold 720K. High-density 3.5-inch floppies, also all double-sided, hold 1.44M; and quad-density disks hold 2.88M, always on both sides. Floptical drives start with ordinary floppy disk technology and a laser-control track that enables more tracks to be squeezed onto every disk, pushing the capacity of a 3.5-inch floppy all the way up to 21M.

The biggest question in adding a floppy drive to your PC is what kind of drive to choose. The question can be daunting because there are so many types of drive—each with its own compatibilities and incompatibilities. Capacities range from 160K to 2.88M—or all the way to 21M. But the "what" question—what kind of drive to upgrade to—is more easily solved by answering a more fundamental "why": Why do you want to add a floppy disk drive to your PC?

There are three basic reasons for considering a floppy disk transplant:

- Adding 3.5-inch compatibility to an older system

- Installing a 5.25-inch drive for reading floppies made by users with lesser PCs than your own

- Increasing your floppy disk storage capacity because you need more room for backups or distributing data

Each of these scenarios has its own best advice, but, before you make your choice, consider what works with each standard—and what doesn't.

Floppy Drive Compatibility

Generally, newer drives of a particular size are backwardly compatible with disks made with older technologies. Whatever you create with a primeval drive is readable on a newer system so long as the disk fits in the drive. Even Floptical drives read ordinary 3.5-inch diskettes.

Going in the other direction varies, however. For example, Floptical disks only work in Floptical drives. With other formats, cross-compatibility varies. For example, you can force DOS to make

Whatever you create with a primeval drive is readable on a newer system so long as the disk fits in the drive.

single-sided disks that work with single-sided, 160K-capacity drives by adding the /1 option when formatting new floppies.

Floptical disks only work in Floptical drives.

Although single-sided disks can be read and written in double-sided drives, double-sided disks can neither be read nor written in single-sided drives. You can't read just one side at a time when you put a double-sided disk in a single-sided drive, because DOS alternates sides when it reads the disk—half the sectors in a file are on each side of the disk. This arrangement is more efficient because it requires less drive-head movement, but it makes single-sided drives useless. Virtually no commercial program disks are single-sided, and none of your friends are likely to have single-sided disks, either. (The odds are better than 600 to 1 against—in a universe of tens of millions of PCs, the number of single-sided drives is in the tens of thousands.) Nearly every software publisher assumes that you have a double-sided drive. If you don't, you should get one, because the increase in capacity and convenience is well worth the $50 price and minimal trouble of upgrading.

A double-density drive cannot read high-density disks.

A bigger problem arises with high-density disk drives. Although double-density disks can be read in a high-density (or quad-density) drive, a double-density drive cannot read high-density disks. The /4 option is supposed to enable you use a high-density drive to format disks to be readable in double-density drives, but high-density 5.25-inch drives use narrower heads than double-density units to squeeze in more tracks—80 per high-density disk versus 40 for double-density. In writing double-density disks, the narrow head leaves a band of unaltered disk around the information it does write, and a double-density head reads the band as extraneous noise, often producing errors. The problem should not arise with 3.5-inch disks because the width of the heads used for double- and high-density drives are the same. Instead of more tracks, high-density 3.5-inch drives squeeze more information on each track.

For true compatibility with all IBM disk formats, you need at least three different floppy drives: a double- and a high-density 5.25-inch and a high-density 3.5-inch drive. Most PC floppy disk controllers operate only two drives. Therefore, you are forced to choose your favorites.

The double-density 5.25-inch drive is the universal exchange standard. If you want to move information reliably to the widest reach of PCs, you need one. If you care more about capacity—particularly for backups—consider a high-density drive. The size depends on what other computers you have (or plan to have) and what your plans are for the future. If you have a laptop computer or are planning to purchase one someday, consider a high-density 3.5-inch drive. Consider single-sided 5.25-inch and double-density 3.5-inch disk drives obsolete.

Floptical drives are intriguing because of their large capacity and backward compatibility. Despite a trade association bearing the Floptical name and a variety of available products, Floptical technology remains essentially proprietary. The capitalized name alone hints that it may never be a mainstream technology. Although the large capacity of Floptical disks hints that the technology could become important for data exchange and distribution, CD-ROM is the top candidate to replace the floppy for distributing software, and larger-capacity cartridge media have more potential for information exchange (see Chapter 8). Only time will tell if Floptical drives will become a valuable PC peripheral, or yet another forgotten technological detour.

Only time will tell whether Floptical drives will become a valuable PC peripheral, or yet another forgotten technological detour.

Floppy Disk Compatibility

Outwardly, all floppy disks appear to come in two sizes. Any 5.25-inch disk fits into any 5.25-inch drive, and any 3.5-inch disk fits into any 3.5-inch drive. Yet, despite the visual similarity in floppy disks, the price differential for disk formats varies by factors as large as 20 to 1. To some people, this is a major scam. Others know better.

If you upgrade your floppy drive, you also have to upgrade the type of disks you buy.

The differences between floppy disks are more than a matter of marketing, brand names, and quality control. High-density disks are physically different from low- or double-density disks. If you upgrade your floppy drive, you also have to upgrade the type of disks you buy.

The magnetic media used for storing information on floppies are scientifically described by several properties. Among the most important is coercivity. Measured in Oersteds, the coercivity of a floppy disk indicates how strong a magnetic field a drive read/write head must generate to write data to the disk.

High-density floppy disks have higher coercivity media, and high-density floppy drives generate stronger signals to write to the disks. Higher coercivities increase the strength of the recorded signal (which compensates for the smaller disk area to which each bit is written on a high-density drive) and make storage less likely to be erased accidentally.

In general, you can't tell high-density and double-density disks apart without reading their labels. To the naked eye, the particles of magnetic medium look identical. Your drive can't see the difference, either. If you tell your drive to format a 5.25-inch double-density disk as high-density, it tries to follow your command. You're apt to get a lot of bad sectors or the disk may be rejected entirely because the first track tests bad. Worse, because of the coercivity difference, any data you do store may deteriorate over time.

The same concepts apply to 3.5-inch disks, but with two differences. First, the difference in coercivity is not as great between double- and high-density 3.5-inch floppy disks as it is with 5.25-inch disks. Second, many 3.5-inch disk drives can differentiate between double- and high-density disks because high-density disks are coded with a special hole in their plastic shell, located opposite the hole used for write-protection. But some machines, notably IBM PS/2s, ignore the signal from the hole sensor and let you format double-density 3.5-inch disks as high-density—with dismal results. Their machines assume every disk is high density unless a complex option is added to the format command.

A double-density disk may format fine as a high-density disk, but it is more prone to go bad over time.

Entrepreneurs have taken advantage of the disparity between prices and coercivities in 3.5-inch floppy disks by developing special punches that slice a high-density sensing hole in double-density 3.5-inch disks. In theory, this subterfuge could save you between $1 and $5 per disk, but you will sacrifice reliability. A double-density disk may format fine as a high-density disk, but it is more prone to go bad over time. In six months or so, you may encounter read errors. Eventually you will lose an important file, and the time you spend recovering the file—if you can—will offset the savings you made by punching the hole. In other words, don't use altered disks for serious data storage.

A worse strategy than buying the expensive hole punch is to try doing it yourself. You could take an electric drill and bore the sensing hole in the disk shell, but you will ruin your disk and your disk drive with the detritus of the drilling. The tiny shards of plastic that inevitably get shorn off during drilling can lodge in the shell, under the read/write head of your drive, or in the drive mechanism itself. Don't risk it to save a few cents.

A safer cost-saving trick is to buy cheaper, single-sided disks and format them as double-sided. This strategy is often successful because there is no physical difference between single- and double-sided disks. All floppy disks have magnetic media on two sides. Single-sided disks are only tested for use on one side—or may have been tested on both sides, with only one side found to be good. In the former case, you may be able to cash in by formatting the disks double-sided and seeing whether you encounter any errors. Be forewarned, however, that disk makers vow that their testing is more rigorous than anything you can do. Your PC may find a marginal disk sector good enough, even though it might go bad at a later date.

Extra high-density (2.88M) floppy disks pose similar issues as 720K and 1.44M floppy disks do. While they are the same size and shape as normal and high-density floppy disks, extra high-density floppy disks use a different magnetic material (barium-ferrite) with a much higher coercivity than even high-density disks. Moreover, the magnetic particles of medium are aligned vertically—perpendicular to the disk surface—rather than laterally as with other floppy disks. Consequently, ordinary floppy disks cannot be formatted at extra high-density capacity. Extra high-density drives are, however, backwardly compatible with older floppy formats and media when used at the rate capacity of each medium.

DOS Considerations

When upgrading to a new floppy format, make sure that the version of DOS you plan to use supports your new drive. Fortunately, nearly every revision of DOS has included changes to accommodate new floppy disk formats (as well as incorporate other advanced features), as you will see in the brief history of DOS and floppy disks that follows.

The whole PC and floppy disk story began with DOS 1.0, introduced along with the original IBM PC in 1981. Its principal claim to fame was that it booted up the PC and let the world see what personal computers could do. As far as floppy disks were concerned, though, it handled only single-sided, double-density 5.25-inch disk drives and stored 160K per disk. Each side was formatted with 40 tracks of 8 sectors with 512 bytes in each sector.

DOS 1.1, introduced later in 1981, opened a new world to the floppy disk—the second side. It enabled the use of single- or double-sided drives with double-density disks. The maximum capacity per disk was 320K, with the same storage format as DOS 1.0 used on each side.

In 1982, when IBM introduced the XT with its 10M hard disk, DOS 2.0 was introduced. More than an upgrade, DOS 2.0 was reworked from the ground up to include tree-structured directories and other features useful in running a hard disk. DOS also grew substantially, rudely cutting into the capacity of DOS system disks. To counteract the larger disk space requirements, the capacity of floppies was increased by altering the disk format. Although floppy disks still packed 40 tracks per side, a simple timing change enabled DOS 2.0 to squeeze nine 512-byte sectors into each track. The capacity of a single-sided disk was thus increased 12.5 percent to 180K, a double-sided disk to 360K.

Unlike previous upgrades, the move to DOS 2.1 in 1983 brought no additional floppy disk capacity. However, changes were made in the operating system to allow the use of half-height floppy disk drives. Timing requirements were relaxed because early half-height floppy drives were not as precise as their larger forebears. The motivating factor in this change was the introduction of the PCjr, which was equipped with a half-height drive.

In 1984 DOS went through another major alteration with version 3.0. Introduced to support the new 286-based IBM PC AT, DOS 3.0 supported high-density, 5.25-inch drives. The track count of each disk was increased to 80 per side. This closer spacing of tracks required a narrower read/write head, leading to the backward compatibility problems mentioned previously in writing double-density disks. Each track was split among 15 sectors to achieve a total disk capacity of 1.2M.

DOS 6 adds no new floppy hardware capabilities, but its DoubleSpace technology potentially doubles floppy disk capacity once again.

DOS 3.1, promised at the same time DOS 3.0 was introduced, made no changes in floppy storage, instead adding file control facilities for network operation. DOS 3.2, on the other hand, broke new ground, being the first DOS to support 3.5-inch diskettes. DOS 3.2 was introduced in 1986 to accommodate the IBM Convertible, an unlamented laptop computer. DOS 3.2 supported double-sided, double-density 3.5-inch drives with a total capacity of 720K. (IBM fortunately ignored single-sided 3.5-inch disks.) Each side was formatted with 80 tracks with 9 sectors each.

To accompany IBM's new PS/2, first introduced in 1987, DOS 3.3 made its debut. DOS 3.3 supported a new format, high-density 3.5-inch disks. The capacity of the little disks doubled (to 1.44M) by increasing the number of sectors per track. The track count was kept at 80 per side. As a result, there were no backward-compatibility problems as with double- and high-density 5.25-inch floppies.

DOS 4.0 added a user-friendly shell and extended support for larger hard-disk partitions. The floppy capabilities of DOS 4.0 remained unchanged from DOS 3.3. But DOS 5.0, introduced in 1991, brought extra-density 3.5-inch floppy disks into the DOS fold, along with added memory-management capabilities. DOS 6 adds no new floppy hardware capabilities, but its DoubleSpace technology potentially doubles floppy disk capacity once again.

Digital Research published several of its own versions of DOS (called DR DOS) to compete with the Microsoft/IBM operating system. DR DOS would mirror the floppy disk capabilities of the Microsoft/ IBM DOS available at the time. All versions of DR DOS were introduced subsequent to 1987 and support all IBM-standard floppy formats through 3.5-inch high-density disks.

If you have kept up with all of the DOS upgrades, you won't have any compatibility problems.

The point to remember from this history lesson is that if you have kept up with all of the DOS upgrades, you won't have any compatibility problems. If, however, you are pulling a computer out into the light for the first time in five years, upgrade any old DOS to Version 3.3 or later if you want to move up to high-density, 3.5-inch floppy disks (the most common floppy upgrade). Any version of DR DOS also works. For extra high-density 3.5-inch floppies, you'll need to notch that cobweb-covered PC up to DOS 5.0 (or later) or DR DOS 6.0. For a Floptical drive, you need only the drive software supplied with the drive itself.

PC Compatibility Issues

If sorting through such an array of drive types and DOS versions is the flu, making them work together is the plague. Most older PCs—the kind you'll most often upgrade to a 3.5-inch floppy drive—don't operate all floppy formats. Current generation PCs with high-density 3.5-inch floppies generally don't have such compatibility problems. The floppy-compatibility problems in older machines, though, range from the understandable—early PCs were designed before 3.5-inch floppies—to the outrageous—except for the latest models, IBM PS/ 2s don't recognize high-density 5.25-inch floppy drives. Between is a vast middle ground of system compatibilities. Some PCs accept any floppy drive type; others seem to work but bestow a generous share of disk errors.

Some PCs accept any floppy drive type; others seem to work but bestow a generous share of disk errors.

Most computer systems have the hardware needed to operate any standard floppy disk drive, specifically a type 765 disk controller chip. The latest PCs, built using Application Specific Integrated Circuits (ASICs) usually emulate a 765 disk controller in one of their VLSI chips. Systems with compatibility problems don't take advantage of all the features of this chip.

Rather than a hardware omission, floppy problems arise from a firmware shortcoming. The primary culprit is generally your system BIOS. The BIOS stores the instructions for matching the 765 to different floppy disk types. If your BIOS lacks the instructions needed to make a 3.5-inch drive work, for example, such a drive won't work with your PC.

The code in your PC's BIOS contains the values needed by the 765 chip to understand the storage formats of different styles of floppy disks. If your BIOS contains the correct values for the type of floppy drive that you want to install, your system can operate the drive. If not, you need to compensate.

Most modern PCs have the values they need for all earlier drive types.

Note that this omission was probably unintentional on the part of the manufacturer of your PC. The necessary values for the various kinds of floppy drive have been introduced one-by-one throughout the history of the personal computer. If your PC's BIOS was engineered before a specific kind of floppy drive was accepted as a standard for IBM-style computers, then it is unlikely to accommodate that type of drive. Most modern PCs have the values they need for all earlier drive types.

Determining whether your PC is compatible with a given type of floppy drive can be as easy as checking your system's owner's manual or as difficult as trial-and-error experimentation. The simplest case is when you just want to duplicate a drive already installed in your system. In almost every case, PCs accept a second drive of the same format—having one working drive ensures that you have BIOS support for its type.

The only likely problems are a lack of space—for example, a smaller PC may have given over its second drive bay to a hard disk—or lack of an extra floppy disk controller channel if the second channel of the system's floppy disk controller has been given over to a tape backup system.

If your system already has a high-density drive of a given size, the odds are favorable that your system can control a double-density drive of the same size. With 5.25-inch drives, this was the most popular upgrade until the introduction of 3.5-inch drives. The double-density drive provided complete compatibility with double-density floppies from other machines, something the high-density drive could not do. With 3.5-inch drives, however, this strategy is pointless. The high-density drive can read and write double-density disks as well as a double-density drive can. With the price difference between double- and high-density 3.5-inch floppy disk drives averaging about $10, opting for lower density and half the capacity doesn't make sense.

Extra high-density floppy disks require special drives. To cope with the special recording medium, extra-high density drives require an extra erase head. The extra head is fixed to the same actuator as the read/write head and moves with it track-to-track. When writing data, the erase head prepares the area by aligning disk flux transitions in the same direction. The read/write head can then change their orientation to record data. The operation of these drives is so different that your PC requires a special floppy disk controller and special BIOS. Any PC factory-equipped to handle extra-density floppies includes everything it needs. However, an upgrade requires more hardware changes than other floppy changes. Floptical drives, too, require different controllers from ordinary floppy drives.

Any PC factory-equipped to handle extra-density floppies includes everything it needs.

Adding a drive that uses a different disk size is a chancy upgrade. You must first determine the inherent compatibility of your system. Start your investigation with the date your system was made. Computers designed before the IBM AT was announced in August, 1984, are likely to recognize only double-density (360K) 5.25-inch floppy drives, because high-density 5.25-inch drives were introduced with the first AT. Systems designed before the PC Convertible laptop computer are unlikely to use double-density 3.5-inch drives because IBM introduced the 720K format with that machine. IBM began using high-density 3.5-inch drives with the introduction of its PS/2 series in 1987, although a few manufacturers anticipated this format.

If you don't know when your system was designed or introduced (most people don't), you're not out of luck. Take a look at your PC's setup procedure (either the procedure you select from the keyboard when your computer boots or the disk-based program that accompanied your computer when you bought it). Check the options it gives you for floppy disk drives.

The setup program used by most computers after the AT lets you select the style of the floppy drive installed as drive A: and B:. If the style of the drive that you want to install is listed in setup (you might have to step through all the options to see it), then you're home free—your floppy disk upgrade will work. If your system does not use a setup procedure, you have a computer designed in the days before the AT. Consequently, your system probably knows about double-density 5.25-inch floppy drives only.

Laptop Compatibility Issues

Laptop computers present their own compatibility issues. Most laptop manufacturers recognize the problem of media incompatibility and provide some means of connecting an external 5.25-inch floppy drive—internal drives of this size just don't fit the tight confines of the typical laptop. Most of these add-on drives attach to dedicated proprietary ports, usually a large connector on the rear of the laptop PC. The manufacturers of these machines offer their own (expensive) products for this upgrade. For these systems, the upgrading chore is trivial—just plug in the drive. The rest of the process has been integrated into a simple procedure by the manufacturer so you can't go wrong.

Third-party products for laptop floppy-drive upgrades are rare because of the nature of the interface. A manufacturer would have to engineer a different connection scheme for each laptop computer for which it wanted to offer upgrades. With the individual sales of each laptop model being tiny compared to the huge volume of generic desktop machines, third-party floppy drives for laptops don't make economic sense. Eventually, everyone will convert to 3.5-inch disks, and the value of clunky 5.25-inch drives for laptops will plummet.

Eventually, everyone will convert to 3.5-inch disks, and the value of clunky 5.25-inch drives for laptops will plummet.

If you need to share disks between your desktop and laptop computers, add a 3.5-inch drive to the desktop machine instead of a 5.25-inch drive to the laptop. The drive will be cheaper because of common interface standards and competition among suppliers. Instead of buying an engineered add-on system, you often can add a raw drive to your desktop machine. A proprietary laptop floppy drive might cost $300 or more, but you can add a floppy drive to your desktop PC for about one-sixth that. Plus, you have more room in your desktop PC—room to fit the drive in place and working room when you make the upgrade—and your installation is permanent, with no need to plug and unplug an external drive when you head for the road. At least you won't have to play musical cables when packing your laptop into an attaché case.

Improving Compatibility

The lack of direct support for a given drive type by your PC does not mean that you are forever banned from adding that kind of floppy as an upgrade. It merely means an extra step—you have to teach your computer how to handle the renegade drive. Fortunately, educating your PC is not traumatic. In fact, three different strategies can give your PC the remedial education it needs:

- Adding driver software to compensate for BIOS shortcomings

- Upgrading your floppy disk controller

- Upgrading the BIOS chips in your PC

The first is the universal approach, the least expensive, and the one that requires the least tinkering with the solid-state secrets of your PC. But it is also the most limited and, occasionally, the most irritating. Conversely, adding new BIOS chips to your PC makes up for the deficiencies, but a new BIOS can affect the other compatibilities of your system adversely. For many people, the optimal solution is the insertion of a new floppy controller—it can add its own bit of BIOS without tinkering with chips or disturbing the inherent compatibilities of your system.

Software Drivers

Software drivers alter the code contained in your system BIOS with special instructions for handling a new type of drive. DOS loads the driver software through your system's CONFIG.SYS file as it would any other device driver. That's the first limitation of driver software—your system has to boot up with DOS before the driver can be read. Consequently, driver software is not useful for drive A: (your boot drive), because your system wouldn't know how to operate the new drive type until it used drive A: for booting up.

Because the driver loads after DOS takes control of your PC, driver software is also operating-system specific. If you don't use DOS, you may be out of luck. You need a different driver for DOS than for OS/2 or UNIX, and you may not be able to find driver software for operating systems other than DOS. If your dealer says that no driver for an operating system is available today but one will be released shortly, wait until it is. Never rely on anyone's promise that such a driver will become available—you want to use your floppy drive now, or at least sometime during your lifetime.

If your dealer says that no driver for an operating system is available today but one will be released shortly, wait until it is.

All told, software drivers are the least desirable way of matching a foreign floppy drive to a PC.

Driver software also raises compatibility concerns. Some software, such as some disk utilities and backup programs, takes direct hardware control of floppy drives and ignores software drivers. These applications thus may not work on floppy drives that use software drivers.

Software drivers also add petty irritations. For example, they take on drive letter identifications further down the alphabet than the last BIOS-based drive. Your new driver-based floppy likely is recognized as drive D: rather than drive B:. You can use DOS facilities to rename the drives, but frequent error messages will tell you a given DOS utility won't work on a renamed drive. You'll grumble that using software alone for the upgrade was false economy.

All told, software drivers are the least desirable way of matching a foreign floppy drive to a PC. Unfortunately, they are the only universal method of doing so, sometimes the only method permitted by a given PC.

Many floppy disk upgrade kits include a software driver to help you upgrade systems that need one. Note that this driver is used in addition to the DRIVER.SYS program that comes with recent versions of DOS. The driver that comes with the floppy disk drive tells your PC how to operate the floppy drive; DRIVER.SYS tells your system how to recognize the new drive. You must make two entries in your CONFIG.SYS file. The driver supplied with your disk drive should be listed first, because it must tell DOS that the drive is there before DOS can deduce what to do with it.

In some cases, a few middle-aged PCs (generally between AT-class machines and 486 systems) not originally designed for 3.5-inch floppy disk drives can be coaxed into operating using DRIVER.SYS alone. Boot your system normally—possibly with error messages and odd sounds from the floppy drive. DOS then reads the DRIVER.SYS entry in your CONFIG.SYS file and reconfigures the floppy to work properly. The only catch is that you then have two drive letters assigned to the new floppy—the drive's hardware assignment which doesn't work and a software assignment which does.

Some (but not all) versions of MS-DOS and DR DOS—but importantly not IBM's PC DOS—include an additional driver program called DRIVPARM.SYS that sidesteps this drive-letter duplication. DRIVPARM.SYS resets the drive type information provided by your system BIOS. The drive on which

DRIVPARM.SYS works keeps its original assignment but assumes a new personality—one that works. DRIVER.SYS also can be used to give you greater system flexibility. You can give the same drive several names to make normal system usage easier. Note that some manufacturers include DRIVPARM.SYS with the DOS that accompanies their systems when sold; other manufacturers using the same DOS version may not include it. The inclusion of this utility is the manufacturer's choice and is not linked to a specific DOS version number.

When you give multiple DRIVPARM.SYS commands for the same floppy drive, the last command listed in your CONFIG.SYS file prevails. If you give multiple DRIVER.SYS commands for the same floppy disk drive, you end up with multiple drive letters, one for each time you include DRIVER.SYS in your system's CONFIG.SYS file. These drives take their drive letter assignments in alphabetical order according to the order they are listed in CONFIG.SYS. The first entry gets the first available letter.

The options for DRIVER.SYS and DRIVPARM.SYS are the same and are listed in figure 6.1. You should specify three options: drive number, as /d:, form factor, as /f:, and the 3.5-inch indicator, /i:. In most cases, that is enough for DOS to understand what kind of floppy disk drive you have installed.

The drive number indicates which channel of the floppy disk controller is connected the drive that DOS is to act on. As with most computer things, counting starts with zero. Hence, use /d:1 to indicate the B: (second) floppy drive.

Four principal form factor options describe the most common floppy drives: /f:0 for double-density 5.25-inch drives, /f:1 for high-density 5.25-inch drives, /f:2 for double-density 3.5-inch disk drives, and /f:7 for high-density 3.5-inch floppy disk drives. The default settings for these form factor options take care of the necessary head and sector settings.

The /i: option indicates that you are using a 3.5-inch floppy disk drive that is connected to your existing floppy disk controller as either drive A: or B:, but for which your system lacks BIOS support. This option may not be available (or work) with all PCs. In systems in which it does, using DRIVPARM is the easiest way to get a new floppy disk drive running. If this option is not available, you'll need to try other upgrade methods.

Figure 6.1

DRIVPARM.SYS
and DRIVER.SYS
command options.

Options under DOS 3.3:

/d: Physical drive on which to act, numbered starting with 0 as the first floppy disk drive (A:). This is the
        only mandatory parameter. You must specify on which drive the driver is to work.

/f: Form factor option, which specifies drive type as follows:

        0 Double-density 5.25-inch floppy drive
        1 High-density 5.25-inch floppy
        2 Double-density 3.5-inch floppy drive
        7 High-density 3.5-inch floppy drive
        If not specified, DOS assumes a value of 2 for /f

/h: The number of drive heads, which corresponds to sides of a floppy disk drive. Although DOS accepts
        any value from 1 to 99, the default is 2.

i/:   Indicates that the drive is an electrically compatible 3.5-inch floppy. You must use this option if your
        system does not have internal support for 3.5-inch drives.

/n: Indicates that the drive does not use removable media. Do not use this option with floppy disk drives.

/s: The number of sectors per track on the disk. DOS will accept any value between 1 and 99 with the
        default being 9.

/t: The number of tracks on each side of the disk. DOS will accept any value between 1 and 999 with a
        default of 80.

Options under DOS 5.0:

/c: Indicates that the drive can detect when drive door is closed. This can speed up some operations with
        floppy disk drives that support the feature. Check your floppy disk drive's manual to see whether it
        supports this feature.

/d: Physical drive on which to act, numbered starting with 0 as the first floppy disk drive (A:) and going
        upward to number 255. This is the only mandatory parameter. You must specify on which drive the
        driver is to work.

/f: Form factor option, which specifies drive type as follows:

        0 Double-density 5.25-inch floppy drive
        1 High-density 5.25-inch floppy
        2 Double-density 3.5-inch floppy drive
        5 Hard disk drive
        6 Tape drive
        7 High-density 3.5-inch floppy drive
        8 Read/write optical disk drive
        9 Extra-density 3.5-inch drive (2.88M)
        If not specified, DOS assumes a value of 2 for /F:

/h: The number of drive heads, which corresponds to sides of a floppy disk drive. Although DOS accepts
        any value from 1 to 99, the default varies with the form factor (/f: option) you select.

i/:   Indicates that the drive is an electrically compatible 3.5-inch floppy. You must use this option if your
        system does not have internal support for 3.5-inch drives.

/n: Indicates that the drive does not use removable media. Do not use this option with floppy disk drives.

/s: The number of sectors per track on the disk. DOS will accept any value between 1 and 99 with the
        default varies with the form factor (/f:) option that you select.

/t: The number of tracks on each side of the disk. DOS will accept any value between 1 and 999 with a
        default that depends on the form factor (/f:) option that you choose.

Floppy Controller Upgrades

In many PCs, you can match an odd floppy disk drive by upgrading your floppy disk controller. Many—but far from all—modern floppy disk controllers come equipped with an add-on BIOS that adds the necessary instructions to your system's existing BIOS to allow it to control any standard floppy drive type. In most PCs, this add-on BIOS is detected automatically when the system boots up. Its extra code is added to the rest of the BIOS to endow your system with support for newer floppy drive types.

But when you shop for a new floppy disk controller that can add BIOS support to your PC, you have to be careful. Older floppy disk controllers, many combined floppy-and-hard disk controllers, and the cheapest controllers do not have the necessary BIOS code built in. Ask before you order a particular controller whether it has its own BIOS. Better yet, check when you order a floppy controller upgrade to be sure that it enables you to use a specific drive type with your PC. Be sure that the vendor allows you to return the controller (without a restocking charge) if it does not work the way the salesman assures.

Not all PCs accept the BIOS of a new floppy disk controller, so this upgrade option may not be available to you. In particular, IBM's first batch of PCs—those that could accommodate only 64K of RAM on their system boards—have a primitive BIOS that cannot be extended by the add-in BIOS on a floppy controller. (Although you used to be able to upgrade the BIOS of these PCs to an extendible BIOS, IBM no longer offers this upgrade.)

Computers that have their floppy disk control circuitry built into their system boards require you to disable that circuitry before adding a new controller card. If you cannot do so, you may not be able to add a new controller. Even if you can, the existing circuitry takes precedence, putting drive letters A: and B: off-limits to your new floppy disks.

Micro Channel PS/2s also foreclose on the possibility of controller-based BIOS upgrades because Micro Channel-based floppy controller cards are virtually impossible to find. That's not a great loss because all Micro Channel computers can handle both double-density and high-density 3.5-inch floppy disk drives. However, most IBM Micro Channel computers lack the capability to control high-density 5.25-inch floppies. The first IBM Micro Channel computers to support this format were the PS/2 Models 90 and 95. Consider high-density 5.25-inch drives off-limits to older PS/2s.

Older floppy disk controllers, many combined floppy-and-hard disk controllers, and the cheapest controllers do not have the necessary BIOS code built in.

Consider high-density 5.25-inch drives off-limits to older PS/2s.

New floppy disk drive controllers are available in an amazing array of designs. Most have two channels—meaning you can connect only two floppy drives to them. Some have more, typically up to four. If you are planning to add a tape backup system someday (or already have one), the four-channel controllers offer a place to plug in QIC-40 and QIC-80 tape drives directly.

When purchasing a new floppy controller, your first concern should be the BIOS. You want to be sure that the controller supports the floppy drive formats that you want to use. Next, consider how many channels the controller offers and verify that you can get up to four channels in your PC, either on one new card or through a combination of your new and old controller cards.

When purchasing a new floppy controller, your first concern should be the BIOS.

Size and interface design are not major issues in selecting floppy controllers. Nearly every board you can find is a short card that fits any expansion slot. That's because today not much circuitry is necessary for controller a floppy disk drive—and there's no point in wasting board space. Bus interface is not an issue; floppy drives operate so slowly that even the vintage eight-bit PC expansion bus is not challenged to pass through the data as fast as the drive reads it. At the other end of the connection, there are no interface compatibility worries, either. Floppy disk connections are standard throughout the world of PCs.

Adding a New BIOS

The most satisfying solution to the floppy incompatibility problem is adding a new BIOS to your PC so that all the needed floppy disk instructions are built into your computer. This change requires that you remove one, two, or four large integrated circuit chips from the system board of your PC and replace them with new ones. That part of the job takes only a few minutes (after you open and disassemble your PC). The more difficult part is finding a BIOS upgrade that works with your computer.

Although several companies manufacture BIOS chips, they aim to sell their chips directly to computer makers. They don't ordinarily deal in single-piece quantities with individual end users like you. Moreover, unless a BIOS upgrade is available from the original maker of your PC, you have no guarantee that a new BIOS actually works with your computer. Contact the dealer who sold you your computer and ask whether the manufacturer offers a BIOS upgrade. If so, your dealer is the best (and likely only) source of supply.

A number of aftermarket suppliers offer what purport to be generic BIOS upgrades for PCs. The problem with these is that they may or may not work, depending on your PC. The only way to be sure is to try one out—but vendors are unlikely to extend this privilege because chances are good you'll destroy the replacement installing it, removing it, or just shipping it. The next best strategy is to get the vendor's absolute assurance that a given BIOS works with your PC—and be sure he stands behind that assurance with a money-back guarantee.

BIOS chips come in varying numbers and chip types. The number of chips your PC uses does not have to be absolutely matched. For example, many IBM ATs have four BIOS sockets but usually have only two filled with chips.

A more important consideration is the width of the BIOS memory. An 8-bit PC uses an 8-bit BIOS; a 16-bit PC usually uses a 16-bit BIOS. But most 32-bit PCs use a 16-bit BIOS, and some of these machines use just an 8-bit BIOS, which they remap into 32-bit memory using ROM shadowing.

You're best off asking for a BIOS that matches the make and model of your PC.

Fortunately, you don't have to worry about most of the 32-bit machines because they have code for 3.5-inch floppies built in. But make certain that you get the right width of BIOS to match your earlier computer. Usually you're best off asking for a BIOS that matches the make and model of your PC. Failing that, figure you need an 8-bit BIOS for a computer based on the 8088 microprocessor and a 16-bit BIOS for a PC based on the 80286 chip.

Finding the BIOS chips inside your PC is merely a matter of looking for the labels. Most BIOS chips are packaged in EPROM chips. Unlike normal integrated circuits which have solid black cases, EPROM chips have a small round window in the center, which enables you to erase the chip by shining ultraviolet light into it. In most cases, this window is covered with a label, identifying the chip and shielding it from inadvertent erasure. Among the nomenclature on the label is the copyright notice of the company that wrote the BIOS.

In most IBM-compatible PCs there are three chips with such labels. One chip is by itself somewhere near the back panel of the machine, usually very close to the keyboard connector. This chip holds the keyboard BIOS and is of no concern when upgrading your BIOS to handle new floppy drive types. The other labeled chips are usually found in pairs somewhere near the microprocessor. These are the ones you will upgrade.

Finding the BIOS chips inside your PC is merely a matter of looking for the labels.

In 16-bit PCs, note that one of every two chips is labeled "odd" in some way, the other "even." That's because the 16-bit addressing range is split between two chips, one handling the odd addresses, the other the even. When substituting chips, be sure to place the new "odd" chip in the socket from which you removed the old "odd" chip, and vice versa.

In other machines you are challenged to match "U" numbers. Most integrated circuits are identified by silk-screened legends on the system board with names in the form of the letter "U" followed by a number, for example U47. Replacement BIOS packs should tell you which chip numbers to switch with which upgrades. If not, call and verify. Trial and error has no place in BIOS upgrading.

Also be sure to match the alignment of new BIOS chips to the old. Figuring which is the proper direction (and telling one end of a chip from the other) is easy. All EPROM chips are notched at one end. Make sure that the new chips have their notches pointing in the same direction as the old chips did.

The orientation of old chips is a better guide for proper alignment than the chip socket.

Normally, you can depend on the chip socket to tell you which direction the notch goes. The socket has a notch or some other distinguishing mark at one end. However, this method is sometimes unreliable. For example, some early IBM ATs had their sockets installed backwards by automatic insertion machinery. Put in a chip aligned in what looks like the proper direction, and these machines summarily blow it up with a brief but bright flash in their erasing window. The orientation of old chips is a better guide for proper alignment than the chip socket.

Physical Considerations

How to install the drive depends on the layout of your PC and its unfilled drive bays.

After you've established what you need to get your upgrade running, you need to decide where to put it. Somehow the drive must attach to your PC, preferably fitting inside your computer as if factory installed. How to install the drive depends on the layout of your PC and its unfilled drive bays.

Internal Versus External Installation

All else being equal, the best place to put a floppy drive is inside your computer's chassis. If your system has an open drive bay large enough to fit a new floppy drive, you're all set. Today the magic size is a half-height, 5.25-inch bay. Most of today's floppy drives are designed to fit such a bay or can be adapted readily to fit one. Of course, 3.5-inch drives also perfectly fit a 3.5-inch bay. Just don't plan to slide a 5.25-inch drive into a 3.5-inch bay—you'd have an easier time fitting a peck of peaches in a two-quart basket.

You usually need one bay for every floppy drive in your system. You can save a bay if you replace your old drive when you add a new floppy format. Two manufacturers, Canon and Teac, offer special two-drive units that slide into a single 5.25-inch bay. Each includes a 3.5-inch and 5.25-inch high-density floppy. Better still, each pair of drives requires you to plug in only a single cable.

All else being equal, the best place to put a floppy drive is inside your computer's chassis.

External floppy drives are available if your system can't accommodate the one you want. For example, all PS/2s except the new Models 90 and 95 are designed for the external mounting of 5.25-inch floppy disk drives. Opt for an external chassis and you can connect just about any floppy drive to any PC (though there are other complications for such installations, discussed later).

In most cases, you want to buy an external floppy-drive system as a complete kit—drive mounted in an external chassis, cables, and software. Although several vendors offer cases to create own external system, you're likely to encounter more problems than the savings justifies. For example, few floppy controllers provide jacks to plug in external cables. In addition, to connect the chassis to your PC, you'll have to get a shielded cable to minimize interference. And you'll need specialized wiring for the inside of the external drive unit. Plus a power supply. A ready-made external drive system eliminates all these worries—for a price—and gives you a streamlined installation job.

Mounting Hardware

If you choose to use a ready-made external floppy disk system, be sure when you order that you get everything you need to install and secure the drive. The necessities include the following:

- A drive of the right format and capacity

- A case, preferably with a built-in power supply

- Hardware to mount the drive in the case

- A connecting cable long enough to install the completed drive unit in a convenient place

- A floppy disk controller or other means of adapting the signals from your existing controller for external transmission (including a mounting system for the required cable jack, such as a card-retaining bracket)

- The software to ensure BIOS compatibility

Be certain that the vendor can supply the hardware or adapter you'll need, even if at extra charge.

Internal floppy disk upgrades bring their own concerns. Although a small drive may have plenty of room to fit in a larger bay, mounting the drive properly requires more than just space. You need mounting hardware; in addition, putting a 3.5-inch drive in a 5.25-inch bay requires an adapter. Sometimes you're lucky—many 3.5-inch floppy disk drives come packaged with adapters or have them available at a small charge (typically less than $10). Some drives are even sold as complete kits that include front panels of black and beige (to match the XT and AT color schemes) in both 3.5-inch and 5.25-inch sizes. Other times you don't fare so well, however. The cheapest drives are often sold bare, without even the screws to attach them to your PC's drive bays. Most advertisements don't tell you what's included, so you'll have to ask when you order. Be certain that the vendor can supply the hardware or adapter you'll need, even if at extra charge.

The mounting hardware you need varies with your computer. In general, you need four 6/32×1/4-inch screws to mount most floppy disk drives in the typical drive bay. Binder-head screws are best for drives that screw into the sides of the bay; the flattened heads give you maximum clearance. If you're going to mount rails to the drive, use flathead screws instead. These fit flush into the recesses in most drive-mounting rails.

If you have an AT-style computer that uses rails for mounting drives, you'll need rails for your new floppy disk if spares didn't come with your PC. Many vendors can supply rails at a modest charge (if any). Sometimes AT rails are included in the drive-mounting kit.

Mounting hardware for PC compatibles is another story. Because different manufacturers often use rails of uncommon sizes, you may not be able to get rails from your vendor. Let your salesperson know the kind of computer you have and see if he can supply the right rails. If he can't (and with obscure brands of PC, that is likely), contact the dealer who sold you your computer to get the rails. Before you go to all the trouble, however, check whether the maker of your computer has anticipated your problem and included extra rails with the system. Extra rails sometimes are packed with computers loose—typically rattling around in a plastic bag with other extra parts—or already installed in drive bays. Save yourself, the vendor, and your wallet some trouble by being sure you need rails before asking for them.

Floppy Drive Cables

If you're replacing an existing floppy drive with one of a different format or greater capacity or if you're adding a second drive to your PC, you shouldn't need a cable. Most PCs come with one designed to handle two floppy drives. Most also have a spare power connector for a second drive.

Most PCs come with a cable designed to handle two floppy drives.

Of course, every rule has its exceptions, and your PC might be one of them. To avoid unpleasant surprises when you start your installation, check the resources inside your PC. Remove the lid from the case and examine the floppy drive cable for a connector for the second drive.

The floppy cable is easy to find—look at the back of the floppy drive already in your system. There you'll find a wide, flat ribbon cable leading to an expansion board or to the system board itself (depending on the location of your PC's floppy disk control circuitry). In systems equipped for two floppies, you'll find a connector in the middle of this cable, ready and waiting for the additional floppy drive.

In systems equipped for two floppies, you'll find a connector in the middle of this cable, ready and waiting for the additional floppy drive.

To check for an additional power supply cable, look for the power supply in your PC. In most cases, it is a shiny, chrome-plated box in the right-rear corner of the chassis. Several bundles of wire emerge from inside, typically from the left side. Some of these bundles are made from groups of four wires—a red, a yellow, and two black wires—leading to a white nylon connector. One of these groups leads to your existing floppy drive, where the connector is plugged in. Check the wires emerging from the power supply for a set of four wires and a nylon connector not attached to anything—the extra power cable your upgrade needs.

If you're adding a third or fourth floppy to your system, you absolutely need a control cable.

If your floppy disk control cable doesn't have a second connector, you need a new floppy cable that does. If you don't have a spare power cable, you'll need a Y-cable (sometimes spelled "wye-cable") or splitter—a wire that plugs into the nylon power connector and yields two duplicates of that connector. If you're adding a third or fourth floppy to your system, you absolutely need a control cable. Order them when ordering your drive.

Connecting Cables

Floppy disk drives usually require two connections to your computer. A wide, flat ribbon cable carries control and data signals to and from the drive, while a four-wire power cable supplies the drive with the current it needs to run.

To avoid surprises, be certain that your PC has a spare power connector before you order your floppy drive. If it doesn't, order a Y-cable to add another connector. The cable has a jack that plugs into one of the power connectors from your PC's power supply at its base and two plugs suitable for disk drives, one at the end of each "Y" branch (see fig. 6.2).

Figure 6.2
A sample Y-cable.

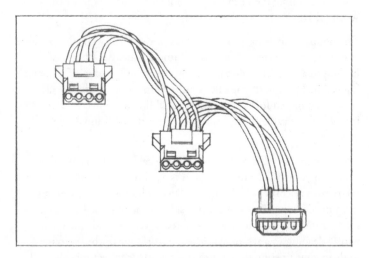

Plug the female end of the cable (the lowest in the drawing) into one of your system's power connector. The Y-cable then provides two male power connectors for drives and other devices. Beveled corners on drive power connectors prevent you from inserting them improperly. If you cannot fit a power plug into a jack on a floppy drive, try turning it over.

Most computers are wired with a signal cable for two floppy disk drives, so if you're just adding a second drive you won't need any other cabling. If you're adding a new floppy disk controller, however, you may require a new cable.

Two types of connectors are used to link floppy drives to their controllers. The original IBM design used by the controllers in PC and XT computers (as well as nearly all 5.25-inch disk drives) was an edge connector, a short extension of a printed circuit board etched with gold-plated contacts. AT and newer controllers and many 3.5-inch floppy disk drives use pin connectors (sometimes called headers), short, sharp, gold-plated pins in two rows that project up from the circuit board. Edge connectors and pin connectors are not interchangeable, so the cable you get must match the style used by your drive and controller. Figure 6.3 illustrates the two connector types.

If you're adding a new floppy disk controller, you may require a new cable.

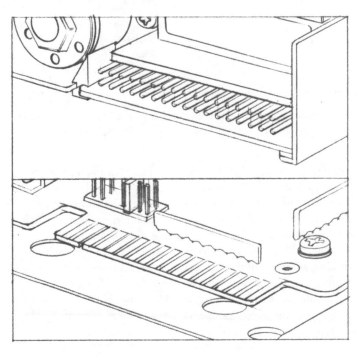

Figure 6.3
Most 3 1/2-inch floppy drives use pin connectors (top) for their signal cables, and most 5 1/4-inch drives use edge connectors (bottom).

Floppy-drive signal cables typically have three connectors—one plugs into the controller and the other two fit disk drives. One drive connector is in the middle of the cable, the other is at one end. The controller connector resides at the other end. You can distinguish the drive end from the controller end by the section of cable that is twisted near the end holding the drive connector (see fig. 6.4). Note

You cannot substitute a floppy drive signal cable for a hard disk cable or vice versa.

that this twist looks similar to the one in a hard disk cable, but it occurs on different wires. You cannot substitute a floppy drive signal cable for a hard disk cable or vice versa.

Figure 6.4
A floppy-drive signal cable.

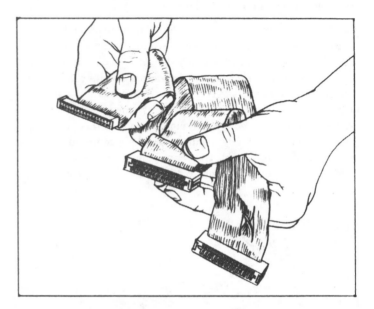

The connector with the twist always goes to the first floppy drive in a computer system, drive A:. The connector in the center goes to drive B:.

Signal cables are keyed so that you can't plug them in improperly. The key is a thin plastic tab wedged into the plug, positioned for the key to mate with a slot cut in the edge connector. Sometimes, however, the tab falls out or cable manufacturers neglect to include it. Without the key, of course, you could slide the connector in backwards. This is not a fatal error, but it prevents the drive from working. Inversion of this connector is the first thing to look for if a floppy disk upgrade does not work. To avoid problems, plug in the signal cable properly by keeping the side of the connector nearest the red (or, sometimes, blue) stripe on the cable on the side of the edge connector nearest the tab slot.

Do your homework before ordering your new floppy drive so that you get all the supplies that you need.

Upgrade Mechanics

The actual mechanics of upgrading your PC with a floppy drive are easy, just a matter of getting your system ready, setting the drive inside, and going to work.

Readying your system means making sure you have space and connectors available for your new drive. This means doing your homework before ordering your new floppy drive so that you get all the supplies that you need. Turn off your PC, disconnect its power cable, and open it up. Count the power connectors and check the drive signal cable. Examine the bay where you plan to put the drive. Check to see whether it requires mounting screws or new drive rails. Make a list of what you'll need and order the hardware when you order your new drive. After your inspection is over, put your PC back together until your new floppy disk arrives.

When you finally get the new drive and its mounting hardware, it's time to dig into your PC again. Follow the same procedure as before—switch off the computer, unplug the power cord, and remove the cover from the case. After you're inside, the first step is to prepare a drive bay for the new floppy disk drive. If you are replacing an existing drive, remove the old drive. Remove the screws holding it or its rails in place. Slide the drive slightly forward, then remove the two cables from its rear (see fig. 6.5). Finally, slide the drive out of your PC. If the drive is mounted on rails you plan to reuse, remove the rails, too.

Make a list of what you'll need and order the hardware when you order your new drive.

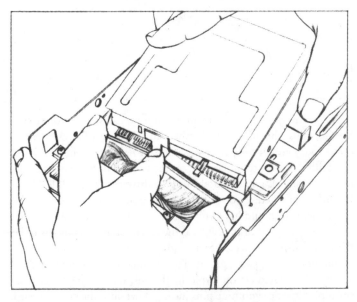

Figure 6.5
Removing the cables from a floppy drive to be replaced.

Most 3.5-inch drive bay adapters include cable adapters to convert the pin connectors on the drive to the edge connectors used in the rest of the system. Attach the cable adapter to the drive before you screw the drive into its bay adapter.

If you're planning to slide your new floppy disk drive into a vacant bay, prepare that bay, too. If the bay has rails in it, remove the rails. If the bay requires you screw the new drive directly into the side of the bay, ensure that no cables protrude into the bay to impede you.

After sliding your floppy drive into its bay but before screwing it in place, connect the signal and power cables to it. The floppy with the connector nearest the twist in the signal cable is drive A:, here shown as the lower of two drives (see fig. 6.6).

Figure 6.6

Attaching a signal cable to an upgraded floppy drive.

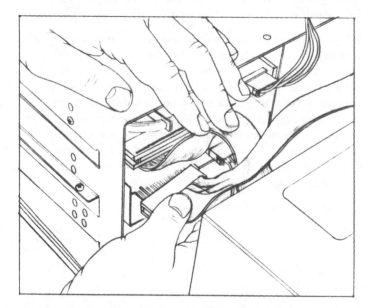

Next, prepare your new floppy drive. In most cases, you shouldn't have to adjust the drive—the jumpers and switches (if any) on most drives today are set to operate with PCs. However, you may need to deal with the drive terminator. A terminator is a package of resistors that keeps signals going to and from the drive at the proper level. Regardless of whether you have one or two floppy drives connected to a cable, you should have only one terminator, located on the drive attached to the end of the cable. If the drive you're installing is to be the second drive connected to a controller, you should remove the terminator resistor pack from it. The terminator either looks like a socketed integrated circuit (typically the only one on the drive) or a small plastic strip with nine pins jutting down into the circuit board. One peripheral manufacturer claims that with recent PCs and controllers you no longer have to worry about terminators—just leave them in place. That's the easy way out, and if your drive works okay there's nothing to worry about. But you may want to remove the extra terminator now, because if you do get many errors from your new floppy drive, the first thing to check would be the terminator—which would mean pulling the drive back out of your computer again.

After the cables are connected, push your new floppy drive into its bay and screw it in place (see fig. 6.7). Then run your system's setup program to tell your PC what kind of drive you've installed.

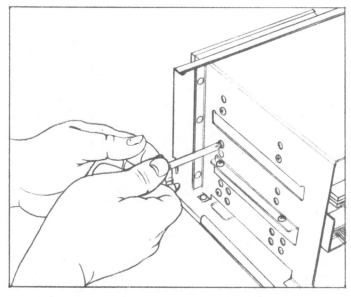

Figure 6.7
Finally, screw down your new floppy drive.

If you're installing a 3.5-inch drive in a 5.25-inch slot, the first thing to do is get the drive ready by mounting it in its drive-bay adapter. Two kinds of adapters are popular. One comprises two angles of sheet metal that mount on either side of the drive to extend its sides. The other is a U-shaped piece that attaches to the side or bottom of the drive. In either case, install the adapter now (see fig. 6.8). Be sure the bezel on the front of the adapter matches the color scheme of your PC—black or beige.

You also may have to adapt the signal connector of a 3.5-inch drive to match the connector cable used by 5.25-inch drives. Some 3.5-inch drives use pin connectors and a miniature power connector. Their adapter kits usually include a small circuit board that converts the connectors. If this converter is just a board that plugs into the back of the drive, install it after you've mounted the drive in its bay adapter. If, however, the converter is a board mounted on the bay adapter, connect its short cables to the drive before you screw the drive into the adapter. After you've made the necessary connections, put the drive in place inside its adapter, line up the screw holes, and start each of the four (or so) screws that hold it in place, then tighten them one-by-one. When you're done, make sure that you haven't distorted the drive by screwing it in too tightly. Slide a disk into the drive and make sure that pressing the release button on the front of the drive ejects the disk. If not, loosen the screws and adjust them until the release button operates smoothly.

Figure 6.8

Inserting a 3.5-inch floppy drive into an adapter for a 5.25-inch bay.

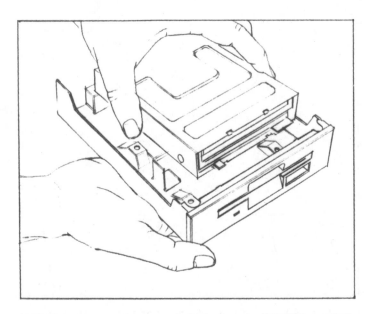

At this point, you can treat an adapted 3.5-inch drive and a true 5.25-inch drive interchangeably. If your PC uses drive-mounting rails, install them on the drive or its adapter. Then slide the adapter-drive unit into your PC. Connect the power and signal cables before permanently screwing the drive in. Then slide the drive into its final position in your PC. When using drive-mounting rails, push the drive back as far as it goes in the bay. In direct-mounting systems, line up the holes on the side of the drive with the holes in the side of the drive bay.

By leaving the drive loose before you tighten the screws, you can adjust its position more easily to get all four screws properly started.

With rail-mounted drives, you can screw the rails into place immediately. With a direct-mount drive, you'll want to start each of the four (or so) screws that hold the drive in place without tightening them completely. After all four are started, tighten the screws one by one. By leaving the drive loose before you tighten the screws, you can adjust its position more easily to get all four screws properly started.

After you've tightened all the screws, test the drive. When you're sure it is working properly, reassemble your PC.

PS/2 Considerations

Because of their case design, most PS/2s require you add 5.25-inch floppy disk drives externally. To do so, you first must install a connector somewhere on or in the system into which you can plug the drive. Companies that offer external drives for PS/2s sell kits that make the job easier. The installation process described here is based on a particular manufacturer's kits, although other kits are similar.

To install a floppy disk drive (or other 3.5-inch device) in a PS/2, you must mount a sled on the bottom of the drive (see fig. 6.9). The sled secures with four screws. After the sled is attached, you can slide the drive right into your PS/2.

The installation process described here is based on a particular manufacturer's kits, although other kits are similar.

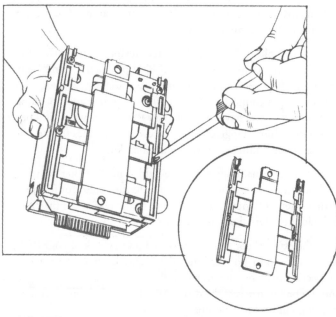

Figure 6.9
Attaching a mounting sled to a floppy drive. The sled alone is shown in the inset.

The various PS/2 models use different drive connection systems that can complicate installation. For example, the PS/2 Model 30 286 uses a cable from the system board to the drive; the Model 50 uses an interposer board, a T-shaped circuit board that floppy drives plug into. Signals from these interconnection schemes must be routed to a rear panel connector into which you can plug the external drive unit.

Some external PS/2 floppy drives require you to plug in an extender cable, then route it to the back of the machine when you add the external connector at the rear of the expansion slot. After you reassemble your PS/2, just plug the external floppy into the new connector.

All the adapters, cables, and connectors should be supplied in a PS/2 floppy disk upgrade kit.

In systems that use cables, you'll need to plug an adapter into the existing drive B: cable (the unused one) and run an extension cable to the rear panel of the system's expansion slots. Then screw into place the retaining bracket holding the external drive connector. In systems with interposer boards, you'll need to plug an adapter into the interposer board, then plug the extension cable into the adapter. Finally, install the external connector in an expansion slot. All the adapters, cables, and connectors should be supplied in a PS/2 floppy disk upgrade kit.

Note that some PS/2 upgrade manufacturers put a single integrated circuit on their cable adapters for floppy disks. This is a buffer chip that ensures sufficient signal strength to traverse the extension cable without errors. It is powered by the electricity supplied to the floppy drive through its connector cable.

IBM has complicated ordering adapter kits for external drives by using different connectors in various PS/2 production runs. Early PS/2s used floppies with edge connectors. More recent designs use drives with pin connectors. The division is by time and not along model lines, so you have to check your PS/2 to see what kind of connectors it uses. Upgrade manufacturers sometimes sidestep the problem by including converters with their kits.

Some PS/2 external floppy upgrades add a small adapter board with buffer circuits on it. Plug the adapter into the connector for the second internal floppy, route the cable to the rear of the machine, and add the external connector to the rear of an expansion slot.

After the external connector is installed on the back of your PS/2, plug in the external drive. Screw the connector in; otherwise, the connection may loosen and you will get error messages when you boot up or try to access the drive. An ounce of prevention is worth several pounds of frustration.

Final Steps

After you've performed the mechanical installation, complete the software part of the procedure. If you have a modern PC with a setup program encoded into its BIOS or loaded from a floppy disk, run the setup procedure. If your older PC requires you to use a software driver, follow the instructions that came with the driver and add the driver to your system's CONFIG.SYS file. PS/2s, of course, require you run the setup procedure on your system's Reference Diskette and add a driver to use a high-density 5.25-inch floppy. After that's done, you can use your floppy for exchanging data, backing up your hard disk, or accessing the greatest range of software available for any kind of computer in the world.

7

Hard Disks

With many applications, your hard disk determines overall system performance. In all systems, the hard disk determines your maximum on-line storage capacity. Upgrading your hard disk can give you more speed, the ability to handle more and larger files, and the satisfaction of building your PC into something better.

Think of your hard disk as your PC's closet, and you will begin to understand why almost everyone contemplates a hard disk upgrade sooner or later. No house known to mankind has ever been built with enough closet space. Therefore, anyone who plans a home renovation without paying attention to the need for closet space is assured unhappy results.

A hard disk is just as essential as any closet and just as likely to be overfilled long before you have outgrown the rest of your PC. Planning ahead and adding excess hard disk capacity only postpones the eventual need for an upgrade. Your files will inevitably overwhelm however much hard disk you choose to install, just as your possessions soon crowd out of your closets. Fortunately, adding extra disk storage is easier than knocking out walls and hammering closets into place.

In a couple of years, even the best hard disk drive outlives its usefulness.

The simple fact of hard disks is that they run out of speed and capacity long before they run out of life. In a couple of years, even the best hard disk drive outlives its usefulness. So no matter how large the hard disk that you bought with your PC, no matter how close to the top of the performance spectrum it rated when you bought it, if it is more than a few years old it can be outdated.

Today's PCs come already equipped with hard disk drives as large as those in servers a few years ago—and even those are beginning to seem puny. The standard measurement of the hard disk has climbed from simply megabytes to hundreds of megabytes. Gigabyte-size

If your vintage PC came without a hard disk, consider a hard disk a mandatory upgrade.

drives will soon find their way into PCs—soon as standard equipment; already as unremarkable upgrades. If your vintage PC came without a hard disk, consider a hard disk a mandatory upgrade.

A hard disk will make any PC faster, more powerful, and above all, easier to use. In fact, there is only one good reason not to add a new hard disk to an old PC: if your PC is so old that it probably came without one.

Most people, however, can live with a slower hard disk. The software cache program SMARTDRV.EXE that comes with the latest MS DOS and Windows versions can do wonders in making an old, slow drive act like a newer one. But if you have tried to keep pace with state-of-the-art software, your old hard disk drive is certain to have become too small for your needs. You need more megabytes, with which you will gain improved performance that will make you wonder how you got along without them. Indeed, a new hard disk drive can be a win-win situation.

But as with any PC upgrade, the toughest part about replacing a hard disk is matching the perfect product to your PC and your needs. The task can seem formidable, because hard disks seem to have their own unintelligible language. But after you sort through the gibberish, finding the best buy means just a little fingertip shopping. Order the drive and the easiest work is ahead of you: installing a disk in your computer.

There are, however, many complicating factors. You need to determine the capacity of the disk you want to add to your PC; the performance level you require—from the slowest, to the fastest disk drives; and the issues that seem tangential but actually govern many of your other choices. These include, which interface and interconnection architecture do you need? Do you need a hardware cache or similar technological speedup? And, how much of what you could possibly add to your PC you can actually afford? These decisions are not easy. But by learning the basics about disk designs and options, you will be on your way.

Hard Disk System Components

Although most people discuss hard disks as if they were a single, well-defined thing, they are not. Hard disks must be considered as a system made from a number of interrelated and interworking parts. These constituents are spread throughout your PC. Part of the hard disk system is locked in your systems *BIOS* (Basic Input/Output System), either *hard-coded* as part of the ROM (read-only memory) chips on your system board or as an add-in extension ROM carried on your systems hard disk controller—if that is a separate element of your PC. The drive mechanism is linked to your system through a connection called an *interface,* where the signals of your PC and hard disk take a common, mutually understandable form. This interface may be related to a separate *disk controller* that translates the demands of your PC for data into instructions that tell the hard disk how to operate, or, those functions may be built into the disk itself as *integrated drive electronics.* With the latter style of drive, you may need a *host adapter* to match the drive's circuitry to that of your PC.

The hard disk itself is a multi-faceted entity. The hard disk, which gives the product its name, is more appropriately called a *platter,* and it is simply a solid circle of aluminum or some other foundation material (to engineers, a *substrate*) that offers a rigid support and can serve as a carrier for a magnetic medium, upon which a digital code can be stored. The substrate is inflexible, hence the name hard disk.

Tiny areas on the medium on the surface of the platter called *magnetic domains* are magnetized to store bits of digital code. The disk platter itself has no means of putting those bits in place, nor can it do anything with those that are already present. For those operations to be usefully accomplished, the platter also requires a reading and writing mechanism and a locating mechanism. Together with the electronics required to operate those additional parts, the complete unit makes up a hard disk drive.

Three separate electronic and mechanical functions are required in the operation of the hard disk drive. First, signals—that is the weak logic pulses in the computer—must be amplified up to a level that will change the magnetic medium during a write operation (putting information on the disk), and the tiny signals created in reading the stored magnetism must also be boosted to the level necessary for the operation of digital circuitry. Second, a mechanism called a *head actuator* must be able to move the head at any point along a radius of the disk to pick out a particular magnetic domain for reading or writing. Third is the spindle motor. This mechanism spins the disk, usually at a constantly and carefully controlled rate, so that the second dimension of the location of a magnetic domain—along the circumference of a circle traced by the head actuator—can be pinpointed.

Differences in each of the parts of a hard disk system affect the performance it can give to your system as well as how and whether it can be connected to your PC.

In many cases, you do not even have to worry about all the details, because you will not have a choice. Moreover, the manufacturer may not reveal some of the innermost secrets of its drive construction to you. In fact, today's hard disks keep their inside operations secret even from your PC, electronically translating the details of their internal construction into a form more readily understood by your PC. The number of heads, sectors, and tracks that your system sees may have no correspondence to the actual disk mechanism.

> *The number of heads, sectors, and tracks that your system sees may have no correspondence to the actual disk mechanism.*

In the last few years disk makers have gone to great lengths to wring as much performance as possible from their products. Where once every hard disk spun at about the same speed—3,600 rpm—today's quickest drives spin almost twice as fast, from 5,400 to 6,300 rpm. The typical hard disk has an average access time of less than half of the fastest drives of only a few years ago. Nevertheless, few of these electromechanical changes make any difference to your system. Most drives today are so fast that the delays caused by the normal operation of your PC—its overhead—overwhelm most of the slowdown caused by their mechanical operation.

The two most important issues that you have to worry about are size and capacity. Size determines whether a specific hard disk drive will fit into your PC, while capacity determines whether what you want in your PC will fit on the drive. Size is measured in inches and fractions; capacity in megabytes.

> *The two most important issues that you have to worry about are size and capacity.*

If you want to connect a hard disk drive, you also must consider its electrical signals and how they match with your PC. In computer lingo, that means you need to know what disk interface you need. Selecting an interface requires you to look at what your PC wants and what any prospective hard disk uses.

Interface Designs

By itself a disk drive is a clever curiosity about as useful as a locked treasure chest; you may believe the chest has potential, but it cannot be tapped until you unlock it. Rather than a mass storage device, a disconnected hard disk would be nothing more than a curiosity, a sealed time capsule holding a record of the long-forgotten past.

To be useful, a hard disk drive must connect with your PC to transfer information from its vast repository to the microprocessor. To get the most value from that storage, the transfers should be as quick as possible so there is no waiting time.

More than just a pathway for data, the hard disk requires other links to your computer. Without some means of telling the drive which bytes were wanted, the digital output of the hard disk drive would be an unintelligible flurry of random pulses. The disk drive thus requires control signals to tell it which bytes to discharge and where to store those sent to it.

Disk Interfaces

Where these two groups of signals—the data and the control—link between the hard disk drive and its computer host is the disk interface. Its physical embodiment is a connector of some sort, which is logical because if the drive and computer could not be detached they would be one unit that would not require an interface. The drive and computer could be one assembly, crafted together as a single piece.

The existence of the disk interfaces are important because the connection scheme gives you a choice. But it also makes matching the drive to your PC critical. If the interfaces used by your PC and a hard disk do not match, no useful information can be passed between them. The mismatched situation would be like connecting your electric line to the tap on your sink: If you expect it to work, you may be shocked at the outcome.

If drives were a permanent part of your PC, you would not have any upgrade problems, because an upgrade would be impossible.

Unlike most developments among PCs, however, progress has simplified the matter of disk drive interfaces. A few years ago roughly four interfaces were widely used in PCs. Nowadays deciding between interfaces for a new hard disk is as easy as a coin toss; there are just two choices. In many cases a coin toss may deliver the right decision. With all but the most demanding installations, the interface does not matter as long as your drive gets properly connected.

Modern Interfaces

The two connections schemes are the *AT Attachment* interface—often called IDE for Integrated Drive Electronics, the technology behind the interface—and *SCSI*, the Small Computer System Interface. Both are major improvements over the older interfaces

If you are upgrading your old PC, consider adding either an AT interface or SCSI drive rather than anything else.

used by PC hard disk systems. In fact, the AT interface and SCSI are such great advances that no disk drive company is currently developing products based on the old interfaces. So, if you are buying a new PC it will have either an AT interface or a SCSI drive inside. If you are upgrading your old PC, consider adding either AT interface or SCSI drive rather than anything else.

There are two good reasons for choosing the modern interfaces: speed and convenience. AT interface and SCSI drives can transfer information substantially faster than the older interface designs, pushing your PC up to its overhead limits. And, for the most part, both SCSI and AT interface hard disks are easier to install. Consider the old interfaces (ST506 and ESDI) only if you need to add a drive to your PC using your existing hard disk controller or if you get a drive with one of those interfaces at a bargain price.

Old versus Modern Disk Interfaces

Philosophical and technical differences separate the old and new disk interfaces. The old designs date back to a time when controller and interface electronics required more space, and the nature of the systems to which they would be connected was uncertain. Disk drives were designed to connect to any electrical device from computer to crockpot. The modern interfaces take advantage of *microminiaturization* and application-specific integrated circuits, and they are tailored to the needs of PCs and workstations.

The older interfaces pass the data pulses generated by the disk drive head directly to the computer host without any processing (except conditioning and buffering to bring them in line with accepted digital standards). The computer host is then charged with creating the data format that is written to the hard disk. In this design, an external disk controller takes care of the details of these chores. Because the signals appearing at the interface—where the signals from the disk and the controller meet—are a function of the device that generates and uses them, the signal arrangement is peculiar to that device. Consequently, this connection scheme is called a *device-level interface*.

The modern interfaces require the disk drive to process the data stream from its read/write head using its own, built-in controller. The controller (the drive electronics) are integrated into the disk drive itself, hence the name integrated drive electronics (IDE). The processed signals are sent to the computer host in a more organized standard digital format as data bytes, rather than pulses. The interface then appears between the on-board disk controller and the host computer system. Because the signals are those normally used by the host system, the connection system scheme is termed a *system-level interface.*

The first of the two connection systems, the device-level interface, might also be distinguished as a low-level interface because of its intimate connection and the lower level of sophistication of its signals (much as a hardware-specific language like an assembler is a lower-level language). Correspondingly, a system-level interface also can be called a high-level interface.

Device-level interfaces were the first to be introduced for PCs, mostly by default. At the time the first hard disks were integrated with PCs the only drive standard available was the device-level interface called ST506. Pragmatic considerations made this device-level connection necessary. The electronics required for signal processing would not have fit on the drive mechanism using the technology available at the time. Moreover, because a device-level interface is essentially system independent, this connection choice enabled drive makers to maximize their market. Because the drives did not match any particular computer, they were equally adept (or inept) at working with any computer. Because there was no truly dominant personal computer standard before the first PC, the use of a device-level interface broadened the market for a disk maker's products.

In fact, the design effort in connecting a hard disk to the small computers was originally backwards from today's perspective. PCs, and their software in particular, were engineered to match hard disks. Consequently, PCs were tied tightly to device-level interfaces. Part of this heritage resulted in a system design in which some PC software takes direct control of the most intimate aspects of hard disk hardware. This software expects any hard disk drive (and its interface) to react in specific ways upon the software's command. For example, some software might examine the sector formatting bits on the disk by prying into the circuits of the disk controller. (Old copy-protection schemes, for example, worked in this way.) DOS itself was designed to best process disk information when it is delivered in the form that a device-level interface packages it.

Although the original ST506 disk interface was more than a match for the speed capabilities of the IBM XT and about equal to the performance of the original AT, faster computers raced far ahead of its capabilities to handle data. To cope with the demands for increased performance, the hard disk industry created ESDI, which is for the most part a better ST506.

The chief difference between ESDI and ST506 is performance, but the standard also encompasses a host of standardized design improvements. These include new commands and special reserved areas on the disk for storing setup parameters and bad track data. An ST506 connection was limited to a data transfer rate of five million bits per second, today's best ESDI hard disks can quadruple that.

ESDI drives cannot be interchanged with ST506 hard disks.

ESDI's ancestry is easy to see. ESDI drives use the same wiring system as do ST506 drives, the same connectors, the same pair of cables, and more. This ancestry, however, does not follow through with compatibility. ESDI drives cannot be interchanged with ST506 hard disks. Although the cables match, the signals do not; consequently, what may look like a simple upgrade is not. You will need a new EDSI disk controller to match the new drive.

As an intermediary upgrade step, however, ESDI no longer makes sense. For one very practical reason, the system-level interfaces are more reasonable choices as upgrades; they are inherently faster because they transfer information in parallel, eight (or more) bits at a time. Because the information is being moved out of the drive through a parallel connection, the actual operating frequency of the link can be lower for a given *throughput* (with eight data paths, for example, information need only travel at one-eighth the speed of a serial interface like ESDI to achieve the same throughput). Moreover, because the formatting information is sorted out in the data separator, this digital chaff need not waste the valuable bandwidth of the disk-to-PC connection. All device-level interfaces must move data serially because that is how the information is read from the disk read/write head. Moreover, extra baggage in the form of formatting signals must accompany the desired bits in the device-level signal, slowing the system further.

Device-level interfaces require the use of an external *hard disk controller,* typically an expansion board separate from the hard disk drive itself, to process their signals. Because the control functions are built into a drive that uses a system-level interface, no external controller is required. Instead, these interfaces use a *host adapter* board that may do little more than adapt one kind of connector to another.

Nearly simultaneous with the development of ESDI, disk companies began working on the first accepted system-level interface used with PCs, SCSI. Compared to ESDI, SCSI represented a complete rethinking of how peripherals should be attached to PCs. SCSI was designed to be more intelligent and more independent. For example, transfers can be made across a SCSI connection without the need for the host computer to control them. To bring this design to life, SCSI embodies an entire language of its own to its connection scheme. Because it is a higher level interface, it permits the connection of not just hard disks, but of almost any other device to a PC.

So far the most intriguing aspect of SCSI from a hard disk user's perspective is its performance. It has the potential to outrun both ST506 and ESDI, and a new revised version of SCSI—SCSI-2—includes options that give the interface far higher peak throughput possibilities than any existing drive mechanism. These options include Fast SCSI, which doubles the clock speed of the SCSI bus, pushing it up from 5 MHz to 10 MHz. Because basic SCSI is an 8-bit parallel interface, these speeds correspond to peak data transfer rates of 5M/sec and 10M/sec. Another SCSI-2 option is Wide SCSI, which broadens the 8-bit bus to 16 or 32 bits, potentially doubling or quadrupling the peak data transfer rate of the system to a maximum of 40M/sec. Should that not be sufficient for future systems, SCSI-3 is waiting in the wings.

In the past, SCSI has fallen short of being an ideal PC expansion standard for several reasons. PCs were not designed for hard disks with system-level interfaces; as a result, early SCSI host adapters took a performance hit in translating between SCSI and PC data formats. SCSI also was plagued by compatibility difficulties. Some SCSI systems do not work with some PCs. Worse yet, some SCSI products do not work with other SCSI products.

Some SCSI products do not work with other SCSI products.

The underlying problem was that much of the original SCSI design was optional. Manufacturers could choose to implement just a few, many, or all of its features. As a result, one SCSI product might have expected something that a second device was incapable of delivering. SCSI-2 helped solve this problem by making more of the SCSI command set mandatory. SCSI, however, is essentially a hardware standard, and it does not define all the software hooks required to control a variety of hardware devices through the connection. The details of implementation are left to the system designer. Because each designer tends to go in his own direction, different devices connected to a single SCSI host adapter may not operate; they just may not speak the same language.

Connecting multiple SCSI devices to a single SCSI host adapter is an invitation to multiple problems.

In theory, you can connect up to seven SCSI devices to a single SCSI host adapter; in reality, connecting multiple devices is an invitation to multiple problems. This difficulty, too, is being solved by the availability of "universal" SCSI software drivers. The pre-eminent set is Corel SCSI offered by Corel Designs, Montreal.

If you stick strictly with hard disks, SCSI is less problematic. The SCSI disk interface is well-designed and, contrary to popular opinion, can actually be easier to connect than any other interface— providing you ensure that your SCSI host adapter emulates a standard PC-style ST506 hard disk controller. This feature is usually termed *WD1002* emulation, which means that the host adapter emulates the standard Western Digital WD1002 ST506 hard disk controller.

The AT Attachment interface is the most recent addition to the PC disk connection family, and it is the only one designed around the PC standard. AT Attachment essentially is the ISA expansion bus slightly reworked (by eliminating unnecessary connections) for linking hard disk drives. AT Attachment combines higher speed with a design that is optimized to match with PCs that follow the IBM standard, building in the compatibility that is necessary for software that wants to take direct hardware control. Because it uses an 8-bit or 16-bit parallel data connection and operates at the same speed as the ISA expansion bus, AT Attachment can deliver data at exactly the same rate your PC can handle. Not all AT interface systems are equipped for 16-bit transfers, however. Even some 32-bit computers provide only 8-bit connections for AT Attachment drives.

Disk Controllers and Host Adapters Issues

One of the most important considerations when adding a hard disk to your PC is that you have something to plug the disk into. With ST506 and ESDI drives, the place to plug in is the disk controller. With SCSI and AT Attachment (and other IDE) drives, you plug into a host adapter. In any case, you are dealing with more than a mere connector. Each of these links to your system has its own particular design features that you need to consider.

If you do not plan on upgrading to a drive that uses a different interface than the hard disk currently in your PC (for example, simply to increase the storage capacity of your system), your only controller concern is making the match. That is, the new drive must use the same interface as your existing controller (or host adapter). After you have made the match, you should be able to plug the new drive in without altering the rest of your system.

If you plan to upgrade your controller along with your hard disk, however, you have more issues to think about, such as your system's floppy disk drives. From a brief period (from the introduction of the AT in 1984 to the introduction of the PS/2 series in 1987) IBM combined floppy and hard disk control functions on a single expansion board. Many compatible computer makers have continued to do so until today. If you plan on replacing the hard disk controller in such a PC, you need to get a controller or host adapter that also includes floppy disk circuitry—or you will have to buy and add a separate floppy disk controller. Not all hard disk controllers or host adapters have floppy disk control circuitry built in, so be careful when you shop.

Not all hard disk controllers or host adapters have floppy disk control circuitry built in, so be careful when you shop.

Also, match the expansion bus connection of the controller or host adapter to your PC. That is, the kind of expansion slot the controller or host adapter plugs into. If you have an old, 8-bit system, you need an 8-bit controller. Classic AT-bus computers should get 16-bit controllers. And EISA and Micro Channel computers need controllers and host adapters that match their advanced circuitry *if* you want to get the best possible performance. (Many EISA systems get by with simple 16-bit ISA host adapters.) The best choice today is, of course, a host adapter with a local bus connection, either VL Bus or PCI. Local buses assure that your system suffers no bus-imposed throughput bottlenecks.

Beyond these common concerns for all disk interfaces, controllers and host adapters for each of the various disk interfaces add their own particular match-up and buying concerns. Each of the popular hard disk interface raises its own particular issue that you must consider when searching out the best product with which to build your upgrade. The following sections look at the most important of these considerations for the different varieties of controllers and host adapters.

ST506 Controllers

The archaic ST506 interface is something to upgrade from and not to. But there are still some compelling reasons to consider ST506 systems and thus their controllers. First is the goodbye syndrome. Because ST506 technology is waving its last farewell, you can find some intriguingly good buys available on the market. Pore through the advertising in the backs of magazines, and you find a wonderland of aging, obsolete products at prices that make yesterday's technologies finally make sense. Drives that once cost $500 can now be found for $50. If you are not mesmerized by performance numbers and are looking for nothing more than good, safe storage ST506 certainly deserves consideration.

The archaic ST506 interface is something to upgrade from and not to.

There is another reason to consider the ST506—it may be exactly what your PC wants. If you have an older AT-class computer that already has a hard disk controller (for example, you want to upgrade to a bigger drive or add a second drive to your system for more capacity), you probably need to buy an ST506 drive to match the controller. Certainly you can upgrade the controller at the same time to advance to a newer interface, but then you will have to put your old disk to pasture or struggle to try to make two unmatched controllers work in the same PC. It can be done, but you can pound nails into your head, too. Whether either is a good idea depends only on how much suffering you are willing to endure. Trying to get disk controllers to cohabitate is enough to make grown programmers weep. Besides, in an AT-class PC you do not stand much to gain from the higher transfer rates of newer interfaces. Buying into new technology will be paying for performance you can see.

Most ST506 hard disk controllers can handle two drives, and in most cases those drives can have different capacities. Old ST506 controllers are an exception. For example, ST506s in the original IBM XT work only with 10M hard disks. Others were designed for particular disk drive units and match only those. In such circumstances, a new drive may require a new controller.

Another worry is when you acquire a large ST506 drive that you want to add to your old, generally agreeable controller. Many vintage ST506 controllers do not understand hard disks that have more than 1024 cylinders or tracks. While that omission is understandable (the PC BIOS does not allow for more cylinders), it can mean wasted space on your hard disk. Cylinders capable of storing extra megabytes may be available on your hard disk yet inaccessible to your controller. To get the full value from your purchase of a larger hard disk, you may need to buy a more up-to-date controller. That is not necessarily bad—you may gain some other benefits such as caching at the same time—but you will have to add the price of the controller to that of the hard disk to calculate the true cost of your upgrade.

All ST506 controllers are not created equally. Hard disk drives that use device-level interfaces never look at the actual pattern of digital code that is being scribbled on their surfaces. The information coding process is carried out by the controller, which means that the controller could use any pattern it wants to represent data. It could, for example, use 10110101 to signify a single bit of data. Certainly that code is inefficient, but the example does show the extent of freedom that a disk controller designer has.

The ST506 standard does not specify what code is to be used for storing data. In fact, a new generation of hard disk controllers has been designed to use a code that is more efficient, allowing more data to be packed on a given disk.

The standard form of data coding used by most ST506 disks is called Modified Frequency Modulation (MFM), which specifies that data can be transferred between the disk drive and its controller at a rate of five million bits per second (5 MHz). Each bit of data is coded as the presence or absence of a flux transition on the disk.

You do not need to know what MFM means. All that is important is that MFM is actually the *least* dense way that information is coded and stored on hard disks today. Therefore, hard disk drives that use the ST506 interface and MFM data coding store less information in a given area and transfer data more slowly than any other current drive technology.

RLL Controllers

Many (but hardly all) ST506 drives also can use a more advanced form of data coding called 2,7 *Run Length Limited* coding or RLL for short. This is a special modulation method that allows information to be packed 50 percent denser on the hard disk surface. Because 50% more data passes under the read/write head with every spin, RLL increases the peak data transfer rate of ST506 hard disks by 50 percent to 7.5 MHz. It also increases the capacity of a given disk drive by 50 percent. An advanced form of RLL, cleverly termed Advanced RLL (ARRL) coding, puts 100 percent more data on a given disk.

To use RLL in your PC, you need an *RLL controller* and a hard disk controller specifically designed to use RLL. You cannot just reprogram your ordinary controller to use RLL because the data coding is set by the actual controller hardware. Most disk controller makers that still offer ST506 products also offer RLL controllers. Note that an RLL controller that has both floppy and hard disk functions uses

RLL only for the hard disk. If you used RLL for floppies (which you cannot), you could not read distribution disks or exchange floppies you make with other people.

To use RLL in your PC, you need an RLL controller and a hard disk controller specifically designed to use RLL.

Although the data coding used by a system is determined by the disk controller (which actually does the translation), you must also be certain to get an RLL-certified disk to match the controller. RLL demands disks with wider-bandwidth electronics and better-quality magnetic media. Disks that are not RLL certified may work initially with RLL controllers but may gradually or catastrophically lose data. On the other hand, RLL-certified disks do work with ordinary MFM coding without a problem.

The issue of RLL also raises one caveat when shopping for hard disks. Of the few RLL-compatible ST506 disks still being sold, vendors often list only the RLL capacity of RLL-certified drives. This is a misleading practice because it can distort the available storage you might expect to get if you do not hook the drive to an RLL controller. When ordering an ST506 hard disk, be sure to ask whether the drive is RLL-certified and whether the listed capacity is with MFM or RLL data coding.

Data coding is not a concern with other hard disk interfaces. The ESDI standard specifies the data coding to be used, so with an ESDI drive you do not have to worry about such mismatches. With system-level interfaces (AT Attachment and SCSI), data coding is irrelevant because neither you nor your PC ever see the raw signals on the disk.

Just as ordinary ST506 systems are archaic, so are RLL systems. Although RLL yields some improvements in speed and capacity over ST506, the concept is essentially obsolete as an individual product. The technology, however, remains important. Hidden deep inside most AT interface and SCSI drives you will find RLL (or more likely, Advanced RLL) data coding.

ESDI Controllers

If you plan on upgrading to a larger drive, be sure that the controller you choose can handle it.

The issues in selecting an ESDI controller are much the same as selecting one that uses the ST506 standard. Most ESDI controllers handle two drives, and for the most part, they are insensitive to drive capacity. However, as with ST506, some early ESDI controllers were incapable of handling drives with more than 1024 cylinders. If you plan on upgrading to a larger drive, be sure that the controller you choose can handle it.

While you do not have to worry about data coding, with an ESDI hard disk, you do face another issue: matching the transfer rates of disk and the controller. Not all ESDI hard disks transfer information at the same speed. The first ESDI drives moved data at ten million bits per second. Later generations of equipment upped that speed to 15, then 20 MHz.

Your ESDI controller must be capable of operating at least as fast as your drive does if you want to get all the performance that you pay for. If you opt for a 15 MHz ESDI hard disk, you need a controller rated to transfer data at 15 MHz or higher. A higher-speed controller—for example 20 MHz—will work, too, but it will not increase the transfer rate of the slower drive. If you do use a higher-speed controller with a slower EDSI drive, you certainly pay for performance that you do not need, but you will also be hedging against the future should you later want to upgrade to a still faster hard disk.

Match speed ratings of ESDI drives and controllers.

The general rule is to match speed ratings of ESDI drives and controllers. Otherwise, the slower component will limit the maximum transfer rate of the entire system.

AT Interface Host Adapters

Because the control electronics of AT interface hard disks are built into the drive mechanism itself, these devices need no separate disk controller that you would have to plug into an expansion slot of your PC. But you cannot plug one of these drives into a slot even if you could find a way to physically squeeze it in. The AT interface still requires you use some kind of host adapter—either an expension board or circuitry built into your PC's motherboard—to match them to your PC's expansion bus. Such a host adapter is often substantially less expensive than a true disk controller, although high performance host adapters can demand a price premium.

Under the AT Attachment IDE standard, up to two hard disks can be connected to a single host adapter. One drive is described as the Master; the other, the Slave. Ordinarily the master does not control the slave. The terms are just a convenience for distinguishing the two drives, better perhaps than calling them Drive 0 and Drive 1.

All new drives that follow the AT Attachment standard can be interconnected in the master-slave relationship, two drives per AT interface circuit.

New on the market are AT Attachment host adapters that enable you to connect up to four hard disk drives. These use clever subterfuge. Each has an on-board BIOS that substitutes for the code built into an ordinary AT Attachment system. This code has no effect on the first two drives you connect to the host adapter but takes over for one of the last two drives. It substitutes new addresses for accessing the last two drives, sidestepping communications problems. The last two drives then act as a second master-slave pair, independent of the first two.

Today, all new drives that follow the AT Attachment standard can be interconnected in the master-slave relationship, two drives per AT interface circuit (four-drive host adapters have two distinct AT interface circuits). But this cooperation does not hold true for all AT interface hard disks. Early units were particular about any other drives that might be connected to them. Typically, an AT Attachment drive from one manufacturer would refuse to share a host adapter with a drive from a different manufacturer. Note that this is a characteristic of the drives and not the host adapter. All host adapters deliver essentially the same signals to one- or two-drive systems. Incompatibilities limiting expansion on the host adapter arise between the drives, the drive-to-drive connection not in the host adapter-to-drive link.

If you are buying a second AT interface drive for your PC, this lack of compatibility between older hard disk can be an important issue. About the only way to be absolutely sure a second drive will work with your existing drive is to duplicate what you already have. The next best choice is to get a second drive from the same manufacturer as your first.

Fortunately, there is no need to resort to this strategy if your system is less than about four years old. With current products, compatibility between the products of different manufacturers is no longer an issue. Any AT interface drive old enough to suffer compatibility problems is likely to be so slow and low in capacity you would not want to consider it as an upgrade.

SCSI Host Adapters

The job of an SCSI host adapter is much more complex than that of other host adapters and controllers because SCSI effectively functions as an expansion bus in its own right. Moreover, SCSI was not particularly tailored for PCs; rather, it was designed as a universal interface, one that serves not only different computer architectures but also a variety of peripherals, from hard disks to scanners and operating systems. The SCSI host adapter must match the signals designed for its universal bus to the particular requirements of the PC bus and DOS. The required translation is more challenging than the work required of other controllers and host adapters because

SCSI structures information in the form of blocks and DOS thinks in terms of clusters. Other interfaces work directly with DOS and clusters.

The translation capabilities of the host adapter imposes a limit on transfer speed of SCSI systems. This limit can be either above or below the inherent speed limit imposed by the design of an SCSI hard disk. Consequently, the performance of an SCSI host adapter is as important or more important than the speed of the hard disk it is connected to. Early SCSI host adapters choked on the conversion process, and system throughput suffered. In the last few years, however, the efficiency of SCSI systems has improved immeasurably. When you shop for an SCSI host adapter, look for newer products. Although old, laggardly host adapters may turn up occasionally, they can impose a drastic performance penalty on your SCSI hard disk and your PC.

Besides performance issues, your choice of SCSI host adapter will determine whether and how any hard disk you connect to it can boot your PC. Some host adapters have on-board BIOSs with boot capabilities (though this potential may be limited on one of the many devices attached to the SCSI adapter). Older SCSI host adapters often have no booting potentials. If you need to boot from an SCSI disk, be sure the host adapter you buy has this capability.

If you need to boot from an SCSI disk, be sure the host adapter you buy has this capability.

SCSI host adapter choice also will determine your flexibility in assigning device identifications and priorities to the peripherals you attach to it. Some host adapters require that your boot drive have a particular SCSI identification. Others boot from any device connected to the SCSI host adapter. Although it is normally no trouble to assign an SCSI hard disk to the identification number that is predesigned to boot the host PC, the ability to easily change boot assignments can make your life easier (particularly if you have multiple hard disks set up with different operating systems).

The use of blocks rather than clusters as storage units in SCSI devices also has its benefits. It isolates your system from the details of disk data. Your PC simply does not care about the physical configuration of the disk or its data storage format. As with new AT interface drives, drive manufacturers are free to use any exotic drive geometry and data coding they want. You simply do not have to worry about what is going on inside the drive.

One of the greatest promises of SCSI is its capability to serve as a high-speed, universal interface. Its design allows up to seven

One of the greatest promises of SCSI is its capability to serve as a high-speed, universal interface.

The SCSI host adapters shipped with CD-ROM players are some of the most sluggish available.

disparate devices to be connected to a single host adapter. Already SCSI-based CD-ROM, magneto-optical rewritable optical disk, tape drives, and scanners are available in addition to hard disks.

Most of these peripherals come equipped with their own host adapters, so you may have to squeeze three or more SCSI host adapters into your PC. That may seem wasteful, because it is. You may be tempted to try to connect all of your SCSI devices to one host adapter. In theory, you should be able to, but in reality you cannot. SCSI host adapters differ widely in performance. The SCSI host adapters shipped with CD-ROM players are some of the most sluggish available. They handicap most anything else you plug into them. If you are going to try to plug every SCSI device into one host adapter, use the one that accompanied the highest-performance SCSI device you have—generally your hard disk drive.

Software compatibility is a major issue with SCSI host adapters and drives. Two major SCSI software standards have appeared for PCs. These include ASPI (Advanced SCSI Programming Interface), originally created by Adaptec and now has the widest industry support, and CAM (Common Access Method), the work of an industry committee (which includes Adaptec) that has yet to gain momentum. A few vendors follow neither standard.

CAM-compliant SCSI host adapters have on-board BIOSs that link with your operating system. Programs written to take advantage of CAM can then make requests to your operating system and have them carried out by the appropriate SCSI device. Unfortunately, DOS is not currently CAM-compliant, although OS/2 versions 2.0 and later are.

ASPI uses a layered approach to the software interface using driver software. Programs communicate and send commands to SCSI devices through an individual software driver for each device. An overall ASPI driver links the individual device drivers to the SCSI system hardware. The BIOS on an ASPI-compliant host adapter merely provides fundamental services that establish the link with the ASPI driver.

In general, this BIOS gives you WD1002 emulation, which means it lets you connect one or two SCSI hard disks to the host adapter, and without further ado or drivers the first SCSI disk is able to boot your system as drive C: and the second as drive D:. Under ASPI, that is about as far as the BIOS support goes, and without the loading software drivers, your system cannot recognize further hard disks or other SCSI devices.

To completely set up an ASPI system, you must install all the required device drivers in your PC's CONFIG.SYS file. You will have to install the ASPI driver when you install your host adapter and install a driver for each SCSI device you connect (except the first two hard disks). Because the device-specific software drivers need the ASPI driver to link to the SCSI system, you should ensure that the ASPI driver entry precedes that of other SCSI device drivers in your PC's CONFIG.SYS file.

ASPI and CAM products do not readily mix, although some developers are working on software to bridge the two systems together. If you have ASPI and CAM products in one PC, it is still often the best idea to install two SCSI host adapters, one for each standard.

Caching Controllers

At the top of the line for most hard disk controller and host adapter manufacturers are the *caching controllers*. These are specialized devices that do more than just match a drive to your PC. In addition, they incorporate a large block of RAM, often megabytes, as a hardware disk cache to make the connected hard disk drives appear faster.

A disk cache works like a memory cache. Information once read from your disk is stored in the cache so that if it is ever needed again, it can be retrieved at the fastest possible speed. Some caching systems actually make your hard disk read more data from your disk than your computer wants, anticipating that your PC and its programs will want what comes next on the disk. The memory used by the cache can be located in any of three places: on the drive itself, on the drive controller or host adapter, or in your system's RAM.

The on-disk cache holds several advantages. It is easy to install and use—just plug in the drive and everything is already in place. The on-disk cache also is designed to perfectly match the drive. The on-disk cache, however, suffers two drawbacks: Most on-disk caches are small, and if your hard disk drive does not have an on-disk cache, you don't have an on-disk cache.

A caching controller or host adapter adds a memory-based buffer with intelligent control electronics to the board that adapts your hard disk's signals to your PC. Board-based disk caches hold several advantages. They work with any drive with a compatible interface. Their dedicated electronics are fast and steal no time from your PC's

You pay a big premium for the extra memory and control circuitry on the board-based disk cache.

microprocessor. The memory in the board-based disk cache is not drawn from your PC's endowment or even its range of accessible addresses. However, this form of caching can be expensive. You pay a big premium for the extra memory and control circuitry on the board-based disk cache.

In many systems, a software disk cache can be as, or more, effective than a hardware caching controller or host adapter. The software cache buffers not only the connection between disk and host adapter but also the bottleneck imposed by the bus connection between the host adapter and your PC. But the software cache takes some of your PC's microprocessor bandwidth during disk operations and robs your system of some of its RAM.

The most effective cache is the hardware disk cache linked to your PC through a local bus connection. With such a system you gain the reduced overhead of the hardware disk cache and still minimize the bus throughput bottleneck. In any case, more memory—megabytes of it—will make either form of cache quicker. The bigger the cache, the more likely disk-based data can be duplicated in the cache. (If a cache were as large as your hard disk, all of the disk's data would be in RAM and there would never be a miss!) More is better but, of course, more costly, too.

Caching control-lers are for people who want the ultimate in disk performance and are prepared to pay a premium price for it.

Buying a caching controller is much the same as with any other disk controller. You need to match the interface used by the controller with that of the hard disk you want to use: ST506, ESDI, IDE (AT Attachment), or SCSI. At one time, hardware caching host adapters exhibited compatibility problems with some disk utility software that required direct hardware control. Although these problems have essentially been eliminated with current host adapters and software, be careful if you have older disk utility software.

Capacity Issues

You should be willing to change interfaces should you find a large drive with a particularly attractive cost per megabyte.

Capacity and host adapter choice are often related issues in choosing a hard disk for an upgrade. Most often, you will want to decide on a host adapter first. (Sometimes the decision is already made for you by the equipment that is inside your PC.) You want to get a disk that matches the interface available. But if your goal is solely to add storage capacity to your system, it often pays to keep an open mind about the disk interface. You should be willing to change interfaces should you find a large drive with a particularly attractive cost per megabyte.

When capacity is your motivation for upgrading your hard disk, the proper place to begin is by considering how much hard disk you need. After all, if the primary reason you are making an upgrade is that your present drive is too small, you should have some idea of what size is adequate.

Odds are that if you had your druthers, you would rather have the largest possible hard disk. Even when you plan for the future, so called spare disk space can disappear at a surprising rate. What once was a generous amount of disk space can become niggardly indeed. Imagine trying to make do with the 10M that came standard in an XT or the 20M IBM originally packed in an AT. Those capacities are becoming impossible to find today except as special-purpose products—removables, hard disk cards, and laptop drives. Today's top-selling hard disks average from 100 to 200M, and the most sought-after size soon will reach from 300 to 500M. If you have a real need for hard disk storage space, you can find drives with a gigabyte or more that fit into a 3 1/2-inch drive bay.

With capacity the primary tradeoff is price. Larger drives cost more, but as capacities increase, the cost per megabyte of storage falls. If you are just counting bytes and not trying to match a budget, a drive with greater capacity is a better buy. It is also likely to be faster because the largest drives are top-of-the-line products on which manufacturers concentrate their development efforts.

Even if you disregard the huge prices demanded for the most capacious hard disks, you have one good reason for not buying a huge hard disk. You might not want to "put all your eggs in one basket" and opt for a pair of smaller drives instead. Putting half a gigabyte of your most important data on a single hard disk is an invitation to disaster. If you keep regular backups, you might not lose everything with a head crash, but your hands will be tied until you can get the disk repaired. Spread what you have across two disks and make your most important files redundant, then you will be better able to weather such emergencies.

Going a step further, in a two-drive system you could use one drive to backup the other. This is now an accepted strategy in networking and deserves consideration even in single-user applications when your time is more valuable than the often-minimal expense of a second hard disk.

As the capacities of hard disks have increased, the drives themselves also have become physically smaller. Just a few years ago, the physical size of a disk drive determined how much it held and how much storage capacity you could stuff into your system. Today, the disk drive manufacturers have increased the density of data that can be written to a disk to the extent that 3 1/2-inch drives hold more than 5 1/4-inch units used to. Readily available 3 1/2-inch drives, which fit in all but the smallest of laptop computers, can hold 2000M—more than you need for anything but a high powered workstation.

Performance Issues

Getting more performance from your system is another reason to upgrade your hard disk. In some cases, a faster drive can make more of an improvement than adding any other accelerator to your system. And the difference is more tangible. When you press a key, your computer will react more quickly to your wishes—loading programs, listing directories, carrying out simple DOS commands with noticeably less hesitation.

By accepting a slower drive, you acknowledge that your time is not so valuable.

For many people, speed is more than an issue of hard disk performance; it is also a measure of technical savvy—on the part of the designer and manufacturer of equipment and the buyer. In these days in which technical breakthroughs strike like lightning, the newer, better machinery is always faster. Moreover, PC elitist see buying anything other than the fastest products as an admission of your inferiority. By accepting a slower drive, you acknowledge that your time is not so valuable.

Do not buy performance that you cannot measure.

Actually, there is some truth to those contentions. But that does not mean that you absolutely need the fastest hard disk in all situations and inside every PC. The better strategy is to find one with performance that matches your needs. Do not buy performance that you cannot measure.

Access Time

The speed factor that determines the response of a hard disk is called *average access time*, a self-explanatory name. This term refers to the average time it takes the drive to find or access any given byte stored on the disk (usually expressed in milliseconds). A disk with an average access time of 15 ms can locate a given block of data in about 15 ms, with the actual time stretching from instantly to about 30 ms. The average access time is the speed you will find listed in nearly every advertisement you can find in computer magazines. The lower the figure, the faster the drive.

The average access time is more than just a measurement of how snappy your disk responds; it also determines how quickly the drive can perform when it must gather a lot of data that is dispersed across the disk (as in sorting through a data base).

In the past, computer power users worried over what kind of head actuator their disk drive used. The head actuator is the mechanism that moves the read/write head. The speed of the read/write head determines the average access time. In today's hard disk market, you do not have to worry about such details. The speed of all head actuators has improved; besides, when you are interested in performance it does not matter how the head gets where it is going as long as it gets there—fast. If a disk delivers a faster average access time, it will be more responsive no matter what technology it uses.

One good reason not to worry about head actuator technology is that there is not a lot of difference between better drive mechanisms anymore. To get speed ratings below the 28 milliseconds expected in today's marketplace (as well as squeeze more data into a smaller drive), manufacturers have had to refine their mechanisms and choose the better technology: servo-controlled head actuators. Certainly there are differences of quality between mechanisms, but the average access speed that they deliver is one of the best indications you have of that quality.

Any hard disk with an average access time greater than 28 ms cannot be considered state of the art, and the dividing line is quickly slipping down to 20 ms. In fast 386- and 486-based PCs, you probably want a hard disk drive that has an average access time of 15 ms or less.

If you want to upgrade an older PC, you might not need all that speed. You can find some older hard disks at bargain prices on the direct market. To match the performance of one of these vintage drives to your PC, you need to know how much speed you need. The answer depends on what kind of PC you have, on what kind of controller you have, on what software strategies you are willing to adopt, and on what you expect.

Some guidelines can be drawn from the drives that IBM has offered with its products. For example, the hard disk of the original XT was rated at an average access time of 80 ms (and often delivered performance closer to 100 ms). The AT got a hard disk rated at 40 ms to match its 8 MHz 286 microprocessor. The 386-based PS/2 Model 70 got a 28 ms drive, and the 486-based Model 90 got a 16 ms hard disk. If you match the microprocessor in your PC with a hard disk at the speed chosen by IBM you will get performance that

If a disk delivers a faster average access time, it will be more responsive no matter what technology it uses.

In fast 386- and 486-based PCs, you probably want a hard disk drive that has an average access time of 15 ms or less.

is somewhere between satisfactory and the minimum that is acceptable. On the other hand, a faster drive will not hurt anything if you do not mind paying for it.

That is not to say that you should never attach a slower drive to your Pentium PC. Because they are older and more rare, slower drives are less expensive. That price advantage makes slow drives useful in many circumstances. For example, if you want to use a second hard drive as a backup system, a slower drive may be an excellent choice. And if you go through dollars faster than bytes, a slower drive may be the best you can afford—any hard disk drive is usually better than none.

A faster hard disk often responds quicker regardless of whether you have a disk cache installed.

Hardware and software disk caching help minimize the differences in hard disk performance. But no cache helps the first access to a file. Consequently, a faster hard disk often responds quicker regardless of whether you have a disk cache installed.

Data Transfer Rate

If you need to process information, finding a byte is not enough. You also must be able to move it from disk storage into your computer's memory, where it can be worked upon. Therefore, average access time in itself is only half of the speed story. Another measurement, the *data transfer rate*, tells the rest: how quickly a hard disk drive can move information into memory. Customarily, the data transfer rate of a hard disk drive is reported in megahertz.

A drive with a higher peak rate will likely operate faster than one with a low rate and will thus be more desirable.

The data transfer rate, which is most often quoted for hard disk drives, may be the most misleading figure in the computer world. The number that is universally published is the peak transfer rate, the fastest that information can possibly move if nothing stands in its way. The path is never so clear, however, and the actual transfer rate that a hard disk can achieve when moving real data rarely approaches even half the peak rate. Nevertheless, the peak data transfer rate is useful as a relative figure. A drive with a higher peak rate will likely operate faster than one with a low rate and will thus be more desirable.

For most hard disk systems, the peak transfer rate is governed by two factors, how fast the disk spins and how tightly information is packed on the disk. Disk makers are pushing up spin speeds and squeezing information tighter to gain more transfer performance. But other constraints make the ultimate transfer rate of the complete disk system. For example, the disk interface you choose may affect system throughput.

Today's drives have transfer rates higher than ever before. But most of the figures you see for disk transfer times are misleading. Many advertisements include only the rated transfer rate of the disk interface. For example, an SCSI drive may boast a 5M/sec or 10M/sec data transfer rate. Those numbers describe the peak speed that a single byte (or at most, a few bytes) can be passed through the disk interface. Those figures do not in any way indicate how quickly information can be continually read from the disk. The actual throughput from a disk is much lower, but the interface can nevertheless influence actual disk throughput because of other overhead it imposes. Because the potential transfer rate through one of the modern disk interfaces (SCSI or the AT interface) is much higher than the speed at which information actually can be read from the disk, the interface would appear not to constrain disk throughput. Actual testing, however, reveals that interface choice can result in substantial throughput differences. For example, disk mechanisms coupled to a host system under SCSI proved twice as fast as AT interface systems in testing. Although some of the difference might be attributable to the individual interface implementations, such results do imply that SCSI is a better high-performance choice for top-of-the-line PCs.

Not all personal computers need the high transfer rate performance of one of the newer high performance disk interfaces. Older, slower computers cannot deal with the data supplied by a hard disk with a fast interface, so added performance would be wasted on them. However, most modern PCs—those based on 486 microprocessors—benefit from a faster disk system. If you are seeking the highest system throughput, you need the quickest hard disk drive available.

If you are seeking the highest system throughput, you need the quickest hard disk drive available.

In most cases, an AT interface will deliver acceptable performance. The interface will not slow the responsiveness of the hard disk (which is controlled by interface-independent access time), and the difference in disk throughput will be masked by other system overhead. However, if you use your PC for disk-intensive operations, it can benefit from a fast SCSI disk system.

Drive Size and Form Factor

Matching the size of a drive to your PC can be more important than matching its capacity. After all, you can still work with a hard disk that is somewhat over (or under) the storage capacity you need. If a drive is too large to fit inside your PC, connecting it may be more than troublesome.

Today, a large capacity hard disk can be small indeed. The latest gigabyte-level hard disks fit neatly into a 3 1/2-inch form factor; half-gigabyte drives are typically only one inch high. Drives fitting a new 2 1/2-inch form factor now hold 120M and more. Although this size drive is not popular for desktop PCs (it is the centerpiece of most laptop PCs), it may find a role as computer downsizing trims space allowed for drive bays.

The only advantage older, larger drives hold over today's tiny units is price. Oftentimes you can find big drives priced lower than more compact units with the same capacity as older models near the end of their lives. If you have the space for them, there is no performance or capacity reason to look down on king-size drives. Most were flagship products at the time they were first introduced.

The only advantage older, larger drives hold over today's tiny units is price.

Beware that big drives tend to be old drives—old in data of design and manufacture. And that is not good. Although some people correlate size and reliability, do not be misled. The latest, tiny hard disks are built using the newest semiconductor technologies—surface mount components, application-specific integrated circuits (ASICs), and very large scale integration (VLSI)—which reduces the number of parts in the electronics of a hard disk to a handful. The fewer components, the less there is to go wrong—and the more reliable the drive can be. Some new drives have rated times between failures from 30 to 50 times longer than first generation hard disks. Some products sport MTBF (Mean Time Between Failures) firgures of 500,000 hours—that's 57 years!

In addition, a small drive has the laws of physics on its side. Because all the parts of a tiny hard disk are smaller, they have less inertia when they move. Today's small drives are simply quicker than even the best big drives of days of old. Moreover, today's small drives are less likely to rattle themselves to death as they operate. Their smaller, lighter-weight heads are also less apt to destroy their disk media should they crash.

Although moving a hard disk outside your PC's case enables you to use a big, cheap old drive, it does not eliminate all issues of drive expansion. Even though you can find external chassis in which to mount an expansion hard disk, making your own external drive system is not easy. Most of today's hard disk controllers make no provision for external cables, so you will have to find your own way of getting control signals out of your PC. Worse, the cables themselves can be hard to get. Although there are many ready sources of supply for internal hard disk cables, vendors of those for external hard disk drives are rare.

Laptop and notebook PCs make size constraints an insurmountable issue, but one that you do not have to worry about. Most laptop and notebook PCs are designed with proprietary hard disks (if they have hard disks at all). The only products that match a particular make and model of laptop PCs are those offered by the computer's maker. Most notebook PCs are not even field-upgradable, so there is no reason to look in the aftermarket for new hard disks.

Most notebook PCs are not even field-upgradable.

Hard Disk Cards

When you install a new hard disk you may wish you had three hands. Balancing the hard disk in its drive bay with one hand, while holding a mounting screw in place with the other, and twisting a screwdriver can be tricky. While there is no easy way to acquire three hands, there is another alternative: the hard disk card.

A hard disk card is a clever idea. It combines a miniature disk drive with the expansion board that is needed to control its operation and to adapt it to a PC slot. The entire assembly slides into an ordinary expansion slot like any other expansion board.

This system has several virtues. The hard disk card is easier to install: it plugs in as easily as any expansion board and does not require extra hands to wrestle the drive and its cables into place. The hard disk card also saves a drive bay. If your computer does not have an extra bay for adding a new disk drive, the disk card still enables you to add up to 120M to your system's storage. Moreover, because the controller and disk drive are sold together as a single assembly, you do not have to worry about matching them; an engineer has already done that for you.

The thinnest, fastest, and best integrated hard disk cards are made by Quantum Corporation.

The thinnest, fastest, and best integrated hard disk cards are made by Quantum Corporation. (This situation is certain to continue, because the company has a patent on putting hard disks in single expansion slots.) The product embodying this technology is called the HardCard.

The original model of this product line was the first trend setting disk that fit into an expansion slot. With each generation (HardCards are currently on their third) the Plus drives have gained more capacity and speed. In regards to performance, they are within their capacity ranges equal to any drive that you can fit into a bay today.

The price of the convenience and bay-saving capacity of the HardCard line is the cost. You will generally pay more for such a slotable hard disk card than for a unit you install in a disk bay.

A number of companies have developed their own versions of hard disk cards by matching 2 1/2-inch and 3 1/2-inch disk drives to short controller cards so that they, too, will fit into your system's expansion slots. Typically, however, these packages are two slots thick, robbing your PC of its valuable expansion room. Although they lack the sleekness of a true HardCard, they can be effective, bay-saving storage add-ons for your system. But these more generic hard disk cards are readily available and relatively inexpensive, typically costing little more than a drive and its associated controller or host adapter.

The same considerations that apply to buying a hard disk card apply to purchasing any hard disk: You need to match the capacity and speed of the drive to your needs and budget. More importantly, you must have the right kind of space available inside your system to accommodate the drive. Some hard disk cards require 16-bit slots, some work in 8-bit slots. Others have particular requirements on which expansion slots they will fit into in particular computer models.

Should you want to buy a hard disk card from a mail-order supplier, describe exactly the slots in your system that you have available to accommodate it. Some hard disk cards are made to overflow slots behind the power supply in your system; others steal a bit of extra space from the left-hand side of the expansion area. Make sure it will fit before you waste your time and money.

Hard Disk Arrays

When shopping for a new computer, a term you are sure to run into is *drive array*. Although hard disk manufacturers continue to improve the capacity and throughput of their products, the gains are modest, matters of refinement rather than breakthrough. Drive arrays, on the other hand, can deliver massive improvement—and do so immediately. However, they are currently so costly and pack so much capacity that you are unlikely to need one with a single-user system. The technology, however, is working its way into the mainstream.

The premise of the drive array is elementary: Combine a number of individual hard disks to create a massive virtual system. But a drive array is more than several hard disks connected to a single controller.

In an array, the drives are coordinated, and the specially-designed controller allocates information between them. The spin of each drive in the array is synchronized, and any single data byte may be spread among several physical hard disks.

The obvious benefit is capacity. Two disks can hold more than one, and four more than two. Drive array technology can also accelerate mass store performance and increase reliability. The secret to both of these innovations is the way the various hard disks in the drive array are combined. They are not arranged in a serial list where the second drive takes over after the capacity of the first is completely used up. Instead, every byte of data is split between drives. For example, in a four-drive system, two bits of every byte might come from the first hard disk, the next two bits from the second drive, and so on. The four drives could then pour a single byte into the data stream four times faster; moving all the information in the byte would only take as long as it would for a single drive to move two bits.

Drive array technology can also accelerate mass store performance and increase reliability.

Sacrificing part of the potential speed and capacity of the drive array can yield greater reliability, even in *fault-tolerant* systems. The key is redundancy. Instead of a straight division of the bits of each byte the array stores, the information split between the drives can overlap. For example, in the four-drive system instead of each drive getting two bits of each byte, each drive might store four. The first drive would take the first four bits of a given byte, the second drive the third, fourth, fifth and sixth bits; the third, the fifth, sixth, seventh, and eighth; the fourth, the seventh, eighth, first, and second. The overlap allows the correct information to be pulled from another drive when one encounters an error. Better yet, if any single hard disk should fail, all of the data it stored could be reconstituted from the other drives.

This kind of system is said to be fault-tolerant: a single error or failure does not shut down the entire system. Fault-tolerant drive arrays are extremely valuable in network applications because the crash of a single hard disk does not bring down the network. A massive equipment failure thus becomes more of a bother than a disaster.

The example array represents the most primitive of drive array implementations. Advanced information coding methods allow higher efficiencies in storage, so a strict duplication of every bit is not required. Moreover, advanced drive arrays even allow a failed drive to be replaced and the data that was stored upon it reconstructed without interrupting the normal operation of the array. A network server with such a drive array would not have to be shut down even for disk repairs.

Just connecting four drives to an SCSI controller will not create a drive array. An array requires special electronics to handle the digital coding and control of the individual drives. The electronics of these systems are proprietary to their manufacturers. The array controller then connects to your PC through a proprietary or standard interface. SCSI is becoming the top choice.

Drive arrays are invariably external boxes that plug into your PC like external hard disks. For all intents and purposes, your PC considers the entire array to be just one uniquely blessed hard disk drive. Such drive arrays are typically bought as plug-in systems. Upgrading your PC with one means nothing more than installing a host adapter and a cable. Although you could create your own drive array, the need to match controller to drives makes the matter more than most folks want to deal with.

Reliability Issues

Reliability means many things when referring to a hard disk drive. Most important, a reliable drive is one from which you can read your data whenever you want to. One that does not deliver data on demand does not belong in your PC— or any computer.

A reliable drive is one from which you can read your data whenever you want to.

The gremlins, goblins, and glitches that can interfere with the smooth transfer of your data are many and arise from diverse sources. Some problems are purely electrical in nature. Something could go awry with the electronics of your drive, preventing it from processing data, garbling what is found, or fouling the operation of the mechanism by failing to issue the proper commands. The mechanical parts of the drive can also break. The motor may stop spinning, a head can come loose, connectors can separate. The media itself can even suffer the ravages of time, simply by self-erasing or by becoming physically flaky.

Looking at a drive might seem to tell little about its long-term prospects. However, you can get a good idea from weighing a product in your hand and carefully examining it. Moreover, knowing a bit about the technology can lead you to products that are inherently more reliable.

The most general guideline to the reliability of a hard disk drive is the MTBF figure given in its specification sheet.

The most general guideline to the reliability of a hard disk drive is the MTBF figure given in its specification sheet. The "mean time between failures" of the product may sound precise, but it is less than it seems. No drive is guaranteed to run trouble-free for the entire period given for its MTBF rating.

An indication of the inaccuracy of the MTBF is the disk warranty. Although a given drive may last more than 50 years under the most continuous use possible according to its MTBF, it is likely to be backed only by a five-year warranty. Such a manufacturer obviously does not put much faith in MTBF, and neither should you.

Remember that MTBF is only a calculated value. After all, how can a manufacturer hang a 50-year rating on a product that has been on the market only for a few weeks? To determine MTBF, the drive maker looks at each individual component that goes into making the drive, takes the published life expectancies of each one, and mathematically combines these values to achieve a number, the MTBF. In theory, this figure should be a reasonable representation of what you should expect from your hard disk drive, but there are so many variables that the MTBF figure does not take into account that it is no assurance that your drive will actually run halfway through the next century without difficulty.

Yet the MTBF has some relevance, because the factors going into it do influence drive life. For example, the fewer, more reliable parts a drive has, the higher the MTBF. Or, the less there is to go wrong, the less-likely something will go wrong.

Even if you are not privy to the manufacturer's specification sheet, you can still see potential differences in reliability that parallel MTBF. A drive that is covered with printed circuit boards is likely to be less reliable than one that has a few square inches of circuitry. Compare a vintage drive, some of which have three boards arrayed around them, to a recent 3 1/2-inch product. You could count the chips on the new drive but could do little better than guess at the component count on the old unit.

Common sense can sometimes be misleading. A big, hefty, sturdy drive would seem to be built to last longer than a flyweight laptop unit. That is not necessarily the case. Old drives had to be big because of the state of technology when they were designed, thus storage densities limited miniaturization. Physically large drives required robust mechanisms to get anywhere near acceptable speed. Jerking a heavy head mechanism around requires powerful components. Feel an old full-height hard disk in operation. Some can make a whole PC hop around like Mexican jumping beans on a sizzling afternoon when they sort a database. You might expect something to rattle loose, and inevitably it will. Consequently, there is no particular reliability reason to favor a full-height drive (5 1/4-inch) over a half-height (3 1/2-inch) or smaller unit.

No drive is guaranteed to run trouble-free for the entire period given for its MTBF rating.

In the developing days of hard disks, there were several features that improved a products long-term prospects that were worth looking for. Among these were hard, plated disk media instead of softer oxide-coated platters and an automatic park-and-lock mechanism that assured a drive would not crash when it was turned off or moved. If you are buying a drive with an older design through a mail-order service, check for these features. Newer drives almost universally make these features standard equipment.

Although the potential for disk head crashes has not been eliminated, newer drives are much less likely to suffer from them. Miniaturization is a primary reason. To achieve the high data-densities needed for packing hundreds of megabytes into a laptop-size package, drive makers have been forced to more exotic recording media. These sputtered and plated magnetic surfaces are inevitably harder than more conventional, lower density recording compounds. In addition, as the drive mechanism is reduced in size, its mass decreases, cutting the momentum of a crashing head and reducing its destructive force. Finally, so many people complained about disk disasters that drive makers had to listen. Park-and-lock style mechanisms in which the read/write heads automatically retract when the drive shuts down have become a standard feature of most hard disks. Unlike days gone by, no single disk model is particularly prone to head crashes any more.

There is one value that is more misleading than the MTBF number: MTTR (the mean time to repair). Typically this figure is 15 to 30 minutes. Even at the $75 to $100 per hour computer service people charge, that would seem to make hard disk repairs amazingly affordable. Actually, however, the MTTR number is better read as "mean time to replace"—simply how long it takes to pull your old drive out and shove in a new one. To estimate the cost of fixing your PC after a disk failure, add the price of a new disk to the labor charge for pulling out your old drive and sliding in a new one.

Buying a Hard Disk Drive

The reliability of your vendor is one of the most important issues when buying a hard disk. Given enough time—and you will want to use your hard disk drive as long as possible—something is bound to go wrong. It is, therefore, necessary to know what to do when the inevitable sneaks up on you. You need to know who you can call for help, what kind of help you will get under the warranty terms of your drive, and what to do when you discover that your warranty has run out long before your luck.

Choosing a Vendor

Most hard disk makers require you to travel to the dealer, so when reliability is your concern, where you buy your disk is more an issue than how it is made. You should shop for a vendor as critically as you shop for the drive. Check the vendors' policies in regards to the big initial headaches: incompatibility with your system and dead-on-arrival drives. The vendor should allow you to return the failed product without delay or charge.

The vendor should allow you to return the failed product without delay or charge.

If you tell the dealer what kind of computer you intend to install the drive in (and what host adapter or controller you are going to use, if you do not buy one with the drive), by law the dealer is obligated to stand behind your success in getting it to work. The dealer telling you that a drive will work in a particular situation creates a warranty of fitness for a particular purpose, which gives you certain rights under the terms of the Uniform Commercial Code. With an uncooperative company, enforcing those rights may be more trouble than it is worth, so it pays to find a company that stands behind what it sells.

Although the hard disk manufacturer is not your first line of defense against failure, it can be a good backup. Low-ball hard disk vendors often go out of business, which means that you can be left with no one to turn to when your hard disk crashes. If you are worried about such possibilities, choose a drive manufacturer who will offer some help. The quality and availablility of manufacturer-based assistance varies widely—from complete toll-free telephone support to the get-someone-else-to-do-it philosophy. See what is offered before you commit to a particular manufacturer's product; you may save yourself a headache later.

See what is offered before you commit to a particular manufacturer's product; you may save yourself a headache later.

Evaluating Costs

Finding out the actual cost of a hard disk can be challenging. The hard disk prices you see in some advertisements may be only part of what you will end up paying for a new drive for your PC. Remember, a working hard disk is a complete system, but disk vendors often

To calculate the actual cost of upgrading your hard disk, you must also consider the cost of the rest of the disk drive system.

list the price of only the drive part of the system. To calculate the actual cost of upgrading your hard disk, you must also consider the cost of the rest of the disk drive system.

Typically, a hard disk drive is sold simply as a mechanism—exactly as it came out of the factory. You get a box, unopened and uninspected throughout its journey from factory to your doorstep. You do not get any of the necessary equipment for connecting the drive to your PC, either.

The first thing a raw drive needs is a way to connect, or put simply, cables. While some PCs come with the cables they need for connecting a hard disk, do not count on it. Check to see what your PC offers before you order a disk.

If you are upgrading to a new disk interface, odds are you need new cables. The lack of extra cables built into your PC is a pardonable sin on the part of your computer maker. After all, the manufacturer of your PC has no way of knowing what obscure things you might plug in. But do not forgive a disk vendor who slights you on cables. He should know that you need cables and should, therefore, include them in what he sells. If the vendor does not do so, do not forget to add cabling costs into the price of the raw drives.

Move to a new interface or add a much larger drive, and you are likely to face an additional charge.

But cables are no good by themselves. In general, that means a disk controller or host adapter. If you are simply adding a second drive of the same type to your PC, you might not need a new controller or host adapter. Move to a new interface or add a much larger drive, however, and you are likely to face an additional charge.

Many of today's latest PCs have built-in support for IDE hard disks. Older machines require a host adapter board that may add $20 to 50 to the total cost of the system.

AT Interface Hard Disks

Adding a second AT interface hard disk is more problematic if your system or the prospective drive predates the AT Attachment standard. Under such circumstances, your ability to connect a second drive depends on the hard disk drives themselves, not the host adapter. With first generation AT interface drives, there is no guarantee that two drives will work with one another, particularly if they are made by different manufacturers. Check AT interface drive compatibility before you buy if you have an older PC or are looking at an older, smaller drive (roughly 40M of storage). If your PC is less than three or four years old and the drive you want to buy is of a reasonable capacity (say 100M or more) you should not have to worry about inter-drive AT interface compatibility.

SCSI

With SCSI you also need to factor a host adapter into the purchase price. But, you probably want to be critical about the host adapter you acquire. If you are particularly worried about compatibility— something that is becoming less of an issue with each new generation of host adapter and drives—you can assure yourself of getting a working drive system by buying a matched host adapter from the same source as your hard disk.

If your system already has an SCSI adapter, you might think you can get away without adding another SCSI host adapter (after all, an SCSI host adapter can handle seven devices). However, each SCSI device you hook onto a host adapter increases the potential for incompatibilities. Unless you choose an SCSI drive that matches the software standard of the one already attached to your SCSI host adapter, you may run into compatibility headaches.

You may be better off getting a new host adapter. Chances are you will even get better performance, as host adapter performance standards have gone up in the last couple of years. The best choice is a host adapter with WD1002 emulation, so you will not have to worry about software drivers when connecting your first two hard disks.

Software Issues

Software is also an issue when it comes to pricing hard disk drives. Depending on your PC and DOS version, you may absolutely need a hard disk preparation program for larger hard disks. If you plan to connect non-disk devices to your SCSI host adapter, you will need SCSI software to make the match.

Many PCs do not have drive tables that support all available hard disks that use the ST506, ESDI, and AT interface standards; that is, the drive parameters listed in the setup programs for most PCs do not list all possible or available arrangements of heads and cylinders.

If you plan to connect non-disk devices to your SCSI host adapter, you will need SCSI software to make the match.

Many modern PCs have a special setup entry for user-defined disk parameters (typically drive type 47). If you acquire a drive that does not match parameters available in your system and your PC does not offer a user-configured drive type, you face two choices: Either give up some capacity and opt for a listed value that is close but smaller, or use a proprietary program to match the drive to your PC.

The latter strategy offers two important benefits. It enables you to put more of the disk capacity for which you paid to work, and it can allow greater flexibility in configuring your drive. You can partition the disk in a greater number of ways, even with multiple operating systems.

But straying from the officially sanctioned setup procedure can lead to problems later on. In particular, proprietary setup programs may be incompatible with some software, such as operating environments that try to take lower-level or direct control of your system's hardware. In addition, you may have to pay extra for the proprietary setup software, another thing to factor into the price of the new hard disk.

Of course, that price often buys you more than a way to exploit the full capacity of your hard disk. The proprietary setup programs often include disk formatting, optimization, and diagnostic utilities. These side benefits by themselves may be worth the price of the setup program.

Upgrade Method

Before you begin to install a hard disk upgrade, take three preparatory steps: back up your old hard disk, reconfigure your system's setup memory, then remove your old hard disk from your computer.

Backing up can be the most time-consuming part and, unless you have or can borrow a tape drive, requires a big stack of floppy disks. If you do not have any special backup software, use the DOS BACKUP program, or to play things safe, use XCOPY instead.

If you have an AT or more recent computer that is configured using a setup program, configure your system for your new hard disk before you remove your old hard disk. This eliminates the lengthy wait and error message that inevitably pops up when you switch drives without telling your PC.

To configure your system, run its setup program either from disk or by pressing the appropriate keys, whichever way your computer accesses its setup utility.

If you are planning on using an automatic setup program such as On Track Computer System's Disk Manager or Storage Dimensions SpeedStor, check the program's instructions for the proper hard disk type for which to set your system. If you do not plan on using proprietary software, change the hard disk listed in setup to match the parameters of your new drive (or the one that most closely matches it without exceeding its capacity, head or cylinder count) unless you are changing controllers. In the latter case, check to see what parameters the new controller requires. Some disk controllers—particularly SCSI systems—require you to set your system to think that it has no hard disks.

After you save your new configuration, turn off your PC and disconnect all cables from it. This is a safety step that ensures that no stray electrical currents can get into your computer and harm its circuits (or you) during your installation. It also will give you greater freedom in installing your drive should you need to cant your system unit to get at a hidden screw—or should you need to turn your PC upside down and shake it to retrieve a loose screw. (You will only want to shake your computer after you have removed your old disk and before you have installed a new one. Never violently shake your computer when it has a hard disk inside it.)

Remove your hard disk by first unscrewing all the hardware that holds it in place. Even after the screws are out, the drive's cables will hold the drive loosely in place. You will be able to shift the drive a bit, which will make disconnecting its cables easier.

If you are going to upgrade to a new hard disk that uses the same interface and controller as the old one, only disconnect the cables from the drive itself. Leave them attached to the controller. If you are replacing both drive and controller, you can safely remove both ends of the cables.

Finally, remove the hard disk from your PC. You also must remove the old controller if you are going to replace it.

Mechanical Installation

The easiest part of upgrading your hard disk is physically installing the drive in your computer. All the work is mechanical, and what you have to do is obvious. You can put a screwdriver to work and almost put your mind on hold.

The most complex issue is determining the means by which your drive should be secured to your computer's chassis. This should become obvious when you remove your old hard disk.

A number of mounting schemes are used by various computer makers. The most straightforward is the direct mounting scheme used by the IBM XT and a wide number of compatible manufacturers. The drive is directly screwed into the disk bay using either of the sets of screw holes on the sides or bottom of 5 1/4-inch and 3 1/2-inch drives. Although some PCs use only two screws on one side of a drive to hold it in place, one-side mounting usually is not very secure. The original 10M IBM XT, for example, hides a third screw that fits into the bottom of its hard disk. Do not overlook this screw when removing your old hard disk from your XT or when you install an upgrade.

IBM introduced a new, more secure mounting scheme in the AT, and many compatible manufacturers use the same scheme or a variation on it. In the AT, mounting rails are attached to the sides of the drive that enable you to slide it into place. The rails fit into guide slots that hold the drive assembly securely on both sides. Many hard disks come with AT mounting kits or with the rails already installed on the sides of the drive.

Some AT-compatibles—notably Compaq Deskpros—use a similar mounting scheme with slightly wider rails that are incompatible with standard AT rails and the AT chassis. If you have one of these machines or a similar computer, you either have to reuse the old rails from your old drive in your new drive or attempt to get new rails to match your computer.

Another variety of AT-compatibles use drive-mounting rails that are narrower and, thus, incompatible with IBM rails. Most machines that use these narrow rails pre-install a set in each drive bay of the computer, even those without drives. In this case, you only need detach the rails from the chassis, screw them to your disk, and slide the disk into place.

Rails are held in the computer chassis in one of two ways. IBM-style systems use small brackets that push the rails to the end of their travel in the bay. Some compatibles make the brackets part of the drive rails. In either case, one screw holds each bracket in place. Just unscrew to slide the old drive out and screw the bracket back in to hold your drive upgrade in place.

Tower-style IBM PS/2s are the same width as those used in the AT, so AT rails will work in their internal 5 1/4-inch drive cages. To loosen a drive in one of these computers so that you can slide it out of the chassis, press down on each of the large blue daisy-like knobs above the drive and turn it counter-clockwise with the palm of your hand until the drive can be slid out.

Desktop PS/2s use plastic sleds to hold their 3 1/2-inch drives. The drive screws into the sled using the screw holes in its bottom, then the sled slides into place. A plastic tab at the end of the sled locks the whole assembly in place. To remove one of these drives, press down the wide tab under and at the front of the drive, then slide the sled forward.

In most systems, you will find it is easier to plug the cables into your new hard disk upgrade after you have put the drive near its final position but not secured it into place. For example, in ATs, slide the drive part way back into its bay, connect the cables, then slide the drive all the way back and screw the rail brackets into place.

If you need to install a new disk controller or host adapter, you can put it into an expansion slot before or after you have installed your hard disk. The best slot to use is the one closest to the hard disk bay that has a connector that matches the one on the bottom of the controller.

For example, ensure that a 16-bit controller is installed in a 16-bit expansion slot. Similarly, 32-bit Micro Channel controllers should only be installed in 32-bit expansion slots, and EISA controllers should only be installed in EISA expansion slots.

Cable Connections

The interface your hard disk upgrade uses determines the number and kind of cables you will have to connect. In most cases, you will need to connect two or three cables to your upgraded hard disk. Figure 7.1 illustrates some of the types of cables there are to connect.

All drives require a power connection, the white nylon modular connector at the end of the set of four wires (sometimes three) that emerge from your computer's power supply. You cannot make a mistake plugging in this connector; two of its beveled corners prevent you from doing so.

The only difficulty you may encounter with a drive power connector is the great effort that is sometimes required to push the connector into its jack. Try to put a finger or thumb under the jack when you push the connector in so you do not unduly stress the circuit board on the disk drive.

Figure 7.1

ST506 and ESDI hard disks use two cables in addition to a power connector. Each drive gets its own signal cable (narrow cable in illustration), and two drives daisy-chain to a control cable (wide cable).

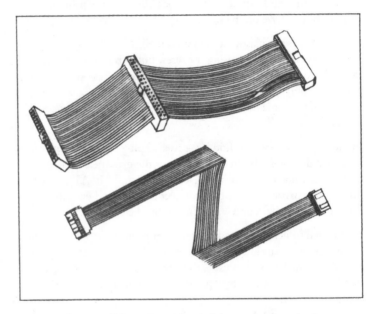

Some modern small form factor hard disks use miniaturized power connectors. If your PC does not have a matching connector, you will need an adapter cable. These are available from direct vendors for less than $5.

ST506 and ESDI hard disks require two additional cables: a wide, flat control cable and a narrow, flat data cable. In theory, the connectors on these cables are keyed to prevent you from attaching them improperly. A thin plastic tab inside the cable connector fits into a slot cut in the edge connector on the disk drive. On the controller end, one of the holes in the cable connector is usually plugged and the corresponding pin on the controller connector is missing.

Sometimes, the plastic key or the plug is absent from a connector. Although putting a connector in backwards should not harm your new drive or its controller, it will prevent the drive from working. You can avoid such mistakes by ensuring that the (usually red) stripe on the edge of each cable is on the same side as the slot in the edge connector on the drive. The stripe also corresponds to the side of the connector that mates with pin one on the connector on the controller. Pin one is usually marked with a silk-screened number.

Each ST506 or ESDI drive in a computer requires an independent data cable run to a separate connector on the disk controller. When upgrading a drive, be sure that you connect the data cable to the same connector that the old drive was attached to. In most cases, J4 on the controller connects to the first disk drive (see fig. 7.2) in your computer (drive C:); connect J3 to the second drive (D:)

Control cables are daisy-chained, that is, a single cable attaches to the disk controller and has two additional connectors to accommodate two disk drives. In the IBM system, the first hard disk (C:) gets attached to the connector at the end of the cable (the one nearest the twisted section of the cable); the second drive (D:) attaches to the connector in the middle of the cable. If there are two twists in the cable—one on either side of a connector—that connector goes to the first drive.

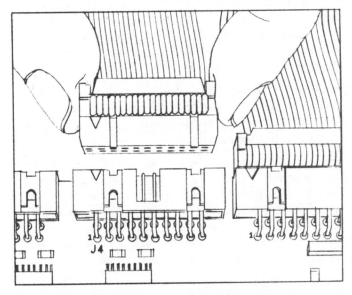

Figure 7.2
Connecting a data cable to the J4 outlet. In most cases, J4s on ST506 and ESDI controllers provide signals for the C: drive.

For this system to work properly, each hard disk in your system should have its drive select jumpers or switches set to indicate that it is the second hard disk in your system. On most hard disks, you will find a set of jumpers or switches labeled DS0 to DS3, DS1 to DS4, or something similar. The correct setting is the second in the series. That is, use DS1 when the labels start with DS0; DS2 when the counting starts with DS1.

AT interface drives require only a single cable in addition to the power connector. Just plug one end into the system board or host adapter board and the other into the drive. If the connectors on the cable are not keyed, make sure that the (usually) red stripe on the cable is nearest pin one on the adapter and hard disk connectors.

In systems that accommodate two AT interface drives, the two are daisy-chained together. Either drive can be connected to either cable connector—a switch or jumper on each drive determines whether it will operate as either the first or second hard disk. You will have to refer to the drive's instruction manual to find the proper settings.

Under the AT interface specification, the first drive in the chain— the Master—becomes drive C:, and the second drive—the Slave—acts as drive D: Be sure to check that only one drive is set as Master and only one as Slave; otherwise, both drives will try to operate at the same time and produce drive errors. (If you have only one drive, it must be configured as the Master.) Every manufacturer uses his own method (and often, nomenclature) for setting Master and Slave status. Check the instruction sheet accompanying your drive to determine the proper settings.

Internal SCSI drives use a simple daisy-chain cable but add several complexities. Again, you must be sure the colored stripe at the edge of the cable aligns with pin one on the drive, host adapter, or other device connector when plugging in.

The first and last device in an SCSI chain must also be terminated. (The host adapter is usually considered the first device.) On most SCSI disk drives, you will find a row of three terminating resistors packs. If the SCSI hard disk is not the last in the daisy-chain, remove all three of these resistor packs. More recent drives have termination switches or jumpers. Turning the termination switches off is the same thing as removing termination resistor packs.

Each device in the SCSI chain must be assigned its own, unique SCSI identification number, zero through seven. The host adapter is invariably assigned a value of seven. Most SCSI host adapters require you to set the boot disk in your system to a particular value (usually zero). The boot drive is then recognized as drive C:. These host adapters require the second hard disk to be set with an ID of one, which is then recognized as drive D:. On the other hand, IBM often sets its SCSI boot drive as device six. Check your host adapter owners' manual if you have any doubt about the best SCSI ID number to assign your hard disk. And check your hard disk drive manual to determine how to set its SCSI identification and which value to use.

You can connect up to seven devices to a single SCSI host adapter, all of which can be hard disk drives. However, no SCSI host adapter automatically recognizes all seven disks. Most only know how to find two hard disk drives (as devices 0 and 1). All the others require software drivers to be recognized.

Using ASPI software for your SCSI system—which is the most common system among PCs—you will need to install in your PC's CONFIG.SYS file a device driver for the SCSI host adapter and one or more drivers for the hard disks. Some host adapters may require individual drivers for each hard disk. With some software, every device that is not a hard disk will require a separate driver. Other SCSI programs use a single drive for all devices. Check your SCSI software manual. Although host adapters with WD1002 emulation will recognize your first two drives without the installation of driver software, you should nevertheless install the software drivers to prevent future surprises.

To properly reinstall your drive, slide it part of the way into its bay. With the drive still loose, plug in its cables. Be sure the red or blue stripe on ST506 and ESDI cables goes to the side of the drive connector closest to the notch in the connector. Power connectors (see fig. 7.3) have two beveled edges, so you cannot insert them improperly.

After you have all the connectors plugged in, slide the drive all the way back into its bay, and screw it into place. With AT-style systems, small metal brackets (see fig. 7.4) hold the drive rails in the bay.

Figure 7.3
Installing the
upgraded hard drive.

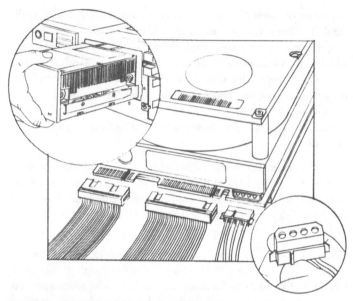

Software Setup

Figure 7.4
Completing installa-
tion of the upgraded
hard drive.

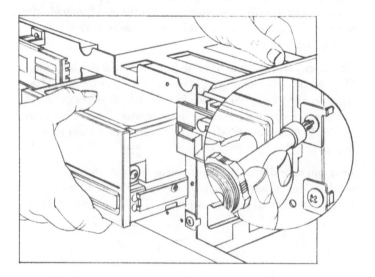

After your hard disk upgrade is physically installed, you face the challenge of software setup. This process involves several steps: matching the new drive to your computer, low-level formatting the drive, partitioning the drive for DOS, DOS formatting the drive, and restoring your file backups to the drive.

The easiest way to get through these steps is to use proprietary disk installation software. One of these programs, which is often supplied with hard disks sold for upgrades, automatically handles all the necessary installation steps except restoring your files to your new disk. Their step-by-step prompted menu systems need little explanation.

The easiest way to get through these steps is to use proprietary disk installation software.

System Configuration

If you do not have automatic installation software, you should have configured your system to accept your new hard disk before you removed the old drive. If you did not, run your system's setup procedure and make sure the hard disk parameters listed there match those the drive manufacturer lists for the model of hard disk you have installed or that your disk controller requires. Check the number of heads, cylinders, and sectors of your hard disk, and match those numbers to the listing in the setup disk chart. If you cannot make an exact match, get as close as possible, with the numbers listed in your PC being lower than the actual configuration of your drive. In most cases a drive with 12 heads will work if you set up your system as if it had 11 but not if you set it up for 13. You may lose capacity but you will make up for your loss with compatibility.

Many newer AT interface drives now offer a feature called automatic translation mode. Thanks to a microprocessor in the disk drive electronics, the drive can determine what configuration hard disk your system expects and adjust accordingly (within the limitations of the drive's capacity, of course). Your system is isolated from the actual layout of heads and cylinders on the drive and only can see the logical configuration the drive wants your PC to know about. You still have to specify a number of heads, cylinders, and sectors. But as long as the indicated values produce a capacity within the range the drive can handle, the drive will operate properly.

The isolation of the physical format of the drive from what your PC sees has another important implication. It allows the drive maker to use any geometry he pleases, free from the BIOS and DOS restrictions on disk architecture. For example, DOS does not understand disks with greater than 1024 cylinders. Most AT interface drives have excess cylinders that are translated to a value within the range of your PC.

Most AT interface drives are limited to 512M capacity because that is the maximum configuration most PCs support. It corresponds to 1024 cylinders with 16 heads and 64 sectors of 512 bytes each. This is a system limit but most drive makers do not exceed it so that they have the largest possible market for their products. However, some drive makers now offer larger hard disks. For example, the one-gigabyte Micropolis 2112 drive is available with the AT interface. To avoid the system limit, Micropolis provides special setup software and a hardware option that allows the drive to act as if it were two separate 512K drives.

SCSI hard disks do not suffer these limitations. In most cases, when installing an SCSI hard disk you should set your system configuration to indicate that the SCSI drive is not present. That is, if the only drive in your PC is SCSI, indicate that you have zero hard disks. The BIOS on the SCSI host adapter gives your system the information it needs to operate the hard disk without other configuration information. The BIOS actually reads the hard disk you have attached to the host adapter and relays its parameters to your PC. Consequently, if you follow the SCSI rules for termination and ID number, you can plug an SCSI hard disk into your PC without the need for other setup. You can pull out one SCSI drive and substitute another, different drive without altering your PC's setup.

Low-Level Formatting

The next step is low-level formatting. This requires a special program, not the FORMAT utility that is part of DOS. Drive vendors usually supply such a program if it is necessary—and if you ask for it. You do not need one if you have a PS/2, a compatible that includes a low-level formatting utility with DOS, a controller or host adapter with the procedure built in, or a PC with a BIOS with built-in hard disk utilities (such as the AMI BIOS).

IBM's formatting program is hidden on the Reference Disk that is included with all PS/2 models. To access it, press the Ctrl-A two-key combination at the main setup menu you see after you boot up from the Reference Disk.

The low-level formatting program included with DOS by IBM-compatible computer manufacturers is typically called LLFORMAT, HDINIT, HDPREP or some other obscure name. Consult your MS DOS manual to find out the magic word.

Many PCs now have hard disk utilities built into their BIOSs. You can access these functions by selecting normal system setup, then hard disk utilities. Often the low-level format procedure is called *disk initialization.* Choose the function from the menu and follow the on-screen instructions.

Most new disk controllers and many SCSI host adapters include a low-level formatting utility as part of their ROM BIOS. (Not all SCSI host adapters have format utilities in their BIOSs; most AT interface host adapters lack BIOSs entirely, so they do not have built-in formatting utilities.) Running these utilities is easy once you know the trick. First you must run the DOS DEBUG utility. After DEBUG loads, you will see a new prompt on the screen, a simple flashing hyphen. In general, typing G=C800:5 or G=C800:6 then pressing Enter starts the program with most popular disk controllers. But these numbers may be different if you have more than one disk controller in your PC, and they may vary with different manufacturers' host adapters.

Which of these two commands to use depends on the perversities of the controller manufacturer. You can be sure only by checking with the (often indecipherable) instructions accompanying the controller. You also can try both commands. If you give the wrong instruction, your system will lock up or crash. Simply reboot (you probably will have to switch off your system and start it over again) and try again with a different value.

If none of these low-level formatting options are available to you, you will need to get a special program to accomplish the chore. Most disk diagnostics packages include the necessary utility along with their other performance enhancing options.

Generally, the makers of AT interface hard disks advise that their products *never* need to be low-level formatted. The format is set forever at the factory. Trying a conventional low-level formatting utility with one of these drives only emulates a true low-level format. In most cases, you will not do any damage. In fact, try it and you are likely to find that the data on the disk will not even be disturbed by the emulated format. According to drive makers, there is no need to low-level format these drives. Although early AT interface drives did demonstrate problems that might have been repaired by low-level formatting, most newer drives do not suffer such problems. The lack of need for low-level formatting is thus a blessing and not a detriment.

When you low-level format a disk, you often must choose a disk interleave. Some formatting utilities test your drive for optimum transfer rate and suggest the best value. In other cases, you can select a default or guess what is best.

With today's latest SCSI and AT interface drives, an interleave of 1:1 is nearly always the best choice. The same holds true for ESDI drives with track buffering. Only old technology drives require a higher interleave. Fast PCs—anything better than a 16 MHz 386SX—and hard disks without full track buffering usually work best at 2:1 interleaving. Only if you have a very old drive and very old PC will you want a higher figure. The IBM XT uses 6:1 interleaving, the AT, 3:1.

Disk Partitioning

All disks require partitioning to be used by DOS. The partitioning program sets up markers on the disk so that your operating system knows how large the disk is and how to read its features.

Partitioning is ordinarily handled by the DOS FDISK program. Different partitioning options are available under the various versions of DOS. You will find it is a good idea to upgrade to a more recent version of DOS when you upgrade your hard disk so you can take advantage of the latest partitioning options.

Upgrade to a more recent version of DOS when you upgrade your hard disk so that you can take advantage of the latest partitioning options.

In any case, you will want at least DOS 3.3, which allows you to install multiple DOS partitions on your hard disk. With DOS 3.3 you will have to divide any disk larger than 33M into at least two partitions. You will also be limited to virtual drives no larger than 33M. DOS 4.01 allows you to partition most drives as a single, large disk or to subdivide them into virtual drives of whatever size you like.

DOS 5 and DOS 6 allow you to create up to four disk partitions with up to 512M in each. Most SCSI host adapters allow you to create even larger partitions, often a gigabyte or more, skirting the DOS limits.

The choice of partition size has a major effect on disk storage. DOS provides for a limited number of disk storage units called clusters. DOS versions since 4.0 allow for a maximum of 65,536 clusters in any given partition. To handle larger partitions requires that the size of each cluster be increased. For partitions up to 128M, DOS makes each cluster 2K long; for each doubling of capacity above that, DOS doubles the cluster size so that a 512M partition uses 8K clusters. Partitions between 128M and 256M use 4K clusters; those between 256M and 512M use 8K clusters.

Generally, smaller clusters are better when you have many files because DOS requires every file to occupy disk space in multiples of clusters. The smallest file or subdirectory requires one cluster of storage no matter its size. And, on the average, every file wastes half a cluster. When you have multiple files, larger clusters waste more space. Keeping clusters small maximizes the storage you have available. Note that DOS begins to use 4K clusters with a 128M partition size, so to maximize storage make your partitions just under 128M.

If your disk is fragmented, smaller clusters can slow performance, because reading individual files may require more head movement—up to four times more. Your disk's read/write head might need to move between four times more clusters to read any given file. You can avoid this slowdown by regularly defragmenting your hard disk.

DOS Formatting

The final step in disk preparation is DOS formatting, which only requires running the DOS FORMAT program for each of the virtual drives created by your upgrade hard disk. Choose the /S option for the drive C: disk.

Restoring Files

After your new hard disk is fully configured and formatted, you can restore all the files from your old hard disk back to it. If you have had some hardware experience, you can speed up this step by first installing your new hard disk as a second drive without first removing the drive you want to replace. Use XCOPY with the /S option to copy all the files from your old disk to the new one. Then remove your old disk from the system and reconfigure your new disk as the first drive.

Not counting the waiting time—the ordeal of backing up, formatting, and restoring—you can probably install a hard disk upgrade in less time than it took to read this chapter. That is certainly quicker than it takes to achieve unlimited wealth and weight loss. And you'll reward yourself with something nearly as valuable—more storage capacity and speed for your PC.

8

Cartridge Disk Drives

Faith is trusting your most treasured possessions to a sealed black box filled with machinery you don't understand. Write your data to a hard disk, and that's exactly what you're doing. Your faith can be misplaced as easily as your data—except that on a hard disk, your data also could be stolen, erased, corrupted, or locked outside the reach of those who need it.

Removable cartridge drives help you keep your faith *and* your data safe. Instead of leaving your files hermetically sealed in a disk drive, the removable cartridge enables you to lock everything away for security, make backups of every byte that's important to you, or mail megabytes of files anywhere a courier dares to tread. Removable cartridge drives also push the mass storage capacity of your PC up to infinity. Fill up one cartridge, and you only need to slide in another. Removable mass storage enables you to archive and exchange hundreds of megabytes of files at a time.

Some cartridge drives are better used for specific purposes, and others can substitute for a traditional hard disk. Upgrading with any adds versatility to your PC.

For the last several years, you've had a choice of three very different technologies that can put your data directly onto removable disk cartridges:

- Purely magnetic drives, the offspring of conventional hard disks

- Optically enhanced magnetic (magneto-optical) drives, which sacrifice some speed for higher data densities and cartridge capacities

- Purely optical write-once drives, which produce permanent
  records of the data you send to them

Although these three designs work on different recording principles,
they produce the same result: your information is encapsulated on a
disk inside a plastic cartridge that you can hold in your hand or hide
under your pillow.

Cartridge disk systems have several advantages over other types of
mass storage:

- *Convenience.* You can take your files anywhere you go without
  having to lug your PC around. Data cartridges are smaller and
  lighter than the tiniest notebook PC and store more information.

- *Exchange.* Some cartridge disk systems have become standards
  in their own right. They can be a top choice when you have to
  send large files to outside parties. For example, service bureaus
  that make presentation slides and prepare color separations
  and typesetting usually accept files stored on SyQuest disk
  cartridges.

- *Capacity.* A cartridge disk system's storage capacity is limited
  not by the drive but by the number of cartridges you acquire.
  When you run out of storage space, you buy a new cartridge,
  not an entirely new drive. On the other hand, the entire
  capacity of your cartridge system is not on-line. Only one
  cartridge fits in a drive, so you have access to only one
  cartridge at a time. Of course, you can always add two or more
  drives to your PC, but the maximum single file size that the
  system can handle is limited to the size of one cartridge.

- *Cost.* When you need to store hundreds of megabytes,
  cartridge storage becomes quite affordable. Although removable media drives generally cost more (often substantially
  more) than non-removable media drives, the cost per megabyte of additional cartridges is much lower than adding
  non-removable storage. The more cartridges you add, the
  greater the savings.

- *Speed.* Tape cartridges have many of the same advantages of
  cartridge disks, but they lack the access speed of disk-based
  media. To find any given file, most tape systems must scan a
  full length of tape, often taking 30 seconds or more. Cartridge
  disk media are random access and can find a given file in
  milliseconds; some approach the speed of conventional hard

disks. Consequently, these systems can substitute as primary storage in a pinch. In fact, you can use a cartridge disk in lieu of a conventional hard disk if you don't mind losing an iota of access speed.

- *Security.* You can remove your vital files from your PC and put them out of harm's way. If you deal with confidential information, you can lock it up or at least remove it from the place where it's most likely to be taken—your PC.

For reasons known only to God and PC marketers, removable cartridge drives are available in just two capacity classes: around 100M (a range of 88M to 150M) and 650M and up (to about one gigabyte). Each range gives you a choice of two technologies. The smaller-capacity cartridges rely on either pure magnetic or magneto-optical technology. The high-capacity cartridges use either magneto-optical or pure optical technologies. The former enables reading and writing of the disks as often as you want. The latter is generally uneraseable—you can write data only once, although reading it is not limited in any way.

Magnetic Cartridge Drives

On the surface, magnetic cartridge technology appears to be little more than a conventional hard disk, except that the cartridge sets the traditional disk platter free to venture off into the world.

In actuality, the resemblance between cartridge drives and traditional hard disks is only superficial. Both have rotating media with a read/write head that moves radially across the disk surface, and both record data as a series of flux transitions in a magnetic medium. But that's about it.

Although nearly all hard drives have multiple platters to increase their capacity, magnetic cartridge drives have only a single platter to keep the cartridges compact and simplify the drive mechanisms. Although the hard disk designer goes to great lengths to exclude contamination from within and around the platters, the cartridge designer knows the task is hopeless and designs his products instead to withstand normal contamination. Where the hard disk designer seeks speed above all else except capacity, the cartridge designer pays more attention to robustness and reliability.

Technical Background

Engineers have created two very different technologies for removable cartridge drives: the Bernoulli Boxes made by Iomega Corporation and the removable cartridge Winchester disk drives manufactured by SyQuest Technology. Although the two systems are based on designs as dissimilar as ravens and writing desks, their capacities and capabilities are parallel.

SyQuest uses conventional magnetic hard disk technology, and Iomega turns traditional designs on their head. The SyQuest mechanism is based on ordinary Winchester hard disk principles, differing chiefly by using special actuator and mechanical design.

SyQuest drives trace their heritage back to the first Winchester hard disks developed at IBM's Hursley Lab. Like all Winchester hard disks, the SyQuest units use lightweight read/write heads that "fly" above and below the surface of the inflexible (thus "hard") disk platter. The head is held airborne by a cushion of air raised by the spinning disk. In the SyQuest drive, the actual flying height of the disk head is between 6.5 and 8 microinches, about the same as many conventional hard disk drives.

Flying the head in a SyQuest cartridge (or conventional hard disk) brings several advantages. Because the head is not in contact with the drive itself, friction cannot wear out the medium on the disk platters. The lack of friction also eliminates one of the major limits on spin speed, which can raise throughput potentials. In fact, the SyQuest drive spins at 3,220 rpm, slightly slower than conventional hard drives—old hard disks were designed to rotate at about 3,600 rpm, although newer drives now spin up to twice as fast.

The SyQuest drive has evolved over more than a decade. Originally, it was a breakthrough in miniaturization (using hundred-millimeter cartridges) and construction (its platters were plated, not coated, with medium). The modern SyQuest drive has drifted into the hard disk mainstream. SyQuest platters are now a standard 5.25 inches in diameter and most conventional hard disks have converted to plated platters. Although other companies have attempted removable Winchester hard disks, SyQuest is the sole survivor that uses that technology.

Iomega took an entirely different tack. Its Bernoulli Box is a radically rethought floppy disk that turns hard disk technology upside down, essentially flying the disk instead of the read/write head. The

Bernoulli drive itself is named after the Swiss physicist Daniel Bernoulli (1700-1782), best known for his book *Hydrodynamica* and the discovery of the Bernoulli Principle. This fundamental law of fluid flow states that the pressure of a fluid is inversely proportional to its velocity.

In Iomega's Bernoulli drives, this principle is used to stabilize a rapidly spinning floppy disk. Ordinary floppy disks spin at 300 to 600 rpm because friction with the liner in their plastic shells otherwise would cause wear and heat. Removing the liner eliminates that problem, but at higher speeds the floppy would become unstable, flapping like a flag in its own wind. Air pressure over a small defect would create lower pressure that would pull on the defect, exaggerating it further.

By taking advantage of the Bernoulli Principle, however, Iomega can spin floppies at higher speeds—2,368 rpm in the case of the company's popular 90M units. The trick is to spin the disk adjacent to a "Bernoulli plate" and use the air pressure between the disk and plate to stabilize the system. The air dragged by the disk increases in velocity and the lower pressure sucks the flexible disk close to the Bernoulli plate. But because the fast-moving air remains between the two surfaces, they never touch but remain locked close together. The result is a floppy disk with a stable high-speed spin.

The read/write head of a Bernoulli drive adds additional stabilization by forcing the flexible disk to bend around the head, again without touching it. The pressures, the disk's elasticity, and other variables work together to keep the disk and head out of contact but in close proximity—within 8 to 10 microinches in the case of the 90M drive.

A chief advantage of the Bernoulli disk system is that the thin floppy disks have little mass. The mylar disks in each cartridge are only 2 mils thick. Consequently they neither cause nor suffer from head crashes should the drive be jarred during operation. Moreover, the cartridges themselves are tough because there's little to break free and rattle around inside them. The cartridges are rated to withstand forces of 1,000 G—that's a drop of 8 to 10 feet (3 meters) to a concrete floor.

Any archival, storage, or backup medium must be able to be called upon in dire circumstances to recover from disaster. The storage medium consequently must be able to withstand environmental hardships and still be usable. Moreover, disk cartridges are often used as a data exchange medium, mailed across continents and oceans. Shipping is rarely kind.

A chief advantage of the Bernoulli disk system is that the thin floppy disks have little mass.

The two styles of cartridge are quite different in endurance. The Bernoulli cartridge design is more forgiving of abuse because of the lower mass of its disks, but it does have its vulnerabilities. Iomega drives are rated over a wide temperature range (from -22 to 52 degrees Celsius in storage) but require a non-condensing atmosphere. Dampness quickly destroys the floppy disk medium by degrading the binders in the disk coating. A damp disk could be torn apart by the read/write head.

You can load and run a Bernoulli disk cartridge as soon as you open its package.

On the other hand, because the floppy disk medium has little thermal inertia, you don't have to wait for disks to acclimatize to the drive when you bring one in from the cold. You can load and run a Bernoulli disk cartridge as soon as you open its package. Slide it into the drive—providing no moisture has condensed on the disks inside. The disks warm up in about the time it takes them to spin up.

The massive platter of the SyQuest cartridge requires acclimatization before it can be used in its drive. The disk needs to warm to room temperature before use. That means waiting for about an hour. However, the SyQuest platters are plated rather than coated and hence are more resistant to condensation. Still, don't use a wet disk.

The massive platter of the SyQuest cartridge requires acclimatization before it can be used in its drive.

When it comes to impact damage, the Bernoulli cartridge is clearly the sturdier. The 1000 G rating of the bare cartridge should withstand shocks equivalent to a fall from 8 feet (about 2.5 meters) to a smooth concrete floor. The more complex and larger SyQuest cartridge is much more delicate. SyQuest rates it as able to withstand a drop of 30 inches (0.75 meters) to a vinyl-covered concrete floor. SyQuest supplies a padded vinyl case for each cartridge, and when inside the case the cartridge's shock resistance rises to withstand a fall of 48 inches.

The Bernoulli system does have its downside, however. The flexing disk is subject to fatigue and eventually wears out. But Iomega designed the Bernoulli drive to minimize fatigue, and they warrant each cartridge for five years, which should exceed the needs of a backup or exchange (rather than primary storage) system.

Capacities

A tiny gap between the read/write head and the disk medium is important because the height of the flight of the head governs how densely data can be written on the disk. The greater the distance from head to disk, the more the magnetic fields of each can spread. Higher storage densities require closer flight.

By juggling design factors, engineers can adjust the head altitude, but the closeness of the head to the medium is ultimately limited by the roughness of the medium. On a microscopic scale, even a smooth platter surface looks like a mountain range. For all their technological differences, the Iomega and SyQuest drives achieve the same data densities.

Both manufacturers use extra tricks to get more from each cartridge. SyQuest puts a head on each side of the rigid disk. Large-capacity Bernoulli cartridges are also recorded on two surfaces, but each is a separate floppy disk. The two disks spin adjacent to their own Bernoulli plates.

The SyQuest drive uses zone-bit recording, dividing the disk into two zones, each of which is recorded with its own format. The outer half of the disk is zone zero, which accommodates 26,624 bytes per track in 512-byte sectors; the inner tracks constitute zone one, recorded with a density of 18,432 bytes per track in 256-byte sectors. The embedded SCSI controller in the drive translates this odd geometry into a form compatible with DOS storage.

Both the Iomega and SyQuest systems use closed-loop head actuators and embedded servo (track-finding) systems. Unlike conventional disk drives that devote an extra surface to servo information, both Iomega and SyQuest locate the necessary data on the same surfaces used for recording information. The only shortcoming of this system is that servo tracks are written on disks at the factory and cannot be altered. Zap one of these disks with a bulk degausser, and the disk cannot be used again.

Thanks to these tricks, the cartridges used by the two systems appear to be closely matched in available storage capacity. Iomega offers drives with capacities up to 150M. SyQuest offers drives that hold up to 105M. Both companies also offer products at around 90M.

This capacity range is shared by another removable media technology. Compact 3.5-inch magneto-optical (MO) disks have a rated capacity of 128M per cartridge. Because 3.5-inch MO cartridges offer the same read/write capabilities as magnetic recording systems, they can be used in many of the same applications. MO cartridges are just as rugged and more compact than their magnetic equivalents but MO recording is slower than magnetic.

The Iomega and SyQuest drives come with partitioning software that determines the size of the file allocation units used on the cartridge. SyQuest conforms to the DOS 6.0 standard for disks up

For all their technological differences, the Iomega and SyQuest drives achieve the same data densities.

The cartridges used by the two systems appear to be closely matched in available storage capacity.

to 128M and allows 4 sectors—that's 2,048 bytes—per allocation unit. Iomega (for reasons unknown) allows 8 sectors (4,096 bytes) in each allocation unit on its drives, even those with less than 128M total storage.

Performance Differences

When any disk drive is used for primary storage, it must be able to access data as quickly as possible. Should you choose to use a removable cartridge drive in lieu of a conventional hard disk, you don't want to suffer a performance penalty.

As with conventional hard disk systems, removable cartridge systems are rated by access time, the average time it takes the read/write head to move from one track to any other. Typical hard disk access times range from the 80 ms required by the original hard disk in the XT to the 15 ms required by the latest hard drives.

The two different magnetic removable cartridge technologies are well matched. Each performs about on par with a conventional hard disk—but one four years old! The cartridge drives are rated with average access times as low as 22 ms, but they actually work more slowly. Actual measurements showed a typical 90M Bernoulli Box to access DOS files at a 30.36 ms average rate. A SyQuest 88M drive was tested with a 33.18 ms average rate for accessing DOS files. You'll notice the difference should you try to use one of these cartridge disk systems as a replacement for a state-of-the-art hard disk. This level of performance is generally acceptable but noticeably slow, particularly if you want the best possible performance from your PC. However, the cartridge disk speeds are no detriment for a backup, security, or data exchange system.

The one place the Iomega drive is truly handicapped is response after a period of inactivity. When the Iomega drive is not used for a short period, the head unloads to prevent undue wear on the medium. Loading the head again takes about 100 milliseconds. That's about what you can expect from a floppy drive coming up to speed. As a result, you should expect a slight pause when accessing the Iomega drive intermittently. Again, this is no handicap for secondary storage. If you do use a cartridge disk system as secondary storage, the data transfer rate is more important because you'll want to copy megabytes from hard disk to cartridge whenever you need data from the cartridge.

Both the Iomega and SyQuest drives use a SCSI interface, so they suffer the same interface bottlenecks. Neither drive strains the 5M per second capabilities of an ordinary (non-fast, non-wide) SCSI connection. The SCSI speeds of these systems are influenced more by the choice of host adapter than any other factor. The higher performance of the SCSI host adapter, the greater the throughput you'll see from the drive.

Of greater concern—and the principal limit on data throughput— are the internal limits of the drive unit, the rate that information can be read from the drive platters and absorbed by the embedded control electronics. Iomega and SyQuest rate the disk-to-electronics speeds of their 90M products quite differently. SyQuest claims a burst rate of 13.953 megabits per second while Iomega posts its drive at less than half that figure, 6.67 megabits per second.

When tested writing data to disk, an 88M SyQuest proved itself quicker than a 90M Bernoulli—but hardly by a two-to-one ratio. The measured difference was so small that it's not a major purchasing criterion. In fact, the Bernoulli appears faster on normal DOS chores because a hardware disk cache is built into its electronics. This small (16K) cache gives the Bernoulli system an advantage over the SyQuest drive should you want to use your cartridge disk as your primary mass storage system.

The one place the Iomega drive is truly handicapped is response after a period of inactivity.

The higher performance of the SCSI host adapter, the greater the throughput you'll see from the drive.

Drive Units and Packaging

The physical embodiment of a drive determines how easily you can add one to your PC as an upgrade. Both Iomega and SyQuest offer their drives for internal installation and as complete external packages. Iomega Corporation offers end-user products under its own name, while SyQuest sells drives under its name only to other companies for repackaging. However, SyQuest also offers its products to end users through its SyDOS division. The end-user products normally are sold complete with matching SCSI host adapters.

The drive units themselves each fit a conventional half-height 5.25-inch drive bay—tightly. Because you need to slide cartridges in and out, these internally mounted drives require bays with front panel access. Each drive has a slot nearly the full width of the drive and covered by a swinging door waiting for you to slide in a cartridge. The Iomega drive is built around a filled-plastic frame; the SyQuest has a cast aluminum frame surrounded by a steel shell.

The Bernoulli drive has but a single rectangular button flanked by two LED indicators. One LED cautions you when the drive is coming up to speed, the other serves as an activity indicator. Pressing the mushy blue rubber button stops the drive so you can extract the cartridge. The cartridge itself protrudes about an inch from the drive even when fully inserted.

When the disks in the Bernoulli cartridge are spinning or the power to the drive is switched off, the cartridge latches in place inside the drive and cannot be removed. In fact, you can extract a cartridge only when the drive is turned on. Note, however, that after a period of inactivity, the drive automatically stops spinning, enabling you to extract the cartridge.

The SyQuest drive also has two LED indicators that duplicate the functions of those on the Bernoulli. The SyQuest cartridge-loading mechanism is more elaborate than that of the Bernoulli Box, however, involving a locking and release lever.

For external installation, both companies put their basic 5.25-inch, half-height drive mechanism on the right side of a compact, attractive package. Iomega's measures 2.5×9.75×10.75 inches; SyQuest's measures 2.5×9.75×9.75 inches. Although both companies paint their external chassis the universal pale white-beige pioneered by IBM for making PCs look bland, SyQuest uses a steel case, while Iomega uses plastic (lined inside with interference-absorbing silver paint). To help you carry around the Bernoulli Box, Iomega styled a handle into the top-front edge of its case. Actually, the handle is almost too clever, such a good fit that it's hard to extract. The SyQuest drive offers no handle.

Inside the case, both drives have essentially the same components, although arrayed somewhat differently. The entire left side of the Bernoulli case is filled with a fully enclosed power supply. Except for its rearmost 2.5 inches, the right side of the case is filled with the drive itself. A small fan, held in place by plastic tabs, dissipates heat through the rear panel. The SyQuest drive puts an open-frame power supply at left. The fan blows down through the bottom of the case.

Installation

The first step in taking advantage of a cartridge disk system is installing it in your PC. Both of these drives require a two-step installation process. First, the hardware is physically installed in your PC. Then you add driver software to your system and prepare each cartridge for storage.

Preliminary Device Setup

Before you begin, set the SCSI identification number of your cartridge driver, whether it mounts internally or externally (see fig. 8.1). Every device in a SCSI chain requires a unique SCSI ID number, zero through seven. The host adapter is invariably assigned a value of seven. Most cartridge drives come preset with the proper number for use with the host adapters accompanying them. However, if you plan to install other devices to your SCSI host adapter, you may have to alter this number. Check the manual to determine whether a particular ID number is required. SyQuest gives you the freedom to select between zero and six—the cartridge disk software automatically locates the drive during setup. Iomega also lets you select device seven on the drive, but you should never use this ID number because it conflicts with nearly every SCSI host adapter. Avoid SCSI identification numbers zero and one because these are preferred by most host adapters for hard disks (and eventually you might want to add a hard disk to your SCSI chain).

The first and last device in any SCSI chain must also be terminated. With internal installations of a single cartridge drive, this is not normally a problem. Because most host adapters and internal cartridge drives come with terminators preinstalled, you only need to

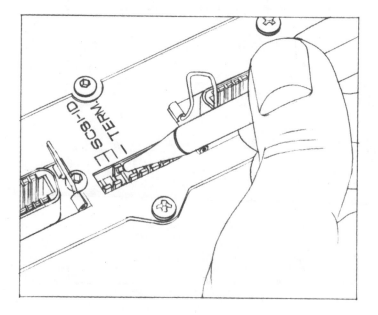

Figure 8.1
Setting a SCSI ID on a drive. SCSI devices use DIP switches (shown), rotary switches, or jumpers to set their IDs.

*The last internal
and last external
device should be
terminated.*

check for the presence of terminating resistor packs. If you're
connecting more than one device to your SCSI host adapter, you'll
have to follow the SCSI termination rules—only the first and last
devices in the chain are terminated. (The host adapter is usually
considered the first device.) However, the Iomega and SyQuest
drives differ in termination method. To terminate the Iomega
Bernoulli Box, just slide the switch on the rear panel of the drive to
the Term position. To terminate a SyQuest drive, plug the terminating connector supplied with the drive into the back of the last device
in your SCSI chain. Again, the first device will be the host adapter—
providing you don't plan on installing internal and external SCSI
peripherals at the same time. If you do, the host adapter shifts to the
middle of the chain, unterminated. The last internal *and* last external
device should be terminated.

Remove terminations by throwing the appropriate switch or
removing the resistors (see fig. 8.2). Some SCSI devices use external
terminations that plug into the second SCSI connector on the last
device in the SCSI chain (see fig. 8.3).

Figure 8.2
Removing termina-
tion resistors.

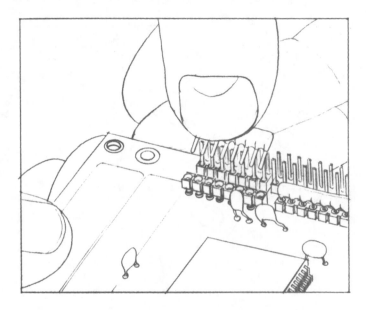

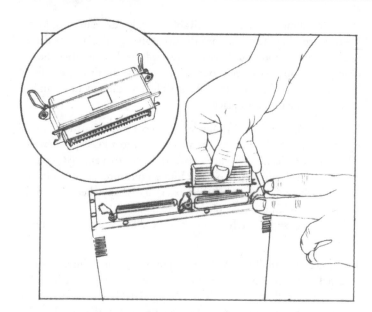

Figure 8.3

An external termina-
tor (inset). External
terminators plug into
the second SCSI
connector on the last
device in the SCSI
chain. Clip the
termination plug in
place so that it
doesn't loosen.

Mechanical Installation

Hardware installation varies with the model you choose. Because
both drives are identical in form, installation of the bare drives is the
same as for any other 5.25-inch half-height device. The degree of
difficulty depends on the mounting scheme used by your PC—
directly screwing the drive to the sides of the bay, using AT-style
rails, or attaching the drive to a mounting tray. Iomega and SyQuest
drives have standard drive-mounting holes on each side and their
bottoms. You also have to slide the host adapter board into a
matching expansion slot and route a SCSI cable from host adapter to
drive.

If your PC uses a direct-mounting scheme in which the drive is
screwed directly to its bay, you can use either set of screw holes—
those on the sides or bottom of the drive unit. Be careful in your
choice of screws. If they are too long, they may interfere with the
operation of the drive. They should pass through the side of the
drive bay and about one-eighth of an inch into the screw holes in the
drive—just far enough to hold it securely without the screw projecting through the drive chassis. If your PC uses AT-style rails, install
them as you would for a normal hard disk, again watching the length
of the screws.

When installing an internal removable cartridge drive in most PCs, it's easier to plug the cables into the drive after you've put the drive near its final position but have not screwed the drive in place. For example, if you have drive-mounting rails, slide the drive partially back into its bay, connect the cables, slide it all the way back, and then screw the rails into place.

External cartridge drives are always two-piece systems—the drive case itself and the host adapter which slides into a PC expansion slot. The only significant difference between the Iomega and SyQuest external units is physical size—the Iomega measures about an inch longer. Otherwise you can put the external case anywhere within reach of the SCSI cable supplied by the manufacturer. With typical units, Iomega supplies a five-foot cable, and SyQuest includes a four-footer.

If you need to install a SCSI host adapter to match an internal or external cartridge drive, it doesn't matter whether you slide it in before or after sliding in the drive (see fig. 8.4). However, it is easier to plug the SCSI cable into the host adapter for an internal drive before putting it into its slot. External cables must be plugged in after host adapter installation.

Figure 8.4

Installing a SCSI host adapter. Screw the host adapter in place and then plug your SCSI cable into it (inset).

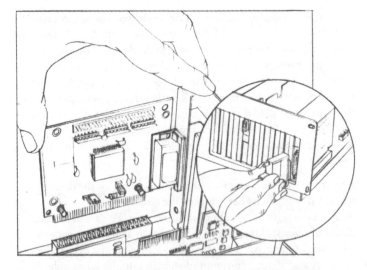

Most SCSI host adapters (including those used by internal drives) have large 50-pin connectors on their rear panels for installing with external drives. These connectors have locking wires at top and bottom which often interfere with mating the board to an expansion slot. The best strategy is to remove the top wire before installing the board, then snapping the wire back in place. If your cartridge drive comes with a host adapter that requires a particular type of slot—16-bit, EISA, or local bus—be sure to slide it into a slot that supports the highest possible performance connector.

If your internal cartridge drive is the only SCSI device in your PC, cabling is simple. Ensure that one end of the SCSI cable is attached to the host adapter and plug any other connector in the cable to your drive. Make sure that the colored stripe at the edge of the cable aligns with pin one on the drive, host adapter, or other device connector.

With external drives, the cabling is standard SCSI. Both the Iomega and SyQuest external drives follow the SCSI connector convention, providing two 50-pin jacks to allow the daisy-chaining of multiple SCSI peripherals. Connect all the other SCSI devices in turn. Each SCSI device except the last (see fig. 8.5) will have two cables—one leading to the device and one going to the next device in the chain.

If your internal cartridge drive is the only SCSI device in your PC, cabling is simple.

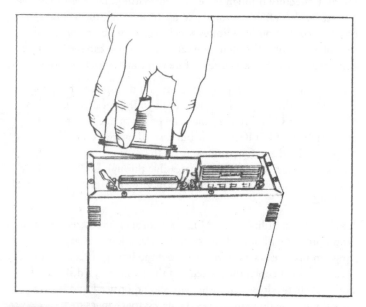

Figure 8.5
Each SCSI device in a chain except the last (shown here) has two cables—one leading to the device, and one going to the next device in the chain.

Software Setup

After your cartridge drive is properly installed, Iomega and SyQuest require a special software installation. Because they are SCSI products, neither drive system requires you to alter your PC's configuration by running your PC's setup procedure.

Both Iomega and SyQuest supply software drivers which allow the drives to be properly recognized by DOS. To install these drivers, both companies provide a menu-driven setup utility.

The SyQuest setup program is called SYPREP. It begins by scanning your system for installed disk resources and listing them (including your PC's native hard disk). It then asks you to confirm what it has found by activating the drive indicator on the SyQuest drive. After you've made your choice, you are led through a procedure that takes the place of DOS's FDISK and FORMAT programs. The system automatically prepares the cartridge as a single partition of 84M or enables you to split it up in the same manner as with DOS FDISK. After the disk is partitioned, the SyQuest software formats the drive and installs the operating system (as a default even if the drive is not in boot position).

The entire procedure, from initializing the file allocation tables and the root directory through the end of formatting, takes less than five minutes with an 88M cartridge. While formatting, the SYPREP program continuously indicates which sectors are being prepared (out of a total of 172,000 on the cartridge) so you can see how long you have left to sip your coffee before you can get back to work.

Next, the SyQuest setup program gives you the option of copying the SyQuest driver, SYDRIVER.SYS, to your boot drive as well as SYDOS' own CONFIG.SYS file. The program does not modify your original CONFIG.SYS file but instead overwrites it. You'll find it easier to let the SyQuest software do the work. After it's done, reboot and the SyQuest drive is accessible through DOS. The drive can be reformatted using the DOS FORMAT command as a normal hard disk drive.

Iomega's setup utility, INSTALL, steps through the system configuration process with forced choice and explanation screens. The program first creates a directory to hold the Iomega files on your hard disk, then copies the contents of the two Iomega diskettes. It explains what it does—and what you should or need to do—as it goes along. The program makes the necessary changes to CONFIG.SYS to install its own driver, edits your existing file and likewise modifies AUTOEXEC.BAT to add the path to its utility files. When finished, it reboots your PC and gives you DOS access to the Bernoulli disk. The Iomega drive responds to the DOS FORMAT command as a floppy disk drive.

Magneto-Optical Cartridge Drives

Familiarity breeds content. Designers are familiar with magnetic storage and are content to design mass storage systems around it. Magnetic technology thus earns its place in the mainstream of storage by default. Other technologies have advantages in their own right, however—some of which put magnetic storage to shame.

Light beams, for example, can be focused more tightly than the magnetic fields of hard disk read/write heads. That sharper focus equates to the potential for higher storage densities—more bytes on every square millimeter of storage medium.

Besides density, optical storage has another advantage. The scourge of magnetic disks is also absent from optical storage—optical recording is a non-contact sport. The only thing that ever touches the data on a disk is a light beam. Consequently, optical disks do not wear out (as flexible magnetic media do) nor do they suffer head crashes. The assembly that reads or writes to the disk can be located a safe distance from the disk surface instead of flying precarious microinches above as magnetic systems require. Moreover, while magnetic disks put the actual recording medium in harm's way directly under the head (and in many cases the medium is devastatingly soft), optical disks protect your data behind a transparent plastic shield through which a laser beam can be focused precisely.

The scourge of magnetic disks is absent from optical storage—optical recording is a non-contact sport.

But optical storage is far from perfect. Turning optical technology into something manageable and reliable has taxed the cumulative brain power of the world's electronic engineers. The perfect optical system—one that does everything that a magnetic storage system does but better—has yet to be developed. Although several technologies are available for making read/write optical disk systems (most commonly called *rewritable optical disks*) the list of trade-offs required for purely optical recording reads almost identical to the list of features for a magnetic drive—access speed, transfer rate, price, medium life. Although not hopeless, making workable optical storage systems is a real challenge.

Optical disks do not wear out (as flexible magnetic media do) nor do they suffer head crashes.

One trade-off has proven to be the most important development in moving optical storage from the lab into your PC. By combining magnetic technology with optical technology and creating a hybrid, the advantages of both optical and magnetic storage can be put to work.

This hybrid, the magneto-optical disk drive, is now available for upgrading any PC. These MO drives (as they are known to their friends) put hundreds of megabytes of storage onto convenient 5.25-inch cartridges (or about 128M onto 3.5-inch cartridges) with the same read/write capabilities of magnetic hard disk drives. If you have to move or backup megabytes by the hundreds, you should take a serious look at magneto-optical storage. In fact, magneto-optical storage appears to be the strongest contender to wrest the storage laurels from the Winchester family. Its rewritable optical technology promises the same massive storage capabilities along with removable cartridges and greater reliability of other optical media. Alas, rewritable has its own drawbacks. Currently, the drives are substantially more expensive than Winchester hard disks, and current products are notoriously slow, midway in the continuum between floppy disks and the best hard disks.

New developments promise to minimize the disadvantages of rewritable optical. Performance is being improved thanks to new mechanisms with integral hardware caches as well as new software for both operating the drives and linking them with your PC. New designs are also increasing cartridge capacities. Costs, although still higher, are becoming more favorable. Although still not replacements for hard disks, magneto-optical drives are strong contenders for secondary storage.

Technical Background

Magneto-optical isn't the only rewritable optical technology to be proposed for PCs. Two others, dye-polymer and phase-change, have also been tried. But the mix of features with these technologies has not proven as compelling as those for magneto-optical storage.

Dye-polymer systems rely on translucent disks with a dye-tinted inner layer that swells into a bump when heated by a laser. The bump changes the reflectivity of the disk and can be detected by the same optical system as is used by a CD player. A second laser can make the bump relax, effectively erasing the data that has been previously written.

The premiere example of the dye-polymer system is Tandy's now-infamous CD-compatible THOR system, promoted as a compact disc on which you can record. Oddly, with products seemingly imminent, the system slipped quietly into obscurity.

In phase-change rewritable optical systems, the recordable material can arrange itself into the ordered lattice of a crystal or into a form in which its molecules are randomly organized like a compressed powder. Although the chemical make-up of the medium remains the same as it changes between states, its reflectivity is altered. The medium is made into tiny light and dark patches used to encode digital information. Some commercial products use this technology to function as dual-purpose units—a single drive can handle rewritable and write-once cartridges.

In contrast, the recording medium in a magneto-optical disk is basically a magnetic material, relying on a magnetic field rather than optical properties to store information. The difference between MO drives and conventional magnetic disk drives is that the MO product uses a laser beam to supplement a magnetic field to write data onto the disk. The laser itself is used without the magnetic assist to read the disk.

The combination of optical and magnetic technologies results from necessity. Because the MO medium must be used over and over again, it poses problems in writing data. The most common optical recording systems—those that make CDs for audio playback and data distribution—use a laser to blast pits or holes in the MO medium. After the laser mars the disk, the medium is difficult to reuse. But other than blasting away the medium and its magnetic field, a laser alone cannot alter the magnetic alignment of a material, just as writing magnetically cannot deliver the unique advantages of optical storage. If a magnetic head were used to write data, it could pack information no more densely than the information would be packed on a conventional Winchester disk. There would be no incentive to use the fine probe of a laser beam to read the disk—no reason for optical technology to be used.

A technological twist allows a laser to read magnetic fields. A laser's photons are aligned in one direction. When the polarized beam strikes the magnetically-aligned particles of the disk, the magnetic field of the media particles causes the plane of polarization of the laser to rotate slightly, a phenomenon called the *Kerr effect*. While small (as little as a one percent shift in early MO media but now reportedly up to seven percent), this change in polarization can be detected as reliably as the direct magnetic reading of a Winchester disk.

Another important difference separates MO from both phase-change and dye-polymer technologies. The latter two rely on a physical change in the properties of the optical medium that results in a change in reflectivity. The magnetic field reversal used by MO drives, however, is not a physical change of state. The magnetic particles never change or even move. Materials that undergo physical changes of state suffer stress that can reduce the effective life of the material because of fatigue. It's like the metal shell of an airliner that must expand and contract each time the cabin is pressurized. After too many cycles, the material may fatigue and fail. The media used for dye-polymer and phase-change rewritable optical disks have limited lives because of such fatigue. Magneto-optical media do not.

Whether these fatigue-prone technologies can be used successfully as computer storage depends on their use and the number of state changes they can endure safely. Typical phase-change media are rated for lives in excess of ten thousand cycles. While just a few thousand cycles may sound sufficient for use in computer disk storage, even a million cycles may be woefully inadequate in a conventional PC mass storage system. While you may not erase and rewrite the entire contents of your disks very often, DOS rewrites the file allocation table (FAT) on the disk every time you create or add to a file. That may happen thousands of times a day. If used like an ordinary magnetic disk, state-change optical media may fail quickly, with errors occurring first in the most important storage area on the disk, the FAT.

That's not to say phase-change and dye-polymer media are unworkable. They're just not amenable to normal DOS operations. By clever engineering, FAT changes can be minimized, such as by moving the FAT before it becomes overwrought. State-change disks also can be effective when buffered by traditional magnetic hard disk media—ongoing changes are made to the hard disk and only occasionally are those changes spooled off to the optical drive. State-change disks are also suitable for specialized applications that require a limited number of write cycles. A writable digital disk storage system for home audio is an example, the purpose for which the Tandy THOR system is primarily targeted. Because most people will record only a few times on a given part of a disk, the medium would not be unduly stressed.

Changes in magnetic polarity are well understood and generally believed to be completely reversible. That's how traditional magnetic media—hard disks and floppies—work. Because MO drives are based on this well-understood principle, they are considered to be capable of an unlimited number of write/rewrite cycles. There's no worry about stress, fatigue, failure, and data loss.

Instead of using optical or magnetic principles alone, MO drives combine them. They use a conventional magnetic field, called the bias field, to write data onto the disk. In a regular magnetic drive, this field would be much larger than the size of a spot created by a focused laser. To get the field down to truly minuscule size, MO drives use the laser beam to assist magnetic writing.

This optical-assist in magnetic recording works because of the particular magnetic medium used in MO disks. This medium differs from that of ordinary Winchester drives in having a higher coercivity, a resistance to changing its magnetic orientation. In fact, the coercivity of a MO disk is about an order of magnitude higher than the 600 or so Oersteds of coercivity of the typical Winchester disk.

High coercivity alone gives MO disks one of their biggest advantages over traditional Winchesters—they are virtually immune to self-erasure. All magnetic media tend to self-erase. With passing time their magnetic fields lose intensity because of the combined effects of all external and internal magnetic fields. But MO disks, with their high coercivities, maintain data more reliably over a longer period than Winchester disks. The quoted lifetime for MO disks is ten years. While that's difficult to prove because MO drives have not *existed* for ten years, many industry people view that claim as conservative. Traditional magnetic media require refreshing every few years to guarantee the integrity of their contents. Mainframe computer data tapes are typically refreshed every two years. MO media promise to extend the time between refreshes substantially.

The high coercivity of MO media also makes the disks resistant to the effects of stray magnetic fields. Although a refrigerator magnet means death to the data stored on a floppy, it would have little effect on a MO disk (but you still wouldn't want to clamp your MO disks to your system unit with refrigerator magnets).

However, the higher coercivity of MO media also presents a challenge: obtaining a high enough magnetic flux to change the media while keeping the recorded domains small. Reducing this high coercivity is how the laser assists the bias magnet in an MO drive. The coercivity of the magnetic medium used by MO disks, as with most magnetic materials, decreases as its temperature increases and becomes zero at a value called a medium's *Curie temperature*. By warming the MO disk medium close to the Curie temperature, the field strength needed to initiate a change is reduced to practical levels. The magnetic medium used by MO disks is specifically engineered for a low Curie temperature, about 150 degrees Celsius.

The same laser used for reading the MO disk can be increased in intensity to raise the recording medium to its Curie temperature. Although the magnetic field acting on the medium may cover a wide area, only the tiny spot heated by the laser actually changes its magnetic orientation.

The design of many MO drives has one intrinsic drawback. The bias magnetic field must remain oriented in a single direction during the writing process. It cannot change because the high inductance of the electromagnet that forms the field prevents the rapid switching of the magnet's polarities. Consequently, the bias magnet in some MO drives can align only magnetic fields in a given area of a disk track in one direction each time it passes beneath the read/write head. For example, when the bias field is polarized upwards, it can change downward-oriented fields on the disk to upward polarity but it cannot alter upward-oriented fields.

To work reliably, the MO recording process requires all fields on a writing area to be oriented in a single direction before the data is written—a given disk area must be erased before it can be recorded. In classic (or two-pass) MO drive designs, this erasure process requires a separate pass under the bias magnet with the polarity of the magnet temporarily reversed. After one pass for erasing previously written material, the actual information is written on a second pass, changing only the areas to be changed with laser heating.

Check the access time for reading and writing when comparing MO drives.

The penalty for this two-step process is an increase in the average access time of MO drives when writing data, which is already slow. Although speeds vary, many MO drives spin their disks at a leisurely 1,800 to 2,400 revolutions per minute, roughly a third slower than Winchester disks (which typically operate at 3,600 rpm and above). Each turn therefore requires 25 milliseconds. Discounting head movement, the average access time for writing to an MO drive cannot possibly be faster than 37.5 milliseconds. (On the average, the data to be erased will be half a spin away from the read/write head, 12.5 milliseconds, and a second spin to write the data will take an additional 25 milliseconds.) Understandably, most MO manufacturers are working on or have developed one-pass drives. Consequently, you'll want to check the access time for reading and writing when comparing MO drives.

To cut the latency of their drives, several makers now offer high-speed MO drives that spin their platters at 3,600 rpm. Note high-speed drives require special disk cartridges to deliver the improved performance. With ordinary cartridges, high-speed drives spin at the same speed as other MO drives.

The MO drive also suffers another performance handicap. While Winchester read/write heads are typically flyweight mechanisms weighing a fraction of a gram, the read/write heads of MO drives are massive assemblies of magnetic and optical parts. Typically this MO head mounts on a sled that slides on parallel steel tubes. Moving that massive head requires a robust mechanism and, thanks to inertia, it takes substantially longer to speed up, slow down, and settle compared to a Winchester head. In fact, when it comes to average access time, there is almost no comparison to a Winchester, which can write data as quickly as 15 ms between random bytes. MO drives, at their current best, are no faster than 60 ms—not counting the twice-around write penalty.

MO drives, at their current best, are no faster than 60 ms—not counting the twice-around write penalty.

The optical sled used by MO drives isn't without its redeeming qualities, however. Unlike the Winchester drive head, which must fly microinches above the media surface to pack data, optical heads can work at a distance. The guide rods fix a distance between head and disk that's huge compared to Winchester's. With that distance comes safety. Head crashes are impossible on MO drives because the head cannot move close to the media. In fact, only the laser beam touches the disk surface (or should—keep your fingers out of the protective door!). As with CDs, the optically active surface of the disk is sealed beneath a tough layer of transparent plastic. Because the beam is out of focus at the surface of the disk and only converges on a spot underneath the clear layer, the effect of scratches or dust on the top of the disk have little effect on accurate disk reading or writing. Of course, MO drives also incorporate error-correction to minimize errors.

Media

Clearly, speed is not a compelling reason to upgrade to an MO drive. You get better performance from a good Winchester magnetic hard disk. And Winchesters will always have a performance advantage over MO products, at least if you believe the predictions made by hard disk manufacturers. However, MO drives have their own distinct advantages that can make them an excellent choice for some applications.

Capacity is often cited as one advantage of MO products. That's not necessarily true.

Capacity is often cited as one advantage of MO products. That's not necessarily true. Today, 3.5-inch MO drives offer no dramatic capacity difference from run-of-the-mill magnetic hard disks. They allow only about 128M of storage per cartridge side. Direct comparisons between Winchester and MO capacities are misleading. The quoted capacities of both types of drive are in the same ballpark, but the technologies are playing different games. Drives using 5.25-inch disks may quote similar capacities for either technology, a maximum of about a gigabyte. Winchester drives might use up to 8 internal disks or platters (15 recordable surfaces) to achieve that capacity while the higher density of MO drives reaches the same figure with a single platter in a cartridge.

The capacities quoted for MO cartridges are misleading, however. Although MO drives are quoted with capacities in the range 600M to 1,000M, only half of the figure that manufacturers commonly quote is on-line storage. The disks in today's cartridges arrange their storage on two sides, and only one side of a cartridge can be read from or written to at a time. To access the other side, you have to remove the cartridge from the drive, flip it over, and slide it back in. Consequently, only half of the total capacity of the cartridge is on-line at a time. The smaller 128M, 3.5-inch cartridges use only one side for storgae.

Although MO drives usually are rated with capacities per cartridge, a single drive has an effectively unlimited capacity. Run out of space, and you only need slide in a new cartridge or flip over the one that's in the drive. You can stock up on as many cartridges as you can afford (the price per cartridge currently is about $250). Of course, only about 300M of that unlimited total can be accessed at a time.

Most makers of MO drives also offer jukebox systems, sometimes termed *autochangers*. These units shift between several disks to achieve astonishing near-line storage capabilities of 50 to 100 gigabytes. It's called near-line storage because you have to put up with a slight wait as the autochanger finds the correct cartridge and spins it up to speed. However, the jukeboxes are not priced for most individual PC owners—they are products for information servers.

Standards

The ISO standard guarantees that any ISO-standard cartridge can be used in any drive supporting the standard.

Data exchange depends on standardization. The cartridges written on one machine must be readable by others. The International Standards Organization (ISO) has proposed specifications for 5.25-inch and 3.5-inch MO cartridges. The ISO standard guarantees that any ISO-standard cartridge can be used in any drive supporting the standard. Although that sounds like a straightforward statement, it has its complexities.

For 5.25-inch MO disks, the ISO standard is actually a dual standard. It allows cartridges of two types, those that store data in 1,024-byte sectors and those that store data in 512-byte sectors. Because larger sectors mean less overhead—among other things, fewer sector ID markers are required—1,024 byte per sector cartridges can store more data, about 650M per cartridge (about 325M per side) versus 594M (often rounded to 600) for 512-byte per sector cartridges (about 297M per side). The actual capacity of each cartridge varies and is inevitably smaller than these figures because, as with hard disks, magneto-optical cartridges may have bad sectors.

Under the ISO standard, a drive must be able to read and write both types of cartridges. Drives produced before the standard was adopted (or by companies not recognizing the standard) may be limited to one or the other size. Some manufacturers offer drives that support not only ISO cartridge standards but their own proprietary storage formats. For example, the Tahiti drive produced by Maxtor augments its ISO capabilities with a special format and data storage method that packs up to one gigabyte per cartridge. Using constant linear velocity recording, it fills the longer, outer tracks of each disk with more sectors full of data. The ISO standards call for the disk spinning at a constant rate, which puts the same number of sectors—and the same amount of data—on every disk track.

As with all too many personal computer "standards," the ISO standard is *not* a panacea that guarantees cartridges written in one MO drive will be readable by another. Although the ISO standard does specify the physical format in which data is stored on the disk, it does not indicate the logical format. Different system integrators may opt for their own partitioning schemes, and software drivers used by one MO system vendor may not recognize the partitioning used by another. Note that few MO drive integrators use standard DOS partitioning.

Compatibility is not the only issue that partitioning affects in MO drives. Capacity has an unexpected effect on the data throughput performance of a drive. A cartridge partitioned for standard 32M DOS volumes may deliver half the effective throughput of a drive using a proprietary partitioning scheme that allows the entire capacity of one cartridge side to be addressed as a single volume. This performance effect arises because of larger volumes on MO cartridges result in larger DOS storage clusters, and larger clusters reduce the overhead involved in extended data transfers. Performance of MO drives also varies more widely than conventional hard

With many of today's MO systems, installation can be a headache, particularly if you try to connect devices from more than one manufacturer to a single SCSI host adapter.

disks because the ISO standard specifies that MO drives use the Small Computer System Interface (SCSI) to connect to their hosts. While this interface choice has its advantage in flexibility (for example, up to seven SCSI devices can be connected to a single host adapter), SCSI also can be a handicap for DOS users. ISO magneto-optical drives, like all SCSI devices in DOS-based computers, can be constrained by the SCSI host adapter used. A good adapter allows an MO drive to transfer data at the speed data can be recovered from the spinning disk, on par with a today's best Winchester hard disks. A poor SCSI adapter may limit mass storage throughput to 10 percent of its possible peak rate and make the overall system look painfully slow. Worse, SCSI systems do not integrate seamlessly with today's PCs and DOS. With many of today's MO systems, installation can be a headache, particularly if you try to connect devices from more than one manufacturer to a single SCSI host adapter.

The strongest point of the ISO standard is that it defines the MO cartridge and the media it contains. This ensures physical compatibility of cartridges and that multiple sources of supply will be available, potentially making media less expensive.

The strongest point of the ISO standard is that it defines the MO cartridge and the media it contains.

Despite their common name, most 5.25-inch cartridges are filled with optical disk platters that actually measure 130 mm (5.12 inches) in diameter. The cartridges themselves measure 0.43 by 5.31 by 6.02 inches (HWD) and resemble 3.5-inch floppy disks in that the disk itself is protected by a sliding metal shutter.

The magnetic medium on an MO disk is constructed from several layers. First, the plastic substrate of the disk is isolated with a dielectric coating. The actual magneto-optical compound—an alloy of terbium (a rare-earth element), iron, and cobalt—comes next, protected by another dielectric coating. A layer of aluminum atop this provides a reflective surface for the tracking mechanism. This sandwich is then covered by 0.30 millimeters of transparent plastic. Disks are made single-sided, then two are glued back-to-back to produce two-sided media.

Unlike conventional Winchester disks that store data on a number of concentric tracks or cylinders, under the ISO standard MO drives use a single, continuous spiral track much like the groove on a vinyl phonograph record. The spiral optimizes the data transfer of the drive because the read/write head does not need to be moved between tracks during extended data transfers. It instead smoothly scans across the disk.

Applications

Optically assisted magnetic drives aren't for everyone or every application. The spiral tracks of MO cartridges demonstrate that designers of the drives recognize that the technology is not at its best when randomly accessing data but favors large sequential transfers. Consequently, current MO drive systems are not aimed at replacing Winchester hard disks as primary mass storage media. Their role is seen as secondary mass storage—the uncharted territory that lies between hard disks and streaming tape.

MO drives are not for every application, but they have significant strengths when a safe, secure means of storing hundreds of megabytes is required. Graphics and audio/visual systems are particular candidates because MO cartridges provide the capacity needed for exchange of extremely large files. Engineers, for example, can put huge CAD files on disks to archive them.

MO drives also make an excellent backup medium, particularly for network applications. A single cartridge can back up all but the largest hard disks. Moreover, the capability to rewrite cartridges allows them to fit traditional backup arrangements in which media are recycled. Compared to tape media, restoration of files from MO disks is fast and easy. However, MO cartridges are more expensive than open-reel or cartridge tapes of the same capacity by a factor of at least two. MO disks also serve as an excellent archival medium. Cartridges are compact enough to carry several in a briefcase or lock securely in a safe. Data stored on them is safe for long-term storage.

In some systems, MO drives could replace hard disks as the primary mass storage system. With suitable caching software, the apparent performance of MO disks can be hoisted nearly to the level of a conventional hard disk. The lag in access time will still become apparent during cache misses, however.

Writing an obituary for hard disks is probably premature. Rewritable magneto-optical disks probably won't displace Winchester technology soon. Like most new technologies, MO likely will achieve its greatest success in a new role, one that it will likely define itself. As it stands now, MO technology is both useful and available, and it affords possibilities that may change the way you use your PC.

MO drives make an excellent backup medium, particularly for network applications.

Installation

Note that your system needs an array of other equipment to take advantage of your MO drive. A rewritable optical drive can substitute for a hard disk, but in nearly all practical applications you'll use the MO drive to supplement rather than replace a magnetic drive.

In addition to the hard disk, you'll want a substantial amount of memory. The multiple megabytes of most new PCs are quite sufficient, but if you have an older machine, you'll want to start with the DOS maximum of 640K and expand to accommodate the SCSI drivers and other software that accompanies the drive. You'll also want an up-to-date version of DOS—no problem with a newer PC but something to consider if you want to add MO capabilities to a system more than a few years old. Consider DOS 5.0 the minimum from a partitioning standpoint.

Because the ISO standards for MO drives specify a SCSI connection, you can follow the same procedure to install any manufacturer's drive unit. You only need understand the ins and outs of SCSI connection. Before you begin the mechanical work, set up the details of your SCSI system. Check the documentation that accompanied your drive to determine whether it requires a particular SCSI ID number to be recognized by its software driver. If so, set the number on your drive. If the driver does not require a specific number, still check the SCSI ID number of your MO drive to ensure it does not conflict with any other SCSI device you plan to connect. Anyhow, you need this number later during the software installation process, so write it down. A good place to record it is the title page of the manual.

Next, check the SCSI termination on your new drive. If you plan to make it the only SCSI device to connect to the host adapter, or if you want the new drive to be the last device in your SCSI chain, you should set the drive to Terminate. Otherwise, it should not terminate the SCSI line.

In most cases, you'll be installing an external MO drive, so you adjust the termination by either setting a switch or plugging a dummy plug into the drive. To use external termination, slide the dummy termination plug into one of the two SCSI jacks on the back of the drive, then snap it in place. Otherwise, remove the termination resistors from the drive or switch the termination off. Because the easiest way to install an optical drive is as the only SCSI device connected to a host adapter, you probably want to terminate the SCSI connection at your hard disk.

MO drives delivered bare for internal installation usually have termination resistors already installed on the circuit board on the drive itself. In single-drive internal installations, you shouldn't need to alter the drive or system terminations.

After you've set the drive terminations, check the instructions accompanying your optical drive to see whether your SCSI host adapter requires any hardware setup. Most SCSI host adapters come already set up to work in PCs that have a single hard disk controller. If you've added a lot of disks or expansion boards to your PC—or another SCSI controller—check to see whether you need to change jumper settings to accommodate the new SCSI host adapter. If such adjustments are, in fact, required, follow the drive's installation manual in making them. Generally, you'll throw a DIP switch or two or alter some jumper settings.

After you set up the host adapter, you're ready for the mechanical part of the installation. Start by switching off your PC. You never should install an expansion board or drive in your computer while the power is on. For safety's sake (for both you and the host adapter), disconnect your PC's power cable. Now open your PC's case so you have access to its expansion slots and, if you are installing the drive internally, its disk drive bays.

For internal drive installations, position the drive in an open bay, but do not secure it. Connect the power cable—one of the cables made from four wires coming from your PC's power supply—but not the SCSI cable to the drive. Because the white nylon connector is keyed, you cannot install it improperly. If it doesn't fit the jack on the back of the drive, invert the connector and try again.

Next install the SCSI host adapter in a vacant expansion slot in your PC. You usually can plug the host adapter into any expansion slot into which it fits. Be certain to twist the board's retaining bracket screw firmly in place.

Should you choose to install your magneto-optical drive internally, the best slot to use is the one adjacent to your hard disk controller, the right-most free slot, or simply the one closest to the hard drive. Your principal concern is to make routing the SCSI cable from the host adapter to the drive as easy as possible.

Now attach one end of the SCSI cable supplied with your optical drive to the host adapter. If you are installing a MO drive externally, screw the cable in place to the jack on the back of the host adapter. Connect the other end of the SCSI cable to your optical drive.

If you're making an external installation and you plan to connect other SCSI devices, plug the SCSI from the host adapter into one of the jacks on the drive and plug the cable leading to the next SCSI device to the other jack on the drive. If your drive uses an external termination and is the only SCSI drive to be connected to your host adapter, the jack to use should be obvious—it's the only one free because the other SCSI jack is filled with the termination.

If you're making an internal installation, fold the SCSI ribbon cable so that it flows from host adapter to the drive. Plug the connector (the last connector on the cable if there is more than one) into the SCSI drive. Professional installers make hard right-angle and 45-degree bends in the ribbon cables, folding the cable tightly against itself so that it doesn't bush out all over everything like honeysuckle. Because you haven't secured the drive yet (at least if you're following these instructions), you should be able to pull it out slightly to reach the jack on the drive. After both ends of the SCSI cable are connected, secure your internal drive.

It's safe now to plug the power cable back into your PC. If you've made an external installation, also connect the power cable to your drive and plug the other end of the cable into utility power.

Some drives are shipped with "dummy" disks installed to protect the mechanism from shipping damage. Sometimes you must release this disk before you switch on the power to your drive. Others eject the dummy disks—automatically or upon your command—after you power up the drive. Check the instructions accompanying your drive.

Turn on your drive (if you've installed it externally) and boot up the computer. While you're waiting for your computer to come up, follow the manufacturer's instructions for loading a disk or cartridge into the drive. (Most optical drives must be turned on to load and unload disks.)

Your PC may boot differently from the way you've become accustomed. The first time you boot up after you've installed a SCSI host adapter you'll probably see new messages on your monitor screen, possibly even an error message alerting you that your new drive isn't ready for use. Often—but not always—these messages can be ignored the first time because you have to run some setup software. If, however, you keep getting an error message after performing the entire software installation, definitely check out what's causing the messages.

Follow the procedure in the drive's instruction manual to configure the system and install any necessary software drivers. Typically you receive a diskette with an automatic installation program on it. Most of the time you can slide this disk into your A: floppy drive, log onto that drive, and run a program called SETUP or INSTALL. These programs are usually self-explanatory. Check the instructions that came with your drive to find out the proper name of the setup program.

After installing the software driver, reboot your computer to put the driver into memory. You should see a new boot message informing you that the drive has been installed properly. If the software of your drive supports DOS directly, verify that the new drive operates properly by using the DIR command on it, ensuring that you have a disk in the drive. Otherwise, follow the instructions for using the drive to verify that it works.

After you've verified that the drive is working properly, turn off your PC and replace its cover. Your drive is ready to use.

Pure-Optical WORM Drives

WORM drives are an orphan technology. They have no close kin— cousins, maybe, but no real brothers and sisters, no parents, and likely no offspring. They are related to other optical technologies like people are related to jellyfish and birds of paradise.

You would think that WORM drives and rewritable optical units would be very similar. Both use light beams to read and write by changing the reflectivity of disks held in cartridges. But they're not. Although the functional difference is the number of times a part of the storage medium can be written to, the two systems use fundamentally different technologies. Most erasable disks rely on a medium that can be shifted between two states of reflectivity (which may differ only by a few percent) under the joint influence of the laser and a magnetic field. The WORM drive uses a laser to ablate a hole in a thin metal film (actually, the laser only pokes a tiny hole in the medium—surface tension enlarges it to its final form).

When used in the right applications, the unalterable nature of WORM data is a virtue, not a weakness.

WORM records cannot be changed or manipulated accidentally or purposefully.

Barring cataclysm, a WORM cartridge should outlast its host computer.

When used in the right applications, the unalterable nature of WORM data is a virtue, not a weakness. A WORM disk provides a permanent archive of the information it records. The WORM works when you want to grow huge, enduring databases, need to maintain a full audit trail through months and megabytes of bookkeeping records, or demand step-by-step backups covering the full evolution of a project. WORM records cannot be changed or manipulated accidentally or purposefully.

WORM disks do not suffer the ravages of time. While everyday phenomena like the magnetic fields of telephone bells and aurora borealis conspire against all forms of magnetic storage, today's optical WORM disks are safe from just about everything. The claimed life for WORM cartridges is 10 years, versus 3 years for magnetic media. Barring cataclysm, a WORM cartridge should outlast its host computer.

If you regularly create records you need to preserve for posterity or the prying eyes of the auditor, WORM makes an excellent choice. You can dump hundreds of megabytes on a disk and know that no one can sneak into the office in the evening and make changes. The large capacity of WORM cartridges means that you can put a year of files on one disk.

Because of its removable cartridge nature, recordability, high capacity, and permanence, WORM media are excellent for data exchange. You can send hundreds of megabytes across the country as easily as dropping a cartridge into a Federal Express envelope. The data that's distributed will remain the same, no matter how creative the workers at the destination office may be. On the downside, however, each WORM disk must be individually written and the disks themselves can be costly. While neither factor is an obstacle when you're sending one copy across the continent, distributing information to a thousand dealers is another matter.

Technical Background

Despite their common design elements—lasers and small plastic-encapsulated disks—WORM drives differ from other optical storage devices. WORM drives store data as physical changes in the disk surface, using a laser to darken the medium. The laser is used to burn a hole in the shiny disk medium. There's no danger—you won't even smell anything burning—because the medium itself is sealed in clear plastic. Typically, the laser makes only a tiny pinhole, and tension on the medium stretches the hole to the desired size.

Generally, the cartridges used by WORM systems consist of a thin metallic film encased in a clear plastic disk. The disk is further protected by a high-impact plastic shell with a sliding metal door that allows access to the read/write head.

Every WORM disk must be written individually, as the optical surface of a WORM disk is sealed by a plastic coating laid on the disk during the manufacture of blanks. Each disk is therefore an original or that wonderful oxymoron, an original copy. If there ever was a million-selling prerecorded WORM disk, you wouldn't want to be responsible for duplicating it. The darkened or evaporated surface does not lend itself to mass production. It doesn't have texture needed to make a master that could stamp out copies like cookies, phonograph records, or CDs.

Thus WORM drives are more expensive than optical disk systems that only can read data (that is, CD-ROM players), if only because of the WORM's recording circuitry. Although you can find CD-ROM players as cheap as $300, WORMs list for up to about $4,000. The huge difference—much more than could be justified by a couple bucks worth of recording circuitry—results from quantities. CD-ROM players are made by the million while a few thousand WORM drives might be sold every year. WORM drives also need higher powered lasers to do their work.

Because WORM is a specialized, niche technology, the range of available products is small. Although about a dozen manufacturers are active in the area, the majority of drives currently sold are made by Literal (formerly Information Storage Inc.) and Panasonic. Normally, you wouldn't have to worry about who made a disk drive because the various products would be interchangeable, the way that CD-ROMs, rewritable optical cartridges, and floppy disks have been standardized. The WORM industry, however, is not guided by a single standard. Instead you have your choice of a number of incompatible "standards," each advocated by its particular manufacturer or a small group of manufacturers.

Although two standard-setting organizations have embraced the optical field, the leading WORM manufacturers follow their own proprietary standard.

The confusion is exacerbated by standards organizations. Although two standard-setting organizations have embraced the optical field—the ISO and the American National Standards Institute (ANSI)—the leading WORM manufacturers follow their own proprietary standard.

The differences aren't easily resolvable things like sector size or the color of the cartridges. The size of the cartridge, the capacity of the cartridge, and the data storage format on the cartridge all may vary.

For example, most WORM cartridges use disks measuring about 5.25 inches in diameter, but the protective shell wrapped around these disks varies in thickness and mechanical accouterments, rendering different manufacturer's products incompatible. You can't slide a cartridge meant for one drive into a drive made under another WORM standard.

The digital contents of the cartridges also varies. The ISO standard allows for a total cartridge capacity of about 650M. Among others, Pioneer, Laser Magnetic Storage, and Hitachi make drives that conform to ISO specifications. Literal makes drives that conform to the ANSI standard and hold about 1.2 gigabytes per disk. Another Literal product uses a thicker cartridge (with the same disk inside) that meets the ISO standard but packs an incompatible capacity of 1.2 gigabytes. Panasonic follows the beat of its own drummer and fits about 940M into its cartridge. While you might be tempted to follow the standards organization of your choice rather than a proprietary system, note that the Panasonic standard yields the lowest cost per megabyte.

Besides the 5.25-inch WORM drives most often used by PCs, larger systems are also available for applications that are even more specialized. Among the most popular are 12-inch disks that provide the basis for immense digital libraries and information retrieval systems. A single 12-inch cartridge can hold 6G—3.2G per side. Those prodigious amounts can be multiplied by juke boxes and WORM cartridge changers. The leading manufacturer of 12-inch WORM systems is Sony. WORM disks are sold with the optical equivalent of a low-level format already in place. Some of the first WORM drives formatted their cartridges with grooves that the laser beam tracked to write and read information. This style of formatting has been superseded in nearly all existing drives by flat disks on which servo information is blasted onto (and through) the disk with a laser. As with floppy disks, WORM disks can be single-sided or double-sided. Unlike magnetic media, WORM cartridges must be flipped over to access the second side, as you would a phonograph record.

WORM drives themselves conform to the 5.25-inch form factor used by older hard disks (except, of course, those that use 12-inch and other size cartridges!). Nearly all available WORM drives require a full-height drive bay, although a half-height model is available from Ricoh. While at one time all WORM drives used proprietary interfaces, the SCSI connection now dominates the field.

Applications

Today's WORM technology lends itself best to three applications: data acquisition, archival backup storage, and data retrieval systems. In that all WORM drives deliver much the same physical virtues (cartridges, archival integrity, and so on), software best distinguishes different products and how they are better suited to one application than another.

If you are among those who need a backup system, you probably need a WORN—Write Once Read Never—system more than a WORM. Backups are something that you hope to never, never, never need.

In that you hope you won't have to pry your data back off your WORM, the most important aspect of the WORM when backing up is how fast you can transfer information to it. The critical elements in forming your purchase decision should be the ease of use of the software (if any) and its speed in transferring information to disk. Although you need assurance that the restoration process works, restoration time won't be too important to you unless your disasters come with painful regularity—in which case you may need other forms of therapy than a WORM drive.

When you need to work with your archives—searching them for a particular phrase or drawing—speed in the other direction becomes more important. You need a system that reads from the disk quickly. For instance, if you plan to file your boilerplate forms and contracts on optical disk or build a database of magazine articles, you'll want to be able to recall files fast.

Explore the ease of use of the systems, whether all functions require you to type commands or just select from a menu. Installation can be bothersome, but you only do it once. Besides, this book should help you find your way through the worst of it.

Because a WORM drive is such a specialized and expensive proposition, explore the products thoroughly before you buy. Try them out if you can. In particular, get a demonstration of the software accompanying the drive.

Installation

Nearly all WORM drives now use a SCSI connection, so standard SCSI installation procedures apply. Pull out the manual and check whether the system requires you to set a particular SCSI ID number. If so, set the number on your drive. Even if the WORM drive has no specific ID number requirement, check the SCSI ID number to avoid conflicts with other SCSI devices connected to the same host adapter. You also may need to use this number during the software installation, to tell the software where to find the drive or to pick out which drive to use, so write it down. A good place to record it is the title page of the equipment manual.

Next, check the SCSI termination requirements of your SCSI system and WORM drive. If the WORM drive is the only device you plan connect to its host adapter or if you want the new optical drive to be the last device in your SCSI chain, set the drive to terminate. Otherwise, it should not terminate the SCSI line.

If you're installing your WORM drive externally, adjust the termination by setting a switch or sliding an external dummy termination plug into the drive. Typically you need to slide the plug into one of the two SCSI jacks on the back of the external WORM drive, then snap the retaining wires toward the center of the connector to hold it in place. Some drives simplify the process by using a single switch (or several) to adjust the termination. Because the easiest way to install an optical drive is as the only SCSI device connected to a host adapter, you'll probably want to terminate the SCSI connection at your hard disk.

If you're installing your WORM drive internally, it should have a set of termination resistors already installed on the circuit board on the drive itself. Nearly all new drives come with these terminations installed. In single-drive internal installations, you shouldn't need to alter the drive or system terminations in any way. In multiple drive systems, you'll want to remove these terminations (typically three resistor packs) if the WORM drive is not the last device in the SCSI chain.

After you've set the terminations, check your WORM drive's manual to see if your SCSI host adapter requires any hardware setup. Most SCSI host adapters come set up to work in PCs that have a single hard disk controller. If you've added a lot of disks or expansion boards to your PC—or another SCSI controller—check to see if you need to change jumper settings to accommodate the new SCSI host adapter. If such adjustments are required, follow the drive's installation manual in making them. In general, you'll throw a DIP switch or two or alter some jumper settings.

After you set up the host adapter, you're ready for the mechanical part of the installation of your WORM drive. As always, begin by switching off your PC—never install an expansion board or drive in your computer with the power on. For safety's sake (for both you and the SCSI host adapter), disconnect your PC's power cable. Now open your PC's case for access to its expansion slots and, if you are installing the drive internally, its disk drive bays.

For internal WORM installations, position the drive in the bay you choose to use, but do not secure it. Connect the power cable—one of the cables made from four wires coming from your PC's power supply—but not the SCSI cable to the drive. Because the white connector is keyed, you cannot install it improperly. If it doesn't fit into the jack on the back of the drive, invert it and try again.

Next, install the SCSI host adapter in a vacant expansion slot in your PC. You usually can plug the host adapter into any expansion slot it fits. Be certain to twist the board's retaining bracket screw firmly in place.

If you have chosen to install your WORM drive internally, the best slot to use is the closest to the drive. Your biggest worry is finding the least obtrusive route for getting the SCSI cable from the host adapter to the WORM drive. Fold the SCSI ribbon cable so it flows from host adapter to the drive.

Attach one end of the SCSI cable to the host adapter. If you are installing the WORM drive externally, clip the cable in place to the jack on the back of the host adapter. Connect the other end of the SCSI cable to your drive.

If you're making an external installation and plan to connect other SCSI devices, plug the SCSI from the host adapter into one of the jacks on the drive and plug the cable leading to the next SCSI device to the other jack on the WORM drive. If your drive uses an external termination and is the only SCSI drive to be connected to your host adapter, the jack to use should be obvious—it's the only one free because the other SCSI jack is filled with the termination.

If you're making an internal WORM installation, plug the drive into your SCSI cable. Because you haven't secured the drive yet (at least if you're following these instructions), you should be able to pull it out slightly to reach the jack on the drive. After both ends of the SCSI cable are connected, secure your internal drive.

After all cables are plugged in and the internal drive is screwed in securely, it's safe to plug the power cable back into your PC. If you've made an external installation, also connect the power cable to your drive and plug the other end of the cable into utility power.

As with MO drives, most WORM drives are shipped with dummy disks installed to protect the mechanism from shipping damage. Check the instructions accompanying your WORM drive for the proper method of removing any dummy shipping disks.

After you've gotten everything all plugged in and the drive slot free, turn on your WORM drive (if you've installed it externally) and boot your PC. After the drive is powered up, insert a cartridge, following the manufacturer's instructions.

Because of the new SCSI host adapter, your PC may boot differently from the way you've become accustomed. You may see new messages on your monitor, possibly even an error message alerting you that your new drive isn't ready for use. Unless there's something really nasty on your screen, you can ignore these initial errors. But check the manual to be sure.

Follow the procedure in the drive's instruction manual to install the drive's software. In most cases, the entire installation process is handled by a single program—you can slide the first disk of the stash that comes with a WORM drive (usually labeled "INSTALL" or "SETUP") into your A: floppy drive, log onto that drive, and run a program called (amazingly) INSTALL or SETUP. If you don't like to experiment, check the instructions that came with your drive to find out the proper name of the setup program.

After you've completed the software installation, reboot your PC. Any earlier error message should have gone away and now you should see a new message informing you that your drive has been installed properly. Your WORM drive is now ready for whatever you plan to do with it. Just be careful—like diamonds, WORM storage (and any errors you write on it) are forever.

9

Backup Systems

A backup system is your insurance against data disaster. It gives you hope when everything looks blackest. You can use a number of media for making backups, but the leading choice remains one of the constants of computing—tape. Not only can a tape drive provide an excellent backup medium, it can also serve as an exchange medium, letting you share information as conveniently as with floppy disks but in quantities measured in hundreds of megabytes. Unlike disks, a number of different tape systems are available, each with its own advantages. The right tape or backup system upgrade means not just installing a drive but installing the right drive for your PC and purposes.

A backup system is your second chance. When something goes awry—your hard disk crashes from neglect, power failure, or physical damage; when a software upgrade makes running your PC a bigger gamble than betting double-zero in Monte Carlo; when your brain fades and important files evaporate—you can return the world to exactly where it was before the error by making a fast file restoration.

You have a lot of alternatives in your choice of machinery to give you your second chance. Several technologies can provide the backups you need—duplicate hard disks, cartridge drives, piles of floppy disks, even ancient, arcane technologies like punched paper tape. Today, the premier backup choice remains the same as it was a decade ago—lowly magnetic tape. Today's tape system, however, is hardly the same as it was when the first PC was introduced. Between then and now, the tape system has evolved so far that yesterday's drives have all the virtues of real dinosaurs—huge, lumbering beasts with enormous appetites for your time and cash. Today's tape systems are adroit and quick and cost less per megabyte of backup

The right tape or backup system upgrade means not just installing a drive but installing the right drive for your PC and purposes.

Today, the premier backup choice remains the same as it was a decade ago—lowly magnetic tape.

storage than ever before. Yet behind the faceplates of the drives, the technology and philosophy underlying tape has remained unchanged through the ages.

Scrutinize what you want for your PC, however, and you'll see that it's not really tape that's the necessity. What you need is what tape does—fast, easy-to-manage copies of your most valuable data that can be preserved for the ages against all adversity. In many applications, nothing does it better.

Examined as nothing more than a means to make backups, tape is not the only available system nor is it always the best. After all, it *is* the oldest storage medium used by computers, and a number of better ideas have come along since (for instance, the Winchester hard disk). Newer isn't always better, however. Even the backward biplane has its advantages in some applications—think of the barnstorming aerobatics that kept your eyes glued to the sky at the last air show you enjoyed—the ancient technology of tape has still to be topped in the applications it handles best.

Tape and computers go back a long time. In fact, they grew up together with magnetic recording and mainframe computers both teething through the 50s. The association of tape and digital signals goes back even further—punch tape, with holes popped out to signify the forerunner of ASCII, Morse code, for telegraphic transmissions. Long, thin ribbons of tape offer the perfect medium for recording long, single-file trains of data.

Magnetic tape was the first successful mass storage medium for mainframe computers—the one that kept computer operators hopping, lifting, and mounting reel after reel of heavy tape. Tape also keeps popping back into the personal computer industry as primary storage, usually with bad results. The original IBM PC was designed for wielding cassette tapes. Toy manufacturer Coleco tried to cheap out in the storage system for its ill-fated Adam home computer and used oddly modified cassettes. That tape helped seal that machine's ill fate. With all that history going for it, you probably wonder why you should even bother thinking about upgrading your PC with a tape system.

Magnetic tape has a few virtues that keep it in the engineer's eye. In cartridges, tape is convenient and rugged. For example, most people still prefer cassette tapes to digital Compact Discs for music in their automobiles. Tape has been around for a long time, so it is well understood and supported. You can buy tape drives (though perhaps not of computer quality) for a few dollars. The tape itself, although a precision product, is cheap to make. In some widths, you can find it retailing for under $20 per *mile*.

Tape has its weakness, too. Although tape drives can write, read, and transfer information as quickly as disks, they are definitely handicapped when it comes to *finding* a random byte because tape is strictly a sequential medium; the long ribbon stores information in a long stream with no shortcuts to find the one particular byte you need. In that most personal computer applications take a random approach to their data needs, tape just doesn't serve well, particularly when compared to the quick response of disk drives. What a disk can locate in a few thousandths of a second, a tape drive may take a few thousand seconds to find.

Tape would be nothing more than a curious footnote in the history of personal computing were it not that two very important applications don't require random data storage or retrieval. These applications are system support functions that require copying large blocks of data and storing the results or sharing them with someone else. *Backup systems*—what you think of first when you think of tape—need to be able to make an exact copy of data stored on disk, maintaining the order laid onto the disk. Tape can make the one-for-one copy quickly and easily. *Exchanging data* also requires an exact copy of the contents of a disk to be transcribed byte-for-byte. Consequently, tape makes an excellent backup and data exchange medium.

> *What a disk can locate in a few thousandths of a second, a tape drive may take a few thousand seconds to find.*

As disk drives get ever bigger and faster, the value of a tape system thus increases rather than decreases. Tape can earn its keep because the more you depend on your hard disk, the bigger the threat the failure of your disk becomes. In effect, your disk is a time bomb, waiting to self-destruct and take your data along with it. A tape drive won't prevent the inevitable disk crash, but it will make recovering from disaster easier—instead of a miracle, you'll just need some time to restore your files.

> *Your disk is a time bomb, waiting to self-destruct and take your data along with it.*

You don't need a complete disaster to show you the value of tape. Accidentally write over an important file—for example, copy an old version over a new version—and no file recovery program will help resurrect your data, but a tape backup will.

The same applications that demand huge hard disk drives also require some way of conveniently exchanging files. Suppose that you're designing a new ocean liner—the QE3—and you need to send your preliminary CAD drawings for approval to the Royal Family. You can spend 15 days plotting them all out and invest in

12 cartons of floppy disks and a two-day backup session, or you can slide a single tape into your tape drive and issue a single command.

Certainly, you have other technologies, such as optical disk cartridges, to choose for these same functions. Tape, however, remains one of the least expensive (in terms of cost per megabyte stored) and most convenient backup media available.

Backup Philosophy

Viewed pragmatically, the primary application of the backup is as insurance against the inevitable. All mechanical devices are subject to failure. Even ignoring deliberate mischief and vandalism, your system is prey to human frailties and error. One errant keystroke, and the command to rid your disk of garbage, DEL *.BAK, will wipe away every batch file if typed as DEL *.BAT. Whenever you write a program that POKEs to memory or writes bytes to your disk, you risk sending your system on a random seek-and-destroy mission, perhaps sliding extra little end-of-file markers every fifth byte on your hard disk or just dropping your bookkeeping records on top of both copies of its file allocation table.

In its most basic form, the backup is just a duplicate copy of all the vulnerable data (and, often, programs) that you have. By keeping everything in two places, you have a greater chance that one will survive when your most dreaded nightmares come true. However, the usefulness and protection of the backup system doesn't stop there. Multiple backups can give you multiple layers of security. Stored off-site, perhaps at a commercial data repository or in your bank safe-deposit box, you can keep your most valuable files alive even when a conflagration or similar catastrophe strikes and annihilates your office and the surrounding neighborhood.

In addition to the extra measure of protection that they afford, some backup systems can also be used as data interchange systems. After you've distilled your important files into a backup, you can send them anywhere in the world, in a single small package, for nothing more than the price of postage or a courier. Choose the right backup system, and you can even interchange data with different computer models and even different operating systems, from Macintoshes to minicomputers to mainframes.

If you're a PC manager or are foolish enough to volunteer for similar duties by setting up systems for friends, the backup system can make your job a breeze. After you've obtained the proper software licenses (or only use your own, homegrown programs), you can save a whole hard disk environment on a cartridge and then transfer everything to another system, setting up the most complex arrangement of files and directories as easily as plugging in the interface card and typing *restore*.

Backup Alternatives

By now, you may be harboring thoughts like, "Cartridge disks can do all of that." Tape, however, brings a combination of virtues that cartridge disks lack: low cost and huge cartridge capacities. A cartridge disk will do for 100 megabytes, but only tape will keep a couple of gigabytes in one cartridge. Although storing that 100M on disk cartridge will cost upwards of $100, you can put five times that amount of data on a tape cartridge at one-fifth the cost.

Tape, however, brings a combination of virtues that cartridge disks lack: low cost and huge cartridge capacities.

Actually, nearly any medium that can hold data is a candidate for a PC backup system. Each one has its own strengths and weaknesses. Consequently, a look at all the various backup alternatives is in order before you commit your cash to a tape drive. The simple truth is that tape and disk cartridges aren't the only choices, and tape is not always the best choice.

For most people, tape is a single-purpose medium that serves to copy the contents of an active hard disk. For such simple copying, tape works well. Copying is a sequential operation—one file is transcribed at a time into the next blank area on the storage medium—and tape is by its nature a sequential medium. Its magnetic ribbon spools continuously past its read/write head, ready to accept or disgorge information in sequence as it goes along. This single-minded purposefulness of tape is also tape's undoing. Other backup media can serve other functions besides backing up, potentially something important like primary storage. For example, cartridge-based disk systems offer the same data-exchange capabilities of tape but have an inherent speed advantage for many system functions.

Cartridge-based disk systems offer the same data-exchange capabilities of tape but have an inherent speed advantage for many system functions.

Disk systems hold this advantage because they step beyond tape by providing random access to data. Disk read/write heads can quickly move tangent to normal data flow to get into the middle of things almost instantly. The heads of a disk drive can immediately scoot over to find a file, even when that file is part of a backup. Not only does such instant access benefit normal storage operations, it can be helpful even when using a disk as a backup system. For example, a disk system can compare an archived file with one you're thinking of backing up to see whether you even need to bother with making a copy of an unchanged file. The whole operation might take a second using a disk drive, although a tape system might have to scan the whole tape just to find the file. A file that's backed up to a disk is also usually faster and easier to recover than one on tape.

Each disk cartridge generally holds less and costs more than a tape cartridge.

Disk drive mechanisms are by their nature more complex—and consequently more expensive—than tape drives. The capacities of the typical cartridge-based disk system also pales in comparison with tape. Although cartridge disk systems allow virtually unlimited off-line storage as do tape cartridges, disk cartridge capacity also tends to cost more per megabyte. Each disk cartridge generally holds less and costs more than a tape cartridge.

Disk backup systems need not use cartridge-based media, however. In fact, simple redundancy ranks as the most straightforward disk backup method—just keep two disks spinning with the same files written on each. Odds are that one will survive the erroneous erasure or simple head crash. Most network operating systems support such built-in disk backup systems and use a technology called *disk mirroring* to automatically ensure that changes made to one disk are reflected in the contents of the other.

Even in a single-user PC, double-disk systems can be an excellent backup strategy, one that is surprisingly inexpensive. Because a second, backup drive needs neither high performance or an additional controller (most hard disk controllers take care of two different disk drives), adding an extra 340M hard disk to your system can cost as little as $300 to $400.

All multiple-megabyte magnetic disk cartridge systems suffer from standardization and compatibility problems.

Although effective in some situations, the double-disk technique affords no protection against the more wide-ranging disasters—like tornadoes—nor does it give the convenience and security feature of removable media. The removable cartridge disk systems that eliminate these problems cost more. Moreover, cartridge capacity and the resultant amount of on-line data is also more limited than that available with conventional hard disks because most disk cartridges contain only a single platter. Most non-removable hard disk systems use multiple platters. In addition, although removable cartridge hard disk systems are faster than most other backup systems, they are generally slower than conventional hard disks.

All multiple-megabyte magnetic disk cartridge systems suffer from standardization and compatibility problems. You cannot exchange information on disk cartridges between different manufacturers' systems. Even systems that use physically identical cartridges are often incompatible. Optical cartridges, WORM, and MO drives suffer similar problems. The cartridges are standardized, but partitioning and operating software is not. The end result is that you're not guaranteed that a cartridge made in one manufacturer's drive will work in that made by another. Although tape used to be the same way, standards have emerged that allow some systems from different manufacturers to exchange tapes.

You're not guaranteed that a cartridge made in one manufacturer's drive will work in that made by another.

Tape is far from the lowest cost backup system from a capital investment standpoint, however. As long as you're willing to put up with the inconvenience of shuffling floppies—stuffing your disk drive with a fresh floppy every 30 seconds to one minute—floppy disk backup can be a viable alternative, particularly when your equipment budget is tight and when you have the discipline to organize a real (but manual) backup system. Daily incremental backups can often be confined to a single floppy disk. Floppy disk drives are the most affordable backup systems available because every PC already has a floppy disk drive of one sort or another. You only need pay for the storage medium, not additional equipment.

Floppy disk drives are the most affordable backup systems available because every PC already has a floppy disk drive of one sort or another.

Although scoffed at by equipment snobs, floppies (particularly high density, 1.2M and 1.44M diskettes) can back up files on par with some more exotic streaming tape technologies when you use a high-performance backup programs. Of course, diskettes also remain the preferred file interchange medium for PCs. If you work on only a few short files at a time, your floppy disk drive may be the only backup system you need.

Compared to floppy disks, the big advantage of cartridge tape backup is that it's convenient. Instead of dealing with boxes of floppies (a complete uncompressed backup of a full 340M hard disk requires at least 236 high-density floppy disks), you can keep everything on one compact tape cartridge smaller—although thicker—than an audio tape cassette. More importantly, with tape you don't have to shuffle disks like an arthritic blackjack dealer, baby-sitting your system for half an hour or more while your hard disk slowly deals out its files.

Tape is also more reliable than floppy disk backup. Judged by the claimed error rates, backups kept on some cartridges actually are more secure than even the hard disk-based originals.

Moreover, the per-megabyte costs of tape typically is less than floppy-based backup. Even if you were to pay just a quarter per high-density disk—low even by mail-order standards—storing backups on tape cartridges can cut your costs to a fraction of the disk price. Figure $59 for 340M of floppies and about $20 for a tape that can hold 10 times more (DAT). Indeed, tape is generally conceded to be the least expensive file archiving medium available.

All tape backup systems, however, do not offer the same protections or potential. Some are faster; some offer more compatibility options; and some are cheaper. The first step in finding the right one to suit your own particular needs is to consider all the backup options and technologies that are available to you.

Tape is also more reliable than floppy disk backup.

Primary Tape Alternatives

A variety of tape systems are now available for use with PCs, and additional models will soon be offered as creative manufacturers and standards organizations dream up new products. Although the number of choices continues to expand, the number of useful tape formats is actually diminishing as disk capacities climb skyward. The variety of currently available tape systems is wide and includes open reels of half-inch nine-track tape cartridges using half-inch, quarter-inch, 150-mm, eight-mm tape, cassettes, videocassettes, and digital audio tape (DAT) cartridges. However, if you have a modern-size hard disk with more than 200M of capacity, your choices are far fewer. You can get by cheaply with mini-cartridge backup, but if you demand fast performance and the ability to fit all your data on a single cartridge (as well as the lowest cost per megabyte), you'll be most interested in quarter-inch cartridge tape and DAT. Other tape media are best considered for special-purpose applications and situations.

Mini-Cartridges

Most mini-cartridge systems work with the floppy disk controller already built into your PC.

The clear price leader in today's backup market is the mini-cartridge. Some mini-cartridge drives are available for under $200 retail, low enough to lure even the most parsimonious PC person into purchasing. The price is low, and installation of the drives is among the easiest because in most cases you don't even need a host adapter. Most mini-cartridge systems work with the floppy disk controller already built into your PC.

The most affordable mini-cartridge systems are the ones you are least likely to want. Mini-cartridges are strapped to keep up with the climbing capacities of hard disks. The cheap drives pack as little as 40M per cartridge. Currently, the most popular advertised capacity is 250M, about the same as today's most favored hard disks, but achieving that capacity takes some imagination and a willing PC and hard disk. Although the cheap drives may suffice if you have an older, low-capacity (under 120M) hard disk drive, they're not a good bet for the future. As soon as you upgrade your hard disk, your tape capacity may prove to be inadequate.

The cheaper mini-cartridge systems are also the slowest tape backup alternatives available. In retailers' lingo, the bottom line mini-cartridge drives are loss leaders. They lure you into the marketplace and encourage you to examine mini-cartridge backup, but the hope is that you'll buy up to a more realistic product. Several viable mini-cartridge alternatives are available.

First, a definition of terms. A mini-cartridge earns its name because of the compact size of its tapes. Individual mini-cartridges measure just under 3 $\frac{1}{4}$ x 2 $\frac{1}{2}$ x $\frac{5}{8}$ inches. A typical cartridge holds 205 feet that measures just under a quarter-inch wide tape (nominally 0.248 inch). The cartridges themselves are often termed *DC2000*-style because that was the designation hung on them by their originator, the 3M Company. Most cartridges on the market use the positions of the last three zeros to indicate the cartridge capacity in megabytes. Thus, a DC2120 cartridge stores about 120M. The small size of the DC2000-style cartridge endows the mini-cartridge system with one of its greatest virtues: tape drives that fit into a standard 3.5-inch drive bay.

The most prevalent mini-cartridge systems on the market follow the standards promulgated by an industry organization called the Quarter-Inch Cartridge committee or *QIC*. The two most popular of these standards are QIC-40 and QIC-80. As the designations hint, QIC-40 aims for 40 megabytes per cartridge; QIC-80 for 80M. Most drives that advertise capacities of 250M follow the QIC-80 standard.

That anomaly results from technological tricks. The QIC standards define the number of tracks spread across the tape and the manner in which data is recorded onto each track (including data density and format). By the clever subterfuge of stocking a cartridge with more tape, its capacity can be increased. A DC2120 cartridge holds 50 percent more tape than a DC2080 cartridge; thus it can store 50 percent more data, 120M, under the same standard.

The other technological trick is data compression. Just as the capacity of a hard disk can be doubled by storing information in a denser form, so can the data on cartridge. Because an average file compresses at about a factor of two to one, the capacity of a single cartridge can be increased by a like amount using compression. For good measure and a round number, tape drive makers rounded the doubled capacity of DC2120 cartridges up to 250M. Despite the compression, the data actually written to a 250M cartridge still follows the QIC-80 standard.

Just as the capacity of a hard disk can be doubled by storing information in a denser form, so can the data on cartridge.

Another part of the QIC-80 standard is the interface used by the drives. As noted, QIC-80 requires a floppy disk interface. That does not necessarily mean that you have to unplug a floppy disk drive to plug a QIC-80 drive in. QIC-80 tape drives will work with a vacant channel on your floppy disk controller, but they need not. Drives may come with special cables or cables and boards that enable you to use two floppies and a tape drive from the same floppy disk controller. Before you order a floppy-interfaced tape system, you should assay your system to determine what you'll need to link up the drive and to get a product to match.

Even if you have a spare channel on your floppy disk controller, not plugging into the controller can add speed to some tape systems. Not all floppy disks operate at the same speeds. Old, low-density drives require an old, slow data transfer rate of 250 Kbps. High-density drives operate at 500 Kbps. Some tape manufacturers have individual products to match one or the other speed. Understandably, 500 Kbps drives are to be preferred (if your PC supports them) because they operate at double-speed. However, a growing number of tape drive makers now offer products that double the high-density rate to 1 Mbps, making them twice as fast again. These drives use special controller boards based on floppy-disk style circuitry but implemented for the exclusive use of the tape drive. Although they are costly (you need the controller board as well as the drive) and take up an expansion slot, the added speed makes these 1 Mbps systems worth the dual penalties.

Unfortunately, you can't tell the speed difference in mini-cartridge systems by looking at the drive. You must get a tape system that's compatible with the speed of your floppy disk controller—or, if you're getting a new controller along with your tape drive, you must make sure that their speeds match. This speed difference is sometimes described in terms of host compatibility. A tape system that's only PC-compatible is probably rated at 250K bps. A tape system that's classed as AT-compatible but not PC-compatible operates at 500K bps.

Using a floppy disk controller for the tape interface slows things down. Most mini-cartridge systems don't even approach the raw throughput that the interface allows. Figure that a contemporary mini-cartridge system will be able to transfer from one to three megabytes per minute to a DC2000 cartridge. This floppy connection scheme limits the data transfer rate of DC2000 systems to about one-tenth the rate of hard disk drives. Your hard disk and your computer have to spin their wheels while waiting for the tape drive to catch up.

In practice, however, the performance penalty of miniature cartridges is not so severe, particularly because after you start the tape drive running, you can wander off and get into trouble some other place. In fact, most tape systems allow you to set a time (for example, during your lunch hour or after 5 p.m.) to make backups unattended by your physical presence. When a tape drive operates without occupying your time, it shouldn't matter how long a backup takes.

That 250M capacity of today's most popular mini-cartridge systems seems right on target for today's 200 or so megabyte hard disk drives. With the advent of DOS 6 and built-in data compression, however, don't count on having enough storage on a single mini-cartridge to handle everything you have on disk. After you compress your 200M hard disk, you'll have 400M or more of storage, more than will fit on a mini-cartridge using compressed. You can't compress data twice (you actually can, but you won't compress it to any smaller size) so there's no way the drive can deal with all that data. If you use data compression on your hard disk—DOS 6 or otherwise—the only way to judge whether you can back it up onto a single cartridge is to compare the *uncompressed* capacity of your hard disks with the *uncompressed* capacity of the tape cartridge. Because QIC-80 systems max out at 120M uncompressed, that's the largest physical hard disk capacity you can fit on a cartridge (when both disk and tape use compression).

That's not to say that you cannot use a QIC-80 tape drive with larger, compressed hard disks. You can with the simple expedient of spanning mini-cartridges. Your disk files will need to be spread across multiple mini-cartridges when you make a full backup. You'll have to baby-sit your tape drive to change tapes, but otherwise you should encounter no difficulties.

The moral is not to be misled by the 250M claim of QIC-80 backup systems, and don't be confused by the capabilities (and limitations) of data compression.

Mini-cartridges are not inherently limited to 120M per tape. Only the QIC-80 standard imposes that limit. The QIC organization is developing other standards to increase mini-cartridge capacity. The immediate step up from QIC-80 is QIC-500M, now currently available, which packs up to 500M on a mini-cartridge *without* data compression. QIC-500M achieves its higher cartridge capacity by packing data more tightly in more (but skinnier) data tracks across the width of the tape. This tighter packing requires the use of special tapes that have a higher coercivity, a servo-tracking mechanism for the tape read/write head to ensure that the track and head are correctly positioned, and high-powered error-correction to bridge over defects in the tape medium itself.

QIC-500M drives are patterned after the QIC-40 and QIC-80 systems and are designed to be backwardly compatible with those older formats. A QIC-500M drive can read tapes written using the old formats, although tapes made on the new drives are not compatible with older drives.

Data compression can push per-tape capacity of the QIC-500M system to one gigabyte.

As with QIC-40 and QIC-80, QIC-500M drives can connect to PCs using a floppy disk interface. However, the standard also allows for the drive to use the same AT Attachment interface that's called IDE in the realm of hard disks. Data compression—exactly the same algorithm used by QIC-80—can push per-tape capacity of the QIC-500M system to one gigabyte.

A higher speed alternative to QIC-500M is QIC-410M. To gain speed, this format substitutes a SCSI-2 connection for the floppy interface but uses the same high-coercivity tape as QIC-500M. The QIC-410M standard is not backwardly compatible with existing standards and packs only 410M per cartridge (potentially doubled with compression). However, the SCSI interface promises higher speeds.

In the future, you can expect to buy mini-cartridge drives that follow the QIC-875M standard. Again designed to use the same high-coercivity tape as QIC-410M and QIC-500M, this future standard promises to pack 875M on a single tape by pressing bits closer together. Drives conforming to QIC- 875 are expected to read QIC-410M and QIC-40/80 tapes. QIC-875M drives will also use a SCSI-2 connection.

Farther in the future is QIC-3GB, the step up from QIC-410M, with which it will be backwardly read-compatible. QIC-3B will use another new tape type in its cartridges (which will be designated QIC-138). As the name indicates, the standard will fit three gigabytes of uncompressed data on each cartridge, double that with compression. The QIC Committee has also proposed a 10-gigabyte mini-cartridge standard and is dreaming about one for 35-gigabyte mini-cartridges.

Perhaps the principal disadvantage of these mini-cartridge standards from QIC-40 onward is that they require that the cartridges be formatted before they are used, much as you must format floppy disks. Although formatting is a small bother with floppy disks, it can be a hardship with QIC-40 tapes, a nightmare with larger capacities. Typically, the process takes about one minute to format one megabyte of tape, up to 40 minutes for the full capacity of a single QIC-40 cartridge, and 80 minutes for QIC-80. (Some tape systems allow you to save time by formatting tapes for lower capacities.)

Although the formatting process can be time-consuming, it has its upside. It adds flexibility and speed during backup and restoration. Moreover, it helps to identify bad spots on tapes and to ensure that they won't be used for storing your valuable data. To allow you to avoid the painfully long formatting wait, many tape manufacturers sell their DC2000 cartridges preformatted. If you opt for the laudable strategy of buying preformatted tapes, you'll want to take care to be sure that the tapes use the same format as does your tape drive.

Other mini-cartridge formats have appeared in the past but no longer see wide application. You probably won't want to upgrade to any of these, but you should be aware of their existence (if just to avoid them) and their strengths (if you find a deal that's too good to resist).

The QIC-100 standard was developed to break through the floppy disk controller speed barrier, but it has proven unpopular in comparison to the other standards. Tapes made on QIC-100 systems are not compatible with other QIC standards, so this choice is not a good one for data interchange. The drives are now difficult to find and probably are not worth the effort.

Tapes made on QIC-100 systems are not compatible with other QIC standards.

Irwin Magnetics at one time sold about half the tape drives inside PCs and became an industry standard in itself—though not one adopted by any recognized standard-setting organization. Although Irwin did produce a QIC-compatible drive, current products continue to follow the older Irwin proprietary standard. As long as you don't want to exchange tapes with people using QIC, these drives can function as superb backup systems with the same strengths and weaknesses as QIC products. (Both Irwin and QIC use floppy interfaces, write to the same kind of cartridges, and require the tapes be formatted before use.)

If you've been turned off by mini-cartridge tape systems in the past because you read about them or tried them and discovered that they were quirky and slow, take another look at a newer drive. The technology has come a long way in the last few years. Today, mini-cartridge tape drives rank as a top backup choice, at least for smaller hard disk capacities.

Today, mini-cartridge tape drives rank as a top backup choice, at least for smaller hard disk capacities.

Quarter-Inch Cartridges

Strictly speaking, a mini-cartridge is a quarter-inch cartridge (measure the tape). But quarter-inch technology started among larger tapes, and the name quarter-inch cartridge (without the "mini ") is usually used to refer to these larger, older cartridges.

Because quarter-inch cartridges are bigger than mini-cartridges, you might expect them to hold more, and you may be right. When quarter-inch cartridge technology first was put to work more than two decades ago, however, a single cartridge held less than one of today's floppy disks. Today, however, quarter-inch cartridges hold 2.5 *gigabytes* and more. If you have a larger hard disk, that makes a quarter-inch cartridge worth considering for backup or data exchange.

Quarter-inch cartridge technology differs in several significant ways from mini-cartridges. First and most obvious, the quarter-inch cartridge is larger. Although the tape is the same width (about a quarter inch), the cartridge spreads out almost to the size of a paperback book, a full 6 x 4 x ⁵/₈ inches. Each one holds 450 to 600 feet of tape. The cartridges are so large, in fact, that there's no possible way to fit a drive that handles one into a 3.5-inch drive slot. Fitting a drive into even a 5.25-inch bay requires sliding the cartridge in sideways.

Quarter-inch cartridges operate at higher speeds than mini-cartridges, so conventional floppy disk interfaces aren't sufficient to handle their high data rate signals. The systems introduced when the PC was young used interfaces that were standardized by QIC. However, because the early quarter-inch cartridge drive interfaces were only designed to handle tape drives, from an upgrade viewpoint, these were best considered proprietary interfaces. Most current quarter-in cartridge systems use SCSI connections.

The speed of a quarter-inch cartridge system can be considerable. From the beginning, many drives could read and write data as fast as the hard disks that they were meant to backup. In fact, the PC that they were connected through was their principal performance bottleneck. Even today, the latest quarter-inch cartridges systems rank as the fastest backup media available—expect throughput to start at about 10 megabytes per minute. They don't just transfer information quickly. They are also among the fastest sequential media devices at finding needed information. Many are able to locate any given data block in an average of about 30 seconds, given the proper control software.

Quarter-inch cartridges have two chief shortcomings—price and compatibility. Quarter-inch tape systems cost about twice as much as mini-cartridge systems, and they have even less compatibility between manufacturers, notwithstanding that all current quarter-inch cartridge systems fall under the purview of one or another QIC standards. For the most part, only the tape hardware and media are standardized by QIC. Software issues, like tape formats, are generally left to individual manufacturers to develop. Consequently, the chances that you can exchange quarter-inch cartridges between drives of different manufacturers are slim.

The quarter-inch cartridge can trace its origins back to 1973 when 3M Company developed the first system as a recording medium for data acquisition applications, such as transcribing seismological information in the laboratory. Externally, today's cartridges look identical to those of the lost ages. Inside, however, the mechanism has been refined, and the tape substantially improved. Capacity has increased several thousandfold along the way. The passing years have proved the cartridges with their clear plastic shells, rugged aluminum bases, and clever internal belt-drive mechanisms to be a reliable and adaptable backup medium. Quarter-inch cartridge systems are often described by 3M's part number designation for the cartridges themselves, DC6000. (This number has evolved from DC300 to DC600 before finding its present value.)

Old quarter-inch cartridge systems for PCs held as little as 60M. Today, the lowest capacity drive you're likely to find is 525M. Multiple-gigabyte products are currently on the market. QIC is planning for drives with capacities of tens of gigabytes within the next few years.

The latest quarter-inch cartridges systems rank as the fastest backup media available

Quarter-inch cartridges have two chief shortcomings—price and compatibility.

The chances that you can exchange quarter-inch cartridges between drives of different manufacturers are slim.

All of these capacities are quoted for uncompressed storage. The data compression rage has yet to strike this medium.

The DC6000-style of cartridge is clever enough to be patented (see fig. 9.1). It's built around a thick, rigid aluminum baseplate that ensures accurate alignment of the tape with the drive mechanism and with the tape driven by a friction band rather than the pressure roller used in audio tape systems. Only the read/write head touches the recording surface of the tape. A clear plastic shell with a hinged door over the head entrance protects the tape.

Figure 9.1

DC6000-style tape drives are two-piece systems comprising a tape drive and a host adapter. Get them as a matched pair to ensure easy installation and smooth integration.

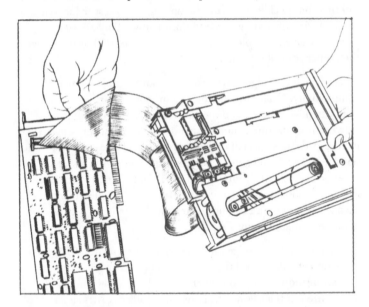

In most older implementations of quarter-inch cartridge systems, information was written in nine tracks across the width of the tape. Newer systems use 18, 30, or more tracks. Unlike the parallel recording used for half-inch tape, however, most quarter-inch systems use serpentine serial recording. Data bits are written sequentially, in one direction, on one track at a time, continuing for the length of the tape. At the end of the tape, the direction of its travel reverses, and recording moves down to the next track until all nine tracks are filled. Old systems often had to read all the data on all the tracks to find a desired block. Modern software links a directory to each tape to help the system find each file and block. The drive needs to scan through only one track and, on the average, only halfway through. Consequently, the high tape speed and large number of tracks results in relatively quick (for a sequential medium) access times.

Quarter-inch cartridge systems have other advantages. Although the complete drive systems are necessarily more expensive than smaller tape drives (if only because they use their own dedicated host adapters), the big cartridges can be an economical storage system. In their larger capacity formats, today's quarter-inch cartridges can cost less per megabyte of backup capacity than smaller cartridges although the tapes themselves might be individually priced a few dollars higher. The big cartridges have also been available longer, and familiarity generally means a better understood, more reliable medium. Moreover, the less dense storage of older quarter-inch systems also helps ensure greater data integrity. Of course, mini-cartridges compensate for their disadvantage by using error correction which (in theory) nearly eliminates the chance that you won't be able to restore a backup you've made, but error-correction is now applied to quarter-inch systems.

Digital Audio Tape Systems

The newest backup alternative is Digital Audio Tape or DAT. Patterned closely after the slow-to-catch-on audio DAT system, computer DAT systems use the same tape and recording method as the machines that can be connected to your stereo system. That's because both systems were designed from the ground up to store digital information.

DAT cartridges are amazingly compact, hardly a couple inches long, smaller even than mini-cartridges, yet each one holds upwards of a gigabyte of computer data. Some systems claim four gigabytes, thanks to data compression that's built into the drive hardware.

The trick underlying their high capacity is helical scan recording. This recording system represents a refinement of consumer video recording equipment with its roots in the original Beta videocassette recorder developed by Sony in 1973. In traditional tape systems, the read/write head is held stationary while the tape zips past it. If it makes any movement, the head rises or falls a fraction of an inch to access different tracks on the tape. During actual reading and writing, however, the head does not move. In helical recording, the read/write head spins at a high rate while the tape travels past. The head is mounted on a spinning cylinder around which the tape is wrapped at a slight angle, giving it the shape of a section of a helix, hence the name.

The relative speed between head and tape determines the highest frequency a tape system can record, which translates directly into data density. The spinning head of the helical systems substantially increases the tape-to-head speed and helps helical media be the most densely pack of commercial data recording media.

As a result of this spinning head technology, the data cassettes and the tape they contain used by a DAT system for gigabyte capacities are physically small. DAT tape is four millimeters wide and packed inside 3 by 2 inch cassettes about three-eighth inch thick. Two lengths are generally available, 60 meters and 90 meters. The shorter DAT cassettes store (without compression) 1.35G at 1,869 tracks per inch; the longer ones, 2.0G.

DAT drives are also compact. Most will fit into a 3.5-inch drive bay. They also use the industry-standard SCSI interface, so connecting them is easy—or difficult, depending on your personal view of SCSI.

A philosophical difference separates quarter-inch cartridge from helical-scan. The former emphasizes simple, low-cost mechanisms and more precise, robust media. Helical-scan uses a complex mechanism that can tolerate more tape variations. Without data compression, DAT systems are not as quick as quarter-inch cartridge systems of similar capacity. DAT was originally designed for audio recording, which requires relatively low transfer rates. Hardware data compression effectively doubles the throughput of DAT systems that use it (with compressible data) and pushes transfer speed up to par with quarter-inch cartridges.

On the other hand, audio systems require fast access to musical selections, and DAT systems carry through the same quick access designs. In a typical DAT system, your data is never more than about 15 seconds away.

The multiple-gigabyte capacities of DAT systems may seem superfluous for today's PC hard disks that store only about one-tenth as much. But at the rate hard disk capacities (as well as storage needs) are ballooning, DAT capacity will soon become a necessity.

Special-Purpose Tape Systems

Although the preceding trio will take care of most backup needs, sometimes a more particular, even peculiar need will overrule one of the standard backup choices. For example, you may need a backup system and a means for exchanging large databases with scientists addicted to DEC's VAX series of minicomputers. Although you could try a direct connection, you might find it easier to transfer information using a common tape format—and the most common format being old-fashioned (even ancient) open-reel tapes. A number of other tape systems have been used for backup in the last decade. Each has its own virtue, often of the type that only a mother would understand. All are still available in one form or another for connecting to your PC.

Nine-Track Tape

The grandparent and progenitor of all computer tape technologies is the nine-track open-reel system. Based on reels of tape half an inch wide and up to 3600 feet long, the first of these systems were developed for mainframe computers in the 1950s. No picture of the primordial computer was complete without a reel of tape jerking back and forth inside the closet-size tape drive of a computer that took control of the world—at least until the climax of the movie.

Open reel tape and its associated drives have evolved through the years. First able to record 800 bytes of data on every linear inch of tape, the latest of these systems can squeeze nearly eight times more, 6250 bytes, into the same space. Tape drives have shrunk to desktop size (not a size to fit on a desktop but in some cases the size of the desktop itself).

Despite the evolution of the equipment, half-inch tape systems are remarkable in how little the tapes themselves have changed through the years and how standardized the data format they use has become. Twenty-year-old tapes that were made with mainframe computers can be read by drives attached to PCs today.

In many ways, open reel tape is the only interchange medium available that standard throughout all sizes and styles of computer. The recording format and data structure are essentially the same for open reel systems no matter who makes them or where they are used. Connect a nine-track tape drive to your PC (no easy feat), and you'll be able to read and write tapes that can be exchanged with DEC minicomputers, IBM mainframes, and even the most powerful supercomputers.

Open reel computer tapes use nine tracks arranged laterally across the width of the half-inch tape. Eight of these tracks record data, and one holds a parity-check bit. Each byte of information is written at the same time, in parallel across the width of the tape, and successive

Twenty-year-old tapes that were made with mainframe computers can be read by drives attached to PCs today.

bytes are written sequentially along the tape. The tape has effectively only one side and is written from one end to the other and then rewound. Flux reversals, the equivalent of data bits, are spaced anywhere from 800 to 6250 per inch, with the most common density being 1600 bits per inch.

The data density, reel size, tape thickness, and a parameter called inter-record gap (the distance between two blocks of data on the tape) all affect how much information will fit a single reel. Capacities around 60M are commonplace.

Software for nine-track systems can usually cope with the variables of recording format. For example, most nine-track control programs allow for various inter-record gaps and even converting the EBCDIC data coding method used by IBM mainframes into the ASCII code used by PCs. About the only nine-track format variable not completely under control of software is data recording density. Higher data densities are available only on nine-track transports that support them. Consequently, lower data densities are used for storage when data interchange is the goal. Lower density tapes are readable on a wider variety of tape machines. The penalty of using lower densities is, of course, that more tape must be devoted to store a given number of megabytes.

Compared to other technologies, open reel tape is an ungainly back up medium.

For strictly making backups, using higher densities will lower storage costs; however, nine-track tape is a particularly poor choice. Compared to other technologies, open reel tape is an ungainly back up medium. Tape reels can be more than 10 inches in diameter and nearly an inch thick (counting their flanges), yet that reel may store no more information than a two-by-three inch cartridge. Moreover, most open reel tape drives themselves dwarf a PC system unit, in size and price. The cost of an open-reel system designed for connection to a PC starts at $3,500 and can reach above $10,000—which may be more expensive than the computer you want to back up. The flip side of nine-track backup issue is data integrity. Just as a battleship can suffer through storms on the high seas better than a rowboat, the large size of open reel tapes earns them an extra measure of long-term security. Data is stored less densely and is less likely to degrade with time or through environmental effects.

The real value of the nine-track tape systems is in data interchange, however. Tape acts like "sneaker-net" taken to the nth degree. Although exchanging diskettes can operate as a rudimentary data-sharing network, nine-track tape moves megabytes as easily as diskettes move kilobytes. Although diskettes are forever linked to one operating system (except through the use of format conversion software), nine-track tapes know no such bounds.

The big tapes are often used to move databases between systems and to distribute information, such as mailing lists. Connected to a PC, the open reel system can function as a backup and as data interchange system. Factor in cost, however, and nine track is a curiosity for all but the wealthiest PC users.

3480 Cartridges

After more than 20 years of dominance in the mainframe world, open reel tape is slowly being replaced (or augmented, depending on your point of view) by a new cartridge system developed by IBM. Usually referred to by the model number of the tape drive, 3480, these cartridges are little more than open reel tapes stuffed into a protective shell. The tape is still half an inch wide and runs through the drive much like open reel tapes. The drive mechanism pulls the tape out of the cartridge, winds it onto a tape up spool, and rewinds it back into the cartridge when it is done.

The difference is more than the convenience of cartridge loading, however. IBM has doubled the number of tracks (doubling them once or twice more is promised) and increased the data density so that a single cartridge, less than a quarter the volume of an open reel tape at $4\,^3/_4$ x $4\,^1/_4$ x $4\,^3/_4$ inches, can hold hundreds of megabytes. In addition, current implementations write two parallel sets of nine tracks simultaneously, doubling data throughput.

Packing more data on tape has its penalties, however, and with the 3480 system, the price you pay is the price. Currently, the tape drives are big ticket ($20,000-plus) products designed for the mainframe market.

Several companies have worked at adapting the 3480-style cartridge into systems that would be practical (and affordable) for PC applications. However, these new 3480-style cartridge systems use different data formats than the true IBM 3480 tape drive. They lack the big advantage of open-reel tape—its capability to exchange information with mainframes.

DC1000 Cartridges

Out of today's tape mainstream but aiming at getting in are several other tape formats. Some of these have already seen their short day in the sun; others are rising in prominence.

Among the former are DC1000 cartridges. About the same size as standard mini-cartridges, DC1000 cartridges use narrower tape measuring 150 mils (thousandths of an inch) wide. Each cartridge holds 10 to 20 megabytes.

As with mini-cartridge tape drives, the DC1000 systems typically interfaced through an extra channel in a PC's floppy disk controller. That, of course, made them slow. Figure in the modest capacities that were quickly dwarfed by fast-growing hard disks and the lack of the blessing of a standards organization, and you'll understand why DC1000 failed to catch on. Today, consider such a unit advertised at an unbelievably low price a curiosity. Consider a unit installed in your PC a liability.

Data Cassettes

Economies of scale and common design make data cassette mechanisms among the least expensive tape drives that you can plug into your PC.

Computer data cassettes have matured from an ungainly youth as a slow, modem-speed, audio technology-based system for sequentially storing the outpourings of home computers to high-speed competitors to more exotic cartridge systems. Using special high-grade computer cassettes and drives, the new systems can pack up to 600M on one tape at rates comparable to mini-cartridge and quarter-inch cartridge technology. Although cassettes are not quite as compact as mini-cartridges, they are a familiar package that holds promise as a strong backup alternative.

Cassette-based systems are priced inexpensively. One reason is that they share their heritage with ordinary audio cassettes. The mechanisms are similar, although data-storing machines require greater precision in manufacturing and entirely different electronics. Nevertheless, economies of scale and common design make data cassette mechanisms among the least expensive tape drives that you can plug into your PC.

Cassette drives are relatively fast—on the order of mini-cartridge systems—and they are economical in their cost per megabyte of storage. All-plastic cassettes are cheaper to make than precision aluminum-based cartridges, and they cost less, about $10 each. Even that relatively low (by computer standards) price might seem high compared to the $2 or so you probably pay for audio cassettes that look pretty much identical to the digital variety. But data cassettes and audio cassettes are *not* interchangeable. Data cassettes use tape media with entirely different magnetic characteristics than the audio variety. Moreover, data cassettes have a special notch on their backbone to distinguish them from audio tapes. Audio cassettes lacking the notch won't even fit into a data cassette drive.

Two factors have prevented data cassettes from gaining greater acceptance. Today's data cassettes lack one virtue enjoyed by mini-cartridge systems—standardization. Data cassettes essentially are a proprietary storage system promoted primarily by Teac Corporation. In addition, makers of mini-cartridge tape systems don't view cassettes as being as reliable a medium as their own products. (Teac obviously feels otherwise.)

Eight-Millimeter Tape

The offspring of the compact videocassette system that uses the same tape width, eight-millimeter tape has been adapted to data storage where huge capacities are required. The smallest eight millimeter systems pack two gigabytes, but five and ten megabyte drives are now de rigueur. Although the cassettes are compact—not much larger than standard audio cassettes—drives tend to be larger, often requiring a full 5.25-inch bay. Because these systems use dedicated high-speed host adapters, they are fast. Some transfer data faster than the quickest quarter-inch based backup systems.

If you have the gigabytes, however, eight-millimeter can pack them away for you.

Today, eight-millimeter cartridge backup is viewed as one of the better high-end backup systems. However, it is costly (what do you expect at the high end?) Moreover, its huge capacities are unnecessary for most single-user PCs. Consequently, eight-millimeter backup is most suited for network server and other commercial applications with huge hard disks. If you have the gigabytes, however, eight-millimeter can pack them away for you.

Choosing a Backup System

No one backup system rates as best for everyone. Each has its own combination of features that can recommend it for a given host PC environment. For most people, the most important factor in guiding their backup choice is cost. Generally, more buys more—speed, capacity, compatibility, and convenience, but price isn't the only way to shop. Other considerations can overrule the price differences between systems. For instance, when you absolutely need access to mainframe tapes or want to interchange information, you'll have to bite the bullet and budget for an open-reel tape drive.

The backup system that's easiest and most convenient to operate is the one least likely to be ignored.

The best backup system is the one that you're most likely to use—and use routinely. No matter how good or expensive it may be, a backup system is worthless if you never bother to put it to work. The backup system that's easiest and most convenient to operate is the one least likely to be ignored—and the one most likely to help when disaster strikes.

No matter the backup hardware you choose, you still need a backup system. That system requires more than just hardware, even more than software. To make it work, you must adhere to a strict backup routine after you make one overall backup of all the files on your hard disk.

The absolute best backup system is one in which you make a duplicate copy of each file as soon as it is made. Finish a worksheet and immediately copy it to your backup medium. Without disk mirroring software, this can also be the most bothersome to use because the onus is on you to do all the backup work. For the most part, software won't matter because you and not the PC will handle all the details of backing up.

For this kind of backup system, your best choice is a random access backup system—floppy disks, a duplicate hard disk, a cartridge disk or a tape system that attempts to emulate a disk device. The last will be very slow—don't say you weren't warned. A device that's designed for random access—that is a disk drive—will speed the backup process so that you can quickly make your copy and get on to something else. If you don't like the bother of constantly making copies, you may want to investigate disk-mirroring software.

The majority of PCs are still best served by a mini-cartridge system.

The second major backup system is one with which you make file copies at regular intervals. For instance, every day at an appointed time, you duplicate all the files that have changed that day by copying them onto the backup medium. This sort of routine is the backup choice in systems where data is really important—most mainframes are backed up on such a daily schedule.

Large capacity media are often best for this kind of backup because the number of files to backup may be great, and you won't want to stick around the whole time shuffling floppy disks in and out of the disk drive. Traditionally, tape systems have been the choice for these regular backups, although there is no reason that cartridge or duplicate hard disks can't be used. Removable cartridge media (tapes or disks) are usually preferred because they permit storing several copies of the entire system setup for recovery when the worst disaster befalls you. Because of its price advantage and proven technology, however, streaming tape is the traditional medium of choice for this kind of backup system. For minicomputer systems and PC users with very large hard disks coupled with very little patience, the quarter-inch cartridge is particularly favored. Today, however, the majority of PCs are still best served by a mini-cartridge system.

Software Considerations

Backup software will determine how convenient the system is to use. The BACKUP command that comes with DOS will not control a tape backup systems. It only works with floppy disks (and in some DOS versions, particularly those older than 3.3, it doesn't work very well.) So you'll need control software for your backup system. Thankfully, most —but not all—backup hardware is accompanied by the software needed to operate it. You'll want to check when you order the hardware to be sure that the software you need is included.

But getting software may not be enough. You also want to be sure that the software does what you want it to. Most backup software packages give you a choice between command-driven and menu-driven modes. To take direct control of your backup session, monitoring it every step of the way, or if you don't want to learn yet another set of commands, you should look for a backup system with the menu-driven software. To automate your backups through batch files that you build yourself, a command-driven backup program is best. With the latest software, you don't have to give up ease of use for automating your backups. The best packages include a *batch mode* that allows you to use the menu system to automate your backups. The important issue is to be sure that backup software that comes with whatever backup device you choose works the way you want it to. You'll probably want a set of command-driven backup utilities or a program that has its own batch mode. Ask when you order to be sure.

A few of the latest independent backup utility packages such as Norton Backup (from Symantec) and PC Tools Backup (from Central Point Software) are able to control some tape drives as well as floppy disk drives. You may prefer to use these programs because they are generally easier to use and more complete than the free programs that come with tape systems. If you choose to use such third-party software, make sure that the hardware you buy will work with the software you want to use. Again, the best method is to ask the person who is selling—for your peace of mind ask both the software and the hardware vendor.

> *To automate your backups through batch files that you build yourself, a command-driven backup program is best.*

The most important selling point for backup software— and backup systems in general—is speed.

The best backup system is the one that enforces the routine that you're most likely to follow.

Sometimes, backup systems, particularly older ones, allow you to choose among different backup methods. Typically, your options are image or file-by-file backups. The image backup is a bit-for-bit copy of the original disk. Bytes are merely read from the disk and copied on tape without a glance to their content or structure. Because little processing overhead is involved, these image backups can be fast. File-by-file backups add structure to the information as it is backed up. Although processing overhead tends to slow down file-by-file systems, finding files within the structure (and hence, individual file restoration) is easier.

In most current systems, these two techniques have merged or image backing up is totally ignored. Because file-by-file backups have become as fast as image backups, there's no incentive for putting up with the greater hassles of the image backup. Even systems that still offer image backup modes have smarter restoration software that can make sense of the inherent structure of image backups so that individual file restorations can be made from them. Consequently, if you buy a current backup system, you shouldn't have to worry about backup modes.

The most important selling point for backup software—and backup systems in general—is speed. After all, if you plan on overseeing all of your backups as they happen, the fastest backup system is always the more endurable. Even when you run in batch mode, a faster system will steal a smaller chunk of your working day. Some backup systems give you a better alternative, automatic backups made at an appointed time. If you don't mind leaving your PC running overnight (and have the faith that it will, indeed, continue to run overnight), you can take advantage of such programs to ensure that you always having a recent backup without spending half your lifetime to make it. The automated backup systems have two key elements: the control software, which is often included in better backup programs, and backup hardware with sufficient capacity to hold all the backups to be made in the wee hours. After all, no one is going to be around to change tapes.

Remember the Golden Rule of backing up: The best backup system is the one that enforces the routine that you're most likely to follow. A backup system that does not get used (or used often) is not a backup system at all.

Media Considerations

In removable media systems, the price of tapes or disks can be a major factor in overall cost. Be sure to consider how many tapes you need and what they cost when investigating the price of backup systems. For instance, you may be able to buy an entire tape drive for the price of a couple Bernoulli cartridges.

You will want sufficient media capacity to hold a minimum of three complete backups.

For most backup scenarios, you will want sufficient media capacity to hold a minimum of three complete backups. For greater peace of mind or more elaborate backup rituals—such as keeping a separate backup for each day of the week—your media needs increase. Most people actively use between 6 and 10 tapes in their regular backup routine.

Exactly how many tapes you'll require depends on how you want to carry out your backups. For the utmost in security, make a complete backup at the end of each business day. You'll need at least five tapes to cover such a scenario. That way, you'll have a week in which to discover you've accidentally erased something important. Some people advocate an even more complex strategy—one tape for each day of the week, with a separate tape for each Friday (or whatever) in the month (to add a month's worth of "What happened to that file?" security). You can even use a separate tape for every first Friday of the month in a year to have a snapshot of your system over a long period at regular intervals.

The alternative game plan is to make an overall backup and then at the end of each day append only the files that have changed to the tape. One tape could thus hold several weeks (even months) of backups. This also saves time because you have less data to backup in each session. The weakness of such a strategy is that you have only one backup of every file—perhaps enough—but then again, you bought your backup systems so that you don't have to take such chances. You'll probably want to supplement such a system by making a new complete backup (on a different tape) once every couple of weeks. With such a system, you'll want at least four tapes.

Remember when determining how many tapes you need to calculate the cost of periodically replacing any media that wear out. All tape media and all disks except for cartridge hard disks will eventually wear out because of the magnetic coating of the tape constantly rubbing again the head (or in the case of flexible Bernoulli cartridges, the media constantly flexing around the head). The exact amount of life to expect from a particular medium depends on your own personal paranoia. According to one major media manufacturer, quarter-inch cartridges should last 5,000 to 6,000 passes across the read/write head. On the other hand, cautious mainframe managers may routinely replace open reel tapes after they've been used as few as 50 times. A good compromise, according to the media manufacturer, would be annual replacement of your backup tapes.

Practical Backup Systems

After you decide on the size of cartridge you want to use, you need to settle on a standard. Standards are important because they determine what software will work with your tape drive and whether you can exchange tapes.

If you have no plans to ever use your backup tapes to distribute data, if the tape drive you buy comes with its own software, and if you have great faith that the maker of the tape system you buy will support it until Gabriel blows his horn, you need not concern yourself with standards. Otherwise, you should ensure the tape drive you buy for your upgrade conforms to one or more of the industry standards.

Software compatibility is the reason that standards are important when you shop for a tape backup upgrade. Adding a tape upgrade is different from adding a disk. A hard disk will work with DOS alone, but you'll need some kind of special software for your tape drive. Remember that the BACKUP command that accompanies DOS doesn't know how to deal with tape.

It's not that the authors of DOS are stingy or retrograde in their thinking. It's just that there are so many different tape drives available—many of them with their own particular commands and features—that accommodating them all through DOS would be about as easy as trying to speak a dozen languages at the same time.

Most—but hardly all—tape drives come complete with their own backup software. When you order a drive, make sure that you ask about its software—does the system include its own backup program? If it does not, you'll have to factor in the cost of backup software to the tape drive cost. Be sure to check what commercially available programs will operate the drive. A discontinued drive

The BACKUP command that accompanies DOS doesn't know how to deal with tape.

A discontinued drive without software that requires you to dream up your own backup program is not a bargain at any price.

without software that requires you to dream up your own backup program is not a bargain at any price.

If the tape drive follows one or more of the industry standards, you have a better chance that third-party software will be available for the drive. The standards you should be most concerned about are those agreed upon by the QIC committee. All of these standards are easily identified by the name of the group as their preface, such as QIC-40. Generally, the number indicates the primary storage capacity of a cartridge that follows the standard. These capacities are only nominal, however. Some cartridges are stuffed with more tape to stretch QIC-40 drives to 60M and QIC-80 to 120M. Of course, tapes can be used to store less than their full capacities. Table 9.1 lists some of the different tape cartridges available.

Table 9.1 Data Cartridge Tape Types

Model	Nominal Length (ft)	Tracks (FTPI*)	Data Density	Nominal Capacity (M)
DC2000-style				
DC2000	205	24	12,500	40
DC2080	205	32	15,000	80
DC2110	205	32	20,000	86
DC2120	307.5	32	15,000	120
DC2165	307.5	32	20,000	128
DC6000-style				
DC300A	300	4	3,200	2.9
DC300XL/P	450	9	3,200 -10,000	45
DC600A	600	16	10,000	60
DC615A	150	16	12,500	15
DC600HC	600	16	10,000	67
DC600HW	600	11	10,000	60
DC6150	620	32	12,500	150
DC6250	1020	32	12,500	250
DC6037	155	32	12,500	37
DC6320	620	26	20,000	320
DC6525	1020	26	20,000	525

Drives that opt for proprietary standards may be insupportable without their manufacturers' software.

Among quarter-inch systems, most of the QIC standards don't specify the exact format to store data on tapes, so they don't guarantee that tapes can be exchanged between different makers' systems. However, the standards are worth looking for because they help to ensure software compatibility. That, in turn, helps you when you want to exchange tapes. Two tape systems that follow the same cartridge standards and use the same software are likely to be able to share tapes with one another. The most popular standards you'll see for quarter-inch cartridge systems are QIC-02, QIC-36, and SCSI. Each of these standards is supported by a third-party software such as Sytron Corporation's SYTOS. Be careful when you buy. Although nearly all currently manufactured tape drives follow one of these standards, close-out products do not. Drives that opt for proprietary standards may be insupportable without their manufacturers' software.

The bottom line is that when you consider tape backup, you need to think of it not just as a drive unit but as a complete system—you need both the hardware and software.

Installation

Installation procedures for mini-cartridge, quarter-inch cartridge, and DAT systems differ because of the different size of the drives and different interfaces they use. Moreover, installation will vary with the system that you install them in. In particular, IBM's PS/2s used a novel floppy disk mounting scheme that simplifies tape drive installation. Each of the installation variations will be covered separately.

Before you begin *any* tape drive installation, however, prepare a place to work. Switch off the power to your PC and remove the power cable from your PC to ensure that you don't inadvertently switch the machine on while you're working. You'll also need to remove the cover from your system's case and, with some systems, the front fascia panel.

Mini-Cartridge Drives

Installing a mini-cartridge system is invariably the easiest job because you need not tangle with odd adapters and complex system interactions. All that is usually required is plugging in a cable and screwing in the drive.

Because most mini-cartridge systems use the floppy disk interface of your PC, you've got to make electrical room for the drive before you can hope to install it. You need to have a free channel on your PC's floppy disk controller.

In most systems, that means that you can have only one floppy disk drive in addition to your tape backup system because most floppy disk controllers can handle only two drives. There are exceptions, of course. For example, the original IBM PC floppy disk controller can handle four floppies—although you probably won't want to install a tape backup system in a PC because PCs don't have hard disks.

Some mail order vendors offer work-arounds for people who need more than one floppy disk. You can add a special additional floppy disk controller that provides connections for a pair of extra drives, or you can replace your old floppy disk controller with one capable of operating four floppy disk drives. An elite few tape drives offer *disk multiplexing*, which allows the tape system to share a channel of your disk controller with a floppy disk drive.

Adding extra floppy disk control channels to your PC can be complicated. For example, if you have a PC with its floppy disk electronics built into its system board, you'll have to defeat your system's existing floppy disk control circuitry before you can install a four-drive controller. If you cannot defeat these circuits, you'll have to suffer with one floppy. Check your PC's instruction manual. Typically, you'll find what you need to know where the instructions list jumper or DIP switch settings.

Outside of finding a free floppy controller channel, you shouldn't have any hardware worries with readying your system for a mini-cartridge drive (see fig. 9.2 and 9.3). If the controller works for one floppy disk drive, odds are greatly in your favor that it will also work for the tape backup system.

In general, the only time you'll need to adjust your PC's setup when installing a mini-cartridge tape system is when you replace an existing floppy disk drive with the tape drive. In that case, just run your computer's setup program and inform your system of the number of floppy disk drives that are actually installed. Don't count your tape system as a floppy disk drive even though it is connected to the floppy controller. If you do, your PC's power-on diagnostic will assume that the tape drive is a floppy disk drive—which, of course, it isn't—and report that the properly functioning tape drive looks like a broken floppy disk drive. To your system, your new tape drive should appear not to exist.

All that is usually required is plugging in a cable and screwing in the drive.

If the controller works for one floppy disk drive, odds are greatly in your favor that it will also work for the tape backup system.

Figure 9.2

Most DC2000-style tape drives must be adapted to fit 5.25-inch drive bays. The first step is to install the proper bezel on the front of the drive to fit it to a 5.25-inch or a 3.5-inch drive bay.

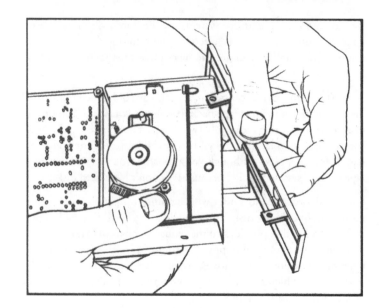

Figure 9.3

To make a 3.5-inch DC2000-style drive fit a 5.25-inch bay, you need to install adapters (inset) to make the drive wide enough to secure in the bay. Secure the adapters to the sides of the drive, taking care that the adapters fit properly against the bezel.

IBM's PS/2s make the addition of a mini-cartridge tape backup system easy. First, you'll need to prepare your second floppy disk bay for your new tape system. Simply remove the blank front panel from the bay. These panels snap into place, so you just snap it out.

Next, ready the drive. You'll need to attach the mounting sled to the bottom of the drive. The plastic sled has four places for screws that match the mounting holes on 3.5-inch drives. Put a screw in each.

In PS/2s, you don't have to worry about cabling because the tape drive, like a second floppy disk drive, plugs directly into a waiting connector at the back of the drive bay. Some drives need adapters to match their electrical connections—the edge connectors on the backs of the drive—to the special connectors used by PS/2s. If your drive requires an adapter, install it before you put the drive in your computer.

Next, slide your new tape drive into the vacant floppy disk bay. As it reaches the end of its travel, you'll have to increase the force you apply to mate the connectors together. The sled will lock itself into place with a slight snap when the drive is fully inserted. Cover the drive with the new fascia that accompanied it, and you're finished.

If you've replaced a floppy disk drive in your PS/2 with the tape drive, you'll have to run the system setup procedure on your computer's Reference Diskette to tell your PS/2 that you've cut down to only one floppy disk drive. After setup completes, you're ready to run your backup software on your new drive.

After setup completes, you're ready to run your backup software on your new drive.

Installing a mini-cartridge drive in systems with 3.5-inch drive bays is only a bit more complicated than PS/2 installation. First, you'll mount the appropriate fascia on the front of the tape drive or the front panel of your computer. Then put the drive approximately in place and connect the cables to it. The drive will require both a power and signal connection (see fig. 9.4). Then screw the tape drive into the drive bay. Depending on your computer, you'll either attach the drive by its side or its bottom. In either case, you'll want to use all four screws to insure a secure mounting.

When your PC has only 5.25-inch drive bays, installation is complicated by one additional step, attaching a drive-bay adapter to the drive. These adapters are usually included with all mini-cartridge tape drives, but to be sure that you get one, make certain that your source of supply knows what size bay your tape system must fit into.

The adapter typically comprises three pieces that may fit together as a single assembly. Two of these are U-shaped metal channels that extend the width of the tape drive; the other piece is a front fascia panel to match the small drive to the larger 5.25-inch opening in your computer's front panel. Screw one of the adapter channels onto each side of the drive. Once the adapter is installed, the mini-cartridge drive is effectively a 5.25-inch half-height device that installs in a drive bay exactly like a quarter-inch tape drive.

Figure 9.4

Before you slide the DC2000-style drive into its bay, plug the drive into the B: drive floppy disk connector. The B: drive connector will generally be in the middle of the floppy disk signal cable. Next connect a power cable to the drive.

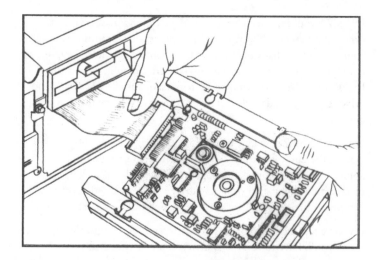

Quarter-Inch Drives

Physically installing a quarter-inch tape drive or a mini-cartridge drive adapter to a 5.25-inch bay is as straightforward as installing a hard disk drive. The hardware you need depends on the mounting scheme used by your PC, but the mechanics are easy to figure out in any case.

No matter what mounting hardware you use, the first step in mounting any tape drive is to put the drive approximately in place. Attach its cables to it before you screw the drive into place. This will give you more working room and save the skin on your knuckles. You need to plug in a power connector from your PC's power supply and the signal cable from the tape drive controller or, in the case of mini-cartridge drives, your floppy disk controller. One rule applies to the signal cable: the stripe on the edge of the cable goes to pin one on the tape drive connector.

What to do in the next step—securing your drive inside your computer—depends on the drive mounting scheme used in your PC. The most straightforward is the direct mounting method used by computers since the original PC. Drive units—disk or tape—are directly screwed into the disk bay using either of the sets of screw holes on the sides of the 5.25-inch device.

Mounting drives in IBM PCs and XTs and many clones using this direct approach has one disadvantage: the drives are held only on one side. For tape drives, this mounting method is particularly inadequate because of the high force require to insert a tape cartridge in the drive—this insertion force is high enough that you may bend the bay or break mounting screws when you try to cram a cartridge into the drive. Should your system provide access only to one side of the drive, you'll want to be certain that your new tape unit is held as securely in place as its screws permit.

Better compatible computers (particularly tower-style cases) provide access to both sides of their 5.25-inch drive bays. Be sure to take advantage of the security offered by these computers and use all four screws to hold your tape drive in place, two on each side.

If you have a modern system that is patterned after IBM's old AT, you'll find secure tape drive installation is easy. Standard 5.25-inch drive users are installed using mounting rails attached to their sides that allow you to slide the drives into place. The rails fit into guide slots that hold the drive assembly securely on both sides. Many 5.25-inch tape drives—both quarter-inch and mini-cartridge units with adapters already installed—come with AT mounting kits or with the rails already installed on the sides of the drive (see fig. 9.5).

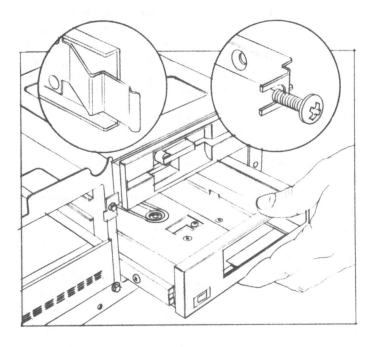

Figure 9.5
The final installation step is to slide it all the way into its bay. Check the connections, screw the drive in place with AT-style brackets, one-piece brackets (right inset), or snap-in brackets (left inset) as required by your system.

Some AT-compatibles—notably Compaq Deskpros—use a similar mounting scheme with slightly wider rails that are incompatible with standard AT rails and the AT chassis. If you have one of these machines or a similar computer, you'll either have to scavenge rails from a device you'll be retiring from your system or attempt to get new rails to match your computer, which can sometimes be a challenge.

Another variety of full-size systems uses drive-mounting rails that are narrower and, consequently, also incompatible with IBM rails. Most machines that use these narrow rails pre-install a set in each drive bay of the computer, even those without drives. In this case, you only need detach the rails from the chassis, screw them to your disk, and slide the disk into place.

Rails are held in the computer chassis in one of two ways. IBM-style systems use small brackets that push the rails to the end of their travel in the bay. Some compatibles make the brackets part of the drive rails. In either case, one screw holds each bracket in place. Just unscrew to slide the old drive out and screw the bracket back in to hold your drive upgrade in place.

Tower-style IBM PS/2s use rails that are close enough to those used by the AT. AT rails will work in the internal 5.25-inch drive cages of these PS/2s. To loosen a drive in one of these computers so that you can slide it out of the chassis, press down on each of the large blue daisy-like knobs above the drive and turn it counter-clockwise with the palm of your hand until the drive can slide out.

You must use the front bay in these computers so that the front of the drive is accessible through the fascia panel of your computer. You'll also have to remove the factory-installed blank panel from in front of the drive bay. To do this, pry off the entire fascia assembly (it should come off easily enough that putting your fingernails behind it will be sufficient). After you've removed the fascia, just push the blank panel out through the back of the panel. If you have a quarter-inch system, the next step is to install the tape controller. Put it in an expansion slot as close as possible to the tape drive. Most tape controllers use eight-bit interfaces so that they will fit into any expansion slot that will physically accommodate the board. Usually, the best slot to use is the one adjacent to your hard disk controller. After the board is in place, route the tape drive's signal cable to the controller as best you can and plug it in.

Using a quarter-inch tape system with a modern small-footprint computer that has only 3.5-inch bays will require an external chassis. Some mail order vendors offer drive units already installed in their own chassis with power supplies. Alternately, you can buy an internal drive and another vendor's case. Cases with room for two half-height 5.25-inch drives complete with its own power supply are available for under $50.

If you opt for the external system, ensure that the tape drive controller offers an external connector so that you can conveniently plug in the drive. You'll also want a cable with connectors at either end that match the drive and the controller.

DAT Drives

Although their technological underpinnings are entirely unlike mini-cartridge and quarter-inch cartridge drives, DAT system installation follow exactly the same steps. First prepare your drive and then prepare your system for it. Add-in the cabling, physically mount the drive, test everything out, and reassemble your PC.

Because most DAT drives are designed to fit the 3.5-inch form factor, physical installation is exactly like that of mini-cartridge drives. A DAT drive will screw right into a 3.5-inch bay.

PS/2s pose greater problems because few DAT kits are designed for their particular style of 3.5-inch bay. That's understandable because the PS/2s that only have 3.5-inch bays are unlikely to need the capacity of DAT. Larger PS/2s with enough capacity to justify DAT all have 5.25-inch bays into which a DAT drive will happily slide once you add a bay adapter.

Prepare your system for DAT installation by switching it off, unplugging it for safety's sake, and removing its cover. When you can peer inside, find a suitable bay for the drive. If you're adding a SCSI host adapter at the same time, scout out a vacant expansion slot with a bus interface that matches the SCSI board.

Prepare your DAT drive by setting its SCSI ID according to the manual for your backup software. The software will need to know where to find the drive, so it demands for ID number control. Next, adjust the termination of the DAT drive following the standard SCSI termination rules: the first and last device in any SCSI chain are terminated. All other SCSI devices are not terminated. In most cases when you want to operate your DAT drive unterminated, you'll want to remove three terminating resistor packs from the DAT drive. If your DAT drive requires a bay adapter to fit a 5.25-inch drive bay, install it now.

> *A DAT drive will screw right into a 3.5-inch bay.*

If you're adding a new SCSI host adapter for the DAT drive, ensure that its jumpers are set according to its manual for proper operation in your PC. Attach one end of your SCSI cable to the board and slide the board into the expansion slot you've chosen for it. Route your SCSI cable—either from your new host adapter or from your existing SCSI system—into the bay you've chosen for your SCSI drive.

Next slide the DAT drive into the bay you've chosen for it. Plug in a drive-power connector and the SCSI connector. Then screw the drive into place.

Before reassembling your PC, plug it in and turn it on. Install your backup software per its manufacturer's instructions and test your backup system. When you're sure that everything is operating properly, switch off your PC and reassemble it.

Cabling Concerns

Mini-cartridge tape drives follow the same cabling rules as floppy disk drives. That is, as with all devices, the red strip on the cable indicates the edge of the cable associated with Pin One on the connector. Disk drive and tape drive signal cable edge connectors have a small slot between their contact fingers, and this slot is always nearer the Pin One edge of the connector.

In a system that has a floppy disk controller that handles two drives, tape drives must always be installed using the Drive B: cable connector. If you use the Drive A: connector, your computer would try to boot from the tape drive, which is generally impossible.

In the standard IBM-compatible cabling scheme, Drive B: is determined by the signal cable. Drive B: uses the connector in the middle of the two-drive daisy-chain floppy disk signal cable. Drive A: uses the connector at the end of the cable that has a twist in the cable right before the connector.

You'll also have to deal with the signal termination of your mini-cartridge tape drive. Tape terminations are handled as with floppy disk drives. When you install your tape drive using the Drive B: cable connector, you'll want to remove the termination resistor from the disk drive.

Each quarter-inch interface standard uses slightly different cabling. With QIC-02 and QIC-36 systems, the only important issue is that you ensure that the red stripe on the connecting cable is on the same side of the connector as pin one on each end of the cable. Pin one is usually marked with a small "1" on the circuit board itself. With these interfaces, you don't have to worry about cable terminations.

SCSI drives require that you set a unique SCSI ID on the drive (see fig. 9.6). The manual that comes with the software you will use with the tape drive will tell you what SCSI ID to use. In addition, you must terminate the first and last device in the SCSI daisy chain but not the middle devices. Most SCSI devices have three terminating resistor packs, all three of which must be removed when a termination is not to be made. Chapter 13 includes more details about connecting SCSI devices.

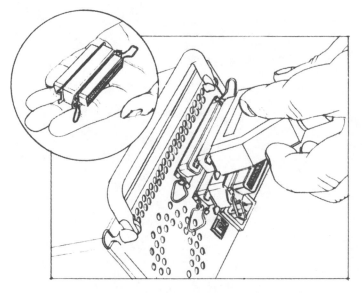

Figure 9.6
Some terminators are external devices (inset) that plug into one of the SCSI ports on the back of the drive. Just insert it into the port the cable is not plugged into.

When your tape drive is in place and its cables are connected and before you put the cover back on your PC, you should install your backup software. Most backup programs have built-in test procedures that will confirm that all went well with the installation of your new tape backup upgrade. After everything checks out, reassemble your PC. You can now make your first backup—and sleep easier knowing that disk disasters can no longer rob you of your valuable files.

10

Video Boards and Monitors

Your display system is the window into the mind of your PC. Peer through it and you can see a lot of the excitement in today's software. Your PC can even think up more colors than your eye can detect. But seeing it all requires a video board or graphics adapter capable of generating high-resolution images and a monitor with matching capabilities. In addition, the speed of your PC's video system can cap the capabilities of your PC. Thus, a full video upgrade includes a display adapter (or graphics board) and a monitor to match its potential.

Images distinguish the biggest innovation in PCs. Where once computers worked only with numbers, then words, a modern machine sees the world and shows it to you in images. From tiny icons you can recognize more quickly than a gray band of text to full-page drawings, electronic photographs, and colorful presentation slides, graphic images enable your PC to communicate a thousand times better than before.

A poor image on your screen is more than just bothersome when it comes to getting the details of a printout right; it can be a big headache—the kind caused by eye strain, squinting, and plain frustration. Full-screen, full-color graphics too often mean wasting minutes of waiting time as every detail is painted on the screen. Too often a PC races through its work only to wait while pixels shift and shimmer across your screen. A graphics upgrade can change all that, giving you and your PC the power to work more smoothly and produce snappier graphics in less time and with less heartache.

A full video upgrade includes a display adapter (or graphics board) and a monitor to match its potential.

The ultimate quality of what you see on your screen depends on the monitor and display adapter working together.

If your display adapter is just a few years old, you may still be able to make a substantial improvement in your PC with an upgrade.

Every PC's display system has two vital parts, the display adapter and monitor. The display adapter converts the abstract thoughts of your PC into an electronic form of an image called a memory-map, in which every dot that makes up the final displayed picture is represented by one or more bits stored in RAM. The display adapter then takes apart that electronic image and sends a copy of each piece to the monitor. The display adapter then tells the monitor which pieces go where, and the final product is what you see on screen.

Each of these two parts of the display system plays a role in the quality of the image you see. The monitor sets the ultimate limit on image quality that cannot be exceeded or improved upon, but the display adapter determines the detail and hues that the monitor will display. The ultimate quality of what you see on your screen depends on the monitor and display adapter working together. The best value results from matching the capabilities of each.

Display Adapters

To see something on your monitor, your PC needs a display adapter of some sort. But just because a display adapter is a necessity does not mean that the display adapter in your PC is good. There are a wide variety of display adapters, stretching from poor to acceptable. Really great display adapters—the kind that do everything you want them to—remain in the realm of the imagination. Moreover, display adapter technology has changed more over the last couple of years than just about any other part of the PC industry. If your display adapter is just a few years old, you may still be able to make a substantial improvement in your PC with an upgrade. In fact, if you want the best possible image and performance from your PC, you will have to make a video upgrade.

All display adapters are limited by industry standards that set the ultimate resolution or sharpness of the image along with other quality-determining factors, such as the number of colors that can be displayed and how stable the image is. Standards are followed because they guarantee a good match between software, the display adapter, and the monitor at the lowest possible cost—in dollars when it comes to the monitor and in performance when it comes to the software.

Currently, the defining characteristic of the various display standards used in the PC environment is resolution. All else being equal, a higher resolution image appears sharper on the monitor screen.

Resolution is generally measured by how many individual picture elements or pixels, roughly corresponding to the dots in a halftone magazine or newspaper photograph, it takes to fill the screen horizontally and vertically. For example, the first display system used by PCs, the Monochrome Display Adapter (MDA), had a resolution termed 720 by 350 pixels because the image was made from 720 pixels laid across the screen horizontally and 350 vertically.

Monochrome Display Adapters

The MDA system is essentially obsolete, left behind by technology because it yielded great text but poor graphics (a result of being a *character-mapped display*). The screen was divided into individual character positions, and one cell of memory was devoted to each character. On-screen information was saved in the form of a single character for each screen position. MDA chopped the screen into 80 rows and 25 columns of characters—2,000 distinct positions—and reserved two bytes of memory to hold the data for each position. MDA is thus amazingly frugal with memory, needing only 4K for a full screen with two bytes (16 bits), storing the information needed to display a character made from 126 pixels, a matrix measuring 14 pixels down and 9 across. Unfortunately, graphics were not the MDA's forte. The MDA system could only make use of block graphics, in which chunky images were made from special graphics characters.

Intermediary Display Adapters

After MDA came a series of intermediary display adapters. First in 1982 came the Color Graphics Adapter (CGA) and then in 1984 the Enhanced Graphics Adapter (EGA) came along, both of which are now obsolete products to upgrade. In 1987, IBM introduced what was to become the minimum standard to be expected in any PC, the Video Graphics Adapter or VGA.

The system improved on the preceding standards in several ways. First, it enables you to connect either a monochrome or color monitor to any VGA board. The board, through special signals, can detect the color capabilities of the monitor and tell your PC which you have. As with preceding display adapters, VGA retained a character-mapped mode but forms images slightly sharper than those of the MDA system, achieving resolution of 720 by 400 pixels when displaying text.

Most important, VGA also uses bit-mapped graphics. Although both the earlier CGA and EGA systems had bit-mapped modes, VGA made them sharper with 640 by 480 pixel resolution. In fact, on a 14-inch monitor at normal viewing distance this resolution is about as sharp as most human eyes can resolve.

Nearly all graphical software uses bit-mapped technology through which the display adapter can individually control each and every pixel on the screen. A bit-mapped system can produce any shape with a grain as fine as a single pixel. Each pixel then plays the same role as the dots in halftone newspaper and magazine illustrations.

A bit-mapped graphics display requires more memory than a character-mapped image.

A bit-mapped graphics display requires more memory than a character-mapped image. Because each pixel must be controlled individually, at least one bit of memory must be assigned for coding each pixel. Whereas 4,000 bytes of memory sufficed for the character-mapped MDA screen, the same resolution with a monochrome bit-mapped image would require 31,500 bytes. Adding shades of gray or color multiplies the amount of memory required. As on-screen resolution and color increase, the memory required for bit-mapped graphics becomes prodigious. For example, the capability to display any of 256 colors on the screen requires eight bits of memory for each pixel. Achieving realistic color images (which computer graphic experts define as being able to make any pixel any of 16.7 million colors) requires 24 bits of memory for each pixel. Increasing resolution similarly pushes up memory requirements. Moving to 1024 by 768 pixel resolution—today's favored level—requires about two and one half times more memory than ordinary VGA. In contrast, the memory required for a character-mapped display increases only with the number of colors to be displayed but does not change as the screen is made sharper. Only when you add more characters on the screen do the character-mapped memory demands go up (at a given number of colors).

The huge memory needs of bit-mapped systems are the primary reason why traditional display adapters have not kept pace with today's PCs. In a conventional display system, the memory on a video board that actually stores the on-screen image—a part that is called the *frame buffer,* because it temporarily stores the entirety of a single image frame as it is scanned onto the screen—is directly controlled by the PC's microprocessor. Having no processing power or intelligence of their own, these conventional display adapters are often called *dumb frame buffers.*

With a dumb frame buffer, moving part of an image from one place on the screen to another—an operation programmers call BitBlTs (for Bit-Block Transfers)—requires the microprocessor to carry out the memory operations. On a conventional video board the microprocessor is connected to the memory in the dumb frame buffer through the PC's expansion bus. Ordinary expansion buses like the ISA (AT) bus, which is most common among PCs, operate at a fraction of the speed of today's microprocessors.

The major determining factor in display performance is bandwidth—how fast characters and images can move to your display system from another part of your PC (such as its RAM or disk storage). The faster that this data can be moved, the quicker it will appear on screen, and the more responsive your PC will be. The bandwidth of PC display systems traditionally have been limited by the underlying design of the PC hardware. Modern display adapters use two technologies to break through this bandwidth bottleneck. The direct approach is the local bus video connection. By using a high-speed expansion bus connection that approaches the performance level of the host microprocessor, local bus systems ship data to your PC's dumb frame buffer memory about as fast as your PC can handle it.

The other speedup technology is the graphics accelerator. An outgrowth of graphic coprocessor designs, the accelerator sidesteps the bus bottleneck. Instead of a dumb frame buffer, the accelerator adds intelligence to your display adapter. An on-board graphics engine that handles most of the image manipulation functions, an accelerator is a special VGA chip that is designed to speed up moving and drawing images in Windows and other graphics programs. Even when installed on an ordinary ISA graphics adapter, an accelerator makes a startling performance improvement.

Even when installed on an ordinary ISA graphics adapter, an accelerator makes a startling performance improvement.

The graphics chip is connected directly to the frame buffer (no bus in between) and uses its processing power for making BitBlT and other graphic operations. Most of the time the accelerator works with data in the frame buffer, so the system need not slow down for bus transfers. This design alternative could be called a *smart frame buffer* but is usually referred to as an *accelerated graphics system*.

Local bus and graphics acceleration are two pathways to improved performance. The techniques differ fundamentally in how they work and the tasks which they speed up. An accelerator alters the kind of information that is shifted between your PC's microprocessor and its display system. A local bus system changes the means by which the display information is transferred. Although there is some overlap in what local bus and graphic acceleration achieve, the two technologies are essentially complementary, and their benefits add up rather than cancel one another out.

Local bus technology actually speeds up the operations that accelerators slow down. By combining bus and graphics acceleration, you get the fastest video available for today's PCs.

Where the two differ is in the mechanics of the upgrade. You can add a graphic accelerator to your PC as easy as plugging in any other display adapter. Adding a local bus is more difficult but still possible. You first must replace the motherboard in your PC with one that has the required local bus expansion slots built in.

Adding a graphic accelerator may give your PC the best combination of graphics speed and low upgrade price.

Which of the two technologies adds the most performance to your PC's display system depends on what you do with your PC. A local bus excels at moving bit images from memory or disk to the screen. Typical applications that need this kind of speed include making slide shows of presentations graphics and multi-media displays. Graphic accelerators outshine local bus designs when creating new vector images—for example, in CAD and drawing programs. Local bus alone will outperform almost any dumb frame buffer display system, and it can beat some of the less-effective graphic accelerators. But a good graphic accelerator alone can deliver better on-screen performance than local bus alone. Although combining the two produces the best results, you may find that adding a graphic accelerator may give your PC the best combination of graphics speed and low upgrade price.

If your PC does not have a local bus or a graphic accelerator, it cannot perform on par with a modern PC. That is why you should be considering an upgrade.

Local Bus

Local bus systems are nothing more than a new connection scheme. Ordinary display systems link display adapter circuitry through your PC's ordinary ISA, EISA, or Micro Channel bus interface. In the case of ISA, that means the megabytes of data meant for your screen—generated by your system's high-speed, 32-bit microprocessor—are marshaled through a narrow 16-bit bus that operates at one-quarter or less of your microprocessor's clock rate.

Older PCs with designs that moved display circuitry to the motherboard did not improve matters. These machines still relied on the same old bus interface logic—complete with its performance bottlenecks—to connect microprocessor to video circuitry. Local bus systems sidestep the expansion bus slowdown by adding a separate high-speed connection directly to the microprocessor—"local" because no distant bus control circuitry intervenes.

In effect, any local bus is like punching a couple extra holes in a funnel—everything runs through, but faster. Local bus accelerates all software without regard to display mode or anything else. Because local bus simply acts like a faster wire—it only moves information more quickly—you do not have to modify your programs or add special software drivers to gain the local bus performance advantage. Nor does local bus ever slow the response of your PC's display system.

Electrically, a local bus system has three buses. One is the traditional expansion (or I/O) bus, into which you can slide your familiar peripherals. Number two is the high-speed memory bus most machines have to prevent the I/O connection from slowing memory operations. Local bus is the third.

Because local bus requires a fundamental change in a PC's motherboard, adding one to your PC requires a two-sided investment. Not only do you need to get a local bus display adapter, but if your PC does not have a standard local bus built in, you also will need local bus slots on your motherboard to plug the adapter into. That means replacing your PC's motherboard, as discussed in Chapter 3. You also will need a local bus display adapter. Today, that is no big investment because most manufacturers price their local bus graphics boards at about the same price as those that use conventional expansion buses. A local bus, therefore, looks like a deal—until you figure in the cost in cash and time of installing a new motherboard. In that the graphics accelerator can boost your PC's video performance to approximately the same level as local bus, you have little reason to opt for a motherboard upgrade to add this technology to an existing system.

When shopping for a new local bus graphic adapter (or any local bus product), you are likely to have two choices: VL Bus and PCI. Only VL Bus approaches a true local bus design. PCI is something else, a combination of a standard for linking together motherboard components and a new-technology, high-performance expansion bus so that some of those components can be moved to separate boards. Despite the technological difference, however, VL Bus and PCI push up the speed at which plug-in peripherals can operate to near the level of today's microprocessors.

VL Bus and PCI slots are not compatible with boards made under the other standard.

If you are looking for a local bus PC, you will have to choose the standard to follow. Today you have a greater choice among video expansion options with VL Bus, because VL Bus has been around longer than PCI. VL Bus has enough industry support that you face little risk that it soon will be abandoned as a standard. If you have a PC with local bus slots already built in, your choice of bus is already made. When you look for local bus upgrades, you will have to confine your choices to the standard your PC uses. VL Bus and PCI slots are not compatible with boards made under the other standard.

Graphic Accelerators

Local bus upgrades are best suited to machines that already have local bus sockets installed. In that such systems already come equipped with local bus graphics adapters, you might seem to have no reason to deal with local bus graphics boards. If technology were unchanging, that would indeed be true. Graphic accelerators is one area in which you can expect changes to happen almost faster than you can install upgrades. The local bus graphics adapter that came with your PC already is likely to be second-rate compared to current products. And, the graphic accelerator chip on your existing board is probably slower than the current crop of chips—probably by a factor of two or more. If you want the best graphic performance, upgrade your local bus graphic adapter. All you have to do is find a new board with the right graphic accelerator.

Graphic accelerators have evolved, and the story begins with the introduction of the first graphic coprocessors. The idea behind the concept was to make the display adapter work as an isolated subsystem that communicated with a PC's microprocessor using a high-level interface—essentially a programming language. The graphics coprocessor was the basis of a smart frame buffer in the guise of a coprocessed graphics adapter expansion board. The graphic coprocessor, rather than the host PC's microprocessor, carried out most of the instructions for calculating where dots were placed on the screen.

By using their higher-level interfaces, coprocessor boards lightened the display processing load on the microprocessor. The high-level languages used by graphics coprocessors enabled the PC's microprocessor to simply send out compact commands to create complex on-screen shapes—such as draw a line or circle, or fill in an area. Issuing a command to a graphics coprocessor involves transferring only a few bytes, compared to the millions required by the dumb frame buffer, making communications within the computer quicker. Moreover, the high-level command leaves the graphic coprocessor to do the actual computation work of generating a display, taking a load off the host system's microprocessor and speeding up its overall operation. It even gives PC hardware parallel-processing capabilities. After the graphic coprocessor receives an instruction from the host PC's microprocessor, it can go about its work while the microprocessor does something else. But the graphic coprocessor and the coprocessed display adapters made from it earn their performance advantage not just by working in tandem with your microprocessor but actually by doing its job better. Graphics coprocessors were specially designed for pixel work, and they can carry out the graphic computations many times faster than most general purpose microprocessors.

Another way the graphic coprocessor earns its speed is through its high-level communications. Instead of the PC system sending a huge bit image across the expansion bus, it only needs to send the graphic coprocessor a few bytes of commands in a high-level language. To draw a screen-width line in color, for example, the graphic coprocessor requires only a few bytes of instructions instead of the 1,000 (or so) bytes that make up the line.

Graphic coprocessors have other tricks, too. For example, they can do *display-list processing*. After they do the math to calculate an on-screen image, they save the results (as a "display list") so that they do not have to recalculate everything to regenerate the screen image. The difference reduces the waiting to zoom into and out of a screen detail from a minute or more to a few seconds. In addition, graphics coprocessors often have other special hardware features that can accelerate image-making speed. For example, hardware zooming and panning relieve the need for recalculating pixels during many fundamental display operations.

The most popular of the graphics coprocessors were the TMS series of chips produced by Texas Instruments. First of these was the TMS34010, a 32-bit microprocessor that was optimized for manipulating graphics. An update, the TMS34020, delivered greater performance.

The essence of the graphic coprocessor was that, like the microprocessors they were patterned after, they are entirely programmable. With the appropriate program, they could do anything—not just draw circles but calculate square roots if need be. Nearly every display parameter could be changed with the right instructions.

Although programmability is wonderful in itself—if nothing else, it provides jobs for the programmers—hardware engineers took a hard look at what graphics coprocessors were called upon to do. Most PC software (read: Microsoft Windows) demanded only a small fraction of the capabilities built into the coprocessor. By hardwiring those functions instead of programming them, the engineers discovered that they could simplify the coprocessor. That meant that they could make smaller, cheaper chips that would deliver equivalent performance (at the sacrifice of the flexibility programmability allowed).

These hardwired chips were designed specifically to handle the operations that stall most dumb frame buffers when running Windows. One of the first and the most familiar of the fixed-function graphic accelerators was the S3 Corporation 86C911. This first-generation chip boasted a hardware implementation of the features of IBM's Extended Graphics Array (XGA) coprocessor that were most relevant to Windows applications. Designed to match the ISA bus, the S3 86C911 used 16-bit architecture all around—internally and linking it to its 1M maximum of VRAM. Although it could handle resolutions up to 1280 by 1024, its color capabilities were limited by its 8-bit connection with its RAMDAC.

S3 has since updated its accelerator line-up with several new chips. To make accelerator performance affordable, S3 designed its 86C80X series to use inexpensive DRAM (rather than Video RAM, VRAM) chips, up to 2M of them. To push its performance up, the company used 32-bit internal architecture with a 110 MHz pixel clock. The 86C801 uses 16-bit architecture to match ISA systems. A step-up version, the 86C805, is designed to link to 32-bit local bus and EISA systems but uses exactly the same video architecture.

For top performance, S3 offers its 86C928 that takes with the same 32-bit internal architecture but a 64-bit link to its RAMDAC and prowess to handle up to 4M of VRAM.

Western Digital entered the accelerator field with its WD90C31 chip with a 32-bit processor but capable of handling only 1M of DRAM and a more limited repertory of functions. The same company's WD90C33 expands the data path between chip and memory to 32 bits and adds more functions (for example, clipping, line drawing, and polygon fills) not supported by the earlier product. ATI Technologies' Mach 32 accelerator chip delivers full 64-bit processing power and the ability to handle up to 4M of either DRAM or VRAM. With its maximum 135 MHz pixel clock, it can easily handle 1280 by 1024 non-interlaced images in 16.7 million colors.

A number of new accelerator chips also promise a 64-bit internal structure: the Weitek Power9000 (which goes all the way to 1,600 by 1,280 non-interlaced resolution thanks to a maximum 210 MHz dot clock) and the Matrox Electronic Systems MGA (which reaches 1,600 by 1,200 with a 160 MHz clock and also handles up to 10M of VRAM).

Weitek also offers two modest 8-bit accelerators, the W5186 (1024 by 768-pixel maximum resolution with 16-bit path to memory) and W5286 (1280 by 1024 max with 32-bit memory path), each rated for 1M of DRAM or VRAM.

Other new graphic accelerators include two 135 MHz chips from Integrated Information Technologies, the 16-bit AGX-014 and 32-bit AGX-015, both of which handle up to 2M of VRAM and even support IBM's XGA standard. Trident Microsystems offers another pair of accelerators, the DRAM-based Storm DG and the VRAM-based Storm VG, each capable of using up to 2M at 108 MHz with full 32-bit architecture.

Other accelerators you may find include Avance Logic's 32-bit pair, the GUIEngine ALG2101 (1M DRAM, 16-bit color) and the GUI-Ultra ALG2201 (2M DRAM, 24-bit color), both rated for 1280 by 1024 interlaced maximum resolution. Primus Technology also offers two products, the P2000 and P3000 with similar features to Avance's GUI-Ultra.

Comparing the relative performance of the various graphics accelerators is difficult. Not only do the various chips accelerate different operations but the same chip also performs differently depending on the software driver supplied with it. A fast chip and a bad driver deliver only mediocre speed. Getting the best performance means optimizing both the chip and its software.

Graphics experts argue over which of the various coprocessors and accelerators is fastest and best. The important point is that a coprocessed display adapter can help the performance of some applications and that having a graphics coprocessor (one that can be used by the applications that you run most often) is immensely better than a high-resolution graphics board that lacks a coprocessor or accelerator.

Graphic coprocessors and accelerators minimize the need for local bus.

Graphic coprocessors and accelerators minimize the need for local bus. After all, the link between the actual graphic accelerator chip and display memory is essentially its own local bus. So most video operations are not restricted by the speed of your PC's expansion bus when an accelerator is operating.

But accelerators do not totally eliminate the advantage of local bus. For example, stored bit-images—found in many multi-media displays—must still traverse the bus. Every byte on disk must be moved by your systems microprocessor to the frame buffer. Once there, of course, the accelerator manipulates it quickly.

You can see the effect when scrolling up a bit image—most of the image moves up the screen rapidly until near the bottom. Suddenly, the scroll stalls to a crawl. The fast-moving part of the image was stored in the frame buffer; that involved in the slow crawl came from disk or main memory.

Drivers

All smart frame buffer systems, whether based on graphic coprocessors or hardwired graphic accelerators, have one need that differs fundamentally from dumb frame buffers. All require high-level instructions to activate their functions. In the case of the graphic coprocessor, these instructions are effectively a programming language of their own. Graphic accelerators have a command set that elicits their functions. The microprocessor in your PC must send the appropriate instructions to the graphics chip to create and move the images on your monitor screen.

Unfortunately, most programs are written assuming the least common graphic denominator in your PC. They are designed to control your PC's microprocessor as if it were connected to a dumb frame buffer. Fortunately, nearly all accelerated graphics adapters work as dumb frame buffers. However, when working as dumb frame buffers, accelerated graphics adapters do not speed up anything. In fact, they can be slower than a plain old VGA adapter.

Every graphic accelerator is different. Even though some manufacturers allow many of their chips to understand commands meant for other models, there is no common ground in the commands for controlling the graphic accelerators of different manufacturers. Every chip family requires different commands to speed up your graphics. If a software company wants its product to work with all possible graphic adapters, it must include code to control them all. If you are a programmer looking for work, that is excellent news: It means job security for the foreseeable future (until the next great graphics invention, at least). But that is bad news if you are trying to make money selling graphical programs. The need for so much code would bloat the size of the program and the budget for developing it.

The bad news for programmers is that there is a better way, one that is prevalent in the PC industry. Programs are written with hooks to link with graphic accelerators. The makers of accelerators then provide driver software that translates the program hooks into the commands needed by the accelerator chip. One program can then link to many accelerators. Better still, if the hooks are standardized, one driver can link a graphic accelerator chip to many programs.

In the real world, there is one additional link: the operating system or environment such as Microsoft Windows. Software companies write their programs with hooks that link to Windows, and graphic accelerator makers develop drivers that link Windows to their boards. As a result, most programs can be made to work with most graphic accelerators at full speed.

This whole assumption is based on the existence of drivers. Without a driver, a graphic accelerator is useless as a performance enhancement (but it does still work as an ordinary VGA board). An out-of-date driver or dysfunctional driver is as bad as—perhaps worse than—no driver at all. So you are dependent on the maker of any accelerated graphics board that you buy to keep its driver software current. Look for a board maker with a good track record. Before you buy an accelerated graphics adapter, make sure that driver updates will be available as necessary. Most board makers operate bulletin board services that you can dial into with your PC and modem to download driver updates.

Most board makers operate bulletin board services that you can dial into with your PC and modem to download driver updates.

In that Windows appears to be the universal standard, you can almost assume that all accelerated graphic adapters will come with drivers to match Windows. If you want to accelerate a specific DOS program, however, you will need a driver particular to that program. Many accelerated graphics adapters include special drivers for the most popular DOS programs—AutoCAD, Lotus 1-2-3, and WordPerfect. Other programs and operating systems (for example OS/2) are less common. If you expect to use such software, be sure that the required driver software is available.

Driver software also adds another consideration in buying a new video card. The efficiency of a driver has a major affect on accelerator performance. Boards using essentially the same hardware can deliver wildly different performance—one twice as fast as another—because of a driver difference.

Without the right software driver, an accelerator does nothing and operates as a dumb frame buffer.

Worse, drivers can be mutable beasts. Some manufacturers change their drivers every few days, and with every change comes new (usually better) performance—and new compatibility problems. Buy a board from a manufacturer that operates a BBS (bulletin board service) so you can get updated drivers as they become available.

Without the right software driver, an accelerator does nothing and operates as a dumb frame buffer. Worse, many accelerators actually slow down when used as dumb frame buffers, offering no benefit to most DOS applications—particularly those that operate in text mode.

Other Video Performance Issues

Several other factors influence the speed of your video displays to one degree or another. Most of these effects are minor compared to the radical difference between accelerated or unaccelerated systems. But if you often operate under DOS without Windows, these factors may have a major effect on how fast your display system operates.

Bus Width

If your PC does not support local bus, you will be forced to use a graphic adapter that plugs into a traditional expansion bus. In that case, get a display adapter that uses the widest bus possible (the most bits) consistent with your PC's expansion slots. With most PCs, that means a 16-bit graphics adapter. Most current products have 16-bit connections. However, low-priced VGA and SuperVGA boards may only have 8-bit connections. These run at less than half the speed of a wider graphics adapter, because most PCs add extra wait states when they access 8-bit expansion slots. Avoid 8-bit boards if you can.

A few graphics adapters are available with 32-bit bus interfaces using either the EISA or Micro Channel standards. These often perform on par with local bus boards. If you have the option, they make a good choice for display systems. A better choice is to get a graphics adapter that incorporates one of the normal advanced expansion buses (EISA or Micro Channel) and local bus.

BIOS Issues

Display speed under DOS is influenced by the software and firmware of your display adapter. Every display adapter since IBM's now-archaic EGA adapter has included its own on-board BIOS to tell your system how to handle its advanced display modes. This BIOS affects the speed at which some programs can change your display. A more efficient BIOS is faster.

The display BIOS also faces issues of bus width. Many graphics adapters—particularly older designs and cut-rate products—have 8-bit BIOSs; others use 16-bit. The former, of course, executes more slowly in all but 8088-based systems (in which a purely 16-bit BIOS does not help at all).

BIOS shadowing minimizes the effects of narrow-width BIOS code on advanced graphics adapters. Some PCs have built-in provisions for automatically shadowing the video BIOS, no matter its origin. Some graphics board manufacturers also include utilities to allow the BIOSs on their products to be shadowed on systems lacking their own shadowing capabilities. In either case, you can gain a performance advantage by shifting to shadowing.

Note, however, that shadowing does not affect most graphics applications because most of these either write directly to the memory on the graphics adapter or use one of the drivers supplied with the graphics adapter. Drivers automatically run in fast RAM memory, so shadowing does not have any effect on driver performance.

Drivers automatically run in fast RAM memory, so shadowing does not have any effect on driver performance.

Shadowing becomes most important if you use your graphics adapter for text-mode work, not exactly what you are buying a graphics board for. Do not worry about shadowing or BIOS matters if you plan on doing most of your work in graphics mode.

Many PCs are designed to move the BIOS code that is shadowed to just under the 16M addressing limit of the ISA bus. Using this location for shadowing can prevent your PC from making use of memory beyond 16M. If your PC demonstrates this problem, switch its shadowing off using its advanced setup procedure. The loss of video shadowing will not have any affect on Windows or OS/2 performance but may slow down the rate that directories scroll down the screen at the DOS prompt. Most people regard the loss of video shadowing as a small price to pay to extend beyond 16M.

Memory Apertures

A new feature you are likely to find on VL Bus video cards is the *direct memory aperture*, a change in the way your PC sees its monitor screen. The aperture is a range of extended memory that can be used to directly address each bit that appears on your monitor screen.

PC-standard display systems with resolution at the EGA or higher level use paged addressing. That is, a 64K area of memory in the high DOS area—typically the first 64K block above the 640K limit nominally assigned to DOS—is reserved for accessing the frame buffer. High resolution display systems require more than 64K of memory, however, so designers had to resort to memory paging to control the entire range of video memory. This technique breaks video memory into several pages, each of which fits within the available 64K address range, and switches one page at a time into the reach of the microprocessor. Paged addressing is sometimes also called *bank-switching*.

This paged addressing not only adds extra overhead to screen updates—the display adapter has to shift to the correct range when reading or writing memory—but it also complicates system and software design. Software and its programmer must track every page change to ensure proper image control. Moving an image across the screen is equivalent to tracing a trip across multiple pages of a map, forcing you to leap forward and backward when you want to check your progress.

A direct memory aperture, which first achieved prominence in IBM's Extended Graphics Array (XGA) display subsystem, overcomes these problems. The entire screen fits one contiguous range of memory. Elaborate screen manipulations require only simple math. However, getting a large enough address range to handle all the memory locations of a high resolution screen requires more space than is available in the confines of the traditional PC video memory area. Therefore, these direct memory aperture systems move the aperture into high (extended) memory.

Moving video memory is problematic. First, the aperture can be reached only by advanced microprocessors (286 or better) because old 8088 and 8086 chips do not have sufficient address range. Moreover, because most programs are written for paged display systems like standard VGA, you will need special software drivers to take advantage of the features of direct memory aperture technology. Ordinary DOS applications cannot use the aperture without drivers.

Local bus adds a unique advantage to direct memory aperture products. ISA boards can address only 16M of memory, part of which must be devoted to the aperture. If you try to use 16M of system RAM as well as a direct memory aperture on an ISA machine, the memory conflict can result in random system crashes. VL Bus has access to the full 4G (that's four gigabytes, about four billion bytes) address range of 32-bit microprocessors. The aperture can be moved higher in memory where it will not cause conflicts with programs.

Resolution

Since it was introduced, the VGA standard has gone from an expensive complex proprietary system into the minimum expected from any PC. The circuitry has been simplified to a few chips, so inexpensive that many manufacturers build it into their computer system boards. Nearly all graphics software now expects a VGA board and will operate in that mode without further ado.

VGA isn't enough anymore. With ordinary VGA resolution, you get only a screenful of data. While that was sufficient when you did only one thing at a time—one screen equals one task—with Windows and OS/2 now becoming the environments of choice, you're not limited to one thing at a time. You may want to see two or more programs running at the same time. Switching from one screen to another might be okay if you have a photographic memory, but odds are you need to see a bit of each of the screens you want to compare. Or you want to see both where you're moving an image from and where it's going. Or you may just want to cram all the data you can into a single screen. You simply need more pixels so that you can see more.

Almost since IBM dreamt up the VGA system, other manufacturers have been struggling to go one (or a thousand) better. Nearly every VGA board has pretenses of higher resolutions. Some just inch up, others reach for the stratosphere. Any graphic adapter made in the last few years claims *at least* 1024 by 768 pixel resolution. Most now aspire to 1280 by 960—four times as many pixels as under VGA.

Until the last couple of years, these higher resolutions were little more than come-ons, promises to get you to buy a product but features you probably would not use. Several obstacles stood in the way of greater acceptance of these higher resolutions. The two most important roadblocks were the lack of standards and the lack of need. Windows and OS/2 have created the need. The standards were more difficult to achieve.

The standards problem became all too apparent when people plugged their monitors into their new high-resolution display adapters and saw the image slide off one side of their screen. One side of the image would be cut off while the other side of the monitor showed a broad black band.

The problem was in the timing of the signals from the display adapter. If the information on each displayed line was delayed from what the monitor expected, the image would unavoidably shift right and off the screen. If the data came too early, the image would shift left—and off the screen. At best, you'd be forced to twiddle a handful of knobs to bring the image back into control in the center of the screen whenever your switched into or out of 800 by 600 pixel mode.

The underlying problem was the lack of a standard. Every maker of a high-resolution display adapters used its own arbitrary timing for its video signals. The adapter makers could use proprietary timings with impunity because the makers of monitors rather than the video boards took the heat. After all, the monitor was the place where the problem occurred, so it was the natural device to blame.

As you might imagine, monitor makers were not delighted by this situation, and one of them decided to do something about it. NEC Technologies, the maker of the MultiSync monitors that gave promise to high-resolution displays (and suffered the indignities of its timing problems) banded together the most prominent manufacturers of high-resolution display adapters in 1988 to create the Video Electronics Standards Association (VESA). (Jim Schwabe of NEC claimed to have coined the VESA name while standing in his kitchen amid dishes packed for moving from California to Chicago.) Within the first three years of its existence, VESA came to embrace literally every maker of display adapters, most monitor manufacturers, and even large computer companies like IBM and Compaq.

The first challenge facing the organization was to straighten out the disheveled high-resolution situation among products proclaiming themselves as SuperVGA. The problem was more than just timing, however. Every display adapter maker created its own SuperVGA display mode to link with software. Each SuperVGA display adapter has its own BIOS and its own name (mode number) for its 800 by 600 mode. Drivers to link boards to software had to be individually written for each display adapter. SuperVGA did you no good without appropriate drivers, and few software publishers were willing to write separate drivers for a dozen different boards.

VESA conquered this problem by creating a "phantom" mode, number 6A, that would be universally recognized as SuperVGA. Calling that mode automatically triggers every conforming SuperVGA's adapter's 800 by 600 pixel mode.

The original signal timing problem proved less tractable because VESA members had two conflicting goals. Graphics adapter makers saw a high refresh rate as desirable because it would minimize image flicker. Monitor makers rallied for a standard that more suited their stocks of existing multiscanning monitors, one with a lower refresh rate.

The result of these conflicts was VESA's great waffle. It adopted not one standard but three: an official hardware standard and two manufacturing guidelines.

The standard pegs 800 by 600 pixel refresh at 72 Hz. This high rate insures the elimination of flicker, a degree of compatibility with whatever European standard may arise, and compatibility with 1024 by 768 pixel displays that use a 60 Hz refresh rate. (Both 800 by 600 at 72 Hz and 1024 by 768 at 60 Hz operate with 48 kHz horizontal scanning frequencies.) For compatibility with older monitors, VESA has set its two manufacturing guidelines with 56 and 60 Hz refresh rates at 800 by 600 resolution. The first is compatible with older dual-frequency monitors and limited bandwidth multiscanning displays designed for 8514/A's 35.5 KHz horizontal frequencies. (As the NEC 2A and 3D fit this class, you can guess the company that lobbied hardest for this guideline!) The 60 Hz guideline is a compromise that allow less expensive electronics with a reasonable refresh rate.

These guidelines are not superfluous but serve a valuable purpose. They define the exact timing of all aspects of the video signal. As a result, the images produced by a display adapter that follows the VESA guidelines will appear at the same place on the screen—no more moving margins.

With the standardization of SuperVGA behind it, VESA has moved into other territories. It started to develop a standard to match IBM's 8514/A display adapters but abandoned that effort to work on conforming to the newer XGA standard, then XGA-2 and other higher resolution standards. Along the way, VL Bus was developed.

Few DOS programs can take advantage of 800 by 600 pixel displays.

As a result of the efforts of VESA, graphic adapter and monitor makers have come together on signal timings for 800 by 600 and 1024 by 768 pixel images. The frequencies used by systems at these resolutions have been brought together. Higher resolution is now not just viable but desirable. But higher-than-VGA resolutions are not without their problems. If you do not use Windows or OS/2, resolutions beyond VGA may be worthless. You may not be able to take advantage of the sharpness of SuperVGA using the software your normally run. Few DOS programs can take advantage of 800 by 600 pixel displays. Although DOS is independent of the resolution of the display system because it operates in text mode, which can readily adapt to any display systems, most graphics adapters don't give you the option of booting and running DOS in 800 by 600 pixel mode. (You may wonder why graphics adapter makers don't allow you to set their boards to boot up in their high-resolution modes with a super-sharp 15 x 10 text font. So do a lot of people.)

If you're committed to Windows or OS/2 Presentation Manager, push your display system to the maximum resolution.

If you're committed to Windows or OS/2 Presentation Manager, however, you'll probably want to push your display system to the maximum resolution it can display. You'll see more on your screen, and the image will appear sharper. But there are some caveats.

The image may be sharper, but you might not be able to see the difference. On a standard 14-inch monitor, you have to squint hard indeed to see the improvement wrought by going beyond 800 by 600 resolution. Remember, VGA is already close to what people with normal acuity can resolve at normal working distances. If you opt for 1024 by 768 pixel resolution, you'll want at least a 16-inch display. Today, 17-inch tubes are becoming preferred.

Once you shift to 1024 by 768 pixel or higher resolution, you'll notice that the rest of the world may not be entirely ready for such sharpness. Under Windows, for example, you'll find at times fonts shrink to nose-on-the-screen size. If you don't have larger fonts to substitute, you may need to get your bifocals tuned up or your resolution tuned down.

For optimum viewing, non-interlaced signals are preferred.

Shift higher, to 1280 by 960 (or to the 1280 by 1024 that some products have picked as a standard), and you'll run into an old bugaboo—*image interlacing*. Most display standards operate non-interlaced—they use *progressive scanning* in which one horizontal line of pixels is lighted on the display after another in sequence from screen top to bottom. Interlacing take two passes, alternating every other line. It gives the illusion the image is being scanned faster (twice as fast) than it really is, so graphic adapter makers can cut corners and run their products at lower speeds. Unfortunately, the illusion is not always completely successful. In the computer industry, interlacing is viewed as inherently evil, something to avoid, because it compromises image quality on some monitors.

The primary image defect with interlaced display systems is image flicker. For optimum viewing, non-interlaced signals are preferred—providing, of course, you have or acquire a monitor that can use them. Interlacing will be described more completely in the discussion of monitors, later in this chapter. If the graphic adapter in your PC cannot generate SuperVGA or better images, you're a candidate for a display adapter upgrade. Even if you have SuperVGA circuitry, you still might want to upgrade to get more out of your PC—more speed from a graphic accelerator or more colors.

Color Issues

Resolution means nothing if the color on your display looks like your monitor got bruised in a blueberry pie fight. All too often, high-resolution color images are mere caricatures of reality. The selection of colors can be so slight you might expect the screen to have been generated less by expensive graphics software than a toddler with a budget box of eight Crayolas. All you get is a few basic colors (red, blue, green, maybe even orange and pink) but none of today's high-fashion in-between shades (taupe, berry, blush, hemorrhage, and contusion). The color limit is imposed not by the device you're most apt to blame—the monitor—because the analog-input monitors with which the latest graphics adapters work have essentially unlimited spectra. Rather, the short-hued rendition is a result of your choice of display adapter—and more particularly, its memory.

The color capabilities of display adapters are measured two ways, by the maximum *palette*, the range of colors that any particular on-screen pixel can be, and by the actual number of colors that can be simultaneously displayed. This duality arises from the way graphics boards deal with colors. A given number of bits (sometimes called *color-planes*) are assigned to code the color of each pixel in the storage system of the graphics adapter. A one-bit code can specify one of two colors, whether any given pixel is on or off. Two bits can specify four colors; eight bits, 256 colors. Memory is thus the limit of the number of colors that a graphics board can store. For a 1024 by 768 pixel image in 256 colors (eight bits), a graphics board needs at least three-quarters of a million bytes of video memory. That's a lot of bytes and not much color. It's also today's minimum to demand from a graphics adapter. This level of color performance will require at least one megabyte of memory on your graphics adapter.

When a display system is limited solely to 256 predefined colors, however, its images look artificial and cartoon-like. Getting realistic or photo-quality image would require even more megabytes. To achieve what computer people consider realistic color—16.7 million different hues—you need 24 bits of storage per pixel.

To broaden their color range without demanding more memory, graphics adapters use *color look-up tables*. Instead of defining a color, the board's video memory stores codes. Each code is matched to any one of a much wider-variety of colors that make up the board's palette.

In VGA-derived systems the palette stretches for 262,144 colors because the VGA system relies on a device called a *Digital-to-Analog converter* (DAC, also rendered as *RAMDAC* because it works with random-access memory) that can use 18-bit codes in its color map. The subtle variations allowed by such wide palettes can create reasonably realistic images under the VGA standard even though only 256 different colors may be displayed on the screen at a time. (Most images are made from a limited number of tones, often all drawn from the same family, so often a small number of different hues can suffice.) In that a couple hundred thousand colors is close to the number of hues that the typical color picture tube can unambiguously generate, the VGA palette is a good compromise between color and cost.

It's not good enough for some people. The human eye can distinguish millions of colors, and so they want the ability to store millions of colors to accommodate realistic tones in devices with better fidelity than a cheap computer monitor. In general, the computer industry has converged to a single high-end color standard: that 24-bit color in which eight bits is used to store brightness information for each of the three primary colors.

The problem with 24-bit color its that it requires three bytes of storage for every pixel on the monitor screen. At high resolutions, that can be a prodigious amount of memory, over two million bytes (2,359,296 to be exact) at 1024 by 768 pixel resolution. Manipulating that much memory dozens of time a second can slow your system down. It also can extract a cost, particularly for display adapters that use more expensive (but faster) video RAM or VRAM chips.

To keep memory requirement in bounds, many graphics adapters use 16-bit color patterned after the system IBM developed for its original XGA. In 16-bit color, both the blue and red signals are allocated 5-bit resolution and the green signal gets 6-bit resolution (because the eye is most sensitive to green and because the green signal is often used on monochrome monitors to make shades of gray). This 16-bit color system yields 65,536 simultaneous on-screen hues or 64 shades of gray.

Some display adapters compromise and use DACs capable of handling full 24-bit color but minimize memory down to the level for 256 on-screen colors. You get a realistic, wide palette but no way of displaying anything but a fraction of its potential. When 256 simultaneous on-screen colors is the limit for a display adapter, a palette wider than 256K is superfluous.

When you go shopping for a graphics board upgrade, you'll find that the color potential of the board can be described in several ways. Specifications may simply list the number of colors—that's simple. But the number of colors may be complicated by wider selection that makes up the palette that those colors may be drawn from—for example, 256 colors from a palette of 262,144. Worse, the specifications may list only the number of color planes that the board can store.

The number of color planes is the same thing as the number of bits used to store color information for each on-screen pixel. One bit per pixel can code only whether a particular dot is on or off, white or black. Two bits per pixel allows four gray levels or colors, with two of the choices typically being black and white.

Figuring out the number of simultaneously displayable colors from the number of bit-planes or bits per pixel is easy. Just calculate two to the number of bit-planes (2^n where n=bit-planes).

Monitor Matching

Perhaps the most important issue when shopping for a display adapter is that it matches your monitor. In other words, you must ensure that the monitor that you own or plan to buy as part of your graphics upgrade will work with the display adapter that you choose. You must make a match in three areas to guarantee success: frequencies, signal type, and color capability.

Frequencies

The signals produced by all display adapters are not the same. They have different characteristic frequencies that describe how often they update each full-screen image (a measure called the *frame rate*, vertical synchronizing frequency, or just vertical frequency) and how often each of the lines of the image is drawn on the screen (called the line rate, horizontal scanning frequency, horizontal synchronizing frequency, or just horizontal frequency). The frequencies produced by a display adapter must match those accepted by the monitor for successful operation.

The frequencies produced by a display adapter must match those accepted by the monitor for successful operation.

With the now-obsolete ordinary graphic systems, matching monitors was easy—just follow the bouncing standard. CGA board required a CGA monitor. An EGA board needed an EGA monitor. And a

VGA board plugged into a VGA monitor. (You can also force a CGA monitor to work with an EGA board and an EGA monitor to work with a CGA monitor, nice to know if you deal in obsolete technology.) The problem is that the ordinary display standards aren't good enough anymore. Nearly all display adapters and even all new PCs come equipped to handle resolutions far in excess of ordinary VGA. Unfortunately, once you pass the VGA level, simple standards-matching falls. Even the standards themselves unravel. For example, the Video Electronics Standards Association (or VESA), has two "manufacturers' guidelines" and one "standard" that determined monitor compatibility at the 800 by 600 resolution level alone. As a result a monitor that may be legitimately called "VESA compatible" might not work with a display adapter claiming to abide by the same standard.

Monitor manufacturers have tried to tip-toe around this issue by building so-called *multi-scanning* monitors (discussed in depth later in this chapter) that can accommodate a range of frequencies. Of course the range of each multi-scanning monitor model is different. As a result of this confusion, you must count frequencies. The range of frequencies accommodated by the monitor you plan to use must include the frequencies produced by the display adapter in the mode that you want to use. Table 10.1 lists the frequencies your monitor must support to accommodate the various display standards.

Table 10.1. Synchronizing Frequency Range

Standard	Vertical Sync	Horizontal Sync	TTL or Analog
	720 X 350 Resolution		
MDA	50 Hz	18.3 KHz	TTL (one color)
	640 X 200 Resolution		
CGA	60 Hz	15.75 KHz	TTL (16 colors)
	640 X 350 Resolution		
EGA	60 Hz	21.5 KHz	TTL (64 colors)
	640 X 480 (also operate at 720 X 400, 640 X 400, and 640 X 350)		
MCGA	60 & 70 Hz	31.5 KHz	Analog
VGA	60 & 70 Hz	31.5 KHz	Analog

Standard	Vertical Sync	Horizontal Sync	TTL or Analog
		800 X 600 Resolution	
VESA guideline	56 Hz	35.5 KHz	Analog
VESA guideline	60 Hz	37.8 KHz	Analog
VESA standard	72 Hz	48 KHz	Analog
		1024 X 768 Resolution	
8514/A	87 Hz*	35.5 KHz	Analog
XGA	87 Hz*	35.5 KHz	Analog
VESA	60 Hz	48 KHz	Analog

*This is the field rate that 8514/A and XGA monitors must be able to synchronize to; because these signals are interlaced, the actual frame rate is one-half the field rate or 43.5 Hz.

Signal Type

The universe of electricity is divided into the analog and digital domains, depending on how signals encode information. *Analog signals* code data as a varying of the strength (amplitude) or frequency of the signal. *Digital signals* code information as discrete state changes. The two don't usually mix—at least not happily.

Nearly all of today's monitors that work at VGA resolution and better use analog signals. Older standards used digital signals. You only need to worry about the difference if you plan to connect up an older display and display adapter—hardly an update you'd want to make. But if you harbor several computer systems in your home or business and you hope to move monitors between older and new systems, then the signal difference can be important. Digital and analog signal systems differ in how they code color and brightness information, and the analog system has a pronounced advantage in color range.

Digital signals use a digital code. Colors and brightness levels are identified by a pattern of signals carried on several distinct connections between the display adapter and the monitor. One wire in the connecting cable is used to carry each connection and thereby each bit in the digital code. For example, IBM's original Color Graphics Adapter (CGA) standard used four digital signal connections; the Enhanced Graphics Adapter (EGA) standard required six, all tucked in a single connecting cable.

Analog signals code brightness levels in voltage levels. A higher voltage of the signal corresponds to (or is the analog of) a brighter on-screen image. In that a single wire can carry any voltage, a single analog connection suffices to transmit an infinity of brightness levels.

Color information can also be coded in analog signals. For example, the National Television Standards Committee (NTSC) video standard, usually termed "composite video," that is popular in televisions, video, and multi-media systems does exactly that. To distinguish color from brightness information on the signal NTSC connection, color information is encoded on a subcarrier—essentially a special radio signal, also analog—that is combined with the brightness voltages.

The NTSC system has a major drawback, however. The frequency of the subcarrier sets an upper limit on the detail that can be contained in the brightness information. Consequently, NTSC is unacceptable for use with computers, except for inexpensive 40-column systems, the kind that connect to television sets and deliver image quality on par with regular television programming. However, many new display adapters offer NTSC outputs so that you can create multi-media images that are compatible with traditional video systems—television-style monitors, videocassette recorders, and videodisc players.

Analog display adapters that follow the PC and proprietary standards separate three signals corresponding to the primary colors of light—red, green, and blue. One connection is assigned to each, and each carries a separate analog signal without limits imposed by subcarriers. The three color signals, each able to indicate an infinity of brightness levels, combine in various mixtures to produce an infinity of colors, at least potentially.

It's important that the digital display adapter you choose and the monitor that you plan to use follow the same color coding.

Most color graphics adapters are limited to far fewer colors than are possible in theory (an infinity fewer, in fact, leaving the paradoxical result that an infinity subtracted from another infinity yields a non-zero number—we'll leave the philosophers to haggle over that one!). In analog systems, then, the number of displayable colors is determined by the display adapter that produces the signals rather than by the monitor that's connected to it. In digital systems, both the display adapter and the monitor may limit color potential. The various digital display standards use different codes for their color outputs. It's important that the digital display adapter you choose and the monitor that you plan to use follow the same color coding. The principal codes are termed eight-color, which was used by early

Apple computers and can pretty much be ignored in the PC environment, 16-color or RGBI which is used by the CGA system, and 64-color which is used by the EGA system.

In today's world, where SuperVGA is the minimal display standard you should expect in a new display adapter or PC, you shouldn't have to worry about analog and digital signals. However, if you go bottom-fishing for a bargain monitor, you may encounter old digital-signal displays at too-good-to-be-true prices. Avoid problems by avoiding such monitors. Ensure that any computer display you buy for your upgrade has analog inputs.

One or Two Displays

Some display adapters—typically those designed for high-end CAD systems and multi-media image manipulation—give you the choice of viewing everything that your PC does on one screen or two. In the latter case, your system will typically boot up on one screen and display high-resolution graphics on the other.

Using a single monitor gives you one big advantage—it's cheaper simply because you only have to buy one monitor. The alternative, connecting the high resolution graphics board to a separate monitor, brings somewhat more versatility—for example, some programs can devote one screen strictly to graphics and the other to text-based control—but at a high cost in dollars and desk space. Then again, most single-board systems don't preclude you adding a second monitor later when you find the need, the desk space, and the cash.

To bring together DOS and super-pixelated graphics, single-monitor graphics boards either incorporate their high-resolution abilities into an otherwise ordinary VGA board or operate as *pass-through* graphics adapters. That is, they connect directly to your existing VGA board through its expansion connector and pass its VGA signals through to your monitor when not operating in their high-resolution modes (see fig. 10.1).

A few display adapters also offer the option of adding VGA capabilities to the basic high-resolution graphics adapter by plugging in a daughter card. Although the daughter card may save a slot and bind display functions tightly together, it's not necessarily the lowest-cost solution. Note that these daughter cards often cost $300 or more while you can purchase an entire VGA board (if your system doesn't have VGA built in) for under $100. On the other hand, the daughter card implies that the high resolution board manufacturer tested

Ensure that any computer display you buy for your upgrade has analog inputs.

When you mix and match VGA and high-resolution display adapters yourself, you can sometimes run into uncooperative combinations.

the VGA daughter and is sure that it will work properly with the high-resolution section. When you mix and match VGA and high-resolution display adapters yourself, sometimes you can run into un-cooperative combinations.

Figure 10.1

The expansion connector on a graphic adapter.

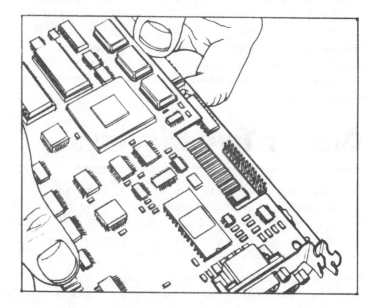

Figure 10.1

The expansion connector on a graphic adapter.

Connections and Connectors

At heart, the installation of a display adapter board of any type appears trivially easy.

At heart, the installation of a display adapter board of any type appears trivially easy. You only need to plug an expansion board into your PC. But display adapters and particularly the coprocessed ones are rarely so straightforward—installation only begins with getting the board into your system.

With pass-through such coprocessed adapters, you'll need a special cable (most coprocessed board makers supply one gratis with their products) and a compatible VGA board. This cable connects between the VGA feature connector—an edge connector at the top of most VGA boards—to a similar connector on the coprocessed board. Its purpose is to send the video output of your VGA board to the coprocessor and thence to your monitor.

When installing a coprocessed display adapter in a PS/2 with VGA circuitry built into its system board, you ordinarily don't have to worry about such cables. Instead, you must be certain to plug the coprocessed board into the expansion slot in your system that has the video extension connector, which is identifiable by the connector on the system board extending slightly further toward the rear of the system than the other expansion connectors.

Classic bus and EISA computers that have their VGA circuitry built into their system boards should (but don't always) have a VGA feature connector on their system boards for connecting with coprocessed display adapters. According to the IBM design, a VGA feature connector is an edge connector similar to those on the lower edges of expansion boards. Sometimes, this feature jack is a header—two rows of square, gold-plated pins, instead of an edge connector. This is the format specified by VESA for video extension connections. If your PC has system-board VGA, examine it before you order your display adapter because the cable you need will depend on the connector that's on your system board. (Some graphic adapters now come with VESA feature connectors, too, so you should check your VGA board to determine the cable it requires.)

When you order a display adapter, you'll need to specify the connectors you'll require at both ends of the cable.

The cable at the other end of your display adapter—the one that links the board to your monitor—is also critical. Even at ordinary VGA resolution, monitor cables are far from standard. Certainly most monitors now accept the 15-pin high-density D-shell connector that IBM chose for VGA, but many monitors use 9-pin connectors—or different 15-pin D-shells (dare we call them "low density?"), 25-pin D-shells, or even three to five BNC jacks more like you'd expect on an over-the-horizon radar set. Similarly, display adapters that venture beyond VGA may use different connectors. For example, some boards use a nine-pin D-shell like a CGA or EGA connector but with an entirely different pin-out.

When you order a display adapter, you'll need to specify the connectors you'll require at both ends of the cable. If you have a choice of what to use, the separate BNC cable approach is the best because it better isolates the signals. Some monitor makers actually rate the BNC inputs of their products with higher bandwidths (and thus, more resolution) than their all-in-one connectors.

Of course, with a multiple-BNC cable you're left with three to five identical-looking connectors for a matching number of jacks. Fortunately, most BNC cables meant for computer monitors are color coded (either with actual color bands near their connectors or with simple designations such as R for Red, B for Blue, G for Green, H for Horizontal sync, V for Vertical sync, and C for Composite sync).

The number of connectors used is a function of the way the synchronizing signal is delivered to the monitor. Three cables are used for "sync-on-green"; four, "composite sync"; and five, "separate sync." Some all-in-one connector systems give you the same options. You'll have to match your monitor to the connections provided by your display adapter using the facilities the monitor provides (automatic sensing, a switch, or whatever), which you should find described in the manual accompanying your monitor.

Once you make the connections, you need to install the software accompanying your display adapter to match the applications you want to run. Today, this installation process is usually managed by an automatic program and you only need to make a few choices from menus. Once that's done, reboot your system, start your application, and prepare yourself for the speed, resolution, and colors of your new display adapter.

Installation

The hardware installation of a display adapter is usually the easiest part of the upgrade job. You merely need to slide the board into the appropriate slot of your PC. Of course, there are complicating issues such as which slot to use.

The first step in the installation process is to open up your PC and scout out the slots that are available for the installation of a display adapter. If your system already has a display adapter that you want to replace inside it, the old display adapter slot is a likely candidate. Before you automatically steal the old slot, however, examine your new display adapter and the slot. Most of the latest display adapters use 16-bit interfaces. The performance of these boards will be compromised if they are installed in an eight-bit slot. Some 16-bit boards may not even work in an eight-bit slot. If your new display adapter is 16-bit and your old one was eight-bit, remove the old board and install the new one in some other slot, one that has a 16-bit interface. Sixteen-bit ISA display adapters will also work in 32-bit EISA expansion slots.

In Micro Channel computers, you should install any display enhancement product in the slot has that the VGA feature connector extension. The VGA feature connector extension is an added part of a 16-bit slot connector that projects toward the rear of the computer's case. If your PC does not have a display adapter in an expansion slot (because the circuitry is built into the system board) or if you are adding a second adapter (such as a coprocessed board), find a slot for the new board that matches the bus width of its edge connector.

In any case, don't install the board yet. You have to set it up first. You may have to change jumpers or switch settings on the board or even on your system board (see fig. 10.2).

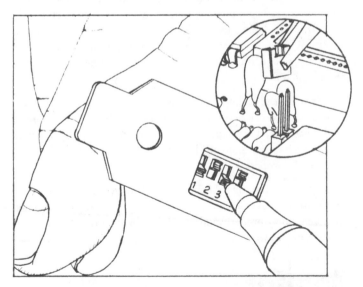

Figure 10.2
Be sure to set any jumpers or DIP switch settings before you install the board.

The first adjustment to make is in case you have a 16-bit display adapter and no 16-bit slots available. Many display adapters have adjustments to allow you to use a 16-bit board in an eight-bit slot. If that's what you plan to do, make the adjustment.

Experiment with alternate addresses only if the default addresses don't work.

Check the memory addresses used by your display adapter. If you're replacing your system board video circuitry or your old display adapter, you can use the default range of most upgrade display adapters, in general the range from A0000(Hex) to BFFFF(Hex) or a narrower selection within that range. Experiment with alternate addresses only if the default addresses don't work.

Many coprocessed display adapters require a second address range and sometimes an Input/Output port address. In general, you should first try the defaults recommended by the manufacturer of the display adapter. If your system does not boot up properly once the installation is complete or if it crashes when you try to start a high-resolution mode, you should experiment with changing these addresses. If your PC has system-board video circuitry that you want to replace, check your computer's owners' manual on how to switch it off. Some systems require that you move a jumper to turn off this circuitry. Others automatically sense the addition of another display adapter and make the appropriate switch themselves.

If you're installing a coprocessed display adapter that needs to link with your system's existing VGA circuitry, prepare the connection now, before you install the new board. PCs with system board VGA circuitry typically provide a header or edge connector to which you can plug in the new coprocessed adapter. Most VGA and better primary display adapters have a VGA feature connector you can plug in to. In any case, you'll want to plug in one end of the VGA connecting cable before you slide in the display adapter so you have room in which to work.

Finally, you're ready. Slide the display adapter into the appropriate slot. Screw it into place. If you need to make a VGA feature connection, do that now. Then plug your monitor into the display adapter. Turn on the monitor and your PC and verify that the display adapter works properly.

If it does not, try resetting the jumpers or switches on the display adapter board to one of their alternate settings, then try again. When your system boots properly and you determine that the higher resolution modes work, you can reassemble your PC.

Monitors

If you're not happy with what you see, you'll want to upgrade your monitor.

Your monitor is simply the most important visual element of your PC. The image on its screen is all that you can see of what your computer does until (and if) your work is committed to paper. You continuously call upon your monitor to reveal your PC's innermost and tiniest thoughts. And the monitor's screen must be something that you're willing to look at for hours on end. If you're not happy with what you see, you'll want to upgrade your monitor.

If any rule dominates all your other cares and concerns in finding the right monitor upgrade for your PC, it is to please yourself. The best monitor is the one that yields the most pleasing image to your own eye. Maybe you don't require the utmost in resolution. Maybe you are so attuned to interlacing that a flicker-free refresh rate dominates all other concerns. Maybe you like off-color, out-of-convergence displays because you suffer from Sixties nostalgia and the creative color scheme gives you a drug-free high. Whatever the case, remember that your monitor is your portal into your personal computer. If you don't like what you see there—if you strain your eyes and credulity—you won't be happy with your work or your PC.

If any rule dominates all your other cares and concerns in finding the right monitor upgrade for your PC, it is to please yourself.

Finding the right monitor upgrade requires more than looking, however. You've got to match the monitor to your display adapter, to your PC, and to your software. The concerns are manifold.

Selecting a Monitor

As with other computer equipment or nearly anything else, a monitor is not difficult to buy. Write a check or read your bank-card number over the phone and await the delivery truck—it's easy. But getting the sharpest monitor, the one with the best color, the one that's the best value, and one that will work with your PC is more of a challenge. You have to match the monitor to your display adapter to ensure that it will work with your PC. Whatever standard or non-standard you elect to follow, you must be certain that your software can take advantage of it. And your monitor choice must be agreeable both to your eyes and your purse.

You'll have a number of technical concerns in making these matches. But your first choice is philosophical. You must decide where your plans for your PC fit in with the designs of the monitor manufacturers.

Scanning Range

The philosophical starting place in considering a new monitor is with the three different kinds of monitors that you can connect to your PC. Monitors are a lot like people—some march in step with a common standard, some stroll in syncopation with their own drummers, and some just don't care either way, accepting a dance from whoever offers. The banners under which the common-standard monitors rally are the well-known display standards used by most display adapters—MDA, CGA, EGA, VGA, and XGA. The different drummers of the display world use their abilities to go beyond the common mien, linking up with their own proprietary display adapters to become complete video systems. And those that don't care are the uniquely adaptable multi-scanning displays.

From these three major classes you must select your next monitor. The choice can be easy, even preordained, but you should consider all the alternatives before you commit your cash.

The common standard has a lot in its favor—safety in numbers and the low prices that come with near-commodity merchandising. Any VGA monitor you find should plug directly into a VGA display adapter and give you an image. You don't have to pore through manuals for timing specifications, mix and match frequencies, or tangle with adapter cables. When you decide to follow one of the popular standards, you have an unbelievable range of monitors to select among, from tiny monochrome screens to 31-inch multi-hued monsters.

Pick any display standard, and you'll find the prices are unbeatable. For example, nearly every computer hardware company—seemingly anyone with the ability to write—puts its name on a VGA monitor of some kind. And this competition has driven prices down below the level where lesser standards were lodged back at the time VGA was announced. Shop around and you'll discover monochrome VGA displays under $100, color under $250. Monitors that owe their allegiance to other standards are even cheaper—with close reading of the ads, you can probably find TTL monochrome displays for little more than $50.

The big drawback in selecting one of these systems is that standards are made for the masses, and for many people the popular choice means mediocrity. By selecting a monitor that transcends the mundane industry standards, you can get higher resolution, faster operation, more information on each screen, perhaps even a screen shape more commensurate with the vertically-oriented letterheads and newsletters you've spent most of your life dealing with.

The price you pay for the benefit beyond the common standards is, of course, measured in dollars. Not only are proprietary monitors themselves more expensive, but also you have to pay for the matching proprietary display adapter that makes a complete display system. When you do, you may suffer compatibility problems with some PCs and applications. Some proprietary display systems won't work with your favorite programs. Some even have difficulties with plain old DOS. Even when you find a proprietary display system that can function with DOS, you may find that your dearer investment doesn't deliver any greater quality on most of the work that you do. Often even the highest resolution proprietary systems step back to the VGA standard—or worse, back to CGA—when DOS scrolls down the screen.

The flexibility of multi-scanning monitors gives you possibly the best of both worlds, the ability to follow the standards when you must but also transcend them when you can. A multi-scanning display can adapt to several standards as well as to some proprietary display modes that give you more colors and resolution than more commonplace monitors allow.

Multi-scanning monitors have their limits, too. No multi-scanning display will work with all possible display adapters. They may fall short at either the high or low end or may simply lack a special input capability required by an esoteric display adapter. Moreover, when you want only to make a modest improvement on today's standard, perhaps to boldly go forward to VESA quality multi-scanning displays often isn't the most affordable solution.

Which style of monitor is best to buy depends on what you have and what you want. If your concern is only the matter of matching a monitor to the display adapter that's already in your PC, you can probably play the standards game. If you want to hedge against future standards, however, the multi-scanning display may be a better choice. In fact, you will need a multi-scanning monitor to take advantage of today's 800×600 and 1024×768 accelerated graphic systems.

No matter which direction you choose, you need to know the signposts that will help point you on your way. All monitors have certain distinguishing characteristics that make some better than others and otherwise define the applications for which they are best suited.

No multi-scanning display will work with all possible display adapters.

Input Type

When you've made your philosophical choice, you need to consider all the technical matters that separate monitors from one another. The best place to start is where monitors start—with the signal provided by your PC. Display adapters under different display standards as well as proprietary display systems that produce signals may use digital or analog signals. Correspondingly, monitors may accept one, the other, or both signal types.

You must match the type of signal produced by your display adapter with the monitor that you buy.

Analog monitors just do what they are told. If they receive the right combination of signals, they can produce nearly any color you want. While analog signals offer a potential for coding an infinite number of colors, the monitor spectrum isn't quite infinite because of limitations in the phosphors in the tube and even the discrete number of electrons that must light each pixel. Even so you can expect to get about 256,000 different colors from a good analog display according to monitor makers. Some makers claim even more. No one will argue that any monitor today can produce the 16.7 million individually distinguishable color produced by a true 24-bit display adapter. But computer monitors still do as well in reproducing color as the primary gauge on civilization—the television set. In fact, computer monitors usually do better.

Digital monitors are more limited. Their spectrum is limited to the square of the number of connections provided for the digital signals. The four connections characteristic of the original CGA system allow 16 colors. The six connections of the EGA make up to 64 colors possible. Today, the available selection of digital-only color monitors is primarily limited to units that conform to those two video standards. Beyond 64 colors, the number of connections required become ungainly at best.

You must match the type of signal produced by your display adapter with the monitor that you buy. Proprietary video systems do this matching for you. After all, when you buy a complete package, you should expect the pieces to work together.

If you choose a monitor that matches a recognized display standard—TTL Monochrome, CGA, EGA, or VGA—you'll also be sure of getting a product that handles the right signal type. Multi-scanning monitors are the only ones that will likely cause you problems, and you can avoid them by selecting one with both analog and digital inputs.

Required Frequencies

Prominent as horsepower ratings in muscle car days are the number of hertz, kilohertz, and megahertz in the specifications of every monitor. These numbers describe the frequencies at which the monitor is designed to operate. Unlike horsepower ratings or even microprocessor speeds, however, bigger numbers here aren't necessarily better—or even necessary.

If you stick with industry display standards or a packaged proprietary display system, you need not worry about the irksome need to match frequencies. When you step beyond the standards or try to connect up a multi-scanning monitor, suddenly these frequencies will haunt your daydreams and nightmares with the same evil inevitability as your boss standing over you at work. There are just so many frequencies and so little sense to them.

Two frequencies determine what signals a monitor can recognize and work with, the *horizontal scanning frequency* and *vertical scanning frequency*. For brevity, the "scanning" is often dropped from the names.

The first of these figures describes how often the lines of the video image are formed. For example, a horizontal frequency of 15 kilohertz (thousands of cycles per second) means that lines appear on the screen at a rate of 15,000 per second. Vertical frequency describes how often a complete full-screen image (or frame) is produced. Consequently the vertical frequency is often termed the *frame rate* or monitor *refresh rate*.

Sometimes these frequencies are referred to as horizontal sync and vertical sync—sync standing for synchronizing—because pulses at the beginning of each line and each frame are used to synchronize or lock the displayed image with the expectations of the display adapter. If the image cannot be locked, the result is akin to the rolling image of an old television with a misadjusted vertical hold control or a torn image that needs its horizontal hold adjusted. (Remember when televisions had vertical and horizontal hold knobs? Remember when televisions had knobs? Feeling old?) The important thing about these frequencies is that any monitor you buy must be rated to operate at the frequencies produced by the display adapter in your PC.

Monitors that can lock to only a single horizontal and vertical frequency are called *fixed-frequency displays*. Those that can lock to two or more sets of frequencies are termed, logically, *multiple fixed-frequency displays*.

A special case of the multiple fixed-frequency display are *dual-frequency monitors* which are designed to latch onto two fixed horizontal frequencies. The pre-eminent example is IBM's now-discontinued 8514 monitor, its model 8515 replacement, and other manufacturer's products compatible with the IBM units. These displays are capable of locking to VGA frequencies as well as the 1024 by 768 interlaced images created by IBM's 8514/A and XGA graphics systems. Some of these dual-frequency displays also can lock to the SuperVGA signals defined by the VESA specifications. Newer multiple fixed-frequency displays may be aimed at making SuperVGA images under the more advanced versions of VESA.

Multi-scanning monitors work with any frequency within a wide range so they can accept the signals of a variety of display adapters. The specification of most multi-scanning monitors list the frequencies of signals the products can accept. The lowest range of horizontal frequencies that should be of interest to you are those of CGA, about 15 KHz. The MDA system requires horizontal frequencies of about 18 KHz; EGA, 22 KHz; VGA, 31KHz; 8514/A, XGA, and some 800 x 600 pixel VESA systems, 35 KHz. High-resolution graphic coprocessor boards may require horizontal frequencies of 48 KHz and higher (check the manual of your graphics adapter). Proprietary display systems can push horizontal frequencies even higher. Note that if you have a VGA board, when it operates in its CGA and EGA modes, even when it simulates those displays it maintains its own nominal 31 KHz horizontal frequency. You only need a monitor that dips down to 15 KHz if you have a CGA or EGA display adapter.

The frequencies generated by the display adapter must match those at which your monitor is designed to operate or be within the range accepted by your monitor.

The range of vertical frequencies that monitors are required to handle is somewhat more modest. Few display systems are as slow as the 50 Hz used by MDA. Monitors that range down to 56 Hz will handle most color display standards including SuperVGA under VESA but not MDA. Most multi-scanning monitors easily adapt to frequencies in the range of 60 Hz (used by CGA, EGA, and some VGA and VESA modes) to 70 Hz (other VGA modes). But a higher top end is required for newer standards such as the high-refresh VESA standard (72 Hz) and interlaced 8514/A signals (87 Hz) All of these frequencies are summarized in table 10.1.

When buying a monitor, the scanning frequency rule is simple. The frequencies generated by the display adapter in your PC must either match those at which your monitor is designed to operate or they must be within the range accepted by your multi-scanning monitor.

Autosizing

Although multi-scanning monitors can do wonders when you have to mate with odd signals, the matching frequencies may not be your only worry. The monitor also must be able to cope with varying image heights. Even within the VGA standard, the height of images displayed on the screen can vary when your software switches between display modes. Along with image height, the *aspect ratio*— the relationship between the height and width of the image—changes, making your graphics look out-of-shape. Squares become rectangles, and every circle will seem to have a slow leak.

The problem is that the VGA standard created by IBM is actually three separate standards, each one differing by the number of lines making up each image. The basic VGA graphics mode makes images 480 lines high. In text mode and the VGA's double-scanned CGA-compatibility mode, images are built from 400 lines. EGA graphics on VGA monitors are drawn with 350 lines. All else being equal in a monitor, the greater the number of lines it displays, the taller the resulting image will look. If a VGA monitor does not have provisions for adjusting its image height to match the three different line counts, aspect ratio and image shape may go from fat to thin to fat again.

To avoid such endo- to ectomorphic and back again graphics, IBM endowed its VGA monitors with a unique system that automatically adjusts the heights of image to match the different modes of the threefold standard. The VGA graphics adapter in your PC tells your monitor how tall to make its image, indicating the number of lines that comprise each image by coding the polarity of its horizontal and vertical synchronizing signals. A truly VGA-compatible monitor detects the polarities of the two synchronizing signals and adjusts its internal electronics to maintain a constant height across all three VGA standards. The fourth possible sync signal coding is used by IBM to indicate interlaced 8514/A and XGA signals that are made from 768 lines.

The most desirable monitor is one that can autosize to match any standard.

Beyond VGA and 8514/A, this sync-indicated system falls apart. No additional codings of sync signals are available beyond the basic four. Even if there were, it would be hard to imagine the monitor industry deciding on an acceptable standard for them. Consequently, monitor makers must either develop their own broader-based autosizing method, stick with the VGA standard and only autosize for four image types, or just let the image height vary with the signal standard. Each of these three approaches have been adopted by a number of monitor makers.

The most desirable monitor is one that can autosize to match any standard. Least desirable is a monitor that entirely lacks autosizing. Most (if not all) VGA monitors can autosize for the three VGA signal types. Most multi-scanning monitors make provisions for setting image height to match different standards. Before you buy, make sure that a prospective monitor can maintain a constant image height with all the graphics standards you plan to use.

Monitor Controls

Even when a monitor lacks autosizing, it need not be impossible to use—as long as its controls are located conveniently. When a monitor manufacturer puts the knobs that control the sizes of its on-screen image—typically those controls labeled horizontal size, gain, or width and vertical size, gain, or height—where you can readily reach them, then you can manually adjust any picture for the proper perspective.

If you often jump between operating modes—text and graphics—or occasionally leap back to EGA graphics, the manual method of image sizing will prove to be tedious and time-consuming, forcing you to twist the controls every time you shift between programs. But if you stick with a single standard, for example running only Windows 3.1 programs or never exiting Lotus 1-2-3, you'll need to make image size adjustments but once.

With some monitors, you may discover that the manufacturer has worked hard to make all the important image controls difficult to find or impossible to adjust. They may put the image controls on the back of a big-screen set so you need gorilla arms to make an adjustment and caterpillar eyes to see the effect. You'll want to avoid such monitors.

Some monitor manufacturers believe they know what you want far better than you do so they seal all the image controls inside their products. Just to make things interesting, they usually emblazon the monitor with a warning to the effect that there are no user serviceable parts inside and you will inevitably die if you try opening the case. If such a monitor-maker has perfect aesthetic judgment—which means it agrees with your own—this simplification can work out. But if beauty to you is in the eye of the beholder and you're beholden to your own views, you're out of luck. You'll be condemned to suffer with a picture from purgatory for the duration of your ownership of the monitor. In other words, make sure you get ready access to the size and positioning controls of any monitor you buy.

Besides location, you also may have your choice of the type of control used for image adjustments. For example, NEC has substituted digital pushbuttons for the more conventional analog knobs or shafts for the size and positioning adjustments of many of its monitors. Pressing one button makes the image larger; another makes it smaller. These digital controls are often coupled with memory so that monitor can recall the settings you've made for each frequency range at which it operates. That way, the monitor can adjust the image to your own personal degree of perfection as you skip between display modes.

Pushbutton digital controls are not for everyone, particularly when they invade everyday functions like brightness and contrast. Pushbutton controls don't tell you how close to the middle or end of their range they are set, nor can you tell from knob position approximately where the control is set. Before you buy a monitor with digital controls, you may want to try one and see whether it works the way you do.

No matter whether a monitor has pushbuttons or knobs, the range of the image size controls can also be important. You'll want a monitor with sufficient control range that you can fill the entire screen with image. If it doesn't, you won't get everything that you've paid for. Some monitors are parsimonious with their pictures and confine the active video area far within the margins of the picture tube face. You can lose as much as an inch all the way around the screen, making a 14-inch monitor the equivalent of a 12-inch display. If you pay for a big screen, make sure you get a big image area to go along with it.

Before you buy a monitor with digital controls, you may want to try one and see whether it works the way you do.

Sharpness versus Resolution

For most people, the most important characteristic of a monitor is its sharpness. On a sharp display, every character is clearly chiseled against the background like the lettering of the cornerstone of a new building. With an unsharp display, you can't tell the difference between a lower-case "m" and a gnat smashed against the screen. Unsharp characters tend toward formlessness and ambiguity, a definite disadvantage when you try to discern the values in cramped spreadsheet columns or the fine print in an on-screen contract you're construing.

Worse, a fuzzy screen can be bad for your eyesight and may sow seeds that blossom into a full-fledged migraine as your workday winds down. Working with an unsharp display can provoke eyestrain. It may cause you to unconsciously squint at the screen to try to make the display look sharper—which means you'll get a headache but no sharper view—no amount of eyeball gymnastics can make up for sharpness that's not there.

Sharpness is the final product of the monitor—what you see on the screen—but it is affected by everything in your display system. If the signals sent to the picture tube lack detail, then the sharpness of the tube is wasted. Resolution is the figure familiar to those who want the sharpest possible image on the screen. But the figure that many monitor makers give as resolution in a product's specifications often does not reflect the actual amount of detail on the screen. That's because what many manufacturers call resolution actually amounts to a measure another monitor parameter, one more properly termed *addressability*.

The difference between resolution and addressability is the difference between strolling across the rusty red surface of Mars and knowing that you could find Mars through your telescope as the fourth planet from the sun. Resolution is—or should be—the reality of the situation, the measure of actual image sharpness. Addressability is a promise or conception of what could be. It merely refers to a monitor's ability to light up a dot on the screen at a particular location.

Addressability is the ultimate limit on how sharp an image can be on the screen, but other factors in the design and manufacture of the monitor may limit its sharpness far below its addressability. For example, any monitor that claims to be VGA compatible has an addressability of 640 by 480 pixels. But the actual resolution of the display might be much less, perhaps more in-line with the 320 by 200 pixels promised by medium-resolution CGA. In the case of better monitors, addressability and on-screen resolution converge and become the same figure. But with inexpensive monitors, the on-screen image may only aspire to be as sharp.

Addressability is determined by the signals generated by your display adapter. The board inside your PC sets exactly how may lines will sweep across each image frame and how many individual dots will be in each line. Your monitor needs only to be able to decode the signal sent by the video adapter to achieve that level of addressability. The resolution of a display is a function of its quality, the results of its electronics, mechanical construction, and the quality of its components.

One of the biggest influences on resolution is the cathode ray tube, the picture tube of the display. Because the picture tube is usually the most expensive part of a monitor, it's often the place where manufacturers cut corners when designing inexpensive displays. A cheap picture tube can easily tempt a monitor maker. The price difference between a good tube and a cheap one may amount to $100 or more—effectively a $200 price difference in the finished product. At current market prices, that's nearly enough to double your cost of a VGA display.

Among the most important factors in the price and quality of a picture tube is the *shadow mask* or slot mask that with current display technology is required between the electron guns and screen inside the tube. The shadow mask is a thin sheet of metal perforated with holes or slots. Its purpose is to assure the purity of the colors on the screen by preventing the electrons meant for the green phosphors from hitting the red and blue phosphors (and the red from blue and green, etc.).

Most picture tubes in monitors have three color "guns" which shoot electrons at the screen to make it glow. The guns are arranged in a triangle, with one assigned to illuminate each color on the screen. The mask is designed so that unwanted phosphor colors fall into the shadow of the mask cast by the electron beam meant for the desired color. The holes in the shadow mask thus determine how closely spaced the dots of color can possibly be on the screen. Color dots of one hue must be spaced at the same distance apart as the holes in the mask. The term that describes this hole spacing—and thus the spacing of color dots on the screen—is *dot-pitch*.

A special kind of color picture tube called the *Trinitron* uses a different arrangement of its electron guns. Instead of a triangle, its three guns are aligned in a straight line, or they may be compressed into what is essentially a single-gun unit. Instead of circular holes in the shadow mask, the picture tube uses a series of vertically-oriented slots to help control each electron beam. Rather than spacing between dots, the resolution limit on these tubes is set by the spacing between slots, the *slot-pitch*. Note that in one dimension—along the axis of the slot—the electron beam in a Trinitron picture tube is essentially unlimited. Nothing mechanical stands in the way of the color spacing except for one or two *tensioning wires* which can sometimes be faintly seen running across the width of a Trinitron screen. To some people, the dark shadow of these tensioning wires is a grave image defect, one that is most apparent on light backgrounds such as the white Windows uses as a default. Before you buy a Trinitron-based display, take a look at the screen with a light background and assure yourself that the thin horizontal shadows won't bother you when you use the monitor.

You're apt to see an increasing number of Trinitron-based monitors offered in coming years. Sony Corporation developed the technology and patented it. In 1991, the initial Trinitron patents expired, opening the market for other manufacturers.

For many monitors, the dot-pitch of the picture tube sets the ultimate limit on sharpness. Unlike resolutions, which are given in the number of lines or dots that can be discerned across the face of a monitor tube, dot-pitches are customarily given in terms of the spacing of holes in fractions of a millimeter. It's easy to convert these dot-pitch numbers into an equivalent resolution figure, however. All you need to do is divide the dot-pitch into the dimensions of the display area.

For example, a fourteen-inch VGA monitor might have an active image area that measures about ten inches wide by eight inches high. In metric, that's 254 millimeters by 203 millimeters. In this case, the minimum required dot-pitch would be just under 0.40 millimeter (that is, 254 mm width divided by the 640 dots stretching across it). Most—but hardly all—VGA monitors in the 12 to 14-inch size have dot-pitches in the vicinity of .031 mm to comply with the rigors of this math.

A display with a finer dot-pitch will produce a sharper, more pleasing image. A display with a coarser dot-pitch (higher numbers) will produce unacceptably fuzzy images.

Some manufacturers offer what they call VGA monitors with 0.50 mm or coarser dot-pitches. Although these displays accept VGA signals, they cannot produce the resolution required for VGA images. They are VGA displays solely because of their 640 by 480 addressability. They will work with your VGA adapter but images they make will likely be unacceptable. Avoid them if you can.

The dot-pitch required by a given video standard is a function of monitor size. Large-screen displays don't need dot-pitches as fine as smaller screens at the same resolution level. However, because most larger monitors are designed to produce resolutions beyond VGA, they usually have dot-pitches comparable to those of smaller-screen displays.

Note that dot-pitch is important only for monitors that use multiple electron guns and shadow masks or slot masks. Monochrome displays use a single electron gun because they need to produce only a single image color. They do not need shadow masks. Consequently monochrome monitors do not have dot-pitches. Any listing of a dot-pitch for a monochrome monitor is simply an error.

When buying a monitor that complies with a display standard, the required addressability is a given. The resolution will be anyone's guess. But the dot-pitch will tell you how sharp the monitor could possibly be. If the dot-pitch of a monitor is not high enough to support the standard under which the monitor is to operate, the monitor is likely to be unacceptable. Consequently, for most people dot-pitch is the most important figure when shopping for a monitor.

Convergence

But dot-pitch is not the only influence on the sharpness of the image on the screen. The three electron beams in the color tube must be properly aimed before they are shot at the screen—or they need some kind of mid-course correction to ensure that they arrive at the proper destination dots. If not, the beams may not line up properly. One color may be offset from the others and give any image a rainbow of outlines instead of a single bold color.

When the electron beams of a color display don't line up, every line drawn on the screen will become two or three lines of different colors. Every dot will become a cloverleaf or multi-color glob. The effect is worse with text. Reading becomes a guessing game with each letter a speckled, multi-colored pox on the screen.

The term *convergence* defines how closely the three electron beams in a color monitor actually converge on a single point (actually, the correct dot in an individual pixel). When a display is badly converged, individual pixels are no longer sharply defined but become two- or three-color blurs as one electron beam spills over onto the phosphors of another color. Monochrome monitors are inherently free from such convergence problems because they have but one electron beam.

Convergence problems are a symptom rather than a cause of monitor deficiencies. Convergence problems arise not only from the design of the display but also from the construction and set-up of each individual monitor. They can vary widely from one display to the next and may be aggravated by damage during shipping.

The result of convergence problems is most noticeable at the screen periphery because that's where the electron beams are the most difficult to control. When bad, convergence problems can be the primary limit on the sharpness of a given display, having a greater negative effect than wide dot-pitch or low bandwidth (discussed below).

Many monitor makers will claim that their convergence is a given fraction of a millimeter at a particular place on the screen. If a figure is given for more than one screen location, the center of the screen will invariably have a lower figure—tighter, better convergence—than a corner of the screen. The number given is how far one color may spread from another at that location. Lower numbers are better. Typical monitors may claim convergence of about 0.5 (one-half) millimeter at one of the corners of the screen. That figure often rises 50 percent higher than the dot-pitch of the tube, making the convergence the limit on sharpness for that particular monitor.

Note, however, while dot-pitch is a global phenomenon across the screen, mis-convergence is a localized problem. Moreover, mis-convergence problems may be confined to individual monitors that have been jarred, jostled, or generally maltreated in shipping.

Unlike a coarse dot-pitch, mis-convergence problems often can be corrected by adjustment of the monitor. Many monitors have internal convergence controls. A few high-resolution (and high-cost) monitors even have external convergence adjustments. But adjusting monitor convergence is a job for the specialist—and that means getting a monitor converged can be expensive, as is any computer service call.

Monitor Bandwidth

Dot-pitch is purely a mechanical limit on monitor sharpness. Convergence is a combination of mechanical and electronic limits. Purely electronic factors also influence the sharpness of images appearing on a monitor's screen. Chief among these electronic factors is bandwidth.

The picture formed by your graphics adapter is sent to your monitor as an electrical signal in which each dot on the screen is represented by a tiny time segment. The duration of that time segment is a function of the horizontal and vertical scanning frequencies of your monitor. The shortest possible time segment that the electronics of your monitor can define clearly sets an upper limit on the resolution of your display system.

The length of this shortest time segment is measured in microseconds but is usually expressed as its reciprocal value, megahertz, as the bandwidth of the monitor. The more megahertz in a monitor's bandwidth, the shorter time that can be devoted to each dot, and the sharper the image that the monitor can display (within the limits of its dot-pitch and the quality of its construction).

The quality of the electronics inside a monitor determine its bandwidth. Better monitors have bandwidths with higher megahertz ratings. In theory, you could compute the bandwidth required by any video standard from the resolution and frame rate of the standard. For example, VGA's 640 by 480 resolution and 70 Hz frame rate multiplied together yields 21,504,000 MHz. While that calculation gives a rough indication of required bandwidth, other factors must also be considered.

The resolution numbers apply only to the active viewing portion of the screen. A substantial fraction of the time, the video signal is not being displayed. At the end of each line of the image, the electron beam turns off, then races back to the other side of the screen to start the next line. This process is called *retracing*. At the end of each frame, the beam must retrace from the bottom of the screen back up to the top to begin the next frame. In addition, blank areas are left on each side of the screen, and the corresponding part of the video signal must also be left the equivalent of blank. All of these factors tend to increase the bandwidth required for properly processing a video signal.

Compensating in the other direction—reducing required bandwidth—is the actual on-screen pattern of pixels. The image that requires the highest resolution would be a pattern of alternating on and off pixels. But this toughest pattern actually has a frequency of one-half the product of resolution time frame rate. Thus, the actual demand for bandwidth is one-half the resolution-times-frame rate once the inactive video periods are added in. In other words, the actual bandwidth required by a video standard is approximately equal to the first rough resolution-times-frame rate calculation—and is one of those strange cases where you can come up with the right answer for the wrong reasons.

Interlacing

One way of circumventing the bandwidth limitations in the electronics of a monitor is to cut the vertical frequency or frame rate of the signal. However, frame rates cannot be arbitrarily reduced because high frame rates—generally above 60 Hz—are required to eliminate image *flicker* on the monitor screen.

Flicker arises when the on-screen image flashes at a rate below which your eye would blend the intermittent illumination of each pixel into the illusion of continuous light. Minimizing image flicker requires higher frame rates, and higher frame rates push up the bandwidth required in a monitor which, in turn, pushes up the price.

Some video standards use a trick called *interlacing* to try to minimize the effect of a lower frame rate. Interlacing allows a higher frame rate to be simulated with a narrower bandwidth.

The idea behind interlacing is simple—slice the image in half and alternate showing each half at half the normal flicker-free rate. Rather than alternating sides of the screen, interlacing involves alternating scan lines. First the odd-numbered lines are scanned creating a zebra-striped half-image called a *field*, then the even-numbered lines are scanned to fill in the dark places with the rest of the picture's detail. The two interwoven fields make up a single image *frame*, hence the derivation of the term "frame rate."

Because the lines are so closely spaced, your eyes can sometimes be fooled into thinking that the whole image is refreshed at the rate of one field. Consequently, a high field rate suffices instead of a high frame rate. Since the frame rate is effectively half of the field rate, the bandwidth required for the system is cut in half.

Interlaced displays suffer the free-lunch problem. In effect, interlacing appears to be giving you something for nothing, which should automatically lead you to believe that there must be some strings attached. There are. The illusion of a continuously-lit image is often not successful. The image tends to flicker, a barely-perceptible flashing of the screen that appears to travel down the screen as mysteriously as the aurora borealis. Worse, obtaining the full claimed resolution from an interlaced image requires that the alternately-illuminated scan lines mesh perfectly together. Often they don't, resulting in a loss of up to half the detail in an image.

People vary in their ability to detect flicker and thus tolerate interlacing. Moreover their susceptibilities may vary with the ambient lighting around the interlaced monitor and even how the individual viewer feels (Are you having a good day?) when looking at the display. Flicker is most noticeable when you view the monitor screen out of the corner of your eye rather than directly. It is also more apparent the larger the screen. Consequently, nearly everyone has different feelings about the effectiveness and palatability of interlacing.

The best rule is that a non-interlaced display will always appear better than an interlaced display. But a higher-resolution interlaced display may be more useful than a lower-resolution non-interlaced display, particularly when the former is substantially less expensive than the latter.

Whether a display is interlaced depends on the graphics adapter you use. Most monitors will handle both interlaced and non-interlaced images. However, a monitor must be able to synchronize to the high field rate (rather than frame rate) used by the interlaced system. Some multi-scanning monitors do not have the range required to display interlaced 8514/A or XGA images. So if you plan on using interlaced signals, be sure that the monitor you choose explicitly supports them.

Monitor Colors and Phosphors

One way that monitors designed specifically for interlaced signals cope with flicker is through the use of long-persistence phosphors. *Persistence* is a term that describes how long the screen phosphors of a monitor glow after they have been struck by the beam from the electron gun. Ordinary screen phosphors are short-to-medium persistence. Long-persistence phosphors permit the glow of each pixel on the screen to linger a little longer, bridging over the low frame rate. However, long-persistence phosphors often cause image *lag*—ghostly afterimages that linger after screen changes—which can be more irritating than flicker.

Phosphor type can be an issue in buying a monitor for other reasons. Phosphor type also controls the color of the image and brightness of the image displayed on a monitor.

With monochrome monitors, phosphor type will determine the overall color of the screen—typically green, amber, or white.

Green is the color of old-fashioned radar sets and oscilloscopes because it is believed to be easiest on the eyes in dark surroundings. Common wisdom holds that green is the preferred color for cave-dwelling monitor viewers, the kind who switch off every light in their offices so every business meeting becomes a seance.

Amber, which actually ranges from yellow to nearly neon-orange, is supposed to be better when the surroundings are bright. Against a dark screen, amber yields higher contrast than green and doesn't easily wash out from splashes of sunlight.

The trend today, however, is to white screens. With graphics, white screens produce grey-scale images reminiscent of familiar black-and-white photographs and television—and hence, more realistic in appearance to all of us in the television generation. White screens also mimic the paper on which so much of the world's work is carried out.

One white is not the same color as another, however. Each monochrome monitor manufacturer brews his own combination of faint shades into its nominally white screens. The result is that the white on monochrome screens ranges from bluish (like black-and-white television) to the yellowish of bleached white paper. The term "paper white" is not critically defined, however, so one manufacturer's paper white monitor can be an entirely different shade of white than another's.

Phosphor color also is important in color displays, as you might expect. While most of today's color monitors use essentially similar blends of phosphors—the most popular is designated P22 (or B22)—you'll still find a range of color cast to different manufacturer's products.

One of the variables is *color temperature*, which refers to the general cast of all the colors in the spectrum. White light is a single color, but a mixture of all colors. And as with the whites of monochrome displays, all whites on color monitors are not the same. Some are richer in blue, some in yellow. The different shades of white are described by their color temperature, the number of kelvins (degrees Celsius above absolute zero) that a perfect luminescent body would need to be to emit that color. Like the incandescence of a hot iron horseshoe in the blacksmith's forge, as its temperature gets higher the hue of a glowing object shifts from red to orange, then yellow and on to blue-white. Color temperature simply assigns an absolute temperature rating to this spectrum of colors.

For example, ordinary lightbulbs range from 2,700 to 3,400 kelvins and are obviously orange. Most fluorescent lights have non-continuous color spectra rich in certain hues (notably green) while lacking others that make assigning a true color temperature impossible. Other fluorescent lamps are designed to approximate daylight with color temperatures of about 5,000 kelvins, a yellowish to pure white. When the sun is obscured by clouds, the outdoor color temperature shifts dramatically higher, toward blue, because the blue sky provides most of the brightness. The outdoor color temperature may rise to 10,000 kelvins.

Normally your eyes automatically adjust to accommodate the temperature of available light. As a result trees, grass, and fleshtones look the same under the noonday sun and at sunset, in direct sunlight or in the shade, even though the color temperature may vary thousands of kelvins.

In theory, then, any color temperature would do for a monitor screen. And if the monitor were the only thing you ever looked at, that would be true. You'd never have to worry about kelvins. But a problem related to color temperature arises when you do critical work such as color desktop publishing with your monitor—and you expect the ideal WYSIWYG. Screen colors don't look anything like what comes out of your color printer or film recorder.

The underlying problem has to do with forms of illumination and the perception of color. Monitor colors just aren't the same as colors on paper or film.

You've faced the underlying problem before, perhaps in elementary school. Once you were weaned from eating crayons to actually drawing with them, you learned about the primary colors—scribble enough wax on newsprint and you'll get a dark, dingy mess. With a little sophistication, you learned that red, blue, and yellow will do for a nice ugly mess teachers claimed was actually black. In high school physics, however, you had to unlearn those lessons because the exam answer for primary colors mysteriously becomes red, blue, and green which, when mixed, yield white instead of black.

The difference is between two different kinds of primary colors, the subtractive and additive, the primary colors of pigment and light. The two are not the same. When you try to match monitor colors on paper, the difference becomes painfully obvious. Your monitor spews out light while your printer fuses down pigment. You cuss up a storm when the match is about as close as two socks slipped on in the dark.

Because pigments only reflect light, their actual color depends on the light illuminating them and its color temperature. On the other hand, your monitor screen emits light, so its color is independent of illumination. To get the best match between your display and your hardcopy, you have to ensure that you view the output of your printer under the same temperature as the light generated by your monitor.

The colors and blend of the phosphors used to make the picture tube screen and the relative strengths of the electron beams illuminating those phosphors determines the color temperature of a monitor. Originally, color television tubes were designed to reflect a perfect sunny day with a color temperature of about 6,000 kelvins. Evidently some engineers felt that the ideal day was actually rather soggy and overcast, suited only to ducks, Englishmen, and ending California droughts. So an alternate color standard was developed with a color temperature of 9,300 kelvins, which is reflected in most commercial computer monitors.

For most purposes, this high color temperature is fine. Your eyes accommodate to it, and you never notice its overcast quality. For critical work like photographic retouching and color desktop publishing, however, color temperature may be crucial. You'll want to look for a monitor with a color temperature equivalent to your normal workplace surroundings or one that has an adjustable color temperature.

Monitor Brightness

Although rarely disclosed by specifications sheets, other important differences mark one monitor more suited to specific applications. Brightness is a particular example. Some monitors are capable of generating brighter images than others, making them more suited for use in environments with high illumination.

Sometimes brightness comes at a penalty. When brightness is increased on some monitors, the *spot size* (the footprint of the electron beam) increases. That is, as it gets brighter each pixel on the screen becomes a fuzzy glob instead of a sharp dot. A better monitor will preserve its fine spot size over a wide range of brightnesses.

When a monitor is operated at a brightness level lower than its maximum, other problems can show up. The relationships between colors can shift with different brightness levels. This problem arises from non-linearities in the amplifiers that are used to increase the input voltage of the monitor to the level necessary to drive the electron beams inside the monitor. These amplifiers must be exactly matched and absolutely linear. That is, the input and output of each amplifier must be precisely proportional, and this linear relationship must be exactly the same for all three amplifiers in a color monitor. In other words, the three must precisely track one another.

If the relationship between the signal strengths of the individual colors varies, the hue of the on-screen image will shift as its intensity varies. At some level, one color will be more intense than the others, lending its cast to the screen. At other levels, another color may be dominant so the hue of the the on-screen image varies with brightness. This shading effect is usually most pronounced in grey displays—each dominate color tinges the grey.

The effects of such poor color tracking in monitor amplifiers are all bad. You lose precision in your control of color. The screen can no longer hope to be an exact preview of what will eventually appear on paper or film. You may even lose a good fraction of the colors displayable by your video system. The end result is that color of the image on the screen won't be what your software had in mind.

A similar problem can occur in monochrome monitors (which have but one video amplifier) and in color monitors when all three video amplifiers are exactly matched. If the input and output of each amplifier do not vary in a precisely linear relationship, the brightness of the image won't reflect the image that your software attempts to generate. The relationship between different grey levels will shift; some grey levels may even disappear from the monitor's repertory. In a perfect monitor, each grey level will exactly track the intensity of the input signal to the monitor. That is, a signal twice as strong should cause a grey level twice as bright.

Nothing on the specifications sheet of a monitor will reveal to you how well the colors and greys of a monitor track. You'll have to observe this with your own eyes. One general rule holds: If you can't see a problem, then don't worry about it. If you can see a problem, it will only bother you more as time goes on.

Tilt-Swivel Base

A tilt-swivel base should be considered standard equipment in any monitor. The base elevates the monitor about two inches to a convenient viewing height and allows the easy adjustment of the screen for comfortable viewing. Some tilt-swivel bases are permanently attached. The better alternative is the removable base which allows you the option of using the monitor without it. If a tilt-swivel base is not included with a monitor, figure an extra $20 to buy a universal tilt-swivel monitor stand from a mail-order vendor.

A tilt-swivel base should be considered standard equipment in any monitor.

Monitor Connections

Installing a monitor upgrade is easy once you've found the right unit. Just plop it atop your PC (if it fits), plug it in (to the wall and to your display adapter) and turn everything on.

Plugging in may be the only challenge. The biggest problem you'll face is the cable, and with the many monitors the cable is not a simple matter. Some monitor manufacturers and vendors try to make things easier for you and include the necessary connecting cable with their displays. That's generally okay for single-standard monitors (CGA, EGA or VGA displays) but can be limiting for multi-scanning units. The cable that comes packed with your monitor might not fit the obscure display standard you've chosen.

Before you buy, check that the proper type of cable accompanies your monitor choice. If the monitor cable requires a 9-to-15 pin adapter, ensure that one accompanies your purchase. There's nothing so frustrating as unpacking a new toy at 9 p.m. and discovering you have no way of plugging it in.

Some monitors come with cables permanently attached (see fig. 10.3)—a great idea if you're afraid of losing the cable but worrisome should your cat confuse the cable with the licorice she's fond of chewing or should you break the connector on the end. The permanent connection can make a simple accident expensive. You'll have to take the whole monitor in for repairs. The loose cable supplied with the monitor wins when you worry about such prospects—should your model train run over the monitor cable and cut it in half, you pay only for a new cable, not a technician's time to replace it.

Figure 10.3

Monitors use any of a variety of input connectors. Shown here are (from top left clockwise): a nine-pin D-shell; a 25-pin D-shell; a 15-pin high density D-shell; and a set of five BNC connectors. All connectors shown here are male.

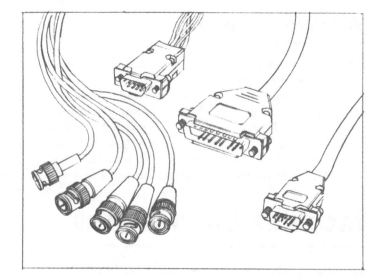

A few vendors make bargain-hunting more of a challenge by making the monitor-connecting cable an extra-cost option. When comparing monitors, be sure to factor in such incidentals.

If you have to buy a cable separately or if you're subverting the reigning standards, you'll have to worry about the type of connectors on the cable. Display adapters matching the popular standards all use the same style of connector—9-pin D-shell connectors (female on the display adapter) for MDA, CGA, and EGA, and special high-density 15-pin D-shell connectors for VGA. But monitors are known to use anything from 9-pin connectors to full 25-pin connectors that you can confuse with serial and parallel ports. Some use three to five video-style BNC connectors. Even monitors with permanently attached cables may have odd connectors at the end, for example some VGA displays may offer retro-mode 9-pin connectors.

Connect the cable between your monitor and your display adapter first. Then plug the power cable into the back of the monitor (if necessary), and finally plug the monitor power cable into a wall outlet. (If your monitor has a switch to select 115 or 230 volt operation, verify it is in the correct position before plugging in the monitor.)

If you're downgrading your display system instead of upgrading or just trying to get by cheaply with a MDA monochrome, a CGA or an EGA color system, pause before you connect your new monitor. All three of these standards use nine-pin D-shell connectors on their display adapters, but the signals used by the color and monochrome systems are completely different. In fact, plugging an MDA monitor into a CGA or EGA display adapter can destroy the monitor (and plugging a CGA or EGA display into an MDA isn't advisable either). Verify the adapter type and display compatibility before you make the connection. Be vigilant when you turn one of these systems on for the first time, too. If you don't see a cursor flashing in the upper-left-hand corner of the monitor or hear a squealing noise come from the monitor when you turn it and your computer on, turn them both off immediately! Those symptoms warn of a mismatched display.

Once you've got your monitor plugged into your display adapter and wall, switch on your PC and let it start booting up. Again, check the upper-left corner of the monitor for a cursor or some other indication that all is well—such as a memory count-up or copyright message.

When you're sure your monitor type and display adapter match but you still don't see anything on the monitor when you switch on your computer, first make sure that both the monitor and computer are actually plugged in and turned on. Listen for signs of life inside your computer; check the power indicator on the monitor.

The next troubleshooting step is to adjust the brightness and contrast controls to their full speed (clockwise) positions. If the monitor screen doesn't light up at all, the monitor may be bad. If you see a mess of lines on the screen highlighted with bright dots, odds are your monitor can't cope with the signal produced by your display adapter. If you see a few zig-zag lines tracing down the screen, suspect your display adapter or the connection between it and your monitor.

With color displays, one family of colors missing from the display indicates a loose or bad signal cable. Failure to display color on a color screen can also be the symptom of a bad cable or a monitor that doesn't support IBM's automatic sensing scheme. If the cable is good, you can often force your VGA monitor to work in color by issuing the command `MODE C080` to DOS.

Odds are, however, that your monitor upgrade will come to life immediately, rewarding you with a sharper, more colorful view of your computer's innermost thoughts.

11
Multimedia

Multimedia brings the PC, video, and stereo sound together and lets them work interactively with each other and you. To give your PC the capability to handle the latest multimedia software (which includes presentations, training, and games), you'll need a sound board and a CD ROM player.

Although the term *multimedia* is dripping from every PC prophet's lips, you'll have to turn your attention elsewhere to hear the truth. As with previous technological promises, you won't find a multimedia in every garage, pot, or PC. Remember, Windows was introduced in 1984 and took nearly a decade to win general acceptance. Desktop publishing has yet to make it into the mass market. Public acceptance moves more slowly than technology, and it will take more than one year for multimedia to make it into most PCs.

Look at the analogies, however, and you'll see reason to explore multimedia technology today. It has the same potential market as Windows—nearly every PC in the world—yet it shares many characteristics with desktop publishing. As with publications you prepare with your PC, the work of multimedia has two sides—sending and receiving. The receiving side suffers the old color television problem—no network wanted to broadcast color until there were more television sets, but no one wanted to buy televisions till there were more color programs. The big explosion in multimedia will come when the receiving end catches momentum and most households has a multimedia PC.

Today's multimedia opportunities lie on the other side of the transaction—making the presentations. The dearth of multimedia software is, in fact, a bonanza for anyone fancying himself a creative type—someone who wants to learn the new communications means,

Public acceptance moves more slowly than technology, and it will take more than one year for multimedia to make it into most PCs.

Multimedia may be the biggest revolution in consumer electronics since the personal computer.

someone who wants to stay ahead of technology, someone who wants to get in on the ground floor of what may become the biggest revolution in consumer electronics since the personal computer.

The multimedia PC has a lot going for it. By combining still and moving text and graphic images with sound and making it all interactive, your multimedia-equipped system will suddenly be more interesting, more fun, more informative—and more expensive. You can get a lot out of multimedia, but you'll also have to put something more into your PC. That means upgrading it to meet the official multimedia PC standards.

The obvious upgrade need is for a CD ROM player.

The obvious upgrade need is for a CD ROM player. You've got to get that hot new multimedia CD out of your hands and into your PC. The CD ROM player provides the necessary slot and playback mechanism.

But the multimedia CD is only the delivery vehicle. You also need the means to experience all facets of multimedia. Although most PCs are already equipped with display systems that put ordinary video to shame, sound comes up short. Most PCs make do with a tiny speaker that can but hoot and toot tones akin to alien love calls. Multimedia requires high fidelity (or at least intelligibility), and that means adding a sound board. If you don't want an ear-ache from atrocious audio, you'll need speakers or a stereo system to plug into.

Odds are if you're running Windows 3.1, your PC is up to the multimedia chore.

You will want to upgrade your PC's video system, too, for higher quality and to help it work in reverse—not just for displaying images but also for capturing them so that you can manipulate them and add them to your presentations. Video upgrades are covered in Chapter 10. Video capture—and other graphics input systems—are up next in Chapter 12.

If you have an older PC, multimedia means more. You'll also need to upgrade your older system to meet the minimum multimedia requirements in processor power, memory, and storage. According to the Multimedia PC Marketing Council, you'll need at least a 16MHz 386SX PC equipped with 4M of RAM, a 40M hard disk, a color VGA system, and a mouse. The council terms systems and products fully ready for multimedia (and that pay a hefty licensing fee) Multi-Media PC compatible or *MPC*-compatible. Even without the label, you probably have all the necessary equipment in your computer already to support the MPC standard—all but the lowest end PCs sold in the last couple of years meet or exceed that standard. Odds are if you're running Windows 3.1—the standard interface for today's multimedia software—your PC is up to the multimedia chore.

If you have a multimedia-capable PC, upgrading with the required CD ROM player and sound board is easy—even in the most difficult installations, you should spend no more than an hour on the job. Moreover, the bulk of the work is mechanical rather than electrical—handiwork rather than brain work. The whole process involves nothing more than sliding the CD-ROM player into a vacant drive bay, plugging the sound board into an expansion slot, cabling the two together, and connecting them to your speakers or a stereo system. Rather than a special computer knowledge, you only need the urge to upgrade and enjoy.

CD ROM Players

Multimedia needs megabytes, a surprisingly large number of them. For example, every full-screen, high-resolution, true-color image needs two to three megabytes. Multimedia, however, is more than pictures. You'll want sound, too, and with quality audio you're listening to nine megabytes per minute. You'll also want data, and the more megabytes there, the merrier. Somehow, you've got to get all that data into your PC. If you want to produce a successful multimedia extravaganza, you'll want to make millions of copies of your millions of bytes.

Multimedia is more than pictures.

When megabytes must be sown to the four winds, today's premiere solution is a thin slice of aluminized plastic—the Compact Disc or CD. Originally designed to store the megabytes needed for the distribution of top-quality stereo sound, the storage capacity of the CD medium was easily adapted to computer data. Today, it is the most affordable computer data distribution alternative. Duplicate CDs can be stamped for under $10 in modest quantities. Make a million copies of a CD ROM, and you can figure the cost as a dollar or two a copy. An equivalent stack of floppies—450 of them—will set you back at least 10 times as much (at a deal).

The storage capacity of the CD medium was easily adapted to computer data.

The easy duplication and low cost that made CDs the stereo medium of choice make the computer equivalent, the CD ROM, the premiere digital publishing medium. Already hundreds of CD ROM titles are available, each one holding an encyclopedia of data. To give yourself nearly instant access to any word, image, or song on disk, you only need to upgrade to a CD ROM player.

To give yourself nearly instant access to any word, image, or song on disk, you only need to upgrade to a CD ROM player.

Background

The very name CD ROM brings together the two concepts that give the medium its power. Like the ROM chips inside your PC, CD ROM is a source of digital code designed for delivery and not alteration. Rather than stamp-sized slices of silicon, with CD ROM, the delivery vehicle is the small, silvery platter of a Compact Disc, about five inches in diameter, with a more than superficial resemblance to the CDs that spin in your stereo system. The resemblance is hardly a coincidence. The essence of your stereo's CD system is that music is stored digitally. CD ROMs merely substitute other data for the melodic digits on the disks.

As with audio CDs, digital data is written to CD ROM master disks using special recording equipment that makes microscopic pits on the surface of a disk. The information encoded in the pits can be read by detecting changes in reflectivity (the pits are darker than background of the shiny silver disk). Because these data pits are a mechanical feature, merely dimples in the disk, they can be duplicated millions of times with pressing equipment similar to that used to squeeze out old-fashioned LP albums. After a CD-ROM disk is pressed, however, the data it holds cannot be altered. The pits are present for eternity.

The capacity of the typical CD ROM disk—300,000 pages of text—is about the equivalent of 150 full-length books.

The audio CDs and CD ROM discs are so similar that most CD ROM systems that work with your PC will, in fact, play the music CDs in your collection—providing you have the right software. Music capabilities are built into most computer CD ROM players. They even have headphone jacks on the front or audio outputs on the back to provide for your listening as well as data processing enjoyment. The software you need to make one of these CD ROM players do double-duty playing audio should be included with any audio-capable CD ROM drive that you buy.

The similarity between stereo and computer CDs extends further. As with music CDs, the digital CDs for your computer are a publishing medium. Like newspapers, books, videos, and records, CD ROMs provide a means through which you can carry home entertainment and information in a convenient form. You cannot write to a CD ROM disk; you buy each one already filled with the information that you want. The CD ROM medium is perfectly suited to this application. The disks themselves are easy to manufacturer—they can be made on the same presses as music discs—and inexpensive compared to more traditional publishing processes. The capacity of the typical CD ROM disk—300,000 pages of text—is about the equivalent of 150 full-length books. At today's bookstore prices of $20 to $30 per volume, publishing the information on one CD ROM on paper might cost $3,000 to 4,500. The retail price of a commercial CD ROM disk that holds the same words would costs between one- third and one-thirtieth of that.

The downside of CD ROM is that using the disks requires that you add a special piece of equipment to your PC, that CD ROM player with an earphone jack. More expensive than its stereo-only equivalent, a CD ROM player can cost from $300 to more than $1,300, depending on how it is meant to be installed (internal or external), the accessories that come with it, and even how many disks it accommodates.

Cost can be a problem when purchasing CD ROM. Although neither the drives nor the compact discs themselves are inordinately expensive—in mass-market quantities, CDs cost no more than a hardcover book to make—the data they contain is valued (by the publishers) in the thousands of dollars. If you're used to paying $15 for an audio compact disc, the $300 toll for a popular CD ROM seems outrageous—notwithstanding that the same information in paper form would cost many times as much. Fortunately, you need only one CD ROM player for as many disks as you want to use. Much like the one in your stereo system, the computer CD ROM player allows you to interchange disks, so that one player allows access to an entire library of CD ROM media.

Computer CD ROM players are more expensive than stereo models because the computer-connected equipment must be more accurate. A tiny musical flaw that might pass unnoticed even by trained ears could have disastrous consequences in a data stream. For example, a single bit error can change the "not" in the Seventh Commandment to "now" and provide an entirely new meaning to an electronic Bible (not to mention your life). To minimize, if not eliminate, such problems, computer CD ROM players have error correction circuitry that's much more powerful than that built into stereo equipment.

A tiny musical flaw that might pass unnoticed even by trained ears could have disastrous consequences in a data stream.

Another difference between stereo and computer CD ROM players is that latter must be connected to and controlled by your PC. By itself, the computer CD ROM player does nothing but spin its disk. Your computer must tell the player what information to look for and read out, and your computer is needed to display—visually and aurally—the information the CD ROM player finds, be it text, a graphic image, or a musical selection.

A CD ROM player is one of the easiest additions you can make to your computer.

The bottom line is, of course, that you have to buy a CD ROM player and attach it to your PC if you want to take advantage of the hundreds of disks that are already available—and the thousands that will undoubtedly be published in the coming years. A CD ROM player is one of the easiest additions you can make to your computer. If you've ever plugged in an expansion board, you can probably accomplish the mechanical part of the installation in a few minutes.

Media

If you can manage to play music on your stereo, you can use CD ROMs.

The best part about CD ROM disks is not their huge storage capacity but that they combine that capacity with familiarity. You don't have to be a genius to deal with the mechanism as you do when loading a computer tape on a mainframe. If you can manage to play music on your stereo, you can use CD ROMs.

The disks themselves store information exactly the same way it's stored on the CDs in your stereo system only instead of getting up to 75 minutes of music, a CD ROM disk holds about 600 megabytes of data. That data can be anything from simple text to SuperVGA images, to programs, and the full circle back to music.

The silver disk puts digital data into optical form. The digital data on CD ROM is coded as a pattern of bits represented by the presence or absence of those pits blasted into the surface of the CD. The overall CD is shiny and reflects light well; the pits don't. A laser beam is focused on the disk and reflects back into a photodetector, which can tell the difference in the brightness of the reflection of a pit or unharmed disk. The pattern of bits codes digital data.

Because CDs are non-contact media—the data pits are sealed within layers of the disk itself and are never touched by anything other than a light beam—they never wear out and acquire errors only when you abuse the disks themselves purposely or carelessly (for example, by scratching them against one another when not storing them in their plastic jewel boxes.) Although error correction prevents errors from showing up in the data, a bad scratch can prevent a disk from being read.

Data weighs more in book form, so those who buy by the pound think books are the better value.

Music and data CD disks are manufactured in the same way. First, a master is recorded on a special machine with a high-powered laser that blasts the pits in a blank recording master. The master is made into a mold that is then used to stamp out copies of the original CD much like dies are used to stamp out coins. The principal differences are that a CD has only one finished side and much finer detailing than does a quarter or half dollar—and they cost more.

Actually, the precision of the CD manufacturing process isn't a significant part of the cost of the disk. Most of the price is attributable to the cost of the data on the disk, the royalty that's paid to the people who create, compile, or confuse the information that's to be distributed. You pay a similar price for the data that's stored in books, only for your book purchase you get something bigger and more tangible—it feels like it should be worth more. Although the cost of manufacturing a single book or CD ROM disk are on the same order of magnitude, CD ROMs appear to give you less for more because they hold so much information. Data weighs more in book form, so those who buy by the pound think books are the better value. On a fact-for-fact and pennies-per-fact basis, however, CD ROMs are substantially less expensive than books. The data is just as valuable, it's just less tangible.

Drives

Perhaps the most welcome feature of a new CD ROM player is that you don't need to learn anything new to use it. You probably already know all the ins and outs of CDs from playing them on your stereo. Many CD ROM players accept disks exactly like stereos do—with drawers that slide out at the press of a button. Just lay your disk in the drawer, press the button again, and it's loaded.

Some CD ROM players make the job even easier. You load your disks into a special carrier that resembles the plastic jewel-box case that most commercial music CDs come in. When you want to load a disk into the CD ROM player, you slide the whole carrier into a waiting slot. Most people buy a carrier for each CD ROM disk they have because of this convenience and the extra protection the carrier affords the disk—no scratches and no fingerprints, guaranteed (see fig. 11.1). CD ROM changes use multiple-disk cartridges exactly like those used by audio CD changers.

When a CD ROM player is properly installed in your computer system, you can access the disk you slide in as if it were just another DOS drive. The CD ROM player will have its own drive letter, and you can check what's on the disk as easily as executing a DIR command.

You might not have access to the data that's stored on the disk so easily, however. Most CD ROMs contain their own searching software that you must run to read the data stored there, but don't worry about having to learn to use another software package. Most of these programs will give you a menu-driven interface that's easy to use and completely intuitive.

Figure 11.1
Many CD ROM
Drives are now
designed to use disk
carriers that prevent
smudges and
scratches to the disks.

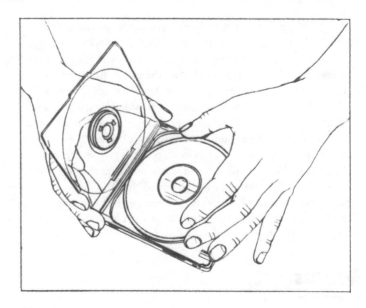

*Each CD ROM
disk you have will
likely require its
own data access
software.*

Although easy on you, these programs are not easy on your system.
They may require a huge amount of memory to run. Most will
demand your system be filled to its full DOS 640K limit. In fact,
these memory-hogging programs may even require you to eject your
favorite TSR programs before you can start to use your CD ROM.

The CD ROM programs may carve their own storage space from
your hard disk, hundreds of kilobytes of it for their files. To compound the misery, each CD ROM disk you have will likely require
its own data access software. If you get several CD ROM disks,
you'll need quite a lot of storage just for the programs that accompany each one.

If you want to install and use a CD ROM player without going the
full multimedia route, you'll have to start with a PC with a full dose
of DOS memory—640K—one that includes a hard disk drive. CD
ROM driver and retrieval software will also require that you use
DOS 3.10 or later on your system.

*The best of today's
CD ROM players
have access times
on the order of
350 milliseconds,
many scoring as
high as 500
milliseconds.*

Although CD ROM players are built around laser beams and optical
technology, don't expect to get data at the speed of light. Compared
to hard disks, most CD ROM players are glacial in their access
times—that is, how long it takes the drive to find the information
you want after it receives a command. For example, with today's
better hard disks drives, the average access time is about 25 milliseconds. The best of today's CD ROM players have access times on the
order of 350 milliseconds, many scoring as high as 500 milliseconds.
Those numbers mean that after you press the Enter key to tell your

CD ROM player what to do, it will delay about half a second on the average before it locates the first bit of information you need.

After the information is found, it must be transferred to your PC. This additional step can take even longer. Although text might pop up on your screen, graphics can take painfully long to display. Although a screen of text comprises only about 2000 bytes of data, a screen image may take a million. Each one has to be transferred individually from the CD ROM player into your PC. After the transfer, the images have to be processed before they can be displayed, eating up more time. As a consequence, painting a full-screen high-resolution image on a 286-based computer can take 10 seconds or more, which is one reason why the MPC standard demands at least 386 sx.

Although text might pop up on your screen, graphics can take painfully long to display.

Compared to the alternative, finding the right book and paging through to the entry you want, CD ROM is lightning-like indeed. For example, searching through the 150 books in the disk *U.S. History on CD ROM* for a keyword takes but a few seconds. You can zoom in on what you need to know in less time than it takes to get to the bookshelf. For those who need answers quickly, CD ROM still rates among the fastest ways of getting them.

Compared to the alternative, finding the right book and paging through to the entry you want, CD ROM is light-ning-like indeed.

The good news is that making a fatal mistake in software compatibility is just about impossible with CD ROM players. You don't have to worry about software compatibilities. All CD ROM players are able to read all standard CD ROM disks just as the CD player in your stereo will play any CD you find in the music store. But all CD ROM players are not the same. They differ both in interface and performance.

Your interface choice is twofold—some CD ROM players use the industry-standard SCSI connection, but a few plug into proprietary interfaces. Speed is not an issue with CD ROM player connections—either kind yields the same level of performance. The actual drive interface is much slower than the rate at which information is read from the disk—SCSI, for example can carry data at more than 30 times the rate that a CD ROM player reads it. In fact, after you've made the connection, the two styles of drive are indistinguishable. All use the same software commands and work the same way.

All CD ROM players are able to read all standard CD ROM disks just as the CD player in your stereo will play any CD you find in the music store.

The interface becomes important only when you install and connect a CD ROM player with the rest of your PC. SCSI players are more versatile because the host adapter they use can be shared with other

SCSI devices. You can plug a SCSI hard disk, magneto-optical disk drive, or fast streaming tape drive into the same host adapter, stretching the expansion capabilities of a single slot to up to seven peripherals.

If you can get them all to work together, that is. SCSI makes the connection more complicated as well as expanding its reach. With SCSI, you have to worry about issues like drive ID and termination for each device. In addition, to make multiple peripheral cohabitate on a single connection, you can spend hours sorting through the options and software.

Proprietary interfaces are typically plug-and-play—attach the power and signal cables to the drive, and you're done. Most proprietary interfaces, however, require that you buy the sound board and CD ROM player as a matched pair, which can limit your expansion options. For example, you might not be able to update later to a faster CD ROM player without buying a new sound board as well.

Performance

The difference in access times between old CD ROM models and new ones is the best argument for avoiding the ancient units.

As with hard disk drives, performance is a twofold issue with CD ROM players. You have to be concerned with finding and getting. That is, the various available CD ROM players differ in the time required to locate data (the *access time*) and the time required to move information from the disk to your PC's memory (the *transfer time*).

Compared to hard disks, CD ROM players are slow by either measure. For example, older CD ROM players require half a second (500 milliseconds) or more to access a given track while a good hard disk does the job in less than a twentieth the time (15 to 25 milliseconds). With these CD ROM players, you often have to wait half a second or more to see a response after you press the Enter key. Newer CD ROM players are better, with access times as quick as 150 milliseconds. In fact, the difference in access times between old CD ROM models and new ones is the best argument for avoiding the ancient units you find in close-out catalogs.

The transfer rate of most CD ROM players is fixed by the hardware standard established by audio CD systems. To play back music at the proper speed, CD ROMs have to deliver data at about 150 kilobytes per second, which is exactly the rate most CD ROM players read information to your PC. In that a true-color VGA image requires 900K of data, you have to wait at least four seconds to get a full-screen image from disk onto your monitor.

The newest and best CD ROM players cut the transfer time in half by kicking the drive into high gear and doubling the speed at which it spins the disk. Information is read twice as fast, making the response of the entire CD ROM system twice as quick. (With enough buffering, sounds and music can be played at normal speed even though they're read double-time.)

Multimedia makes one additional requirement on the CD ROM player you install in your PC. It must have an extra audio connection to send sound in analog form from player to sound board.

You might think an audio connection unnecessary. After all, audio CDs store information digitally, and your PC should be able to handle the recorded sound information as if it were any other data. In fact, your PC could—but it likely won't be able to manage the data fast enough. The two channels of high-quality compact disc audio would require your PC's microprocessor to read, convert, and output data at a rate in excess of 1.4 M/second (two 16-bit channels with a 44 MHz sampling rate). When your PC is juggling a full-motion video and half a dozen hypertext references at the same time, the additional workload can slow performance to a crawl. Passing along audio intact keeps things moving closer to full speed.

Standards

Unlike other peripherals that you might want to add to your PC, the CD ROM player and its media have been completely standardized. The same CD ROM disks will fit the currently available mechanisms so that you're ensured that your new digital library will be readable and should remain so far into the future. You don't have to worry about how a given brand may affect the compatibility of your CD ROM system.

You do have to ensure that the CD ROM disks that you buy are compatible with your computer's software architecture. Many disks are sold in special versions for PCs or Macintosh computers, with different access software to match the target computer. Hence when you order a disk, it is important to specify the kind of computer on which you plan on using it.

The data on CD ROM disks is stored in a particular format—an arrangement of tracks and sectors similar to that of hard disks—and, thankfully, one format has become a standard across the industry. Nearly all CD ROM disks and CD ROM players available today conform to the *High Sierra format* or its more recent upgrade, the ISO 9660 specification.

The only practical difference between these two standards is that the driver software supplied with some CD ROM players, particularly older ones, meant for use with High Sierra formatted disks may not recognize ISO 9660 disks. You're likely to get an error message that says something like `Disc not High Sierra`. The problem is that the old version of the Microsoft CD ROM extensions—the driver that adapts your CD ROM player to work with DOS—cannot recognize ISO 9660 disks.

Ensure any CD ROM player you purchase comes with Version 2.0 or later of the Microsoft CD ROM extensions.

To meld CD ROM technology with DOS, Microsoft Corporation created a standard bit of operating code to add onto DOS to make the players work. These are called the DOS *CD ROM extensions*, and several versions have been written. The CD ROM extensions before Version 2.0 exhibit the incompatibility problem between High Sierra and ISO 9660 already noted. The solution is to buy a software upgrade to the CD ROM extensions that came with your CD ROM player from the vendor who sold you the equipment. A better solution is to avoid the problem and ensure any CD ROM player you purchase comes with Version 2.0 or later of the Microsoft CD ROM extensions.

If you take the installation step-by-step, you should run into few difficulties.

The connection between CD ROM players and your PC also has been, for the most part, standardized. Nearly all CD ROM players that you can buy today use the Small Computer Systems Interface or SCSI to link with your computer. A few CD ROM players connect through a serial port, but when you're talking about moving 600 megabytes of data around, a 9600 bit-per-second connection amounts to trying to drain a lake using a sponge. You won't want to mess with serial-linked CD ROM players unless you have from now till the glaciers come home to wait for your data.

But life isn't easy with SCSI, either. Although the SCSI connection is quicker than serial—by a factor approaching one thousand—it can be ornery. In fact, SCSI is one of the most complicated interfaces to get operating properly, particularly with a PC. However, if you take the installation step-by-step, you should run into few difficulties.

Installation

The typical CD ROM player installation makes the otherwise complex issue of SCSI termination simple.

When you're certain that your new CD ROM player hasn't suffered shipping traumas, check to be certain that it is properly set up to match the requirements of your PC. If your CD-ROM player uses a proprietary interface, the drive itself should not need any preparation. The interface design eliminates the installation variables.

SCSI-based CD ROM players may require some setup or at least a bit of checking of setup variables.

As with any SCSI product, you'll need to set a SCSI ID number and check the termination of a SCSI-based CD-ROM player. On internal SCSI players, the ID number is usually set with a number of jumpers or DIP switches. Most drives that you buy packaged together with their controllers come preset with the proper value. In any case, you'll want to jot down the ID assignment of your drive for future reference. The typical CD ROM player installation makes the otherwise complex issue of SCSI termination simple. Because most CD ROM players are the only SCSI devices connected to their host adapters, they should be terminated. Most CD ROM players arrive with their terminations already in place, so you ordinarily need not make any adjustments to your drive.

If, however, you plan to connect more than one SCSI device to your host adapter, you'll want to remove the terminations from the devices in the middle of the SCSI chain, leaving the terminations on your host adapter and the last drive in the chain. Most internal SCSI drives use a set of three terminating resistor packs to supply their terminations. Leave these packs in place to maintain the termination of your drive; remove them if you do not want the drive to be terminated.

When your CD ROM player is properly prepared, next ready your PC for the installation. Switch your system off and disconnect its power cable. Slide the lid of your PC's case forward and off.

Most of today's internal CD-ROM players require a half-height 5.25-inch drive bay with front panel access (you do need to slide disks into the drive). Any bay that fits that form factor will do; the mounting requirements of CD ROM players are no more stringent than other drives. You mount a CD ROM player in a drive bay exactly as if it were a floppy disk drive.

If you don't have a vacant bay suitable for a CD ROM player, you have several choices. You can opt for an external drive—which will drive up the cost of your upgrade substantially, often $100 or more. Alternately, you can remove a floppy disk drive to gain space. Better still, consolidate your floppies by replacing two drives with a combo unit that fits a 1.44M and 1.2M floppy into a single half-height slot (see Chapter 6).

If your PC follows the old AT standard and uses mounting rails, install a pair of rails on your CD ROM player. Be sure that you install the rails at the proper height and with the proper orientation in relation to the player.

After you screw in the rails, try fitting the player into place. The rails should stop the player so that its front panel projects the same distance forward as your floppy disk drives. In addition, your CD ROM player should fit in the bay with about a one-sixteenth inch gap between it and the drive above or below it. If the drive doesn't seem to fit properly, try re-orienting the rails—turn them 180 degrees around one of their axes until they are arranged to make your drive fit properly into a bay.

Before you install the drive check the path through which you'll have to route your interconnection wiring. The cables will need to run from the drive bay, across the tops of your other expansion boards, and down to the host interface or sound board. Just lay the cables in their approximate places and examine the situation (see fig. 11.2). You'll have to judge whether it will be easier plugging the cables in before or after you slide the drive into place. In most installations, you'll want to connect the audio cable to your CD ROM player drive before you slide the drive into place (see fig. 11.3). If that scheme works best, you'll also want to install the control cable to the drive at the same time.

Figure 11.2

Attaching cables to your CD-ROM drive is almost exactly like attaching cables to a floppy disk drive.

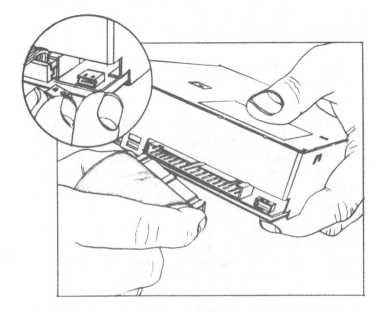

Before sliding the drive into its bay, slide the wires through the bay to its rear with one hand and then grab the cabling from the rear of the bay with your other hand. As you slide the drive into place, pull the cables through the bay at a matching speed. Lay the cables out in their final position across the tops of your other expansion boards.

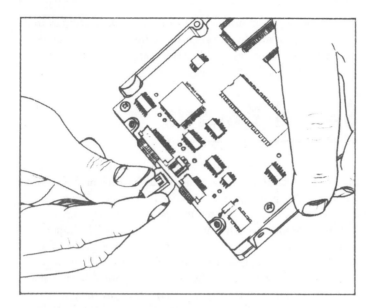

Figure 11.3
Connect the audio cable to your CD-ROM drive before you slide the drive into place.

With your CD ROM drive almost in its final place, plug a DC power cable into it. The power connector for an internal CD ROM player matches the style used by larger floppy disk drives. Slide the plug into the jack on the drive. The jack and plug are keyed to guard against improper insertion. If the plug does not slide into place, twist it around by 180 degrees and try again. These connectors fit tightly together. When the plug initially mates into its jack, it may require extra force to push it all the way into place.

Slide the drive the rest of the way into its bay and secure it in place. If you've used AT-style drive-mounting rails, screw the end brackets in place at the front of your PC. If the drive mounts directly, screw it into the sides of its drive bay.

Now concentrate on installing the software. You'll want to verify that everything works before you reassemble your PC so that you don't have to take everything apart again to find the errors of your ways.

Plug your PC in and boot it up. To bring a CD ROM player to life, you'll need to add a device driver to your system's CONFIG.SYS file. This drive enables your PC to recognize that the CD ROM player is connected. Then you must run the Microsoft CD ROM extensions program (preferably from within your PC's AUTOEXEC.BAT file) so your computer knows how to manage your new CD ROM player.

To bring a CD ROM player to life, you'll need to add a device driver to your system's CONFIG.SYS file.

All the other details in using your CD ROM player (as well as your sound board) for multimedia are handled from within Windows. Slide a disk into your new CD ROM player, load Windows, and await the multimedia revolution.

Sound Boards

A bad sound board shrieks and crackles worse than a radio in a thunderstorm; a good one can rival the best audiophile stereo system.

Sound boards serve several functions. They convert stored sounds from digital to analog form so that you can hear them; they record sounds for later playback; they create sounds of their own with built-in synthesizers; they mix the results together; and they amplify the final audio product so that you can actually hear it. The important differences between sound boards are twofold—the quality of what they deliver to your speakers and the compatibility with your software. Of the two, the latter is the more important because if a sound board cannot make noise, you can't hear anything no matter how well it might be able to do its job. When you have the basic compatibility that you need, however, your ears will prefer the better sounding board. A bad sound board shrieks and crackles worse than a radio in a thunderstorm; a good one can rival the best audiophile stereo system.

Sound boards have three primary jobs: creating sounds from instructions sent them by your programs, playing back sounds created by some other source, and controlling other sound-making devices. The best example of re-created sounds are those sampled by the board itself and recorded on your hard disk. Sound boards control other devices through the *Musical Instrument Digital Interface* or MIDI, a connection that is required on all MPC-compatible products.

Synthesis

Compatibility is most important when you call upon a sound board to create sounds from program instructions.

Compatibility is most important when you call upon a sound board to create sounds from program instructions. If a given sound board is not completely compatible with your software, it cannot produce the sounds that the programmer originally intended. The key words to look for in judging the compatibility of a sound board are Sound Blaster and Ad Lib.

One of the first sound boards to gain popularity was made by a company, no longer in the sound-board business, called *Ad Lib*. Because it had the widest user base early when noisy games were becoming popular, many game programmers wrote their products to take advantage of the specific hardware features of the Ad Lib board. The capability to mimic the Ad Lib hardware became the minimal standard for sound creation compatibility.

Another company, Creative Labs, entered the sound board business and built upon the Ad Lib base. Its *Sound Blaster* product quickly gained industry acceptance as a superset of the Ad Lib standard—it did everything the Ad Lib board did and more. The Sound Blaster found a huge market and raised the standard for sound synthesis among game products. Because programmers directly manipulated the hardware registers of the sound Blaster to make the sounds they wanted, to run most games, and to produce the proper sounds, you need a sound board that is hardware compatible with the Sound Blaster. Several iterations of Sound Blaster hardware were produced; the minimal level of compatibility to expect today is with Version Sound Blaster 1.5.

The Sound Blaster found a huge market and raised the standard for sound synthesis among game products.

The Sound Blaster generates sound using a technology called *FM synthesis*. It works by combining pure frequencies together. Even the most complex sounds can be perfectly simulated by the proper combination of pure tones—providing the combination includes infinitely fine variations in frequency and strength. Practical products have finite limitations, so FM synthesis cannot quite duplicate real-world sounds. The sounds created through FM synthesis are recognizable—both as what they are supposed to represent and as synthesized sounds.

The Sound Blaster relies on a particular integrated circuit to produce its array of synthesized sounds, the Yamaha YM3812. This chip has a single output channel, so it can produce only monophonic sound even when it is installed on a sound board that's otherwise called stereo. Some sound boards use two of these chips to produce stereo. The YM3812 has a fixed repertory of 11 voices, six of which are instrumental and five for rhythm.

A newer FM synthesis chip has become popular on better sound boards, the Yamaha YMF262 or OPL3. Not only does the OPL3 have more voices—20—but it also uses more sophisticated algorithms for synthesis. It can also produce a full stereo output.

An alternate technique used for creating sounds is *wave table synthesis*. Also known as sampling, wave table synthesis starts not with pure tones but with representative waveforms for particular sounds. The representations are in the form of the sound's exact waveform, and all the waveforms that a product can produce are stored in an electronic table, hence the name of the technology. The waveforms for a given instrument or sound are only templates that

Wave table synthesized notes all have the same frequency mix and consequently have an unreal sameness to them.

the synthesizer manipulates to produce music or what is supposed to pass as music. For example, the wave table may include a brief burst of the tone of a flute playing one particular note. The synthesizer can then alter the frequency of that note to play an entire scale and alter its duration to generate the proper rhythm.

Although wave table synthesis produces sounds that are more life-like than FM synthesis, they are not entirely realistic. The particular mix of frequencies produced by a musical instrument—its timbre—varies with the note that is played. So the waveform of one note differs from that of another not only by frequency but by frequency mix. Wave table synthesized notes all have the same frequency mix and consequently have an unreal sameness to them.

Digitization

Reality cannot yet be synthesized.

Reality cannot yet be synthesized. Even the best synthesis systems only approach the sound of real-world musical instruments and not-so-musical noises. The best—or most real—sound quality produced by a sound board is thus not synthesized but recorded. As with Compact Discs, sound boards use the high-tech high-quality high-fidelity digital sound recording system.

Digital recording of sound turns music into numbers. That is, a sound board examines audio waveforms thousands of times every second and assigns a numerical value to the strength of the sound every time it looks. It then records the numbers. To reproduce the music or noise, the sound board works backward. It takes the recorded numbers and regenerates the corresponding signal strength at intervals exactly corresponding to those at which it examined the original signal. The result is a near-exact duplication of the original audio.

The digital recording process involves several arbitrary variables. The two most important are the rate at which the original audio signal is examined—called the *sampling rate*—and the numeric code assigned to each value sampled. The code is digital and is defined as a given number of bits, the *resolution* of the system. The quality of sound reproduction is determined primarily by the values chosen for these variables.

The sampling rate limits the frequency response of a digital recording system. The highest frequency that can be recorded and reproduced digitally is the half the sampling frequency. This top frequency is often called the *Nyquist frequency*. Higher frequencies become ambiguous and can be confused with lower frequency values producing distortion. To prevent problems, frequencies higher than half the sampling frequency must be eliminated, filtered out, before they are digitally sampled. Because no audio filter is perfect, most digital audio systems have cut-off frequencies somewhat lower than the Nyquist frequency. The compact disc digital audio system was designed to record sounds with frequencies up to about 15 KHz, and it uses a sampling rate of about 44 KHz.

The number of bits in a digital code determines the number of discrete values that it can record. For example, an eight-bit digital code can represent 256 distinct objects, be they numbers or sound levels. A recording system that uses an eight-bit code can thus record 256 distinct values or steps in sound levels. Unfortunately, music and sounds vary smoothly rather than in discrete steps. The difference between the digital steps and the smooth audio value is distortion. This distortion also adds to the noise in the sound recording system. Minimizing distortion and noise means using more steps. High-quality sound systems—that is, CD-quality sound—requires a minimum of a 16-bit code.

Sampling rate and resolution determine the amount of data produced during the digitization process, which in turn determines the amount that must be recorded. In addition, full stereo recording doubles the data needed because two separate information channels are required. The 44 KHz sampling frequency and 16-bit digital code of stereo CD audio result in the need to process and record about 150,000 bits of data every second, about nine megabytes per minute.

Many older sound boards were not powerful enough for full CD-quality.

For full CD compatibility, most newer sound boards have the capability to digitize at the CD level. However, to save disk space and processing time, most give you the option of using less resource-intensive values. Moreover, many older sound boards were not powerful enough for full CD-quality. Consequently, you'll find sound boards that support intermediary sampling frequencies and bit densities. Many older sound boards also limit themselves to monophonic operation. The MPC specification only requires eight-bit digitization support. Most sound boards support 22 and 11 KHz sampling; some offer other values such as 8, 16, or 32 KHz.

Many older sound boards also limit themselves to monophonic operation.

If you're making original recordings of sounds and music, you'll want to use as high a rate as is consistent with your PC's resources. If you want to play back sounds recorded on another PC (or pre-recorded), you should choose a sound board that supports the original recording format. Don't expect to get the quality of a recording studio from a sound board even though it may boast full CD-level digitization. In operation, the electronic noise rattling around inside your PC will leak into the sound board and its signals, degrading your recordings with an electronic background cacophony.

Control

A sequencer is nothing more than a memory and messaging system with editing capabilities.

Another way you and your PC can make beautiful music is by controlling external electronic musical instruments. Instead of generating sounds itself, your PC becomes a *sequencer*, a solid-state surrogate conductor capable of leading a big band or orchestra of electronic instruments in the cacophony of your own creation. A sequencer is nothing more than a memory and messaging system with editing capabilities. The memory required by the sequencer is supplied by your PC's hard disk. The editing is the software for you music making. The messaging system is a MIDI interface. MIDI is the standard connection for plugging electronic instruments and accessories together. In essence, MIDI is hardware (a special kind of serial port) and software (a protocol for transferring commands through the port). Amazingly, it's one of the few sound board standards that's actually standardized enough that it works with just about everything that says MIDI without compatibility worries.

A MIDI interface is electronically and logically simple. It merely provides a moderate-speed port to pass commands between musical interfaces (see fig. 11.4). Its data rate measures 31,250 bits per second. Because every byte transferred is framed with a start bit and stop bit, it allows information to be exchanged at 3,125 bytes per second.

Figure 11.4.
A set of typical MIDI ports from an external MIDI device.

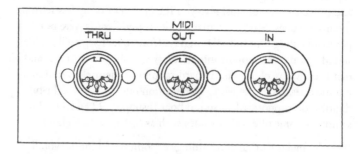

The MPC specification requires that your PC have a MIDI interface for controlling external devices. Most sound boards incorporate MIDI so that you won't need anything else to achieve that level of MPC compliance.

MPC also requires a game port, a 15-pin connector into which you can plug a joystick or other device into your PC. Most multi-function port boards now include a game port as standard equipment. (See Chapter 13.) If your PC lacks a game port, look for a sound board that includes one.

Sound boards also include connections for CD ROM players to link them into a single multimedia system. These connections are of two types, sound and control. The MPC specification requires the direct audio output of the CD ROM player to feed into the sound board so that your PC can playback true CD-quality audio without the need to pass through the sound board's digitizer.

In addition, many sound boards include CD ROM interface connections. These connections are of two types, proprietary or SCSI. Most boards will include one or the other. Both are useful, but you may want to avoid them. The reason to avoid the proprietary connection is because it's proprietary. The most important examples are on Creative Labs' products, which link directly to Panasonic CD ROM players. Although the connection is simple, it prohibits you from plugging in a better CD ROM player—one with faster access or a higher transfer rate. The SCSI connection on sound boards is best avoided if you want to attach more than one SCSI device to your PC. Sound board SCSI connections lack the high performance attributes of dedicated SCSI host adapters. If you try to plug in a hard disk or other peripheral to your sound board in addition to your CD ROM player, you'll be disappointed. You'll probably have difficulty getting it to work, and if you do get it to work, its performance will be on the shy side of satisfactory, at least if you're used to the potentials of today's hard disks.

Most of the time, you can switch (or jumper) off the CD ROM interfaces on sound boards and use a separate SCSI host adapter. If your sound board came with software drivers for CD ROM aimed at taking advantage of the on-board port, you may need another drive to connect a CD ROM player to a different port. You'll want to check out this driver situation before you purchase your sound board and CD ROM player.

Features

The final consideration in choosing a sound board is the array of features that it offers beyond those listed above and the minimal requirements of MPC.

If your PC lacks a game port, look for a sound board that includes one.

The reason to avoid the proprietary connection is because it's proprietary.

The SCSI connection on sound boards is best avoided if you want to attach more than one SCSI device to your PC.

Most boards include software that links to the board's hardware so that you can mix and manipulate sounds. You'll need the ability to combine the audio output of your CD ROM player with digitized disk files and even external inputs. The latter is particularly important if you plan on adding external sounds to your multimedia productions. Many sound boards provide a microphone input to allow the recording of speech. The software should also give you control of the recording process, allowing you to set the quality level (sampling rate and resolution) and length of the recording. You should also be able to edit the recording later.

When you have the potential quality of a sound board, you've got to be able to get it out of your PC and into your ears. Most sound boards provide speaker-level outputs for you to plug in to. As with stereo equipment, these outputs vary in quality and power.

Most sound boards will produce several watts, which is sufficient for small speakers but may not adequately drive your stereo system. You can get or make adapters that allow you to plug the speaker output of your sound board into the auxiliary input of your stereo so that you can fill a room or neighborhood with your PC's musical misgivings.

Although sound boards have hi-fi potentials, they often slight you in the low-frequency range. It's not unusual to see sound board specifications that limit low-frequency response to tones of about 100 or 150 Hz. Only a few sound boards go down to the limits of human hearing to a room rattling 20 Hz. Because of the low-frequency cut-off of most sound boards, there's little penalty in using small, cheap speakers with most of them.

Installation

You should check to see what your options are in the ports used by the board and what ports other devices in your PC use.

Proper preparation is the first step in installing a sound board inside your PC. Your new sound board will require that you assign it a series of input/output ports to control its functions. Most boards come pre-configured to use an otherwise idle set of ports, but sometimes conflicts can arise with other peripherals in your PC. You should check to see what your options are in the ports used by the board and what ports other devices in your PC use.

Prepare your sound board by setting the jumper and switch values of other peripherals in your PC on the board that assigns the port address (see fig. 11.5). Most of the time you won't know which addresses are used in your PC but familiarizing yourself with the port assignments and jumper locations will aid you should you later need to troubleshoot your board.

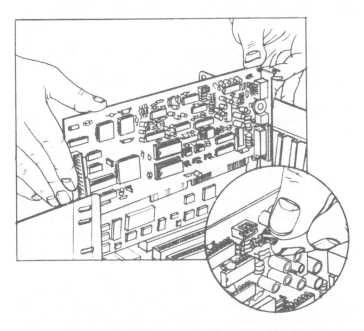

Figure 11.5
Make sure that all jumpers are set correctly (inset) before sliding your new sound board into place.

The one compatibility problem you may face arises when setting up the MIDI system. Most MIDI ports prefer to use the input/output port address of 330(Hex), as most MIDI software expects to find MIDI there and often refuses to recognize MIDI at other locations. That's not ordinarily a problem except that many SCSI host adapters are just as single-minded about using the same port for their own purposes (like operating your new PC's hard disk). By putting your MIDI adapter in your recycled PC (which likely does not have a SCSI disk) you sidestep any such issues. This is one case where the SCSI port on the sound board is an advantage—the sound board SCSI port and MIDI port automatically co-reside in your PC without problems.

If you're adding a MIDI connection to your PC that's not part of a sound board, you may run into compatibility difficulties. Many MIDI boards don't give you a choice of port location, locking you into 330 (Hex). If yours does give you a choice, make sure that the value you set for it will mate with your MIDI software. The MIDI sections of many sound boards default to an address of 220(Hex), so either the board or your software will require adjustment for compatibility. As with other expansion boards, you'll set these values with jumpers or DIP switches.

When your sound board is properly prepared, ready your PC for the installation. Switch your system off and disconnect its power cable. You'll find the system easier to work on if you also unplug all the other cables from it. Mark where each was connected so that you can later replace it without confusion.

Rotate your system around so that you face its rear panel and remove the screws holding on the top of its case. Turn the machine back facing you again and slide the lid of its case forward and off.

Scout your system for a vacant expansion slot to use for your upgrade. Although most sound boards use eight-bit interfaces and should fit comfortably in any full-length expansion slot, you may be able to reduce the noise level in the audio your sound board produces by putting the board as far as possible from the electrical noise-generating elements of your PC—that is, its power supply and hard disk drive. In most systems, this means that you'll want to put the sound board in the leftmost slot of your PC (when you view it from the front) or as close to the left side of your PC as possible. If you can, you'll also want to move other expansion boards away from the sound board.

Before you install your sound board, check the path of your interconnection wiring between it and your CD ROM player. The cables will need to run from the drive bay, across the tops of your other expansion boards, and down to the sound board. Lay the cables in their approximate places.

At this point, you'll have to make a judgment: whether you'll have an easier time plugging in the cables before or after you slide the sound board into place. In most installations, you'll want to connect the audio cable to the board (and probably to the CD ROM drive) before you put it into place. If that scheme works best, you'll also want to install the control cable from sound board to drive at the same time.

Most sound boards use a small nylon connector for their audio. This connector is keyed so that you cannot insert it improperly, but the connector is delicate, and the orientation is difficult to determine after the drive is installed in the tight confines of a PC. This is another good reason for plugging in the audio and control cables before installing the board. Hold the board in one hand over its designated slot, slide in the audio and control cables, and then push the board into its slot. Screw the retaining bracket of the board into the rear of your PC.

External Connections

When you've finished with your sound board's connections inside your PC, you'll need to plug in speakers or your stereo system to its audio outputs. Powered speakers are available in several styles. An increasing number of speaker systems designed specifically for multimedia are becoming available. Some are individual satellite speakers that you can place anywhere, but others come pre-installed in a cabinet that matches your PC and fits on top of your system unit between it and your monitor. Ordinary powered speakers that you might plug into your Walkman-like portable stereo will also work, although you may need an adapter cable to match the jack on your sound board to the plugs on the speakers.

If you already have a stereo system and want to connect your multimedia system directly into it, check the plugs and jacks at both ends of the connection. Most stereos use pin-plugs (also called RCA or phono plugs) for their inputs. Although pin plugs are standard on some sound boards, others use miniature phone plugs and will require an adapter to plug in.

Connecting your stereo to a sound board is just a matter of sliding the plugs into jacks (see fig. 11.6). If your sound board gives you a choice of outputs—speaker or low level—choose low-level for your stereo connection. Connect this output to the auxiliary input of your stereo receiver, preamp, or integrated amplifier. If your stereo doesn't have an auxiliary input, other usable input choices (in order of preference) include tuner, CD, or Tape 2. Do not use "phono" inputs because the level and equalization of the signals will be mismatched.

> **Warning:** Before you try out your sound board for the first time with your stereo, first turn down the volume on your receiver to prevent big surprises and blown speakers. Barely crack the volume control on and then select the proper input on your stereo receiver and boot up your PC.

When the physical installation of your sound board is complete, you'll need to finish by installing the software accompanying it.

Wiring together a MIDI system is as easy as plugging in hi-fi or video components. MIDI devices link with special cables that have male 5-pin DIN connectors at either end.

Connecting your stereo to a sound board is just a matter of sliding the plugs into jacks.

Figure 11.6
Connecting your
stereo to your
sound board is just
a matter of sliding
the plugs into the
jacks.

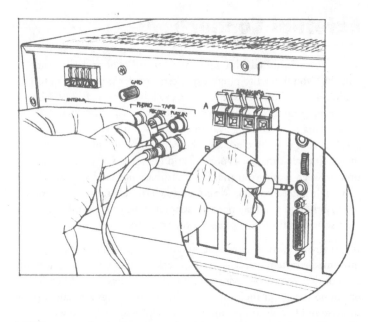

*Wiring together
a MIDI system is
as easy as
plugging in hi-fi
or video compo-
nents.*

MIDI ports come in three types—input, output, and through. You
connect the output of one MIDI device to the input of another. A
through MIDI connection just duplicates the wiring at the MIDI
input of a device. It acts like a wye-cable, allowing one output to
connect to several inputs—plug an output into a MIDI input and
then run another MIDI cable from the MIDI through connector to
another MIDI input.

After you've made all the connections, install your software and
prepare for the challenge. Mastering a MIDI system is like learning
to play any musical instrument—a lot of practice that can be as
enjoyable as you want to make it. Without further ado, you and your
PC can make beautiful music together.

12
Input Devices

Computers don't process data; they process the data in the commands that you give. The only way to get your commands inside your PC is with an input device. The range of input devices is wide, stretching from keyboards to mice and graphics tablets. Each input device has its own best function and purposes, and each has its own upgrade concerns. This chapter examines the range of input devices and what you need to know to add or upgrade those with which your PC is equipped.

A house without a door misses the point. A house is supposed to be a home, a private place to relax and a shelter against the elements, wild animals, insects, and process servers. Without some way of getting in, you can hardly enjoy those benefits.

A PC needs an input device for the same reason. Without a means of getting your commands into your computer, it could never give you answers that were relevant to what you do. It would be as impenetrable as a brick house without a door. Just as the monitor serves as a window to give you a look at what your PC is doing, an input device is your door through which you can enter your PC and command it, tell it what you want and what to work with.

The classic input device is the keyboard. What you type on it gets entered into the computer's memory, to be analyzed, acted upon, or stored. Keyboards are ubiquitous, and they are the most efficient way of sending your thoughts to your PC, but they have a drawback. They are lousy at handling graphics. Drawing a picture with a keyboard is cumbersome—you can either use a corner of the keyboard to scratch an image into loose sand (which won't help your PC understand it much) or you can type in a series of commands that tell the machine what to draw (which isn't how you think in images).

This chapter examines the range of input devices and what you need to know to add or upgrade those with which your PC is equipped.

Each of these input devices has its own strengths and features, and each is a subtly different upgrade to make.

Optical character recognition will add the capability to read printed text to the scanner's otherwise autistic talents.

For handling graphics, you need a graphic input device, one that can translate shapes into computer-digestible form, one that can let you manipulate images naturally—by pointing. In the PC realm, there are now several common pointing devices. Among the most used and most useful are the mouse, the trackball, and the digitizing tablet. When you need to convey a complete picture in its original form, the scanner is a handy addition to that trio. Optical character recognition will add the capability to read printed text to the scanner's otherwise autistic talents.

Keyboards

Before you venture off into graphic territory, you almost always need to get started with a keyboard. Even if you configure your PC to boot up into a graphic environment, you must somehow first program the boot-up process. That programming inevitably means plunking your fingers down on a keyboard.

The real reason that keyboard upgrades can be mind-boggling is that the selection of a keyboard is not a technical issue.

Keyboards are tricky upgrades—but not because the upgrade process is difficult. In fact, it only requires that you unplug your old keyboard and plug the new one into its place. The real reason that keyboard upgrades can be mind-boggling is that the selection of a keyboard is not a technical issue. It is a matter of personal preference, and there's no accounting for tastes. After all, some people like liver. Others like IBM's 101-key enhanced layout. Decisions about key layout have to be left to your own preferences.

Only two technical issues enter into your choice and installation of a keyboard change or upgrade. Any new keyboard must match the hardware and firmware standard used by your PC, and the keyboard needs to have the correct connector to mate with your system.

Currently, the world is plagued only by two PC keyboard electrical standards, the XT-style and the AT-style. These two styles use different internal firmware, and they respond differently when your system tries to communicate with them. They cannot be interchanged.

An XT keyboard follows the original IBM keyboard standard laid down in 1981. On the surface, it has 83 keys and no illuminated indicators. The AT standard took over after 1984 with a new electrical design. Hardly incidentally, it added a key (bringing the

total to 84) and illuminated indicators. The IBM Advanced Keyboard, the current 101-key model, follows the AT standard
electrically and is interchangeable with it but of course brings along
at least 17 changes, moving function keys to the top row, adding an
additional cursor keypad, hiding the Ctrl key, and shrinking the
Enter key.

The moral of this story is that if your system has an XT-style
keyboard, you need an XT-style replacement to match it electrically.
Most modern PC systems use the AT-style of keyboard. The layout
of the keys does not distinguish the two standards, so you can plug a
101-key keyboard into an XT if the keyboard follows the XT
electrical standard.

A few replacement keyboards give you your choice of electrical
standards—a switch (typically hidden on the bottom of the keyboard) allows you to select between the XT and AT electrical
interface. All you have to do is be certain that you have the switch
properly set for your PC.

If a replacement keyboard does not work with your PC, the first
thing to check is this switch. If you find a switch (typically labeled
XT-AT) try sliding it to its alternate position to get the keyboard
working.

The other difference between keyboards is the connector used to
plug into your PC. Two connector styles are used by current
keyboards. One follows in the tradition of the original PC and uses a
large, five-pin DIN connector (see fig. 12.1). IBM abandoned that
connector style with the introduction of its PS/2 series, which uses a
smaller six-pin miniature DIN connector. Compatible computer
makers follow whichever standard they please.

The good news is that there is no electrical difference between the
signals on these different connector types. A simple adapter will
allow one type of keyboard to plug into the opposite kind of
connector. The bad news is that such adapters can be difficult to
find.

After you match the connector on your PC to that of your keyboard
replacement, you only need to plug in the replacement to get typing
again. Be sure to turn your PC off before you plug in a new keyboard, however. To work properly, the keyboard must be initialized
by signals from your PC which are sent out while the machine is
booting up. Besides, it's also good practice never to plug anything
into your PC while its power is on.

*If your system has
an XT-style key-
board, you need
an XT-style replace-
ment to match it
electrically.*

Figure 12.1
A large, five-pin DIN connector (left) and a smaller six-pin DIN connector (right).

Mice

Apple's Macintosh, the first personal computer with a graphic interface to make any real impression on the marketplace, introduced the *mouse*. The idea was a gem: people don't normally select items or operations by typing. Rather, they point, and the mouse was designed as a pointing device. (The only weakness in this argument is that people don't naturally point by rolling an odd-shaped plastic object around their desks, but that's another story entirely).

You need a mouse or one of its kin if you plan on moving to a graphic environment.

The mouse was elegant in its conception. It was only a hand-holdable hunk of plastic that could measure how far you shoved it. Your PC could detect the motion you made, thanks to some kind of transducer hidden in the mouse. Based on the distance the mouse moved, the PC could move an on-screen cursor correspondingly. Although difficult to explain, the mouse has proven effective—so effective that you need a mouse or one of its kin if you plan on moving to a graphic environment.

The problem is that mice come in different races—in different shapes and colors with differing numbers of buttons—and each works a little differently. Not all mice speak the same language, and not all will crawl into the same holes, because some require their own particular interfaces. Finding the right mouse requires that you take all of these issues into consideration.

Motion Detection

In that the entire purpose of a mouse is to detect movement, the motion detection mechanism is the most essential element of each product. Not all mice use the same technology to detect motion, however. Some are purely mechanical; others rely on optics. There's something to be said for each.

The most common form of mouse is the *mechanical mouse.* It features a small ball hanging down from its lower surface. As you push the mouse around, the ball spins. Two metal wheels inside the mouse contact the ball and spin as the ball rolls. A sensor inside the mouse detects how far each wheel spins. Because the two wheels are mounted at right angles to one another, they can detect motion in two directions—X- and Y-coordinates—anywhere across the plane surface.

The mechanical mouse design is reasonably simple. More importantly, it works on any surface that you can move the mouse across. In a pinch, you can pick up the mouse and spin its ball with your fingers, but the ball rubs against everything in its way—dirt, grease, and leftovers from the pizza you ate sometime last year. The mechanism can gum up. Fortunately, you can usually remove the ball from inside the mouse, wash it, and replace it (see fig. 12.2).

The advantage of the optical mouse is that it doesn't collect grime like its mechanical cousin.

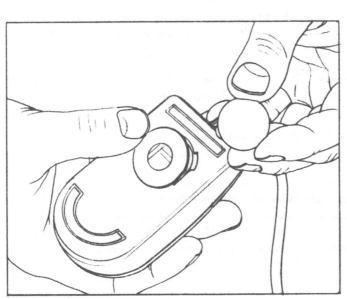

Figure 12.2
The ball in a mechanical mouse can be removed for cleaning.

The *optical mouse* is actually simpler mechanically than is a mechanical mouse. In fact, an optical mice has no moving parts (if you don't count the mouse itself). Instead, the optical mouse relies on optical sensors and light-emitting diodes. The light from the diodes is bounced off a specially patterned surface called a *mouse pad*. As you move the mouse over the surface, the nature of the reflections changes, and these changes can be detected by the optical sensors.

The advantage of the optical mouse is that it doesn't collect grime like its mechanical cousin (providing you keep your pizza off its pad), and it has no mechanical parts to wear out. On the other hand, it requires its specially patterned surface to work. To some people, that need can be a disadvantage. To others, it's a blessing because it forces them to keep a clean area for their mice to run on. Even folks with mechanical mice often invest in special pads to run them on.

Buttons

Besides detecting motion, a mouse needs to have some way of determining when you've found a choice spot—for instance, when you've finally got the mouse positioned over an icon you want to select. For this indication, mice rely on pushbuttons. Different mice may have one, two, or three pushbuttons.

The purest form of the mouse—the prototype mouse used by the Macintosh—has only one button. One reason underlying this design was that you, the fallible human, are less likely to mistakenly press the wrong mouse button. Two mouse buttons, however, give you more flexibility. One button can select while the other de-selects. A third button adds another option—and the chance for more confusion.

In truth, the number of buttons is important for only one reason: software. Some programs are written to use one button; some require two. Very few require three. Thankfully, most applications make allowance for other button counts than their primary preference (for example, by ignoring all but one button). Still, you're best advised to check the number of mouse buttons your application requires before you select a mouse. Generally, a two-button mouse will work for most applications, often with one button to spare.

Protocols

Mice convert the motions they detect into a digital code that can be processed or analyzed by your PC. The only loose end is what code the mouse uses. A standard mouse code would help software writers craft their products to better take advantage of mice. A standard mouse code would be so useful, in fact, that the industry has come up with four distinct standards. Called mouse protocols, these standards were developed by four of the major forces in the mouse industry, and each bears its originator's name. These include Microsoft, Mouse Systems Corporation (for a period known as MSC Corporation), Logitech, and IBM Corporation. The first three were designed for individual mouse products created by the respective companies. The IBM protocol was introduced with the PS/2 series of computers, which came equipped with a built-in jack that accepted a mouse.

In truth, you don't need to know the details of any of these protocols. You only need to know that they exist—and that they are different. You need to match the protocol used by your mouse to your applications.

Today, the Microsoft mouse protocol is the most prevalent. Many applications have been written to directly accept code from Microsoft-compatible mice. For example, Windows 3.1 will make direct contact with any mouse that's compatible with the Microsoft mouse protocol. You can use other mice with these applications, although setting things up is a bit more difficult because other mice will require the use of software drivers to convert their protocols into a form that the applications will understand.

Note that PS/2 mouse ports are more hardware specific and require the use of mice that use the IBM protocol. A growing number of applications are being written to directly accept this protocol as well.

Most mice sold today are capable of emulating the Microsoft mouse protocol. Those that have this emulation built into their hardware can be directly substituted for a Microsoft mouse. Others require the use of drivers to make the match.

The important issue is to check your applications for what mouse protocols they will accept. You can then use any mouse that can match those protocols.

You need to match the protocol used by your mouse to your applications.

Interfaces

If you have a spare serial port, a serial mouse is the least expensive way of adding a pointing device to your PC.

Your PC faces another barrier in understanding what your mouse has to say—your mouse must make hardware contact with your PC to transfer its signals. Mice connect with PCs in any of three ways: through a serial port, through a built-in dedicated mouse port; and through a special adapter that plugs into an expansion slot. Mice that use these methods are called (respectively) serial mice, proprietary mice, and bus mice.

From a performance standpoint, which style of mouse you choose makes little difference. All three kinds of mice interfaces use the equivalent of a serial connection. The principal factors in choosing one over the other are the resources of your PC.

Obviously, you will need a serial port if you want to attach a serial mouse that plugs into such a port. If you have a spare serial port, a serial mouse is the least expensive way of adding a pointing device to your PC.

Most people, however, have designs on all their serial ports and consequently don't want to tie them up with a mouse cable. The bus mouse provides an out. The bus mouse host adapter does not steal a COM port from DOS nor does it share one of the serial port interrupts, the sharing of which often causes problems with modem communications. The only problems associated with using a bus mouse are finding a spare slot into which to slide the host adapter and finding the extra cash to pay for the additional hardware. A bus mouse and a serial mouse work effectively the same way. Which you choose makes no difference to your software.

If your system has a built-in mouse port, you may be stuck needing a proprietary mouse. Although your source of supply may be more limited (and the mice consequently more costly), a proprietary mouse is the easiest of all to install. You only need to plug it in.

Resolution

A higher resolution mouse is a faster mouse, not neces-sarily a more precise mouse.

Mice are sometimes rated by their resolution, the number of Counts Per Inch or *CPI* that they can detect. When a mouse is moved, it sends out a signal indicating each increment of motion it makes as a single count. The number of these increments in an inch of move-ment equals the mouse's CPI rating.

The higher the number of CPI, the finer the detail in the movement that the mouse can detect. Unless the mouse driver compensates, higher resolution translates into faster movement of the mouse pointer on the screen. That's because the screen pointer is controlled by the number of counts received from the mouse, not the actual distance the mouse is moved. Consequently, a higher resolution mouse is a faster mouse, not necessarily a more precise mouse.

Installation

The installation procedure for a mouse depends on what kind of mouse you have. A dedicated mouse plugs into the appropriate jack on the back (or front) of your PC. A serial mouse, for example, is nearly as easy to install. Just plug the mouse into a vacant serial port. The only catch is that you may need to install a driver in which case you may have to specify (as a command line option) which port you have chosen. If you have more than two serial ports in your PC, you'll also want to be certain that your mouse doesn't share an interrupt with another device that may be operating at the same time, such as a modem port. If you do, you may suffer a problem when running Windows. If you run a communications program in the background, it may try to access your modem while you're pointing with your mouse in the foreground. Modem and mouse may try to use the same interrupt and collide, crashing your system. To avoid any such problems, ensure that mouse and modem don't share an interrupt. That means if you attach your mouse to serial port one, don't use serial port three for a modem; if you connect your mouse to serial port two, don't use serial port four for a modem.

Be certain that your mouse doesn't share an interrupt with another device that may be operating at the same time.

Bus mice are the most difficult to install, but they are still easy enough you need not fear them. Their host adapters slide into your PC exactly like any expansion board (see fig. 12.3). Then the mouse plugs into the host adapter.

The first step in installing a bus mouse requires that you determine which of your system's resources you want to assign the host adapter. In most cases, the host adapter will require one or more input/output ports as well as an interrupt. The instruction or installation manual accompanying the bus mouse should list the choices of resources that you can assign. In addition, the manual should outline what the factory default values are, suggested alternatives, and how to change the defaults.

Figure 12.3

To Install a bus mouse, set the configuration DIP switches or jumpers on the board. Then slide the host adapter into an expansion slot, screw it into place, and plug the mouse into the board.

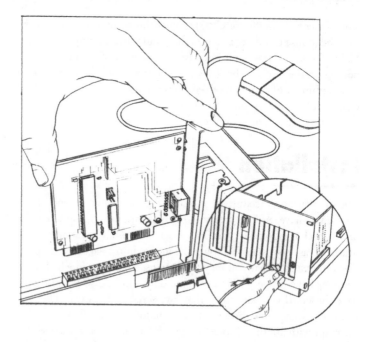

The first setting you should try are the factory defaults. You'll find that using the defaults is easier because you don't have to change anything. In addition, these are the settings that the manufacturer has found to work in the majority of PCs. If you find you need to alter the factory defaults, write down the changes you had to make in the instruction manual where the choices are listed so that you can refer to them in the future. On most host adapters, you'll change these settings by altering DIP (dual in-line package) switches or jumpers (see fig. 12.4).

Perhaps the most demanding part of installing a bus mouse is choosing which interrupt to use, particularly if you want or need to vary from the factory default. Your choices will vary with the kind of PC you have. If you have a computer with an eight-bit expansion bus, your choices will be limited because these machines have only eight hardware interrupts available to them. Of these, only three or four are available for expansion accessories, and these are typically already used in the average PC. Hardware interrupt 0 (computer people always start with zero, don't they?) is used by your system's timer; 1 is assigned the keyboard; 2 is used by some display adapters and network adapters; 3 is used by the second serial port in your system; 4 is used by your first serial port; 5 by the hard disk; 6 by your floppy disk drives; and 7 by the printer port. The port used by your mouse cannot (or should not) be used by another peripheral. In 8-bit bussed machines, interrupt 2 is the most common choice.

Sixteen-bit PCs are more generous with their interrupts, having a total of 15 for input/output devices. The likely candidates are interrupts 10, 11, 12, and 15. A good choice is interrupt 11, the default choice of many bus mice.

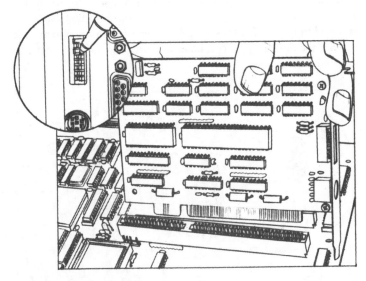

Figure 12.4

Many host adaptors for mice require that you set the interrupt with a DIP switch.

Generally, you can tell if your mouse's bus adapter board can use these higher interrupts by examining its expansion connector. Those that have only a single edge connector about four inches long can address only the lower eight interrupts. Boards with two edge connectors—a long one near the card retaining bracket and a short one from one to two and a half inches long—usually have all 15 interrupts of the 16-bit expansion bus available to them. Of course, you'll have to install such a 16-bit board in a 16-bit expansion slot to use the higher numbered interrupts.

After you've properly set up the host adapter to take advantage of your system's resources, you're ready to begin the rest of the hardware installation process. Start by switching off your PC, disconnecting the power cord for safety's sake, and removing the cover from the system.

Find a vacant expansion slot in which to install the host adapter. It is very important that you properly match the interface of the slot to the host adapter. Most bus mouse host adapters are designed to use 8- or 16-bit expansion slots, but some of their settings will be functional only in 16-bit slots. The reason is that 16-bit slots have more interrupt signals available on them. If you plan to use a higher numbered interrupt (which you should to avoid conflicts with other serial ports in your system), you'll need to use a 16-bit expansion slot. When you've firmly seated the host adapter in its expansion slot, be sure to screw the board securely in place.

After you've securely screwed the host adapter into your PC, you can attach the mouse cable to the host adapter. Just plug it in (see fig. 12.5). Before you reassemble your PC—plug all the cables you removed from your PC back in again. Then switch your system back on with the case open. After it boots up, install the software that came with the mouse.

Figure 12.5

After installing the host adapter, just plug in your mouse.

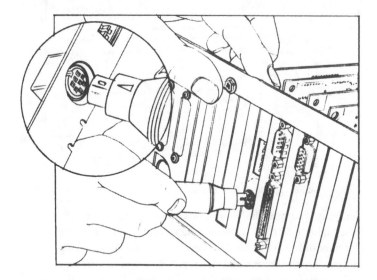

The typical software installation will require you to put a driver in your CONFIG.SYS file (or rely on the automatic installation procedure supplied with the software) and to copy some files to your hard disk. You may be able to run a mouse driver from the DOS command line. Either way, when your mouse software is installed, test the mouse and be sure it works. If it does, switch off your PC and reassemble it. If your bus mouse does not operate properly, switch off your PC, remove the host adapter, and try setting it to use different system resources. When you're successful, reassemble your PC.

Trackballs

Just as Jinx the Cat hated "meeses to pieces," so does anyone with a cluttered desktop. When there's no vacant spot on the Formica to give a mouse a good run, that pointing device becomes pointless.

When the mouse is trapped by untidiness, the graphic operating environments that should help make PCs accessible to non-technical users become nearly useless.

But the desk-in-disarray is only one of the problems faced by mousekateers. The arm movements required to push a plastic rodent require clumsy, wasteful, and tiring whole-arm movements. They are inefficient and exhausting.

The leading mouse alternative, the trackball, eliminates these problems (see fig. 12.6). Essentially a mouse turned upside down, the trackball is much like it sounds—a big ball that is rotated to cause a screen icon to move correspondingly. In addition, two or three pushbuttons duplicate the selection functions of mouse buttons. As with mice, trackballs send out the same signals as mice and work with the same software. And, like most mice, trackballs are powered directly through the serial interface (or other connection that they use) so there's no need for an external power supply.

When there's no vacant spot on the Formica to give a mouse a good run, that pointing device becomes pointless.

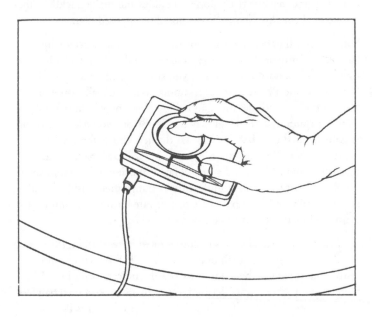

Figure 12.6
A typical PC trackball.

Types

The species diversification of trackballs is nearly as wide as that in the Rodentia. In crafting a product, each trackball designer goes his own direction. Various products range in dimension from shooter-size to cue ball; the arrangement of pushbuttons is confined only by the imagination (and definitely not by human dexterity); and the assembly itself can take on just about any shape or form. The ancillaries, too, go their separate ways—cable lengths, emulations, even data translations.

There's no definitive perfect trackball because there's no standard way of holding and using one. Some trackballs appear designed for alien hands with sixteen thumbs or fingers arranged in a full circle. Others seem like natural extensions of your own digits. Like beauty, the trackball depends on the beholder—the hand that's laid upon it, the way the hand holds it, even the way the user works.

A right-handed trackball isn't always the best choice for a right-handed person.

There's even conflicting research on whether it's best to move a trackball with the thumb or fingers. According to a company that makes trackballs, these devices operate best with the fingers, the fingers are more agile so they're more precise at spinning the ball. A competing company that makes a trackball designed for thumb control says that the thumb has more muscle control than the fingers. Some makers wisely don't take sides and make trackballs that can be used equally adeptly by the posed or opposed digit.

Some trackball deficiencies are obvious. One brand is decidedly handed one way or the other—you have to order the trackball for right- or left-handed operation. If you switch hands when you tire from using one all day long for spinning your trackball, you won't want a product with definite handedness. Moreover, that natural hand for spinning a trackball may not be the one you use for writing. A right-handed trackball isn't always the best choice for a right-handed person. Before you order a one-handed trackball, be sure that you know which hand you will favor in using it. To avoid such variables, most trackball manufacturers arrange their pushbuttons symmetrically and offer hardware or software button redefinition to swap the functions of the two sides.

As with mice, trackballs are sometimes rated in resolution, the number of Counts Per Inch of movement (CPI). As with mouse resolution, these numbers don't necessarily indicate precision. A higher number of Counts Per Inch can actually make a trackball less precise to use. A trackball with a high number of Counts Per Inch will move your on-screen pointer a greater distance for every degree of spin you give the ball. As a result, the high CPI trackball will make the on-screen cursor move faster but with less control. A low number of Counts Per Inch means you have to spin the ball further to move the cursor, giving you *greater precision* in your control.

Most trackball manufacturers now give you several choices for the effective resolution of their products so that you can tailor its actions and reactions to match the way you work. In addition, most trackball makers offer *ballistic operation* in which the translation of ball movement to on-screen cursor change varies with the speed of the ball's spin. This yields fast positioning without loss of precision. The only problem is getting used to such non-linear control in which the speed at which you spin the trackball has as much (sometimes more) effect as how far you spin it.

Probably the most important issue in a trackball is what software it works with. The great majority of trackballs emulate the most common mouse interface, that used by the Microsoft Mouse, in the PC environment. For PS/2s, they duplicate the protocol used by IBM's own mouse. Most trackballs also include menuing software to help the trackball take command of almost any software.

Unlike most other peripherals, there's no one trackball objectively better than the rest. Operating any of them is an acquired talent, like brain surgery, piano-playing, or hair-combing. Any judgment must be subjective, and which is better suited to a particular user depends most on personal preference and familiarity.

Installation

Trackballs are for all intents and purposes just mice turned upside down. They send out the same signal as mice do, using one of the familiar mice protocols, and they install exactly like mice install. Often they use proprietary mouse ports like those on PS/2s. In that case, just plug your trackball into the appropriate port.

As with serial mice, serial trackballs plug into unused serial ports. If you have a free serial port, a serial trackball is a quick, easy, and cheap way of adding a pointing device to your PC. Remember that trackballs are just upside-down mice and avoid sharing a serial port interrupt between trackball and modem.

Trackballs that use dedicated host adapters install just like bus mice. Their host adapters slide into your PC exactly like a bus mouse host adapter. The trackball then just plugs into the host adapter.

When you install a trackball host adapter, your first step is to determine which of your system's resources you can dedicate to the use of the host adapter. As with a bus mouse host adapter, a trackball host adapter will require one or more input/output ports as well as an interrupt. You'll find the resources needed and a list of the assignments you can make in the instruction or installation manual accompanying the trackball. The trackball manual should also outline what the factory default values are, suggested alternatives, and how to change the defaults.

Trackballs are just upside-down mice; avoid sharing a serial port interrupt between trackball and modem.

The factory settings are always the first choice because they are the ones that the manufacturer has determined work with most PCs. Besides, you won't have to change anything. If you do decide to alter the factory settings, be sure to write down whatever changes you make. The best place to record this information is in the instruction manual where it documents the choices. Most of the time, you'll adjust the setting of a trackball host adapter by altering DIP (dual in-line package) switches or jumpers.

After you've properly set up your trackball host adapter to take advantage of your system's resources, you're ready to begin the hardware installation process. Start by switching off your PC, disconnecting its power cord for safety's sake, and removing the cover from the system.

Find a vacant expansion slot in which to install the trackball host adapter, one that offers the proper interface. As with bus mouse host adapters, trackball host adapters are designed to use 8- or 16-bit expansion slots, but some of their settings will be functional only in 16-bit slots. If you plan to use a higher numbered interrupt (which you should do to avoid conflicts with other serial ports in your system), you'll need to use a 16-bit expansion slot because only 16-bit slots have interrupts numbered higher than eight available to them. After you've slid the trackball host adapter into the correct type of slot and firmly seated it, screw the board in place.

Next, plug the trackball cable into its host adapter. Before you reassemble your PC, plug all the cables you removed from your PC back in again so that you can test your installation. Switch your system on with the case still open.

After your system boots up, install the software that came with the mouse. The typical software installation will require you to put a driver in your CONFIG.SYS file (or rely on the automatic installation procedure supplied with the software) and copy some files to your hard disk. Some trackball drivers are installed as programs that you run from the command line or inside your system's AUTOEXEC.BAT file. Either way, once your mouse software is installed, test your trackball and verify that it works properly. When all seems well, switch off your PC and reassemble it.

Digitizing Tablets

Although they often resemble a deformed mouse coupled with an over-designed pad and sometimes work the same way, digitizing tablets represent an entirely different pointing technology. Digitizing tablets can be distinguished from mice in two ways. In its native mode of operation, the digitizing tablet indicates absolute locations, that is, you point to a particular location on the tablet. Later, by putting the tablet's pen or cursor back in the same location on the tablet surface, you can repeatedly identify the same point. In effect, the identified point is logically fixed to its location on the surface of the tablet. A mouse is a relative pointing device. It indicates displacements between locations rather than absolute locations. Roll a mouse across a pad, lift it up, and you have no guarantee that moving it back to its original location will identify the same on-screen point.

Whether absolute or relative positioning is preferable depends on how you work. If you draw with your eyes locked on the screen, relative locations may be all you need. If you want to trace an existing drawing, however, absolute positioning is a must. It's perfect when you need to make the on-screen (and in-file) digital image an exact analog of the on-paper artwork. Tape a blueprint to a digitizing tablet, and you can transfer every one of its lines into your favorite drafting program. The absolute/relative distinction between tablets and mice is blurring, however, at least from the tablet perspective. Most of today's digitizing tablets include mouse drivers that allow them to emulate one or another mouse (Microsoft's mouse is the most popular emulation). Equipped with such an emulation, the digitizing tablet becomes more versatile than the mouse because it can deliver absolute and relative positioning information, depending on what the application software requires.

If you want to trace an existing drawing, however, absolute positioning is a must.

Most of today's digitizing tablets include mouse drivers that allow them to emulate one or another mouse.

Digitizing tablets also differ from mice in the way you use them. Typically, digitizing tablets give you a choice of using a *digitizer pen* (or stylus) or a *cursor*. Some manufacturers also call digitizer cursors pucks or tracers. A pen makes using a tablet almost indistinguishable from ordinary drawing. In fact, you can draw on paper with the ink in a digitizer pen as you digitize information for your applications. You hold the tablet pen the same way as you would a Rapid-o-Graph or ballpoint. Only the long tail—the cable leading back to the tablet—will make you aware that you're connected to your computer. An increasing number of tablets even eliminate the need for this umbilical.

On the other hand, you manipulate tablet cursors the same way you would a mouse. A cursor is a hand-size pointing device with one to 16 buttons on top and a reticule with crosshairs that allows you to identify exactly a particular point to digitize. Compared to mice, cursors are more accurate (thanks to the advanced technologies used by tablets, the reticule, and absolute positioning) and less comfortable to use. Although the latest and best mice are ergonomically designed so that you can rest your hand on them and relax most of the muscles in your forearm, cursors are generally gripped with your fingers extended as if you were picking up some kind of odious insect that threatened to crawl up your leg. Cursor design is perhaps one aspect of digitizing tablets that requires some rethinking.

Digitizing tablet is an amazingly straightforward term in the otherwise confusing corpus of computer cant. Digitization is the function, the process of converting positions on a plane (classic Cartesian X-Y coordinates) into digital values that can be used by applications such as Computer-Aided Design (CAD), drawing, and painting programs. The term "tablet" indicates the physical embodiment of the device and its metaphor. The digitizing tablet resembles the classic paper drawing tablet, a flat surface upon which you can sketch. The latest digitizing tablets are even close in size and heft to drawing tablets.

Underneath their simple, flat surfaces, however, the digitizing tablet is a complex electronic miracle that can pin-point a specific location with an accuracy as fine as one-thousandth inch. Although as cheap as $499 or less retail, they use technologies as sophisticated as those that locate Soviet submarines or stealth bombers.

Types

Current digitizing tables range in size from the dimensions of a paperback book to a full drafting table. They differ in the accuracy and resolution they deliver, the speed at which they transmit information, and the freedom that they afford you in using them. At heart, they use a variety of technologies to determine the co-ordinates of their pointing devices, and the pointing devices have their own spectrum of differences.

Size

Bigger means bulkier and more expensive—and more expansive.

Size is the most visible and perhaps the least important dimension to digitizing tablets. Many manufacturers offer tablets identical in all features except for the available drawing area. A given product line may embrace a range from 12-by-12 inches to 36-by-48 or more. This size difference is mostly a matter of preference. How much you need is guided by the application you plan to use, the images you wish to digitize, and how much you can afford. Bigger means bulkier and more expensive—and more expansive.

Big also means more precise because tablet precision is measured by the number of lines that can be resolved within a inch. A 48-inch tablet will resolve four times as many points as a similar 12-inch one. The bigger tablet will also be more tiring to use because you may have to stretch back and forth across the whole surface to draw what you want. Then again, applications often allow you to set the size of the digitizing area you want to use. You can do your coarse drawing on a small tablet section and work on details full-size.

Size does not necessarily translate into working area, however. The useful space on a tablet varies with several outside factors. The application you run and the digitizing tablet driver you use with it control how much of the work-surface is put to work. For example, AutoCAD provides its TABLET CFG command that allows you to shrink the tablet space actually devoted to screen manipulation and to define portions of the tablet as menu areas.

Resolution and Accuracy

Resolution and accuracy describe how well a given tablet can identify a point on its surface. Resolution indicates how far from one another two points must be to be individually distinguished. Accuracy indicates how closely the digitized data comes to the correct representation of the cursor position. The more lines of resolution per inch, the better. The smaller the accuracy specification—usually given in fractions of an inch—the better. In theory, at least. A larger variable is your own accuracy in positioning the cursor on the drawing you wish to trace. You'll need a steady hand and sharp eye to strain even the 0.025-inch accuracy of the worst of available digitizing tablets. Moreover, when precision counts you may rely on the resolution of a tablet and the co-ordinate data supplied by your application (or a "snap-to-grid" facility) to zero in on the precise point you want to digitize.

The more lines of resolution per inch, the better.

The smaller the accuracy specification—usually given in fractions of an inch—the better.

Speed

If you're drawing freehand, speed may be the most important digitization issue to you. A tablet must be fast enough to follow the quickest motions of your hand. Most digitizing tables are rated in the number of points- per-second they can transmit back to your PC. This points- per-second speed is dependent on the communications rate of the connection between tablet and host (you'll want to use the fastest data rate possible, serial speeds of 9600 bits per second or quicker). A slow tablet may not be able to keep up with fast freehand drawing. If you're merely sampling individual points from a blueprint, however, even a slow tablet will suffice.

Proximity

Proximity indicates how far a pointing device can be lifted above the digitizing surface for a given tablet to recognize its location. The larger the proximity range of a tablet, the more freedom you have in drawing—and the thicker the art you can successfully trace through.

Software and Emulations

Make sure that the tablet you choose emulates something your software supports.

Two factors are important to determine whether you can use a given tablet at all: software and emulations. The software included with a digitizing tablet may include specific drivers to allow the tablet to work with specific applications. For example, mouse support usually (but not always) takes the form of a driver.

Many applications already have built-in support for digitizing tablets. With these programs, it's important that the tablet you choose works like one that your favorite applications know. Most tablets can emulate one or another of the more popular data formats used by digitizing tablets. Make sure that the tablet you choose emulates something your software supports.

Cursors and Pens

The pointing devices that accompany digitizing tablets run a wide range—differing in size, shape, even color. From a usefulness and versatility standpoint, however, the most important distinguishing characteristic is cordlessness. Most pointing devices must be tethered to the tablet by a cable that is used in communicating position information to the tablet electronics. Some of the most recent tablet designs are now cordless. This can be a great convenience. Not only is there no cable to tangle, snarl, and resist your drawing efforts but also cordless operation allows you to instantly switch between using a pen and a cursor. Moreover, a cordless pen can be as elegant to draw with as a Waterman fountain pen.

Of course, cordlessness can be a problem, too. Just as the life of a Bic pen in the corporate environment must average around 13 minutes—before it's pocketed and disappears from the known universe—cordless pens and cursors can travel just as quickly. Not that a cord will prevent a thief from liberating the pointing device (and at prices up to $250 the prospect may be tempting)—the cord serves only as a reminder not to put the pen in your pocket and stroll off. The umbilical can also prevent an expensive pen from dropping and self-destructing on the floor or from being trodden upon. Some people actually tape strings to cordless digitizing pens to prevent them from traipsing off.

The shape and feel of a cursor or pen is the most subjective aspect of using a digitizing tablet. Generally, a pen feels like using a bloated ballpoint, not unlike the typical technical pen. For the most part, the cursor is simply a hunk of plastic you can conveniently hold that provides a vehicle for pushbutton switches. Although no cursor is as hand-pleasing as a Microsoft or KeyTronic mouse, they range from an okay grip to a cramp and a gripe about style over function.

The number of buttons you need on a cursor depends mostly on how many your favored applications support; pattern is a matter of preference. A 16-button cursor will mean that you might rarely have to go back to your keyboard to elicit functions. You'll probably still have to squint at the cursor or scratch your head to remember which button does what.

Pens differ in the number of buttons they offer, too. Generally, all pens give at least one switch that's activated by pressing down on the point, the *tip-switch*. A second button (and sometimes a third) on the side of the pen near the tip may also be available. How useful additional buttons are depends on the software you use.

Many digitizer pens have internal ink supplies so that you can draw on paper as you transmit data back to your PC. Sometimes, a manufacturer distinguishes its digitizer pens from a digitizer stylus in that the latter doesn't contain an ink supply. With few exceptions, pens can be equipped with dummy inkless cartridges to make them into styli.

A new kind of pen, the pressure pen, is rapidly becoming popular. Instead of merely indicating on or off, the pressure pen sends out a digital value corresponding to the effort applied to the pen tip. This force can then be used by an application to indicate the width, weight, or color of a line drawn in that application, a feature particularly useful in freehand sketching. Pressure pens vary in the range of forces they can detect and the number of pressure levels they can digitize, typically from 64 to 256.

Templates

Templates put menu-selectability on the tablet in the form of a usually-laminated plastic sheet that defines and identifies areas on the tablet that will elicit particular functions in an application. Move the pen or cursor into an area, click a button, and a function is carried out.

Using a template means that you end up watching the tablet and not the screen.

Templates also have their drawbacks. Using one means that you end up watching the tablet and not the screen. Your head is apt to bob up and down as you work with your eyes shifting from template to screen. Templates also shrink the active area of the tablet that you can actually use for drawing, increasing speed and convenience but slighting on accuracy.

Still, templates can be useful. In fact, AutoCAD includes its own template for tablet users. Many tablet makers offer their own improvements on this or additional templates for commonly used applications like Windows.

Technology

Technology indicates the operating principal a tablet relies upon to find its pointing device. For the most part, the technology of a tablet is academic—as long as a tablet is accurate, it shouldn't matter to you whether is uses radar or telepathy. However, some technologies have some specific advantages and disadvantages. For example, the resistive decoding permits some tablets to be built as see-through sheets of glass. More exotic sonic technology allows some digitizers to turn virtually anything into a tablet.

Ergonomics

A more comfortable tablet will make everyday work more pleasant.

The importance of ergonomic issues depends on how you work. If you're the regimented engineer, you may prefer a heavy-duty tablet that stays put on your desk or drafting table (or even substitutes for a drafting table). Free-wheeling artists may want the freedom of a lightweight tablet that can be cradled in your arms or on your lap. Moreover, some people like to suffer. Almost any tablet will do for them. For most people, however, a more comfortable tablet will make everyday work more pleasant—and every little bit helps.

Installation

As with trackballs, digitizers are mouse variants. They install in much the same manner with two exceptions. There are currently no proprietary digitizers, and bus-style digitizers may use other interfaces besides serial-port derivatives. The only difference is that many digitizing tablets require their own source of AC power, typically an external transformer.

For the most part, you only need to plug a serial-based digitizer into a vacant serial port, plug in its power cord, and then run the software accompanying the digitizer. If you plan on using the digitizer as a mouse substitute with a multi-tasking system, be sure that the tablet's serial port does not share an interrupt with the serial port used by your modem.

The digitizers that use their own interface cards are installed exactly like bus mice. Their host adapters slide into your PC the same way as does any expansion board. Then the digitizer plugs into the host adapter.

With a digitizer host adapter, you'll again have to determine which of your system's resources you want to assign to the digitizing system. In most cases, the digitizer will require one or more input/output ports as well as an interrupt to control it. Check the instruction or installation manual that came with your digitizer to find out its needs. You'll set the resources used by the digitizer system using DIP switches or jumpers on its host adapter board. Most of the time, it makes the most sense to stick with the factory default settings. Change them only if you encounter an incompatibility with your PC (meaning that your digitizer doesn't work). Don't forget to write down the changes you make for future reference.

After you've set the digitizer's host adapter to take advantage of your system's resources, begin the hardware installation process. Switch off your PC, disconnect the power cord from your computer for safety's sake, and remove the cover from your system.

Find a vacant expansion slot in which to install the host adapter. Again, be sure to use an expansion slot with the same interface as the digitizer host adapter, an 8- or 16-bit slot as the board requires. Remember, a 16-bit slot is necessary if you want to exploit a higher interrupt. After you've chosen a slot and firmly seated the host adapter in it, be sure to screw the board in place.

After the host adapter is installed inside your PC, attach the signal cable between the digitizer and its host adapter. Plug the digitizer into an AC outlet if it requires external power.

Before you reassemble your PC—plug all the cables you removed from your PC back in again. Then switch your system back on with the case open. After it boots up, install the software that came with your digitizer so you can test it out.

The typical software installation will require you to put a driver in your CONFIG.SYS file (or rely on the automatic installation procedure supplied with the software) and copy some files to your hard disk. Some applications, like AutoCAD, have built-in drivers for most digitizers, so in those cases you'll only need to run the setup procedure for the application. Whatever is required, carry out the installation and then test the digitizer to be sure that it works. When you're sure all is well, put your PC back together again, and you're ready to use your digitizer.

Scanners

If you're impatient, aesthetically impaired, or if phosphorous isn't your medium, you have hope in the scanner.

Getting great graphics from a PC is child's play—providing you let your child tinker with your PC. Getting those graphics into your PC is another matter. Professional artists hover over their monitors pushing their mice around for hours and days crafting the images they want. If you're impatient, aesthetically impaired, or if phosphorous isn't your medium, you have hope in the scanner.

With a scanner, you can capture as an electronic graphic image anything you have on paper—or, for that matter, anything reasonably flat. Dot-by-dot, a scanner can reproduce photos, line drawings, even collages in detail sharper than your laser printer can duplicate. Better yet, equip your PC with optical character recognition software, and the images your scanner captures of typed or printed text can be converted into ASCII files for your word processor, database, or publishing system. Just as the PC opened a new world of information management to you, a scanner opens a new world of images and data to your PC.

The best part of today's scanners is that they are affordable.

The best part of today's scanners is that they are affordable. A hand scanner that can convert almost an infinity of graphic images into electronic form costs little more than a single disk of electronic clip art—prefabricated drawings in electronic form. Instead of buying an expensive mapping program (with layouts of cities you've never heard of, let alone need for your reports) you can draw your own on paper or copy an atlas (with the publisher's permission, of course) for a pittance.

Although they are technically sophisticated, scanners are operationally easy. If you can use a photocopier, you can master desktop scanning technique in a couple of tries—and without wasting a sheet of paper. Hand scanners are nearly as easy.

In fact, the only problems you face in upgrading your PC with a scanner are selection and connection. You need to find the one right scanner from the wide variety of products available. Then you need to connect it to your PC so that its signals can be converted into files that will be accepted by your graphics or publishing software.

Of the two, the selection process is the one that will give your brain the biggest workout. Although all scanners accomplish basically the same task, the various scanning products are hardly identical. Not only do they work differently, they excel in different tasks. What you want to do with a scanner—capture simple drawings, duplicate color photos, or read printed text—is one of the chief factors in deciding which product is best for you.

To complicate things, you need to match a scanner technology with the way you work and what you can afford. You'll find that there's a scanner design for everyone except the miserly sort who won't begrudge $100 or so for the least expensive models.

Your first chore is getting a bit of technical background so that you can discover what kind of scanner is best for you. Your PC will also need to be capable of using the scanner. In most cases, that means you'll need a hard disk drive to handle the huge files the scanner will create, a graphics-capable display system to let you see what you've scanned, and often additional extended or expanded memory to speed up the scanner's operations.

Types

The essence of a scanner is elementary. It uses an array of light sensors that detect the brightness of the reflection off the image being scanned. In most cases, the scanner has a linear array of these sensors, typically charge-coupled devices or CCDs, squeezed together hundreds per inch in a narrow strip that stretches across the full width of the largest image that can be scanned. The width of each scanning element determines the finest resolution the scanner can

The narrower the scanning element, the higher the resolution and the finer the detail that can be captured.

detect within a single line. The narrower the scanning element, the higher the resolution and the finer the detail that can be captured.

This line-up of sensors registers a single, thin line of the image at a time. Circuitry inside the scanner reads each sensing element in order to create a string of serial data representing the brightness of each point in the line being scanned. After it has collected and arranged the data from each dot on the line, the sensing element can advance to read the next line.

How the scanning sensor moves to that following line is the fundamental design difference between scanners. Somehow the long line of sensing elements must shift their attention with extreme precision over the entire surface of the image to be captured. The scan typically involves a mechanical sweep of the sensors across the image. Two primary strategies have emerged in scanner technology. One requires the image sensor to move across a fixed original; the other moves the original in front of a fixed scanner.

Drum scanners exemplify the latter technology. They work like printing presses in reverse. You feed a piece of paper bearing the image to be scanned in, and it wraps around a rotating drum that spins it past the sensor string that's fixed in place inside the machine.

Two designs take the opposite tack and use the moving- sensor concept. The *flatbed scanner* is named for the flat glass surface it gives you upon which to place the item to be scanned, face down. The scanning sensors are mounted on a bar that moves under the glass, automatically sweeping across the image. The glass surface allows the sensors to see up to the image. *Hand scanners* make you the motive force that propels the sensor over the image. You hold the T-shape hand scanner in the palm of your hand and drag it across the image you want to scan. The string of sensors peers through a plastic window in the bottom of the hand scanner.

The sweep of your hand is not nearly as controlled as the movement of scanning mechanisms.

Flatbed and drum scanners are designed with precision mechanisms that step the sensors or image a small increment at a time, each increment representing a single scan line. The movement of the mechanism, which is carefully controlled by the electronics of the scanner, determines the width of each line (and thus the resolution of the scanner in that direction).

Hand scanners present a problem. The sweep of your hand is not nearly as controlled as the movement of scanning mechanisms. If you move your hand at a speed other than that at which the scanner expects, lines will be scanned as too wide or too narrow, resulting in image distortion—at best the aspect ratio may be off; at worse, the scanned image will look as wavy at the Atlantic under the influence of an errant typhoon.

To keep track of the image, the hand scanner uses a feedback mechanism. For example, the Logitech ScanMan uses a rubber roller that senses how fast you drag the scanner along. The rate at which the roller spins gives the scanner's electronics the feedback it needs about scanning speed. From this information, the software that controls the hand scanner can give each scanned dot its proper place.

For most people, the hand scanner is the most appealing because it is the least expensive. It needs no precision (and expensive) scanning mechanism. Moreover, the hand scanner is compact and easy to carry. You could plug one into a laptop PC (if your laptop has an expansion slot to accommodate the scanner's interface board or if you have an external adapter to match the scanner) and carry the complete system to the neighborhood library to scan from books in its collection. Hand scanners can also be quick because you can make quick sweeps of small images instead of waiting for the lumbering mechanism of another scanner type to cover a whole sheet (see fig. 12.7). Hand scanners may also adapt to some non-flat surfaces and three dimensional objects. For example, most will easily cope with the pages of an open atlas or gothic novel—although few can do a good job on a globe or watermelon.

Each of these three technologies has its advantages and disadvantages. Some scanner designs are suited to some applications more than others.

Hand scanning is a learned skill.

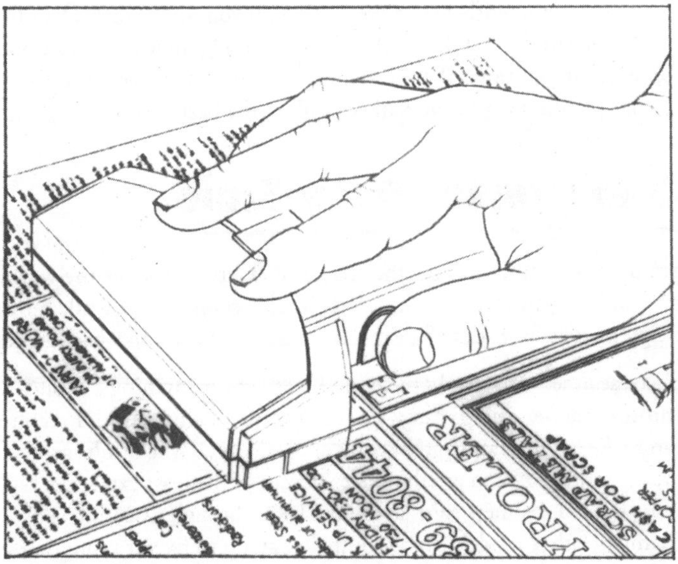

Figure 12.7
A hand scanner is ideal for scanning small images from flat surfaces.

The convenient size of the hand scanner can also be a disadvantage. To avoid being absolutely unwieldy, most will scan in a single pass areas only about four inches wide. Although that's enough for a column of text and most scanners offer a means of pasting together parallel scans of larger drawings and photos, the narrow strips of scan make dealing with large images inconvenient. Then again, because a hand scanner is not limited by a scanning mechanism, it can allow you to make absurdly long scans, typically limited only by the scanning software you use. Hand scanning is also a learned skill. You have to move the scanner at the right rate—very slowly at high resolutions—and doing so smoothly and reliably requires practice.

The big drawback of the flatbed scanner is price.

Drum scanners are moderate in price and compact in size because their mechanisms are relatively simple. However, that mechanism imposes a stiff penalty—only thin, flexible images can be scanned. Generally, that means normal paper. Books (at least while intact) and solid objects are off limits. Only certain sizes of paper may be accepted. While this may be no disadvantage in a character- recognition application, it may be frustrating when you want to pull an image off a large sheet without resorting to scissors or a photocopier first.

Flat-bad scanners are like copying machines in that anything that you can lay flat on their glass faces can be scanned—books, magazines, sections of poster, even parts of your anatomy. Of course, the scanned image can be no larger than the scanner bed. The big drawback of the flatbed scanner is price. Their precision mechanisms make them inherently expensive. Although you might find a hand scanner for under $100, you'll be lucky to find a new flatbed scanner for less than ten times that—even more if you want color. But for regular graphics work, the flatbed is often the best choice.

Color versus Grey Scale

Scanners also differ in how they perceive reality. Some see the world only in black and white, others have Technicolor vision, while most weigh matters in shades of grey. Which to get depends on what you do.

Color scanners are clearly the best. They can do anything a monochrome scanner can do but with full spectral fidelity. A color scanner can make an amazingly good copy of any image—the results are breath-taking, and so are the prices. Prices of the least expensive color flatbed scanners start at about $1000 through discount channels; other models can work their way up to five or more times that price. Color hand scanners are also more expensive than their monochromatic kin.

Because they are high-end engines, color scanners don't skimp when it comes to their abilities. Most can register anywhere from 256 thousand to 16 million different hues. While that may be more than you or your software wants to manage, their palettes can easily be scaled back, either through hardware controls or through software. Some scanner programs even optimize the scanner output so that those hundreds of thousands of colors can be accurately represented by a sampling as small as 256. Similarly, the color images are easily rendered in grey, again either in the scanner hardware during the scanning process or by software processing after the fact.

Many color flatbed scanners impose another penalty besides price. They can be slow, requiring a separate pass of their image sensors for each primary hue. On such machines, a complete color image takes three passes—three times as long as monochrome or as much as five minutes for a full-page image. Single-pass color scanners trim the waiting time. Just as color scanners have different spectral ranges, grey-scale scanners differ in the number of shades they can detect. At the bottom are the plain black and white machines that recognize no intermediary tones. From there, the grey-scale range increases as powers of two. A few years ago, a scanner with a range of 16 greys was top of the line. Today, the figure is 256. That's a good place to be because 256 greys gives good results on most monitors (the VGA monochrome standard actually allows for only 64 greys) with a manageable amount of storage, one byte per dot in the image.

Today, you'll want at least 300 dots per inch as the minimum in your scanner.

Most grey-scale scanners can also be set to recognize fewer grey tones, usually the selection is between 2 (black and white) 16, 64, and 256 greys. The more greys you select, the larger the resulting image file will be but the more realistic the image will appear. A limited grey range is useful for text recognition and for capturing line drawings, but you'll want a wide range of greys to capture photographs.

Scanners also differ in the resolution that they support. All scanners have a maximum mechanical limit on their resolution. It's equal to the smallest step that their sensor can be advanced. Today, you'll want at least 300 dots per inch as the minimum in your scanner.

As with colors and shades of grey, a scanner can easily be pro-grammed to produce resolution lower than its maximum. Lower resolution is useful to minimize file size, to match your output device, or simply to make the scanned image fit on a single screen for convenient viewing. Many scanners shift their resolution in distinct increments—75, 150, and 300 dpi, for example—although others make resolution continuously variable.

Illumination color becomes important when you want to scan from color originals.

Color can be an issue even with monochrome scanners. Most scanners provide their own sources of illumination for scanning images (this eliminates one variable from the scanning process and makes for more uniform and repeatable scans). Although the color of illumination might seem immaterial for a monochrome scanner, that's not necessarily true. Illumination color becomes important when you want to scan from color originals.

For example, some hand scanners use red light-emitting diodes (LEDs) for illumination. LEDs have long, troublefree lives. But when colored objects are illuminated in their red light, the brightness reflected from the image does not correspond to the brightness the human eye would perceive in white light. Green illumination gives a better approximation of the human eye's perception of tones. Colored images captured by a scanner that uses red illumination may seem tonally incorrect. Fleshtones, in particular, scan too lightly. For line drawing and text recognition applications, however, red can sometimes be better. Red pencil or ink marks on an image won't reproduce, so you can sketch or comment in red and not have it show in your scans.

Optical Character Recognition

Scan a newspaper clipping into your PC, and you can read it on the screen, paste it into other documents, and print it out just like any graphic image. But you can't edit it with your word processor. And when you press "Save," you might end up with a half megabyte file even though the article in question only contains a few dozen words.

The difference is data types. Your word processor uses text files in which each character is stored in a one-byte code called the American Standard Code for Information Interchange or *ASCII*. Every letter is represented by a single distinctive byte value. When a page is scanned, characters are treated as graphics, stored as patterns of bits the order of which corresponds to the dots found by your scanner. One character might require a hundred bytes to store.

You can translate text into graphic form into ASCII codes in two ways—by typing everything into your word processor or by optical character recognition. Add character recognition software to your scanner, and you can quickly convert almost anything you can read on your screen into word processor, database, or spreadsheet files.

Once the realm of mainframe computers and special hardware costs tens of thousands of dollars, optical character recognition is now within the reach of most PCs and budgets, available from direct vendors from $100 to $400. Just two years ago, a breakthrough—the introduction of feature-matching software—made fast, accurate character recognition possible with any PC scanner.

Previously character recognition systems used a technique called *matrix matching.* The computer would compare small parts of each bit image it scanned to bit patterns it had stored in a library to find what character was the most similar to the bit pattern scanned. For example, a letter "A" would be recognized as a pointed tower 40 bits high with a 20 bit wide crossbar.

The problem with matrix matching was that there's a world of variation to printing—different fonts, type sizes, and styles. For example, an Italic "A" has a completely different pattern signature from a Roman "A," even within the same size and type family. Consequently, a matrix-matching OCR system must have either an enormous library of bit patterns (requiring a time-consuming search for each match) or the system must be limited to matching a few typestyles and fonts.

Feature matching software can thus race through a scan very quickly while making few errors.

In the latter (and most common) case, you often have to tell the character recognition system what typeface your were trying to read so it would use the correct pattern library. Worse, most matrix matching systems depended on regular spacing between characters to determine the size and shape of the character matrix, so these systems worked only with monospaced printing such as that generated by a typewriter. *Feature matching* character recognition overcomes all of these problems by working smarter. Instead of just looking, it analyzes each bit pattern. When it sees the letter "A," it derives the essential features of the character from the pattern of bits—an upslope, a peak, and a downslope with a horizontal bar across. In that every letter "A" has the same characteristic features—if they didn't your eyes couldn't recognize each one as an "A," either—the feature matching system doesn't need an elaborate library of bit-patterns to match nearly any font and type size. In fact, feature matching recognition software doesn't need to know the size or font of the characters it is to recognize beforehand. Even typeset text with variable character spacing is no problem. Feature matching software can thus race through a scan very quickly while making few errors.

Although more straightforward than ever before, character recognition is still demanding when it comes to system resources. For example, the highly regarded OmniPage program from Caere Corporation requires Windows 3.0 and a wealth of memory—four megabytes of RAM and eight megabytes of hard disk space. You'll also need one of the scanners supported by the program to scan interactively or any scanner that can produce line-art TIFF files with a resolution of at least 200 dots per inch.

Today the range of available recognition software is wide. Better programs use feature-matching algorithms and know how popular word processors, databases, and spreadsheets format text and data in their files. You'll want to be sure the recognition program you choose can generate files compatible with the other applications you use.

Character recognition programs work either interactively with your scanner or from standard bit-image file formats. Some will even recognize text that your PC has received through fax transmissions. Be sure that the program you choose is compatible with your scanner or your scanner can generate the required file type. As with anything else, the best programs tend to be the most costly, but they more than pay for themselves in the time you save.

Connections

Getting acceptable performance from a scanner means using a high-speed connection because scanners generate prodigious quantities of data. For example, a full-page scanned at 300 dpi with 256 shades of grey requires over seven megabytes. You wouldn't want to move that through a standard serial port. At least three different interfaces designs are used by different scanners—SCSI (the Small Computer System Interface), GPIB (General-Purpose Interface Bus), and proprietary.

Although some scanners do give you a serial option, in most cases you'll want to use a faster interface—one with substantially higher speed. For example, the Microtek MSF-300Z can move data 10 to 100 times faster through its proprietary interface as through a standard serial port. In hand scanners, the proprietary connections dominate because the tiny devices have neither the room nor the need for standardized interface circuitry. Desktop scanners often opt for one of the standard interfaces. These, too, are best treated as proprietary designs when you're connecting up a new scanner.

SCSI presents problems because the "standard" allows for so many variations that getting two SCSI products from different manufacturers to work together can be frustrating (at best). For example, you may have both a SCSI hard disk and a SCSI scanner, but the drive might not work when connected to the scanner's host adapter and the scanner might refuse to operate when connected to the drive's host adapter. You'll avoid some of these headaches if you just connect each device to its own host adapter, pretending that each SCSI board is actually a proprietary interface.

(If you *are* going to try to share a single SCSI host adapter between a disk and a scanner, use the disk's host adapter if you can. Generally, the host adapters that come with SCSI hard disks give much faster performance than scanner host adapters.)

GPIB was originally developed by Hewlett-Packard Company (hence, its original moniker, the Hewlett-Packard Interface Bus) for interconnecting its test and measurement equipment. It provides both a medium-to-high speed connection (fitting neatly between serial and SCSI) along with a structured control system. As with SCSI, multiple devices can be daisy-chained together using GPIB and only one host adapter in a PC. Although GPIB is used a lot in laboratory systems, it's not a common connection for PC peripherals. In that you're unlikely to hook up anything else to a GPIB host adapter, you'll end up connecting scanners that use GPIB as if they had proprietary interfaces.

When it comes to connecting up a scanner, there's nothing inherently bad about proprietary interfaces. Because each scanners are designed specifically to match its own interface and because other devices do not share it, your compatibility worries will be minimal. You should find the connection between the host adapter and scanner is quite straightforward—all you have to do is plug the scanner in.

But there's another place where you can run into compatibility problems—the connection between the host adapter and your PC. The host adapter has to share some of the resources of your PC with other expansion boards and even the system board, so it's possible (and often likely) that conflicts will occur (see fig. 12.8).

Figure 12.8

Scanners using proprietary interfaces require that you allocate system resources. You'll need to make adjustments to DIP switches or jumpers on the board (main drawing) or through a cut-out in its retaining bracket (inset).

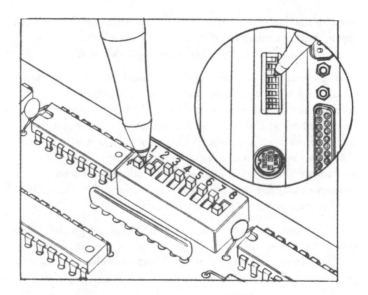

Scanner host adapters often need to use input/output port, memory, and interrupt facilities of your PC just as other expansion boards do. For example, to deliver better performance some hand scanners are interrupt driven, which means they need to take exclusive control of one of the interrupts available in your system. Some desktop scanner host adapters use I/O ports to transfer data and instructions between the scanner and your PC. Some host adapters need to reserve an address range in which they will place their BIOS code. In each case, you must be certain that the facilities used by the host adapter don't conflict with the requirement of other accessories connected to your computer.

Choosing an interrupt to use if you have an eight-bit PC can be daunting because your choices will be limited. Eight-bit machines have only eight interrupts, of which only three are generally usable—and those are often put to work at other chores. Interrupt 0 (computer people always start with zero, don't they?) is used by your system's timer; 1 is assigned the keyboard; 2 is used by some display adapters and network adapters; 3 is used by the second serial port in your system; 4 is used by your first serial port; 5 by the hard disk; 6 by your floppy disk drives; and 7 by the printer port. Your only choice is to use an interrupt that is not needed by another peripheral. Interrupt 2 is the most common choice.

Sixteen-bit PCs are more generous with their interrupts having a total of 15 for input/output devices. The likely candidates are interrupts 10, 11, 12, and 15. A good choice is interrupt 11.

Generally, you can tell if your scanner's host adapter can use these higher interrupts by looking closely at its expansion connector. If you see only a single edge connector about four inches long, then the board can only handle the lower eight interrupts. If the board has two edge connectors—a long one near the card retaining bracket and a short one (which may be very short, perhaps only an inch long), the card likely can handle the 15 AT interrupts. In order to use interrupts higher than 7, you must install the scanner host adapter in a 16-bit (or 32-bit EISA) expansion socket even though the board itself may look like an eight-bit short card.

I/O port addresses are more numerous than interrupts—in most systems you have a choice of 1024 ports. But ports are more numerous because they are needed for more functions. Some expansion boards use several ports for their functions. For example, the Microtek scanner uses 16 ports and a Direct Memory Access (DMA) channel.

The trick is to find a range that other accessories in your system do not use. For the most part, common peripherals stick to certain well-defined values. For example, the first two serial ports in most systems use 3F8(Hex) and 2F8(Hex). In most cases, the default chosen by the scanner manufacturer should work fine. If you later discover your scanner doesn't work, changing the port address should be the first thing to try. The same is true for the memory addresses that may be used by host adapters.

If you discover that your scanner doesn't work, changing the port address should be the first thing to try.

Installation

The first step in installing a scanner is determining which of your system's resources it will need. The instruction or installation manual accompanying the scanner should tell you exactly what the product requires. The instructions also should outline what the factory default values are, suggested alternatives, and how to change the defaults.

Always try the factory default first. It's easier because you don't have to change anything. Moreover, these settings are those that have been found to work with most PCs.

If you find you need to alter the factory defaults, write down the changes you had to make in the instruction manual. That way you can always refer to them. (You'll find out how important this bit of forethought can be when you install the scanner software. It may demand to know the settings you made. If you didn't write them down, that may mean tearing apart your PC all over again.)

In most cases, these values will be set using DIP (dual in-line package) switches or jumpers on the host adapter board. In Micro Channel machines and more advanced host adapters, the required settings are made using the installation software accompanying the host adapter.

SCSI scanners may also require that you set a SCSI identification number on the scanner itself. The factory default is the best choice, but you should verify that the setting is proper and has not been jiggled, jostled, or manhandled to some other value. After you've properly set up the host adapter, you're ready to begin the hardware installation process. Start by switching off your PC, disconnecting the power cord for safety's sake, and removing the cover from the system.

Find a vacant expansion slot in which to install the host adapter. Be sure to properly match the interface—while 8-bit boards will fit in either 8 or 16-bit slots, 16-bit boards and 8-bit board using higher interrupt numbers should only be used in 16-bit slots.

After you slide the expansion board in, you'll want to be sure to screw the board securely in place. Because scanners use large connectors (typically 25 pins or more) to plug into their host adapters, you can easily unseat the host adapter when you plug in the scanner's cable to it.

Most scanners can be plugged into their host adapter and into a wall outlet (if necessary) at this point. Connect the signal cable accompanying the scanner at both ends—one connector goes to the scanner, the other to the host adapter. Some scanners that use the GPIB connection may be an exception. These may require that you test out the GPIB host adapter before you connect the scanner. Check your instruction manual to be sure.

Many flatbed scanners have shipping screws or tape strips securing their mechanisms against transportation damage. Before you set up your scanner, be sure to remove these (see fig. 12.9).

Next—before you reassemble your PC—plug your PC in again. Switch it back on, and after it boots up, install the software that came with the scanner. If the installation procedure does not require you have your scanner switched on, turn it on any way so that it can warm up.

The typical software installation will require you to put a driver in your CONFIG.SYS file (or rely on the automatic installation procedure supplied with the software) and copy some files to your hard disk.

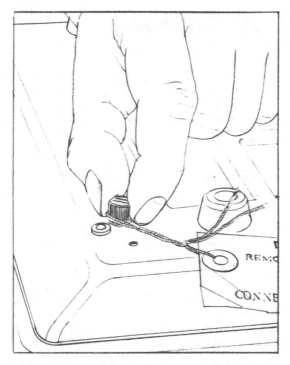

Figure 12.9
Check the bottom of
the scanner for a
shipping screw like
the one shown here.

After you've installed the software, reboot your PC and try out the
scanner with its control program or other scanning software. Your
scanner should magically come to life. Typically, when you select the
software command to scan, the scanner should light up as if by
magic—that is, if you and the software have carried out all of the
installation process properly. Make a scan to verify that all is well. If
you're able to complete a scan and see an image on your PC,
congratulate yourself on a job well done, switch off your PC, and
reinstall its cover.

If the scanner doesn't work, you likely are suffering from a resource
conflict of some kind. Switch off your PC and try changing the port
address, interrupt assignment, or memory address used by the
scanner host adapter until the scanner works properly. Rather than
trial and error, try the alternate suggestions listed in the instruction
manual first.

When your scanner is working, you'll find that its definitely not
child's play. Making a scan may take longer than your kid's attention
span, but you'll cut the time and expense of getting good graphics
and even text into your PC.

Video Capture

If you plan to make multi-media displays, you need to get media from somewhere so that you can multi it. Although static images can be captured with a scanner, motion is what multi-media is all about. So if you would rather have moving images than still-lifes, you to grab some video to stick in your schticks. What you need is a video capture system.

With a one-board upgrade to your PC, you can stock up on both static and moving images. Moreover, the applications of video-in-your-PC transcend over-hyped multi-media shows. With a video capture board, you'll have a tool for bringing real-world images into your presentations, desktop publications, correspondence, even some databases. If you do decide to venture into the tentative territory of multi-media, you'll have one of the tools you'll need to get started.

Video capture is about images and putting them to work. Although you could draw them with Freelance or PC Paintbrush, when you talk about moving images and flashing frames at a several per second rate, you'll need to draw faster than Joyce Carol Oates produces novels. The source of choice is video. In the typical multi-media extravaganza (you do aspire higher than a mere "presentation," don't you?) you'll want to combine video images with computer effects, editing, and emendations and send them back out either as video or on your monitor screen. While the output is easy—video outputs are as easy to get as installing a vintage Color Graphics Adapter, squeezing a video signal into a PC is as tricky as getting a cat back into the bag.

Technologies

Satisfying full-motion results are also beyond the range of today's best PCs.

The big problem you face in adding video capture to your PC is deciding on exactly what you mean by "video." Not only is there a proliferation of video signal types, the video capture process itself yields images in different speeds. That is, your video images can fit into a multi-media presentation in either of two ways—as slide shows of static images or full-motion video.

The latter of these is the more compelling because moving video lets you alter reality, manipulate real images, even do computer animation. Everybody wants to be Walt Disney or Walter Lantz. Reality can temper those dreams. Satisfying full-motion results are also beyond the range of today's best PCs (and, besides, both Disney and Lantz are dead).

For full-motion video, you can choose among three alternative technologies—using your PC to control an analog source such as a videocassette recorder (VCR), using your computer's own microprocessor horsepower to reconstruct images in real-time, or adding a coprocessor board to do same.

The first makes your PC into a simple controller and offers few image manipulation opportunities. Even with today's so-called multi-media PCs, the resolution of the other two techniques in real-time is suitable only for small (about one quarter of a screen) windows. Full-screen full-motion images using today's multi-media technologies are coarse and simply look out-of-place in a professional presentation. The hardware for making computer-generated (or just digitally-stored) full-motion multi-media images has yet to arrive.

Still video is another matter. Today, most PCs can paint true-color still images on their screens with full video resolution, manipulate them, and consign them to a video display system or VCR. Better still, you can quickly and cheaply add the necessary hardware to your PC to capture static video images for multi-media presentations and other purposes. Although the unmoving frame may lack the dynamism of Hollywood movies, they can make a slide show of the highest professional quality. Captured still video images are equally at home in more traditional presentations (such as film-based slide-shows—load up the old Kodak Carousel), desktop publishing in color and black-and-white, even image databases in which you can store a picture of a house (for example) along with a description and other details.

The essential element in getting still video images into your PC is a video capture board, an expansion board that slides into your PC and accepts a video signal input. The video capture board takes an analog video signal and converts it into computer-compatible digital form that can be imported into ordinary graphic applications and stored on disk.

Of course, you'll need more than a video capture board to add still video to your PC's repertory. Even those unmoving images have to come from somewhere, so you'll need a video source. The likely candidates are a video cassette recorder (VCR), video camera, or a camcorder.

The last is your best choice. For example, if you want to make a professional presentation (that is, to the public) copyright law will stymie your using most VCR images—you can't legally grab frames from commercial videos like movies or how-to tapes without first getting permission. On the other hand, the video camera is an endangered species in today's consumer electronics market, both rare and often unaffordable. The camcorder has replaced it, adding its own taping facilities with affordable prices (go figure). Most camcorders have live video outputs suitable for plugging into a video capture board.

Although nearly all video capture products come with their own control programs, you'll typically want additional software for editing your captured images, augmenting them with text and graphics, and presenting them in multi-media or more conventional form. Some video capture boards will also require a preview monitor so you can see what you're doing and what your PC is capturing. Finally, if you want to finish preparing your multi-media production before the next PC revolution rolls through, you'll want powerful PC. Although video capture boards will work in almost any computer (if you're patient), you'll probably want at least a 25 MHz. 386. Image manipulation eats microprocessor power faster than a couch potato consumes popcorn. You'll also want a hard disk with a capacity measured in hundreds of megabytes to accommodate a reasonable library of captured images. Each full-screen color video image will require about half a megabyte of storage.

The heart of the video capture system, the one that determines many of your other choices, remains the video capture board. Unlike SuperVGA boards, memory boards, and port expansion boards, different video capture boards have little in common and are as far from being generic products as Ferraris are from being commodity cars. Although all video capture boards share the same function—an analog image signal goes in and PC-compatible digital data comes out—they use different signals and connectors, follow different standards, and even produce different forms of digital output. You'll find boards with various color capabilities, resolutions, signal acceptances, and file format support. To get the right product for your upgrade, you need to match each of these characteristics with the requirements of your still-video application.

Signals

Generally, most video capture boards will be capable of accepting composite video.

Your first consideration should be signal type—a video capture board is worthless if it won't plug into the video source that you already have or are planning to acquire. Moreover, if you don't yet have a video source, you'll have a choice of signal types, one of which may give you a better quality captured image than the others.

In most cases, when people talk about video, they mean a particular kind of video signal—classic NTSC *composite video*. Composite video scores high because it is convenient to work with—you need only connect a single wire to relay all the information in composite video image. The required wire and its connectors are cheap, and cables are easy to fabricate from them because there's only a single central conductor surrounded by an interference-preventing shield. Moreover, composite video is popular. Most consumer video equipment uses composite video signals; most professional video equipment makes some provision for composite video. Generally, most video capture boards will be capable of accepting composite video.

NTSC refers to the American standard for a special type of signal. Although the engineers may scoff at the quality of these signals and tell you the letters stand for "Never The Same Color" (or sometimes, "Never Twice the Same Color"), they actually stand for National Television Standards Committee, which hammered out the details of the specification in the mid 1950s when the major television networks were arguing over the best way to broadcast color images.

Composite video refers to signal that puts NTSC color onto a single wire, combining brightness information (luminance) with color (chrominance) along with a synchronizing signal into a single composite of the original signals. The combining process chosen by the NTSC (chrominance is loaded on top of the luminance as a subcarrier) has a severe drawback—it limits the resolution of the chrominance signal and even puts a cap on the sharpness of luminance.

In production studios, high-quality video is handled as with three separate signals and three separate connections, one for each color. This has its drawbacks for consumer use for several reasons. For compatibility with other video standards, the separate signals must undergo a complicated conversion process inside equipment. Because three connections are necessary, it's complicated to connect and potentially costly in cabling.

The only drawback to composite video is quality. Because of the way color signals must be processed to squeeze under the composite video definition, resolution is sharply curtailed. Although the image encoded in a composite video signal may look acceptable on a small, misadjusted television set, its shortcomings rapidly become apparent as screen size and quality increase. In particular, colors look smeared because under the composite video standard, color resolution is cut to about one-third that of a black and white image.

The next step up from composite video is *S-video*. Slowly becoming a standard in high-quality video equipment, S-video sidesteps the composite video limit on color resolution to produce dramatically sharper images. The "S" stands for separate. The chrominance and luminance of the composite signal are given separate wires so that they don't suffer the degradations of the composite combining process. Because engineers often abbreviate luminance signals as Y and chrominance as C, S-video is sometimes called Y-C.

Whatever the name, the result is a higher resolution signal. Better VCRs, for instance, use S-VHS standard, which uses S-Video signals for inputs and outputs.

The downsides of S-Video are cost, complexity, and availability.

The downsides of S-Video are cost, complexity, and availability. Only the elite among electronic apparatus is equipped with S-video inputs and outputs. Although processing S-video signals is actually less complex than with composite video, storing and displaying their improved quality takes higher quality components and technology, which pushes up the price of equipment. Moreover, where composite video is simply a single signal, S-video uses two. That means either two wires or complex cables with two isolated conductors and special connectors.

The best quality comes from *RGB video* signals. This is the professional system that assigned each color a separate connection. Often it's best to leave RGB to the professionals because there's no one standard for synchronizing signals. Three ways of handling synchronizing signals are popular in RGB systems. These include *sync-on green* which piggybacks the horizontal and vertical synchronizing signals on the green image signal; *composite sync* which combines horizontal and vertical sync into one signal (called, logically enough, "sync") and gives the combined signal a single wire; and *separate sync* which provides a dedicated connection each for the horizontal and vertical synchronizing signals. To carry image color and synchronizing information, separate sync requires five separate circuits; composite sync, four; sync-on-green, three.

In most cases, you'll want to match the signals used by your video image capture board with your existing signal source.

Note that you only need to aspire to the better-quality video standards when you want color images. Monochrome composite video signals do not suffer from the limitations of color signals. In fact, a monochrome image essentially reduces S-video to composite video because the color component of S-video is absent. Consequently, for monochrome-only image capture, composite video is a completely acceptable standard.

Besides these standards which reign in Japan and the United States, you may encounter other video specifications used in Europe and the rest of the world—*PAL* and *SECAM*. The video standards are built around entirely different frequencies and even color technologies than the NTSC composite. Unless the video capture board you choose expressly indicates that it will work with PAL or SECAM, you can safely assume that it will not. Then again, if you plan to display the output of a capture board on an American video system, you'll only want to work with NTSC signals.

In most cases, you'll want to match the signals used by your video image capture board with your existing signal source. If you have an S-video source, you'll want to take advantage of its quality using a image capture board that accepts those signals. Otherwise, you'll want to work with composite video.

Connectors

The signals used by your video source have another effect that you must consider when you order any video capture product: connectors. Several connector types are used by the various standards. For example, a composite video output might take one of three physical forms: a pin plug (similar to the RCA connector or phono plug like those used in hi-fi equipment), the F connector that's ubiquitous in home video equipment, or the BNC connector widely used in professional video gear. S-Video outputs may take the form of two ordinary video connectors like pin plugs or a special S-Video connector. Most RGB signals use BNC connectors because the equipment that uses them aspires to professional quality.

The type of connector has little effect on the quality of the image that's transferred but has a major effect on whether the image can be transferred. If you can't plug your camcorder into your image capture board, you won't be able to digitize what you see. To avoid surprises that frustrate your capture board installation, you'll want to be sure to order any necessary adapters along with the board.

Before you buy, check your camcorder (or other video source) to determine what form of output connector it uses. Then tell the vendor of the capture board you want to buy what you find so he can equip you with a proper cable to connect camera to board. This bit of forethought will save you a day or two of frustration, the time you'll wait while the afterthought video cable is shipped.

Color Range

The range of image capture boards is wide. At the low end, you'll find monochrome-only products aimed particularly at desktop

The type of connector has little effect on the quality of the image that's transferred but has a major effect on whether the image can be transferred.

publishing but suited to any application requiring video images or their manipulation. At the high end are true-color capture boards that have spectra millions of times wider than the seven hues conventionally attributed the rainbow, far more colors than most mere mortals can distinguish.

Sticking with monochrome offers several advantages, mostly based on its simplicity: easier connections, lower cost, and potentially sharper images. For a given image size (in pixels), monochrome images are much more compact to store and quicker to process because there's less data in a monochrome image. The 256 grey scales that can be coded using a single byte per pixel will be adequate to make a realistic black-and-white image. Even the 64 grey scales of the standard VGA display produce an acceptable level of realism when you look at things in black and white.

Monochrome images are much more compact to store and quicker to process because there's less data in a monochrome image.

True-color systems—those able to match just about any color you can see with a full spectrum of 16.7 million hues—require three bytes of data per pixel (a 24-bit code, eight bits per color per pixel). Storing such a color image takes three times the disk space and three or more times the computer time to process than a monochrome image of the same size and resolution.

True-color is so good that you don't need anything better—but you can often make do with less. Most of today's video capture boards occupy the territory between monochrome and true color.

To make the data produced by 24-bit or 16-bit color systems more managable, many video capture boards are equipped with software that palettizes their color images. By using a color look-up table, the 16.7 million potential hues in an image can be reduced to 256 and yet still give a reasonable approximation of realistic color. Although trimming storage requirements by two-thirds, such palettized images can be acceptable for all but critical purposes, particularly when your goal is not the ultimate in realism but more one of naturalism—making the images look like the real world without true photographic quality.

Resolution

Resolution is an odd issue with video capture. You may think that you want your captured image to be as sharp as possible, but the ultimate in sharpness is not always necessary or desirable. For example, trying to squeeze more than 525 lines of vertical resolution from a captured video image doesn't make sense because a standard NTSC video image has only 525 lines, not all of which are visible. The 480 lines of the standard VGA 640 by 480-pixel graphics mode is actually a very good match. Most (but hardly all) of today's video capture products offer this resolution level.

Some capture products limit resolution to 320 by 200 pixels. This resolution can be acceptable if you plan to use the resulting images only in small windows or to pull them into documents. With full-screen images, you will be able to detect a lack of sharpness, particularly in the monochrome images that don't suffer the degradation of composite video's limitations.

Should you plan to use the images you capture in printing, you'll find you'll often get better results if you capture images at the same resolution that you want to use them. The algorithms used by some programs to scale images often have deleterious effects on image appearance, particularly should you make the mistake of storing an image in dithered form at its captured (rather than printed) resolution. (Dithering is a method of simulating grey scales, used by some programs to approximate halftone output with ordinary laser printers). The moire patterns introduced in the image-scaling process will make the printed images blotchy (if artful, at least to some eyes).

Image Storage and Display

Storing captured images is another concern. All video capture boards convert the images they grab into a graphics file that can later be read by other programs or reconstructed on the screen. The file format supported by the software provided with a video capture board (such as TIF, PCX, and so on) determines what programs can work with the captured images. You'll want to make sure that your software and video capture board speak the same file format language.

Make sure that your software and video capture board speak the same file format language.

A final distinguishing characteristic of video capture boards is how they work with your display system. Some capture boards replace your existing graphics adapter. Others work in conjunction with it. The type you choose will affect the equipment you need in your PC, how you install the board, and whether you may need a preview monitor (and whether you can even use one). For example, although the Publisher's VGA from Willow Peripherals allows you to preview images in near-real time (albeit in monochrome) on your normal VGA display, the SuperVIA from Jovian Logic requires you to connect a composite monitor to its output for properly preview its work.

A composite monitor can be something as inexpensive as a low-cost color computer display or color television with a composite video input. You can also use a multiscanning monitor, provided that your monitor accepts the frequencies used by composite video signals— 15.75 KHz horizontal and 60 Hz vertical—and has the necessary composite input. If you prefer the quality of S-video signals, you'll of course need an S-video monitor.

Installation

Installing a video capture board proceeds much as with installing any expansion board inside your PC. However, you'll need to be armed with some knowledge about how you intend to use the board before you begin. Specifically, you need to know what kind of signals you plan to use and whether you will use a preview monitor, should your capture board allow for one.

Many video capture boards require that you set these options before you install them in your system. As with most expansion boards that work in classic bus computers, you'll be required to adjust DIP switches or jumpers on the video capture board. Simply match the signal type and monitor usage to the settings listed in the manual accompanying your video capture board. Adjust the switches or jumpers on the board accordingly.

If the video capture board you plan to use doubles as a VGA adapter as does the Publishers' VGA, you'll need to prepare your system to accept the capture board's add-in display circuitry. If you have a PC with a display adapter built into its system board circuitry, you must switch off the system-board video to avoid conflicts with the add-in VGA of the video capture board.

Most PCs allow you to defeat their video outputs by simply changing the setting of a single jumper. Better systems will have a label inside advising which switch positions turn their VGA circuits on or off (Compaq, for instance, often puts such a label on the top of the drive bays). Otherwise, you'll need to pore through your PC's instruction manual to find the appropriate switch settings.

Should you intend to replace an old Monochrome Display Adapter with the VGA circuitry on your video capture board, you may also need to change the primary display designation in your PC. (This setting determines whether the PC puts its boot-up image on a color or monochrome monitor—select incorrectly and your computer will come up with a blank screen.) All VGA adapters require you to set your system board for color (vs. monochrome) or CGA/EGA (vs. MDA).

Again, check your owner's manual to determine which switch to use and what position to move it to. Some systems rely on you to select the primary display using their setup procedures (the same ones you use to determine hard disk type—either a setup program on a configuration disk or a procedure built into your PC's BIOS.) Newer systems do not require you make such designations. Check the index of your PC's instruction manual under "monitor" or "graphics."

When your video capture board and system unit are properly prepared, you can slide the new expansion board into almost any vacant expansion slot inside your PC. As with other expansion boards, you should match the bus interface used by your capture board with the connector in the expansion slot. If your capture board uses a 16-bit bus interface, be sure to put it into a 16-bit (or 32-bit EISA) expansion slot.

Exactly which of your PC's 16-bit slots you use does not matter, but because many capture boards (such as the SuperVIA) have daughtercards stacked on them, you'll probably want to arrange your expansion boards so that there is a vacant slot to the right (when looking from the top or front of your PC) of the capture board.

Grounding is important in video systems, so be sure to screw the retaining bracket of your video capture board into the rear of your PC. A bad ground can introduce noise into the captured image, typically a waviness or ripple effect that resembles your view of the world when you have warmed yourself with too many hot toddies. Firmly screwing the capture board to your PC will also ensure that you don't dislodged the board from its expansion socket when you slide in video connectors.

If your capture board provides VGA circuitry, connect your VGA monitor to it. Then boot up your computer to assure yourself that the display section of your new image capture board works properly. After you've confirmed the success of your installation, you can connect your video source to the capture board and install its software. Remember to plug in both ends of the input cable—one end to your capture board and the other to the video source, typically your camcorder.

If your capture board requires a separate monitor, connect your preview display and your video source to your PC. Then boot up your system and install the software that accompanied the capture board.

Finally, test your capture board. If its maker has included a test program with its software, run it. If not, switch on your camcorder. Make sure that you have an image in its viewfinder (this expedient guarantees that you do have the camcorder turned on, that you have adequate light, and that you haven't forgotten to remove the lens cap).

Execute the capture board's software and choose to preview an image. What you see on your VGA display or preview monitor should approximate what you see in your camcorder's viewfinder. If it does, you're all set to start capturing images. If not, it's trouble-shooting time.

Troubleshooting

You can capture whatever your camcorder sees and turn any image you grab today into the multi-media presentation of tomorrow.

The first troubleshooting step is to connect a video monitor to the output of your camcorder or other video source to be certain an image is being sent from the source and down the cable. If not, adjust your camcorder as you normally would to produce an image on the monitor and then reconnect the source to your capture board.

If you get an image when connecting your monitor directly to the source but not through the capture board, the problem is likely with another interface—between you and the video capture software. Make sure that you've properly configured the software and have followed the correct steps to preview an image. Odds are the press of a couple of keys will get your capture system working.

From that point on, your imagination and camera-work are your only limitations. You can capture whatever your camcorder sees and turn any image you grab today into the multi-media presentation of tomorrow.

13
Ports

To link your PC to the outside world, you need a connector of some sort. To the computer, that connector is a port. The two most common ports are serial—which are used for everything from mice to speech synthesizers—and parallel ports—used mostly for printers but increasingly finding application for data transfer. High-speed connections need even more than these ports can deliver, and the choice has increasingly become SCSI, which today has joined the ranks of must-have ports for your PC.

Only in a storm will any port do. PC equipment has its own demands and can be frustratingly particular about the ports it wants to use. Even if you make the right choice within the three most popular families of PC ports, you still can run into frustration. The wrong serial port will shortchange your communications; the wrong parallel port can prevent communications entirely; and SCSI (Small Computer System Interface) ports are a headache of their own. Even though all parallel ports look the same with the same connectors screwed to their brackets, parallel ports can have invisible electronic differences. Serial ports, too, hide subtle variations that have nothing to do with their variations in connector types. SCSI ports are social butterflies, interacting with equipment and software so much you can't make sense of where they are going or even what they are.

The only consistency in PC ports is that you need them—in multitude—to tie your PC to all the peripherals you want and dream about. A mouse, a modem, a plotter, a speech synthesizer, and a file transfer link with your laptop—each those goodies will likely demand a serial connection. Those that abstain from speaking serially will want a parallel port instead. Because most PCs only come with one or two serial and parallel ports, eventually you'll need

Only in a storm will any port do.

If you've never tangled with a port problem, ports may seem like simple additions.

to add more of them. On the other hand, high-performance peripherals are increasingly demanding the speed and versatility of SCSI. Once the realm only of top-of-the-line hard disks and CD ROM players, SCSI is adapting to printers, scanners, and even PC interconnections. If your PC didn't come equipped with a SCSI port, you're certain to be adding one to match a SCSI peripheral within the lifetime of your current PC. Without enough ports, you have to twist into the contortions of a combination switchboard operator and sideshow India rubber man on amphetamines, plugging and unplugging cables every time that you want to connect something to the single serial and parallel port that's standard on most PCs. Little wonder that ports are the most common, most needed—and surprisingly—least expensive upgrades granted PCs.

If you've never tangled with a port problem, ports may seem like simple additions. An extra parallel or serial port may cost as little as $10 to $20 and install in minutes. Just order a board from about any ad in any computer magazine and slide the board into an expansion slot. Only afterward will you discover the truth, in the two evenings you spend figuring out why your new ports won't work. Although serial and parallel ports are among the easiest and cheapest upgrades you can make, they are not without their own idiosyncrasies. You just can't add ports willy-nilly, nor can you expect all port hardware to work in every PC.

Not all serial ports are the same, nor are all parallel ports. Some have different speed capabilities. Some have different computer compatibilities. Some may just not do what you want them to. Moreover, the ports you can add depend on what ports you have. What will work may depend on what software you plan to run.

SCSI is a different situation entirely. You've got your choice of SCSI standards to follow—not just simple SCSI and SCSI-2 but also Fast SCSI, Wide SCSI, and something called SCSI-3 peeking over the horizon. Three different connectors are standard among today's SCSI ports, and more are coming. The host adapters that bring your PC its SCSI ports vary in speed; some even have their own built-in caches. If that is not enough, your SCSI installation only starts when you've mastered the hardware. After that, you've got to untangle a spaghetti-pot of software—drivers to match peripheral to port and make whatever SCSI machine you've bought perform its own prestidigitations.

Faced with all the potential confusions, pawning your PC and purchasing an abacus sounds like the better alternative, but don't give up. With a little insight and planning, you can be sure that your new ports will be the perfect upgrades for your PC. All you need to know is how to pick the right board or host adapter and how to bring all its features to life.

Serial Ports

Serial ports are designed for economical data transfer. The simplest serial ports require only three connections: one wire to send out a signal, one to receive replies, and a third common wire that completes the electrical circuits of the other two. To squeeze information down this narrow channel, data bits must march one-at-a-time in a game of follow-the-leader. Because all the bits in this one-dimensional march of data look the same—electrical pulses—meaning can be coded only by the relative position of each one. The 8, 16, 32, or 64 bits that travel side-by-side down your computer's various buses must be turned sideways so that they move one-after-the-other.

You should be able to see a shortcoming of serial communications already—moving 64 bits one at a time will take longer (all else being equal, of course) than moving them in one big push. Serial communication is inherently slow , but the narrow channel has one big advantage: anywhere a single electrical signal can flow serial communication can follow. Serial signals readily adapt to long transmission distances. The primary problem with long connections is that wires interact with one another and their surroundings with the result that high frequencies drain away. By lowering the frequency of a serial signal it can thus go farther—slowing down a serial signal increases its reach. Moreover, a single signal wire (or pair of them for two-way data flow) is easier to shield from noise, so it's easier to stretch error-free serial data flow than parallel flow.

Anywhere a single electrical signal can flow, serial communication can follow.

The job of the serial port is to convert the parallel data in your PC into serial form. The job is more complex than it sounds, however, because the port must be able to figure out the meaning of each identical bit in the flow of data. It works its magic using a set of marker signals and timing the relationship of each bit to the markers. Although conceptually complex, the job is easily handled by modern silicon circuitry, with the result that serial ports are a quick, cheap upgrade for most PCs.

For the uninitiated, however, difficulties are apt to arise because serial ports link not only the serial communication line but also with the hardware of your PC and your software. The port must make its presence unambiguously known to your PC and its software.

After all, a mouse connected to a serial port does you no good if Windows can't follow its paw prints, nor will your modem be a benefit when your terminal program doesn't know it's connected.

The necessary linkages between ports and your system are made at several levels. The port ties into your expansion slots so that your PC's electrical signals can cross over it its circuits. It logically links to your system's BIOS so that your PC hardware knows at what addresses it can send instructions to the registers on the port expansion board. DOS couples with it by assigning a name to the port. Only after all these linkages are made can programs that take advantage of DOS services know where to go when they want to communicate. More importantly, these linkages conspire together to limit the speed and number of ports that you can attached to your PC. Although you can beat some of the limits, others are more stalwart in the obstinacy.

Maximum Port Allowance

PCs are severely limited in the number of ports that they can recognize.

The number of things you may want to link to your PC with a serial port is potentially huge. Unfortunately, PCs are severely limited in the number of ports that they can recognize. Old-fashioned serial ports may limit you to no more than two connections. Even the most modern serial ports limit you to four ports on any given PC that runs DOS or Windows.

The roots of serial port shortage started growing more than a decade ago. When IBM initially crafted the PC, the company's engineers really had no conception of what the machine would be used for. They had no idea that you might want to connect all manner of external devices to your personal computer because no one had ever attached a PC to anything before. After all, virtually no one (in comparison to today, anyhow) had a PC to link up or anything to connect to one.

If you plan on adding serial ports to stretch your system's quota beyond two, you'll need one of the recent versions of DOS.

The good news is that when they designed the original PC BIOS—which for complete compatibility every clone computer must match—the IBM engineers allowed space for identifying four ports each of both the serial and parallel persuasions. But the bad news was that when they assigned the addresses from which these ports could operate, they allowed for only two serial ports and three parallel ports. This limit applied whether ports were available on the rear panel of your PC or were embedded in internal devices like modems. DOS allowed for an equal number of names to match the assignments. As a result, even though you could load up to four serial port addresses into your system's BIOS, until DOS Version 3.3 was released, only two serial ports could be recognized by the operating system and most applications.

Although some board hardware could add supernumerary serial ports, these could link only to proprietary programs because the logical addresses used by the additional ports were non-standard. For example, a number of internal modems were located at logical addresses recognized by some communications programs but not by other software. Only the software knowing these proprietary addresses would work with these ports. DOS 3.3 and later—introduced with the first of IBM's PS/2s—finally expanded its understanding to four serial ports, and the new machines assigned standard addresses to them. Consequently, if you plan on adding serial ports to stretch your system's quota beyond two, you'll need one of the recent versions of DOS. That's no big deal because you should have upgraded your DOS long ago.

Other operating systems do not have the same limit as DOS. For example, OS/2 recognizes up to eight serial ports.

Just updating DOS is not enough to push up to four serial ports. The circuitry on a serial port adapter determines the identity of the port. Older serial adapter boards only know how to make themselves recognized as either of the first two serial ports. They have no conception that the other two ports can exist. These board can only be used as the first two ports. They will work happily in conjunction with more modern ports that will take any identity, but you can never hope to have more than two ports in a system that uses these older boards alone.

Speed and UARTs

You may encounter other compatibility problems with serial ports. Speed is one. In the original IBM design, serial ports were designed to operate at rates of 50 to 9600 bits per second. This speed was pushed up to 19,200 bits per second in machine designs dating from after 1991. Even that is not sufficient to run today's latest external high-speed modems at full speed. Consequently, some companies have developed special, high-speed serial ports that operate at 38,400 bits per second.

*Some chips are not
fast enough to
keep up with
today's PCs.*

Surprisingly, many programs that use serial ports—in particular data transfer utilities—operate at even higher speeds—for example, 115,200 bits per second or so—using conventional low-speed serial ports. The reason is that these slower speed ratings take into account the overhead of using the BIOS to communicate with the serial port, which imposes severe software overhead. Moving a single character to a serial port requires your PC to execute hundreds of instructions. Data transfer programs that take direct control avoid the use of the BIOS and cut overhead per character to a few instructions. The actual operating speed of a serial port is determined by a divisor that's set in the register of a timing circuit. Using a big divisor, systems may put the brakes on serial circuitry to limit its speed to 9600 bps or so. By reprogramming this time base—essentially eliminating the divisor—fast file transfer programs can accelerate nearly any serial port to its hardware-enforced limit of 115,200 bps. Commercial communications programs and modem applications require the protection and assurances provided by using the overhead-consuming routines and are thus limited to the nominal port ratings that some manufacturers put on their products. Unfortunately, this technique doesn't help slower speed serial ports keep up with today's high-speed modems that are capable of data rates as high as 57,600 bits per second.

Timing circuitry and overhead is not the only speed constraint on the operation of serial ports, however. The actual processing capacity of the chips used to generate the serial signals used by the serial port limits how quickly they can react to the commands sent by your PC. Some chips are not fast enough to keep up with today's PCs. The chips in question are called UARTs (Universal Asynchronous Receiver/Transmitters). Three different UART chips are used in PC applications. They share a family resemblance that allows them to all operate with the same software but differ in their speed capabilities. They even look the same physically.

The UART used by the original IBM PC was termed the *8250*, and it's the slow child of the family. It's not even capable of operating at the speeds demanded by an ordinary 80286-based PC. Although the 8250 will work in the original PC, XT, and most eight-bit "turbo" computers, it can't cut it in ATs and more powerful machines based on the 386 and 486 microprocessors.

For today's faster PCs, the minimal UART chip is the 8250's successor, the *16450*. This chip will work in nearly any computer—although it may not be able to keep up with fast modems, particularly when you use multitasking software. To take advantage of the capabilities of all of today's high-speed communications products, the UART you'll need is an improved 16450 that's called the *16550*. Completely backwardly compatible with the 16450, the 16550 beefs up its predecessor by adding a 16-byte first-in, first-out buffer. This buffer allows the new chip to keep communicating even when a multitasking computer turns its attention to other projects. When properly programmed (and using the right software) the 16550 can carry out its 16 bytes of communications on its own. By the time the 16550 runs out of data, the multiprocessing system will probably have had a chance to restock its buffer. This capability to communicate on its own allows a fast, continuous flow of data even under multitasking systems.

Use of the buffer in the 16550 does not start automatically. It must be turned on by whatever program you use to run your serial port, for example your modem communications program. If your software does not turn on the 16550 buffer, the chip is effectively restrained to 16450 operation. The only way you can be sure that your software will take advantage of the 16550 is to check the manual that accompanies your communication software. Most recent programs do have this capability.

Because the newer, faster UART chips are backwardly compatible with the older ones and because they do not suffer from being operated too slowly, your biggest concern in buying a port upgrade is to be sure that you get a product that uses UART chips fast enough for your PC—or even the fastest possible UART chips. If you ever plan on using a serial port board in an AT, for example, you need a 16450 or better on it. The 16450 and 16550 are pin-for-pin compatible with one another, so you can always upgrade the older chip for the newer one by pulling out the old and inserting the new. If you have even vague plans of trying this upgrade, be sure that any serial port board you buy puts a socket underneath its UART chips.

Some system units and a few aftermarket boards don't use UARTs. They substitute VLSI (Very Large Scale Integration) chips that have several functions built in. For example, the Western Digital 16C552 combines the electrical equivalent of two 16550 UARTs and a parallel port into one chip. Port boards that use VLSI chips are capable of matching the speed needs of any PC.

Many port boards comes standard with a single serial port but provide provisions for you to later add a second one. Usually, all you need to add is a UART chip and a cable. Although any of the preceding three UARTs may fit in the waiting socket, you're best off getting the best. The latest design ensures the highest speeds and most reliable operation.

The only way you can be sure that your software will take advantage of the 16550 is to check the manual that accompanies your communication software.

Port boards that use VLSI chips are capable of matching the speed needs of any PC.

Parallel Ports

Just as the number of serial ports you can install in your PC is
constrained, so is the parallel port total. The original IBM PC and
every subsequent machine that follow the industry standard can
recognize only three parallel ports. For the most part, three ports
isn't much of a constraint. You're unlikely to have more than three
parallel devices to connect to your PC. This three-port limit is
enforced both by boards—as with serial ports, the identity of a
parallel port is determined by the hardware. But the limit is also
enforced by DOS. No matter the version of DOS you have, you can
handle three parallel ports.

Parallel ports are simpler than serial in that no special circuitry is
needed to change data from one format to another. Computers think
in parallel fashion and deliver data that way to their port circuits.
The only translation required may be to reduce a 32-bit bus signal
into one that fits the 9-bit width of a parallel port. This conversion is
relatively simple and commonplace. Your PC needs to do it automatically to allow intercompatibility between 8-, 16-, and 32-bit
expansion boards in one PC.

Although they are simpler than serial ports, not all parallel ports are
the same. The printer ports of the original IBM PC were exactly
that—output-only ports designed to connect to printers. In later
machines, these ports developed bidirectional capabilities so that
they could transmit and receive data. (IBM first announced this
capability with the introduction of its PS/2 line, but the feature was
actually available on earlier machines.)

Nearly all parallel products that come as factory equipment in
today's PCs are bidirectional, and some system accessories take
advantage of this feature for higher speed data transfers. For example, laptop file exchange programs like the more recent versions of
Traveling Software's LapLink can use parallel connections to double
or triple their transfer speed.

Not all parallel ports on upgrade boards are bidirectional, however.
Because two-way parallel ports require bidirectional logic buffers—
which are more expensive than the one-way kind—the least
expensive port upgrade boards are likely unidirectional. Be wary of
these boards. If you want to use your new port for more than just
printing, you'll want it to go both ways. Ask when you order to be
sure that any parallel port you buy is truly bidirectional.

Bus Mastering

In coming years, you may face a new port design choice—*bus mastering ports.* The ports take advantage of a new technology that is only useful in advanced-bus computers, such as those equipped with EISA, Micro Channel, VL Bus, or PCI. These newer buses allow ports to take advantage of bus mastering technology. Ports on these boards can take control of data transfers from your system's microprocessor. With this control shift, your system will be able to speed up data transfers by eliminating most of the work its microprocessor would ordinary have to do, moving the tough part of the transfer to the circuitry of the bus-mastering board. The first computers to use this technology were IBM's Models 90 and 95. Other manufacturers have not been quick to embrace this technology. (IBM wasn't, either. Four years elapsed between the introduction of the technology and IBM putting it to work.) Few bus-mastering port upgrades are currently available, although that may change as designers try to eke more speed for their products.

Few bus-mastering port upgrades are currently available, although that may change as designers try to eke more speed for their products.

Bus mastering is most effective for parallel ports because their data rates—often upwards of 300,000 bits per second—are high enough to strain slower microprocessors. Most serial ports aren't fast enough to cause this kind of slowdown.

Serial and Parallel Addresses

Every serial and parallel port needs a unique identity by which your PC and your operating system can recognize it and send it commands and data. To give the ports in your PC the required identity, they must be assigned input/output addresses through which your system, using its BIOS, can communicate with the registers on the port adapter board. These addresses must be unique for each port so that each one can be unambiguously identified. Typically, you assign the addresses used by most port upgrade boards by changing jumpers on the board or running setup software before you install the board.

When your PC boots up, it checks for these port addresses by querying the board and loads the address values into the PC's memory at a special location. DOS then checks that location to find which ports are available and assigns a name to each port based on its position in memory.

The BIOS rules of loading port addresses are the most important. Your system goes in quest of ports in a particular order. It searches for serial ports in this sequence: 3F8(Hex), 2F8(Hex), 3E8(Hex), and finally 2E8(Hex). It looks for parallel ports in this order: 3BC(Hex), 378(Hex), and 278(Hex). As it finds each port of a particular type, it plugs the corresponding address value into the locations reserved for that purpose in the *BIOS data area*, the lowest reaches of your PC's RAM, which start at absolute memory address 0400(Hex). The first eight bytes here hold the four serial port addresses; the next eight bytes are reserved for parallel port addresses. When DOS loads, it reads the addresses from the BIOS data area and assigns each one a name in exactly the order in which they are listed in the BIOS data—COM1 through COM4 for serial ports and LPT1 through LPT3 for parallel ports, with the name PRN also assigned to LPT1 as a default.

The scheme can result in some perplexing effects when you make an upgrade. For example, when you plug in a second parallel port, its address may occur earlier in the sequence than the port you already have installed. The new port will then pre-empt LPT1 and take that designation itself. As a result, the printer or other device you had connected to the first port won't respond like it used to after you add the upgrade. Your software will still send data out LPT1, but it will go to the new port and ignore the old one (which has become LPT2).

The practical outcome of this switch-hitting of ports is that you may think you've ruined your PC by upgrading it when, in fact, all is well. You just have to let your software know the changes that you've made to your system. Either reinstall your software and advise it of your revised port assignments or rearrange the cables on the back of your PC to match the new port nomenclature.

Worse than this name-changing confusion is when you err in configuring your new ports by inadvertently assigning two ports the same addresses. As a result, one, the other, or neither port may work. In this case, you'll have to change the hardware settings on one of the ports so that each port has its own unique address.

OS/2 uses different addresses for its serial ports beyond the first two. In addition, it will accommodate up to eight serial ports. If you plan on using a port upgrade with OS/2, make sure that it will respond to the addresses used by that operating system. Table 13.1 summarizes the addresses used by OS/2 ports.

Table 13.1 Input/Output Port Assignments for OS/2 Serial Ports

OS/2 Port Name	I/O Port Address (Hex)
Serial 1	03F8
Serial 2	02F8
Serial 3	3220
Serial 4	3228
Serial 5	4220
Serial 6	5228
Serial 7	5220
Serial 8	5228

Most serial ports require that you assign an interrupt for them to work properly. Although some port upgrade boards automatically select the interrupt to use based on the port address you designate, others make interrupt assignment an additional step, seemingly just to confuse you. The serial port assigned to COM1 normally should be given hardware Interrupt Request (IRQ) 4. Serial port COM2 normally uses IRQ3. COM3 shares IRQ4 with COM1, and COM4 shares IRQ3 with COM2. Parallel port interrupts are usually not assignable.

One of the biggest problems you'll face when you want to add another port or two is an identity crisis. Older boards may be reluctant to take on higher port assignment numbers. Many serial port boards allow you to assign their serial ports only as COM1 or COM2. With such a board, you won't be able to get more than two ports to work in your system no matter how many boards you add or how many serial ports are already installed in your PC. Be sure that the serial ports on any upgrade board you buy can be assigned as COM3 or COM4 as well as COM1 and COM2. If you plan on using OS/2, you'll need even greater flexibility.

When assigning names to serial ports, don't forget that internal modems have their own, embedded serial ports that take an address like any other serial port. If you have an internal modem, one fewer port address will be available for your upgrade. The modem's serial port address may also conflict with the address of other ports, so you'll need to know the value that's assigned to it.

Most serial ports require that you assign an interrupt for them to work properly.

Parallel port interrupts are usually not assignable.

If you have an internal modem, one fewer port address will be available for your upgrade.

You'll also want to study up on your system unit because many PCs now have at least one serial and one parallel port installed on their motherboards. Be sure you know which ports are already installed, what addresses they use, and how to reassign their port addresses (or how to switch off the ports).

Serial and Parallel Port Connectors

If you already have something to plug into the port, you'll want to be sure the connectors match.

A seemingly trivial concern with important implications is the connector used by your port upgrades. If you already have something to plug into the port, you'll want to be sure the connectors match. If they don't, you'll need to get the appropriate adapters.

With serial ports, two styles of connector are popular, 9-pin and 25-pin male D-shells. The original PC used the 25-pin scheme. Because the AT put a parallel and serial port on the same expansion board that was limited in size by the original design of PC option retaining brackets (the metal strip on the back of each expansion board), there was not enough room for a full 25-pin jack for each. The parallel port needed all 25 connections and couldn't be shrunk, so the serial port was trimmed to its essentials, nine pins. Port boards that offer a parallel and a serial port attached to the same retaining bracket use the AT scheme. PS/2s reverted back to the 25-pin serial-port scheme because their connectors were mounted on the rear panel of the machine rather than on the retaining bracket of an expansion board. Most port upgrade boards that offer a second serial port usually move the second serial port to a separate retaining bracket and give it a 25-pin jack.

The only difference between 9-pin and 25-pin jacks is that you might need an adapter to match certain peripherals to one or the other. Most mice, for example, use nine-pin connectors but come with adapters to mate them with 25-pin jacks. As long as you have matching cables or adapters, the style of jack used for a serial port does not matter. The two styles use the same signals and work the same with standard serial devices.

Parallel ports are standardized with 25-pin female D-shell connectors. Game ports, when offered by upgrade products, also follow a standard using female 15-pin D-shell connectors. To distinguish game ports from VGA outputs, which also use 15-pin D-shell connectors, look at the arrangement of pins. The pins on game ports are arranged in two rows, and the 15-pin connectors used by VGA adapters use three rows of pins.

Shopping for Serial/ Parallel Port Adapters

Unlike other products such as hard disks and display adapters that you might buy as upgrades, you'll find a glaring lack of brand names among port expansion products. The fierce competition has resulted in low prices—so low in fact that most brand name suppliers can't or won't compete. Most of the port products that you find will consequently be inexpensive, anonymous, and likely Oriental.

That's not to say that they are not very good. Port technology is rudimentary in comparison with today's latest Pentium-based PCs, so it doesn't take a bevy of rocket scientists with silicon slide rules to design the circuits or the latest surface-mount equipment to make the boards. Most port expansion products will work unerringly in most PCs.

Of course, you can still get a bad board, so you need to rely more on vendor support than for brand name products. Because you have no one else to turn to when something goes wrong, pick a vendor whom you trust and upon whom you can depend.

You also need to be sure that the port upgrade that you choose includes the features that you need, for example port addressability and bi-directional parallel ports. You'll want to select a vendor who can answer your questions about his product, deliver what you want, and accept it back if it does not meet your expectations and needs. If you're adding a new serial port, you'll want to be sure to get a 16550 UART on it so that your future communications capabilities won't be constrained.

The one exception to the no-name port board philosophy is the high-speed super serial port that can operate at 38,400 bits per second even when allowing for full DOS overhead. The boards, necessary for the highest speed of today's modems, are available only from a few manufacturers with well-known brand names. They also cost substantially more than the generic off-shore competition. That's the price you have to pay to get the best performance for your PC.

Most port expansion products will work unerringly is most PCs.

The typical port expansion board will be half the length of a standard expansion slot (there's so little circuitry that a lot of board space is not required), the height of an XT expansion slot, and will use an eight-bit bus interface connector. There's little need for a 16-bit interface because the ports themselves limit the transfer rate well below that which the eight-bit ISA bus can handle.

Most of these boards will be equipped as standard equipment with one parallel and one serial port. Some make a second serial port an inexpensive (say $10) option. The second-serial option kit buys you a another UART, a short length of cable, and a mounting bracket. You will inevitably need a second (third or even fourth) serial port, so the option is well worth the price.

> *Although you might not regard having a game port as a big advantage, it's certainly no disadvantage.*

Some port boards also include a game port for connecting a joystick. Although you might not regard having a game port as a big advantage, it's certainly no disadvantage. Consider it a free bonus.

Multifunction boards that combine memory and ports are still available for some kinds of PCs. Some of these are even backed with name brands. A multifunction board that uses an eight-bit bus connection can be a worthwhile addition to a PC or XT if you can also use the memory expansion. Similarly, a 16-bit card will benefit a six- or eight-megahertz AT. However, avoid adding such memory boards to faster, most powerful computers (any machine rated at 12 megahertz or faster) because such a board can slow overall system performance on memory operations.

Serial/Parallel Port Installation

The installation process for serial and parallel port upgrades is little more than plugging a board into your PC. The only tricky part is preparing the adapter board before you slide it into an expansion slot. After that you only need to worry about simple mechanics. You face no software obstacles or setup headaches. Your system takes care of those details automatically.

Adapter Preparation

The first thing to do when you're considering port expansion—even before you buy a board—is to make a list of the port locations used by your existing ports to determine available port address assignments and whether adding another port is even feasible. You have several options in determining the ports already installed in your computer. First, check your system's documentation and that included with all the expansion boards installed inside your PC. These should list the ports already provided (and thus the addresses used) by your PC. You can also use commercial system-reporting software such as *Check It, InfoSpotter,* or *System Sleuth* to determine what port addresses your system already uses and which are available. Be wary, however. These products are not infallible. Sometimes, they make mistakes and miss ports or incorrectly identify them. Another tool that has the advantage of being free is the DEBUG program that's typically included with DOS. DEBUG allows you to check what's stored in your system's memory including the BIOS data area.

To determine what ports are used using DEBUG, first run the DEBUG program. After it loads, it will present you with a hyphen as a prompt. It may not look like much, but that hyphen is the key to a powerful tool. To use it, type the following command at that DEBUG hyphen prompt:

```
D 40:0
```

This tells DEBUG to display the contents of the 40th paragraph of memory (if you count hexadecimally like your PC does). In other words, you are asking to see the contents of your system's memory at absolute address 400(Hex), the part of the BIOS data area where the various port assignments are stored. After you type the command, you should see a block of numbers displayed on your screen, similar to this:

```
-d 40:0
0040:0000   F8 03 F8 02 00 00 00 00-78 03 00 00 00 00 00 00    ........x.......
0040:0010   2D 44 04 80 02 00 00 80-00 00 28 00 28 00 34 05    -D........(.(.4.
0040:0020   30 0B 3A 27 30 0B 0D 1C-06 21 64 20 65 12 67 22    0.:'0....!d e.g"
0040:0030   08 0E 62 30 75 16 67 22-0D 1C 64 20 20 39 00 80    ..b0u.g"..d  9..
0040:0040   AB 00 C0 00 00 00 01 03-02 03 50 00 00 10 00 00    ..........P.....
0040:0050   00 18 00 00 00 00 00 00-00 00 00 00 00 00 00 00    ...............
0040:0060   07 06 00 D4 03 29 30 00-00 00 00 00 50 00 0F 00    .....)0.....P...
0040:0070   00 00 00 00 00 00 00 00-14 14 14 14 01 01 01 01    ...............
```

Your concern is the top line that shows the first paragraph—16 bytes or 10(Hex) bytes—of memory at location 400(Hex). The numbers on the far left are sign posts to tell you where you are in memory. The block of two-digit numbers left of the central hyphen on the first line are eight bytes used for storing the addresses used by serial port assignments, the eight bytes on the right hold the parallel port assignments.

Each port assignment is split among two numbers (actually byte values), the two bytes given in reverse order according to the byte arrangement convention of Intel Corporation. The first pair of numbers is COM1; the second pair COM2; and so on. An assignment of 0000 indicates that no port of that number is present. In the preceding example, two serial ports are assigned, COM1 at 03F8 and COM2 at 02F8, and one parallel port, LPT1 at 0378. The last two byte entries in the parallel port section are irrelevant because only three such ports are allowed. Ignore any numbers you find there.

In most cases, you can switch off the ports that conflict with existing ports.

Rather than relying exclusively on any one of the three methods of port determination—documentation, commercial software, and DOS DEBUG—the best strategy is to use all three to cross-check one another. Generally, the most reliable is DEBUG because it does no interpretation of the facts that might result in an erroneous display.

When you know how many ports you actually have assigned, you can calculate how many you can add. Choose a port expansion product that matches or exceeds your needs. In most cases, you can switch off the ports that conflict with existing ports, either on your system board (for ports originating there) or on your port expansion board (for the ports it provides).

Next is the tough part, finding the one right port board for your needs. You'll end up checking magazine ads, perhaps even visiting your dealer. When you order, be sure that you let the vendor know how many ports you want to add and what locations you have available for those ports. If you need a port at COM3, let the vendor know. Make sure that the parallel ports you get are truly bidirectional and that each serial port is equipped with at least a 16450 UART chip.

Board Installation

When you get your new port board, your first job is to configure it to match your system, to fold the ports it provides around the ones your PC has installed. When you know the addresses that your PC already uses for its ports, you can assign non-conflicting addresses to your new port adapter board. In most cases, you will have to set DIP switches or jumpers on the board to assign its addresses. Because every port adapter board uses a different array of switches and jumpers to make its settings, no general directions apply to selecting the right switch and jumper positions. Check the documentation accompanying the board for the proper switch and jumper settings.

Check the documentation accompanying the board for the proper switch and jumper settings.

If you're adding more than the one parallel and one serial port that's available on most port upgrade boards, you'll need to do a bit more preparation. A second serial port may require that you install an additional UART (which you should order with the board). Fortunately, the chip installation process is easy. A UART is installed like any other integrated circuit. First, prepare the leads (legs) of the chip so that they are at right angles to the body of the chip and so that they fit properly into the chips socket. Hold the chip long-ways between your fingers and press the whole row of pins on one side of the chip down against a smooth, flat surface such as a desktop until the leads form a 90-degree angle with the body of the chip. When the pins are straight, align the chip over the socket that's waiting for it. You must be sure to properly orient the chip, lining up the notch that appears on one edge of the chip with corresponding notch in its socket. Finally, press the chip into its socket (see fig. 13.1). Double-check your work and double-check to ensure that it is oriented properly and that none of the chip's pins have folded underneath the chip or have splayed outward from the socket.

Figure 13.1
Prepare the board before you plug it into your PC by sliding the chip into the vacant slot on the board. First straighten the pins of the chip (inset), ensure that the notch on the chip and socket line up, and then push in the chip.

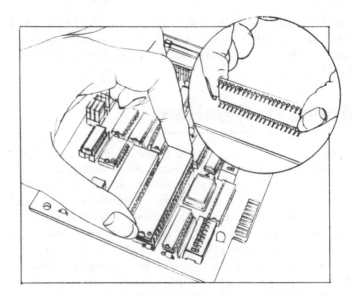

Most port boards only have room for two connectors on their retaining brackets. When you add more than one serial port from a single board or if you have a game port on the board, you'll have to attach the supernumerary jacks to the upgrade board using short cables that should be supplied with the board. The second serial port will likely use a 25-pin jack, and the game port will use a 15-pin jack, each tethered to a short ribbon cable.

To hold these jacks in most PCs, you'll need to mount them on an additional retaining bracket (see fig. 13.2). Sometimes, they are supplied already installed in a bracket. Otherwise, you may have to install them in a bracket yourself. If the jacks and bracket are delivered as separate pieces, put them together by first removing the two screws and nuts at the outer ends of each jack, then push the jack through the matching hole in the retaining bracket, and finally reinsert the hardware you removed to hold the jack securely in place. Some PCs have cut-outs on their rear panels to accept these extra jacks directly. You can save an expansion slot if you use these cut-outs instead of an additional retaining bracket. If you plan to make use of these cutouts, first remove the hardware from the extra port connectors and any small blank panels blocking the cutouts now—but don't yet install the jacks in the cutouts.

As with the UART chip, proper orientation is important.

Before you install the port upgrade board in your PC, attach the extra serial and game port connector cables to it. As with the UART chip, proper orientation is important. The side of the cable with a red (or blue) stripe should be aligned with pin one of the header that the connector plugs into on the upgrade board. Pin one is usually identified by a small silk-screened number on the board.

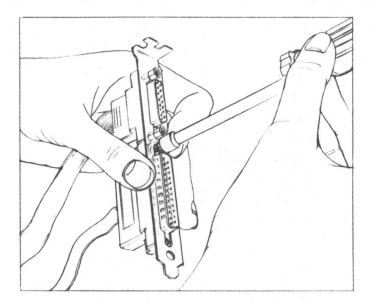

Figure 13.2.
You'll also have to install extra port connectors in a retaining bracket. Slide the connectors through the rear of the bracket and then screw the connectors in from the front. A nutdriver is the best tool.

When the cables are attached, slide the board into any vacant expansion slot in your PC and screw it in place. Any slot will do in most cases (see fig. 13.3). Because port adapters use eight-bit interfaces, you can use 8- or 16-bit expansion slots. Because most port adapters are short cards, you can take advantage of the abbreviated slots behind your disk drives. After you slide the board into the slot of your choice, locate a nearby slot to use for the optional second retaining bracket for the extra port jacks. Remove the retaining bracket from this slot. Finally, install the second port adapter retaining bracket in this slot. If you've opted to install the extra jacks in rear- panel cut-outs, now is the time to do so. Use the hardware you removed from the jacks earlier.

When you've screwed everything in and organized the cables, you've finished the hardware part of your upgrade (see figs. 13.4 and 13.5). Check your work by running DEBUG again to see your new address assignments.

Before you use your new ports, you'll want to verify that you haven't changed the names of any of your old ones. Try using your already-installed peripherals and verify that they work like they used to. If not, reinstall your software—each and every program you normally use that sends something out either a parallel or serial port—to reflect the new port designations or rearrange the peripheral cables you've plugged into the various ports on your PC.

Figure 13.3
If your PC has cut-outs on its rear panel, use them instead of wasting a slot for the extra port connectors. Slide the connectors through the chassis from the inside and then screw in the hardware from the outside.

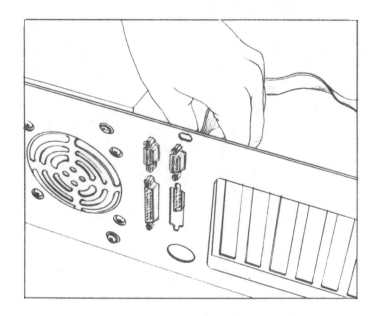

Figure 13.4
Before you slide the port adapter board into an expansion slot, plug the cables from the external connectors into it. Be sure to observe polarity.

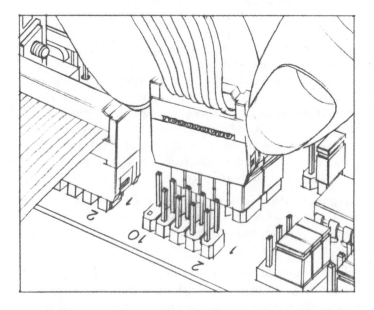

SCSI is potentially the fastest means of connecting peripherals to your PC.

SCSI

SCSI has been tomorrow's interface for about as long as anyone can remember. Back in the 80s it was hailed for its speed; in the early 90s, it was shunned as a headache. Today, it is revered because of its

great speed. That reverence is entirely justified. SCSI is potentially
the fastest means of connecting peripherals to your PC.

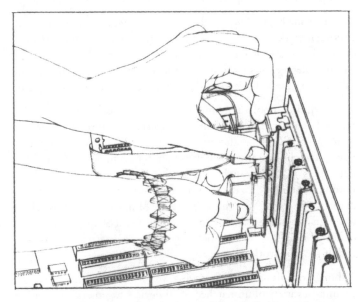

Figure 13.5
Slide the port adapter
board into a vacant
slot. Then slide the
retaining bracket
with the external
connectors into the
adjacent slot. Screw
both the port adapter
and the extra
retaining bracket into
place.

SCSI is more than a simple port. Beyond merely linking a device to
your PC, SCSI functions more like an expansion bus. A single SCSI
host adapter can link up to seven devices to your PC, so even a computer with a limited number of expansion slots could accommodate
more peripherals than would be prudent. In fact, for some Apple
Macintosh computers, SCSI is the only expansion bus available.

But SCSI goes beyond that. Not just a bus, SCSI is an entire
expansion system with a complete protocol and language of its own.
It takes advantage of advanced features like bus mastering and can
even disconnect itself from your PC and manage its own transfers
entirely independently. In linking together peripherals, SCSI's
performance potentials outclass everything but local bus—and then
it can come close to straining even them. Best of all, it has progressed
from assured headache to a connection scheme potentially easier to
link up than any other. Already, SCSI hard disks can be easier to link
to your PC than disks using any other interface. SCSI promises to do
the same for whatever you want to connect to your PC.

Perhaps the reason SCSI is one of the most important upgrades for
your PC is that SCSI is unavoidable. If you want to connect many of
the state-of-the-art peripherals to your PC, you'll probably *have* to
use SCSI connection. Magneto-optical disk drives, for example,
require the use of a SCSI interface. SCSI is part of the ISO standard
for MO drives. Although you can find CD ROM players with

*For some Apple
Macintosh comput-
ers, SCSI is the
only expansion bus
available.*

*Not just a bus,
SCSI is an entire
expansion system
with a complete
protocol and
language of its
own.*

*In linking together
peripherals, SCSI's
performance
potentials outclass
everything but
local bus*

proprietary interfaces, the only standard connection scheme by better drives is SCSI. The bottom line is that if your PC does not have a SCSI port, it isn't equipped for the future—or even for the present.

In years gone by, the big bugaboo with SCSI was that the details of making it work had not been refined to the point that any mixture of peripherals attached to a single host adapter will plug-and-play. To some degree, that's still true. Some SCSI devices get along about as well as a squad of five-year-olds equipped with a single candy bar.

This enduring problem has many sides. When SCSI was first released, it allowed manufacturers to select the features to implement. All SCSI devices did not support all SCSI features, and those that did might take their own direction in how to do it. Worse, the developers of SCSI thought of it as a hardware standard and did nothing to standardize the software needed to control the various devices connected through the interface. Although SCSI ensured that signals could get from a computer host to a SCSI peripheral, the hardware-only standard did nothing to get the device at the other end of the wire working.

Although this situation is improving, you'll still find randomly chaining a variety of unmatched SCSI devices together an invitation to disaster. You need to check the compatibility of the various SCSI devices you want to connect with today's hardware and software standards. If you can make a match, you'll be able to link all your equipment together without a hitch.

If you can't make a match, however, you don't have to give up on SCSI. (And probably you can't. It may be the only expansion system available with the peripheral you want to install.) Instead, give up SCSI as an idea interface and practice practical SCSI. Slide a second SCSI host adapter into your PC to match the equipment that doesn't follow the standard used by the first. Of course, to do this, you'll have to make sure that you can install multiple SCSI host adapters in your PC. Usually, you will have to relocate the SCSI BIOS code on some of the adapters to avoid conflicts. If you have several unmatched SCSI products, you'll find that two SCSI host adapters can be better than one.

If you're only connecting one SCSI device to your PC, you probably won't have to worry about the esoteria of the connection. You can remove all doubt when you get a new SCSI product by opting to buy a matching host adapter at the same time. Shift the decision and potential errors to someone who should know better—the vendor selling you on SCSI—someone to whom you can return the whole mess if something goes awry.

The bottom line is that if your PC does not have a SCSI port, it isn't equipped for the future—or even for the present.

If you have several unmatched SCSI products, you'll find that two SCSI host adapters can be better than one.

The mechanical aspects of SCSI are quite simple. A SCSI system consists of four essential parts. First is the aforementioned SCSI host adapter, which plugs into an expansion slot inside your PC and translates the signals on your PC's expansion bus into commands that can travel across the SCSI connection.

The second essential part of a SCSI system is a SCSI device. It can be a hard disk, CD ROM player, or any of a multitude of other peripherals that rely on a SCSI connection. Up to seven SCSI devices of any type can be connected together to a single SCSI host adapter. In theory, you should be able to mix hard disks, tape drives, CD ROMs, and scanners all on one SCSI connection. The reality of the situation isn't quite so rosy.

You also need a *SCSI cable* to link all the devices to the host adapter and software to link the SCSI system to your PC. Finally, you need *SCSI driver software* to match your host adapter and SCSI devices with your PC. Often, this software comes in two parts: a software driver that loads through your system's CONFIG.SYS file and BIOS code that's built into ROM chips on the SCSI host adapter.

Most of the time, SCSI devices for the PC market are sold as complete kits that include the drive, the host adapter, and the cable. Some vendors sell the various pieces separately, catering to people who want to design their own systems or add a second (third, fourth, whatever) device to the SCSI connection they already have. Avoid surprises and be sure that you get everything you need—the drive player, host adapter, cable, and software—when you order.

Standards

SCSI is an evolving standard. That's good because it means that SCSI is steadily getting better and easier to manage. But that also means that there is more than one SCSI. Worse, when a new version of SCSI is announced, all the products using the old version don't automatically disappear. They linger on the market, which means you can't tell which version of SCSI is used by a given product without scrutinizing the specification sheet. Fortunately, there are only two major SCSI incarnations, and the newer one is backwardly compatible with the old.

The two principal flavors of SCSI are ordinary SCSI and SCSI-2. The important difference between the two is that SCSI-2 is newer, bigger, better, faster, and more standardized. The original SCSI was designed with an eight-bit data path and a maximum speed of 10 megahertz, which calculates to a theoretical 10 megabyte-per-second

In theory, you should be able to mix hard disks, tape drives, CD ROMs, and scanners all on one SCSI connection.

There are only two major SCSI incarnations, and the newer one is backwardly compatible with the old.

SCSI-2 is newer, bigger, better, faster, and more standardized.

throughput. SCSI-2 is a superset of the original specification that allows designers to optionally incorporate data paths as wide as 32 bits and speeds up to 20 megahertz. A SCSI-2 system that takes advantage of all these possibilities might possibly move information as quickly as 80 megabytes per second. More importantly, SCSI- 2 makes more of the features of the SCSI connection mandatory— meaning that you should have fewer problems when connecting up SCSI-2 components.

As this is written, SCSI-2 products are entering the upgrade market in force. For example, hard disks using SCSI-2 have been available for nearly two years. Just being SCSI-2 doesn't guarantee that a product takes advantage of all the high- speed innovations of the standard. A device can be legitimately called "SCSI-2" if it matches the entire range of software commands that are mandatory under the new specification. The higher performance SCSI options are specifically declared. *Fast SCSI* takes advantage of the higher clock speeds permitted under the new SCSI standard. Fast SCSI means anything faster than the original 5MHz clock—either a 10MHz or 20MHz clock speed. *Wide SCSI* takes advantage of the broader data paths the new standard permits. Again, Wide SCSI means anything wider than the original 8-bit data path, either 16-bit or 32-bit.

You can attach SCSI-2 drives to ordinary SCSI host adapter, but you won't realize all of their features or performance. Similarly, an ordinary SCSI drive will work with when connected SCSI-2 host adapter. In either case, you can expect getting the system to work to be no easier or harder than working with a plain SCSI system.

Host Adapters

A slow host adapter can be a roadblock to the performance of a fast hard disk or CD-ROM player.

You add SCSI to your PC using a *SCSI host adapter*, which is similar to a disk or tape controller but is much more complex. In the past (and even now in many cases), SCSI has not been an entirely satisfactory interface for PC hard disks because it was designed as a universal interface, one that serves not only different computer architectures but also operating systems and a variety of peripherals, from hard disks to scanners. The SCSI host adapter must match the signals designed for its universal bus to the particular requirements of the PC bus and DOS. The latter is the more challenging because SCSI structures information in the form of blocks, and DOS thinks in terms of clusters. Early SCSI host adapters choked on the conversion process, and system throughput suffered. In the few years, however, the efficiency of SCSI systems has improved immeasurably, although old, laggardly host adapters may turn up occasionally.

Because the host adapter can so severely limit the performance of a SCSI system, the choice of this adapter is as critical as your choice of hard disk or other peripheral you want to connect to it. A slow host adapter can be a roadblock to the performance of a fast hard disk or CD-ROM player. SCSI host adapters can vary widely in a manufacturer's line. For example, Adaptec offers low-performance host adapters, the 1520 series, and high-performance models, the 1540 series. The latter transfers data about twice as fast as the former, and you'll see the difference in your PC.

Besides performance issues, your choice of SCSI host adapter will determine whether and how any hard disk you connect to it can boot your PC. Some SCSI host adapters have a built-in BIOS that enables them to duplicate all the functions of a conventional hard disk controller. This feature, called *WD1002* emulation, indicates that the host adapter can mimic the function of the ST506 disk controller used in IBM's original AT. With WD1002, your SCSI hard disk operates exactly like an old-fashioned hard disk, eliminating compatibility worries.

The BIOS on your SCSI host adapter also determines your flexibility in assigning device identifications and priorities to the peripherals you attach to it. Most host adapters with WD1002 emulation demand that you identify your first hard disk—the boot drive—as SCSI device 0. The on-board SCSI BIOS may also include advanced features, such as firmware to low level format your hard disk. (See Chapter 7, "Hard Disks," for instructions for using such features.)

All this variety means that when it comes to SCSI host adapters, you'll want to shop carefully.

With WD1002, your SCSI hard disk operates exactly like an old-fashioned hard disk, eliminating compatibility worries.

Installation

The physical installation of a SCSI port requires advance preparation should you want the effort to be trouble-free. Before you link all of your SCSI devices together, you need to sort out the cabling, assign SCSI ID numbers to the various devices, adjust terminations, and set the options of your SCSI host adapter. Only after the prepatory work is done should you slide the host adapter into its slow and plug together your SCSI chain.

Cabling

The very nature of SCSI means that you'll have to worry about cables. After all, SCSI is a means of connecting peripherals to your PC. A cable is a vital part of that link.

SCSI cables come in two types—flat, ribbon cables for internal installation of SCSI devices and round, shielded cables for external devices. Internal cables usually use 50-pin connectors. Two systems of external cables are now used by SCSI devices. Most older SCSI systems, SCSI and SCSI-2, use 50-pin Amphenol-style connectors where space permits. Where space is limited, many manufacturers opt instead for 25-pin D-shells similar to those used by parallel ports. The 50-pin style of connector is normally preferred because it gives each active SCSI wire its own ground return, and a 25-pin connector is insufficient for all the needed signals together with their grounds. Because of space considerations, a number of makers are shifting to new, miniaturized SCSI connectors that include all 50 pins of signals. Figure 13.6 shows several types of connectors.

Figure 13.6
Three different SCSI connectors.

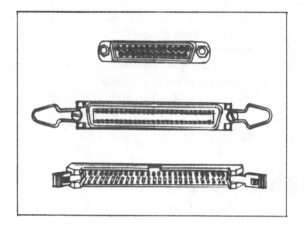

Wide SCSI naturally requires more connections for its broader data path, and only the newer miniaturized connectors provide what's needed.

There's another ramification to these connector types that will be important with more advanced systems. Most of today's SCSI devices use *single-ended signals*, which simply means that all the signals can share a common ground. SCSI also allows for *differential signals* that carry information as the difference between two wires. By definition, differential signals require two wires, so a common ground won't work properly with them. Differential signals have greater resistance to noise than to single-ended signals, so their application will certainly become more widespread as SCSI speeds increase.

New SCSI devices and host adapters are likely to use miniaturized SCSI connectors. These plugs and jacks simple pack more connections into less space so that a full 50-pin connector is physically smaller than a 25-pin D-shell. Wide SCSI naturally requires more connections for its broader data path, and only the newer miniaturized connectors provide what's needed. Wide SCSI requires that all devices in the SCSI chain support all of its signals; therefore all will need wide SCSI if you want to use just on wide SCSI device.

From a function viewpoint, there's no difference between full-size and miniaturized SCSI connectors. They work exactly the same. The little plugs and jacks just fit into tighter confines. Your only worry is making sure that your SCSI cables have the proper connectors on each end to match your SCSI devices.

Wiring together SCSI internal SCSI devices usually requires a single cable with several connectors on it. Each device plugs into one of the connectors. All connectors have exactly the same signals, so it doesn't matter which device you put where in the chain—with one important exception. In most installations, your SCSI host adapter must be at one end of the cable, and another device must be at the other end of the cable. Subsequent devices then can be plugged into any available connector. If you have a single internal SCSI device, it must be plugged into the end of the cable opposite from the host adapter. Internal SCSI devices have only one SCSI connector, so which connector to use is a straightforward choice.

Internal SCSI connectors are supposed to be keyed by plastic tabs on one edge of the plugs matched by cut-outs on one edge of the jacks so that you can't plug them in backwards (see fig. 13.7). If a plug doesn't seem to fit into its jack, try reversing the plug.

Some internal SCSI plugs lack these keys. To ensure yourself that an internal SCSI plug is not in backwards, look for the red or blue stripe on the edge of the SCSI cable. As with other computer wiring systems, the stripe indicates the wire in the cable that leads to pin one on the connectors. Check for the pin one connector on the SCSI jack by looking for the number "1" stenciled onto the circuit board. (You might see a "2" instead of a "1." It indicates the same end— one end of the connector has the low numbers; the other end has the high numbers.)

External SCSI devices are daisy-chained together (see fig. 13.8). That is, each SCSI device has two physical connectors on it. You run the SCSI cable from the host adapter to one of the SCSI connectors on the first device you want to connect. It doesn't matter which of the two connectors on the SCSI device you attach to. Functionally, they are both the same. If you want to connect more than one external

SCSI device to a single host adapter, you attach another cable to the second connector on the first device and run the cable to one of the two connectors on the second device. For three or more SCSI devices, you continue this procedure, running a new SCSI cable from device to device, chaining them all together. You'll need one cable for every device in your external SCSI chain.

Figure 13.7
An internal SCSI connector cable.

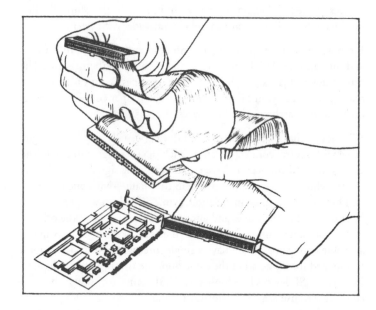

Figure 13.8
Daisy-chaining external SCSI devices.

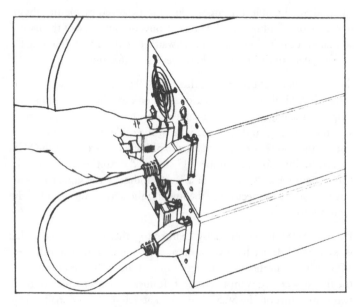

External SCSI connectors are D-shaped. You must orient the plug properly to fit into a jack. Don't force external SCSI connectors into place. If the connector does slide smoothly in, turn it around and try again.

Because all devices in an external SCSI chain are linked in series, breaking the chain can have deleterious effects on data transfer. Obviously, any device in the chain on the other side of the break from the host adapter won't be able to exchange information with the host adapter. Worse, because of the high-speed of the SCSI connection, a single break can disrupt signals throughout the system, so *all* of the devices on both sides of the break may stop working properly. Consequently, it is mandatory to ensure that all SCSI connectors are tightly in place.

> *Don't force external SCSI connectors into place.*

Old-style 50-pin SCSI connectors have locking wires to ensure that your plugs don't pull out of their jacks. After you plug one of these connectors together, lock the wires by squeezing them toward the connector shell. Old-style 25-pin SCSI connectors must be screwed together. New, miniaturized SCSI connectors have latches that automatically snap into place to lock connectors together. However, you'll have to release these latches to *remove* a SCSI connector. Once you know the secret, it's easy to do. Just squeeze into the connector shell the tabs on the two short sides of the connector. The connector will unlatch, and you should be able to easily pull it out.

Terminations

After you've wired your SCSI devices together, you still have more work ahead of you. To prevent spurious signals bouncing back and forth across the SCSI cable chain, the SCSI standard requires that you properly terminate the entire SCSI system. A termination is a bank of resistors that absorb the excess signals on the SCSI line and prevent them from reflecting back across the cable.

> *The SCSI standard requires that you properly terminate the entire SCSI system.*

According to the SCSI specification, the first and last device in a SCSI chain must be terminated. The first device is almost always the SCSI host adapter in your PC. The last device is the one that has a cable attached to only one of its two SCSI connectors.

The only time your host adapter might not be at the end of a SCSI chain is when you install internal and external SCSI devices. This sort of connection typically puts the host adapter in the middle of the chain so that the internal drive and not the host adapter should be terminated.

SCSI products are terminated in a variety of ways. The three most popular are internally with resistor packs, externally with dummy termination plugs, and using switches.

Resistor packs are components attached directly to circuit boards. Most PC-based SCSI host adapters come with termination resistors already installed. You can identify them as being three identical components near the SCSI connector about an inch long and one-quarter to three-eights an inch high and hardly an eighth of an inch thick. Most commonly, they are red, yellow, or black and shiny.

Typically, these terminator resistors are removable—you can grab hold of one and pull it off the expansion board (see fig. 13.9). There's normally no need to do that in the case of your SCSI host adapter because all three resistor packs need to be there except when you combine internal and external SCSI drives in a single chain.

Figure 13.9

Removing a termination resistor from a SCSI host adaptor.

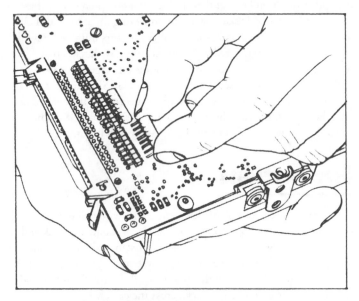

You may also find these terminators on SCSI devices themselves. You're most likely to find them on an internal drive. Some external SCSI devices rely on the terminators on the drive inside their cases, requiring you to take apart the device to access the terminators.

External SCSI terminators are plugs that often look like short extensions to the SCSI jacks on the back of SCSI devices. One end of the terminator plugs into one of the jacks on your SCSI device, and the other end of the dummy plug yields another jack that could be attached to another SCSI cable (see fig. 13.10). Some external terminators lack the second jack on the back. Generally, the absence

of a second connector is no problem because the dummy plug
should only be attached to the last device in the SCSI chain, the
device that has an extra unused SCSI jack.

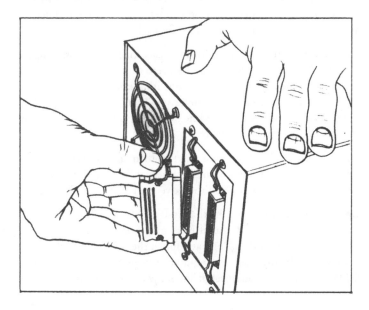

Figure 13.10
An external termina-
tion plug.

Switches, the third variety of termination, may be found on external
and internal drives. Sometimes, a single switch handles the entire
termination, but occasionally a SCSI drive will have three banks of
DIP switches that all must be flipped to the same position to select
whether the termination is active. These switches are sometimes
found on the SCSI drive or on the case of an external unit.

*In most cases, you
should ensure that
only one SCSI
device attached to
a host adapter
uses a terminator.*

Because the rule is that the first and last device in a SCSI chain needs
to be terminated, in most cases you should ensure that only one
SCSI device attached to a host adapter uses a terminator. Remove or
switch off the terminators on all other devices except the last one in
the chain. The termination on the host adapter takes care of the first
device in the chain.

Some SCSI devices give you the option of supplying SCSI termination power. The general rule is that no more than five devices in a
SCSI chain should supply termination power. Generally, two
should—the first and last devices in the chain. With other devices,
you should ensure that termination power is switched off.

*Every SCSI device
connected in a
chain must have its
own, unambiguous
SCSI ID number.*

Identification

Because up to seven SCSI devices can be attached identically to a single chain, your system needs some method of distinguishing which device is which—like a name for each link in the chain.

Never assign the same SCSI ID number to two or more devices in the same SCSI chain.

In the SCSI system, this identification is carried out by assigning each SCSI device a SCSI ID number, zero to six (seven is usually reserved for the host adapter). The one important rule is that every SCSI device connected in a chain have its own, unambiguous SCSI ID number. Never assign the same SCSI ID number to two or more devices in the same SCSI chain.

Most external SCSI devices are assigned their ID number by a switch on the rear panel of the equipment. Internal SCSI devices may have several jumpers or a switch on the drive itself that sets SCSI ID.

Some software drivers require that your CD ROM player have a particular SCSI ID set. Other drivers are more accommodating, accepting any SCSI ID as long as you tell the software which you want to use. In any case, you should check the SCSI ID of your CD ROM player when you install it should you need the number for future use.

If the driver software that comes with your CD ROM player gives you a choice of SCSI ID numbers, you can give it any number when it is the only SCSI device connected to your system. However, higher numbered SCSI devices have greater priority.

Often, SCSI hard disk drives are assigned a SCSI ID of six to make them the most important device connected to the system. Some SCSI host adapters, however, require any device that's connected to the SCSI chain that needs to boot the computer host have a SCSI ID of zero. Generally, a CD ROM player is not a high-priority device, so a lower number is appropriate for it, providing that number is not pre-empted by a hard disk drive.

Host Adapter Configuration

As with other ports, you have to assign system resources to a SCSI port. Specifically, you must adjust your SCSI host adapter for the memory addresses, DMA channel, and interrupts that it will need.

If your SCSI board has an on-board BIOS, you'll need to assign a base address to it. The primary address for hard disk BIOS code is

C8000(Hex). If your PC already has a hard disk installed (including an IDE or AT interface hard disk), you cannot use this value. Choose an alternate address, D8000(Hex) is preferred. If, however, your SCSI host adapter will run the first or only hard disk in your PC, choose the C8000 (Hex) value.

Most SCSI ports require that you assign them a block of port addresses. Again, these should not interfere with the assignments of other peripherals in your PC. Most SCSI boards default to a port address of 330(Hex). Generally, this will work *except* if you have a MIDI board in your PC. Most MIDI boards also prefer the 330(Hex) value. You'll need to alter one or the other assignment.

SCSI host adapters usually will require interrupt and DMA channel assignments for the SCSI port. Generally, most will default to interrupt 11 and DMA channel 5 in ISA or better systems. Change these values only to avoid conflicts.

If your SCSI host adapter also has a floppy disk section, you'll probably find a jumper to enable or defeat its floppy circuitry. Enable it if you plan to connect a floppy disk drive to your host adapter. You may also have to select an interrupt, DMA channel, and base address for the floppy disk drive. In most cases, the best values to use are interrupt 6, DMA channel 2, and I/O port base address 1F0(Hex).

If your SCSI host adapter allows the selection of SCSI parity, switch it on. SCSI auto sense is best left off for most PC installations. Adjust other SCSI host adapter options to suit the needs of your PC.

SCSI auto sense is best left off for most PC installations.

When you've taken care of the connection details, you're read to try out your SCSI device. If it came or its host adapter came with diagnostic software, check everything out. If you've paid attention to all the details, your SCSI system should work right off and deliver excellent performance with a wide range of peripherals.

14

Modems and Other Connections

M oving information is one of the most important functions of a PC—either sharing what you have with others or acquiring it from them for your own purposes. A direct electrical connection is the most efficient way to share data between PCs. Modems span distances. Networks span multiple PCs. In between are links coupling paired PCs and printers. All of these can be an effective means of making your data more useful.

Sneakernet is what the cognoscenti call the most primitive means of moving files from one PC to another. A play of words on the Ethernet local area network system, Sneakernet implies shuffling information from one computer to another with quick, jogs between PCs with floppy disks clutched in your hands. Although such foot-mode networking may benefit you with a good daily workout, it won't do much for office productivity, efficiency, or your shins.

With a simple system upgrade, you can run circles around Sneakernet whether you need to connect two PCs or a dozen, in the next room or on the next continent. Instead of plugging around the office in oxfords or pumps, the better solution is to plug-in, connecting your PCs together with a cable and transferring your files electronically. Add a modem, and your PC can reach out and touch bulletin boards and databases around the world. If you have more than two PCs, you can build a simple peer-to-peer network almost as easily as plugging in your telephone.

A direct electrical connection is the most efficient way to share data between PCs.

If you have more than two PCs, you can build a simple peer-to-peer network almost as easily as plugging in your telephone.

The electrical connection between PCs makes sense for several reasons. After a field trip to the hinterlands, your work may be locked on the hard disk of your floppyless notebook PC. You may have two PCs with floppies of incompatible formats, 5.25-inch disks on one, and 3.5-inch disks on the other; you may want the convenience of sharing files between your system and that of a coworker without the hassle of handing around floppy disks; or you may want the absolute security that comes with keeping important files in two places at the same time. You can quickly back your PC up onto another PC through a hard-wire connection and then never worry again about disk crashes, exploding system units, or thieves with a penchant for PCs.

You're probably familiar with the words used to describe the big business method of making hardware links between PCs—the *local area network* or LAN. Those words inspire fear in many individual PC users, and rightly so. A network can be a true web, tangled beyond mortal comprehension. A full-fledged network is often so complex that most businesses opt to hire experts dedicated to overseeing their network operations, the network managers. Then they hire more experts to figure out what the first few had in mind. All the while, the experts pay other experts to install and test their networks for them.

Should your aims be more modest, however, you can forego the complications of a real network while still circumventing Sneakernet. If, instead of planning to tie together all of the computers in the world, you link together just two PCs, the job becomes plugging in a cable, one end in each PC. The installation can be a breeze. A modem is hardly more difficult to plug into a PC. A peer-to-peer network can be easier than you think (and fear). Any of these connection systems can be easy no matter how far you want to stretch the wires, whether you just plop your laptop atop your desktop machine to move a file, or link computers in two different offices, continents, or galaxies.

Modems

You cannot let your PC and telephone line directly conspire together without a modem to bridge them.

To extend the reach of your PC from its serial ports to link to any other computer in the world through the dial-up telephone network, you absolutely need a modem. More than a matter of manifesto or electrical necessity, it's the law. You cannot let your PC and telephone line directly conspire together without a modem to bridge them.

Although the need for a modem is foregone after you decide on a dial-up telephone link, your choice of modem is hardly a simple decision. In addition to manufacturers and models, you have to pick a standard to follow. Where once all was orderly, and the decision was easy—you had but two choices and both of those dictated by the iron hand of Mother Bell—today, the selection of modem standards is wider than that of long distance carriers.

Distinguishing this surfeit of standards is an alphabet soup of acronyms, an assortment of speeds, and more features than Detroit can list as options on the sticker of the latest highway hog. Today, you can find standard modems that push data through at rates as high as 115,200 bits per second, that can send a fax to the local delicatessen to bring lox and a bagel to your doorstep, or that can field dozens of phone calls while you waste away in your hot tub sipping imported mineral water.

Finding the right one can be as daunting as prospecting for lawrencium in the wilderness. You have only a general idea of what your looking for—wealth, fame, fortune, and saving telephone line charges—but only a faint inkling of an idea what form the object of your quest will take. When prospecting, you can turn over rocks and poke around with a stick, or you can hire a geophysical survey company with a network of linked seismographs to scientifically narrow the search. Fortunately, finding a modem can be easier, with this chapter substituting for the geologist's survey.

Today, the selection of modem standards is wider than that of long distance carriers.

Function and Purpose

Along with the meaning of life, one question has perplexed more computer owners than perhaps any other—Why do I need a modem? After all, the modem seems to be the most contrived computer accessory ever foisted on an otherwise astute segment of the buying public. Your PC and your telephone deal in the same stuff—electrical signals—so connecting them should be a job of nothing more than clipping in a patch cord.

Modems exist for the very good reason that computers and telephone lines get along about as well as crude oil and cormorants. Although computers and telephones use electricity for their communications signals, computers use digital electric signals, and telephones are based on analog technology. Although superficially similar, neither can make sense out of the other.

Noise-free and error-free, digital signals can be transmitted over vast distances without degradation.

Much of that signal difference has to do with history. The first pained words out of Alexander Graham Bell's speaking telegraph were analog electrical signals. Little has changed since then. If Dr. Bell could sneak into the late 20th Century and steal back to the 19th with a $5 telephone, he would have almost no problem getting it to work with his own fledgling equipment. On the other hand, the technology of today is digital. Noise-free and error-free, digital signals can be transmitted over vast distances without degradation. Digital signals are the same electricity that courses through your PC as its brain waves. Yet these same signals are completely incompatible with the century-old telephone system.

(Strictly speaking, digital communications are older than the analog kind. The conventional telegraph predates the telephone by nearly three decades—Samuel F. B. Morse wondered what God had wrought in 1844—but most folks never installed telegraphs in their homes and otherwise failed to take advantage of the certainty of digital technology until the advent of the PC.)

The job of the modem is to accommodate today's digital pulses to a telephone network still firmly rooted in the 19th Century. The modem converts digital data into audio-like signals that can be carried over telephone lines as if they were voice communications. Like electrical goodwill ambassadors, they help hostile signals get along together by making converts.

Modems translate digital signals into analog through a process called *modulation.* In fact, the word "modem" is just a contraction for modulator/demodulator, a functional description of a modem's work. Modulation is the secret. The best of today's modems take advantage of modern modulation methods to squeeze in more than a dozen data bits where only one should fit. Modulation also is the great performance separator between modems. Faster modems, which can operate at up to 28,800 bits per second without compressing data, use newer, more exotic modulation methods.

Modulation, however, is not enough to reach the highest data rates. The latest modems can squeeze information through the telephone line faster by condensing it down to its essence, reducing or eliminating redundant information. By compressing your data, the modem can cut the time your telephone must be connected—and costing you money—to transfer a file of a given size. Because today's high data transmission rates press against (and often beyond) the capability of an ordinary telephone connection to carry them, modems also need some way to detect—and, if possible, correct—any errors that might sneak in.

In addition, modems must carry out a number of seemingly trivial but important tasks in making and continuing the connection. For example, a modem must be able to tell the difference between different transmission speeds so that it can automatically connect with another modem. Such speed-seeking is not a mere convenience. You couldn't tell one speed from another by yourself, even if you had perfect pitch and the hearing of a Pekinese pooch.

Most modems are boxes full of convenience features that can make using them fast, simple, and automatic. The best of today's modems not only make and monitor the connection, but even improve it. They dial the phone for you, remembering the number you want, and trying again and again. They listen in until they're sure of good contact and only then let you transmit across the telephone line.

Most modems are boxes chock full of convenience features that can make using them fast, simple, and automatic.

Understandably, modems are available in great variety, and choosing the right one is more difficult than plugging one in and connecting up. If you know what to look for—and what all of the confusing terms mean—you'll be able to make the right choice as easily as selecting the right candy from the store.

Standards

No modem is an island. One modem would do the world no good—it would just send data out into the vast analog unknown, never to be seen (or heard) again.

But having two modems isn't automatically enough. Like people, modems must speak the same language for the utterances of one to be understood by the other. Modulation is part of the modem language. In addition, modems must be able to understand the error-correction features and data compression routines used by one another. Unlike most human beings who speak any of a zillion languages and dialects, each somewhat ill-defined, modems are much more precise in the languages they use. They have their own equivalent of the French Academy—standards organizations.

Standards are your best assurance that a given modem can successfully connect with any other modem in the world.

In the United States, the first standards were set long ago by the most powerful force in the telecommunications industry—the telephone company. More specifically, the American Telephone and Telegraph Company, the Bell System, which promoted various Bell standards, the most famous being Bell 103 and Bell 212A. After the

Bell System was split into AT&T and the seven regional operating companies (Baby Bells, a situation also known as AT&T and the seven dwarfs), other long distance carriers broke into the telephone monopoly. Moreover, other nations have (not surprisingly) become interested in telecommunications.

As a result of these developments, the onus and ability to set standards moved from AT&T to an international standards organization, the *Comite Consultatif International Telegraphique et Telephoneique* or CCITT (in English, that's International Telegraph and Telephone Consultative Committee). All of the high-speed standards used by modems today and the immediate future are sanctioned by the CCITT. These standards include v.22bis, v.32, v.32bis, v.42, and v.42bis.

Along the way, a modem and software maker, Microcom, developed a series of standards prefixed with the letters MNP, such as MNP4 and MNP5. The letters stand for Microcom Networking Protocol. A few other standards are acronyms for their underlying technologies.

The kind of communications you want to carry out will determine what kind of modem you need.

Standards are important when buying a modem because they are your best assurance that a given modem can successfully connect with any other modem in the world. In addition, the standards that you choose will determine how fast your modem can transfer data and how reliably it will work. The kind of communications that you want to carry out will determine what kind of modem you need. If you're just going to send files electronically between offices, you can buy two non-standard modems and get more speed for your investment. If you want to communicate with the rest of the world, however, you'll want to get a modem that meets the international standards.

The following are the most popular standards for modems that are connected to PCs.

Bell 103

In dire situations, the Bell 103 standard attached with an acoustical coupler can be a safe (if slow) haven.

Bell 103 comes first in any list of modem standards because it was the first widely adopted standard, and it remains the standard of last resort, the one that will work when all else fails. It allows data transmissions at a very low speed.

Bell 103 uses a kind of modulation called Frequency Shift Keying or FSK, in which different tones frequencies signify a digital one and digital zero. Each change in the modem's signal thus carries one bit of digital information. Consequently, the Bell 103 standard is the only one in which the baud rate (the rate at which signal changes) is equal to the data rate. Bell 103 modems operate at a maximum data rate of 300 bps.

FSK signals are so resistant to noise and other line problems because frequency varies little even with disastrous changes in a telephone connection or its routing. In fact, FSK is so reliable and straightforward that sound waves can carry it effectively. Thus Bell 103 signals can be sent down a telephone line without direct electrical connection by putting a loudspeaker against (or near) a telephone microphone, a technique called *acoustic coupling*.

Bell 103 is the one popular modem standard that works most reliably with acoustic couplers, although some 1200, 2400, and even 9600 bps acoustic couplers are available if you look hard enough. In dire situations, where a direct connection cannot be made to a telephone circuit, the Bell 103 standard attached with an acoustical coupler can be a safe (if slow) haven.

Bell 212A

Bell 212A is the next logical step in a standards discussion because it was the next modem standard to find wide application in the United States. It achieves a data transfer rate of 1200 bits per second by switching to phase modulation from FSK.

In phase modulation, a fixed tone called a carrier wave is altered so that the phase of its wave cycles are altered to specific phase angles in relation to the unchanged carrier. For instance, in quadrature modulation (which is used by Bell 212A modems), each state differs from the unmodulated carrier wave by a phase angle of 0, 90, 180, or 270 degrees.

Under Bell 212A, the carrier wave can change up to 600 times per second or 600 baud. The four different phase states are sufficient to encode the four different patterns of two digital bits. Consequently, each baud (signal change) with its four states can carry two bits of information, doubling the actual throughput to twice the baud rate. Consequently, a Bell 212A modem operates at 600 baud and transfers information at 1200 bits per second.

Although once the most widely used communication standard in America (v.22bis now ranks as the probable favorite, but faster standards are gaining followings), many foreign countries prohibit the use of Bell 212A, preferring instead the similar international standard, v.22.

LAPB

LAPB stands for Link Access Procedure, Balanced, an error correction protocol designed for X.25 packet-switched services like Telebit and Tymnet. Some high-speed modem makers adapted this standard to their dial-up modem products before the v.42 standard was agreed upon. For example, the Hayes Smartmodem 9600 from Hayes Microcomputer Products includes LAPB error-control capabilities.

LAPM

LAPM is an acronym for Link Access Procedure for Modems and is the error correction protocol used by the CCITT v.42 standard.

Microcom Networking Protocol

Microcom Networking Protocol is an entire hierarchy of standards, starting with MNP Class 1, a no-longer-used error correction protocol, and including MNP Class 10, Adverse Channel Enhancements, which is designed to eke the most data transfer performance from poor connections. MNP works with modems that may conform to other standards. The MNP standards specify technologies rather than speeds. MNP Classes 2 through 4 deal with error control and are in the public domain. Classes 5 through 10 are licensed by Microcom and deal with a number of modem operating parameters.

MNP2

MNP2 is designed to work with any modem that's capable of full-duplex communications. It works by confirming each byte as it is sent by having the receiving modem echo back each character. The sending modem can compare what it sent out with what came back to see whether any errors occurred during transmission. This two-way street of data cuts effective transmission rates to half of what would otherwise be possible.

MNP3

MNP3 improves on MNP2 by working synchronously instead of asynchronously. Consequently, no start and stop bits are required for each byte, trimming the data transfer overhead by 25 percent or more. Although MNP3 modems exchange data between themselves synchronously, they connect to PCs using asynchronous data links— which means that they plug right into RS232 serial ports.

MNP4

MNP4 is basically an error-correcting protocol but also yields a bit of data compression. It incorporates two innovations. *Adaptive Packet Assembly* enables the modem to package data in blocks or packets that are sent and error-checked as a unit. The protocol is adaptive because it varies the size of each packet according to the quality of the connection. *Data Phase Optimization* eliminates repetitive control bits from the data traveling across the connection to streamline transmissions. Together, these techniques can increase the throughput of a modem by 120 percent at a given bit-rate. Using MNP4, a 1200 bit per second modem could achieve a 1450 bit per second throughput. Many modems have MNP4 capabilities, but newer international standards are subsuming and replacing it.

MNP5

MNP5 is purely a data compression protocol that squeezes some kinds of data into a form that takes less time to transmit. MNP5 can compress some data by a factor of up to two, effectively doubling the speed of data transmissions. On some forms of data, such as files that have been already compressed, however, MNP5 may actually increase the time required for transmission.

MNP6

MNP6 is designed to help modems get the most out of telephone connections independent of data compression. Using a technique called *Universal Link Negotiation*, modems can start communicating at a low speed, and after evaluating the capabilities of the telephone line and each modem, switch to a higher speed. MNP6 also includes *Statistical Duplexing*, which enables a half-duplex modem to simulate full-duplex operation.

MNP7

MNP7 is a more efficient data compression algorithm (Huffman encoding) than MNP5, which permits increases in data throughput by a factor as high as three on some data.

MNP9

MNP9 (there is no MNP8) is designed to reduce the transmission overhead required by certain common modem operations. The acknowledgment of each data packet is streamlined by combining the acknowledgment with the next data packet instead of sending a separate confirmation byte. In addition, MNP9 minimizes the amount of information that must be retransmitted when an error is detected by indicating where the error occurred. Although some other error-correction schemes require all information transmitted after an error to be resent, an MNP9 modem only needs the data that was in error to be sent again.

MNP10

MNP10 is a set of *Adverse Channel Enhancements* that help modems work better through poor telephone connections. Modems with MNP10 will make multiple attempts to set up a transmission link, adjust the size of data packets they transmit according to what works best over the connection, and adjust the speed at which they operate to the highest rate that can be reliably maintained. One use envisioned for this standard is cellular modem communications—the car phone for data.

V.22

Although Bell 212A and v.22 modems speak the same language, they are unwilling to start a conversation with one another.

V.22 is the CCITT equivalent of the Bell 212A standard that delivers a transfer rate of 1200 bit per second at 600 baud. It actually uses the same form of modulation as Bell 212A but is not compatible with the Bell standard because it uses a different protocol to set up the connection. Although Bell 212A and v.22 modems speak the same language, they are unwilling to start a conversation with one another. Some modems support both standards and allow you to switch between them.

V.22bis

V.22bis was the first true world standard, adopted into general use in the United States and Europe. It allows a transfer rate of 2400 bits per second at 600 baud using a technique called *trellis modulation* that mixes two simple kinds of modulation, quadrature modulation and amplitude modulation. Each baud has 16 states, enough to code any pattern of four bits. Each state is distinguished by its phase relationship to the unaltered carrier and its amplitude (or strength) in relation to the carrier. There are four distinct phases and four distinct amplitudes under v.22bis, which, when multiplied together, yield the 16 available states.

V.32

V.32 is an international high-speed standard that permits data transfer rates of 4800 and 9600 bits per second. At its lower speed, it uses quadrature amplitude modulation similar to Bell 212A but at a higher baud rate—2400 baud. At 9600 bits per second, it uses trellis modulation similar to v.22bis but at 2400 baud and with a greater range of phases and amplitudes.

Note that although most Group III fax machines and modems operate at 9600 bits per second, a fax modem with 9600 bps capability is not necessarily compatible with the v.32 standard. Don't expect a fax modem to communicate with v.32 products.

V.32bis

V.32bis extends the v.32 standard to 14,400 bits per second while allowing intermediary speeds of 7200 and 12,000 bits per second in addition to the 4800 and 9600 bit per second speeds of v.32. Note that all of these speeds are multiples of a basic 2400 baud rate. The additional operating speeds that v.32bis has and v.32 does not are generated by using different ranges of phases and amplitudes in the modulation. At 14,400 bits per second, there are 128 potentially different phase/amplitude states for each baud under v.32bis, enough to encode seven data bits in each baud. Because there are so many phase and amplitude differences squeezed together, a small change in the characteristics of a telephone line might mimic such a change and cause transmission errors. Consequently, some way of detecting and eliminating such errors thus becomes increasingly important as transmission speed goes up.

V.42

V.42 is a world-wide error correction standard that is design to help make v.32, v.32bis, and other modem communications more reliable. v.42 incorporates MNP4 as an "alternative" protocol. That is, some v.42 modems can communicate with MNP4 modems, but a connection between the two won't use the more sophisticated v.42 error-correction protocol. At the beginning of each call, as the connection is being negotiated between modems, a v.42 modem will determine whether MNP4 or full v.42 error-correction can be used by the other modem. V.42 is preferred; MNP4 is the second choice. In other words, a v.42 will first try to set up a v.42 session; failing that, it will try MNP4; and failing that, it will set up a communications session without error-correction.

V.42bis

Different from and incompatible with MNP5 and MNP7, v.42bis is also more efficient.

V.42bis is a data-compression protocol endorsed by the CCITT. Different from and incompatible with MNP5 and MNP7, v.42bis is also more efficient. On some forms of data, it can yield compression factors up to four, potentially quadrupling the speed of modem transmissions. (With PCs, the effective maximum communication rate may be slower because of limitations on serial ports, typically 38,400 bits per second.) Note that a v.42bis-only modem cannot communicate with a MNP5-only modem. Unlike MNP5, a v.42 modem never increases the transmission time of "incompressible" data. Worst-case operation is the same speed as would be achieved without compression.

V.fast

V.fast is the name given to the next generation of modems, those that operate at double today's speeds. By adding new levels of modulation to existing technologies, V.fast pushes the basic bit rate up to 28,800 per second. On top of that, V.42bis compression can push willing block of data through at rates approaching 115,200 bps. In fact, most PCs can't even hope to drive their serial ports faster—that's the top-end (for now at least). Although V.fast is not widely used yet, in the next couple of years, it will likely become the high-performance modem standard. With the coming of all-digital telephone systems, it may just be the last modem standard as well as the fastest.

Other Considerations

All of these modem standards support true duplex communication. That is, data can be transferred in two directions at the same speed simultaneously. Before the v.32 standard was adopted, however, the makers of high-speed modems used their own, proprietary modulation schemes—some of which were true full *duplex*; some of which used different speeds for sending and receiving; and some could only operate in one direction at a time, switching the direction of the flow of data as communications needs changed. These modems, once state of the art, have been relegated to "oddball" status by the acceptance of v.32 and v.32bis standards. Newer half-duplex, 9600 bps modems now conform to an international standard, v.29.

That's not to say that products that don't conform to the full duplex standards are totally unusable. As long as you control both ends of the conversation, you can use these other high-speed modems successfully—even economically. Because of the plummeting cost of v.32 and v.32bis modems, however, opting for such obsolete technology makes little sense. The problem with using a non-standard modems—no matter how much a bargain it may seem—is that it will foreclose on access to on-line databases and bulletin boards, which have quickly embraced v.32.

It is important to check all the standards a modem supports.

Note that with the exceptions of v.42/MNP4 and v.32/v.32bis, the various modem standards are independent of one another. That is, getting a modem that uses one standard does not ensure that the modem will work with other (particularly slower) standards. For example, nothing in the Bell 212A standard requires a Bell 212A modem to be able to communicate with a Bell 103 modem. Although most modems do incorporate more than one communication standard, such backward compatibility is not guaranteed by the standards. Should you buy a v.22bis modem to communicate at 2400 bps, you may be surprised if it does not work at 1200 bps and slower speeds. So it is important to check all the standards a modem supports.

Fallback describes a capability with which some modems are endowed that enables them to test the quality of a telephone connection and to negotiate using the highest speed that the connection will allow with the other modem. If, for example, a bad telephone line won't allow a modem to use full 9600 bps v.32 communications, it may negotiate to use Bell 212A instead, falling back from 9600 bps to 1200 bps.

Automatic fallback is important to extract as much communications potential as you can from every dial-up connection.

Modems that support multiple standards are not automatically guaranteed to fallback. They may try the speed for which they are set and, failing that, give you a `No Carrier` error message when they can make sense out of the data on the telephone line. You've got to make the call again at a different data rate. Of course, you may get a better (or worse) line on the second try, so your modem may never be operating optimally for the connection. Automatic fallback is important in any modem you buy if you want to extract as much communications potential as you can from every dial-up connection.

After a modem falls back, it may not leap forward again. Many modems may slow down when a burst of noise or other transient problem temporarily degrades the quality of connection, and then continues to operate at that low speed even if the connection quality improves. Other modems, such as those that follow MNP10, adjust their speed upward and downward to accommodate any change in connection quality. The capability to move up to a higher speed when a connection supports it is sometimes called *automatic fall-forward.*

Modem speed is the major factor in setting the price of a modem. Faster modems are more complex and more exacting; consequently, they cost more—until competition and advancing technology drive the prices down. If you don't need the fastest modem in the world, you can save big. If you rarely transfer files, you probably don't need high speed. But if you are moving dozens or hundreds of kilobytes every day, a 9600 bit per second or faster modem can pay for itself in lower phone bills in a matter of months.

One final note on modem speed: don't think that you'll always get throughput of 9600 bits per second from a 9600 bps modem. The modem world doesn't work quite that way. Modem standards indicate only what signals a modem can deal with under ideal conditions, but not every connection is ideal. Modems vary in their capability to accommodate noise on telephone lines, changing levels, and other signal problems. Check modem specifications to determine how well the product can deal with noise, what its minimum signal is, and other signal recovery features like echo-cancellation.

Over a perfect telephone line, nearly all modems function perfectly—without errors. However, perfect telephone lines are impossible to find, and even getting an acceptable one nowadays seems to require bribing an operator. The performance differences between modems appear as line quality goes down. Better modems are better able to cope with bad connections. They work with worse circuits and can pull data through with fewer errors.

A 9600 bit per second or faster modem can pay for itself in lower phone bills in a matter of months.

Modem standards indicate only what signals a modem can deal with under ideal conditions.

Better modems are better able to cope with bad connections.

One result of newer standards and protocols is that the effective throughput of modems will vary with line quality depending on the technical adroitness of the design of each product. Although two modems may each follow the same standard, one may move data faster than the other because fewer blocks of data must be re-sent because of errors that sneak in the telephone line. Unfortunately, this difference does not show up on the specification sheets; it can only be judged with rigorous testing. If you need to find a modem with the best possible performance, you're forced to depend on test reports and the reputations of the modem manufacturers.

Don't forget hardware reliability. As with other computer peripherals, the more reliable modems are those with fewer components (because there is simply less to go wrong.) Look for a modem that uses the latest electronics (VLSI and Surface-Mount Components). More compact modems by necessity use these space-saving (and reliability-increasing) technologies.

The more reliable modems are those with fewer components.

Rapidly becoming a non-issue in modem purchases is the command set used by a product. The command set is the assortment of instructions that a modem understands that tell it to carry out different functions (for example, to dial the telephone or to hang up). No command set has received official sanction by the CCITT as the one and only world-wide standard. However, most modems today follow a de facto standard, the Hayes command set. Also known as AT commands because each command line begins with the "Attention" characters AT, this standard was originally developed by Hayes Microcomputer Products for use with its line of Smartmodems.

The popularity of Hayes modems led many software companies to incorporate AT commands in their programs. Other manufacturers adapted their modems to AT commands so that they could work with all of the same software as Hayes modems. More communications were written using AT commands because of the proliferation of compatible modems. The result is that a modem that recognizes the Hayes command set will work with the widest variety of software. Modems with Hayes compatibility are more versatile.

A modem that recognizes the Hayes command set will work with the widest variety of software.

Note, however, that the Hayes standard is not immutable. As new modem features and capabilities are developed, the commands set becomes richer. A program that takes advantage of a newer, more advanced Hayes command may be frustrated by an older modem with a more limited command set. Some modems only recognize the most rudimentary of commands, for instance using ATDT to initial the dialing sequence. Others more elaborately mimic the operation of Hayes products and incorporate the same registers as used by

Smartmodems, which permit, for example, setting the number of rings required before the modem answers.

Hayes actually holds a patent on modem control that coves part of the AT command set, specifically the way that a command can interrupt a communication session. Consequently, any modem that claims 100-percent Hayes compatibility must be licensed by Hayes.

The safe bet is selecting a modem that's as Hayes compatible as possible.

Other modem command sets have been used in the past, and modems that use non-Hayes commands are still available. The commands used by a modem are significant only to the extent that your communications program must know what commands to use. The commands have no effect on the data exchanged between two modems. You can use a non-Hayes modem as long as your communications program knows the command set of your modem. Of course, most communications programs understand the Hayes command set best. Unless you have masochistic tendencies or software that is specifically designed for another modem command set, the safe bet is selecting a modem that's as Hayes compatible as possible.

The final consideration in selecting a modem is the features that are offered. Features is a broad term used to indicate all the other differences between modems.

For the most part, the features of a modem determine how easily and conveniently it can be used. Primeval no-frills modems once required that you dial or answer the telephone manually and physically connect the modem to it at the appropriate time. Today, such manual modems are rare, mostly just leftovers of obsolete product lines. All the circuitry required for auto-dialing and auto-answering of your phone are incorporated into the standard integrated circuits used by nearly all modem makers. These features come essentially free to the modem manufacturer, so you should expect them to come free to you, too.

In today's competitive communications worlds, you'll find that nearly all current modems are equipped with a basic minimum of features far beyond the needs of the casual user. Specific applications may demand features that are out of the product mainstream (for example, AutoSync to allow your modem to communicate synchronously with an asynchronous connection to your PC). If you need modem capabilities beyond basic dialing and answering, you should carefully check the features offered by the products you're considering.

Selecting one modem from the hundreds of products currently available is no small task. However, it can be made more tractable by making four separate judgments about each particular modem's performance, compatibility, features, and price. Choose the performance level you need, compatibility with the standards used by the services you plan to regularly connect with, the features to match the needs of your software, and the price you can afford. Although the modem you choose won't likely lead your PC on a quest to take over the world, it will connect you and your PC with the world of data communications.

More than any other PC peripherals, modems are likely to come with software, typically a full-fledged communications program. This software can be more than just a free program—it can be a key to unlocking particular modem features (such as the capability to use higher numbered serial ports). Be sure to ask what you get when you order—and make sure that it comes in the box when you get the modem.

Internal and External Modems

Generally, all modems, regardless of the standards they follow, fall into two classes—internal and external. The difference is, of course, where the modem is installed, inside an expansion slot of a PC (in a laptop, it may be a dedicated modem slot) or external to the computer, connected by cable to a serial port. On the surface, physical appeal may seem the best guiding factor because often exactly the same circuitry is available in either of the packages. Other considerations might lead you to preferring one style of modem over the other, however.

An external modem offers the advantage of portability—you can move external modems between different systems, even those of different architectures. The same external modem can serve a PC, Mac, or Amiga as easily as moving a plug and cable from one system to the other. Even if you have two or more identical PCs (or whatever) moving an external modem between them is easier than swapping an expansion board between different systems.

Another advantage of external modems is that most of them give you a good look at what they are doing, courtesy of front panel light-emitting diodes that monitor vital modem functions. You can see the state of modem control signals and whether data is actually being sent or received. Although you can run some diagnostic programs that will put a semblance of these indicators on your monitor screen when you have an internal modem, this software tends to complicate things and can even slow down communications.

Another reason to look at external modems is that sometimes you might not even be able to find an internal modem for your computer. For example, you might be blessed with an odd, old, discontinued machine (say a Data General One laptop) for which internal modems are not readily available, or your small footprint PC might already be stuffed to its maximum three-slot capacity with a network adapter, SCSI adapter, and GPIB board for your scanner. You might not have room for an internal modem.

The big advantage of internal modems is that they tend to be a few dollars cheaper than external units. Internal modem makers can cut costs because they don't need all of the extra packaging or power supplies (although they do need some extra signal circuitry) required to make external modems.

Internal modems aren't always cheaper, however. Special-purpose internal modems, such as those designed to fit particular notebook-style PCs, often demand a price premium. Typically, the original manufacturer of the computer is the only source for such modems, and because the manufacturer controls the whole market, the manufacturer also can control the price. Then again, with notebook or laptop PCs, the convenience of putting everything in one totable package may offset the price difference. The manufacturer can get away with a bigger profit because you are willing to pay more for convenience. For portable applications, the pocket modem can be an ideal compromise that keeps your costs under control. Small enough to actually put in your pocket (or the pocket of a laptop computer's carrying case), pocket modems retain all the advantages of external modems—in particular, the capability to quickly shift them between different PCs. In addition, pocket modems can save laptop and notebook computer owners something more important than cash: battery power. Many of the internal modems of laptop PCs continue to consume power even when not in use, cutting the effective battery life of the computer. When operating, a modem inside a laptop PC may cut the duration of a charge on the system's battery by a quarter. A pocket modem, which draws no electricity from the battery reserves of the laptop, eliminates that kind of power drain.

All pocket modems are not the same when it comes to power, however. Some require their own batteries, typically a nine-volt transistor radio battery, giving you yet another diminishing resource to worry about while you travel. Line-powered pocket modems eliminate this hassle because they can get all the electricity they need from the telephone line, courtesy of the telephone company.

Power used to be an issue with internal modems in desktop PCs, but modern technology has mostly erased this concern. The only exception to the "Who cares?" rule about internal modem power is the combination of a vintage modem and vintage PCs. If you happen to have an original IBM PC with a 63.5-watt power supply, stay clear of old-technology internal modems, those that take a full-length expansion slot or multiple boards. These modems draw so much current that they can overly strain a PC that has been fully expanded with EMS memory and a hard disk. You're safe with a new modem, however. Most of today's inexpensive internal modems fit on short expansion boards, sometimes as little as five inches long, and draw negligible current from the computer. More than a low-power modem, however, you need a reorientation to see that an 8088-based PC just doesn't make sense in a world where 486 machines cost less than a good stereo.

An external modem somehow needs to connect to a serial port on your PC. Although some pocket modems will plug directly into a port connector, most modems require a cable. Few modems come equipped with the necessary cable, so be sure to order a serial cable when you buy your modem. Almost universally, you will require a straight-through serial cable, although the standard seven connections (rather than the full 25 of the serial connector) are generally sufficient. Pocket modems are so small that they can often plug directly into the serial port on the back of your PC or laptop. You'll just have to make sure that the modem and your PC use the same kind of serial connector—9- or 25-pin—and get an get an adapter if you need one.

With internal modems, you have a different concern. An internal modem incorporates its own serial port and its own UART. If you want the maximum possible communications speed, you'll want a 16550 UART on your internal modem. Most vendors hush up which UART is used on a particular modem—16550 UART cost more—so you have to ask to be sure that you get one. Most high-speed modems won't operate at full speed without a 16550 UART, so it's important to ask.

A final factor to take into consideration in selecting between an internal and external modem is that the price difference between different manufacturers dwarfs the difference between the internal and external modems of any given manufacturer. Exactly how much you should spend depends on what you're looking for and what you're willing to settle for. As with any other PC product, you should carefully consider every aspect of your modem purchase before making your decision—select the one that you're absolutely sure you want and then settle for the one you can afford.

Support Issues

When you have a problem with a data or fax modem, you have two
avenues of support. Most of the time, you'll first want to give a call
to the vendor who sold you the modem. Check what the vendor
offers for support before you buy any modem. A tollfree support line
is ideal, particularly one that's attended 24 hours a day.

Before you buy, ask the salesman about his company's support
policy. Ask whether the company has a support number and make
sure that the support line operates 24 hours a day—or at least into
evening hours. You'll probably test your modem in the evening or
late night when telephone charges are lowest, so you'll want support
to be there when you need it. Check whether the support line is toll-
free and ask whether there are enough people to answer your
questions immediately or whether you'll have to wait—presumably
forever—for someone to call you back. Technical support that
depends only on the salesperson who wrote down your credit card
number is usually as good as no support.

Modem manufacturers differ in their support policies. Although
many will try to help you with your problems (sometimes only after
wending your way through the corporate hierarchy), others may not
even be in business any more—or they may be located in some
foreign land lacking telephone connections with the United States
and the 20th Century. In that you may have to rely on the modem
manufacturer for help when your pleas to the vendor go unanswered,
you'll want the manufacturer of your modem to be at least reachable.
A modem vendor with a consumer support line is a godsend,
particularly if the line is tollfree. Technical support through a
bulletin board service can be helpful, but remember, it will be
difficult to connect to the BBS if you cannot make your modem
work!

Product warranties are given by the manufacturer and the vendor.
However, the latter is usually more important because you'll get the
most direct help with your modem from the vendor. The easy-to-
quantify issue is the length of the warranty. A modem warranty
should extend past the first connection to at least 90 days. You
expect your modem to last much longer than that. So should its
manufacturer. You'll find that better products—and better vendors—will offer modem warranties measured in years. How that
warranty is honored is also important. The easiest to deal with is a
replacement policy under which the modem vendor will send you a
replacement modem when you send yours back. If the vendor elects
to repair your modem instead, you may be disconnected for weeks.

A return policy is also helpful if you cannot get your modem to work with your particular PC configuration. Subtle incompatibilities may make one modem unhappy in your system. If so, you'll want to be able to return the modem and try another model without suffering a restocking fee. Manufacturers' warranties are trickier to get a handle on. Generally, the warranty period starts when the product is sold to your vendor, not to you, so it may expire sooner than you think. Worse, a manufacturer may choose not to recognize its warranty if you don't buy from an authorized dealer. So it's important to clarify whether you get a manufacturer's warranty when you buy your drive. Of course, a manufacturer's warranty is meaningless if the modem manufacturer is out of business or beyond your reach in the depths of the Pacific Basin.

Pre-Installation Considerations

One factor to which most people fail to pay attention when they install modems is port usage. Although an external modem's need for a serial port is obvious, the needs of an internal or fax modem are more subtle. Even though an internal modem or a fax modem with ordinary data (Hayes-compatible) capabilities doesn't connect up to a serial port connector on your PC's back panel, it still needs a serial port to link its signals to your PC. The needed port is actually embedded in the circuitry of the internal modem or fax modem. Although this circuitry eliminates your worries about the serial connections, you still need to be concerned with the usage of the port resources of your PC.

Every serial port in a PC—including the one embedded in an internal modem and the data section of a fax modem—must be assigned internal hardware I/O ports and an interrupt from your PC's innate resources. That means an internal or fax modem will steal one of the serial port names from DOS—COM1 to COM4— limiting the number of other serial ports you can install in your system.

Not all internal modems can adapt to the full complement of serial addresses. Some internal modems, particularly older models, can only be set up as COM1 or COM2. A modem that can also be addressed as COM3 or COM4 will give you more serial port flexibility—providing your communications software can take advantage of a higher numbered port (many older communications programs cannot).

When assigning a COM name to the serial port used by a modem, no matter whether it's an internal, fax, or external modem, you also need to be concerned about what your other serial ports are used for. Serial ports share interrupts in pairs. COM1 and COM3 use hardware interrupt four, and COM2 and COM4 use interrupt three.

If you connect a device that might issue an interrupt while your modem is in operation to the same interrupt line as is used by the modem, the result can be an interrupt collision that could interrupt your communications session or even crash your computer. This might happen when, for example, you have your modem assigned as COM4 and a mouse connected as COM2. Move the mouse while transferring a file, and your computer could lose its mind. The moral is to not share an interrupt between your mouse and modem by being careful about what COM name you give each.

Installation

An external modem is one of the easiest upgrades to install. You only need to make three, sometimes four, connections: plug the modem into your phone line (see fig. 14.3), connect it to one of your PC's serial ports (see fig. 14.4), and plug it into its necessary electrical supply (see fig. 14.5). The optional connection is to your telephone (see fig. 14.2).

Figuring out which cables to use should not be a problem. The necessary power cable should come with the modem. In addition, most modems include a short telephone cable with modular connectors at either end for plugging into your telephone line. If you need to plug a telephone in to the same line, get a two-jack adapter (which should be available in any store that sells telephones—drug store, electronics store, or discount store), plug the adapter into the jack for the telephone line, and plug the modem and the telephone into the adapter. If your external modem has two jacks on its back, run a wire from the one marked "Line" to your telephone line jack. Connect the modem jack labeled "Phone" to your telephone.

You're expected to supply only the signal cable between your PC and the modem. Even this cable should not be a problem. You need a *straight-through* cable to make the connection (see fig. 14.4). So called *null-modem* or *cross-over* cables are unnecessary—they won't even work. For short distances (six feet or so), a straight-through 25-pin ribbon cable will work just fine. If you choose to use a shielded cable, you'll only need the nine connections made on the small AT-style serial connectors (nine-pin). Your modem cable normally should have a male connector on one end (to mate with the modem) and a female connector on the other end (to mate with your PC).

Internal modems and fax modems with direct data transmission capabilities are hardly more difficult. Before you begin installing the internal modem, you should take stock of the serial ports already installed in your system so that you can determine which unused port will be best for the internal modem. Assign the modem to an unused DOS name. To be safe, you'll want to avoid sharing an interrupt with your mouse or other pointing device. If your mouse is connected to COM1, don't define your modem as COM3. If your mouse is connected to COM2, don't define your modem as COM4. When you've decided the port at which location you modem, you should set the modem hardware to use that port. Most internal modems have a switch or jumper to select the port value used. PS/2 modems and some more exotic new modems may make the port selection a software process.

After you've set up your internal or fax modem's port assignment, you're ready for the hardware installation. First, you'll want to power down your PC, unplug its power cord, and remove its lid from its case so that you can locate a vacant expansion slot for your modem. Generally, any slot will be fine (see fig. 14.1). Nearly all modems use eight-bit bus connectors, so any ISA 8- or 16-bit slot or an EISA 32-bit slot should accommodate the modem. Any Micro Channel slot should accommodate any Micro Channel modem. When you've located a slot, just slide the modem in and screw down its retaining bracket.

Next, test your modem before putting the top back on your PC. Connect the necessary cables. Typically, you'll need to plug in one or two modular telephone wires. If there is just one jack on the back of your internal modem, connect it to a standard modular jack to which you would plug in an ordinary telephone. If you need to plug a telephone into the same jack, get a two-jack adapter, plug the adapter into the jack, and plug the modem and the telephone into the adapter. If your internal modem has two jacks, run a wire from the one marked "Line" to your phone jack. Connect the modem jack labeled "Phone" to your telephone (see figs. 14.2).

Figure 14.1

After you've assigned system resources to an internal modem, install the modem in any convenient expansion slot. Modems are so slow that fast 16-bit slots won't help them.

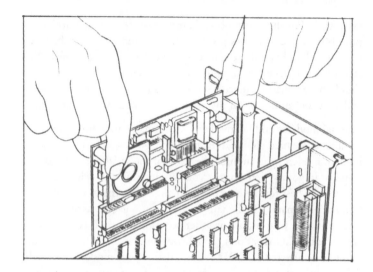

Figure 14.2

After you've installed your internal modem, connect the jack that's labeled "phone" to your telephone. Make the same connection if you have an external modem.

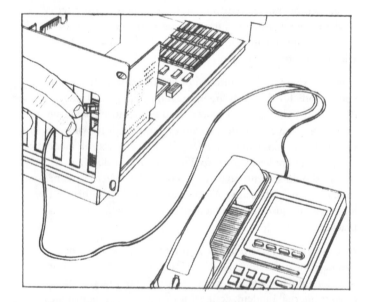

Connect the jack on the modem that's labeled "Line" to your telephone line. This also applies to external modems (see fig. 14.3). With internal modems, your hardware installation is complete

With external modems, your next step is to connect the serial jack on the modem to a serial port on your PC (see fig. 14.4). Use a "straight-through" cable. Do not use a "null modem" cable.

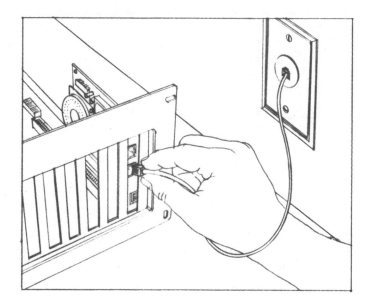

Figure 14.3
Connect the jack on the modem that's labeled "Line" to your telephone line.

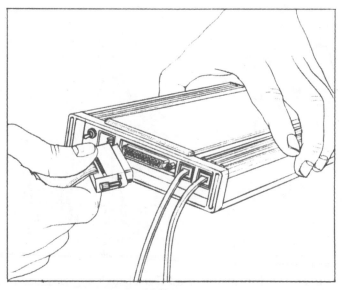

Figure 14.4
Connect the serial jack on the modem to a serial port on your PC.

Finally, plug your external modem into an electrical supply (see fig. 14.5). Most modems use external transformers that you first plug into a wall outlet, and then into the modem.

If your modem has only one jack, and you want to share your modem line with a telephone as shown in figure 14.6, you'll need an adapter (see inset). Plug the adapter into your telephone line and then plug the modem and the phone into the adapter.

Figure 14.5
Plug your external
modem into an
electrical supply.

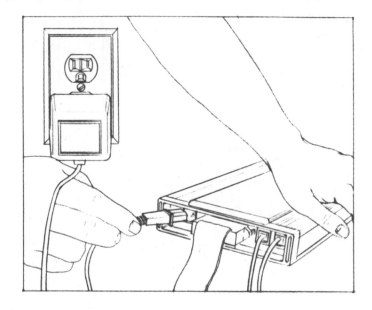

Figure 14.6
Plug the adapter into
your telephone line
and then plug the
modem and the
phone into the
adapter (inset).

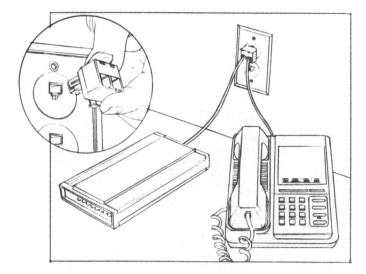

To test the modem, plug in your PC and boot it up. Use your
communications program (or the one that came with the modem) to
make a call. If it works, you know the internal modem is working.
When your modem passes all the tests, you can safely button up
your PC. Turn it off and replace the lid.

If the modem fails to operate with your communications program or
its own self-test software, check to make sure that the modem's
command set is compatible with your software. (You should expect
that the software that came with the modem will use the right

command set.) Be sure that the communications program and the modem are set to use the same DOS port. These simple verifications will solve most of your modem problems. In a few minutes, your PC will be communicating with the rest of the world.

PC FAX

Fax, short for facsimile transmissions, gives the power of Star Trek's transporter system to anyone who needs to get a document somewhere else in the world at the speed of light. Although fax doesn't quite dematerialize paper, it does move the images and information a document contains across continents and reconstructs it at the end of its near-instantaneous travels. The recipient gets to hold in his own hands a nearly exact duplicate of the original, the infamous reasonable facsimile. From that angle, fax is a telecopier—a Xerox machine with a thousand miles of wire between where you slide the original in and where the duplicate falls out. In fact, the now aging telecopiers made by Xerox Corporation were the progenitors of today's fax machines.

PC-based fax certainly isn't for everyone, but it can be a powerful tool.

Functionally, however, fax works like television for paper. Much as a television picture is broken into numerous scan lines, a fax machine scans images as a series of lines, one at a time, and strings all the lines scanned on a document into a continuous stream of information. At the receiving end, another fax machine converts the data stream into black and white dots on another sheet of paper, duplicating the pattern of the original.

In actual application, fax plays the role of a modem for pictures. Although we in the West send our data across wires in digital bytes representing our alphabet of a handful of symbols, the fax machine serves the same purpose where pictograms rule. Quite understandably, the first growth spurt for fax occurred in Japan, a country with a combination of complicated typography and an affection for technology.

A fax board for your PC now costs less than just about any available fax machine.

Today, technology has blended the two wonder products of the 1980s, PCs and fax machines, into one. Add an adapter to your PC called a *fax modem* or fax board, and your PC can become a complete fax sending and receiving system. The allure is so great that digital fax systems are one of the favorite upgrades for PCs. One reason is that most PC- based fax systems are dual-purpose units. In one package and on one board, you get a conventional modem and fax powers. Another reason is price. A fax board for your PC now costs less than just about any available fax machine. In fact, fax adds

PC-based fax requires computer knowledge and an ability to wade your way through software.

as little as $20 to the price of a modem. (Sometimes, it adds nothing.) If you want fax capabilities, you will be sorely tempted to plug them in your PC.

On the downside, however, are a couple of as yet unresolved fax problems. Although fax machines are no more complicated than a telephone to operate, PC-based fax requires computer knowledge and an ability to wade your way through software. Some people see the PC-ization of fax as an impediment to productivity rather than a convenience. Moreover, PC-based fax isn't fast. Many fax boards for PCs operate at half the normal fax rate, and you have to get those fax images out of your computer somehow. Typically, you'll want to use a laser printer—but you won't get laser-like speeds. Printing a fax page may take several minutes.

When performance and ease of use count, most people still prefer stand-alone fax machines. However, the prices of fax boards are tempting. If you consider fax capabilities as a free bonus on a modem (as they so often are), there's no reason not to upgrade to fax in your PC. Moreover, if you do a lot of fax sending rather than receiving, PC-based fax systems can deliver some powerful advantages. For example, you can print to fax as easily as to ordinary paper—if you have the right software. If you need to send a newsletter to 100 clients, you can create it in a desktop publishing program and then squirt it out to your fax board with your PC handling all the details of getting one copy to each person on your distribution list.

PC-based fax certainly isn't for everyone, but it can be a powerful tool. It also can be so affordable that you won't want to pass it up.

Background

The concept of facsimile transmissions is hardly new. As early as 1842, Alexander Bain patented an electro-mechanical device that could translate wire-based signals into marks on paper. Newspaper wire photos, which are based on the same principles, have been used for generations.

The widespread use of fax in business is a more recent phenomenon, however, and its growth parallels that of the PC for much the same underlying reason. Desktop computers did not take off until the industry found a standard to follow—the IBM PC. Similarly, the explosive growth of fax began only after the CCITT adopted standards for the transmission of facsimile data. The first of these, now termed Group 1, was based on analog technology and used frequency shift keying, much like Bell 103 modems, to transmit a page of information in six minutes. Group 2 improved that analog technology and doubled the speed of transmission, cutting transmission time down to three minutes per page.

The big break with the past and breakthrough was the CCITT's adoption in 1980 of the Group 3 fax standard, which is entirely digitally based. Using data compression and modems that operate at up to 9600 bits per second, a full-page document can be transmitted in 30 to 60 seconds using the Group 3 standard. Newer Class 2 fax modems operate under the Group 3 standard and deliver 14,400 bps. The data compression makes the speed of transmitting a page dependent on the amount of detail that it contains. In operation, the data compression algorithm reduces the amount of data that must be transferred by a factor of five to ten. Group 3 modems automatically fall back so that a bad phone connection may slow fax transmissions to lower speeds to help cope with poor line quality.

Under the Group 3 standard, two degrees of resolution or on-paper sharpness are possible (which also affects speed): standard, which allows 1728 dots horizontally across the page (about 200 dots per inch) and 100 dots per inch vertically; and fine, which doubles the vertical resolution to achieve 200 x 200 dpi and requires about twice the transmission time.

In 1984, the CCITT approved a super-performance facsimile standard, Group 4, which allows resolutions of up to 400 x 400 dpi as well as higher speed transmissions of lower resolutions. Although not quite typeset quality (phototypesetters are capable of resolutions of about 1200 dpi), the best of Group 4 is about equal to the resolving capability of the human eye at normal reading distance. However, today's Group 4 fax machines require high speed, dedicated lines and do not operate as dial-up devices. The ill-fated (now discontinued) Zap Mail services offered by Federal Express were based on Group 4 facsimile equipment.

All PC-to-fax modems that you can buy today use the Group 3 standard, Class 1 or 2. Not all have the top speed the standard permits. Many plug-in PC fax modems top out at 4800 bps. Although this lower ceiling makes for more secure communications and lower purchase prices, it also doubles the cost of every document you fax. In a few months, what you save in buying a slower fax modem will be devoured by telephone line charges—if you plan to use your fax modem a lot. If you look at fax as only a luxury that you'll use once or twice a month, however, you probably won't worry about slow-speed, 4800 bps fax modems for your PC.

One of the first PC-to-fax connections was made by Xerox Corporation by tying an ordinary facsimile machine, their modem 895, to a PC. The fax machine functioned as a fax machine, scanning, transmitting and regenerating documents. The PC took control. It sent commands to the fax machine to dial the phone and to deliver transmissions to entire groups of recipients. The PC could also access the fax data stream, recording it on disk, storing documents, or previewing images before they were sent or after they were received. A software utility could convert standard ASCII files into fax-compatible data.

The primary advantage of putting a fax board into your PC is convenience.

Today's approach has refined the idea behind the Xerox creation but does away with the fax machine entirely. Instead, it substitutes a fax-compatible, high-speed modem that installs in an expansion slot inside of your PC. The PC itself creates the fax images—or they can be derived from a peripheral image scanner. The fax board converts the characters in your ASCII files into graphic images that can be received by distant fax machines. In effect, a fax board turns any fax machine into a near laser-quality printer.

At the other end of the connection, when a fax transmission is received, it is displayed on the monitor screen, stored in a file, or printed by using a standard dot-matrix or laser printer. Optical Character Recognition software can even turn the fax image into ASCII files for use with your word processor.

At both ends of the line, incoming and outgoing calls are managed much as they are in the linked fax-and-PC systems. The PC keeps makes the calls, even to multiple recipients, logs them, and answers the phone when a fax comes in.

The primary advantage of putting a fax board into your PC is convenience. Without the connection, you would have to print out a document made by your PC, and then scan it into the fax machine. When you receive something without the PC-to-fax connection, you would have the paper copy as the starting ground for any manipulations you would want to make. Unless you have a scanner, that means pulling out the scissors and rubber cement if you want to make changes. Link PC and fax, and you can work on the screen, editing with painting programs or electronic publishing editors. Going in the other direction, you can create fax documents using your word processor or, with the appropriate conversion software, any other program. Instead of printing the results, you send them out by fax.

Creating fax on the PC confers your work with an added advantage, an apparent increase in resolution. By their nature, scanners have to make do with whatever they are force fed. Unless the edge of a character or line perfectly matches the edge of a scanning cell, the question as to whether the corresponding dot should be black or white will be ambiguous. As a result, scanned characters can have fuzzy or jagged edges. When the character is made by a computer to be printed using a fax machine, however, each dot can be optimally placed to give the sharpest apparent resolution. Fax text and graphics created on a PC look better than anything that's scanned in.

Selecting a Fax System

Standardization doesn't mean that all fax modems for PCs are alike. Certainly, they differ in speed capabilities. More importantly, their control software differs. Two identical fax modems with different control software will act as unalike as a teenager alone and one accompanied by a parent at the mall. The control software deter-mines the speed of the modem (by how efficiently it compresses and decompresses files into fax format), what you can do with the modem, and how easy the modem is to operate. When buying a fax modem for your PC, you should consider not only its hardware features but those of the software that runs it.

You do have to consider the hardware, however. First, the speed. Faster is better, and 14,400 bps is best for a fax modem. Slower 4800 bps products are only for people whose worlds don't revolve around fax or who have time to spare, but little cash. The 9600 bps speed is tolerable and may unlock some big bargains. Of course, you'll want a regular data modem on your fax board so that you don't have to waste two expansion slots on a single telephone connection. Con-sider the data section of a fax modem the same way you would any other modem: check the standards, the speeds, and the port compat-ibility it offers you. Even though your fax modem may ship out fax images at 9600 bps, it may be limited to 2400 bps when you want to make a standard modem connection. Moreover, make sure that the data modem section of the fax board uses the Hayes AT command set. You don't want to abandon your favorite communications software when you use your new modem. Ensure that you can electrically install the data modem section of fax board at a port address unused by any other ports in your system. Remember, the data modem has an embedded serial port just like any other internal modem. It will need the same system resources as any serial port or modem.

The data modem has an embedded serial port just like any other internal modem.

When selecting a fax modem by the software accompanying it, you'll want to ensure that you get all the features you need. Any fax modem will send files down the phone line, but you should check which graphic and text file formats the program will accept. You might not be able to transmit the files created by your graphics software.

Speed is something that you can judge only by trying the software.

One of the best features of fax is that it standardizes the data format that's sent over your telephone. Any fax modem can cope with any Group 3 fax transmission without interpretation problems. However, this compatibility does not extend to the files that fax software stores on your disk. Generally, each fax-board manufacturer's fax program uses its own on-disk storage format. Consequently, you cannot exchange disk files of fax transmissions with people who use a different fax system even if you and your partner follow the Group 3 standard to the letter.

Ensure that the graphic adapter you choose is compatible with the software that controls the fax modem.

Nearly all fax modems allow you to send the same message to a group of recipients and to delay the sending of faxes to a later time, presumably when phone rates are lower. If you really need these features, however, you'll want to assure yourself that the modem you choose offers them. Speed is something that you can judge only by trying the software. The question you need to answer is not how fast the software works but whether you can live with software that prints fax images so slowly.

Before you can install a fax board, you'll need to make sure that your PC is properly equipped to handle it. Most fax boards require at least a hard disk, DOS 3.1 or later, and a lot of memory. You'll also need a graphics adapter compatible with the fax program if you want to preview images before you send or print them. You'll also need to ensure that the graphic adapter you choose is compatible with the software that controls the fax modem.

Installing a fax modem is like installing any other modem. You'll have to resolve any port conflict before you start, slide the modem in, and connect up the phone line. The only additional complication is setting up the fax software.

Installation

Begin installing an external fax modem as you would any other modem. You only need to make three, sometimes four, connections: plug the modem into your phone line, connect it to one of your PC's serial ports, and plug it into its necessary electrical supply. The optional connection is to a telephone deskset.

The cables to use in hooking up a fax modem should not be a problem. The necessary power cable will be standard equipment with the modem. In addition, most fax modems include a short telephone cable with modular connectors at either end for plugging into your telephone line. As with data modems, you may need a a two-jack adapter if you need to plug a telephone in to the same line. You find such adapters in any store that sells telephones—drug store, electronics store, or discount store. Plug the adapter into the the jack for the telephone line and plug the modem and the telephone into the adapter. If your external modem has two jacks on its back, run a wire from the one marked "Line" to your telephone line jack. Connect the modem jack labeled "Phone" to your telephone.

Most fax modem makers expect you to supply the signal cable between your PC and the modem. Even this cable should not be a problem. As with ordinary modems, a fax modem requires a straight-through cable to make the connection. So called null-modem or cross-over cables are unnecessary—they won't even work. For short distances (say six feet or so), a straight-through 25-pin ribbon cable will work just fine. If you choose to use a shielded cable, you'll only need the nine connections made on the small AT-style serial connectors (nine-pin, of course). Your modem cable normally should have a male connector on one end (to mate with the modem) and a female connector on the other end (to mate with your PC).

Internal fax modems with direct data transmission capabilities are hardly more difficult. The fax section of the modem doesn't require the assignation of a COM port, although you may need to dedicate an interrupt to it. Setting up the data section of the internal modem usually is more complex.

After you've prepared your fax modem with whatever setup is required, you're ready for the hardware installation. As with any-thing you install inside your PC, the first step is to ensure your safety and that of your PC. Power down your PC and unplug its power cord. Then to gain access, remove its lid from its case so that you can locate a vacant expansion slot for your internal fax modem.

Generally, any slot will be fine. Because nearly all fax modems use eight-bit bus connectors, any ISA 8- or 16-bit slot or an EISA 32-bit slot should accommodate the modem. Any Micro Channel slot should accommodate any Micro Channel modem. Just pick a slot and slide the fax modem in. Screw down the modem's retaining bracket. Next, test your fax modem before putting the top back on your PC. You'll have to connect it to your telephone line to perform the needed testing, so attach the necessary cables to the modem.

In most cases, you'll need to plug in one or two modular telephone wires. If your fax modem has just one jack on its retaining bracket, connect it to a standard modular jack to which you would plug in an ordinary telephone. If you need to plug a telephone in to the same jack, get a two-jack adapter, plug the adapter into the jack, and plug the modem and the telephone into the adapter. If your internal fax modem has two jacks, run a wire from the one marked "Line" to your phone jack. Connect the modem jack labeled "Phone" to your telephone.

To test the modem, plug in your PC and boot it up. Install the fax software that accompanied your fax modem or whatever fax software you'll be using. Some fax modems come with software that tests and verifies proper operation without a telephone connection. If your fax modem has its own test software, try that now. If not, try your fax software and see whether it works with the fax modem. When your modem passes these preliminary tests, you're safe to button up your PC. Turn off the power to it and replace its lid.

If your fax modem fails to operate with its test software or your fax software, ensure that you've set its jumpers and switches properly, that the modem is properly seated in its slot (if it's internal), and the phone line is properly connected and working. Checking out the details solves most fax problems. More difficult to sort out are incompatibilities between third-party software and fax modems. Questions about these are best answered by the technical support people at the software publisher. Odds are, however, that you won't have to call or fax a service rep to get your fax modem working.

Printer Sharing

In most cases, standard PC printers offer only a parallel connection, so there's no port choice to make. Use parallel.

The most common reason people want to link PCs together is to share a common resource, and that resource almost inevitably is a printer. With a printer sharing device, you can connect two, three, or a dozen PCs to a single printer, spreading the cost of an expensive, feature-laden printer among several people and PCs. If you're not prepared, however, connecting up the printer sharing device itself can become a headache.

In concept, setting up a printer sharing system is simple. You just run a wire from each PC that has to share the printer to the sharing device. Then run another wire to the printer. As soon as you try connecting up the cables, the complexities will be as obvious as the plugs that won't fit the jacks—and often won't work even if they do.

The confusion in cabling a printer sharing system results from all of the port choices available to you. Although simple sharing devices may all use only parallel ports, more sophisticated equipment will offer you the choice (either when you order or when you hook everything up) of either parallel or serial ports. These port choices must be made at two places—going to and from the sharing device.

Port Selection

From the sharing device to the printer is often the easiest port choice to make. In most cases, standard PC printers offer only a parallel connection, so there's no port choice to make. Use parallel.

The other side of the sharing device may give you a choice of using a parallel or serial interface to link to each PC. As with the printer side, the preferred method for making this connection is the parallel port.

DOS and PCs based on the IBM standard automatically default to using the first parallel port as the primary printer outlet. Parallel ports can transfer data much more quickly, as high as about 30,000 characters per second (versus 10,000 for fast serial port modes, about 1,000-2,000 character per second in IBM-supported operating modes). Most PCs also have the capability of giving you more parallel ports. Older PCs and DOS versions support two serial ports and three parallel ports. Even though recent PCs and DOS give you the option of four serial ports, these can be quickly consumed by other system options: mice, modems, and scanners. Only printers usually use parallel ports.

The range of an IBM-standard parallel port is a distinct disadvantage for peripheral sharing.

Parallel ports also are preferred because they are easier to connect and get working. As long as you get the correct cable—the nearly ubiquitous IBM printer cable—you are assured that your printer will work properly with your PC.

The range of an IBM-standard parallel port, however, is a distinct disadvantage for peripheral sharing. In most cases, the maximum permitted length of a parallel data cable is eight feet. Although you may get away with stretching a parallel connection to fifteen feet, going to great lengths quickly becomes chancy. It's not that a long parallel cable won't work. Rather, long parallel cables are subject to picking up stray signals (and emanating them) because of their high data rates.

Even at the highest speeds, serial connections reach much farther than parallel.

Worse, the signals inside of a parallel cable can interact, confusing each other. As a result, you may sometimes find a strange character mixed with the otherwise normal output of your laser printer. Of course, should a stray character find its way into one of the command sequences that tells your printer to switch fonts, the results could be unexpected and dramatic.

Serial connections are slower, more confusing, and probably inevitable because they can reach farther. Unless you and your compatriots wanting to share are willing to cluster in a tight group around your printer as if it were a campfire and there were spirits aprowl in the night, you'll want to extend more than eight feet of cable from each PC.

Even at the highest speeds, serial connections reach much farther than parallel. For example, properly cabled, a 19,200 bit per second serial connection may operate flawlessly over 100 feet. Slower connections can stretch for half a mile.

Even those length limits might seem modest compared to what you're used to with a serially connected modem. For example, a 2400 bps (or even 9600 bps) modem connection may reach for thousands of miles. Ordinary, serial connections can't go that far because they used digital signals; modems translate those digital signals into a variety of analog that can better withstand long-distance connections.

Along with length, serial connections bring their own breed of obstacles—setting up ports, mating connectors, and ensuring the proper flow of data. Conquering these serial connection complexities requires several steps. You must make your PC amenable to substituting serial for its preferred parallel. Then you need to rig up the right cables that provide the requisite flow control, connector style, and connection type.

PC Setup

Your first concern is to get your PC to recognize a serial port as your connection with a printer. IBM saw the serial port only as a secondary printer linkage, treating it as a poor step-child to the parallel port. To make a serial connection work with your printer, you must convince your PC that the serial port is a parallel port, and you must set up the serial port to match the characteristics of the input of your printer sharing device.

The secret to success with serial on your PC is DOS's do-nearly-everything MODE command. MODE enables you to set the speed and other operating parameters of your serial port as well as telling your PC to think serial instead of parallel when it comes time to print.

Readying your serial port for printing is a two-step process. First, set its speed and other communication protocol parameters; then redirect print commands to the port. Remember, you must set the communications parameters first, before you do the redirection.

For proper communication, you must designate the speed at which the port is to operate in bits per second, the parity checking code used on each word of data, the number of bits in each data word, the number of stop bits to indicate the end of each word, and so on. The proper protocol values to use are determined by the needs of the inputs to your printer sharing device. You'll find these parameters given in the instruction manual of your sharing device.

If your sharing device gives you a choice, you'll need to use the highest possible bit rate that doesn't cause errors in transmission. With reasonable cable lengths, 9600 bits per second normally is your first choice.

To use MODE, you type the parameters on the command line at the DOS prompt after typing the MODE command. Better yet, include the command and its parameters in your system's AUTOEXEC.BAT file so that they load every time you boot up.

When using MODE, the syntax of the command (the way you type the instruction) is critical. Here's the proper syntax:

First, specify the port you want to set up (COM1, COM2, COM3 or COM4), a colon, the speed in bits per second to use (110, 150, 300, 600, 1200, 2400, 4800, 9600, and in some systems 19200) using the exact speed or only the first two digits of the speed, the parity (E for even, O for odd, N for none), the number of data bits (7 or 8), and the number of stop bits for each word (1 or 2).

Finally, add a P to the command to designate that it is to be used for a printer port. This instruction tells your PC to continuously retest the port when it gets a time-out error so that your system doesn't give up in the middle of a print job.

The letters used in protocol parameters can be upper- or lowercase. All parameters in a MODE command must be separated by commands.

The proper form for the mode command that sets the first serial port to operate at 9600 bits per second with no parity, eight data bits, and one stop bit would be:

```
MODE COM1:9600,n,8,1,p
```

When the serial port is set up, you need to switch your PC's print commands over the that port. To redirect all the print commands that go through DOS, use the following mode command (assuming that you'll connect your printer to your first serial port, COM1):

```
MODE LPT1=COM1
```

The makers of printer sharing devices often make serial port setup an easy matter, avoiding the need to deal with DOS. Typically, they will supply programs that automatically create a batch file that handles all the mode commands you need. Alternately, the printer sharing device may come with driver software that installs itself and entirely eliminates the need for mode commands.

Take advantage of this software when it is available. Often, it will also add features to help you manage your printer and sharing device more efficiently.

Note that MODE-command port-redirection only works for programs that use DOS to handle their print operations. Many applications ignore DOS and print by sending instructions straight to your PC's ports. These programs will ignore this DOS redirection and leave you scratching your head about why your printer won't work.

To avoid such problems, you must specially configure each such program to use the serial connection. To do this, you need to specify a serial driver when you install the program. Typically, the installation software of each application will ask you what kind of printer you are using and what port it is connected to. Specify a serial port, and the program will either ask you for the communications parameters to use—or tell you which you have to use.

Hardware Installation

The physical part of connecting your PC to a sharing device means that you have to tangle with cables, and it will be a tangle because of all the cable and connector types you must deal with.

One of the primary distinctions between cable types you may encounter is shielded versus unshielded. A shielded cable has a metal braid (sometimes a metal film) encircling the various wires inside it. A plastic jacket usually covers the braid. An unshielded cable lacks the braid. The most common unshielded cables used with PCs are ribbon cables, strips of parallel wires bound together. Ordinary telephone cable is also unshielded; there's usually no braid within the plastic jacket of phone wire.

The purpose of the braid to to stop interference from leaking out or leaking into the cable. Nearly all cables for use outside of your PC's case are now shielded to comply with the strict emissions requirements of the FCC. Shielded cable also helps ensure the integrity of the data transferred through the cable, so they are to be preferred.

Although parallel cables need a full contingent of 25 wires to convey all the necessary data and control information, serial cables often use fewer conductors. In situations where software flow control is used, serial cables can get along with as few as three conductors. With hardware flow control, cables may use only seven to nine conductors.

Your printer sharing device will determine the kind of flow control you'll use; most often it will be hardware. Although software flow control simplifies cabling, it will also preclude the use of graphics with your printer sharing device.

Software flow control works by sending messages between your computer and printer (or printer sharing device) to tell your computer when it's safe to send data and when the printer needs time to catch its breath. In the most common form of software flow control, the ASCII characters with the mnemonics XON and XOFF are used for signaling (hence this kind of flow control is often termed XON/XOFF). These characters are forbidden in the data stream except for flow control signaling. If they should appear in the data bound for the printer, they would disrupt flow control.

If you need to print graphics through a serial port, you'll have to use hardware flow control.

Because most graphics applications use all ASCII character combinations, interference with software flow control would be unavoidable. Hence, if you need to print graphics through a serial port, you'll have to use hardware flow control.

The cables are not the only concern in wiring up your printer sharing device. You need to be certain that the connectors are wired to match the type of serial port that you are using.

It is important to find out whether your printer sharing device has DTE or DCE ports so that you can get the appropriate cable.

Serial ports come in two flavors, DTE (which stands for Data Terminal Equipment) and DCE (Data Communications Equipment). The difference between the two is simple. DTE ports use pin

2 for transmitting data and pin 3 for receiving it. DCE ports do just the opposite, pin 2 receives data, and pin 3 transmits it.

Imagine that you connect two DTE devices with an ordinary cable that connects the pins at one end with those with the same number at its other end. Both DTE devices will try to send on pin 2 and listen on pin 3. Neither device will ever hear what the other device has to say. Consequently, DTE devices can communicate only with DCE devices when you use such a straight-through cable. For two DTE devices to exchange information, their signals must be crossed. This is ordinarily achieved through using a cross-over cable that switches the pin 2 with pin 3 connections (as well as several others used in flow control).

It is important to find out whether your printer sharing device has DTE or DCE ports so that you can get the appropriate cable. Because PC serial ports and most input connectors on printers are set up as DTE, the preferred connection on a printer sharing device will be DCE all around.

Most makers of printer sharing devices sell cables made to match your PC with their sharing devices. When you know the cable type, however, you can order exactly what you need from a mail order vendor. You'll have to specify how long you want the cable, how many conductors you'll need to use (typically 25 for parallel connections and 8 or 9 for serial with hardware flow control), the connector type, and for a serial cable whether it is straight-through or a cross-over cable.

By searching out a mail order vendor that specializes in cables, you should be able to find what you need at a fraction of the price demanded by the sharing device maker. Not only will you save by sharing a printer, you'll also save with lower cabling costs.

PC-to-PC Connections

Figure the savings in not having to install a second laser printer or high-speed v.32 modem, and the PC-to-PC connection can pay for itself tenfold.

If you have two PCs, someday (like yesterday) you're going to want to use one machine to open a file that's stored only on the other. Then you've got to find a floppy, check for enough free space, pull off the write-protect tab, and discover that you've got 16 levels of subdirectories to erase. When you try to reformat it to save time, DOS inevitably replies that Track 0 is bad, and your floppy belongs in the trash. Although what you reach for is another floppy, what you really want is some magical way of getting your file from one machine to the other. You want a direct PC-to-PC connection.

The benefits of such a PC-to-PC connection can be more than the mere convenience of moving files around, however. With most systems, you can also share printers and modems. Figure the savings in not having to install a second laser printer or high-speed v.32 modem, and the PC-to-PC connection can pay for itself tenfold. What you need is inexpensive, costing as little as $100 from a direct vendor.

The trouble involved can be similarly untaxing. In many ways, linking two PCs can be one of the easiest upgrades you can make. You can get everything you need in one box and install it all in a few minutes. From there, you can customize the link to suit your own circumstances, from a temporary setup you pull out only after a business trip to a permanent connection that keeps your systems constantly in touch.

Before you start eyeing the ads looking for the right PC-to-PC connection system, you need to set a goal for your interconnection upgrade. You have to ask yourself what you want to do with your link-up and how you want to use it.

One issue that you must decide upon is whether you want to link your PCs together permanently or prefer to connect and disconnect them as you need to make transfers. You'll find more to the difference than just moving connectors around.

A permanent installation can require a lot more work. You'll need to run wires between your PCs in such a way that you don't trip over them or accidentally tug them out. Moreover, a permanent installation will make permanent demands from your PC. You'll give up some memory (and other system resources) to keep the connection ready and operating all the time.

The permanent link is more convenient, too. The effort you put in to cabling will pay off in not having to touch the wires again. You'll be able to access files on one PC from the other any time you want—no hassles, no hardships, no thinking. In most cases, you'll just use another drive letter or two to access the other computer.

You'll even be able to share other system resources. The permanent connection can make some of the hardware resources of one PC accessible by the other. The two computers can share a single printer and modem without the need for additional hardware or software.

The temporary connection is best for moving files from one computer to another but little else. You won't want to hassle with cables whenever you want to print a letter or phone CompuServe. Then again, you won't pollute your PC with the driver software and other

The permanent connection can make some of the hardware resources of one PC accessible by the other.

terminate-and-stay- resident (TSR) programs needed for file transfer when you're not actually using the connection. This can save your PC valuable kilobytes of DOS memory and all the compatibility hassles of loading yet more memory-resident software on your PC.

Interfaces

When linking PCs, the most important hardware concern is the connection interface. It will determine the kind of wiring you need, the speed of the transfers, the possible length of the link-up, and the growth potential. Your choices are threefold: using parallel ports, serial ports, or dedicated host adapters.

The disadvantages of using a parallel connection are distance, cable complexity, stunted growth, and scant availability of connection software.

One of the biggest advantages of parallel ports is that they are there. Most people connect just one printer to their PCs yet are apt to have two parallel ports, leaving one free for the remote connection. Parallel ports are also quick. Because they move information a byte (instead of a bit) at a time, they can transfer information at astounding rates, about half a megabit per second.

Parallel connections won't work reliably across long distances. Their high speed and multiple parallel wires limit their usefulness to no more than about 25 feet (some experts recommend parallel connections be no more than 10 feet long).

Parallel connection wiring is expensive. A parallel connection requires cables with almost 25 individual wires inside. Not only must you pay for the wires, but if you want to make a permanent installation, you may have to solder, screw, or punch each of those into place—definitely not a job to look forward to when you wake up in the morning.

Moreover, parallel connections have no upward growth path. You can link two PCs through parallel ports and no more. Opt to add a third PC, and you'll be looking for a new interconnection scheme.

Because of these three shortcomings, you are certain to encounter the double-barreled fourth—availability and compatibility. Few PC-connecting programs support parallel ports. Worse, although most PCs come with bidirectional parallel ports that allow you to shift data back and forth, some inexpensive add-in parallel ports work in only one direction. Parallel connection programs are not compatible with one-way ports. Your PC may be able to send data out but not receive it.

Serial ports offer more range than parallel connections but sacrifice speed. Even the top operating speed of a serial connection lacks the performance of a parallel link—possibly one-third the speed or slower. Stretch the serial connection, and the maximum data rate plummets from its 115,200 bits per second top rate to as little as 300 bps. Although those low transfer rates might sound like a disadvantage, their value can be immense because they allow the connection to continue to work—and work for great lengths, perhaps thousand of feet.

Generally, you can expect to get maximum serial performance from cable length of about 100 feet, particularly if you use shielded cable. That's more than enough to stretch from one end of your home to the other or from one office to another in a business. Longer cable runs will require you to operate serial ports more slowly.

Besides allowing for long runs, serial connections make cabling easy. Some systems use as few as three wires (send, receive, and ground), and others may add a few additional connections for flow control of the data. For modestly sized installations, you can use ordinary telephone wire, hardware, and modular connectors for making a serial link-up permanent. Nearly anyone with the ability to keep colors consistent—anyone able to connect the red wire to the red terminal—can install a serial based system armed with nothing more than a screwdriver.

Serial ports also allow a reasonable degree of upgrading. Many serial-based interconnection schemes, often called *zero-slot LANs*, allow you to link several PCs together rather than just two. Although the relatively low speed of serial systems limits their use for large networks, they can adequately serve a work group of half a dozen people.

On the downside, serial ports can be scarce. Although most PCs have serial ports, they are also in great demand for them. Mice, graphics tablets, trackballs, and modems all compete for the available serial connections. As a result of this port competition, you just might not have a serial port available for connecting PCs together.

Proprietary and network interfaces start at about the speed of parallel ports and streak off into supercomputer territory, from below a megabit per second to hundreds of megabits using fiber optic technology. Cables can run to almost any length—kilometers—and can be so exotic that the tools required to tie two wires together can cost more than a whole serial-based network.

You'll also have to give up an expansion slot in each PC for a network host adapter—if you have any free slots. In addition, a dedicated network extra adapter also extracts a price. A single Ethernet adapter, for example, will likely cost you more than an entire two-computer connection package that includes hardware (cable and connectors) and software. Cabling, too, may be more expensive.

Counterbalancing the cost is flexibility. With most such dedicated connection interfaces, the growth potential is essentially unlimited, providing your budget is likewise. After all, you're talking about a real network here, and you'll have real network concerns—probably more than you'll want to bother with for a two-PC link up. Real networks take real work.

DOS Links

You'll find a number of products that offer themselves as complete kits for making the PC-to-PC connection. These offer special proprietary software and a cable so that all you need to do is plug in. Alternately, you can use the *Interlnk* software included with DOS 6 or the PC interconnecting software that's included in most DOS utility packages like the Norton Utilities and PC Tools.

Generally, the principal difference between these alternatives is one of packaging. You can buy a box or can—an all-in-one box that contains everything you need to tie your PCs together or a do-it-yourself can of worms that requires you to mix and match software and hardware.

The truth is that you can probably link PCs together using little more than a home-made cable and the rudimentary utilities included with DOS 2.0. You could also perform brain surgery on yourself with a kitchen knife. If you're skilled and extremely lucky, you might just get away with it. The probability is greater, however, that you'll be in for some severe headaches along the way, no matter the ultimate outcome.

The all-in-one box approach will include the software you need to link two PCs (with a license that reflects operation on two machines simultaneously) and a plug-in starter cable. Open the box, read the instructions (or try to), plug everything together, and you should be on your way. Learning all the details and features will take you some time, possibly weeks, but you should have the basic functions down in a few minutes.

Rolling your own connection system leaves everything to your imagination. First, you need the hardware. That's easy. For serial-to-serial systems, you'll need a standard cross-over cable, the kind required to hook a serial printer to your PC. You should be able to find one of a reasonable length for under $20 from most direct vendors.

When you have the serial ports of two PCs connected, you need to choose software that can handle the functions that you need. For example, if all you want to do is transfer a file, you can use any standard communications program, even one you nab free from your local on-line bulletin board. You can even take remote-control of one PC from the other with the appropriate software choice. If, however, you want the convenience of LAN technology—sharing disk drives between PCs, sharing modem and printer resources— you'll need some kind of LAN-like software. That's when the big surprise will hit you—you want the very same software that comes in the all-in-one box. Interlnk will do the same thing, but without the convenience features such as synchronizing disks, updating files, and minimizing transfer time. The price you pay for the big box is hardly more than you might expect to pay for the cable, but it packs these features and more. For LAN-like functionality, the sensible thing to do is buy a package deal.

For LAN-like functionality, the sensible thing to do is buy a package deal.

Commercial Products

At one time, you had your choice of two ways of handling a file transfer across a PC-to-PC connection. Some packages gave you a program to run on each PC, essentially a specialized communications program, that took complete control of both systems. A menu enabled you to pick a file or group of files to transfer. Other file transfer packages (and DOS Interlnk) run invisibly in the background on each PC and enable you to use the disk drive of one computer as if they were physically attached to the other. The more advanced connection software that incorporates LAN features also follows this latter style.

The choice between these two operating modes is a matter of personal preference. Either will get the job done, and both are limited by the speed of the hardware connection. Odds are that you won't even have to make the choice when selecting software—many PC-to-PC connection packages give you both options. You can try both and select the method you prefer.

The menu-driven approach is easier—you just run a program, and it worries about the details. Drive-emulation programs like Interlnk require that you add a software driver to both of the PCs that you want to connect. Other programs may require this modification in only one of your systems.

In an Interlnk system, your two PCs are not equal. One acts as a server (much like a network server) and the other functions as the client. The client can share the server's resources, but the server cannot use the drives or other resources of the client. The client and the server each run separate software. In a typical application, your notebook PC will be the client and your desktop machine the server.

The server has the easy software to setup and run. You only need to run the program INTERSVR.EXE, which takes over the system and turns it into a vegetable for any purpose other than serving the client.

You must edit the CONFIG.SYS file of the client to give it access to the server. You add the device driver INTERLNK.EXE to the commands in CONFIG.SYS, for example adding this entry:

```
DEVICE=C:/DOS/INTERLNK.EXE /DRIVES=4
```

DOS's on-line help documents the options you can add to the Interlnk command line. Type *HELP INTERLNK.EXE* at the command line while running DOS 6 to review these options.

No matter what kind of software you use to link your PCs together, installing the hardware part of the PC-to-PC connection is a simple matter, at least on a temporary basis. All you need do is plug one of the cables accompanying the software into each of the two PCs you want to link.

Sounds easy until you discover that some packages give you a wide choice of what to plug in. For example, one popular PC-to-PC connection package includes two cables, one of which has four connectors. Use the cable with only two connectors for a fast link through parallel ports. The four-connector cable links serial ports. The four connectors are arranged so that the cable will plug into either 9- or 25-pin serial jacks at either end (see fig. 14.7).

Note that there is a cross-over hidden inside the middle of this cable. That means the connectors at each end are designed to act differently to match PCs. If you're linking two PCs, you must use one of the connectors at one end of the cable in one PC. The other PC must use one of the connectors at the *other* end of the cable. If you try to plug the 25-pin connector from one end into your first PC and the 9-pin connector from the same end into your second PC, the connection system won't work. You've side-stepped the crossover.

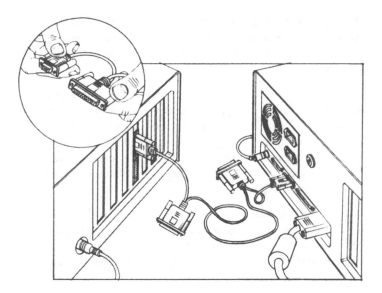

Figure 14.7
A commercial PC-to-
PC serial connection
solution. 9- and 25-
pin connectors are
provided at each end
of the cable (inset).

Other products may come with slightly different hardware. With
one, you get two short cables with a 9-pin connector on one end and
a 25-pin connector on the other. Plug only one of these connectors
into a PC, leaving the other end of the cable dangling. You'll find a
modular telephone-style jack carved into the larger, 25-pin connector of the pair attached to each cable. Plug one end of the
telephone-style flat cable into the modular jack of each of the short
two-connector cables. The short cables are actually only adapters; the
phone wire is the actual PC-to-PC link.

*After you've got
both ends of the
cable plugged in,
the hard hardware
work is all over.*

After you have both ends of the cable plugged in, the hard hardware
work is all over. You next need to set up the software to match the
hardware.

Actually, you have to make a double-match. The first match is to
indicate the port that you've plugged the cable into by its DOS
name—LPT1, COM1, or whatever. With serial connections, you
must make another match, the operating speed of the port. This
speed must match that set at the PC located at the other end of the
connection.

You indicate these matches as part of the software setup procedure of
the PC-to-PC connection program. With interactive, menu-driven
programs, opt for the "Options" choice from the menu and make
your matches there. In the device-driver style of program, the ports
and speeds that you want to use are indicated as command-line
parameters for the device drivers. An installation program will
usually handle this work for you.

When your software also allows resource sharing, you'll have to specify the port and computer to which each shared resource is connected. Again, this process is usually handled by the installation software.

As a final step with this network-style connection software, you'll need to reconfigure your applications to match the new configuration of each of your computer systems. For example, you'll have to reconfigure your word processor to recognize the new port assignment for your shared printer. You may also want to change batch files you've created to execute programs so that you can load software from the second PC.

If the instruction manual accompanying the software does not indicate the new port assignments, the installation program will. Make sure you write down the values noted by the installation software so that you have a reference for reconfiguring your applications.

Small Networks

Computer networks have a knack for knocking even knowledgeable PC gnostics down to size.

File sharing across the network alone will eliminate a major source of data loss, duplication of records, and out-of-sync file updates.

When it's no longer an only child in your business, your PC must learn the same lesson as the infant growing up with siblings—sharing. Sharing among PCs means more convenience, better utilization of expensive resources (such as printers), and fewer mistakes and misunderstandings.

Computer networks have a knack for knocking even knowledgable PC gnostics down to size. They bring the worst of all possible worlds together: impenetrable software, inhospitable hardware, and cabling as confused as a pit of epileptic snakes. Installing a network operating system can take system managers days; deciphering its idiosyncrasies can keep users and operators puzzled for weeks. Network host adapters often prove incompatible with other PC hardware—their required interrupts and I/O addresses locking horns with SCSI boards, port controllers, and other peripherals. As for cabling—weaving the wiring for a network is like threading a needle while wearing boxing gloves during a cyclone that has blown out the the electricity, the candles, and the last rays of hope.

In fact, no one in his right mind would tangle with a network were not the benefits so great. File sharing across the network alone will eliminate a major source of data loss, duplication of records, and out-of-sync file updates. Better still, a network lets you get organized. You can put all your important files in one central location where they are easier to protect, from disaster and theft. Instead of worrying about backing up half a dozen PCs individually, you can easily handle the chore with one command.

Electronic mail can bring order to the chaos of tracking messages and appointments, even in a small office. With network-based E-mail, you can communicate with your coworkers without scattering memo slips like grass seed or felling a forest for paper.

Sharing a costly laser printer or large hard disk (with some networks, even modems) can cut your capital cost of a computers equipment by thousands or tens of thousands of dollars. For example, instead of buying a flotilla of personal laser printers, you can serve the hardcopy need of everyone with just one machine.

Fortunately, you can get all the benefits of network connectivity without its biggest headaches if you keep your needs modest and pick the right technologies.

Although you still won't be able to plug PCs together with the same impunity as with Christmas lights, modern cabling will make the chore little more difficult than connecting a few telephones. Using such a modern smaller network won't require any more PC savvy than copying a file from a different disk drive. Installing the hardware will still take a bit of forethought and knowledge, but you can master those needs relatively easily. That's where this upgrade reference will help.

The most successful small networks today are built by using two concepts—peer-to-peer architecture and 10Base-T twisted-pair hardware. The combination of peers and pairs means simple installation, understandable operation, and low costs.

Peer-to-peer means no dedicated file server as you will find in big, complex networks. Instead, all PCs exist as equals. Generally, one PC is granted access to the disk drives and printers connected to another. The same DOS commands apply to the drives local to an individual computer and those accessed remotely through the network. In that most people already know enough about DOS to change drive letters, they can almost instantly put the network to work.

The twisted-pair wiring of 10Base-T means that you use exactly the same kind of cable as you would when putting in an extension telephone. You can even plug everything together with simple modular connectors. In fact, the biggest 10Base-T cabling trick may be keeping the wires from wrapping around you feet.

Alternatives

Everyone doesn't have the need for a network. If you only have one PC, you've nothing to connect together. If you have more than one PC, you probably would like to link them together—but you may be afraid of the work involved. You have good reason. Even companies with their own computer resource departments typically hire consultants when planning a network. The issues are entirely unlike those of managing individual PCs, and most involve the snarl of wire that's the heart—or at least circulatory system—of the network. For example, the network guru has to worry about such things as coaxial cables, terminations, loop resistance, and (probably) the phases of the moon.

Fortunately with 10Base-T, an entire network can be plug-and-play, linked together with cables you can buy direct. For more complex or permanent installations, 10Base-T lets you take advantage of existing telephone wiring to install the network without blasting holes in walls and ceilings.

Zero-Slot LANs

Zero-slot LANs (Local Area Networks) that take advantage of serial port connections set the low-price limit: no hardware costs and the same twisted-pair wiring as 10Base-T. These add much the same software complication as a small network but suffer from a hardware-imposed disadvantage. The serial ports themselves limit network communications to 115,200 bits per second in most PCs, and lower speeds are often necessary with long reaches of cable because zero-slot LAN signals are particularly prone to interference. Many zero-slot LANs require special cables, making their installation more complex than that of 10Base-T. Others use simple telephone-style wiring, making their installation equivalent to that of a 10Base-T network—except there's no need for host adapters, and they deliver only slow performance.

Arcnet

Arcnet is another low-cost networking scheme for which you can readily acquire components direct. Arcnet systems can be as easy to connect as 10Base-T—it uses the same hub-based architecture—when you use pre-fabricated cables. Moreover, Arcnet components are relatively inexpensive—$50-60 for host adapter boards, $20 for a passive hub, $100 for an active hub. That's about half the price of 10Base-T. But the price of 10Base-T is falling dramatically. Moreover, Arcnet is slow for today's high-performance computing needs in that it operates at 2.5 megahertz. Few new Arcnet installations are made today, so you'll probably want to join the trend away from them.

Ethernet

Ethernet is the signaling system used by 10Base-T; it's effectively a superset that also encompasses other wiring topographies. Ethernet is a formal standard, IEEE 802.3, that allows for several wiring options besides 10Base-T. These include thick Ethernet, which involves cables nearly half an inch in diameter (10Base-5), and thinwire Ethernet, which uses cable less than a quarter-inch in diameter (10Base-2). Both of these systems use a bus architecture. That is, PCs are daisy-chained together. The wiring is complex and persnickety. The network cable must snake through an entire building and get properly terminated at each end. When it does not work, costly network monitors are required to find problems. Although effective for large businesses, these systems tend to be more complex than a do-it-yourselfer will want to tangle with.

10Base-T

10Base-T starts with a combination of the best of the zero-slot LAN and Arcnet and then adds in several of its own virtues. As with a zero-slot LAN, 10Base-T uses cheap twisted-pair wiring. As with Arcnet, you connect 10Base-T PCs in a simple star-configuration—every system links to a central hub. Unlike either the zero-slot LAN or Arcnet, 10Base-T is a formally defined industry standard. That standardization means wide support and prices driven by the mass market. With 10Base-T, you're not susceptible to the failure of a single component manufacturer. Best of all, 10Base-T is fast, as quick as any Ethernet system (see fig. 14.8), operating 10MHz—four times faster than Arcnet and almost 100 times quicker than a zero-slot LAN.

Unlike either the zero-slot LAN or Arcnet, 10Base-T is a formally defined industry standard.

Twisted-pair wiring has several things going for it: it's cheaper to make and sell than coaxial cable; it's more flexible and easier to work with; and zillions of miles of twisted-pair are installed in offices around the world—it's the stuff otherwise known as telephone wire.

Coaxial cable holds the advantage when it comes to distance. Thick Ethernet can extend network reach to more than half a mile, but that's far more than the typical small business needs.

Figure 14.8

Two network cabling solutions: twisted pair (10Base-T) and coaxial cable (Ethernet).

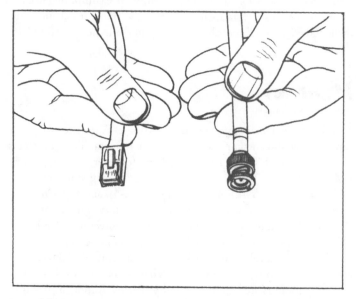

One of the biggest problems faced by the designers of network systems is keeping radiation and interference under control. All wires act as antenna, sending and receiving signals. As frequencies increase and wire lengths increase, the radiation increases. The pressure is on network designers to increase the speed (with higher frequencies) and reach of networks (with longer cables) to keep up with the increasing demands of industry.

Two strategies are commonly used to combat interference from network wiring. One is the coaxial cable used by other Ethernet systems. Coaxial cable is naturally resistant to radiation. As a result, coaxial won out for network wiring early on. Twisted-pair wiring, however, has price and availability advantages, so it has been adapted to higher speeds by using second strategy: special differential signals.

Coaxial cable is special two-conductor wire in which a central signal-carrying conductor is surrounded by a shield (a continuous braid or metalized plastic film) at ground potential that prevents stray signals from leaking out of the central conductor or noise seeping in. Twisted-pair wiring uses two conductors that are wrapped around one another in a loose double-helix, sort of a enlarged, relaxed DNA strand.

Most twisted-pair systems (including 10Base-T) use differential signals. That is, each conductor carries the same information at different polarities (plus and minus), and the equipment subtracts the signal on one conductor from the other before it is amplified (thus finding the difference between the two conductors and the name of the signal type). Because of the polarity difference of the desired signals on the conductors, subtracting them from one another actually doubles the strength of the signal. Noise that is picked up by the wire, however, appears at about equal strength in both wires. The subtraction cancels out the noise. Twisting the pair of wires helps ensure that each conductor picks up the same noise.

In addition, any radiation from the wire tends to cancel itself out because the signals radiated from the two conductors get added together. Again, the twist helps ensure that the two signals are equally radiated.

The coaxial Ethernet wiring schemes have another disadvantage. They connect PCs together as a bus. That is, a the network cable runs from one PC directly to the next, from one end of a building to another. In effect, each system (except the two on the ends of the cable) has two connections: one from the previous machine, one going to the next device.

Of course, that's neither the most convenient arrangement nor how most wiring is installed in buildings. In the typical office building, the most common wiring is used by telephones, and telephone wiring typically converges at one spot (or one location on each building floor), the wiring closet in which likely lives the PBX (Private Branch Exchange, the telephone switching equipment for a business).

Because 10Base-T was designed to mimic the telephone wiring system, it requires only a single cable and connection for each device. Each 10Base-T cable runs back to a central location where all cables converge into a network hub. (It's called that because the network cables radiate from it like spokes that stick out from the hub of a wheel.) Network mavens call this wiring scheme a *star topology*, but all you really need to know is that 10Base-T links PCs together with a central hub. (In reality, 10Base-T is a bus just like any other species of Ethernet, but the wires going to and from each PC are contained inside the jacket of the single cable running to the hub. Consequently, you'll find two pairs of wiring inside each 10Base-T cable.) Larger 10Base-T networks can link multiple hubs together, up to four under the official definition of the standard.

Peer-to-Peer Networking

The physical part—the wire—is only part of a network. The architecture—how the network is logically structured—determines how easy it is to use and administer. The two general classes of network architecture are client-server and peer-to-peer.

Big networks use the client-server design in which one or more powerful, centralized computers hold all the mass storage and common resources of the network. These machines, called servers, are dedicated to providing their resources—typically hard disks and printers—to individual PCs (the clients) connected to the network.

The servers run special software, the network operating system, which compares to DOS as Paradise Lost does an Ogden Nash poem. Understanding and installing a network operating system is a skill in itself, far beyond the ken of the typical PC user. The typical client-server network requires a guru called the network administrator to manage.

Although the client-server network functions like an autocracy with service with the server in command, the peer-to-peer network is a democracy. Each PC is considered an equal, a peer, and none is particularly endowed with overwhelming mass storage or an incomprehensible network operating system. Instead, each system connected to the network uses simple driver software that makes the resources of the other PCs appear as extra disk drives and printers. There's no monstrous network operating system to deal with, only a few extra entries to each PC's CONFIG.SYS file. Although someone does have to make decisions in setting up the peer-to-peer network (such as which PCs have access to which drives in other PCs), day-to-day operations usually don't require an administrator to meddle.

The peer-to-peer scheme has another advantage: you don't need to buy an expensive file server. Not only will that save cash, it can give you the security of redundancy. The failure of a server puts an entire network out of action. The failure of a network peer only eliminates that peer—the rest of the network continues to operate. If you duplicate vital files on at least two peers, you'll never have to fear losing data from the crash of a single system.

Shopping List

Putting together a peer-to-peer 10Base-T network involves software and three hardware parts—the network/host adapters in each PC, a hub, and the wire that links them together.

You'll need one 10Base-T network adapter for every PC you want to add to the network. The network adapter provides the connection between PC and network cable. All 10Base-T network adapters provide the same basic functions, although some are more feature-packed than others.

In a peer-to-peer network, you will be less likely to need to load programs through the network line, so you need not worry about squeezing out the utmost in speed. A minimal host adapter, one using an eight-bit interface and only a single modular jack for plugging in the cable, will usually suffice. Moreover, a 16-bit host adapters doesn't necessarily buy greater speed—that's set by the 10MHz Ethernet rate. (In that some PCs add more wait states when addressing 8-bit boards than with 16, the 16-bit board can sometimes be quicker.) A 16-bit network adapter will give you more installation versatility, however, including a wider range of interrupts (15 for a 16-bit board versus eight for the eight-bit board) that you can assign to the board to avoid conflicts. If you've already got a number of peripherals inside a PC, you may need the wider interrupt selection.

For the utmost in compatibility, you'll want to look for two buzz words when selecting network adapters. NetBIOS compatibility will ensure that the host adapter will work with most network software. Novell NE2000 compatibility ensures that the board duplicates the Novell product and delivers the features expected by the software. Some network adapters allow for optional boot ROMs, which enable PCs to boot up using a remote disk drive, but this feature is more applicable to client-server rather than peer-to-peer networks.

The twisted-pair cabling for 10Base-T has a few of its own requirements. The most important is that it must be truly twisted to properly minimize noise and interference. Ordinary modular telephone cables are inappropriate for 10Base-T because these cables are flat and lack the needed twists. In addition, ordinary modular telephone cables use four-wire RJ-11 connectors that will snap into 10Base-T connectors but won't connect with all of the necessary signals. A 10Base-T jack is designed to accept eight-wire RJ-45 connectors even though only four of the connections are active. Two of these connections use pin numbers beyond the reach of RJ-11.

To make a permanent 10Base-T installation, you can use the phone wiring that's already installed in most businesses. Most multi-pair telephone cables—such as the ubiquitous 25-pair cables—give each cable pair the proper twists and are entirely suitable for 10Base-T use. Of course, you'll need to connect to the trunk cable somehow. The easiest way is to add the appropriate jacks and to use twisted-pair cables with RJ-45 plugs between the jacks and your PC.

If all your PCs are in one room or reasonably close proximity, the best choice is to buy prefabricated RJ-45 cables, which are available direct from several sources, in standard lengths (for example 10, 25, 50, and 100 feet). You can loosely coil up several feet of extra cable without problem. The only restriction imposed by 10Base-T is that the length of cable between PC and hub cannot exceed 100 meters (328 feet).

You'll need at least one hub for your network. You have two principal types of hubs from which to choose available—stand-alone and the Peer-Hub.

The stand-alone hub is a box with circuitry inside and a bunch of jacks for RJ-45 plugs on the back. The circuitry inside links the 10Base-T cables together. Stand-alone hubs are distinguished by the number of features they offer, but most of those features are designed to make the network administrator's job easier and are unnecessary in a small (say five or fewer PCs) peer-to-peer network. For such smaller systems, the minimal hub will be all you need.

The Peer-Hub, made by Artisoft, is a good choice for a smaller network because it fits into the expansion slot of a PC and links to the host adapter for that PC and ties in other network nodes without an extra box. Although the resulting wiring arrangement—with all network cables radiating from the Peer-Hub—will make the system the Peer-Hub is in look like a server, electrically the host computer acts only as another peer. Besides the normal peer connection, the only link between the Peer-Hub and its host is for power. The host PC provides electricity to run the peer-hub's circuitry. In fact, supplied with the proper power, the Peer-Hub board can act as a stand-alone hub.

Because 10Base-T is an formal industry standard, a side variety of software supports the system, including the most powerful network operating systems. Several peer-to-peer network packages compatible with 10Base-T are available. The leading packages include Novell's Netware Lite and Artisoft's Lantastic.

Although the first name is the same as Novell's premiere product, Netware Lite is a completely different package. Ordinary Netware is a true client-server network operating system. Netware Lite is a more modest product that is easier to use and install. Novell doesn't even call it an operating system. Artisoft does call Lantastic an operating system because the product provides all the essential network features. More importantly, Artisoft provides hardware and software in a single matched package for sure-fire installations.

No matter what peer-to-peer software you choose, you'll typically need one copy for each PC you need to connect to comply with licensing terms.

Installation

The first step in setting up a 10Base-T network is getting organized. Take inventory of what you have and what you want to do. Count how many PCs you want to connect and consider where they are located. Then determine the most convenient location to put your 10Base-T hub.

You have two alternatives. The stand-alone hub typically sits alone, usually locked in a closet. Most larger businesses have dedicated wiring closets on each floor in a building or amid a cluster of offices to organize the telephone wiring. The network hub naturally fits the same location.

You don't have to put the hub in a closet. Some people stuff them above suspended ceilings (neither a permanent solution nor likely a legal one; fire codes look dimly on such things). However, you can always sit the hub on or under a desk, adjacent to a PC, wherever is convenient.

With a Peer-Hub, the decision is made for you. The hub sits inside one of the peers in the network.

The important consideration with locating the hub is that you put it in a convenient location, out of the way but easy to access should problems develop. Ideally, you'll want the hub in the exact center of the PCs it serves, to minimize wiring hassles. With a Peer-Hub, choose the most centrally located peer to minimize the length and tangle of the network cabling. As long as you don't violate the 10Base-T wiring limitations, however, you can locate the hub anywhere.

After you've set a location for each PC and the hub, you can configure the wiring. You only need to run one cable from each PC node to the hub.

How you run the wiring and what wire to use is another matter entirely. The easiest route is to strew about ready-made cables. Otherwise, you'll need a special tool to crimp modular connectors on the cables.

How exotic you want to get with 10Base-T wiring depends mostly on your aesthetic sense. You won't gain anything in network reliability by using existing telephone wiring or cleverly hiding your wiring inside walls. In fact, the most reliable wiring you can use are the prefabricated lengths. Every connector you crimp on a cable adds a potential problem. Moreover, you have less control (typically none) over the quality of existing wiring. When the wiring is in place, prepare the network adapter for each peer. Typically, you'll have to select the interrupt, base address, and DMA used by each network adapter.

These settings must be made individually to avoid conflicts with other peripherals installed in the peer into which you want to slide the network adapter. Although you can adjust each peer's vital parameters to different settings, finding a common ground that works for all network adapters makes sense. Maintenance will be easier because you won't have to worry about custom-configuring replacement boards or when moving boards between systems.

As with other expansion boards, you'll make these adjustments using DIP switches or jumpers on each network adapter. The manual accompanying the boards should document these settings. In most cases, the factory default settings should work fine.

When you've configured the network adapters, install one in each PC that you want to act as a network peer. Slide the boards into expansion slots. Of course, the normal expansion issues apply. Switch off each system, unplug its power cable, remove the lid, and remove the blank retaining bracket from the slot you want to use. Although you can put 8-bit boards into 8- or 16-bit slots, 16-bit boards should only go into 16 bit slots.

Be sure to screw the card retaining bracket into each PC. Not only will the screw prevent you from dislodging the board when plugging in the network cable, it will also provide a better ground which will improve network reliability.

Before reassembling each peer, plug it in and boot it up to ensure that the network adapter doesn't inadvertently interfere with some vital system function. When you're sure all is well, turn off the peer and re-install its cover.

Finally, you're ready to plug your network together. Slide each RJ-45 plug into the jack in each peer. Then plug the other end of each cable into the hub (see fig. 14.9).

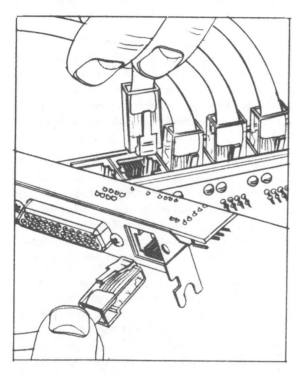

Figure 14.9
Plug each RJ-45 plug into its network card and into the hub to finish the installation.

Switch on the hub and then all of the PCs in the network. Follow the instructions accompanying your network software and install the appropriate drivers on each peer. When the software is properly configured and installed, reboot all of the peers, and your network should be up and running.

Permanent Installations

Few people enjoy tripping over cables or the look of a round, black line streaking across the living room carpet from one room (and PC) to another. Although you could roll out the duct tape to keep the cabling under control, the easy way out may lead directly to the doghouse. If you plan on making your PC-to-PC connection permanent, you might want to find an alternate, more attractive course for the cable to follow.

When your two PCs are close together, you can usually take advantage of the wiring that comes standard in the box. At most, you might want to invest in some wiring clips to hold it out of the way and out of sight. The extra wire can be curled in a loop behind one of the PCs.

To go the extra mile—or fraction thereof—you'll want to do your own wiring. That way, you can be as artistic and professional as you like (or as you can manage). You can hide wires within walls or staple them to baseboards, just as the phone company is wont to do. In fact, one of the best wiring strategies for a permanent installation of a PC-to-PC connection scheme uses ordinary telephone wiring and other supplies.

Telephone wiring has at least three big advantages: it costs very little, is widely available, and requires few tools and even less skill to connect up. If you can't find the supplies you need through the mail-order channel, you should be able to locate what you want in discount, appliance, and electronics stores—nearly anywhere telephones are sold. The only tools you'll need are an ordinary screwdriver and wire-stripper. No soldering is usually necessary.

Ordinary telephone wiring is not recommended for 10Base-T because many modular cables don't actually twist the wiring pairs. They run together parallel for the length of the cable. These flat modular cables should be avoided for 10Base-T, although they may function for zero-slot LANs and direct PC-to-PC serial links where data rates are modest. For 10Base-T, you'll need special round cables, which are sold for the purpose by most computer supply companies. Permanent telephone wiring—the stuff you plaster into the walls—generally does twist the pairs together, so it can be used for 10Base-T. If you have your doubts, check the wire to make sure that the conductors are twisted into pairs.

Perhaps the biggest advantage of telephone wiring is that you don't have to know how it works or what the signals are to connect wires together properly. It's all a matter of consistently matching colors.

Standard telephone cables have four wires, one each green, red, yellow, and black. You'll find that many of the terminal blocks to which you connect the wires are similarly coded G, R, Y, and B. Match the wire color with its initial, and you're sure to get everything right. Eight-wire systems enhance this rainbow w/brown, blue, orange, and violet.

Alternately, you'll find short wires leading from the modular phone jack to the terminal screws. These wires will be properly color coded. All you need to do is match green with green—the green wire from the jack with the green wire from the cable you want to connect—the red with red, and so on, at both ends of the cable.

If you use a cable with a different color coding, all you need to do is ensure that you match each end. If you attach the blue wire with a white stripe to the G terminal (or green wire) at one end of the cable, be sure that it goes to the G terminal (or green wire) at the other end. Modular jacks come in several styles based on the connector type and mounting style. Modular connectors vary in the number of gold-plated wires they use as contacts. The most common—the type you're most likely to find in the drugstore hardware department—is the RJ-11, which has four contacts. Odds are that no one in the store will know it's an RJ-11 jack—count the gold-colored wires inside it to reassure yourself. Mail order vendors will call the jacks by their proper name and expect you to do the same.

RJ-13 and RJ-14 modular jacks have more contacts, which are used by some low-cost networks. You can use these larger jacks for four-wire modular cables, but properly wiring them can be confusing. (You need to connect at least the green, red, black, and yellow wires of the jacks.)

10Base-T wiring requires RJ-45 jacks. These look like overweight RJ11 jacks—they have eight instead of four separate connections. Because 10Base-T only uses four of its possible eight connections, you can use ordinary RJ11 modular jacks *if* you make your own modular connecting cables. Just make sure you are consistent with the color coding of the wires at each end.

Flush and surface-mount styles of jacks of every connector style are available. The flush mount allows you to hide all the wiring inside the wall. Double flush-mount jacks are available; these are great because you can use one jack for your existing telephone connection (to plug in your modem) and the other for your PC-to-PC connection, hiding all the wires in the wall. Surface-mount jacks are for the less fastidious. They allow you to run wires along baseboards, within walls, or wherever you want.

The easy part of a permanent installation is connecting the jacks to the wires at the ends of the cable. You need only strip each conductor of the cable by removing about one-half inch of its plastic insulation, bend a half-loop in the stripped end of the wire, put the bare wire half-loop around the screw terminal so that twisting the screw in place cause the loop to close, and tighten the screw. Getting the wire between PC locations is the big challenge, one that you'll have to suffer through yourself.

Snaking wires through walls, under carpets, above the ceiling, and wherever else you need to will take time. But, thankfully, you only need to do it once. When you're done, you can hang up your sneakers and relax, thanks to the convenience and security of your new PC-to-PC connection.

15

Power Supplies and Protection

Computer circuits need a safe and steady supply of electricity to operate. A power supply gives its circuits safe power; a backup power system helps make it steady. Although all of today's PCs provide more than enough power for frugal modern peripherals, changing your PC's power supply can reduce noise, improve cooling, or repair failures. Backup power will benefit any PC and make your work in progress invulnerable to power problems and outages.

Backup power will benefit any PC and make your work in progress invulnerable to power problems and outages.

Electricity is the life blood of every PC. Every flip and flop of a computer's logic circuits requires a pulse of electricity. Not just any electricity will do, either. It must be pure DC, direct current, not the indecisive alternating current delivered on power lines.

Computer circuits are delicate, too, instantly destroyed by a direct shot from the 120 volts of the power line. Computer semiconductor circuits prefer their DC at a modest level of just five volts, although some disk drives need twelve to make their motors spin.

Not only do PCs require their own particular voltages to operate, they require them continuously. Interrupt the flow of electricity, and your PC will literally lose its mind. Every byte in its memory will evaporate faster than a tear in a hot skillet. The shortest interruption in utility power—a break no longer than the blink of your eye—and all you'll be staring at is the boot-up screen again—if you're lucky. If you're not especially blessed, however, your PC might never recover from a power failure, its circuits seared by the surge that often accompanies the restoration of power.

Delivering exactly the kind of electricity your computer needs is the job of its power supply. Ensuring that there is a constant supply of electricity to run the power is the job of the backup power system. Of the two, the power supply has the simpler job. It only needs to transform the power line downward to the more sedate levels used by your PC's integrated circuits and to rectify the line current, changing its AC into DC. Backup power systems have to detect power failures, generate the right kind of electricity to run your PC, and keep their own internal battery supply (where they get their electricity when your favorite utility decides not to provide it) full charged. The power supply is mandatory; your PC won't run without it. The backup power system is optional; your PC will work without one, but you might not want to risk the consequences.

Power upgrades involve one of two changes: replacing the power supply in your PC to gain a benefit the original manufacturer of your system never thought mattered (or thought you would be willing to pay for). A few ancient PCs even need new power supplies to handle the electrical demands of moderate expansion. Adding backup power removes temptation from the Fates. What you need varies with what you want to do. More or better power inside your PC requires a new power supply. Power protection requires a backup power system. This chapter will examine both powerful upgrades.

The Role of the Power Supply

The electricity your PC demands from its power supply can be copious.

The electricity your PC demands from its power supply can be copious. For example, a 486 microprocessor alone is made from 1.2 million or so transistors, each one thirsty for a few microwatts of electricity. As personal computers and the microprocessor they are built from become increasingly powerful, that need for power inside the PC increases as well. Although today a trend has begun to build "green" PCs that win high ecological marks by being economical in their power consumption, the machines most likely in the need of upgrading still rely on older, power-hungry technologies. One reason is that without a change in underlying semiconductor technology, basic physical laws dictate that the faster a computer's circuitry operates, the more power it will consume. Doing more work in a given time takes more power, exactly as your car needs more gas for every mile-per-hour it travels over the speed limit.

That's one problem that your PC faces. The power resources of the universe are limited, and those of your PC's power supply are even more constrained. No power supply can deliver unlimited amounts of DC to your computer's circuits. The components that make up the power supply face maximum limits beyond which they might overheat and melt down—literally. Fortunately power supplies, like nuclear reactors, have safety shut-down circuits that turn the unit off, usually before any damage is done. Heat still limits the capacity of the power supply.

To keep the heat inside the power supply from shutting things down at an inadvertent moment, most manufacturers try to keep things cool using a fan. The power supply fan literally blows the heat away. Most PC designs rely on the power supply to do double duty—not just cool the power supply itself but also circulate air throughout your PC to moderate the temperature of all of its circuitry.

In this all-cooling role, the fan inside your PC's power supply serves a vital role, one of extending the life of your computer. Most experts agree, the cooler you keep electronic circuitry, the longer it will last. Unfortunately, some power supplies suffer from some shortcomings in the cooling department. Some power supplies don't blow enough air to adequately ventilate a high-power PC. Others waft bushels of air but announce their efforts with all the cacophony of an ill-tuned Hoover. Replacing one of these electrical underachievers with a better role model—the strong, silent type—can make both your microprocessor and your ears immensely happier.

Heat is a particular enemy of the overstrained power supply. If the power supply in your older PC isn't up to the chore of producing all the electricity your system needs, it will overheat and then switch itself off to protect itself. What's good for the life of the power supply will be fatal to the data you're working on in your PC. At some unpredictable time, an overworked power supply is liable to shut-down on its own, leaving you in the dark and angry.

Heat is a particular enemy of the overstrained power supply.

Today, most computers have power supplies able to handle 200 watts or more. That's generally more than enough to satisfy the needs of even a grandly expanded computer. The power supply of the original IBM PC was rated at a modest 63.5 watts, however and that's inadequate to run a typical hard disk in addition to the computer's own circuitry. Other computers, too, were designed and equipped with power supplies of less than 100 watts. Even the 135 watts of the IBM XT can be too small in some situations. If you're building your own PC—or have built one—the watts available from the power supply (and consumed by the PC's circuitry) will similarly be important to you. You, too, may be a candidate for an improved power supply.

Upgrading your computer's power supply if it cools too little, protests too much, or produces too tiny of a current will give your machine the cooling, quiet, and power you'll want for reliable expansion that you can live with.

Power Supply Upgrade Facts and Dangers

First things first. Power supplies deal with potentially fatal amounts of electricity, and a power supply upgrade will mean monkeying with its electrical connections. You'll want to be sure that the jolts put out by the power supply won't end up coursing through your body.

When dealing with PC power supplies, most of your worries of electrocution are groundless.

Fortunately, when dealing with PC power supplies, most of your worries of electrocution are groundless. There's nothing dangerous in dealing with computer power supplies. They are sealed assemblies that have no exposed life-threatening voltages that you might accidentally touch. The likelihood that you might even get a shock during a power supply upgrade is about the same as the probability that a comet will crash down on your house tonight. Nor is there any danger to your computer's delicate electronic components if you're careful and follow the step-by-step procedure outlined here.

Changing a power supply is among the easiest things you can do to your PC.

Moreover, no skill and (generally) only one tool—a screwdriver or nutdriver—is required to make a power supply upgrade. Changing a power supply is among the easiest things you can do to your PC. The entire operation usually can be completed in 10 minutes.

Upgrading a power supply is cheap. Moving from the threshold of pain down to a whisper or up from 63.5 to 200 watts will cost somewhere between $50 and $100 from most vendors. Opting for the top end and a truly premium power supply—one with double fans for extra cooling or special fan control circuitry to keep things quiet—may cost substantially more, but such an upgrade still ranks as one of the less expensive improvements you can make to your PC. Compared to the peace of mind and quiet operation they can bring, however, any power supply upgrade can be a bargain.

About Power Output

The design purpose of every computer power supply, no matter the watts it makes, is the same: convert utility power into a carefully regulated source of the low DC voltages needed for operating computer circuitry. Most books will tell you that there are two chief ways to make the conversion and two corresponding types of power supplies—linear and switching. That's all well and good, but the difference between the types is about as significant to making your upgrade as is the chemical composition of the atmosphere of Jupiter. For the purpose of making an upgrade, a power supply is a sealed tin box that high-voltage AC goes into and low-voltage DC comes out. What goes on inside the box doesn't matter in the least. On a more practical level, you won't have a choice, anyway. Without exception, the replacement power supplies you'll find for upgrading your PC will all be switching power supplies. They are more compact, energy efficient, and (most important of all, particularly to the manufacturer) cheap to make.

The only electrical issue that's relevant to making a power supply upgrade is the number of watts a power supply produces. The more watts, the more power a power supply produces and the more peripherals that it can run.

The more watts, the more power a power supply produces and the more peripherals that it can run.

Computer power supplies are rated in the number of watts that they can deliver before overloading. In direct current circuits, like those of a computer, the number of watts is equal to the product of the volts and current (the amperage or number of amps) delivered. For example, a computer power supply might produce 5 volts at 20 amps and thus achieve an output of 100 watts.

The power supplies for practical PCs must deliver several voltages, however. In addition to a positive polarity of five volts, they also need to produce negative five volts, positive twelve volts, and negative twelve volts. The rating of a power supply is the total of the output at each of these voltages.

Most of a circuitry in a personal computer uses positive five volts, so this potential usually has the highest rating of any of a power supply's output, typically 20 to 30 amperes. Disk drives typically use 12 volts to operate their motors, so the positive 12-volt supply is usually the next highest rated, usually from three to five amperes. The other two voltages are used by some specialized circuitry (for example, serial ports use both positive and negative voltages) but only in small amounts. Consequently, the negative outputs of computer power supplies are normally quite modest, often a fraction of an amp.

That said, just about any power supply that you can buy as an upgrade will be sufficient for powering all the state- of-the-art peripherals any PC can reasonably use.

Once upon a time, that was not true. Every PC was made with what its manufacturer considered to be an adequate power supply. But early manufacturers could hardly anticipate everything that you would eventually want to add to your PC. The original IBM PC was the primary victim of this lack of foresight. IBM never designed that machine to accept a hard disk drive, and consequently it lacked sufficient power to operate one—at least one of the same vintage of the machine.

Time quickly changed, however, and in the modern world inadequate power is a thing of the past. Manufacturers haven't developed any better foresight. Instead purchasers have developed higher standards, and energy efficiency has advanced. Nearly every PC made in the last half dozen years has a power supply of at least 150 watts. At the same time, miniaturization and integration have pared down the power required by most peripherals. Where once a hard disk drive of 100 megabytes demanded nearly 50 watts just to keep spinning, today you can get five times the capacity with one-fifth the power requirement. The needs of expansion boards has not declined quite so precipitously, but new boards nevertheless draw half or less what their slower equivalents would have wanted a few years ago. Equipped with today's circuitry and peripherals, even the meager 63.5 watts of the original PC's power supply is sufficient. After all, the entire energy budget of some laptop computers is under five watts.

Table 15.1. Typical Power Requirements in PCs

Expansion Boards	
Packed AT-size board	15 watts
Full-length board	10 watts
Short card	5 watts

Floppy disk drives (when running)	
Old full-height 5.25-inch	15 watts
Half-height 5.25-inch	10 watts
3.5-inch	5 watts
Hard disk drives	
Full-height 5.25-inch	25 watts
Half-height 5.25-inch	15 watts
High-capacity 3.5-inch	10 watts
Low-power 3.5-inch	5 watts
System boards	
PC or XT	20 watts
Older 286	40 watts
Newer 286	20 watts
Newer 386	25 watts
486	35 watts

Combine old components and an old PC, and power may still be a worry. In most cases, however, 150 watts will serve the needs of nearly any system except servers and the like with extreme disk burdens.

Selection Criteria

Even though you don't have to worry about power reserves when selecting a power supply, you still face sufficient selection consideration. You still have your choice of the number and style of the connectors to which power is delivered, the size and shape of the case in which the necessary power conversion electronics are packed, and the cooling that's provided for your system.

Connections

For a power supply to be useful to your PC and its peripherals, it must deliver its endowment of electricity in a manner that your equipment can accept. That means that a power supply must be able to connect to the system board of your PC and to all the disk and tape drives in its bays. For each device you attach to the power supply, you'll need one or more power connectors.

The connectors for the disk and tape drives are the easy part. All full-size disk (and tape) drives use the same style connector, and all commercially available power supplies use these connectors. About the only difference you'll find in drive power connectors is their number.

Quite simply, more is better. Four connectors are usually—but not always—standard on most power supplies. You probably won't want a power supply with fewer than four drive power connectors—that's enough for two floppies, one hard disk, and a tape drive or CD ROM player or something that's still lurking in the back of a creative engineer's head.

Besides their number, how those connectors are attached to the power supply is also important to consider before you make a purchase. Some power supply makers put multiple connectors on a single set of wires from the power supply. This can be inconvenient because you may have to make odd twists in the cable—even stretch it—to connect multiple drives. The better arrangement is to give each drive power connector its own set of wires from the power supply box.

The connectors that plug into your PC's system board are another story. Every power supply and system board manufacturer seems to have its own standard. Pre-PS/2 IBM computers use two Burndy connectors for the system board link-up. PS/2s often (but, again, not always) combine the two connectors into one. Although other manufacturers use Burndy connectors, many also use slightly different Molex connectors. The two are not 100-percent compatible.

One difference between the two connector types is that the pins of a Burndy are rectangular. Molex system board connectors use smaller, square pins. Only with great effort can you mate dissimilar connectors together. Before you order a power supply, take a close look at the connectors on the system board. You may want to disconnect one (with your PC switched off, of course) to examine the shape of its pins.

Most power supplies come equipped with Burndy connectors. Consequently, power supplies with Molex connectors are rare. You'll have to look harder to find them. Be sure to ask the vendor you order your power supply from what kind of connectors it uses.

Be sure to ask the vendor you order your power supply from what kind of connectors it uses.

Packaging

In fitting a new power supply into your computer, the critical issue is whether the new unit will fit inside your system's existing case. In general, two standard sizes of power supply are available: those designed to fit the original IBM PC, XT and similar-sized chassis, and those made for the AT and its clones. AT power supplies are larger and generally, in keeping with their size, have higher power ratings. AT supplies generally start at 192 watts and are available in 250-watt and higher ratings. About 150 watts is tops for PC/XT power supplies.

The PC/XT power supply is a rectangular box that measures 4.5 by 8.5 by 5.5 inches (HWD). One side features a plastic extension that holds the big red paddle connected to an internal power switch. The jacks and cut-outs on the rear panel are designed to mate with openings in the rear panel of the PC and XT chassis. Consequently, these locations have become somewhat standardized.

AT power supplies are vaguely L-shaped and measure 5.5 by 8.5 by 6 inches (HWD). Part of one corner is notched out to allow room underneath for the larger system boards in AT- size chassis. Again a big, red paddle is brought out from the power switch on the right side of the power supply, and the various jacks and fan opening on the rear panel have been standardized to match the corresponding holes in the AT rear panel.

The major issue in fitting a power supply to a case is height. Some cases are shorter than others. The low height of XT-size cases means only XT-size power supplies will fit. AT and mini-AT cases are taller, meant to accept AT-size power supplies. However, most AT and mini-AT cases will also accommodate XT-size power supplies. If you want to be sure that a power supply that you order will physically fit the case that you have, measure the height that is available. Then check the available width both at the plane of the motherboard and at the top of the case to see whether the AT-size power supply with its notched bottom will fit.

Beware. Some power supply designs take liberties with the normal IBM component layout. In some cases, that's great. For example, adding a bigger fan or pair of fans and altering the shape of the power supply box can help give your PC better cooling abilities. But other modifications are undesirable. Re-arranging the power switch and outlets are particularly problematic. Such an altered arrangement may make it impossible to install the power supply in your PC chassis. Consequently, when you order a power supply for your upgrade, ensure that it is an exact external match for the IBM design—and that the vendor will accepts its return (without restocking charge) if it does not.

Personal computers that don't follow the IBM packaging scheme pose problems when you want to upgrade the power supply. You're likely to have a difficult time finding a power supply that will match the size and mounting requirements of a proprietary case, including those used by Compaq computers. Although replacements are usually available from the original equipment maker (if the original maker is still in business!), the prices will be high and you won't have a choice of special high-cooling or quiet models.

If you want to upgrade an non-standard system—for example to silence the turbo-charged wind-machine noise of a models of the Compaq Deskpro, you may be out of luck. Should you want to replace the power supply in one of these nonstandard computers as a repair measure, you're likely to be stuck depending on the manufacturer of the computer to supply you with what you need. If, however, your system uses a standard-size motherboard, you could always replace the case to make a new, improved power supply fit.

The design of the PC power system is supposed to be idiot-proof, but there is always someone willing to take up the challenge.

Removing Old Power Supplies

The first step in any power supply upgrade is obvious—remove the old to make room for the new. But before you go wild with a screwdriver, you'll want to take a couple of preparatory steps to guard against complications caused by idiosyncrasies in the original manufacture of your PC. The design of the PC power system is supposed to be idiot-proof, but there is always someone willing to take up the challenge.

Begin by ensuring your safety and that of your computer. Remove all cables from all jacks on the rear panel of your PC. This will also give you the side benefit of flexibility—you'll be able to move your PC anywhere you want, turn it upside down if necessary, to make the removal and installation job easier.

Turn your PC off. Then unplug the power cord, the cord leading from the power supply to your monitor (if there is one), and all the cables attached to all of the expansion board retaining brackets at the back of your computer. If you suspect age is taking a toll on your short-term memory, you may want to mark which connectors go into which jacks before you disconnect them all. Just for good measure, disconnect the keyboard cable and mouse.

After you've disconnected all external cables from your PC, disconnect the internal cables to the power supply (see fig. 15.1). In most cases, you'll find two, labeled P8 and P9 (right inset). Then remove the four screws that secure the power supply to your PC's chassis. The screws are located approximately in each of the four corners of the power supply (left inset).

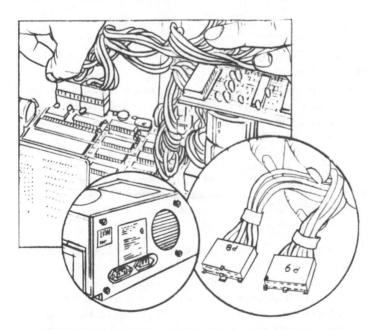

Figure 15.1

After you've disconnected all external cables from your PC, disconnect the internal cables to the power supply.

Once you can freely move your PC around, remove the top of its case. The tops of most PCs, XTs, and ATs are held in place by five screws on the rear panel; the first PCs had only three screws. In any event, these will be the screws closest to the edges of the rear panel—one in the center, one in each of the lower corners, and in machines using five screws, two in the upper corners. Put the screws in a safe place, then pull the top of the computer's case all the way forward, angle it upward, and lift it off (see fig. 15.2).

Figure 15.2

After the power supply screws are removed, push the power supply toward the front of your PC with firm, even pressure.

When you can peer inside your PC, the power supply will be easy to identify. It's the shiny chrome-plated box in the right-rear corner. All of the power cables that you will need to deal with emerge from the left side of that box. You must disconnect all of these cables from the devices that they plug into. You cannot disconnect them from the power supply itself.

You'll find the job easier if you do the disconnecting in two stages. In the first stage, remove the one or two cables that connect the power supply to your system board. At this point, however, take a moment for one of those extra steps to ensure installing your new power supply will be trouble-free.

The connectors on these cables are supposed to be keyed so that you cannot insert them improperly. However, sometimes the keys—tiny tabs that prevent you from inserting connectors in the wrong jacks—break off the connectors. Sometimes manufacturers remove all the keys themselves. In either case, it might be possible to plug the connectors of your new power supply upgrade in improperly.

After you've pushed the power supply as far forward as it will go, you can lift it straight up and out of your PC. If it's still tethered by a cable or two, remove them now. Note the retaining tabs at the bottom of the chassis and matching holes in the power supply itself (see fig. 15.3).

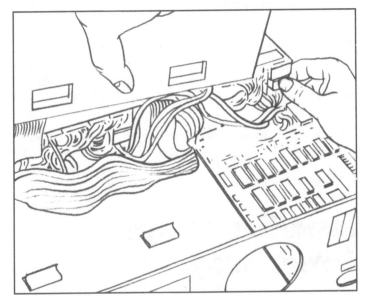

Figure 15.3

After you've pushed the power supply as far forward as it will go, you can lift it straight up and out of your PC.

To avoid dire consequences, take note of the colors of wires and the position of each color while the connectors are plugged into your system board. Write down the color scheme. Only then should you unplug the system board connectors.

You will find it helpful if you partly remove your existing power supply before you remove the power connectors from your disk drives. Consequently, the next step in this upgrade is to remove the four screws that hold the power supply in place. These screws are all located on the rear panel of your PC where they form a rectangle. Unscrew all four (in most cases a nutdriver is the best tool, though some manufacturers use Phillips screws) and put the screws in a safe place.

At this point, your old power supply might not feel the slightest bit loose. That's normal. It's still held in place by two tabs in its bottom. To free up the power supply, put your fingers around the edges of the chassis (taking care to not cut yourself on sharp edges—you may want to put on your mittens just in case!) and push the power supply toward the front of the computer with your thumbs. Don't jab it.

Gradually increase the pressure with your thumbs until the power supply slides forward. The more it moves, the looser it will become.

When you finally push it far enough forward that it lightly touches the back of the disk drive bay, it will be free enough that you can lift it partly out of your computer's chassis. Because the drive cables are still attached, you'll probably have to rotate the power supply forward to lift it completely out.

While holding your old power supply with one hand, use the other hand to remove the power connectors from each of your disk and tape drives. Once these connectors are removed, nothing should be holding the old power supply to your PC anymore. Put the old power supply aside.

You may want to take advantage of this opportunity to clean up the inside of your PC. You can gently vacuum out the dust using a soft rubber attachment to your sweeper—one with a brush on the end will help dislodge the more reluctant dust bunnies.

Installing a New Power Supply

Installing the new power supply is pretty much the reverse of the removal process, but if you take a moment to familiarize yourself with the attachment scheme, the operation will go much easier. Examine the bottom of the power supply and you'll see two slots stamped into it. At the bottom of the chassis of your computer, you should be able to see two matching fingers stamped into the metal work. The fingers slide into the slots and hold the power supply down inside the chassis. When you put the power supply into the chassis, you'll have to make sure that those fingers properly engage.

When you've completed the familiarization tour, hold the new power supply just above the vacant area in which it will be installed. The on/off switch should be on the right side, looking from the front of your PC.

Before you drop the new power supply into place, you'll have an easier time reconnecting the power plugs to your disk drives. Hold the power supply with one hand and connect the power plugs with the other. The plugs are keyed to prevent you from inserting them improperly, so if they don't fit, turn the plug over and try again.

After all the drive power connectors are in place, lower the new power supply into the chassis.

When the power supply touches bottom, push it gently as far toward the front of your PC as you can. It should rest against the back of the drive bays. Now push down on the power supply to press it all the way into the chassis.

Put the new power supply in your PC—lower it as far forward as it will go, then push it back into place, making sure that it catches on the tabs in the bottom of the chassis (see fig. 15.4).

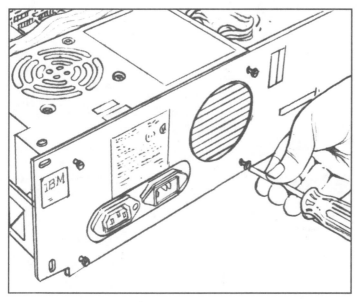

Figure 15.4

Put the new power supply in your PC— lower it as far forward as it will go; then push it back into place, making sure that it catches on the tabs in the bottom of the chassis.

Gently slide the power supply toward the rear panel of your PC while you hold it down. The fingers in the chassis should engage the slots and make it progressively more difficult the farther back you push the power supply. You might not even get it to exactly touch the rear panel of the chassis. As long as it comes within about one-eighth of an inch of the rear panel, you don't need to worry. The screws will tighten it into place.

There's a trick to getting all the screws into your new power supply. First start one screw in the matching hole in the chassis and power supply. Make sure that it turns freely and spin it only one or two turns into place, *not* all the way. Then start the second screw, the third, and the fourth. Don't tighten any of the screws until they all have been started. That way you can shift the power supply around a little bit to get all the screws to fit properly. When all four screws have been started, you can tighten them all in any order.

Finally, reconnect the power supply connectors to your system board (see fig. 15.5). This simple task is the one place where you're likely to run into problems.

Figure 15.5

Note the keying tabs on the connectors.

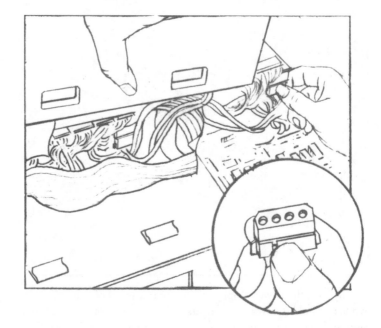

Many power supplies come with all of their plastic-tab keys in place on their system-board power connectors. These tabs will prevent you from inserting either connector into the jacks on your system board. To make the connectors work, you'll have to trim off the excess tabs. Diagonal cutters are the best tool to use, but if you're careful you might cut the extra tabs off with a pen knife or nail clipper. You could even file them off.

The best model you have for getting the keying right is your old power supply. Compare the connectors of the old with the new and make the new match the old.

With some computers, you'll find all the tabs have been trimmed off. You'll probably have to do likewise, but then you'll need to be very careful when you plug the connector in. Make sure that the connectors when plugged in match the color pattern you wrote down before removing the old power supply. That's why you wrote down all those colors.

Before you re-attach all the external cables to your computer, you should make a safety check. Examine the voltage selector slide switch if your new power supply has one. It should be visible through the rear panel of your PC after the new power supply is installed. The switch will have two settings, typically 115 and 230, or 120 and 240. Standard line voltage in the United States is between 110 and 120 volts. You'll want to make certain that you can see the a figure in that range visible on the voltage selector slide switch.

When you're certain the voltage is set properly, reconnect all the external cables to your PC and switch it back on. Your PC should come immediately to life. If it does not, check all the internal cables (and make sure that you've plugged your system into a wall outlet). If you've followed all these installation instructions, double-checked your wiring, and your system still does not operate, chances are your new power supply may not be working. Contact your power supply vendor.

When you're sure that your system is operating properly, install whatever new options you've bought that required additional power. Switch your system back on and check it again before you put the top back on the case of your PC. When you're satisfied that all is well, reassemble your PC.

Power Protection

If goblins and gremlins do exist, they live not in enchanted hollows or haunted houses but in power lines. The most mysterious of the dangers faced by any computer system are the vagaries of the utility-supplied electricity that runs them: the glitches, surges, sags, spikes, and—most dreaded of all—the black-out. An entire industry has developed to make and sell products to protect your PC from these evils. The minimal protection device is called the *surge suppresser*, and its job is to stop spike and surges from reaching the circuitry of your PC. The surge suppresser does nothing to prevent problems associated with brownouts and blackouts. The ultimate power protection weapon is the *backup power supply*. Besides insulating your PC from power loss, better backup power supplies will also ward off the rest of the evils that may be lurking in the electricity you feed your PC.

Surge Suppressers

No matter the cause, the brief jolt of a surge can be unpredictable, unpreventable, and lethal to all electronic hardware.

An electrical surge is nothing more than a higher voltage than your PC's components can handle—miniature lightning on the power line. But a surge is not only like a lightning stoke, they are often caused by lightning. Other surges result from pulses inadvertently generated when electrical equipment switches on and off. Some surges even result from the work of improperly design surge suppressers. No matter the cause, the brief jolt of a surge can be unpredictable, unpreventable, and lethal to all electronic hardware.

Little wonder surge suppressers are so compelling. These inexpensive plug-in creations can short-circuit the worst surges before they reach your PC, stopping the surge dead in its tracks and keeping your hardware and data alive.

Surges are a particular kind of anomaly on your utility power line that are part of a wider class called overvoltages, a condition that arises when more than the expected voltage appears on your power lines. Not all surge overvoltages are the same. They differ in intensity, duration, and mode. The various facets of a surge influence its capability to damage your PC and the kind of protection that you require.

Voltage is one factor in characterizing surge intensity. PC power supplies are designed to deal with moderate overvoltages—a few tens of volts—and automatically compensate to keep the electricity going to your computer components within acceptable limits.

In theory, you want a surge suppresser that would eliminate any surge in excess of the 120 volts that your PC normally uses. In practice, such a surge suppresser would do more harm than good. First of all, in the alternating current circuits that supply your PC, voltage is commonly measured in two different ways. By its nature, alternating current is an evanescent thing of sinusoidal waveforms that switch polarity 120 times a second (making 60 complete cycles in the same period). Line voltage is generally described as the geometric average of the cycling waves and is termed RMS (for Root

Mean Square, the means of calculating a geometric average) which fairly describes the energy content of the electrical flow. Surges, however, are measured at peak values—the greatest excursion of the voltage level of the sinusoidal waveform. What passes for 120-volt utility power actually is a series of 170 volt peaks.

A surge suppresser that starts to work at exactly 170 volts is also a poor idea. Although power companies normally maintain voltages within tight limits, sometimes the power line voltage may sneak up an extra dozen or two volts for periods ranging from milliseconds to several seconds. If a PC-size surge suppresser tried to smooth out these long, powerful, though low voltage surges, it would likely self-destruct.

In fact, there's no need for a PC surge suppresser to worry about a few dozen extra volts on the power line. Most PC power supplies can withstand brief surges—those lasting in the microsecond range—of 800 volts without difficulty. In fact, several computer manufacturers believe that their PCs can withstand any surge that your power line can contain, and they do not recommend that you install a surge suppresser. However, most PC makers see surge suppressers as valuable protection for your PC—or as an extra preventive measure that may not be unnecessary but won't hurt anything.

Except for direct hits by lightning, surges greater than 6000 volts will never reach your PC. Larger voltages are so powerful that they cause the wiring in your home to briefly short out (the insulating plastic sheath around the wire breaks down and temporarily becomes an electrical conductor) and eliminate the surge. Consequently, surge suppressers need not worry about higher voltages.

Any device that works over a range just a bit larger than 800 to 6000 volts will be an effective surge suppresser.

Because of the low resistance of power lines, high voltages are inevitably linked to high currents, with the result that surges can contain huge amounts of power. The maximum surge that might get through to your PC—6,000 volts—is likely to be backed by a current as high as 3,000 amperes. Such a surge amounts to 18 megawatts—on a continuing basis, enough power to run a small city. Surges are thankfully short-lived, lasting a few millionths of a second, so they contain a more modest amount of energy, perhaps a few hundred joules (watt-seconds), about the same amount of energy required to operate a light bulb for a couple of hours.

The problem with surges is that this energy rushes through semiconductor circuits faster than they can dissipate it—silicon junctions fry in microseconds. The job of the surge suppresser is to absorb or reroute the surge energy before it reaches your PC.

Besides intensity and energy, surges also differ in their mode. Modern electrical wiring involves three conductors: a hot, neutral, and ground. Hot is the wire that carries the power; neutral provides a return path; and ground provides protection. The ground lead is obstensibly connected directly to the earth.

Four kinds of devices are most often used to protect against surges: MOVs, gas tubes, avalanche diodes, and reactive circuits. Each has its own strengths and weaknesses. Typically, commercial surge protectors use several technologies in combination.

MOVs are Metal Oxide Varistors, disc-shaped electronic components typically made from a layer of zinc oxide particles held between two electrodes. The granular zinc oxide offers a high resistance to the flow of electricity until the voltage reaches a breakover point. The electrical current then forms a low-resistance path between the zinc oxide particles that shorts out the electrical flow.

MOVs are the most popular surge protection component because they are inexpensive to manufacture and easy to tailor to a particular application. Their energy-handling capability can be increased simply by enlarging the device (typical MOVs are about an inch in diameter; high power MOVs may be twice that.)

The downside to MOVs is that they degrade. Surges tend to form preferred paths between the zinc oxide particles, reducing the resistance to electrical flow. Eventually, the MOV shorts out, blowing a fuse or (more likely) overheating the MOV until it destroys itself. The MOV can end its life in flames or with no external change—except that it no longer offers surge protection.

Gas tubes are self-descriptive: tubes filled with special gases with low dielectric potential designed to arc- over at predictable low voltages. The internal arc short circuits the surge. Gas tubes can conduct a great deal of power—thousands of kilowatts—and react quickly, typically in about a nanosecond.

On the negative side, a gas tube won't start conducting (and suppressing a surge) until the voltage applied it reaches two to four times the tube's rating. The tube itself does not dissipate the energy of the surge; it just shorts it out, allowing your wiring to absorb the energy. Moreover, the discharge voltage of a gas tube can be affected by ambient lighting (hence most manufacturers shield them from light).

Worst of all, after a gas tube starts conducting, it doesn't like to stop. Typically, a gas tube requires a reversal of current flow to quench its internal arc, which means that the power going to your PC could be shorted for up to 8.33 milliseconds. Sometimes, gas tubes continue to conduct for several AC current cycles, perhaps long enough for your PC power supply to shut down. (Many PC power supplies switch off when power interruptions exceed about 18 milliseconds.)

Avalanche diodes are semiconductor circuits similar to zener diodes that offer a high resistance to electrical flow until the voltage applied to them reaches a breakover potential. At that point, they switch on and act as conductors to short out the applied current. Avalanche diodes operate more quickly than other protection devices but have limited energy capacity, typically from 600 to 1500 watts.

Reactive surge suppressers work differently from other types. Although MOVs, gas tubes, avalanche diodes share the same operating principle—shorting out the surge before it gets to your PC—a reactive surge suppresser uses a large inductance to resist the sharp voltage rise of a surge and spread it out over a longer time. Adding a capacitor tunes the reactance so that it can convert the surge into a semblance of a normal AC waveform. Other noise on the power line is also automatically absorbed.

Unfortunately, this form of reactive network has severe drawbacks. It doesn't eliminate the surge—it only spreads out its energy. The size of the inductor determines the spread, and a large inductor is required for effective results. In addition, the device only works on normal mode surges. The reaction may also cause a *common mode surge* in the wiring leading to the device by raising the neutral line above ground potential.

The simplest and lowest cost surge suppressers are nothing more than three MOVs in a terminal strip. These are often short-lived, self-destructing after one or two surges. Unfortunately, they often give no sign that they have failed, so they may leave you inadvertently unprotected. If you worry about surges, you'll want something more complete than a protected terminal strip.

If you worry about surges, you'll want something more complete than a protected terminal strip.

Most better commercial surge suppressers combine several of these technologies along with noise reduction circuitry. They usually incorporate multiple stages, isolated by inductors, to prolong life and improve response time. Heavy-duty components such as gas tubes or large MOVs form the first stage and absorb the brunt of the surge. A second stage with tighter control (more MOVs or avalanche diodes) knock the surge voltage down further. Rarely will one of these more complex unit fail. Most have indicators to warn when they are no longer capable of protecting your PC.

A surge can occur between any pairing of conductors: hot and neutral, hot and ground, or neutral and ground. The first pairing (between hot and neutral) is termed *normal mode*. It reflects a voltage difference between the power conductors used by your PC. When a surge arises from a voltage difference between hot or neutral and ground, it is called *common mode*.

Surges caused by utility switching and natural phenomena—for the most part lightning—occur in the normal mode. They have to. The National Electrical Code requires that the neutral lead and the ground lead be bonded together at the service entrance (where utility power enters a building) as well as at the utility line transformer that's typically hanging from a telephone pole near your home or office. At that point, neutral and ground must have the same potential. Any external common mode surge becomes normal mode.

To completely protect your PC, you'll want a surge suppresser that works in normal and common modes.

Common mode surges can, however, originate within a building because long runs of wire stretch between most outlets and the service entrance, and the resistance of the wire allows the potential on the neutral wire to drift from that of ground. Although opinions differ, recent European studies suggest that common mode surges are the most dangerous to your equipment. (European wiring practice is more likely to result in common mode surges in that the bonding of neutral and ground is made only at the transformer.) To completely protect your PC, you'll want a surge suppresser that works in normal and common modes.

Many surge suppresser manufacturers tout EMI (Electromagnetic Interference) noise reduction circuitry as an additional feature of their products. However, external noise reduction is essentially irrelevant to PCs. All PCs must pass FCC Class B certification (for home use) or Class A verification (for business use). Both standards require PCs to prevent the noise and interference they generate from reaching the power line. The same circuits that prevent noise from getting out of your PC prevent power line noise from getting in. Although additional noise isolation won't hurt your PC or peripherals, there's no reason to pay extra to get it.

The cheapest, most versatile, and least effective surge suppressers are the inexpensive (say $5 to $20) outlet strips you'll find in hardware and discount stores. The surge protection built into these units typically is nothing more than one or three MOVs, and the units often fail when confronted with the first big surge that comes along, giving you no warning that your PC is unprotected. Better surge suppressers are larger boxes with four to eight outlets, an indicator or two, and a fuse or circuit breaker. These cost from $25 to $100. In most cases, they will deliver long, trouble-free surge protection. More expensive surge suppressers are also available, but they are best chosen for any additional features that they offer (such as switched outlets). They don't deliver any more surge protection than do moderately priced units.

Installing a surge suppresser is no more difficult than plugging in an extension cord. Plug the surge suppresser into a wall outlet, then plug your PC and all of its peripherals into the surge suppresser. No adjustments are necessary, you don't have to run any complex software installation, and—for once—you probably can get by without once glancing at the instructions. (As if you were going to anyway!)

> *Installing a surge suppresser is no more difficult than plugging in an extension cord.*

Backup Power Systems

Backup power systems excel where surge suppressers fail. They give your PC the electricity it needs when your local utility decides to take a break. They put-off or prevent blackout and help you get through brownouts, and a good backup power system will also stop other power problems from reaching your PC, functioning as well as (if not better than) a surge suppresser.

The protection afforded your PC by a backup power supply varies with the product you choose, however. The basic protection all backup power systems offer is reserve electricity to power PCs through utility failures. When the utility fails, the backup system takes over with its own electrical supply. Better backup units also protect against other power-related problems—overvoltages, when utility-supplied electricity inches dangerously above its nominal 120-volt level; surges, short bursts of even higher voltage; and noise, a potpourri of hitchhiking signals of various frequencies that can interfere with computer circuits. In effect, one upgrade can protect your PC from nearly everything that can sneak into it through its power connection.

To confuse issues, backup power supplies fall into three types, off-line, on-line, and internal. Off-line systems, more frequently called *standby power supplies*, do nothing until the power blacks out, and then swing into action. On-line systems, usually called *uninterruptible power systems* (or UPSs), break the direct connection between power line and your computer, constantly conditioning the power that's routed to your PC. Hard-to-find internal systems are a cross between standby and uninterruptible systems that installs inside your PC. If you have difficulty distinguishing these three flavors of power protection, you're not alone. The makers of only standby supplies are rather indiscriminate (and misleading) in their labeling, often calling their off-line products UPSs. The standards and testing organization Underwriters Laboratory also uses this misleading nomenclature.

The words aren't nearly so important as what the different types of backup power supplies do. If you want to get the right kind of power protection upgrade for your PC, you'll need to know which type of backup device will give you the security you need. Each of the three types of backup system has its own strengths and weaknesses.

Standby Power Supplies

The primary purpose of any backup power system is to jump into action to fill the gaps in supply of electricity provided by your local utility. A standby power supply does exactly that—it stands watch over the utility power supplying your PC and, when the electric supply fails, it switches on to provide power from its internal batteries.

The operative word in that description is "switches." Ordinarily, the battery current in the standby power supply is not connected to your PC. It switches into action. Making the switch—and even detecting that the utility power has failed at all—requires a short period, a time typically measured in milliseconds. All except a few aged PCs ignore such brief gaps in the power supplied to them, so the standby power system is able to create the illusion (to you and your PC) that electricity is continuously available even during a blackout. The safety margin is wide. Most PCs can withstand outages as long as 300 milliseconds without flinching. Most standby power systems switch over in twelve milliseconds or less.

The elements of a standby power supply are a set of rechargeable batteries to provide power when none is available from your electrical utility, an inverter, a battery charger that keeps power stockpiled in the batteries, and the switch for making the change-over. Better standby power supplies augment that minimum with spike and surge protection, sometimes even power control features such as multiple switched outlets to which you can connect the various peripheral of your PC. You can't tell whether this protection is built into a standby power system just by looking. You'll need to check its specification or ask the salesperson with whom you're negotiating.

The biggest advantage of the standby power system is that it offers affordable blackout protection that's easy to install. Models with surge arrestors will give you the most affordable blanket power protection available.

The biggest advantage of the standby power system is that it offers affordable blackout protection that's easy to install.

Uninterruptible Power Supplies

Exactly as its name implies, an uninterruptible power supply or UPS creates a constant flow of electricity that is never interrupted, even for the briefest fraction of a second. In most elegant form called *double-conversion UPS*, the UPS constantly generates the alternating current required by a PC from its internal batteries. All the while, the batteries are also being charged so the drain on the battery resources is continually replaced. When utility power fails, nothing happens to the output of the UPS because it merely continues to supply battery-backed electricity. The only alteration is that the batteries are no longer being charged, and their reserves slowly drain away.

The important part of this design is that the output and input of this kind of UPS are isolated from each other by the battery. All the evils of utility power are kept out of the supply going to the computer. So the UPS automatically protects against transient high voltages on your power line, the surges and spikes that might otherwise do damage to your PC's electronics. Not only are no additional surge arrestors necessary, the classic UPS yields better protection than just about any ordinary surge protector.

Other kinds of UPS are becoming popular that are crosses between the classic UPS design and standby power systems. They offer switchless output power but don't constantly drain their batteries. These units are often described as *on-line backup systems*.

In one on-line design, instead of the input being directly connected to the output, the backup power system (as it would in a pure standby supply), it can be connected through a transformer. The battery-backed part of the power system is connected to another winding of the transformer. When the utility power fails, the battery power section switches on. The reactance of the transformer—electrical energy stored in the magnetic field of the transformer—bridges over the brief gap caused by the switch. The output of the system can thus continue without operation. Using this design, the battery charging section of the power supply can be trimmed down in size because it never needs to carry the full output load of the power system.

The important difference between on-line and double-conversion UPSs is that the design of the latter guarantees surge suppression, but the former does not. During the period that an on-line device is not supplying battery power, your PC is connected directly to the utility power line and is vulnerable to whatever glitches waft down the line. To make up for this deficiency, most on-line UPSs have built-in surge suppressers. If you're thinking about buying an on-line device, you should check to be sure that it has surge suppression.

If you're thinking about buying an on-line device, you should check to be sure that it has surge suppression.

Double-conversion UPSs are a dying breed because they typically cost about twice as much as an on-line or standby system with the same ratings. Although a double-conversion UPS gives the greatest possible power protection that can be afforded to a PC, a standby system or on-line system coupled with spike and surge protection can be just as effective. Only a handful of first-generation PCs are so sensitive to brief power lapses that modern standby power supplies with quick switching won't work. (Only a fraction of IBM's original production of Personal Computers XT could not tolerate such quick switches.) If you want the best, opt for a double-conversion UPS. Otherwise, you'll likely to be able to get along quite nicely with an on-line or standby power supply.

Internal Battery Supplies

Ask any criminal. An inside job is best, and that advice holds true even when it comes to a UPS. Putting a UPS inside your PC instead of outside offers some unique benefits that cannot be matched by any other power protection system—not just more safety but a lower price, too. But of course, this design has its drawbacks as well.

Thanks to miniaturization and a better technological match, all the circuitry necessary to build a UPS—including the battery supply—today can be packed onto a single expansion card that plugs into one of your PC's expansion slots. On the surface of it, putting a UPS inside a PC makes a lot of sense. The batteries used for backup power naturally produce direct current (DC), exactly the same variety of electricity that's produced by your PC's power supply and used by your computer's circuits. Unlike an external standalone UPS, a UPS-on-a-card approach doesn't require expensive circuitry to convert line power to battery power and back again. That saves both space and the cost of materials.

That's not to say building a UPS on an expansion card is trivial. The match between battery and computer current isn't all that perfect. Computer power supplies generate several voltages—plus and minus five volts as well as plus and minus twelve volts—and each would ordinarily require a separate pack of batteries. UPS's-on-a-card avoid the need for multiple battery supplies by incorporating DC conversion circuitry, which is nearly as complex as that required to build an external UPS.

The real problem with putting the UPS inside your PC is that the UPS won't be able to tell the difference between a real power outage and those caused by you flipping the big red power switch off. The instant your turn off the power to your PC, an internal UPS will detect a power failure and swing into action.

With true computer industry adroitness, the UPS-on-a-card makers have turned this design flaw into a feature—one that can make a UPS-on-a-card an even more valuable product. All current internal UPS cards incorporate state-saving software, programs that automatically save the contents of your PC's memory and state of its microprocessor by copying all that data to the computer's hard disk when the power fails. Restore power to your PC, and the UPS's state-saving software will load everything back into memory so that your system can resume from exactly the place it was when the computer was switched off. Taking advantage of this capability, the internal UPS adds an auto-resume to your PC—whenever you switch a system with an internal UPS, the state of your PC's RAM will be saved. Turn it back on, and its memory will be reloaded, and you can start your work from exactly where you stopped.

The biggest weakness of the internal UPS is that it offers only one kind of power protection—against total blackouts. Because it is located inside the PC after the power supply, the internal UPS is too far downstream to protect the computer's power supply from spikes and surges in utility power. You'll want to add a surge protection of some kind to your system even if you install an internal UPS. Moreover, the internal UPS won't keep a video monitor, external hard disk system, or external modem operating when utility power fails. You might want to keep a flashlight handy.

The biggest weakness of the internal UPS is that it offers only one kind of power protection— against total blackouts.

Backup Power Strategies

All backup power systems have a single purpose—providing electricity when utility current fails—but they don't have the same use. The difference is what you do with your PC and the kind of protection that you want. The classic case of the backup power system is the blackout bridge. The electricity from the backup system keeps your PC going throughout a power failure. Not only don't you lose your work, you won't even lose your train of thought.

In such an application, a backup power system has to be pretty hefty. Not only must it prop up your PC for the duration of the failure, it must also keep your monitor and other peripherals going. And if you want to see what your doing, you might even need a lamp. Moreover, when used in this way the backup power supply needs enough internal battery supply to carry the load across blackouts that stretch for ten minutes or more.

> For the most part, relying on a backup system for completely uninterrupted operation of your PC doesn't make economic sense.

For the most part, relying on a backup system for completely uninterrupted operation of your PC doesn't make economic sense. Few blackouts stretch beyond a few seconds. In most cases, electrical power will return within a minute of a failure. Consequently, long battery life—enough to wait out the longest possible blackout—is not necessarily critical. Lower your goals, and you can get with much less in the line of battery reserves. Most single-user systems can get along with just enough backup power that the computer can be properly shut down—all files saved, applications ended, and temporary files deleted. A minute or two will do. The best of both worlds, and perhaps the best compromise, is to couple enough backup power to carry a complete system through a short blackout—those lasting about a minute—with sufficient reserves for an orderly shutdown.

Server PCs need more. They cannot just switch off while a dozen or a hundred users are depending on the disks inside for storage. The server has to stay alive longer than any of the PCs that it services. Moreover, it must be able to signal the PCs it serves to let them know that the power has failed and that the system may be shutting down in a few minutes. Consequently, a server requires a special type of backup system—one with enough power to assure that all active files being used by all PCs connected to the server can be saved, and one with a built-in signaling system to notify the server of the power failure in a manner gentler than a total shutdown.

A final consideration is the unattended PC, be it a machine waiting to make a backup or waiting to service a telephone call or just waiting. A power failure will interrupt the wait. A backup supply can help keep the system going, but during a prolonged power outage, an ordinary backup system is an invitation to trouble. Once the battery reserves in the backup supply run out, the unattended PC is on its own. If the failure occurs during a telephone transaction, the call will end and will business being handled through it will have to be started anew, hardly a fatal error. But if caught in the middle of a backing up a hard disk, a backup supply shutdown can be just as dangerous as an unprotected blackout. Files may be lost; worse, the disk being backed up could be corrupted. When power returns, the unattended PC may not know how to return to its appointed business. It might just boot up and sit around wearing a DOS prompt until some unfortunate human is rooted from bed to ferret out the problem.

State-Saving Software

The unattended PC needs a particular kind of backup system, one that can save the state of the PC being protected. Every register, every memory location, must be properly preserved so that it can be restored—automatically—when the unattended PC restarts as power is returned.

All the current internal UPS systems use state-saving software and operate similarly. The UPS instantly switches your PC over to battery operation whenever your PC's power supply kicks out because of a blackout or brownout. Battery electricity is supplied for a short period—a second or two—to bridge across brief service interruptions. After that short delay, the UPS assumes that the failure will be a long one, and the state-saving software swings into action, directing your PC to copy the contents of its RAM, video memory, and even microprocessor registers to disk memory.

All the current internal UPS systems use state-saving software and operate similarly.

If utility power returns during the period in which the operating state of your systems is being saved, the UPS control software returns normal control back to you once the state-saving operation is completed. You can resume exactly where you left off. But if utility power still has not been restored, the UPS-on-a-card system parks your hard disk and shuts down the system.

Turn your PC back on, and it will automatically restore itself to exactly the place it was when the power failed—the same software loaded into memory, the same image on the display, everything in place all the way up to the last keystroke. (Of course, since the computer may have been hung in an error condition when it was switched off, for example for a warm boot, the UPS control software also allows sidestepping this automatic restoration.)

State-saving can be a perfect solution for keeping unattended PCs playing. For example, put an internal UPS in a network server, and it will pop back up after a power failure exactly where it left off.

As clever as this concept sounds, it has its drawbacks. As with all state-saving systems, each UPS-on-a- card requires the dedication of at least as much hard disk space as there is RAM to save. An eight-megabyte PC will lose eight megabytes from its disk plus sufficient disk space to store the contents of display memory. Moreover, saving a lot of memory to disk can be time consuming, taking as little as five or ten seconds or as long as several minutes, depending on the amount of memory to be backed up, the speed of your PC's microprocessor, and the performance of your hard disk. The profusion of memory types also complicates matters, particularly with 386 and 486 PCs. While all internal UPSs can automatically save the state of all standard types of memory (DOS, extended, and expanded), some have difficulty with the advanced memory paging abilities of the latest microprocessors. If you have memory in your system managed under the XMS or VPCI protocols (the kind of extended memory used by DOS 6.0 and Windows 3.1, for example), you'll have to be more critical in your shopping. Be sure to verify the internal UPS that you buy can save the state of the memory in your system. Just like any terminate-and-stay-resident utility, state-saving software will steal some of your systems DOS memory from other programs. And it can be sensitive to the order in which it is loaded in relation to other TSR programs. For example, some state-saving software requires that it is loaded only after other software drivers.

Backup Power Supply Ratings

The fundamental difference between backup power supplies of a given type is capacity, how much electricity they can deliver. Capacity is not a single measure but two. You need to be concerned with how much power the backup system can deliver, that is, what is its maximum rating measured in watts or volt-amperes. In addition, you need to know how much energy the supply can provide, that is, how long it can back up your PC. Although energy is measured in ergs, joules, or (more familiarly) watt-hours, the principal measurement you'll want to tangle with is the minutes the supply will run your computer system.

Power

Nearly every backup power system is sold by its power rating. This figure helps you judge how much equipment you can protect with the backup system. Just as power supplies are limited in the amount of current they can handle by their designs and components, so are backup systems. Exceed the rating of the backup system and your protection device becomes an invitation to disaster. It will either fail as soon as your turn your system on or will gradually overload, failing right in the middle of some important calculation you're making.

Backup power supplies are rated in watts or volt-amperes. If you're familiar with Ohm's Law, a basic principle of electrical circuits, you know that power equals current times voltage, that is, watts equals amps times volts. With such an easy relationship between the watts, volts, and amps, you may wonder why the power protection industry needs two different measures. In truth they do, but the reason is surprising. In alternating current (AC) systems, watts don't necessarily equal the product of volts and amps. In AC circuits, the voltage and current can be out of phase with one another—when voltage is at a maximum, the current in the circuit can be at an intermediary value. So the peak values of voltage and amperage may occur at different times. But power requires both voltage and current simultaneously. Consequently, the product of voltage and current (amperage) in an AC circuit is often higher than the actual power in the circuit. The ratio between these two values is called the *power factor* of the system.

What all of this means to you is that volt-amperes (VA) and watts are not the same thing. Most backup power systems will be rated in VA because it appears to be the higher figure because of the power factor. You must insure that the total VA used by your computer equipment is less than the VA available from the backup power system. Alternately, you must insure the wattage used by your equipment is less than the wattage available from the backup power system. Don't indiscriminately mix the two. If necessary, you can change a VA rating to a watt rating by multiplying the VA by the

Volt-amperes (VA) and watts are not the same thing.

power factor of the backup power supply. To go the other way, divide the wattage rating of a backup power system by its power factor to reach its VA rating. (You can do the same thing with the equipment you want to plug into the power supply, but you may have a difficult time discovering the power factor of each piece of equipment.)

Energy

Although the carefully controlled, the continuous power created by a backup power system prevents power-line anomalies from harming computer systems, even the best system can't guarantee an endless supply of pure electricity. When utility supply fails and the backup supply draws upon its internal battery reserves, the watt-hours are limited, typically to a fraction of an hour. As with all good things, the reserves of the backup supply must eventually come to an end. When the backup power supply runs out of backup power, the result is just as deadly to data as the utility failure the UPS is supposed to protect against.

Most manufacturers rate their backup systems for a given number of minutes of operation with a load of a particular size. For example, a backup system may be rated to run a 250 volt-ampere load for 20 minutes. These figures are useful for calculating how long you can expect your system to run on backup power and for comparing different products. If your PC and peripherals draw some other amount of power than that which is given in the duration ratings of a backup power system, how long your PC will run off batteries can be anyone's guess.

You can get an idea of the maximum possible time the backup supply will carry your system by the batteries it uses. After all, the only electricity is has available is hidden inside those batteries. Most batteries are rated in amp-hours, which describes how much current they can deliver for how long. You can convert that rating to a genuine energy rating by multiplying by the nominal battery voltage. For example, a twelve volt, six amp-hour battery could, in theory, produce 72 watt-hours of electricity. That's a theoretical figure because the circuitry the converts battery DC to AC will con-sume some of the power and because ratings are only nominal for new batteries. But the figure does give you a limit. If you have only 72 watt-hours of battery, you can't expect the system to run your 250 VA PC for an hour. At most, you could expect 17 minutes. Realistically, you might expect 12 to 15.

To add greater battery capacity to your backup system, these ratings become useful if not invaluable. You can calculate how much additional running time each battery will add to your system. You can even allow for the efficiency of the backup power supply by calculating how much life you get from the built-in battery of the system.

Buying a Backup Power Supply

The first step in locating the best backup power supply for your PC is to determine the type of protection that you need. If you want blackout protection that allows you to keep working when the power fails and make the decision for yourself when to shut down your PC, a standby power supply is the inexpensive choice. An uninterruptible power supply will give you greater protection from electrical ills at a correspondingly greater price. If all you want is insurance against losing files and work to an unexpected outage, an internal power backup system will give you the least expensive solution, albeit one without surge protection. If you want automatic operation or have an unattended PC, the internal backup supply or an external power supply with state-saving software will be the best choice.

If you want automatic operation or have an unattended PC, the internal backup supply or an external power supply with state-saving software will be the best choice.

External Backup Supplies

If you choose an external backup power supply, your next step is to determine how much power you'll need. The amount required depends on the PC you have and whatever peripheral you would also like to protect. Many backup power supplies are sold in configurations designed for particular styles of PCs—XT-size, AT-size, server-size. In general, such systems make allowance for the connection of a monitor in addition to the PC but for no other peripherals. About 250 volt-amperes of power is sufficient to safe-guard the small-footprint PC including ancient machines like the original PC and XT and desktop PS/2s (along with the typical 12- to 14-inch color VGA monitor). Move up to an AT or a high-performance desktop computer based on the 386 or 486 microprocessors and you'll want to get from 300 to 350 VA from a backup system. Tower computers, because of their larger power supplies and greater expansion potential, may require even larger backup systems, up to 500 VA.

Besides your monitor, the only other peripheral you'll want to connect to your backup systems is an external modem. Generally, these draw a negligible amount of power so you probably won't have to make any allowance for one. Although you may be tempted to connect your printer to the backup system, that's not a good idea. Printers require a lot of power, which means you'll have to move up to a hefty (and expensive) backup system. Moreover, most impact printers use powerful electric motors that require a great deal of start up power—so great in fact that they might over-strain an inexpensive backup system, either blowing the fuse or destroying some of its transistors. In other words, never, never connect a printer to a backup system. When looking for an external backup power supply, you'll want to look at the indicators that are provided. Nearly every external backup supply includes warning bells, whistles, or Sonalerts to warn you that the system has switched over to backup power—just in case you hadn't noticed the lights went out. In addition, they give some warning to indicate when the supply is approaching the end of its electrical reserves. Some backup systems have more exotic arrays of indicators, such as thermometer or bar- graph style LEDs that show the discharge level of the batteries or a similar indication of the amount of current being drawn from the system. Whether these indicators are useful depends on how you intend to use the backup system. In most cases, an impending-doom indication is all that's necessary. Then again, having a full array of blinking lights, whistles, and meters may make you feel like the master of the universe.

Another difference between backup power systems is the waveform of its output power. Normal utility-supplied electricity comes in the form of smooth sine waves, and that's what backup power supplies should produce, too. Unfortunately, sine waves are expensive to make, so many backup systems skimp here. For standby power systems that will operate your PC for a few minutes at a time, you probably need not worry about the waveform. However, prolonged use of square waves may cause some equipment to overheat, so they should be avoided in uninterruptible systems.

Although waveform should be important, it tends to fall near the bottom of purchase criteria because few people understand what it means—and few backup systems deliver exactly what they promise. Part of this situation results from interaction between the backup power system and your PC. The waveform of any power system depends on the kind of load attached to it—highly reactive loads (for example, motors and transformers) cause the waveform to change shape so you never know what's really getting to your equipment. And part of the discrepancy arises because there's no real standard for what a sine wave really is (at least in backup system brochures). You have to take the manufacturer's word for what kind of waveform its equipment produces, and you can bet most backup supply makers have engineers who squint their eyes up to make themselves see sine waves in some strangely abstract shapes.

About the worst danger that non-sine wave current is supposed to pose to your PC is overheating. Square waves have a different energy content than sine waves and they are rife with harmonic distortion. The result of these shortcomings is that the transformers in linear power supplies heat up. Of course, PCs don't use linear power supplies. Moreover, you will probably run your PC for such a brief time from a standby power system so that this heating problem (if it actually is a problem) should not be an issue. Except in odd or unusual circumstances (or with an odd and unusual standby power system), you can safely ignore the output waveform.

In some applications, the output frequency of the backup system can be critical. Ideally, a backup system should produce power at exactly the 60 Hz that utilities supply electricity. For PCs, anything close will work. Most PCs now have power supplies designed to work with a range of frequencies (typically, 50 to 60 Hz.) so they will accept anything reasonable from a backup system. About the only devices sensitive to input power frequency are clocks. However, the clocks in most PCs don't rely on the line frequency to tell time. Instead, they have their own crystal oscillators and thus function independently from power line frequency.

Internal Backup Supplies

If you choose to use an internal backup power supply, your purchasing criteria will be different from those for an external supply. For example, internal systems are more critical about the computers with which they are used. Because they connect directly to the output of your PC's power supply, the kind of connector use there is critical. Some internal backup systems are designed so that they will accept either Burndy or Molex power connectors. Others require that you get an adapter to match the kind of connector used by your PC's power supply and system board. When you buy an internal backup system, you'll want to specify the brand and model of computer you have so that your dealer can make the right match. Alternately, you can tell your dealer what kind of connector that you need. One look will tell you everything that you need to know.

Because internal backup supplies uniformly use state-saving software, in most cases you won't have to worry about the energy reserves of the backup supply. Most have enough battery power to save the state of all but systems with extraordinarily large memories and extraordinarily slow hard disk drives. Other external backup power supply considerations are meaningless. You don't have to worry about output waveform or frequency because internal backup supplies deliver DC—the waveform of which is a flat line. Nor do you need to consider blinking lights—even if an internal backup supplies has them, you can't see them outside your PC.

With internal backup systems, the primary issue is the software packed with the hardware. The software must be compatible with your computer, its memory, and the applications that you use. Be especially critical in verifying that the internal power supply and its software that you want will be able to save all the memory in your system—including XMS if you use Windows 3.1. Saving only part of your PC's memory won't work.

Installing an External Backup Power Supply

An external backup power supply is almost trivial to electrically install. You need only plug the power supply into an ordinary wall outlet (see fig. 15.6) and plug the power cords from your PC and its monitor to the outlets on the back of the power supply (see fig. 15.7). External backup systems that use state-saving software or link with network operating systems add another connection. These systems provide a signal output that is usually connected to a serial port. The backup supply uses this cable to indicate to its PC host when it has switched over to its battery power and when the battery power reserves are precariously low. The necessary cable should be supplied with the backup power system, but is often available only as an extra cost option. Backup systems from different manufacturers use their own connections and cable styles for this warning signal.

Where to put the power supply is the only loose end. With some units—those that are low, flat, and deep, the obvious place is to use the backup supply as a monitor stand. Those designed as power directors with multiple switched outlets lend themselves to such installations, putting all of their power controls right at hand. If your monitor is on top of your PC, however, using a backup system to further increase its height is not a good idea. All backup systems are packed with heavy lead-based batteries. These can actually stress or bend the case of PCs with potentially deleterious consequences. If your monitor is located on a desktop and your PC next to your desk, however, sliding a backup system underneath the monitor should not be a problem.

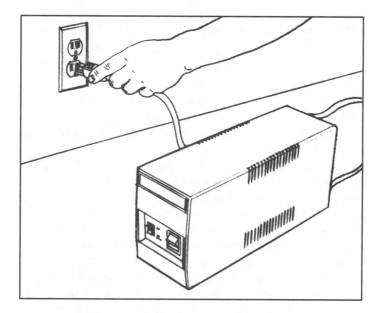

Figure 15.6
The first step in installing a backup power supply: plugging your backup into the wall.

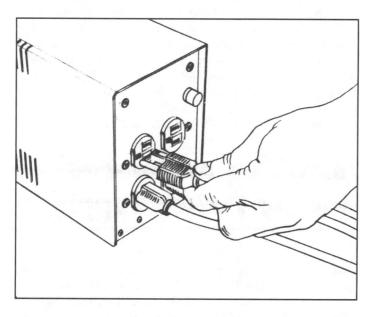

Figure 15.7
The final step: plugging your PC into the backup power supply.

Smaller external backup supplies are designed to be placed next to PC cases. There's no reason not to—unless it puts the backup supply too close to the edge of your desk. A heavy backup system can do substantial damage to itself, nearby equipment, and even you if it plummets to the floor. Be careful.

Bigger backup power supplies should be located as near as practicable to your normal operating position, your desk. You want to power supply within earshot so that you can hear its warning tones, and you want it close enough that you can see and access its controls.

Check the manual that comes with your backup system to see how it recommends you operate the system. In some cases, you'll want to leave the backup system on all the time and switch your PC on and off with its own power switch. Some backup systems prefer that you use its power switch to control the backup system, your PC, and your monitor together with the backup system's own on/off switch. Usually using the backup supply's switch is best. That way if the power fails during the evening or some other time you're not around your backup system won't try to supply electricity to nothing. Working into such a no-load condition can damage some backup systems. One additional hint: most backup systems have several outlets on their rear panels. People who visit occasionally to clean your office typically look for the first outlet they can find to plug in their vacuum cleaners. And the first place they plug in is the back of the backup power system. They switch on the vacuum, and the initial surge its motor draws blows out half the circuitry inside the backup power system. The vacuum doesn't work, so they look for another outlet—and deny they had anything to do with the smoke curling out of the backup power system. Sound far-fetched? It isn't. Someone somewhere somehow will accidentally overload your backup power system if you're not careful. To avoid such problems, cover all unused outlets on the back of your backup power system with masking tape, an evil red color if you have it.

Installing an Internal Backup Power Supply

Only the connections and adapters used by various models of internal backup systems vary.

Conceptually, all internal backup power supplies are installed in the same manner. They intercept the output of your system's own power supply that is bound for the system board and substitute their own protected outputs. Only the connections and adapters used by various models of internal backup systems vary.

In any case, the first step in installing an internal backup systems is to free up enough expansion slots into which to fit the backup system. These slots should be as close as possible to your system's power connections to insure that the adapter or cables will stretch to accommodate the backup system. In some cases, you may get a better fit if you relocate your system's disk controller one slot further away from the power supply and slide the backup supply into the controller's old slot. Remember to keep 16-bit devices in 16-bit slots when you move expansion cards in systems with various slot interfaces.

Next, disconnect your system's power supply from the system board. In most PCs, you'll find two separate cable bundles each going to its own connector on the system board. Often the connectors at the ends of these cables are labeled P8 and P9. To unplug these cables, you simply slide them up and out. Simple, perhaps, but not always easy. The connectors can fit tightly. You may need to rock them a little to get them loose. You might want to press down on the system board around the connectors as you try to pull each connector off so you don't stress the board too much. Although it's tempting to yank out the two connectors together by grabbing the both bundles of wire at once, take your time and remove the connectors individually and carefully. Being too rash may destroy your system board, an expensive replacement proposition.

Next, connect the backup supply to your system's electrical system. Two basic methods are used by internal backup systems for this process.

One kind has two sets of jacks on the backup supply's expansion board. One set of jack will match those in your system, be they Burndy or Molex. The other set will be other style of connector. Determine which set of connectors your PC's P8 and P9 cables (or whatever they are labeled) will fit into *but don't plug them in yet.* Now locate the second set of jacks on the backup card and the short adapter cable that came with the board. The adapter cable should have Burndy connectors on one end and Molex on the other. Plug one end of this cable into the backup supply using the jacks that did not match the connectors on the wires from your PC's power supply. Get the backup supply expansion board into position for installing inside your system but don't slide it into place. Instead, first connect the free end of the adapter cable you just installed into the power supply jacks on your system board. Magically, the connectors at the other end of the adapter cable are guaranteed to match the jacks on your system board. Observe the keying and numbers of the jacks. The positions of the various colors of the new wires should match those of the old. Once that wire is in place, plug the wires from your PC's power supply into the matching jacks on the backup supply expansion board. Finally slide the expansion board all the way into its slot and screw it into place.

The other style of internal backup supply uses a special three-connector adapter cable that's made to match the style of power connector in your PC, either Burndy or Molex. One end of this three-connector cable will fit into the system board power supply jacks. Plug this connector into the system board jacks. In the center of the three-connector cable you'll find a jack that will accommodate the two power connectors that formerly plugged into your PC's system board. Plug these connectors into the central jack on the three-connector cable. Pull the cable out of the way and slide the backup supply into the expansion slot that you have prepared for it. Screw the board tightly into place. Finally, plug the remaining connector of the three-connector cable into the jack on the backup supply.

When the backup hardware is installed, follow the software installation procedures accompanying the product. These will vary with the board you've chosen and even software version.

Check the technical manual accompanying the internal backup supply board to find out whether you must charge the board before you can rely on it. The only way to charge the board is to run your PC because the board draws its electrical supply from your PC's power supply (when it is turned on, of course). When your backup supply is fully charged, you can depend on complete protection for your PC against electrical blackouts.

A

Dealing with Your PC's Case

The real, physical work of upgrading is mechanical—the simple act of plugging in your new peripherals. In the ideal case, it's easy. Few PCs, however, present you with an ideal case. Try installing an upgrade, and you'll suspect that your PC has the case from Hell. This appendix points out the more common complications and helps makes the best of even the least ideal expansion situations.

Every expansion board and every external peripheral worth its salt includes a clever set of line drawings on cracking open the case of your PC and plugging in the board or whatever new miracle you've bought. In a perfect world, these illustrations should make this book entirely unnecessary. Tailored to the specific product, these instructions should provide you with all the guidance you need to get your upgrade going. Providing, of course, you own the one exact machine that the artist who drew the illustrations used as a model and provided every step of the procedure goes by the book—no complications, no surprises, no bloody fingertips, no curses to make the rest of the family run for cover.

When you actually try to follow those instructions, however, you're likely to discover that cables sneak in the way like irascible sidewinders; screws miraculously migrate from the locations so carefully documented in the instructions; and Venus and Mercury align in such a way that tidal forces conspire against your new expansion board fitting into the slot you've chosen. You may breeze through the entire installation as if you've spent the last 15 years designing computer equipment; then, when you switch on your PC, a tiny

This appendix points out the more common complications and helps makes the best of even the least ideal expansion situations.

wisp of smoke curls out of the power supply or, worse, nothing happens when put push up the big red power-switch paddle on the side of your computer.

Although this appendix can't be guaranteed to cover every possible situation you could encounter while making an upgrade, it will point out many of the tribulations that the breezy instruction manuals choose to ignore.

Removing the Cover

For official IBM PCs, XTs, and ATs, locating the screws that need to be removed is fairly easy.

The steps in removing the cover from the chassis of a PC, XT, or AT is probably the most documented PC procedure in existence. Remove the screws, pull the cover straight forward, and then lift its front up and off. Although these instructions sound simple, problems can arise in every step.

What can go wrong in removing screws? First, you have to find the screws and only remove the right ones. Then you've got to be able to thwart the efforts of the assembly gorillas and actually loosen and remove the screws, and you've got to be able to find the screws when you reassemble your system.

Remove more than five screws from the rear of an IBM PC, XT, or AT, and something will be looser than it should be.

For official IBM PCs, XTs, and ATs, locating the screws that need to be removed is fairly easy. All of these machines except the first batch of PCs (the so-called PC1s that allow only a total of 64K of RAM on the system board) use five screws—one located in each of the four corners of the rear panel and one more in the center of the top of the rear panel. PC1s use only three screws, omitting the two at the top corners. Remove more than five screws from the rear of one of these computers, and something will be looser than it should be.

Clone computers make finding the screws more of a challenge. Although most machines stick with the IBM screw arrangement, many others go off in their own directions. For example, Zenith puts four more screws at the lower edges of the side of the chassis. Others sneak screws under the lower lip of the chassis.

A couple of general rules will help you determine whether you should remove a screw. The screws that hold the lid on the case will, in general, be near an edge or corner. A screw in the exact middle of the rear panel—halfway between top and bottom and halfway from the right and left sides—is unlikely to be one of those that holds the lid in place. Second, you can generally see where a tab or edge of the chassis tucks under the lid of the case allowing the screw to fasten everything together.

After you remove all the screws, and the lid still doesn't come off, look again. Keep looking until you find out what's preventing the top from coming off. The first reaction—to force the lid off—is generally ill-advised.

There's a good reason why twisting a screw all the way into its hole is called driving it home. Many screws are like homebodies that love to nestle securely in their dwellings, unwilling to budge out of the warmth and security of their home come what may—including your best efforts with a screwdriver. Coaxing these screws out is never easy. You can make the job easier by using the correct screwdriver and method of removal. Don't just twist the screwdriver. With a reluctant screw, that makes the screwdriver tip likely to pop up and mangle the head of the screw. Instead, press down when you want the screw to come up. Although that sounds counter-intuitive, the added pressure will ensure that the screwdriver tip stays in the slot in the head of the screw. If the screws holding the top on have hexagonal heads that fit a nutdriver, use a nutdriver to remove them. Because you can get a better grip while doing less damage to the head using a nutdriver, it's the better choice. Odds are the factory did, and that's why you have to spend four years pumping iron to get the strength to remove some of them.

Because you can get a better grip while doing less damage to the head using a nutdriver, it's a better choice than a screwdriver.

If a screw resists your best efforts to break it free, you can encourage it along by giving it a gentle tap. Make sure that your screwdriver is properly engaged in the head of the screw and then give the screwdriver a gentle downward rap.

Nevertheless, an unusually large number of PCs show an evil tendency to resist the removal of their lids even after all the screws have been properly removed. For example, my original PC snaps so tightly together that even without screws in place, you might suspect someone had welded the top onto the chassis. This little bit of reluctance is rarely covered in the generic directions accompanying PC expansion products.

If you're certain that you've found and removed all the fasteners holding the top on your computer, and the top does not easily slide off, it's time to gently force it off. Don't yank. Instead, put the palms of your hand on the top and right side of your system so that you can press on the front faces of the disk drives with your thumbs. Now apply firm pressure with your thumbs. Gradually increase the pressure until the top pops free.

As a last resort, grasp the two sides of the lid and give a quick, sharp yank forward.

As a last resort, grasp the two sides of the lid and give a quick, sharp yank forward—the same kind of quick motion that magicians use for pulling tablecloths out from under banquets. If that doesn't work, look again for a hidden screw and assure yourself that your PC is supposed to disassemble in the same manner as a standard IBM PC.

The next step in the pre-fab instructions is to slide the top of the case forward. It should move smoothly. In some cases, however, you'll feel a bit of resistance. If you do, stop. In all too many PCs, the tab that holds the screw in the center of the rear panel dips down and catches on one of the flat ribbon cables running to the disk drives. If you don't pay attention to this, you can yank the cable off with the case lid, bend or break the matching contacts on the disk drive or its controller, or injure the cable by slicing it with a sharp edge of the tab. So if you feel the slightest resistance when sliding the lid forward, reach under the lid and determine whether a cable is caught on the central tab. If one is, push it down out of harm's way. Then continue to slide the lid off.

When the rear end of the lid reaches the front panel, this central tab will stop against the back of the front panel or something else in the way (like a disk drive). At this point, lift the front of the lid up at about a 45-degree angle to the chassis. The bottom of the lid will come free from the case and allow you to lift the lid up so that the tab will clear the front panel. The lid should then be free, allowing you to set it aside and work peacefully on the components inside your system.

As computer manufacturers become more creative, they tend to go their own direction with the cases they wrap around their products. Although many retain the early IBM slide-off-the-front configuration, a growing number have developed alternate designs. Some of these require a deft touch to successfully open.

The standard IBM design has several distinguishing characteristics. The back panel of the chassis is part of the chassis bottom, not the removable lid of the case. The screws that hold the system closed go through this backpanel and attach to tabs at the sides of the lid and one tab at the center of the lid. The front of the case is a decorative plastic bezel that's permanently affixed to the lid (not the bottom of the chassis). The sides of the case curl under the right and left edge of the chassis forming a lip about half an inch wide.

If the lid of the case does not curve around the chassis to form a lip, there's a good chance that the top of your computer will simply lift straight off. This style case also usually has two or three screws at the bottom edge of each of the two sides of the lid. After you remove these screws, try to lift the top of this style of PC straight up. You may have to flex the sides slightly to get it to release. If the front refuses to budge when you lift but the back slides up relatively easily, the front of the lid may tuck under the front-panel bezel. Try pushing the lid slightly backwards before lifting again. You should only need to push it one-quarter to one-half an inch backwards before it frees itself from the front bezel. It should then lift straight up.

Some manufacturers make the very top of the case a separate piece. These systems reveal themselves with a seam or crack that runs across both sides of the case half an inch to an inch below the top edge of the case. These are typically held together by screws in the rear panel. The top has a lip that hangs down over the rear panel, and the screws that hold the top on go through this lip and fasten to holes threaded in the rear panel. The front edge of the lid is held down by tucking it under the front bezel. After you remove the rear panel screws from this style of case, you only need to slide the top backwards far enough that it clears the bezel and then lift it off.

Tower-style PS/2s of the Model 60, 65, and 80 series use a plastic version of this last case style; only the left side rather than top of the case is removable. Instead of rear-panel screws, these machines use a pair of large captured-screws in the middle of the lid to hold the system together. These large screws are designed to be removed with a tool that's out of the standard PC repertory—a quarter (twenty-five cents American). To open a tower-style PS/2 case, loosen the two large screws until they are free but don't try to twist them out entirely and remove them. You can tell that they are free in their holes when they lean a bit to the side and you can press them in and they pop back out at you under spring pressure. When these screws are free, you can pry around the edges to lift the lid off. The front of the lid tucks under the front panel of the system, but lifting the lid will force you to angle it in respect to the chassis. This angling will release the lid from the grasp of the bezel.

Other tower-style PCs use a variety of cabinetry schemes. Some are modifications of the traditional PC case. Some flop an ordinary PC cabinet on its side, making the bottom of the chassis one of its sides. Others modify the traditional case by switching the axis of the case so that the lid is a tall inverted-U that nevertheless slides off rather conventionally.

Fitting Expansion Boards

Sliding an expansion board into a slot is an easy job, at least until you try to do it. By rights, all boards should fit all slots, but more often than occasionally a board won't quite make it. The board may not seat in its socket; its retaining bracket may refuse to slide into place; the board may not fit in the length of the slot.

A few expansion board fitting problems are obvious. A board designed for an AT may not fit into smaller computers. The AT accepts boards nearly an inch taller than the cases of the PC and XT. Slide a tall board into a short computer, and you have a compelling reason to leave the top off the case. Similarly, long expansion boards won't fit into short slots.

Ordinary expansion boards not fitting ordinary expansion slots is more difficult to explain. The causes are probably twofold—the boards and the slots are too ordinary. The machine and expansion board makers may have taken a rather cavalier attitude to such exigencies as tolerances. As a result, the length of the expansion board or the size of your PC's expansion slots vary somewhat from the agreed standard. Expansion boards are invariably a fraction of an inch too long, and slots are a fraction too short.

Any time an expansion board is bent, it and the components on it are stressed.

The widely practiced method of coping with this problem of fit is to make the overgrown expansion board squeeze into the shrunken slot. Often the board may be bent or otherwise slightly curved to fit into the slot. Avoid this practice. Bending an expansion board is an invitation to danger, disaster, and an early demise to the product. Any time an expansion board is bent, it and the components on it are stressed. The copper-foil printed circuit traces on the board can crack, breaking connections or making them intermittent. Worse, the cracks can occur within the inner layers of the board (many expansion boards are made from multiple layers glued together though they appear no thicker than a single printed circuit board), invisible to your eye but just as damaging to the function of the board. Resistors and glass-clad diodes easily crack when stressed. As a result, a single flex of an expansion board can leave it bereft of life, and your budget bereft of cash.

Do not attempt to make an expansion board fit by sanding or filing away at the board.

There is no entirely satisfactory way of dealing with this problem other than returning the ill-fitting board for a replacement of the proper dimension. Even then, you're betting that you got the one board that was made too long when it's more likely only the original prototype was the correct length. Although there's no perfect solution, you can do several things to coax an oversize board into an undersize slot. If the chassis of your computer is flimsy, lightweight metal (and most too-small chassis appear to be), you can slightly alter the size of an expansion slot by bending the metalwork. Don't be too ambitious else you run the risk of nothing fitting inside the chassis again. In some systems, you can remove the plastic card guide at the front end of the expansion slot, earning nearly one-eighth inch of extra slot length. However, because it's not a good idea to leave an expansion board wavering loosely in its slot, you may want to try filing or sanding down the card guide to make it thinner and replacing it. The slenderized card guide will still provide its essential function even after the trim. Do not attempt to make an expansion board fit by sanding or filing away at the board. Several problems could arise. You might separate the various layers of a multi-layer board, or you may get fine shavings of metal from the board mixed into a delicate circuit or, worse, a disk drive.

Problems are apt to arise at the other end of the expansion slot, too. Some card retaining brackets will simply refuse to fit properly in place. Most likely, they will stop about half an inch before they are all the way into place. The problem in this case is usually a failure to fit the tab at the bottom of the board into a matching slot. Before attacking this problem, however, ensure that the reluctant expansion board is actually engaging with the card edge connector at the bottom of the slot. If you don't get the board started in the connector properly, there's no way that the card retaining bracket will fit. Should the board be started in the edge connector, but the retaining bracket won't budge, the next step is to make the retaining bracket fit. Most of the time you can easily bend the bottom of the bracket a fraction of an inch toward the rear of the board. This slight bend is usually sufficient to make the tab on the retaining bracket find its designated slot. Width as well as length is important with expansion boards. Except for the original PC, which had one-inch slot spacing, all IBM-standard personal computers space their expansion boards at 0.8-inch intervals. Some expansion boards come precariously close to that thickness. Multi-level boards—those with their own daughtercards—often exceed that height. Scrunching too many boards too close together can lead to several problems.

Contact between expansion boards in adjacent slots is forbidden. Expansion boards should never touch one another. The biggest problem is the dreaded short circuit. When one of the printed circuit traces on the bottom of one board touches an uninsulated component at the top of another, odd things are apt to happen—and every one of them is likely to be bad. Inadvertent contact between

If you don't get the board started in the connector properly, there's no way that the card retaining bracket will fit.

Inadvertent contact between expansion boards can send voltages onto the wrong circuits, causing data errors.

expansion boards can send voltages onto the wrong circuits, causing data errors, or it could route a supply voltage directly to ground, preventing the operation of the entire computer system.

Boards that touch can cause other problems, too. If there is any pressure put on one board by the other, the result is stress much like putting too long of a board into too short of a slot. The pressure may cause one or both of the boards to flex slightly, dramatically increasing the likelihood of failure.

Boards that are too close together may also cause heating problems. Certainly, there's a cooling airflow inside your computer, but pack a number of boards closely together, and the airflow may be blocked if only in a few small areas. Wherever the airflow is blocked, the result can be localized heating, and heat is the biggest threat to semiconductor circuits, shortening their lives as inevitably as death, taxes, and the obsolescence of your current PC.

If you have a choice, spread your expansion boards across the available expansion area. Don't start by filling slot one, then slot two, then slot three. Although there's something to be said for methodology, your system will be far happier if you first fill slot one, then slot six, then slot three.

Affixing the Cover

Getting all the screws into the back of a PC can sometimes be a headache. You may get three screws nicely seated, and then the remaining two won't even start in their holes. You then end up trying to put the last screws in at odd angles and tapping new threads into the holes, a frustrating and undesirable alternative.

A neat trick will help ensure that you can easily drive all the screws home. Instead of twisting each screw individually all the way into place, make the job a two-step process: first start all the screws, leaving them loose enough so that you can nudge the cover in one direction or another. After you've got all the screws started, drive them home. This two-step process works because tightening any one screw locks the lid into an alignment that is optimal for only that one screw. Leaving the screws loose until you get them all started allows you to adjust the case lid as necessary to get each screw started. This technique works anywhere you have to put multiple screws into a single assembly.

One place three hands would be welcome is starting the two screws at the lower rear corners of the chassis. The flexible lid often flares out at the bottom so that the holes in the rear of the chassis lead to blank metal instead of the tapped screw holes in the tabs in the lid. All you have to do is press the side of the lid of your PC against the chassis with one hand while you hold the screw in place at the hole with your other hand and rotate the screwdriver with your other hand. That's just another reason why nutdrivers are so helpful—they can hold the screw securely enough that you don't have to.

If you don't have a nutdriver, you can substitute ingenuity. Usually, you can force the side of the PC into place with the palm of your hand and twist your fingers around to hold the screw in its starting position. How elegantly you manage this depends on your dexterity. You may have to lift the chassis to get your hand underneath. Of course, utility and not elegance is the issue. No one will know the contortions you go through completing the assembly of your PC.

The Case for Case Screws

Although you have exactly one reason not to replace all the screws in your PC—and not a very good reason at that—you have several other motivations to tighten everything back up. The reason not to replace screws is simple laziness. Omit this step, and you've saved a couple of twists of the wrist and maybe a minute of effort, but you'll make your system vulnerable to a legion of disasters.

Not securing the retaining brackets of expansion boards to the rear panel of your PC is more than potentially dangerous. This omission has caused hundreds of thousands of dollars of damage in systems, one IBM engineer has confided to me. The only way that expansion boards can be electrically grounded to your PC's chassis is through the retaining bracket, and the screw at the top is the only part of the design that ensures a firm mechanical and electrical connection. Certainly, your PC will operate properly (or seem to) without this screw in place, but when disaster strikes in the form of a lightning bolt, you may be putting your life (and that of your PC) at stake.

According to a story related by an engineer at a large computer company (nameless because it's unlikely that the company will officially sanction a report of its product causing a conflagration), a production line was once stopped, and engineers chained to their workstations when a report got back from a fire marshal that one of the company's computers had started a major business fire. After the company's engineers had studied the charred remains for nearly a week, they had found the true cause: lightning struck the power line, wandered through the computer, and tried to find its way to ground through the retaining bracket. The lack of a screw on this particularly bracket caused a high resistance connection that became so hot it started a fire. One screw, properly tightened in place, might have prevented the disaster. Okay, that's a rare occurrence, an act of God, and besides you live in a tank at the bottom of the ocean and are thus immune to lightning. If you're lazy enough, you can come up with a million excuses. If you want to be safe, twist the screw into place.

The lack of a screw holding an expansion board in place also allows the board it's supposed to be holding still to shift. Move the computer, and the loose board can rattle out of its slot. Try to plug a connector into a loose board, and you're likely to push the board partly out of its socket. The board will stop working. Worse, you might angle the board so that some of the contacts on its edge connector cross the contacts on the socket connector, shorting two or more circuits together. In a fraction of a second, you could damage the expansion board or, more likely, your PC's system board.

You should also replace all the screws that hold the top of your PC's case to its chassis. Certainly, you should wait to replace them until you know that your PC is operating properly after you've plugged in (or removed) an expansion board. But when you're certain the system is working, put every screw back in place.

There's no surprise more devastating—at least to your PC—than picking up your computer to move it, grasping it firmly on each side, only to have the chassis slide out of the case and crash to the floor. Potential victims include the PC itself (definitely not designed for such a plummet), the floor that it strikes, your feet that cushion the landing, and your shins that the whole mess is likely to bounce back up into. You won't know the real meaning of the word "sheepish" until you have to explain that accident to the repairman.

The screws that hold the lid on your PC's case also serve to electrically unify the system. This electrical connection helps to contain interference inside the computer, reducing the chance that signals emitted by your PC will creep into your or your neighbor's television pictures or radio programs or accidentally launch ICBMs from a nearby Air Force base.

People who review computer hardware (like this author) and those who must maintain a fleet of PCs for larger corporations are most tempted to forget the necessity of proper mechanical reassembly. Even I admit to not screwing in expansion boards when testing the dozen latest video expansion boards. But the system I depend on for writing is all snugged together, screws in place. Even the cable connectors are screwed into their jacks on the card retaining brackets. After all, my livelihood depends on this machine, and I make every effort to ensure its reliability. You should do likewise with your own PC.

B
Drive Installation

The easiest part of upgrading your disk device or anything that fits into a drive bay (such as a tape drive) is physically installing the drive in your computer. All the work is mechanical, and what you have to do is obvious. You can put a screwdriver to work and almost put your mind on hold.

The most complex issue is determining the means by which your drive should be secured to your computer's chassis. This should become obvious when you remove your old hard disk.

A number of mounting schemes are used by various computer makers. The most straightforward is the direct mounting scheme used by the IBM PC and a wide number of compatible manufacturers. The drive is directly screwed into the disk bay using either of the sets of screw holes on the sides or bottom of 5.25-inch and 3.5-inch drives. Recently, however, IBM and most other manufacturers have developed exotic retaining schemes so complex that they might make Rube Goldberg salivate (if he weren't dead).

PC Disk Drives

The original PC and clones with the same style of case have two drive bays that accommodate only full-height drives—and don't do very well at that. They only accommodate full-height drives because their bays offer only two screws at the bottom, nothing halfway up to secure a second half-height drive in the bay. In fact, the sides of the bay don't even go up high enough to hold an upper drive.

The PC mounting scheme isn't very secure because drives are held in place only by one side. Should you install a tape drive using this mounting scheme, for example, and force a tape into the drive's slot, you are likely to bend the sides of the bay.

You can work around the full-height restriction of a PC bay by using *drive adapter plates*, thin sheets of metal that attach to either side of a pair of half-height drives and convert them into a single full-height stack. The plates work simply—they have four holes or slots to accommodate screws that fit two into one side of each drive, holding the drives together. You can even fabricate them yourself out of thin sheet metal (for example, roof flashing or a piece of flat furnace duct). You can make your own template for the screw holds by stacking two half-height drives and measuring the distances between their holes—about 3 1/8 inch front to back, 2 1/8 inch top to bottom. You should make one plate for each side of a drive pair.

Installing these plates can be a problem because of the tight clearances in the PC chassis. Generally, you must use flathead or binder-head screws. Mount one side first, the side opposite the side of the drive bay into which you will put the retaining screws. After you have one plate installed, slide the drive pair into the full-height bay. You may have to rock the drive to get the screw heads to clear. When the drives are in the bay, slide the other plate between the drive and the side of the bay, lining it up so that you can put a screw through the side of the bay, through a hole in the plate, and into the lower disk drive. Screw in the front screw of the bottom drive loosely, then the rear screw all the way, and then the front screw all the way. Then screw in the two screws to hold the top drive in place.

XT Disk Drives

The vintage XT series of computers showed that IBM could learn a bit from the mistakes in the original PC. Although the first XTs would accommodate only two full-height drives, by the time the model was discontinued, it had learned to accept half-height devices as well by extending the sides of the bay upward. Moreover, even in its full-height configuration, the XT scheme provided slightly more secure mounting for one of its full-height devices.

The left bay of the XT was originally designed to accommodate a full-height, 10-megabyte hard disk drive, commodious in 1982 but paltry, indeed, by today's standards. To replace an original XT hard disk—perhaps with a bigger and faster half-height hard disk that can share its bay with a tape backup system—you're in for a surprise when you try to remove it from the XT chassis. Twist out the two screws on the left side of the drive, and it will not budge. That's because IBM added a third screw that goes through the bottom of the XT chassis into the drive. You must remove this screw to get the drive out of the computer. To access it, you'll have to turn the XT over. Remove this screw *before* you remove the two on the side of the drive so that the disk won't come crashing out of the chassis while you have it upside down. If the hole in the chassis of the XT for this screw matches one in the replacement drive you want to place in the computer, by all means use the screw.

Fitting half-height drives into all but the latest XT models requires the same ingenuity and adapter plate as putting them into a PC. In more recent XTs that allow for mounting holes for half-height drives in the sides of their drive bays, you'll still want to put an adapter plate on the blind side of the drive to hold the top drive more securely in place. The bottom of the drive tray will hold the lower drive more securely. If your new drive choice has a hole on its underside matching the third screw-mounting hole in the XT chassis, you'll want to take advantage of it when installing your drive replacement. The extra screw will ensure a solid mounting.

AT Disk Drives

IBM introduced a new, more secure mounting scheme in the AT, and many (if not the majority of) compatible computer manufacturers use the same scheme or a variation on it. The AT provides space for three drive units. On the left is an internal full-height drive bay designed for a full-height hard disk. The other two bays are on the right side of the chassis and are designed for half-height devices. IBM allows the bottom-most bay to also hold a full-height hard disk or a special optical drive that requires front panel access only to the top of its bezel. Most AT-compatible computers make the extra area below the lower of the two right half-height drive bays into a third half-height bay. Most also allow the full-height bay on the left to be split for two half-height devices. Some systems give all drive bays direct access through the front panel bezel of the system; others restrict bays with front panel access to the three on the right.

In the AT, drives are not directly mounted to the sides of the drive bays. Instead, they slide into place on mounting rails. The rails fit into guide slots that hold the drive assembly securely on both sides. The rails fit the guides tightly and hold the drive firmly in place from both sides. This mounting scheme has become so popular that many hard disks come with AT mounting kits or with the rails already installed on the sides of the drive. These rails may be made from plastic or aluminum. Because both materials provide secure mountings, there's no particular advantage to choosing one material over the other.

The keys to the success of this mounting system are its solidity and the ease with which drives can be replaced. This mounting scheme is solid because the rails are held in place from four directions. The rail guides prevent up or down movement of the drive. A tapered stop at the end of the bay and a retaining bracket at the front of the bay not only lock the drive in laterally, they also press it solidly into place. Note that the pressure is applied to the rail and not the drive, preventing the force that secures the drive from mechanically distorting it.

The ease of using the rail system is obvious. You don't have to be double-jointed to install or remove a drive. All the hardware on the chassis you must monkey with is on the front panel. To mount the rails on the drive, you can put the drive on your workbench and twist and turn it any way you want to get the screws into their holes. You'll appreciate that ease should you acquire a disk or tape drive that comes without AT mounting rails already attached.

If you have to install rails on a drive yourself, the most difficult part of the job is making certain that you have the rails oriented properly when you screw them into the drive. The vital consideration is that you put the tapered end of the rail at the rear of the drive. That is, when you slide the drive into your AT, the tapered end of the mounting rails should be first into the bay. Some rails are not tapered, however. If the rails you use lack a taper at one end, it doesn't matter which end of the rail goes toward the rear of the drive. However, orientation may still be important to ensure that your drive mounts at the proper height within the drive bay.

Although AT rails are a standard size, replacement rails have their own subtle variations. Many have four or eight holes punched in them instead of the two on genuine AT rails. The extra holes allow the identical rail to fit the right and left sides of the drive. You have your choice of two heights to use with these rails depending on whether you use the upper or lower set of holes. Which to use depends on your system. Put your new drive approximately in place in its drive bay and check where its drive mounting holes line up in regard to the slot for the guide rail. Install the guide rail using the holes that put it at the appropriate height.

Because the holes are not in the center of genuine AT rails, these rails may lead you to think that your drive doesn't fit inside your PC—it may either mount too high or too low in the drive bay. If a drive does not properly fit into your AT, try reversing the rails. Move the one from the right side to the left and vice versa while keeping the tapered end toward the back of the system. This will likely change the mounting height of the drive sufficiently to make it fit.

Another important consideration when choosing the screw holes to use when orienting the rails to your drive is to ensure that the rails fit so that the they end about one inch inside the front of the drive. This allows the small brackets that secure the drive to poke slightly into the slots in the side of the bay to hold the rails in place while allowing the drive to project slightly through the bezel in the front of the case.

Securing a drive in an AT requires screwing in the small angular brackets at the front of each rail. The AT has three such brackets. Two are L-shaped; one is U-shaped. The odd bracket secures the right side of the hard disk and the left side of the lower half-height bay.

AT-Compatible Disk Drives

Some AT-compatibles—notably Compaq Deskpros—use a mounting scheme that's similar to that of the IBM AT but, for reasons of their own, use differently shaped rails. For example, the rails of the Compaq line are slightly wider, making them incompatible with standard AT rails and the AT chassis. Compaq rails won't fit into IBM-size guides, and although IBM-size rails will fit Compaq guides, they'll rattle around instead of yielding a secure mounting system. If you have a Compaq Deskpro or a similar computer, you'll either have to recycle your old rails (remove them from your old drive and switch them to the new drive) or attempt to get new rails to match your computer, which can sometimes be a challenge. Your best source of supply is the dealer who sold you the drive upgrade that you want to install, or you can try the dealer who sold you your original computer.

Another variety of AT-compatibles use drive-mounting rails that are narrower and, consequently, also incompatible with IBM rails. Most machines that use these narrow rails pre-install a set in each drive bay of the computer, even those without drives. In this case, you only need detach the rails from the chassis, screw them to your disk, and slide the disk into place.

Rails are held in the computer chassis in one of two ways. IBM-style systems use small brackets that push the rails to the end of their travel in the bay. Some compatibles make the brackets part of the drive rails. In either case, one screw holds each bracket in place. Just unscrew to slide the old drive out and screw the bracket back in to hold your drive upgrade in place.

PS/2 Disk Drives

For larger drives, tower-style IBM PS/2s use the same width mounting rails as those used in the AT, so AT rails will work in their internal 5.25-inch drive cages. To loosen a drive in one of these computers so that you can slide it out of the chassis, press down on each of the large blue daisy-like knobs above the drive and turn it counter-clockwise with the palm of your hand until the drive can be slid out.

Special plastic mounting sleds are used to hold all drives in desktop PS/2s and 3.5-inch drives in tower-style models. The drive screws into the sled using the screw holes in its bottom, and then the sled slides into place. A plastic tab at the end of the sled locks the whole assembly in place. To remove one of these drives, press down the wide tab under and at the front of the drive and then slide the sled forward.

These drives are sometimes reluctant to slide in or out. If a sled-mounted drive is reluctant when you try to remove it, be sure that you've released the latch. Be sure to hold the retaining tab in the center of the drive sled up when you try to slide the drive out. If you face resistance when you try sliding a drive in, ensure that the drive is properly mating with the connector at the back of its drive bay. Try wiggling the drive to get its edge connector to slide into the connector.

C

The PC Toolkit

Doing any job right depends on using the proper tools. Upgrading a PC is no different. Certainly, the tools you'll require are commonplace—in most cases a simple screwdriver is sufficient. Impatient people may even make do with a table knife levered into the screw slots. Using the right tools, however, will likely reduce the number and volume of oaths you'll utter during the upgrade and help preserve the pristine condition of your PC's hardware so that the next upgrade goes equally smoothly.

One reason to rely on the right tools is that computer hardware can be notoriously difficult to manage. Many computer manufacturers apparently capitalize on the free labor available at the primate sections of their local zoos and use gorillas to twist the screws in place in their products. Or they use impact wrenches, Super Glue, and welding torches to ensure that no screw will inadvertently—or purposely—be pulled from its hole. Try to remove one of these recalcitrant fasteners with the wrong tool and you'll grind and mangle the screwheads smooth, into impossible-to-extract shapes destined to haunt you every second you own the PC. Without the right tools, you may never get inside to install your upgrade—and if you do, you may never get in a second time when your upgrade needs a little extra aid.

The minimum tool you'll need for working on your PC is a blunt-tip place knife, the kind you swipe from the kitchen to twist out a screw when you discover that the tiny hands of children have taken your real tools to points unknown. In most cases, a knife and a lot of leverage will suffice because there's nothing complicated or delicate about removing or installing PC hardware. Just the same, using a knife for any chores described in this book is not recommended, and you take your personal safety into your own hands when you use a knife or any improper tool.

To do the upgrade job right, you'll need a certain minimal set of tools. These include screwdrivers, nutdrivers, pliers, and, perhaps, a chip extractor. Often a single screwdriver will suffice for simple chores such as installing an expansion board. However, computer manufacturers have not standardized on the fasteners they use for holding their products together. So if you want to be ready for any upgrade job, you best prepare yourself with a kit.

Screwdrivers

All screwdrivers are not the same. Although you may be familiar with the difference between Phillips and flat-blade screwdrivers, even ordinary flat-blade screwdrivers run a wide gamut. Using the right one is imperative if you want to ensure that you do your upgrade right.

Although most folks would consider one screwdriver to be inter-changeable with any other, the blades can be distinctly different widths and thicknesses. Ideally, the width and thickness of the screwdriver's blade should exactly match that of the screw you want to extract or tighten into place. The proper fit ensures that the screwdriver will have the maximum contact with the slot in the head of the screw and have the least amount of play. A blade that's too thick won't work—you can't get it into the slot in the screwhead. Too small of a screwdriver won't allow you to put enough torque on the job to extract a reluctant screw. A blade that's too wide typically won't be a problem except in close quarters. Two sizes of screwdriver will normally suffice in a PC toolkit, 3/16 and 1/4 inch.

Phillips Screwdrivers

With other types of screwdrivers, the match between tool and fastener becomes even more important. For example, with the Torx screws used by Compaq and several other compatible computer makers, the wrong size of screw driver just won't work. With Phillips screws, the size match may seem less important but is also critical. The wrong size of Phillips screwdriver—particularly one that is too small to properly fit a screwhead—is a guarantee that you will gouge and tear the head of the screw, potentially making the fastener impossible to extract.

Phillips screwdrivers come in a variety of sizes, the most common of which have the numerical designations of 0, 1, and 2. A higher number indicates a larger tool. In most cases, a larger Phillips screwdriver won't work on smaller screws. Although you can sometimes make do with a smaller screwdriver for a large screw, don't risk it. The sharp crosses of the Phillips head will quickly turn into impossible circles, leaving you no choice but the ultimate solution in getting inside your PC. Normally, a number one and number two Phillips screwdriver will handle all your upgrading needs.

Nutdrivers

Some computers, particularly the pre-PS/2 IBM machines, were assembled with hexagonal-headed screws that can be inserted with either a flat-bladed screwdriver or a nutdriver. Instead of a blade, a nutdriver has a hexagonal socket that firmly grips a matching fastener on all six sides. Using a nutdriver offers several advantages. The nutdriver socket more securely holds the fastener (as compared to a conventional screwdriver) so that you can more easily start the fastener into its hole. And the nutdriver's better grip means that you can use more torque to tighten the fastener without damaging its head. That's how the gorillas at the computer assembly plant make PCs nearly impossible to disassemble.

Typically, two sizes of nutdriver are required for work on IBM and closely matched compatible computers. The screws holding the case covering the chassis required a 1/4-inch nutdriver. The screws securing expansion-board retaining brackets use a 3/16-inch nutdriver. Some tool manufacturers color code their nutdrivers for easy identification. Most commonly, the 1/4-inch nutdriver is coded red; the 3/16-inch nutdriver is coded black.

Torx Screwdrivers

The Torx screw is the better screw. Phillips improves on the standard slotted screw by giving a cross-shape, four distinct surfaces of contact, to spread the force you apply. Torx does two better, giving you six points. That also makes it incompatible with standard screwdrivers, and makes Torx screws more choosy about the tool you use on them. Torx screwdrivers come in numerical sizes, and you must have the correct match between a Torx screwdriver and screw to have any success.

From one perspective, that's good. You're much less likely to try to use a sharp knife or other ill-suited instrument to remove a Torx screw. It's also bad, because you probably don't have the right size Torx screwdriver lying around. Even your corner hardware store might be challenged to find the right size for you. Worse, you probably won't know what size you need. And, because you cannot pull out the Torx screw without the right screwdriver, you obviously can't take a sample of the screws to the store with you to make a match.

If you are a harried technician in a large corporation charged with overseeing a flock of a thousand PCs, the drawbacks of Torx screws become an advantage. If everyone who has access to the PCs in your business could simply remove the lid and make changes (or liberate an expansion board or two), you'd have chaos on your hands. Put a little obstacle like a strange screwhead in the way, and you'll be able to sleep better nights (and afternoons, too).

Compaq is the one major manufacturer that has chosen to use Torx screws. Two sizes predominate, T-10 and T-15. Arm yourself with those, and you'll be able to handle nearly any upgrade in a full-size Compaq computer.

Long-Nosed Pliers

For the most part, you won't need pliers, wrenches, or other such high-torque grippers for your work upgrading your PC. Normally, you won't find anything to squeeze or any nuts to grab because at worst everything will screw together into threaded holes.

There is one place where the tight, precision grip of long-nose pliers will be most welcome—when you have to change the jumpers that determine the settings of an expansion board or system board. With long-nosed pliers, you'll be able to easily remove and relocate jumpers with little effort or frustration. Because of the devilish way that most board makers have of locating jumpers between other taller components, you will rarely be able to get a grip with your fingers alone. Tweezers may work, but long-nosed priers will make the job much easier.

If you plan to exchange system boards, you'll need pliers to squeeze the mounting spacers together so that you can remove them, and if you drop a screw into the bowels of your PC, a pair of long-nosed pliers may seem a godsend.

Small electronic pliers are best. These are usually described by their overall length, from handle to tip. Even the tiniest, four-inch pliers will work satisfactorily for the typical upgrade job. If you have larger hands, five-inch pliers may be more to your liking, but six-inch pliers will probably prove too cumbersome for the delicate surgery involved in moving jumpers.

Chip Removal Tools

Some time or other you will be required to remove an integrated circuit in making an upgrade. That is, you'll have to pull an integrated circuit chip, such as a RAM chip or microprocessor, out of its socket so that you can put something else in its place. Sockets are designed to hold chips tenaciously. They have to. The chip must make perfect electrical contact with its socket if it is to work. Moreover, if chips were loose, they might rattle out of their sockets at some inopportune time, like when you're using the machine.

Chips are held in place so tightly that you're likely to be unable to remove them with your fingers. Moreover, the bigger the chip, the more pins it has friction-fitted into the socket and the more difficult it will be to remove. Typically, the biggest chips (microprocessors) are the ones you'll want to remove most.

Inserting chips, on the other hand, is relatively easy. Once you have a chip in place with its leads directed into its socket, you can usually just press them in. Tools are rarely needed for ordinary insertion.

To make the removal process easier, you can invest in an aptly-named chip removal tool. These come in a variety of configurations. The most common are designed for 16-, 18-, and 20-pin dual in-line package (DIP) integrated circuits. This tool looks like a pair of giant, ill-formed tweezers. Simply a U-shaped piece of springy steel about six inches long, its jaws are separated by about the length of a chip. The tips of the jaws are bent at right angles so that you can maneuver them under the chip, squeeze the tool to lock them in place, and pull up.

Pulling large integrated circuits, such as microprocessors in 28-, 40-pin, or 64-pin DIP cases or square pin-grid array cases, requires more effort than this simple tool can usually provide. A number of strange chip removal tool designs are in use. All use a variation on the basic tool—a pair of grippers to slide under the chip and grab it—but add some kind of mechanical aid to pulling the chip. Typically, this will be a screw that you twist to slowly lift the chip from its socket.

Chip removal tools are used rarely enough that most people prefer to improvise rather than buy one. Most commonly, they will use a flat-blade screwdriver to pry chips from their sockets. They hold the screwdriver parallel to the chip and slide its blade under one end of the chip. Then they lever one end of the chip up by lifting the screwdriver or force the chip up by twisting the screwdriver blade. This process often works too well. One end of the chip lifts high while the other is still stuck in the socket, resulting in a steady progression of increasingly bent pins running from one end of the chip to the other. If you want to use this technique, you can minimize the number of bent pins by working from both ends of each chip. Either use two screwdrivers (which is ungainly) or use a single screwdriver to slowly work each chip from its socket. First lift one end slightly, then the other, back to the first, and so on until the chip is loose enough to remove with your fingers.

You can usually repair the damage of bent pins by using your long-nosed pliers to carefully bend them back. Don't be too vigorous, and don't plan on straightening the pins of a given IC more than once. Pins aren't designed to bend all that much, and they typically show their dislike for the procedure by sulkily letting go. A chip so crippled is worthless and will have to be replaced.

Using a screwdriver requires adequate space for prying, and space is usually at a premium inside your PC. You often cannot reach the chip you need to remove with a screwdriver. Fortunately, most PCs come already-equipped with their own chip-removal tools—an expansion slot retaining bracket. Use the the L-shaped bracket as a lever, sliding the tip of its short arm under one end of the chip to pry up and loosen the chip. Just press back on the long arm, prying the end of the chip upward. As with using a screwdriver, you'll need to be careful to avoid bending the lead on the chip. Again, the best strategy is to pry up on one end slightly, then pry up slightly on the other, continuing the back-and-forth process until the chip is free.

Index

J-K

X-Z